To inspire ambition, to stimulate the imagination, to provide the inquiring mind with accurate information told in an interesting style, and thus lead into broader fields of knowledge—such is the purpose of this work

The New
BOOK OF KNOWLEDGE
Volume One

Other Famous Works
of
Popular Instruction
by
the Same Editor

✦ ✦ ✦

PRACTICAL KNOWLEDGE FOR ALL
SIX VOLS.

NEW UNIVERSAL ENCYCLOPEDIA
TEN VOLS.

UNIVERSAL HISTORY OF THE WORLD
EIGHT VOLS.

THE SECOND GREAT WAR
NINE VOLS.

PEOPLES OF ALL NATIONS
TWO VOLS.

COUNTRIES OF THE WORLD
TWO VOLS

WONDERS OF THE PAST
TWO VOLS.

*MANNERS AND CUSTOMS OF
MANKIND*
THREE VOLS.

OUR WONDERFUL WORLD
FOUR VOLS.

WORLD'S GREAT BOOKS IN OUTLINE
SEVEN VOLS.

*MASTERPIECE LIBRARY OF SHORT
STORIES*
TWENTY VOLS.

MADE AND PRINTED IN GREAT BRITAIN BY THE AMALGAMATED PRESS, LTD.

From the painting by Cowan Dobson

FOR you, Dear Reader, we have ventured far into the boundless fields of knowledge, and have filled no fewer than eight capacious treasure houses with riches of a kind compared to which even the fabled spoils of Ali Baba's Cave would be but poor and trashy.

And in the eighth volume you will discover something far more precious than his magic ' Open Sesame ! ' For you are there provided with three master keys which, properly used, will unlock for you every room, cabinet, and coffer in our treasure houses.

It is my earnest hope that you may use these keys to your life-long profit of mind and your continuous intellectual pleasure.

The NEW BOOK OF KNOWLEDGE

A Pictorial Treasury of Reading & Reference for Young and Old

Edited by

SIR JOHN HAMMERTON

COMPLETE IN EIGHT VOLUMES
Alphabetically Arranged

OVER SIX THOUSAND ILLUSTRATIONS
OVER 600 IN COLOUR AND GRAVURE

VOLUME ONE
A1—BON

THE WAVERLEY BOOK COMPANY LTD.
Farringdon Street, London, E.C.4

The Editor introduces the NEW

BOOK OF KNOWLEDGE

THE celebrated Dr. Samuel Johnson answered the question "What is knowledge?" by replying "Knowledge is of two kinds; we know a subject ourselves, or we know where we can find information upon it." While this may seem too simple a division of so vast a subject it is, as I hope to illustrate, an excellent definition in general terms.

Since Dr. Johnson's day knowledge has "grown from more to more" so unceasingly that the whole field of ascertained fact and recorded experience, which science and discovery in the last hundred and fifty years have opened up to human ingenuity—for evil as well as good, unhappily—holds unbounded possibilities for the future of mankind. In saying this, we must pin our faith to the good prevailing.

The first of these two kinds of knowledge can now be divided into hundreds of subsections, any one of which by study we can come to know ourselves. No one human being could hope to *know* them all.

THE NEW BOOK OF KNOWLEDGE has been devised to help its readers in both ways : (1) to acquire a thorough understanding of one or more subjects to which their own inclinations attract them, or (2), no matter whither their fancies lead, to enable them to turn with confidence to its pages for the information they require.

PERHAPS a few words will illustrate what precisely is meant by *knowing* a subject ourselves, or *knowing where* to find information about it. One of the most distinguished books written this century and published only within the last ten years, is Dr. G. M. Trevelyan's English Social History. This masterpiece he was able to write without continually consulting other books as he proceeded with its composition, simply because, through many years of intently studying books about the past ages of English history, exclusively with regard to the social life of the people in each succeeding period of time, he could shape in his own mind a sort of continuous mental pageant of English life in all ranks of society from the time of Chaucer to that of Queen Victoria: a survey of six centuries. And he happened to be endowed with the genius for making his mental pageant as vivid as reality to his readers through the medium of his writing. That is what Dr. Johnson meant by saying "We know a subject ourselves." If one is attracted to some epoch of history such as the Tudor period, or the Georgian, and studies deeply the contemporary accounts of the political and social state of England within that period, then one can acquire a knowledge of the subject, and the pleasure of acquiring this knowledge for oneself, even if one has no literary gift for expressing it, is a great mental enrichment.

NATURALLY, I do not suggest that THE NEW BOOK OF KNOWLEDGE comes to you with the direct motive of your concentrating upon any one period of history, of social life, literature, invention, or the fine arts, as in our day all such branches of knowledge have become the lesser fields of the specialists. But it comes to you with an abundance of invaluable assets by providing information about "everything under the sun," so that the reader who has no intention of bending his mind to any particular line of study has here all the information necessary to the acquirement of a wide *general* knowledge of literature and life which will carry him far beyond what he learned in his school days and equip his mind for the understanding of the life of the world in which he finds himself.

Nay, it will carry his mind back through many thousands of years before he himself made his appearance in the world, while it places him in mental contact with all that is going on in the world of his own day.

And this the reader of THE NEW BOOK OF KNOWLEDGE shall be able to do without any feeling of a task imposed, but with a keen sense of the pleasure which may be derived from acquainting oneself with fascinating knowledge of all the wonder and beauty of the world we live in and the vast universe of which it forms no more than one relatively small unit.

THE NEW BOOK OF KNOWLEDGE is, in a way, no newcomer for public favour, having for more than a generation flourished as an established favourite with the British reading public, equally acceptable to young and old. But editorially it has never been regarded as a finally finished production; it has never stood still; it *keeps unceasingly in step with the growth of knowledge itself*, and each new edition is brought " up to date " in the fullest sense of that phrase.

In the years between the two world wars the work was completely re-shaped, expanded, and revised under its present title and editorship. Now it has undergone an entire change of presentation, largely altered in its literary and pictorial contents to bring it into line with all the latest developments of post-war knowledge in the fields of science, history, literature, the arts, biography, social life and the ever fascinating realm of Nature.

Every page of THE NEW BOOK OF KNOWLEDGE has been set afresh in a new readable type which enables us to present the equivalent material contents of the previous set of ten volumes in the handier form of eight. Every article has been rewritten or revised in the light of the later information at our command following the universal upheaval of the Second World War, hundreds of new illustrations, maps, plans, and colour plates enrich its pictorial contents. No similar work exists in the British Commonwealth at this day.

Readable as a Story-Book

In making this claim for THE NEW BOOK OF KNOWLEDGE I am repeating what I have emphasized in its former editions: that it is " an encyclopedia which is more than an encyclopedia." As its immensely varied contents are arranged in alphabetical order while being couched in a style of writing which is much more attractive than any ordinary encyclopedia ever attempts, it is, for the most part of its four thousand odd pages, as readable as a story-book.

Each volume of the work carries in its introductory pages a carefully compiled series of aids to the ordered study of that particular volume which greatly help the studious reader to attain that knowledge on any subject to which he or she may be attracted, so that the first kind of knowledge specified by Dr. Johnson—*the subject we know ourselves*—may be acquired, and they who, after making acquaintance with these volumes, cannot increase or confirm their knowledge of any subject by knowing where to find it, must surely be regarded as lacking in the first essentials of self-instruction. " Here and There in This Volume " is an aid to knowledge which we offer our readers with that view, and there is no " quiz " you will ever listen to on the wireless that will help you in any way comparable to the questions we have framed for you in the opening pages of each volume.

But mark well our eighth volume. It is a curiously compact volume in as much as it embodies three different sections which serve to extend and amplify the main work and immensely to increase its educational usefulness. Volume Eight is indeed not so much the tail end of our book as its coping-stone, and since a knowledge of our method is vital to the full and satisfying use of THE NEW BOOK OF KNOWLEDGE I am here explaining the particular function of Volume Eight as briefly as possible. Its use is described in fuller detail on page 7.

Our Dual Purpose

The dual purpose of the work has been achieved by relegating to the last volume of the set in the unique " Fact-Index," all the lesser, but still important, subjects of miscellaneous information. Thus in itself it constitutes a minor encyclopedia of the latest information concerning famous persons, world events, and facts of geography, history, science, and general knowledge, additional to those related in the main articles of the preceding volumes. *The Fact-Index is under continual revision.*

Two other unusual features are found in Volume Eight. " Through the Year with the N.B.K.," and " Study Outlines " are of the highest educational value: the one to help our readers each day to particular subjects of reference, and as an attractive method for teachers to impart a topical touch to the lessons of the day; the other a long established favourite with teachers and tutors in planning special studies in about fifty leading subjects; both designed to be quickly serviceable to the student and the general reader.

> There is really no limit to the uses of this work as an educational aid to serious minded students, however advanced they may be in their studies; to the ordinary reader in search of pleasant and profitable reading ; to all young people still at school or, their school days over, still needing to amplify their knowledge for the battle of life on which they are engaging ; and, indeed, for all who are " never too old to learn."

Here, certainly, within these eight volumes is a treasury of essential knowledge for readers and students of all ages in quest of instruction and entertainment while they pursue the path of learning, which leads to knowledge, which in turn can lead to *understanding*. For that is the eventual aim of knowledge acquired by way of book-reading—understanding, without which the fullness of life itself can never be quite realized. That way too lie most of the attributes of the good life where tolerance and an open mind may flourish and personal prejudices can be overcome to contribute towards individual and human happiness.

HERE AND THERE IN THIS VOLUME

When you are just looking for 'something interesting to read,' this list will help. With it as a guide, you may wander through storyland, visit far-away countries, meet famous people of ancient and modern times, review history's most memorable incidents, explore the marvels of nature and science—in short, find whatever suits your fancy at the moment.

HOW MANY QUESTIONS CAN YOU ANSWER?

Here are a few only of the unnumbered thousands which are answered in each one of our eight volumes. You can use this page as a test of your own knowledge, or you can draw up from it a set of 'posers' with which to puzzle your friends. But odd scraps of knowledge are of little value compared with the result of organized study, and you should refer to the Study Outlines in the Eighth Volume for a reading guide.

COLOUR AND GRAVURE PLATES AND PAGES
IN THIS VOLUME

WHEN YOU ARE IN NEED OF READY REFERENCE

In using THE NEW BOOK OF KNOWLEDGE as a work of reference, Volume Eight is indispensable. As regards its contents that particular volume is unique, for it is at once a complete Index to the preceding Seven Volumes and an Encyclopedia in itself. Its purpose is fourfold, as indicated below.

(1) **Through the Year with the N.B.K.** Its opening section takes the form of a Calendar of the Year, giving for each day all the chief events and matters of interest, with references to the pages of THE NEW BOOK OF KNOWLEDGE in which full particulars concerning the event, personality, or other interest of the day may be found. By the intelligent use of this section (a) the young reader can have the daily delight of reading about topics that have special association with the particular day of the year on which he may be making his reference ; (b) father or mother can suggest what would be the most appropriate reading for the day ; and (c) the school teacher can set the lessons for the day with a genuine topical appeal.

(2) **Study Outlines.** This large and important section of the volume provides a simple method of study which should enable any of our young readers to become expert in using THE NEW BOOK OF KNOWLEDGE as an auxiliary manual of home study ; and thus what is learnt in school may be amplified, brought home more vividly, and more securely fixed in the memory.

(3) **The Fact-Index.** Actually this is in itself a complete Encyclopedia. In addition to providing many thousands of references to contents of Volumes One to Seven, it records many more thousands of facts in biography, geography, history, science, the arts, etc.,

that are not mentioned in its seven predecessors. Therefore, if you look in vain for any subject in the alphabetical order of Volumes One to Seven, turn to Volume Eight and you will almost certainly find it there.

It is a good plan, when using THE NEW BOOK OF KNOWLEDGE as a work of reference, always first to look up any subject in the Fact-Index of Volume Eight.

(4) **Thousands of Additional Entries.** In the main body of the work all important terms are explained as they arise ; but the scientist in every field of learning uses a '' shorthand'' of words and terms to convey a more precise meaning and to save repetition. Such words and terms are included in the Fact-Index so as to free the reading pages from a burden of thousands of brief cross-references which a more strict following of the full encyclopedic method would involve. When in doubt, therefore, about the significance of a term, *look it up in the Fact-Index ;* often you will find all the information you want there, but if further explanation is required the Fact-Index will give you page references to that more complete account in the main volumes. Remember that apart from its role as a never-failing source of recreative and entertaining reading, THE NEW BOOK OF KNOWLEDGE is designed to make your school and college learning of treble value by fitting that learning into its place in daily life.

KEY TO PRONUNCIATION

Most of the subject-headings in THE NEW BOOK OF KNOWLEDGE require no special indication of the way in which they should be pronounced. There are also many for whose proper pronunciation it is only necessary to know which syllable is stressed; in these cases the stress is shown *after* the syllable, thus, Armadil′lo. Where further guidance is necessary the following signs are employed.

ah = a as in father
aw = a as in ball
ê = vowel sound in fern, word, girl, curl
ow = vowel sound in now, bout
oi = vowel sound in noise, boy
Unmarked vowels have their **short sound**, as a in hat, e in bet, i in bit, o in not, u in but, oo in book
Marked vowels have their **long sound**, as in hāte, bē, bīte, nōte, tūne, bōōn

Vowels in italics have a slurred or obscure sound as in abet (*a*-bet′), recent (rē′-s*e*nt), conform (k*o*n-form′), nation (nā′-sh*u*n), tailor (tā′-l*o*r)
th = first sound in thing, thank
th = first sound in the, that
zh = s in measure, leisure
g = hard g, as in good, girl
j = soft g, as in gem, ginger
kh = guttural in loch

LIST OF ABBREVIATIONS

The abbreviations most commonly used in this work are noted below; longer lists of abbreviations often met with in reading or conversation are given under the heading Abbreviations in Volume One and also in the Fact-Index that is contained in Volume Eight.

A.D., *Anno Domini* (in the year of our Lord, of the Christian era)
a.m., *ante meridiem* (before noon)
b., born
B.C., before Christ
C., Centigrade
c., *circa* (about)
Co., county, company
d., died
e.g., *exempli gratia* (for example)
etc., *et cetera* (and so forth)
et seq., *et sequens* (and following)
F., Fahrenheit
h.p., horse-power

i.e., *id est* (that is)
lb., pound, pounds (weight)
m., miles
MS., MSS., manuscript, manuscripts
oz., ounce, ounces
p.m., *post meridiem* (after noon)
Pop., population
Pron., pronunciation
q.v., *quod vide* (which see)
sq. m., square miles
St., Saint
U.S.A., United States of America
viz., *videlicet* (namely)
yd., yard

A

A1. Sometimes when you ask someone "How are you?" the reply is "A1, thank you." That term is borrowed from the shipping world. Every ship that is built or owned in this country as well as many foreign ships are insured at Lloyd's (*q.v.*), a London corporation whose members are mainly, though not wholly, engaged in insuring ships and their cargoes. Before a ship can be insured it has to be classified by Lloyd's Register, a committee of shipowners and others whose surveyors examine all ships built to its requirements and classify them according to their seaworthiness, 100 A1 being the highest class.

Aachen, (Pron. ah′khen), GERMANY. It was the year 1000 after Christ, and many believed the end of the world was at hand. Otto III, the ruler of the Holy Roman Empire, had come to Aachen, the old German capital 44 miles west of the Rhine, intending to open the sacred tomb of Charlemagne: there was a legend that in time of dire need the great emperor would return to help his people. The tomb lay under a marble slab beneath the dome of the chapel which Charlemagne himself had built, with marble columns and other materials taken from the classical structures of Rome, Ravenna and some other great Italian cities.

When the royal sepulchre was opened the torch's flickering light disclosed a strange sight. The body of the great emperor, clothed in white, was seated on a huge marble throne. One of the hands held a sceptre and on the head was the imperial crown. The spirit of the man who 200 years before had founded an empire greater than the world had seen since the days of the Roman Caesars seemed to survive in death. Before the commanding dignity of that huge figure the young emperor quailed.

AACHEN'S IMPERIAL THRONE
On this throne in the cathedral at Aachen the body of Charlemagne, with crown on head, orb and sceptre in his hands and the imperial mantle on his shoulders, rested for over 350 years.

The torch fell from his grasp and he rushed out of the tomb, ordering the stone to be replaced. Two years later Otto III died and was buried in that same chapel above the tomb.

One hundred and sixty years later the tomb was again opened, this time by the Emperor Frederick Barbarossa. The marble throne, the c r o w n, and the sceptre of Charlemagne were taken to add dignity and strength to Frederick's imperial projects, and the bones of Charlemagne were placed in a shrine north of the chapel, where they remain today. Between the 9th and 16th centuries 32 emperors and kings of Germany were crowned in that marble chair. The chapel and tomb of Charlemagne, now the central part of the cathedral of Aachen, are the heart of the city. Aachen is believed to have been the great emperor's birthplace, but it owes its historic fame to Charlemagne's fondness for its hot sulphur springs which led him to make it his favourite place of residence. These unfailing springs made Aachen a famous resort for health-seeking visitors from all parts of Europe. Near by Charlemagne built his palace and held his court. Here were gathered the great scholars of the day, teaching in the Palace School, and the gay life of the court went forward merrily.

Two important treaties were concluded at meetings or congresses held at Aachen, or Aix-la-Chapelle (pron. āks-lah-sha-pel′) as it is named in French. The first, signed in 1668, ended a war begun by Louis XIV of France to enforce certain rights claimed on behalf of his wife in what was then the Spanish Netherlands (now Belgium). The other, in 1748, ended the War of the Austrian Succession. Aachen became a part of the kingdom of Prussia in 1815. After the fall of Napoleon, representatives of the allied powers, Britain, Austria, Prussia and Russia, met there to discuss the future of France and European affairs generally.

It was from here that the German surprise attack on Belgium was launched in 1914 at the beginning of the First World War, and it was for a time the headquarters of the Kaiser. Again, in 1940, in the Second World War, it was one of the vantage points from which German armies overran Belgium and Holland; and when on October 20, 1944, Aachen was taken by American forces, after intensive bombardment, only a skeleton of the city remained. Charlemagne's cathedral, from which his shrine and relics had been removed (temporarily) to a place of safety when the attack began, was one of the few buildings still standing.

Aardvark. (Pron. ahrd′vark). Nature must have fashioned the aardvark in one of her playful moods. She arched its body and coated it with yellowish hair; on a short neck she set a long head adorned with great ears and a tubular snout; then she gave it a naked tapering tail.

This grotesque mammal was discovered by the Boer settlers who moved out into the South African veld in the 17th century. There they found it rooting about at dusk among the termite or " white

ant " mounds that dot this region.
Because of this and its habit of burrowing rapidly into the ground when
frightened they gave it the name
aardvark, which is the Dutch for
" earth-pig."

It is a harmless, timid beast, that
feeds mostly by night, sleeping away
the hot daylight hours in a deep cool
burrow. Its strong feet are armed
with blunt, powerful claws, with which
it rips open the stout walls of the termite mounds. As the insects swarm
from their stronghold, the aardvark
sweeps them up with its long sticky
tongue. Aardvark meat is relished by
the African natives and by many predatory animals. Since only one young
is born to an aardvark mother in a
year, it is not surprising to find that
the weird-looking creature is nowhere
numerous. It is about five feet long.

Two species are recognized—the
Cape aardvark of South Africa and the
northern aardvark of Abyssinia and
other parts of north-eastern Africa.
Despite their name they are not related to the pig but are classified in
an order by themselves, the *Tubulidentata*. The
scientific name of the South African aardvark is
Orycteropus capensis ; that of the northern aardvark
is *Orycteropus aethiopicus.*

W. S. Berridge

AARDVARK, ONE OF NATURE'S FREAKS

The aardvark of Africa is similar to the anteaters in that it has a long
slimy tongue with which to catch insects, but is unlike in having teeth. It
can bury itself under the ground very quickly, and sleeps in a deep burrow.

Abbotsford. When Sir Walter Scott
(1771–1832) was a boy he sometimes travelled with
his father from Selkirk to Melrose in Roxburghshire
(border county of Scotland). At a certain spot
the old gentleman would stop the carriage and
take his son to a stone on the site of the battle of
Melrose, fought in 1526 between the Scotts and
their rivals, the Douglases and Kers. Not far
away was a little farm called Clartyhole, and this
the writer of the Waverley Novels and The Lady
of the Lake eventually purchased, in 1812.

In due course the farmhouse was turned into a
wonderful home that has been likened to a veritable
fairy palace. Through windows enriched with
the insignia of heraldry the sun shone on suits of
armour, trophies of the chase, fine furniture, and
still finer pictures. Panelling of oak and cedar
and finely carved ceilings relieved by coats of arms
in their correct colour added to the beauty of the
great writer's treasure-house. More land was
purchased, until Sir Walter Scott
owned nearly 1,000 acres, and it is
estimated that the building cost him
over £25,000. A neighbouring Roman
road with a ford used in olden days by
the abbots of Melrose suggested the
name of Abbotsford for the estate.
(*See* Scott, Sir Walter).

Abbreviations. In writing compositions and in printing
articles in books, magazines and newspapers, certain abbreviations, sanctioned by established custom, are often
used. Lists of abbreviations are given
in the Fact-Index and in all good
dictionaries. Examples are : £ s. d.,
standing for *librae, solidi, denarii,* the
Latin words for Roman money, used
for our pounds, shillings, pence; MS.,
manuscript; Mr., mister; Mrs., mistress; Esq., Esquire; oz., ounce; e.g.,
exempli gratia, Latin for " for example ";
q.v., *quod vide,* " which see "; i.e., *id est,*
meaning " that is."

The following are Latin terms, except
where otherwise stated A.D., *Anno
Domini,* in the year of the Lord; ad
lib., *ad libitum,* as desired; a.m., *ante*

Annan

ABBOTSFORD HOME OF SIR WALTER SCOTT

**Sir Walter Scott was never happier than when he was at Abbotsford, his
beautiful home on the banks of the Tweed near Melrose. Here he passed the
last twenty years of his life, in the midst of the romantic Border country,
dispensing, until the last sad years, a princely hospitality.**

meridiem, before noon ; A.V. (Brit.), *Authorised Version* (of Bible) ; *Cantuar. Cantuariensis*, of Canterbury (Archbishop's signature) ; cet. par., *ceteris paribus*, other things being equal ; Consols. (Brit.), Consolidated Funds ; D.G.. *Deo gratia*, by the grace of God ; D.V., *Deo volente*, God willing.

Ebor., *Eboracensis*, of York (Archbishop's signature) ; *et cetera*, and other things ; fec., *fecit*, he made ; Fid. Def., *Fidei Defensor*, Defender of the Faith ; fl., *floruit*, he flourished ; Gestapo, *Geheime Staatspolizei* (German), Secret State Police ; ib., ibid., *ibidem*, in the same place.

Incog., *incognito* (Italian), unknown ; infra dig., *infra dignitatem*, beneath dignity ; inst., *instante mense*, in the present month ; int. al., *inter alia*, among other things ; Lit. Hum., *Literae Humaniores*, Oxford examination in classics.

Memo., *memorandum*, to be remembered ; N.B., *nota bene*, note well ; nem. con., *nemine contradicente*, nobody expressing dissent ; non obst., *non obstante*, notwithstanding ; non seq., *non sequitur*, it does not follow ; ob., *obiit*, died ; op., *opus*, published work ; PAYE (British), pay as you earn (Income Tax) ; per pro., *per procurationem*, by proxy, on behalf of ; pinx., *pinxit*, he painted ; p.m., *post meridiem*, after noon ; pro tem., *pro tempore*, for the time being ; prox., *proximo mense*, in the next month.

P.S., *postscriptum*, additional writing ; q.e.d., *quod erat demonstrandum*, which was to be shown ; R.V. (British), Revised Version (of the Bible) ; S.A., *Sturm Abteilung* (German), Storm Division ; S.S., *Schutz Staffel* (German), Security Squadron ; T.S.F.. *télégraphie, téléphonie, sans fil* (French), wireless ; ult., *ultimo mense*, in the last month.

Abélard, PIERRE (1079–1142).

All was astir about the cathedral of Paris—not the great Gothic Notre Dame of our day, but its plainer and smaller predecessor of the early 12th century. For the morning bell had rung and from the taverns and hospices and boarding-houses a motley stream of students, laughing and chattering in a mixture of Latin and their mother tongues, was pouring into the enclosures to listen to the lectures of the various masters. In the class-rooms they sat upon the straw-strewn floor, the right knee raised to support the waxed tablets, and for six or seven hours they industriously took notes. In those days books were few and the teaching was almost all by word of mouth.

Of all the masters, Abélard (pron. ab′ā-lar) was the most learned and, too, the most brilliant. The eldest son of a noble family in Brittany, he had left castle, the chase, and the life of a noble in pursuit of knowledge, for his ambition was to become a scholar. For a time he himself had studied in Paris; but he soon surpassed his teacher in learning, and at the early age of 22 he too had become a master and had begun to teach. He was especially interested in logic, or the art of reasoning. Later he became proficient in theology also, and was soon known as the leading scholar of his time. Students flocked by thousands to hear his lectures, and his books in hand-written copies—especially " Sic et Non " (" Yes and No ")—were

read by all learned men. This book was so called because it was made up of such questions as the following:

Should human faith be based upon reason, or no ?
Is God one, or no ?
Is God a substance, or no ?

Then came Abélard's romantic but unhappy love affair with Héloïse, a beautiful and accomplished girl, one of his pupils. As marriage would interfere with his prospects in the Church, Abélard and Héloïse were secretly united. Their marriage soon became known and they separated in circumstances of the greatest pain and unhappiness.

Abélard retired to a monastery, and Héloïse became a nun. He continued to teach, but his popularity made enemies for him among those who were jealous of his influence, and others disagreed with his teachings. For he taught that nothing should be accepted unless it could be *proved* true, while they believed that religious faith should come first. These opponents, led by Saint Bernard of Clairvaux, finally triumphed, and Abélard was condemned as a heretic. Broken in health, he died a year later. But his fame lived after him, and largely as a result of his teachings the University of Paris became the chief centre of learning in Europe.

The noble character of Héloïse, as shown in her letters to Abélard after their separation, has won the admiration of all ages. When she died, after living long as a nun, she was buried by his side

ABÉLARD AND HIS HÉLOISE
One of the greatest and most tragic love-stories in history is that of Abélard and Héloise, and here we see the famous scholar's effigy beside that of his wife on their sepulchre in a Paris cemetery. This imposing tomb was erected in 1817 by admirers of his genius.

at the abbey of Nogent where she had been abbess. Later their remains were removed to Paris, where they now rest in the cemetery of Père-Lachaise.

Aberdeen, SCOTLAND.

Rushing southward every weekday from this third largest city of Scotland, go express trains carrying the catch of the sturdy North Sea fishermen—herring, halibut, sole, and the like—to the markets of London; for Aberdeen rivals Grimsby, the English fishing port in Lincolnshire, as a centre of the British steam trawling industry.

Aberdeen is situated on the North Sea, between the mouths of the rivers Don and Dee, 130 miles north-east of Edinburgh, and is the chief city of northern Scotland as well as the county town of Aberdeenshire. It is sometimes called the " Silver City by the Sea" because of the gleam of its grey granite buildings, especially after a heavy fall of

chief city and by far the largest centre (*see* Aberdeen), is 1,970 square miles in extent, and has, especially in its south-western corner, a beauty and wildness that is difficult to surpass even in Scotland. For it is in this part, near the centre of the country, that the Grampians (Britain's nearest approach to real mountains) send out various branches towards the north-east, including the Cairngorm group, whose highest point is Ben Macdhui (4,296 ft.).

In the valley of the river Dee are Braemar, scene of annual Highland Games, and Balmoral Castle (*q.v.*). The Dee and the other rivers of Aberdeenshire, including the Don and Ythan, are

rain. From the fine-quality granite quarried in the neighbourhood is derived its title of the " Granite City." In addition to its fishing fleet, fish-curing establishments and granite quarries, it has large manufactures of woollen and linen and cotton goods, paper, jams and preserved foods. Other industrial installations include large breweries, distilleries, and chemical and printing works, and shipbuilding yards. The city's most famous street is Union Street, on which are the municipal buildings and other fine public edifices. The First World War memorial, attached to the art gallery and museum, was opened by King George V in 1925. Of the older buildings, the most noted is St. Machar's Cathedral, the remaining parts of which (dating from the 14th century) are in use as the parish church. The docks cover about 97 acres.

Aberdeen University consists of two colleges—King's, in Old Aberdeen, founded in 1494, and Marischal, in New Aberdeen, founded in 1593, the latter being an imposing building constructed in white granite. The population is about 189,300.

Aberdeenshire. The Scottish county of Aberdeen, in which the city of that name is the

ABERDEEN'S NOBLE COLLEGES AND BUSY DOCKS

While it is still in some ways a country town Aberdeen, " the capital of the Highlands," is also a great educational centre. King's College (top), founded in 1494, is the oldest college of the University. Marischal College (centre), which with King's constitutes Aberdeen's University, was rebuilt and enlarged between 1837 and 1841. At the docks (lower) the fishing fleet responsible for Aberdeen's greatest industry is based ; in the centre of this view the spire of Marischal College can be seen. The city formerly consisted of two towns, Old and New Aberdeen, amalgamated in 1891.

well stocked with salmon and trout. Agriculture is carried on, particularly in the fertile north-east, and fishing, stone-quarrying and textile manufactures are important. The largest towns, apart from Aberdeen, are Peterhead and Fraserburgh (on the coast) and Huntly and Inverurie (inland). Population is over 300,000.

Abraham. Some two thousand years before Christ, at a time when the Egyptian and Babylonian civilizations were already grown old, there dwelt at Ur in the land of Chaldaea—which was at the junction of the Tigris and Euphrates rivers —a man named Abram. In Genesis, the

Sir L. Woolley and Joint Expedition; " The Times "

ABRAHAM'S CITY IN BABYLONIA

Ur of the Chaldees in Babylonia was Abraham's birthplace. It has been excavated by archaeologists, and here we see (above) a street called Quiet in the ancient city and (left) a reconstruction of a dwelling-house there.

command of Jehovah and his rescue is one of the best-known stories of the Old Testament. According to the Bible narrative (Genesis xi-xxv) Abraham died at the age of 175 years and was buried at the side of Sarah at Machpelah. (*See also* Ur).

Abyssinia. When Portuguese explorers in the 15th century first made their way from the coast of the Red Sea into eastern Africa, they found in the midst of its wild mountains what they thought was the kingdom of Prester John, a fabled Christian monarch, whose power and wealth were the theme of many a medieval legend.

There was some basis for this belief, for in the 4th century A.D., Abyssinia had been converted to Christianity. Then the Mahomedan Arabs swept over northern Africa in the 7th century, cutting off the country from civilization. What the Portuguese explorers found was a strange remnant of this primitive Christianity. Before its conquest by the Arabs the country was called Ethiopia, but the

first book of the Bible, we have his life-story, and are told how the Lord said unto him:

" Get thee out of thy country, and from thy kindred, and from thy father's house, unto a land that I will show thee. And I will make of thee a great nation, and I will bless thee, and make thy name great."

So Abraham, as he was later named, journeyed westward at the call of God to a new land, and settled in Palestine. There he led a patriarchal life, surrounded by his flocks and herds, man-servants and maid-servants, sons and daughters. Thus he who was " called the Friend of God " became the founder of the Hebrew nation.

Abraham was accompanied in his migration by his wife Sarai (whose name was later changed to Sarah), and by his nephew Lot, whose wife was turned into a pillar of salt at the destruction of the cities of Sodom and Gomorrah. A son Isaac was born to Abraham and Sarah in their old age and became heir, to the exclusion of his half-brother Ishmael. The intended sacrifice of Isaac at the

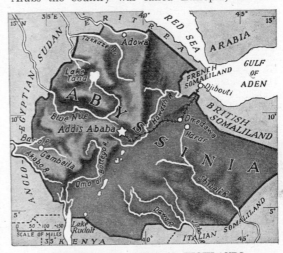

ABYSSINIA IN AFRICA'S HIGHLANDS

This ancient kingdom, cut off from civilization, was rarely visited by European travellers until the 19th century.

13

ABYSSINIA'S GRIM AND BARREN MOUNTAINS

This landscape illustrates the rugged nature of much of Abyssinia. The photograph was taken from the caravan route between Addis Ababa and Dessie, which sometimes rises to a height of 11.000 feet and, despite many bends, takes motor traffic.

Arabs gave it the scornful name of Abyssinia, from their word *habesh* or *habeshi*, meaning a mongrel. The name Ethiopia is now again in official use.

In the 18th and 19th centuries one or two European travellers managed to enter the country, but in general it remained cut off from the outside world very much as described by Dr. Johnson in his book Rasselas. At that time it was divided into the three kingdoms of Tigré, Amhara and Shoa, with the ruler of Amhara as its overlord, a position however, maintained only by constant warfare.

This period came to an end when an Abyssinian adventurer called Theodore secured the supreme power. In 1868 he imprisoned the British consul and other officials, and the British Government sent an expedition to free them. The capital, which at that time was Magdala, was stormed and taken after fierce fighting, and Theodore, deserted by his followers, committed suicide.

After a spell of unrest Menelik II became ruler of the whole of the country, and in his reign occurred the first war between the Italians and the Abyssinians. Italy had established colonies on the coast of the Red Sea and sought to extend her power inland. Abyssinia was invaded, but the Italian army met with disaster at Adowa on March 1, 1896. Peace was made and the independence of Abyssinia recognized. Menelik, who in 1908 founded his country's first boys' grammar school, the Menelik Lyceum, died in 1913 and was succeeded by a grandson, Lij Yasu; but he was deposed in 1916 because of his Turkish sympathies. The next ruler was Menelik's daughter, who reigned under the regency of Ras Tafari, a great-nephew of Menelik, until her death in 1930. Ras Tafari was then crowned emperor, taking the name of Haile Selassie. The " King of Kings " (Negus Negusti), as he calls himself, claims descent from King Solomon and the Queen of Sheba.

In 1906 Britain, France and Italy agreed to respect Abyssinia's frontiers, and treaties were made

with Italy giving her the port of Assab on the Red Sea and the right to construct a motor road to it. The country became a member of the League of Nations in 1923, and in 1931 a system of constitutional government was instituted.

Following incidents in 1934 and 1935 at Walwal, near Italian Somaliland, Italy invaded Abyssinia in October 1935. The League of Nations decided that Italy was the aggressor; and economic

G.P.A.

UNCHANGED FOR CENTURIES

The people of Abyssinia still employ the simple implements used by their forefathers from time immemorial. This Abyssinian farmer is crushing grain with a pestle and mortar, the latter formed from a tree trunk.

" sanctions " were applied against her, but with little effect. The Italians, employing aerial bombardments and poison gas attacks from the air, succeeded in occupying the principal Abyssinian towns, and on May 1, 1936, Haile Selassie fled to England. Four days later Abyssinia was proclaimed an Italian colony, and despite the moving appeal of the emperor to the League of Nations, Great Britain and most of the other great nations had recognized the Italian conquest by 1938.

When Italy declared war on Great Britain in 1940, British and Imperial troops invaded Abyssinia, at the same time organizing bands of Abyssinian patriot " irregulars." The emperor Haile Selassie returned to his capital, Addis Ababa, on May 5, 1941, and by the end of the following November the country was clear of Italian forces. In January 1942 Abyssinia was once more recog ized as a sovereign independent state by a treaty with Great Britain, who sent out technical advisers.

The area of Abyssinia is about 350,000 square miles. Its population has never been accurately determined, and has been variously estimated at between 5,500,000 and 10,000,000. Of these about one-third are of the ruling race, the Amhara,

and more than one-half Gallas; the rest are Somalis, Falashas of Jewish origin, Negroes, and a few Greeks and Armenians. Addis Ababa has about 150,000 inhabitants, the only other towns of important size being Dire Dawa (30,000), the old walled city of Harar (40,000), and Gondar (22,000).

The country has always been backward, the people being chiefly engaged in pastoral pursuits and their agricultural methods primitive. Minerals and oil are known to exist, but have been very little developed. There is only one railway, operated by the French government, and connecting Addis Ababa with the port of Djibouti in French Somaliland. During the Italian occupation great strides

ADDIS ABABA IS ABYSSINIA'S ANCIENT CAPITAL

During the Italian occupation of Addis Ababa, 1936–41, some changes were made in the streets, and new buildings of European design began to appear among the old houses of mud and stone. The upper photograph shows a cinema in Abyssinia's capital. In contrast to such up-to-dateness is the market place (lower), crowded every day by traders who sell or barter local products, including leather goods, baskets, pottery, metal ware, grain, tobacco and cotton.

ABYSSINIA'S MARKET TOWN OF HARAR
The towns of Abyssinia are mostly built of mud and stones, and this photograph of a street in Harar, an ancient market town in the province of the same name, shows the primitive architecture and a typical group of those who have their homes within its massive walls.

were made in road-building, and Abyssinia now has over 4,000 miles of motor-road, linking the principal cities. A network of airlines was started in 1947. The chief river is the Blue Nile, which has its source in Lake Tsana.

The official language is Amharic, although some 70 dialects are spoken. There also exists a classical language, used in the Coptic Christian churches, called Giz.

Acacia. (Pron. *a*-kā'-sh*a*). All over the warmer parts of the earth— especially in Australia, Africa, and South and Central America—are to be found the thorny, pod-bearing shrubs and trees of this great genus of plants. Gum-arabic and gum-senegal are produced by certain African species, while the bark of some Australian ones (known as " wattles ") is used in tanning. The pods of a few African acacias (especially that called " neb-neb ") are also rich in tannin, and the seeds of one species which grows in South America are roasted and used as snuff. Other acacias furnish drugs or timber.

The acacias, of which there are about 550 species, belong to the family *Leguminosae* and the sub-family *Mimosaceae*.

The false acacia, or locust tree, is often called acacia; it belongs to another branch of the family. The name acacia comes from the Greek *akis*, meaning " point " or " barb." Some of the shrubs reach a height of over 20 feet. Many fine acacia trees are to be seen in English parks, where they were planted for their attractive plumes of foliage.

Academy. The original "academy" was founded by the Greek philosopher Plato in ancient Athens, and was so called from the name of the grove Academia where he used to walk and talk with his disciples. The word came to mean an association for promoting literature, philosophy, science, or art, and many such flourished in Italy in the days of the Renaissance. The most famous academy today is the French Academy.

Let us suppose that it is the day of the annual meeting of the French Academy, and the members file ceremoniously into their hall in Paris to occupy the arm-chairs of the " Forty Immortals." They are the most prominent living masters of French literature, and election to their body is considered the highest honour that can be bestowed on a French writer. One of the chairs is vacant, for its occupant in the past year has been removed by the hand of death. Presently one of the academicians rises and introduces a candidate. The works of the candidate are known to all ; he has paid the required visits to each of the members, and the necessary majority vote in his favour has been given. His sponsor wittily—sometimes rather sharply—characterizes him and his work, and the candidate responds good-humouredly, praising especially the deceased member to whose seat he has been chosen. So, with due ceremony, the circle of the Immortals is once more made complete.

Australian Information News Bureau
ACACIA IS AUSTRALIA'S EMBLEM
Of the many varieties of acacia to be found in Australia the wattle, with its masses of fragile golden blossom, is the best known. It is in flower somewhere or other in that vast continent throughout the year, and it is the national symbol of the Commonwealth.

The French Academy was founded by the great Cardinal Richelieu in 1635, and it still serves as a supreme court in all matters relating to the French language and literary style. The award of one of its twenty-three prizes to a French literary work is the supreme recognition of excellence. With four similar organizations—for Inscriptions, Science, Fine Arts, and Moral and Political Sciences — the Academy constitutes the Institute of France, established in 1795. Napoleon valued his membership in this distinguished organization so highly that he put after his name in his proclamations as General-in-Chief the words " member of the Institute."

In Britain there is a British Academy for the promotion of historical and philosophical studies, and the Royal Academy of Arts for painting, sculpture, and architecture. The Royal Academy, founded in 1768, has its headquarters at Burlington

National Museum, Naples   *Alinari*

ACADEMY OF PLATO

The first Academy was the school held by the Greek philosopher Plato in the shaded grove of the Academia, in Athens. This mosaic, found at Pompeii, is believed to show a class of Plato's Academy in session.

Royal Academy of Dramatic Art, the Royal Academy of Music, and the Royal Military Academy (Sandhurst).

Acadia. (Pron. a-kā'-di-a). On September 5, 1755, a group of some 400 men—French settlers in that district of the New World which we call Nova Scotia and which they named *Acadie* —were assembled in the church of Grand Pré, on an arm of the Bay of Fundy. Forty-two years before, France had ceded Acadia to Great Britain; but the inhabitants had clung to their French speech and sympathies, and in recent hostilities some of them had even taken up arms with their neighbours of French Canada against the King. Now they were assembled to hear " his Majesty's intentions " with reference to them.

Briefly those " intentions " included the deportation of the male Acadians who refused to take an unconditional oath of allegiance to the British sovereign. Some 6,000—men, women and children—were thus expelled and settled in the English colonies, from Massachusetts to Georgia. The story of Longfellow's poem Evangeline dea's with the dispersal of these Acadians and the search of the maiden Evangeline for the lover from whom she had been separated on their marriage-day.

Accounting Machine.

The old-fashioned ledgers and other account books, in which entries were made by hand, have very largely been replaced today by loose-leaf records. The leaves are sometimes punched at the margin to fit over studs or screws in a cover or binder; generally they are kept in metal ledger trays. They are arranged in alphabetical order, and old or filled-up sheets can be taken out and new ones put in at will. Above all these advantages over the old-fashioned fixed-leaf book is the one that the sheets can be filled in on a typewriter, and mechanically accurate duplicates taken with carbon paper, speeding up the accounting process and doing away with errors due to indistinct handwriting.

From this it was only a short step to fit the typewriter with an adding device like that used on many cash registers, which totalled the items and, when a lever was moved, printed this total at the foot of the column. So we got an accounting machine, which not only adds and subtracts the items but prints them neatly in a tabulated record like that shown here.

				IN ACCOUNT WITH
Richard Roe				**ANY BANK LIMITED**
1234 High Street				
Longwater				
Somewhere				LONDON, W.1

DATE	PAYMENTS		RECEIPTS		BALANCE
	DESCRIPTION	AMOUNT	DESCRIPTION	AMOUNT	
			BALANCE FORWARD		
JAN 1'47					231.17. 6
JAN 2'47	VINCENT F	21.13.11			
	JONES W	10. 0. 0			
	TURNER G	27.16. 6			
	DEPOSIT ACCOUNT	300. 0. 0			
	CHEQUE BOOK	4. 0			
	GRANT H	1. 1. 0	DIV £234.15.0. HUDSON BAY	19.16. 6	
			CASH	23.17. 0	85. 4. 5OD
JAN 3'47	FOSTER L	49.17. 6			
	VERNON T W	50. 2. 6	CASH	200. 0. 0	14.15. 7

Burroughs Adding Machine Ltd.

ACCOUNTING MACHINE'S NEAT RECORD

Part of the record of someone's banking account, this detailed statement was prepared in one operation on a bank typewriter-accounting machine. A debit balance (here shown ringed) was emphasised in red and followed by the warning letters OD (overdrawn).

House, London, where an annual exhibition is given of works by living artists, for whom election as R.A. (Royal Academician) is a signal honour, as only a limited number are permitted at a time.

The word academy is also used in some countries as a name for schools for boys and girls similar to high schools. Most of these academies were founded before the present system of universal education arose, and were often fostered by churches, religious societies, or organizations interested in military training. Schools for specialized training are also often called academies. Thus we have the

The mechanism of adding machines (most of them do other arithmetical operations besides addition) is explained in our story of Calculating Machines; everything is done by toothed wheels which advance one or more steps according to the number that is being registered. If Britain used decimal coinage our machine would merely need wheels with ten teeth on each; unfortunately, our machine must be able to make steps of one-twelfth and one-twentieth, for pence, shillings and pounds; thence we can go on with ten-toothed wheels for tens, hundreds and thousands of pounds, and so on.

Accuracy Gained and Time Saved

So far we have told how the machine adds together items while it prints them, But we also want to show the customer's payments on the account sheet. Sometimes credits for money received or allowances made are printed in red, this being done by an automatic ribbon-shift device. The accounting machine, when such an item is printed, can be arranged to subtract the amount from the total of debits, and to print the balance underneath (or in a separate column). Customers' statements, as issued by banks, are made out like this ; the account at the end of each day's entries, whether of money paid in or drawn out, is balanced. Banks generally use the red colour for a warning, and if the customer has drawn out more money than stands to his credit, the debit balance may be printed in red, and the letters " OD " or " DR " shown alongside the item.

When invoices, or monthly statements, are being made out on an accounting machine, the machine will keep a running total of all the separate totals, so that we know at the end of the task just how much money we have debited in the various bills or statements. Each individual total, as printed by operating the keys, is added to the grand total by further wheels of the counting mechanism. Laborious and time-wasting calculation is done away with ; as soon as the last invoice of the batch has been typed out, we have the grand total for the day ! Machine accounting has worked wonders in lessening labour and—above all—in bringing about more accurate accounting. But the operator, like the ledger clerk of olden times, must of course do his part accurately.

Acetylene. (Pron. *a*-set'-i-lēn). One of the most active and useful gases, acetylene is produced commercially by the action of water on calcium carbide. (Calcium carbide is made by heating a mixture of lime, chemically named calcium oxide, and coke, which is a form of carbon; the mixture is heated to the required degree in an electric arc furnace.)

Early types of lamp for cycles and motor-cars used acetylene, produced by letting water from a container above

Firth, Brown and Co. Ltd.
OXYACETYLENE CUTTING TORCH
Combination of a special powder with the intensely hot flame of the torch wielded by this goggled operator enables stainless steel plate to be cut to shape as readily as any ordinary steel.

drip into a receptacle containing the calcium carbide ; a pipe from the carbide receptacle led to a jet in front of a reflector, where the gas burnt with an intensely bright flame. Lamps used for lighting streets in foggy weather, or for illuminating road and building works at night, work on the same principle, though the water is admitted in a more efficient manner. Portable generators which make acetylene for welding and cutting metal operate on the same principle, though today acetylene is usually supplied in steel cylinders under pressure, the gas then being dissolved in acetone.

Acetone is made by distilling wood; about 300 volumes of acetylene will dissolve in one volume of acetone, and the gas is more easily and safely transported in this dissolved condition. The cylinders are packed with a porous material such as kapok or charcoal in order to distribute the dissolved gas and thus lessen the danger of explosion.

Acetylene is a compound of carbon and hydrogen (C_2H_2). The flame owes its brilliance to the exceptionally large number of carbon particles that are set free inside the flame. Unable to burn up immediately because air does not reach them, they glow intensely in the flame's heat. If, however, enough oxygen is used with the acetylene to consume this free carbon, the flame loses its brilliance and gains in heat. The oxyacetylene blowpipe or torch is designed to take advantage of this fact. It gives one of the hottest known flames (6,300° F.) which is capable of cutting through the hardest steel by actually burning away the metal in its path. The flame is also much used for welding.

In a cutting torch, the oxygen is fed around the outside of the flame so that it not only helps to burn the acetylene more rapidly but helps also to oxidize or burn the metal to be cut. In a welding torch the oxygen is fed to the interior of the flame and only in such quantity as will be consumed there; thus the metal melts instead of burning. (*See* Welding).

Acetylene is the raw material out of which is manufactured acetaldehyde, which in turn may be made into acetic acid or into ethyl alcohol. Acetaldehyde is the parent also of many vinyl compounds, which are important in Plastics. From vinyl acetylene was produced one of the earliest types of synthetic rubber.

When water is dripped on to calcium carbide a vigorous reaction takes place, and heat is absorbed from the surrounding air or the wall of the vessel in which the carbide and water are contained. The carbide and water combine, producing (1) acetylene gas and (2) calcium hydroxide, which is the chemist's name for slaked lime. When acetylene breaks up again, as it does on burning in the welding or cutting torch, the energy previously absorbed in the chemical reaction between water and carbide is given out once more as heat. This heat, added to that produced by the oxidation of the carbon, is the cause of the very high temperature of the acetylene flame. While acetylene, of course, will burn in air, a more complete burning can be produced if oxygen is fed to the flame — for it is the oxygen contained in air which ordinarily sustains the flame, and the more oxygen we give, up to a certain limit, the fiercer is the combustion.

Achilles. (Pron. *a*-kil′-ēz). Of all the many Greeks who fought in the war against T r o y, the bravest was Achilles, son of Peleus, king of the Myrmidons. His mother, the sea-goddess Thetis, was warned that her son was doomed to an early death, and had sought to ward off this fate by dipping him as a babe in the dark waters of the River Styx, which flows through the underworld, so that no weapon could wound him. Phoenix taught him the art of war, and the centaur Chiron music and medicine.

To prevent him going to the Trojan War, his mother dressed him as a girl and hid him among the maidens at the court of the king of Scyros. Thither came Odysseus (Ulysses), the wisest of the Greeks, disguised as a pedlar. When he had spread his wares before the laughing, chattering girls, he suddenly sounded an alarm of war. The frightened girls ran screaming away, but the disguised Achilles betrayed himself by seizing a spear and shield from

' ACHILLES ' IN A LONDON PARK
This statue in Hyde Park, London, described on its pedestal as Achilles, could well be an impression of the Greek warrior; but it is in fact a reproduction from a Roman monument. It was erected in 1822 as a tribute to the Duke of Wellington.

Fox

the pedlar's stock. So, yielding to his destiny, the young hero joined his countrymen.

Achilles went to war with 50 ships and became renowned as the greatest warrior of all the Greek hosts. During the first nine years of the struggle he captured 12 cities around Troy. Then he quarrelled with Agamemnon, the leader of the Greeks, over a maid Briseis, whom he loved. When she was taken from him, he sulked in his tent, refusing to fight, and the Greeks were hard pressed. At last his friend Patroclus, wearing the armour of Achilles, drove the enemy before him, until he was himself slain by Hector, the leader of the Trojans. Enraged at the death of his friend, Achilles went forth again to battle, equipped with new armour which his mother prevailed upon Hephaestus to make. Achilles drove the Trojans within their walls and in single combat killed Hector, whom he dragged round the walls of the city at the tail of his chariot.

Here ends the account in the Iliad, which deals only with " the wrath of Achilles "; but the story is taken up by other writers. These tell how Achilles was slain some time later while driving the Trojans back to the city gates. The god Apollo, it is said, angered by the death of Hector, guided the arrow to the one spot on Achilles' body that was vulnerable—that part of the heel by which Thetis had held him when she dipped him into the Styx. This part of our bodies is still called " the tendon of Achilles," and we sometimes refer to the weak point in a man's character as " the heel of Achilles."

The SHIELD of ACHILLES

WHEN the grievous tidings were borne to Achilles that Patroclus, clad in Achilles' armour, was slain, he poured dust over his head and tore his hair in anguish. His mother, Thetis, the sea-goddess, heard from afar her son's lamentation and sped to his side.

" My child, why weepest thou? What sorrow hath come to thy heart? "

Achilles made answer: " My dear comrade is dead; Patroclus, whom I honoured above all others as though he were my very self. My soul biddeth

me also live no longer if Hector be not smitten by my spear and die for the slaughter of Patroclus."

Thetis, the silver-footed goddess, sped straight to Olympus, the abode of the gods, to the forge of Hephaestus. In his youth she had befriended the lame god and now he was eager to help her. She told him of her son's trouble, and asked Hephaestus to make for Achilles new armour such as never yet was borne by man.

The divine smith set to work and made a breastplate, and a great helmet ridged with gold, and also greaves to protect the hero's thighs. Most wonderful of all was the shield, whereon Hephaestus wrought great wonders of metal in bronze, gold, tin, and silver wire. There he fashioned cunningly the sea, the earth, the sky and all its stars, the sun, and the moon. There were images of two cities, one at peace and one at war. In the peaceful city was a wedding and happy girls were singing. In the city at war were men defending it, who stood on its walls, while by a stream hid warriors, to spring on the cattle and herdsmen of their enemies as they came to drink.

In another part of the shield was pictured a field with ploughmen at work, while in still another the harvest was being reaped. He also pictured a vineyard with men and maidens going down a path carrying baskets of grapes upon their heads, and a dance of maids and men, most delicately wrought.

Thetis received gladly these god-made arms that no mortal could pierce, and brought and laid them at the feet of her son. Terrible as a god, his glittering armour blinding the eyes of the Trojans, his stature and strength filling their hearts with fear and trembling, Achilles led forth his men to battle.— *Retold from Homer's Iliad, Book xviii.*

Acids and Alkalis.

Acids and alkalis are chemical opposites and cannot get along together. Whenever they meet, there is a disturbance. Yet this very opposition provides much of the world's most useful energy. There is hardly a life process or an industry in which they do not play a part.

To most people acid means something that is sour, and it is true that this is characteristic of most acids. But a chemist defines an acid as a hydrogen compound in which the hydrogen can be replaced by a metal. The other part of the compound is called the acid radical. For example, in sulphuric acid (H_2SO_4) one atom of sulphur and four of oxygen form the acid radical which is joined to two atoms of hydrogen.

If a piece of copper is put into a sulphuric acid solution, a rapid reaction takes place. Hydrogen is set free and copper unites with the acid radical to form copper sulphate ($CuSO_4$).

The strongest acids are the mineral or inorganic acids, like sulphuric, nitric, and hydrochloric. More important to life are the weaker organic acids, like acetic (in vinegar), citric (in lemons), lactic (in milk), and the amino acids (in proteins).

A strong alkali is a caustic, soapy substance. A weak alkali, which chemists usually call a base or a basic compound, is less easily distinguished. But whether called alkalis or bases, all members of this group contain one or more oxygen-hydrogen units (OH). This unit is called the hydroxyl radical and acts in many chemical exchanges as if it were a single element. The other part of the alkali or base is usually a metal or a combination of atoms that acts like a metal. For example, caustic soda is a compound of the metal sodium (Na) with the hydroxyl radical and is called by chemists sodium hydroxide (NaOH).

Now we can see why an acid and an alkali react so readily. An acid has hydrogen to exchange for metal. An alkali has a metal to exchange for hydrogen. When the two meet, the exchange is often so violent as to be almost explosive. For example, if we bring together hydrochloric acid (HCl) and sodium hydroxide (NaOH) we get the following reaction : $HCl + NaOH = NaCl + HOH$. The sodium from the alkali has displaced the hydrogen in the acid and has united with the chlorine (Cl) to form sodium chloride (NaCl) which is common table salt. This displaced hydrogen has teamed up in turn with the hydroxyl radical (OH) in the alkali to form water (HOH). Though water is commonly designated as H_2O, the " HOH " form is often used in chemical formulas to emphasize that water is actually a hydrogen-hydroxyl association.

In this example, we see that common table salt is one of the products of the reaction. Chemists give the name salt to any compound formed from a metal and an acid radical. Thus, the reaction between sulphuric acid and sodium hydroxide produces the salt called sodium sulphate. The reaction between carbonic acid (H_2CO_3) and calcium hydroxide—$Ca(OH)_2$—produces the salt called calcium carbonate. The names of salts indicate the acids with which they are associated, as sulphates (sulphuric acid), sulphites (sulphurous acid), chlorides (hydrochloric acid), nitrates (nitric acid), nitrites (nitrous acid), carbonates (carbonic acid), chromates (chromic acid), and so on.

If all of the hydrogen in an acid is replaced by a metal, the resulting salt is called a normal salt. The formation of sodium chloride, described above, is an example. If only part of the hydrogen is replaced, an acid salt is formed. This takes place, for example, when carbonic acid reacts only partially with sodium hydroxide. The acid salt, sodium bicarbonate ($NaHCO_3$), is formed instead of the normal salt, sodium carbonate (Na_2CO_3). A basic salt is formed when all the hydrogen of the acid has been replaced by the metal, but some surplus metal has carried over hydroxyl into the new combination. An example is basic lead carbonate, $2PbCO_3Pb(OH)_2$.

Measuring Acidity of Solutions

Acids and bases cannot react freely except in watery solutions. Only then do the various units that compose them become loosened. The loosening is called dissociation, and takes place according to the laws of ionization, *see* Ionization. When acids dissociate the hydrogen atoms become hydrogen ions (H^+) with positive electrical charges, while the acid radicals form negatively charged ions. When bases dissociate, the hydroxyl radicals become hydroxyl ions (OH^-) with negative electrical charges, while the metals form positively charged ions. When hydrogen ions and hydroxyl ions meet they form water. This leaves the negative acid radicals and the positive metal ions free to form salts. They may remain in solution or, if the salts in question are insoluble in water, they will be thrown out of solution as a precipitate.

In terms of ions, an acid can be defined as any substance that yields hydrogen ions in solution ; a base is any substance that yields hydroxyl ions. A solution that contains an equal amount of each type of ions is called neutral. Adding one or the other to bring about this balance is called neutralization. The acidity of a solution is often measured by the quantity of alkali required to neutralize it, and vice versa. This process is called titration.

More exact measurements of small variations in acidity and alkalinity than are possible by titration are obtained in terms of what is called hydrogen ion concentration. Up to this point this story has passed over the fact that even the purest water is itself at all times partially ionized and contains some free H^+ and OH^- in addition to its H_2O molecules. Why this should be so is a difficult problem of electrochemistry. But careful computations have established that there is one ten-millionth of a gram of H^+ ions per litre of pure water, and an equivalent amount of OH^- ions, establishing an equilibrium. Addition of an acid to the water disturbs this equilibrium and increases the proportion of H^+ ; addition of a base decreases this proportion.

Since it would be awkward to express these changes of proportion in such terms as ten-millionths, the logarithm of ten million, which is 7 (see Powers and Roots) is used as a base number instead, together with the symbol pH. Thus the hydrogen ion concentration of pure water is indicated by pH_7. This is the neutral point ; numbers smaller than 7 indicating acidity, and larger numbers alkalinity. Particularly useful is this system of measurement in biology and medicine, where very small differences of acidity and alkalinity are of great importance. For example, the pH value of normal human blood lies between 7 and 8 ; if it gets outside this range, disease and death may result.

The most accurate determination of the hydrogen ion concentration in a liquid is made by electrical tests, since the amount of electricity that will pass through a solution depends on the number of ions that are free to carry it. But sufficiently exact for many purposes are tests based on standardized colour reactions, the colour produced in the unknown liquid being matched against the colours shown by liquids of known concentration.

Certain compounds which contain no hydroxyl to begin with, like sodium carbonate (Na_2CO_3), are, nevertheless, alkaline or basic when in solution, because they dissociate the water in such a way as to manufacture an excess of OH^-. Other compounds, like ferric chloride ($FeCl_3$) have the opposite effect, and yield acid solutions by producing an excess of H^+. Such double decomposition between water and another compound is hydrolysis.

The name alkaloid is given to certain organic substances that behave somewhat like alkalis. Caffeine, nicotine, quinine, morphine, cocaine, atropine are among them. (See also Alkali Metals).

Acropolis. (Pron. a-krop'-o-lis). Just as Athens is the centre of interest in Ancient Greece, so the Acropolis (from Greek akros, topmost, and polis, city) interests us most in Athens. Long ago the whole of Athens was confined to this single hill whose top the early inhabitants levelled and fortified against armies from the surrounding plain. The Acropolis was defended by the Athenians for the last time in the second Persian War, in the year 480 Before Christ when certain citizens fortified it with stakes and beams. The oracle at Delphi had promised safety in a " wooden wall," and not everyone believed with Themistocles that this oracle pointed to abandonment of the city to the invader and reliance upon the " wooden wall " of the Athenian fleet.

When the Acropolis was no longer needed as a fortification, Pericles made it a shrine of Athena, the patron goddess of Athens. The great sculptor Pheidias planned the new Acropolis and made the principal statues, and the most famous sculptors, artists and builders all had their part in making it beautiful. The hill rose several hundred feet

ACROPOLIS OF ATHENS IN THE AGE OF PERICLES

Here we see the hill of the Acropolis as it probably looked to an Athenian of 2,500 years ago. The pillared structure on the left of the reconstruction is the Propylaea, which formed a gateway to the upper slopes ; while behind are the Erechtheum temple and the huge bronze statue to the patron goddess Athena. To the right, dominating the whole, is the matchless Parthenon, still standing today in ruined majesty. Slight damage was done by shells and mortar bombs to the ruins during the fighting between Greek government troops and rebels, December 1944–January 1945.

above the surrounding plain, and when Pheidias set a huge bronze statue of Athena upon its top, sailors could see the shining crest of her helmet and tip of her spear as soon as they rounded the point of Sunium, 15 miles away. Her treasure-house, the *Parthenon*— so called from the Greek word for maiden, since Athena was pre-eminently the maiden goddess—was the most beautiful temple in all Greece. Erechtheus, one of the mythical kings of Athens, shared the honours with Athena, and his temple, the *Erechtheum*, was also very beautiful. Its famous little " porch of the maidens " still looks very much as it used to, although one of the supporting maidens is in the British Museum, London, and its place in Athens is taken by a cast.

CREATOR OF ADAM STYLE

Robert Adam was the greatest of a famous family of Scottish architects, and his achievements in domestic architecture are universally admired. He was buried in Westminster Abbey.

The ascent of the Acropolis is made from the *Agora* or old-time market-place. You go up a series of steps and through the *Propylaea* or gateway. This has a picture gallery on one side and the little temple of the Wingless Victory on the other. After going through the gateway you come out upon a marble terrace where the little Athenian girls used to dance dressed up like bears in honour of the goddess Artemis. Beyond that is the precinct where Pheidias' great bronze statue of Athena stood. To the right is the Parthenon, and to the left the Erechtheum temple.

Of all the buildings which the genius of Man has produced, the Parthenon was the most nearly perfect. It was built of Pentelic marble, with Doric columns all round it, perhaps the most beautifully proportioned ever hewn. It was 228 feet long, 101 feet broad, and 65 feet high.

There were three sets of surpassingly beautiful sculptures. First there was the sculpture of the two " pediments," or triangular gables at the ends of the building. The eastern pediment represented the birth of Athena, the western or back pediment the struggle between Athena and Poseidon for the guardianship of Athens. Then there were the " metopes " (squares which in a wooden temple would be the ends of beams), 92 in all, and these were carved in relief each with some separate mythical hand-to-hand struggle —gods against giants, Lapithae against Centaurs, Greeks against Amazons, Greeks against Trojans, and so forth. The third set of sculptures was the " frieze " round the top of the *cella* or chamber wall inside the colonnade. This represented the Panathenaic procession which took place every year for the ceremonial purpose of giving Athena a new saffron gown. The frieze was 39 feet above you, and as you caught glimpses of it between the pillars it seemed to be slowly advancing.

In the shrine beyond the cella was the famous ivory-and-gold statue of Athena Parthenos, which reached to the ceiling. This statue was the work of Pheidias. Everything about the temple was

most exquisitely proportioned, and architects still study its ruins with professional interest.

When the Greek traveller Pausanias visited the Acropolis in the second century A.D. —nearly six centuries after Pericles—it was filled with statues and monuments, some old, some of them as late as the Roman Emperor Hadrian. Now there is little left except the architecture. The sculpture suffered terribly by theft and otherwise in the Middle Ages. The greatest damage to the building came in 1685, when the Turks used the Parthenon as a powder magazine, and it exploded. Many of the sculptured marbles were taken to London for safe keeping in 1825, and may be seen in the British Museum.

Many another ancient city besides Athens had its Acropolis, for, as we have learnt above, the word means the highest part or citadel of a city. Some say it was these flat-topped hills in the Greek plains that made the development of a high civilization possible at so early a date.

Adam, ROBERT (1728-1792). All those who are interested in architecture have lamented the destruction in London of much of the work of the

A ROBERT ADAM INTERIOR

As a designer of interiors Robert Adam (top) stood supreme in his day. This hall at 20, Portman Square, London, is a typical example of his art. He had three brothers, all of whom planned many beautiful buildings.

four brothers Adam—John, Robert, James and William—who in the latter part of the 18th century designed many beautiful buildings. The Adelphi, a terrace of houses just east of Charing Cross, was their joint work (hence the name, for *adelphoi* is Greek for brothers), and was considered to be one of the gems of London architecture, but it was demolished in 1936 to make room for more modern buildings. Robert Adam, most famous of the four brothers, excelled in interior decoration, and

PRESIDENT ADAMS, FATHER AND SON

The noted Adams family, hailing from the State of Massachusetts, counted two Presidents of the United States among their number, these being John Adams (left), who succeeded Washington in 1797, and John Quincy Adams (right), his son and sixth President from 1824 to 1828.

Adam ceilings, staircases and chimney-pieces have a delicate beauty that has led to their being removed and preserved when the houses for which they were originally designed were demolished. Robert Adam designed, among many other buildings, the screen to the Admiralty building in Whitehall, London (screen is an architectural term, applied in this instance to the graceful stone partitions that separate the forecourt of the

A ROBERT ADAM EXTERIOR

Boodle's Club, St. James's Street, London, is another fine example of the work of Robert Adam (see also illustrations in facing page). Ceilings, staircases and chimney-pieces designed by him are much sought after today.

Admiralty from Whitehall); the Royal Infirmary, Glasgow; the Register House, Edinburgh; and Ken Wood House, Hampstead. Perhaps the finest Adam interior now to be seen in London is at the Courtauld Institute at 20, Portman Square.

Adams, JOHN (1735-1826). No family has given more famous men to American history than that of which John Adams was the most prominent member. From the beginning of the struggle of the American colonies for independence from the mother country, he was one of the staunchest upholders of the rights of the Colonies, and in June 1776 he seconded in the Continental Congress the famous resolution of Richard Henry Lee, that " these colonies are, and of right ought to be, free and independent states."

He was a member of the Committee appointed to draw up the Declaration of Independence, and with John Jay and Benjamin Franklin he concluded in 1782 the preliminary treaty with Great Britain which recognized the independence of the United States and put an end to hostilities. Adams became the first American minister to Great Britain, and he was the first vice-president of the United States. On Washington's retirement in 1796 he became President, but was defeated on seeking re-election in 1800. In spite of Adams' great abilities he was never really popular, being blunt, vain and somewhat tactless.

John Adams and his son John Quincy Adams (1767-1848) supply the only instance of a father and son having been presidents of the United States. After representing his country as minister in Holland, Russia and Prussia, John Quincy Adams was one of the negotiators of the treaty of peace with Great Britain in 1812. In 1824 he became sixth President of the United States, but on offering himself for re-election in 1828 and 1831 he was defeated, for, like his father, he had not the art of winning personal popularity. At the end of his presidency he was elected to Congress and was a keen advocate of the emancipation of the slaves.

The Adams family has given other distinguished men to the service of the United States, including Charles Francis Adams, who was minister to Great Britain from 1861 to 1868, and Charles Francis Adams, Secretary of the Navy from 1929 to 1933.

Addison, JOSEPH (1672–1719). Among the famous London coffee-houses which sprang up like mushrooms in the early 18th century, " Button's " holds a high place in the history of English literature. It was a favourite meeting place for the essayist and man of letters, Joseph Addison, and four or five of his boon companions; here they would often sit through the afternoon enjoying leisurely discussions. Addison, the leading spirit of this group, was a gentleman of culture. Save for his last few years, which were marked by literary and political quarrels, his life was tranquil and pleasant. He was born at Milston, Wiltshire, where his father was rector. He spent a studious youth and entered Oxford, where he became known for the charm of his verse. After obtaining a master's degree he entered the political life of the day. His career received great momentum from the publication of his poem The Campaign, celebrating the victory at Blenheim (1704). This won him much popular and political favour, and from then on Addison held many offices, the most important being that of Secretary of State for Ireland in 1717.

It is not, however, for his statesmanship, or, indeed, for his poetry or his tragedy Cato, so famous in their day, that Addison is still loved. It was rather in his essays in the Tatler and the Spectator that he reached his highest powers.

Of Addison, one of the most versatile and gifted of English writers, Macaulay wrote that "he alone knew how to use ridicule without abusing it," and " reconciled wit and virtue."
Painting by Sir Godfrey Kneller

out of closets and libraries, schools and colleges, to dwell in clubs and assemblies, at tea-tables and in coffee-houses."

This combination of editors was ideal. Steele, an Irishman, was brilliant, impulsive, and had a head full of ideas. Addison was of a calmer temperament, and could develop gracefully the ideas and characters suggested by Steele. The Spectator, which contained no news but only light, often gently satirical essays, told of imaginary members of a club who discussed all kinds of subjects, from training young ladies in the use of fans to the appreciation of Milton. Charming characters are introduced, notably the courteous, well-loved Sir Roger de Coverley, whose delineation emphasized a new standard, that of the cultured country gentleman.

He was also the author of a number of popular hymns, of which The Spacious Firmament on High, and When all Thy Mercies O My God, are still well known.

Addison's prose style has always been greatly praised. Samuel Johnson wrote: " Whoever wishes to attain an English style, familiar but not coarse, and elegant but not ostentatious, must give his days and nights to the study of Addison." This may seem excessive, yet Addison deserves high honour for his great part in redeeming literature from the fanaticism of the Puritans and from the bombast and licence of the Restoration, and for introducing into English literature a delightful manner of expression.

A school friend of Addison, Sir Richard Steele, perceived that the growing sociability of the times, as shown by the popularity of the coffee-houses, had prepared the way for a paper which would discuss news, politics and society. So in 1709 he inaugurated such a journal, the Tatler. Addison soon became a contributor, and after the Tatler was discontinued in 1711, he and Steele started another paper, the Spectator. Its purpose was to bring " philosophy

Learn to ADD as Fast as You can READ

Although addition is one of the first things you learn at school, not many people can add as quickly as bank-clerks and accountants. Frequent practice on the right lines will make you a master of the art.

Addition. A boy who knows how to play cricket and keep the score can quickly learn to add up sums of any length. Everyone needs to be able to add figures quickly and accurately. You may be treasurer of a cricket club—of course, your accounts must be right; or you may wish to build a shed, and will have to work out just how much wood to buy and what it will cost.

Addition is simple enough ; it is mostly a matter of practice until you can *add without mistakes*, and then more practice to get speed.

There is always a best way to do anything, and of course each of us wishes to find that best way. In learning to add the first rule is : Keep your mind on addition, and on addition only. Don't let thoughts of anything but addition creep into

your head while you are adding. The second thing to remember is: Practise often, but not long at a time; five minutes is enough for the beginner. But have these five-minute practice periods often, a number of them every day. Try to get some fun out of your practice drills. Ask others to join you. Test each other. In between your drill periods, do something entirely different.

Here are some suggestions that are useful in gaining accuracy and speed in addition:

(1) Write all figures in straight rows and columns, making quite sure that units are under units, tens under tens, and so on.

(2) Some people add going up the column, and some going down. As the answer is placed at the bottom, it is perhaps best to add from the top.

(3) Use as few words as possible In adding 6, 7 and 5, don't say "6 and 7 are 13 and 5 makes 18." Merely give the results, "13, 18."

(4) Master the 100 Fundamental Addition Facts which are shown on the right, until you can give them without hesitation. These combinations are the basis of all addition, for they give every possible combination of the digits.

(5) Don't count on your fingers. In long additions it is sometimes a help to jot down the numbers to be carried; but don't get them confused with the results of the addition.

(6) Cultivate the habit of adding steadily, but at the same time rapidly.

(7) Test all your answers.

A good way to speed up your ability to add is to drill yourself in sums ending in a given number, as for example : 1 and 8, 2 and 7, 3 and 6, 4 and 5, 5 and 4, 6 and 3, 7 and 2, 8 and 1. When you have mastered the 100 Fundamental Facts you will find yourself thinking "13" when you see the problem "7 plus 6," just as you think "cat" when you see the letters c-a-t.

The diagram below affords an excellent drill for rapid work in addition. Draw the diagram on a blackboard or large sheet of paper. Then let someone write a number in the centre circle and point rapidly to one after another of the other numbers. You should be able to give promptly the sum of the centre figure and any outer figures which the pointer indicates. Change the centre figure often.

It is always a good thing to have means of checking or testing the correctness of a sum. The means most commonly used is to *repeat* the addition in some different way. If the columns have been added from the bottom *up* in getting the sum, they are added *down* in order to test its correctness. Every addition should be double-checked.

283		
976		One simple way of testing correctness of addition when columns are long is to write the sum for each column and then to find the sum of these partial sums. A mistake in any one column can then be detected without re-adding all the columns.
428		
396		
478		
896		
397		
248		
52		
55		
35		
4102		In the accompanying example 52 is the sum of the first column, 55 the sum of the second, and 35 is the sum of the third column. Note that the tens column is set over one place to the left and the hundreds

	0	1	2	3	4	5	6	7	8	9
0	0	0	0	0	0	0	0	0	0	0
	0	1	2	3	4	5	6	7	8	9
1	0	1	2	3	4	5	6	7	8	9
	1	1	1	1	1	1	1	1	1	1
	1	2	3	4	5	6	7	8	9	10
2	0	1	2	3	4	5	6	7	8	9
	2	2	2	2	2	2	2	2	2	2
	2	3	4	5	6	7	8	9	10	11
3	0	1	2	3	4	5	6	7	8	9
	3	3	3	3	3	3	3	3	3	3
	3	4	5	6	7	8	9	10	11	12
4	0	1	2	3	4	5	6	7	8	9
	4	4	4	4	4	4	4	4	4	4
	4	5	6	7	8	9	10	11	12	13
5	0	1	2	3	4	5	6	7	8	9
	5	5	5	5	5	5	5	5	5	5
	5	6	7	8	9	10	11	12	13	14
6	0	1	2	3	4	5	6	7	8	9
	6	6	6	6	6	6	6	6	6	6
	6	7	8	9	10	11	12	13	14	15
7	0	1	2	3	4	5	6	7	8	9
	7	7	7	7	7	7	7	7	7	7
	7	8	9	10	11	12	13	14	15	16
8	0	1	2	3	4	5	6	7	8	9
	8	8	8	8	8	8	8	8	8	8
	8	9	10	11	12	13	14	15	16	17
9	0	1	2	3	4	5	6	7	8	9
	9	9	9	9	9	9	9	9	9	9
	9	10	11	12	13	14	15	16	17	18

two places, as compared with the units column. The answer is the same as that obtained by the ordinary method.

An important point to remember is that only *like* quantities can be added. You cannot add yards to feet; the yards must be changed to feet or the feet to yards. The sum of 6 yards and 4 feet equals 18 feet + 4 feet, or 22 feet.

Accuracy and a reasonable speed being required in all calculations, a simple method by which the habit of adding steadily and rapidly can be acquired should be adopted,

9	51
6	42
5	36
7	31
9	24
8	15
7	

as that in which a column of figures is written in any order and the naming of the partial sums is practised in any order, as shown in the margin.

Beginning at the bottom of the column on the left we add 7 + 8 = 15; 15 + 9 = 24, etc. Add rapidly, giving successive sums only.

Additions in which amounts of different denominations are calculated is called compound addition. When sums containing pounds, shillings and pence are added and the total is also given in pounds, shillings and pence, then the calculation to be made is one of compound addition.

Greater accuracy is called for than in simple addition, because the sum of a column of one denomination has also to be converted into a different denomination—pennies into shillings and shillings into pounds—and the sum carried forward to the appropriate column.

The calculation of sums in compound addition takes considerably longer than in simple addition, and it is as well to begin with sums containing only two or three amounts. When these can be added quickly and accurately more addends (amounts to be added) may be included.

Compound addition enters into our everyday life almost more than simple addition, and proficiency at it is essential in book-keeping.

The operation of addition has seen but few changes through the centuries. It is of interest to note that a monk of Constantinople, Maximus Planudes (c. 1340), suggested that—as in pointing to the figures—it is easier to add up than down, the answer should be written at the top. Though machines now add and subtract (see page 17) the ordinary person must still use his head and do it in the old way!

AID TO RAPID ADDITION
As swiftly as possible give the sum of any of the outer figures (as indicated by someone) and the central figure, the latter being changed frequently.

ADELAIDE'S PRINCIPAL THOROUGHFARE
The capital of the State of South Australia is, like other Australian cities, notable for its broad streets, wide open spaces and the absence of slums. The photograph above shows King William Street, which runs through the centre of the city. On the right is the clock tower of the General Post Office.

Adelaide. The interior of the great island continent of Australia is as yet sparsely populated, the vast majority of the population being congregated near the coast, and the capitals of all the States of the Commonwealth are close to the sea. Adelaide, the capital of South Australia, lies near St. Vincent Gulf, seven miles from Port Adelaide, through which its sea-borne commerce is carried. It was founded in 1836 by William Light, then surveyor-general of the State, and named in honour of Queen Adelaide, wife of King William IV. It is a city of wide and regular streets, set beneath a range of picturesque hills, at the foot of which are the suburbs, with many residential villas and houses surrounded by beautiful gardens. Adelaide has many fine public buildings, and extensive parks and gardens. It is an important railway centre and exports wheat, flour, wool, meat, cheese, butter and fruit. It has a thriving motor-car accessory and body-building industry, and air services link the city with the other States of the Commonwealth. The population is over 390,000.

Aden. (Pron. ā'-den). The "Gibraltar of the East," as Aden is frequently called, is a British colony on the south-west coast of Arabia. The town of Aden (capital of the colony), built on a rocky promontory in the crater of an extinct volcano, is strongly fortified. It guards the southern entrance to the Red Sea through the Strait of Bab-el-Mandeb, which is situated 105 miles west across the Gulf of Aden. Aden's military importance increased greatly with the opening of the Suez Canal in 1869, for with control of both Aden and the canal, Great Britain gained complete command of the shortest sea route to India.

Aden, however, was an important trading centre long before the Suez Canal was built. Until the 15th century, when the Portuguese found the sea route to the East round Africa, Aden was the principal market for the shipment of Asiatic products to Western nations. It was held by the Turks until

1630, and captured from the Arabs by the British in 1839 after a quarrel with the Arab sultan over the bad treatment of shipwrecked sailors.

The natives of Aden, chiefly Arabs and Somalis from Africa, speak a form of Arabic. The climate is terrifically hot at times, but, on the other hand, it is so dry that it is unusually healthy for the tropics. Huge and ancient water-tanks which, it is presumed, did at one time serve as reservoirs, were accidentally discovered in 1854, completely hidden by rubbish and debris from the hills. They were cleared out and repaired by the British Government, and to one of the dried-up constructions was affixed a tablet commemorating the discovery. Their origin remains a mystery.

Aden, with an area of 75 square miles, was formerly administered from India, but since 1937 it has been under the Colonial Office, London. In December 1946 a Legislative Council was established, giving the people a share in the government and development of the colony, which includes the island of Perim and the Kuria Muria islands. The Aden Protectorate, a territory of 112,000 square miles, stretches eastward to the sultanate of Oman. Because of its good harbour Aden is an important

ADEN'S ANCIENT WATERWORKS
Nothing is accurately known of the origin of these great water-tanks cut in the hillside above Aden. They have long been dry, and reservoir systems now supply the town. Average annual rainfall is only two inches.

coaling and oiling station, and from the interior of the mainland it exports coffee, gum, salt, hides, tobacco, grain and sugar. There are no railways in the colony, but air services connect it with Cairo and Karachi ; population is about 46,000.

Adjective. Suppose your little brother is lost and you are trying to tell the police what he looks like. You say something like this :

"Johnny is a short, light-haired, blue-eyed, little boy."

Now the words *short, light-haired, blue-eyed, little* you have added to the noun *boy* to make its meaning clearer and more definite. Such words we call adjectives, from the Latin word meaning " added to." They are always "added to" nouns or pronouns and limit or define them.

Adjectives are " compared " to show degree—as *deep, deeper, deepest*. The first form is the positive degree, the second is the comparative, and the last is the superlative. Sometimes *more* and *most* are used, especially when the addition of the syllables *er* and *est* would make the word difficult to pronounce; as, *beautiful, more beautiful, most beautiful.* A few adjectives have irregular comparison—as, *good, better, best; bad, worse, worst; little, less, least; many* or *much, more, most.*

Adjectives which merely describe are called *descriptive* or *qualifying* adjectives. Adjectives which point out or locate (*this, that, yonder,* etc.) are called *demonstrative* adjectives, from the Latin verb meaning " to point out." There are several kinds of demonstrative adjectives: *numeral* adjectives (*two, three,* etc.); *ordinal* adjectives (*first, second,* etc.) ; *articles,* (*a, an, the*). *Interrogative* adjectives ask a question (*Which book ? What man?*). *Possessive* adjectives denote possession (*my* book, *his* pencil).

One of the commonest mistakes in the use of adjectives is to use the superlative degree instead of the comparative when only two objects are compared—as, " John is the *tallest* of the two boys," for " John is the *taller* of the two boys."

There is sometimes a good deal of perplexity as to whether an adjective or an adverb should be used after certain verbs. As a general rule, the adverb should be used if it could be replaced by a phrase denoting manner; the adjective should be used if some part of the verb " to be " could be substituted for the verb. Thus: " He felt *cold* " (that is, he *was* cold); but, " He felt *rapidly* in all his pockets

ADEN'S ROCK-BOUND COAST
Though it is arid and infertile, the small British colony of Aden is a valuable link in Empire communications, for it lies near the entrance to the Red Sea, about two-thirds of the distance between Britain and India. In its fine harbour many ships plying between Europe and the East replenish their supplies of fuel.

for the matches " (here expressing manner). " She looked *shy* "; but, " She looked up *shyly.*" " The man appeared *kind* "; but, " The man appeared *suddenly.*" Sometimes either adjective or adverb may be used with little difference of meaning ; as " They arrived *safe* (or *safely*)."

Adjutant. This is not a handsome bird. Indeed, the adjutant is quite the ugliest of the long-legged stork family, and is appreciated for its worth rather than for its beauty. In Calcutta and other Indian cities adjutants are regarded as true feathered friends and protected by law. Should one of them see a dead animal it promptly eats it, and is therefore a useful scavenger. Frogs, fish, large insects and snakes also form part of its diet.

With its huge beak, bald or scantily covered head, ungainly legs, untidy plumage, and long throat-pouch, the Indian adjutant is one of the quaintest-looking of birds. Members of the species are also found in Java and Africa. The nest is nothing more than a collection of twigs and sticks. The scientific name of the Indian adjutant is *Leptoptilus dubius;* of the African species, *L. crumenifer;* of the Java variety, *L. javanicus.*

The bird gets its name from the grave way in which it stalks about, like an adjutant on parade; an adjutant in the army is an officer seldom above the rank of captain who helps (Latin *adjutare,* to help) or acts in the capacity of assistant to the commanding officer of the battalion, especially in the administrative work of the unit.

ADJUTANT BIRD
This bird is protected by law in many cities which it frequents : it helps to keep the streets clean. It gets its name from the manner in which it walks about—in fancied resemblance to the bearing of an army adjutant.

Admiral. You will be surprised to know that the proudest title of a naval officer is probably a relic of the stirring times of the Crusaders, who sought to rescue the Holy Land from the grip of the infidel. During their wanderings the soldiers came across the Arabic words *amir al*, meaning commander of the (sea, etc.). The first Englishman to bear the title was Sir William Leybourne, who was called " admiral of the sea of the King of England " in a document written at Bruges, Belgium, in 1297. Three years later the first actual commission seems to have been given by Edward I to Gervase Alard, a brave and distinguished seaman, who was styled captain and admiral of the ships of the Cinque Ports (*q.v.*), " and also of all other ports from the port of Dover by the sea-coast, and of the whole county of Cornwall."

There are four grades of admiral in the Royal Navy. Highest is Admiral of the Fleet, and usually

ADMIRALS' GOLD BRAID

In the British Navy officers wear gold stripes round the cuffs of their pilot jackets to denote their rank. Left to right above are the stripes of an admiral of the fleet, admiral, vice-admiral and rear-admiral.

(except in time of war) officers attain this rank only on retirement after very distinguished service; it corresponds to field-marshal in the Army and to marshal of the R.A.F. Next in seniority comes admiral, followed by vice-admiral and rear-admiral, corresponding to general, lieutenant-general and major-general respectively. Admirals are also called flag-officers, because at sea they fly a flag indicating their rank, and the warship wearing the flag is known as the flagship.

Until 1864 the flag ranks below admiral of the fleet were subdivided into those of the red, white and blue squadrons, the rank of Nelson at the battle of Trafalgar (1805) being vice-admiral of the white. In some foreign navies the titles of flag officers are very similar to those in the Royal Navy.

The Board of Admiralty, the governing authority of the Royal Navy, has its offices in Whitehall, London, and consists of the First Lord, who is a member of the Cabinet, and five Sea Lords, with certain civilian advisers. On the Admiralty roof are great wireless aerials through which communication may be made with the fleet.

Adonis. (Pron. *a-dō′nis*). Of all the youths beloved by the goddess Aphrodite (Venus), Adonis, or Tammuz as he was called in Syria, was the most fair, and for him the glorious goddess forsook the heights of Mount Olympus to wander through earthly woods and fields. But Adonis was a bold young hunter, and his rash pursuit of dangerous game caused Aphrodite many anxious moments. In vain she besought him to forgo the hunt and remain with her. Adonis laughingly escaped and continued to take part in his favourite sport.

Then one day he came upon a wild boar especially large and fierce. When he wounded it with his spear, it turned and charged him, burying its tusks in his sides and rending and trampling the poor youth to death. The grief of Aphrodite at this mishap was pitiful. Rushing to Adonis' side, she knelt over him and burst into a passion of tears. A Greek poet, in describing her lament, says :

> As many drops as from Adonis bled,
> So many tears the sorrowing Aphrodite shed :
> For every drop on earth a flower there grows :
> Anemones for tears ; for blood the rose.

Time did not soften Aphrodite's grief, and, going to Olympus, she implored Zeus to restore her lover to earth. And so it was arranged that Adonis should spend one half of every year in

ADMIRALS' FLAGS

The top flag, a plain St. George's cross, is flown by an admiral. Vice- and rear-admirals' flags have respectively one and two red balls next the staff.

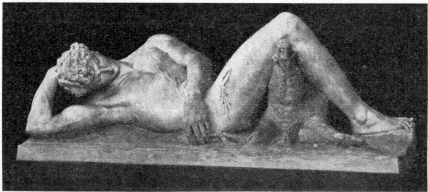

Anderson

ADONIS DYING OF THE WILD BOAR'S THRUST

The story of Venus and Adonis is one of the most famous in mythology, and is the subject of one of Shakespeare's best-known poems. One of the greatest of all artists, Michelangelo, found in the death of Adonis the inspiration for this beautiful sculpture—" Adonis Dying." Beneath the young hunter's knees is a representation of the wild boar that inflicted the mortal injuries. The sculpture is in the National Museum, Florence, Italy.

the upper world. In the glad days of early spring he left the Elysian Fields to join his beloved, and on his path the flowers bloomed and birds sang to show their joy at his coming. But when winter came he returned to the land of the dead, and all Nature drooped in mourning at his departure.

Adrianople (pron. ā-dri-*a*-nō′-pl), OR EDIRNE. Named after the Emperor Hadrian (Anno Domini 76–138) this city, the scene of many important events in the troubled history of the Balkan lands, lies 130 miles north-west of Istanbul. Edirne is the Turkish name, but the older form persists in other countries.

Near it the Visigoths in A.D. 378 won the victory over the Emperor Valens which began the downfall of the Roman Empire. The Turks captured Adrianople in 1360, and made it their capital until they won Constantinople in 1453.

In 1913 Adrianople was taken from the Turks by the Serbs and Bulgarians, but was restored in the peace which followed. After the First World War (1914–18) it was awarded to Greece (1920). It again became Turkish in October 1922 after the defeat of the Greeks in the Greco-Turkish war of 1920–22. Population is about 46,400.

Adriatic Sea. (Pron. ā-dri-at′ik). This great arm of the Mediterranean separates Italy from Yugoslavia and Albania. Its greatest length is 450 miles, and its average breadth about 110 miles. The chief cities that border its shores are Venice, Trieste, Fiume, Ancona and Brindisi.

The dark green water of the Adriatic is very salt, owing to the fact that, with the exception of the Adige and the Po, no rivers of any size flow into it. Tides are almost absent in the Adriatic but gales are frequent.

From the 12th to the 18th centuries the rulers of Venice each year threw a ring into the Adriatic (called " wedding the sea "), in token of their claim to dominion over that sea. The name comes from the town of Adria, in the north of Italy,

once a flourishing seaport, but now 15 miles inland owing to silting-up by the rivers.

Adverb. When your father asks you how you got along in your studies yesterday, you answer : " I did well," or " I did poorly."

You have answered his question by adding the word *well* or *poorly* to the verb *did*. Words that are thus added to verbs to modify their meaning are called adverbs, getting their name from the Latin words *ad* meaning " to," and *verbum*, " verb." Adverbs may also modify adjectives, other adverbs, or prepositions—as, *very* tall (modifying an adjective) ; *too* slowly (modifying another adverb) ; *just* above the house (modifying a preposition).

The most interesting characteristic of adverbs is their great variety of meanings. They may express time (*today*), place (*here*), manner (*quickly*), degree (*very*), number (*once, twice*), exclusion (*but, once, only*), etc. Some adverbs, called *conjunctive* adverbs, also connect adverbial clauses with other parts of a sentence—as, " He left *before* I arrived." Others, called *interrogative* adverbs, introduce questions—as, " *When* did you come ? "

Most adverbs are formed from adjectives by adding the suffix *ly*—as, great (adj.), greatly (adv.) ; real, really ; splendid, splendidly. But some adverbs have the same form as the adjectives ; for example, " a *fast* train " (adj.), and " run *fast* " (adv.).

Adverbs are generally compared (*see* Adjective) by the use of *more* and *most ;* an example is, freely, *more* freely, *most* freely. Some, however, are compared like adjectives by adding *er* and *est*. Thus we say, " John runs *fast*, but Henry runs *faster*." " You and John climbed *high*, but I climbed *highest*." The adverbs *well, badly, much, little*, have the same irregular comparison as the corresponding adjectives, *good*, etc. The chief difficulty in the use of adverbs is confusion with adjectives. *Real* kind, going *slow*, etc., are mistakes for *really* or *very* kind, going *slowly*, etc.

Where CIVILIZATION BEGAN *in* EUROPE

The islands of the Aegean Sea were stepping-stones by means of which civilization passed into Europe from its birthplaces in Egypt and Mesopotamia. Some of the wonders of the island cultures are here described.

Aegean Civilization. (Pron. ē-jē′*an*). In the island-strewn Aegean Sea, European civilization had its birth ; and across its waters, for 5,000 years, the threads of European, Asiatic and African commerce and history have interlaced. Here Europe thrusts southward its easternmost peninsula toward the boldly jutting mass of Asia Minor. Across the narrow basin between the continents, East and West have faced and fought each other since the very dawn of history.

What a panorama unfolds before the imagination when one thinks of the nations whose vessels have ploughed the Aegean ! Ancient Egyptians, Cretans and Phoenicians ; Persians, Athenians and Spartans ; Romans, Goths, Venetians and Arabs ; modern Turks, Greeks and Italians, Germans and British—these are some of the many peoples

who have made history in this sea through 50 centuries—down to the Second World War.

The early inhabitants of Crete had long heads and dark complexions and were rather short. They were essentially a seafaring people and carried on an extensive trade with their neighbours, especially with Egypt. Wall paintings have been discovered which show them paying tribute to the Egyptians (about 1500-1450 before Christ), and by way of return Egyptian civilization was brought to Crete. The golden age of Crete lasted until about 1400 B.C. when invaders from the city of Mycenae, on the Grecian mainland. burnt Knossos the capital, but European civilization remained centred about the Aegean Sea.

This historic sea is the north-eastern arm of the Mediterranean. It is partly shut off to the south by the long narrow island of Crete, which lies squarely in the middle. Look at the map below and see how thickly the sea is sprinkled with islands, which form a natural bridge between Europe and the East.

More than 5,000 years ago, at a time when the ancestors of the modern European peoples were still barbarians—without metals, without money, without writing, without sailing ships, and without comfortable houses—the people who lived in this Aegean basin had taken the first steps upward from barbarism. Under the influence of their highly civilized neighbours of the valleys of the Nile and of the Tigris and Euphrates, they too developed

We call this civilization the Aegean civilization, and the people who developed it we call the Mediterranean race, see Races of Mankind. We know that this people had lived in the Aegean basin from far back in the Stone Age. But they did not begin to progress from barbarism to civilization until about 3000 B.C., when they first came into frequent contact with the progressive Oriental peoples, especially the Egyptians.

This contact first took place between Crete, the southernmost of the Aegean islands, and the Egyptians, who were only a three days' sail to the south. By 2000 B.C. the Cretans had become a highly civilized people. Their war and trading galleys made the Aegean and other parts of the Mediterranean a Cretan lake, and the kings of Crete received tribute from many dependencies. The great legendary sea-king of Crete was Minos, and the term "Minoan" Age has been applied to the whole period of nearly 2,000 years when Cretan influence was dominant in the Aegean.

The first dwellers on the Grecian mainland to feel this influence were the people of the Gulf of Argos, which looks to the south directly toward Crete, and was only a two days' sail for the adventurous Cretan traders. The route is shown on the map alongside. The barbarous inhabitants of Mycenae and Tiryns, the two chief settlements on the

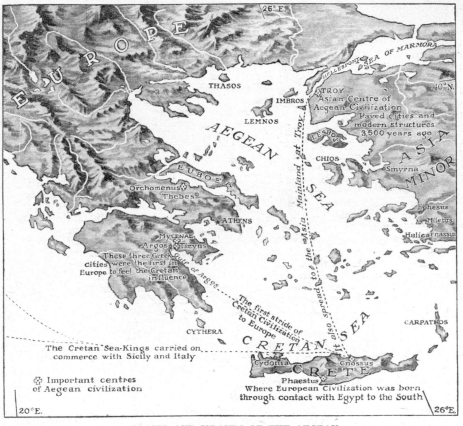

COASTS AND ISLANDS OF THE AEGEAN

This map illustrates how civilization travelled westward in the Mediterranean from its sources in Egypt and on the mainland of Asia. By 2000 B.C. Egyptian influence had spread to Crete, distant only three days' sail; and the wonderful city of Knossos (Cnossus), vast remains of which were disinterred by Sir Arthur Evans during 1900-1908, was a direct result. Then in turn Cretan culture broadened out to all the lands bordering on the Aegean Sea—to Troy and other famous cities in Asia Minor, to Mycenae, Argos and Tiryns in Greece, and across the sea to Sicily and Italy. Thus European civilization found its nursery in the sunny islands that dot the waters of the Aegean Sea.

a civilization worthy to be compared with any that had before existed. In Crete and at Troy and elsewhere on the mainland, they built paved cities with massive fortifications. They raised great stone palaces, richly decorated with paintings and sculptural ornaments, and equipped with running water, bathrooms, drainage, and other conveniences which we regard as typically modern. They developed an art of extraordinary interest, producing work in pottery, metals and carved gems that has rarely been surpassed in beauty.

Argive plain, bought the beautiful wares of the Cretan traders, and in course of time developed a high civilization of their own. The name "Mycenaean Age" was given to the period when Mycenae and Tiryns flourished (1500-1200 B.C.), because of the wonderful gold cups, sculptures and other articles discovered there. Other cities on the Greek peninsula and on the Aegean islands shared in this culture, which was spread as far as Sicily, Italy and Spain by the roving Mycenaean traders. On the mainland of Asia Minor, too, the same

EXQUISITE AEGEAN ART OF 3000 YEARS AGO

While the Greeks were still barbarians the skilled artists of the Aegean were turning out such magnificent wares as those shown above. Top left is a wine cup from Crete dating from about 1350 B.C.; it is of black soapstone with eyes of crystal and jasper. The vase ornamented with an octopus, seaweed and rocks, dates from about 1600 B.C. The tiny ivory statue of the Cretan snake goddess is remarkable for lithe grace: note the flounced skirt. Centre is a piece of Late Minoan pottery showing a cat stalking a bird. Bottom left are shown two gold cups, the lower one being the famous one found at Vaphio in Sparta, Greece, ornamented with a representation of the netting of wild bulls; and right is the marble throne from the great Palace of Knossos (Cnossus), which was the ancient capital of the island of Crete.

general type of civilization sprang up, beginning there 1,500 years before the great palaces of Mycenae and Tiryns were built. The famous city of Troy, in the north-western corner of Asia Minor, near the shores of the Hellespont, was the Asian centre of this Aegean civilization. At first a mere trading village, by 2500 B.C. Troy had become a rich and sumptuous capital, scarcely inferior to its great rival Knossos (Cnossus), the capital of Crete. In another thousand years Troy had spread its power and imposed its rule over its neighbours and had become the mistress of a considerable kingdom. (*See* Troy).

AENEAS TAKES HIS FATHER TO SAFETY

It is related that after the Greeks had conquered Troy, Aeneas escaped with his father, Anchises, and his son. He is here seen carrying the infirm old man on his shoulders, while Anchises is receiving the household gods from Creusa, who was his daughter-in-law.

Painting by L. Spada in the Louvre, Paris

But by the time the use of iron had become common in the Aegean (about 1000 B.C.), the widespread Aegean civilization had received its deathblow at the hands of the Indo-European invaders from the north. These peoples we know as the Greeks. At that time they were still barbarians. In wave after wave they swept down into the peninsula of Greece and across the Aegean. The kingdoms of Mycenae and Troy and Knossos were so completely overwhelmed that their memory survived only in confused traditions.

Less than 100 years ago men knew nothing of this first great chapter in European history. The palaces and vases and weapons and paintings of this pre-Greek epoch lay silted over beneath the sands of the ages. It was not until Heinrich

Schliemann in 1870 began to dig down through the deposits that hid the buried city of Troy that the story of Aegean civilization began dimly to be suspected. Then followed excavations at Mycenae and Tiryns and other places, until today we have many remains of this forgotten civilization.

Nowhere else have such impressive survivals of the earliest Aegean culture been found as in the island of Crete. Sir Arthur Evans started the excavations there in 1900, reconstructing many of the ruins at his own expense, notably part of the palace at Knossos. Evans believed that the Phoenicians borrowed their alphabet from the Cretans (*see* Alphabet). At Knossos, Phaestus and other Cretan cities, excavators have uncovered a wealth of statuettes, weapons, tools and pottery, as well as clay tablets covered with writing which has not yet been deciphered. Pictures of bull fights, festal processions, crowds and acrobats show us what a highly developed civilization they enjoyed, curiously like our own in some respects.

From the dawn of history to the present, most of the people inhabiting the Aegean islands have been of this ancient Mediterranean race. Inter-mixtures, however, have occurred with Greeks and later conquerors. From the Roman conquest of the Mediterranean almost down to our own times, the islands have worn the yoke of foreign domination. When Greece at last shook off Turkish rule (1821–1829) many of the islands were joined to the new Hellenic kingdom. Nearly a century later the Balkan wars and the First World War of 1914–18 restored most of the remainder of the Aegean archipelago to Greek rule. During the Second World War, after their conquest of Greece and Crete in 1941 the Germans occupied the more important Aegean islands until May 1945. Rhodes and the Dodecanese, a group of twelve islands lying off Asia Minor, which had been in Italian possession since 1912, were awarded to Greece by the Italian Peace Treaty of 1947.

Aeneas. (Pron. ē-nē′as). According to the stories which the old Romans loved to tell, their imperial City of the Seven Hills was settled by men descended from the heroes of lofty-towered Troy. Aeneas, son of Anchises and the goddess Aphrodite (Venus), led this little band that reached Italy and settled on the plain of Latium.

Aeneas, so the legend runs, was the bravest of all the Trojans after Hector. When Troy was conquered and burned, he escaped from the city with old Anchises on his shoulders and leading his son Ascanius by the hand. For seven years he and his companions wandered over the Mediterranean in their swift-oared ships. Near Carthage on the African coast Aeneas was wrecked, and the Carthaginian queen Dido loved him and begged him to stay. But the gods sent him wandering again, and Dido killed herself for grief.

After further wanderings Aeneas came to Latium, whose king welcomed him and gave him his daughter Lavinia in marriage. In battle with the Etruscans he vanished, and his subjects, failing to find his body, consequently worshipped him as a god. Aeneas is the hero of the most famous epic in Latin, the Aeneid of Virgil. There he is frequently called " the pious Aeneas " because of his loyalty and devotion to his father Anchises.

A PICTURE PAGEANT OF FAMOUS BRITISH AEROPLANES

While a Pan-American Clipper flew eastward over the North Atlantic on the night of July 5, 1937, the Empire flying-boat Caledonia, of Imperial Airways, crossed in the opposite direction, eventually alighting at Newfoundland 15 hours after leaving Foynes in the Irish Free State (as Eire was still called at that time). Caledonia afterwards flew on to New York, where she is here seen cruising over the numerous skyscrapers on Manhattan Island. These were the first survey flights for a regular Transatlantic air service between Britain, Canada and the U.S.A.

AIRCRAFT THAT WON THE BATTLE OF BRITAIN

British Official: Crown Copyright

It was in the Spitfire (top) and Hurricane (below) that pilots of the Royal Air Force defeated the German Air Force's onslaughts in the summer and autumn of 1940 and thus warded off invasion of Britain. The Supermarine Spitfire was armed with eight machine-guns or with four machine-guns and two cannon. Its engine, a Rolls-Royce Merlin, gave a speed of about 360 m.p.h. A similar engine was used for the Hawker Hurricane, the speed in this case being about 330 m.p.h. Either four cannon or eight or twelve machine-guns were fitted to this famous aircraft.

NIGHT FIGHTERS THAT THWARTED GERMAN RAIDERS

British Official: Crown Copyright

The Boulton Paul Defiant (top) and the Bristol Beaufighter played a mighty part in thwarting Germany's plans for mass night bombing raids on Britain after the failure of Nazi daylight attacks during the Second World War. Both aircraft were also used for daylight operations. The Defiant had a power-operated turret housing four machine-guns, and a Rolls-Royce Merlin engine of 1,030 h.p. In the Beaufighter the armament was six machine-guns and four cannon ; two Hercules engines of 1,600 h.p. gave a speed of over 330 m.p.h., with a range of some 1,500 miles.

TWO MIGHTY LONG-RANGE BOMBERS OF THE R.A.F.—

That Germany's vital industrial areas and certain isolated key factories were put out of action during the Second World War was largely due to Britain's heavy bombers, two of which are shown here. They differed considerably in detail: the Short Stirling (lower photographs) had a single fin and rudder, while the Handley Page Halifax (top) had twin fins and rudders. The cockpit and nose of the Halifax are shown in the top right-hand photograph, with the gun turret and, beneath it, the compartment for the bomb-aimer. There was another gun turret

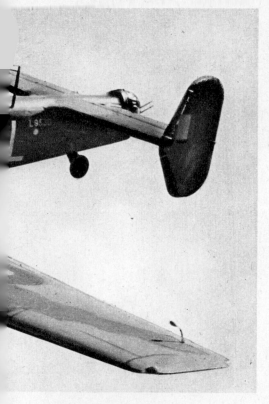

British Official; Crown Copyright

in the tail, to protect this vulnerable part. With four Rolls-Royce Merlin engines, the Halifax was, for its size, fast and easy to handle—well able to dive, climb or turn rapidly when anti-aircraft gunfire or hostile fighters threatened too closely. The Stirling had the same long, overhanging nose, with turret and bomb-aimer's compartment ; its distinctive appearance is well shown in the head on view at the left. Like the Halifax it had a tail turret. The Stirling's power units were four Hercules engines each of 1,635 h.p., or four Wright Cyclones each of 1,200 h.p.

EVER-MOUNTING SPEED IN THE ROYAL AIR FORCE

British Official; C. E. Brown

These R.A.F. aircraft were noted for their speed. The Gloster Meteor (top), first flown in 1943 and the R.A.F.'s first jet' fighter, was driven by two Rolls-Royce turbo-jet units, and on November 7, 1945, established a speed record of 606 m.p.h. The De Havilland Mosquito (centre) was an all-wood machine for various purposes, the one shown being the photographic reconnaissance version; it had a speed of over 400 m.p.h. The Hawker Tempest V (bottom), with a speed of 435 m.p.h. was one of the few aircraft able to overtake the German flying bombs.

FOR OFFENSIVE AND DEFENSIVE SEA WARFARE

British Official; Crown Copyright; Topical

The Bristol Beaufort torpedo-bomber (top) was used by R.A.F. Coastal Command during the Second World War for attacks on enemy shipping. It had two Bristol Taurus engines, of 1,065 h.p., and was armed with two machine-guns in the nose and another pair in a turret on the top of the fuselage. The Short Sunderland flying-boat (centre and lower photographs) had nose and tail turrets, besides guns in the fuselage. With four Bristol engines, totalling nearly 4,000 h.p., it had a speed of 210 m.p.h. Sunderlands were used for convoy work and anti-submarine patrols.

INCREASING SIZE OF OUR COMMERCIAL AIRCRAFT

Charles E. Brown

Designed as a long-range reconnaissance flying-boat the Short Shetland (top) was modified for commercial service, carrying 40 passengers. Four 2,500 h.p. Bristol Centaurus engines give a speed of 267 m.p.h. and a range of some 2,000 miles. All-up weight is 130,000 lb. The Avro Tudor VII (lower), a four-engined airliner, which underwent its trials in 1947, has a designed speed of 330 m.p.h. and accommodation for 60 passengers. All-up weight is about 80,000 lb. Each of its four Bristol Hercules engines develops 1,675 h.p., and its range is 2,000 miles.

HOW and WHY an AEROPLANE FLIES

Behind even the humblest and least romantic looking home-made flying model is a wonderful story. Ranging far back in time, it tells of brilliant but hard-won achievement unsurpassed in human endeavour.

Aeroplane. Today mechanical flight is no mystery. If you place several dried autumn leaves, such as beech leaves, on a flat surface and blow steadily at them on a level, some of them will rise in the air. The dried leaf has something of the same shape as an aeroplane wing, in that it is cambered, or bent, towards one of its broad surfaces. Hang a model aeroplane in the path of a fairly strong air current and the model will, like the dried leaf, rise in the air.

At the Science Museum, London, you can see this very experiment, for in the Children's Gallery there, in a showcase, is a captive model suspended in the airstream from a "wind tunnel." Pressing the button at the front of the showcase turns on the air stream, and in a moment the model lifts, and remains airborne as long as the air stream lasts.

A propeller-driven aeroplane stays up in the air because the propeller, as it screws the aeroplane forward, creates an airstream which supports it under the wings. If the propeller stopped, gravity would pull it towards the ground. The wings are shaped so that they will have a sucking effect on the airstream on top, and a condition of lowered pressure ; beneath the wing there must be the *opposite* condition, one of increased pressure by the air. A kite is an aircraft, and no sensible boy takes out his kite unless there is a wind, for flight is impossible unless the air meets the aircraft with some violence. The force with which an aeroplane itself meets the air is called thrust, and the resistance of the air to the aircraft is termed drag. The kite has usually a tail, which tilts up the nose and makes certain that the kite will meet the air at an angle to its flight path. The wings of an aeroplane also are set at an angle for the same reason, this angle being called the angle of incidence.

The effect of this angular positioning of the wing is to drive the air underneath, and so to force the kite or the wing upwards. The wing of an aeroplane is not flat, like the skin of a kite, but when looked at from the end, as if cut through across the narrow way, the wing is seen to be curved or cambered in section. This is shown in the top diagram above ; the areas of low pressure and high pressure are also roughly indicated. Most of the lift derived from the wing is felt *above*—suction effect—and the rest is due to air pressure underneath the wing. Before an aeroplane could fly, some light and comparatively powerful type of engine had to be found, and the Wright brothers

AIR PRESSURE ON A WING

When an aeroplane wing is driven through the air high pressure underneath forces it up, and low pressure on top has a sucking effect. Arrow indicates centre of pressure.

SHAPED FOR STABILITY

If the aeroplane should roll to the right or left, the increased air pressure on the lower wing will tend to correct this movement.

designed their own petrol engine for this purpose. An aeroplane needs "stability," or the power to fly level when required, without pitching or rolling, or swinging off its course. Lengthwise or fore-and-aft stability is taken care of by the tailplane. The tailplane is so arranged in size and angle of incidence that it balances out pressures farther forward which tend to tilt the aircraft about its centre of gravity. This last is the point in the aeroplane where, if it were possible to balance it on a pivot, it would be in equilibrium.

Directional stability is maintained by the fin in the tail unit, a vertical surface something like a ship's keel in function. The rudder is attached to the fin, and used for steering the aircraft sideways, but the fin is intended to keep it on a straight course without any tendency to "yaw," or swing off sideways from that course.

Lateral (or side-to-side) stability is provided for by a simple angular arrangement of the main planes or wings. The wings meet the body or fuselage of the aircraft at a wide "V," sloping upwards. This is called the di-hedral angle. This arrangement is to prevent rolling. Should the aircraft be pushed over into a banking attitude when flying straight, the wing which is lower for that reason will be at a greater angle to the flow of air (this angle being called the angle of attack); because of this increased angle the lower wing will get more lift from the air than does the upper wing, and this difference of lift tends to move the aircraft back to the normal (*see* diagram opposite).

The aim of designers is to render the aircraft naturally stable in flight, by these devices which relieve the pilot of many small adjustments and alterations of controls. The fact that, once set on a given course an aircraft can almost fly itself, or can be guided and controlled by an "automatic pilot" (*see* diagram in next page) shows how far designers of today have achieved their aim.

Before describing how a pilot controls the flight of a propeller-driven aircraft we must say something about the engine and airscrew. The latter rotates at a high speed—driven by a powerful multi-cylinder petrol engine—and forces back the air behind it. For any given aircraft a certain speed is enough to produce sufficient lift to nullify the downward tendency due to the weight of the aircraft; a *lower* speed will diminish the lift and the craft will be unable to maintain its height.

Let us see now what will happen if we *increase* forward speed instead of diminishing it. Generally the aeroplane begins to climb instead of flying on a level course. We now have greater thrust, due to increased speed, than is sufficient to balance the weight of the machine ; and the aircraft now takes up a climbing attitude, with the nose tilted upwards. By this change of attitude the aircraft has got back again to the state of equilibrium which it lost for a time when we increased the engine speed and the thrust.

If the pilot wants to fly quicker and on a level, at the same height, he must manipulate the aircraft so as to reduce the angle of attack, at the same time as he increases the speed. Then the aircraft will have very little or no increase in lift, because the new attitude as compared with the original one has cancelled out the added lift given by greater speed.

On the other hand, if the pilot desires to reduce speed without losing height, he will increase the angle of attack ; this works, up to a certain point, but speed is lost as the angle is increased, and a stage is reached when the angle cannot safely be made larger to make up for the drop in speed, or the aeroplane will "stall." This means that the air flow over and under the wings no longer behaves as it did in ordinary flight; lift is very much reduced by the stall. If the machine is too close to the ground it may fall, out of control. Given sufficient height, however, the aircraft nose

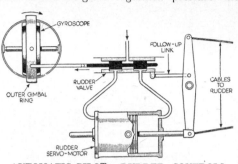

AUTOMATIC PILOT : RUDDER CONTROLS

After setting his aeroplane on the desired course the pilot can switch on the automatic pilot, which then takes over control.

drops, the machine goes into a dive, and the speed increase thereby brought about may enable the wings to acquire again enough lift to support the machine in time to prevent a crash.

The pilot has three sets of main controls: rudder, elevator and ailerons. The rudder is hinged to the fin, and cables or rods connect it to a bar on which the pilot's feet rest. When he pushes the left foot forward, the aeroplane turns to the left, and so on. The elevators are two hinged extensions of the tailplane—horizontal rudders, in fact. They are connected to the control column. If he pulls back the column, the elevators rise, catch the air stream, and the tail is forced down by the greater pressure thus brought into play : the machine tends to climb. Pushing the control column forward lowers the elevators and makes the aeroplane dive. (*See* diagram below).

Now for the ailerons, which is the name given to hinged portions of the wings set at the rear. They are connected to the control column so that, when the aileron on one side rises, that on the opposite side is lowered. Movement of the control column sideways to the left raises the left (or "port" side) aileron and lowers the right (or "starboard") one. Air pressure then forces the right wing up and the left wing down. This operation is called banking, and is used in conjunction with the rudder when making a turn—for the same reason that a cyclist banks when going at speed around a bend in the road.

In page 43 is a picture of the cockpit instruments on a training aircraft. The numbered diagram accompanying the picture gives the names of the controls. Most of them explain themselves : here are some notes about the others. The flaps are hinged to the rear or "trailing" edge of the wings; unlike the ailerons, the flaps move downwards only, or back to the normal line continuing the surface of the wing. Again unlike the ailerons, both flaps go down or return together ; when lowered, according to the amount they go down they increase the effective angle of attack. In coming in to land, the lowered flap permits the aircraft to come down more steeply and at a slower speed; at a later stage, just before touching down, the lowered flaps act something like brakes, cutting down the speed quickly and shortening the run needed for safe landing.

The directional gyroscope is set by the compass and then keeps the aircraft on its course. It is quite a different instrument from the gyro-compass, which is mentioned in the next page. The

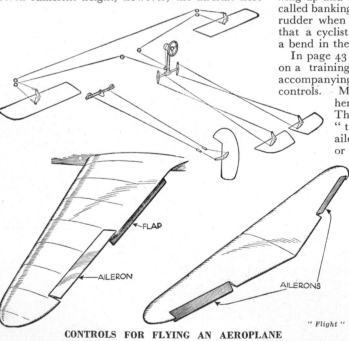

CONTROLS FOR FLYING AN AEROPLANE

In the upper diagram is shown the way in which the rudder, elevators and ailerons are controlled, the rudder being drawn separately for clearness. Flaps (lower left) on the rearward or trailing edge of a wing reduce speed and steepen the gliding angle. When one aileron (lower right) is pulled down (increasing lift on that side) the opposite one goes up (decreasing lift).

artificial horizon is for giving information to the pilot about the attitude of the aircraft in relation to the horizon. (You can read more about such devices in our story of the Gyroscope.) These instruments and the " automatic pilot " depend on a peculiarity of a heavy wheel set spinning very quickly on an axle mounted in a ring so that the ring itself can swing freely in a U-shaped yoke or support. The axle stays in the same plane—this means that if we start the wheel with the axle horizontal, for instance, the axle will keep horizontal and will strongly resist any attempt to push it out of the horizontal. If we try to press one end of the axle downwards, the result is a kind of jerk or kick which *makes the ring move round*, carrying the wheel and its axle. This move-

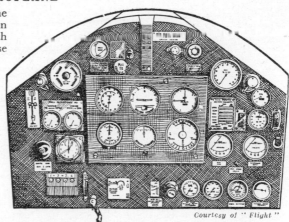

Courtesy of " Flight "

COCKPIT INSTRUMENTS OF MILES MASTER TRAINER

1. Flaps indicator ; 2. Airspeed indicator correction card ; 3. Speaking tube ; 4. Reflector sight lamp ; 5. Reflector sight dimmer switch ; 6, 10. Cockpit lamps dimmer switches ; 7. Undercarriage indicator ; 8. Instrument flying hood release ; 9. Revolution indicator ; 11. Signalling switchbox ; 12. Main magneto and undercarriage indicator switches ; 13. Oxygen regulator ; 14. Air speed indicator ; 15. Artificial horizon ; 16. Rate of climb indicator ; 17. Oil thermometer ; 18. Oil gauge ; 19. Boost gauge ; 20. Fuel gauge ; 21. Cockpit lamp ; 22. Landing lamps switch ; 23. Time of flight clock' ; 24. Altimeter switch ; 25. Directional gyroscope ; 26. Turn and bank indicator ; 27, 28. Fuel contents indicators ; 29. Fire extinguisher switch ; 30. Bomb selector switches ; 31. Radiator flap indicator ; 32. Bomb jettison switch ; 33. Oil cock ; 34. Starting magneto switch ; 35. Engine priming pump; 36. Pneumatic pressure gauge ; 37. Radiator temperature gauge ; 38. Fuel contents indicator switch ; 39. Brake triple pressure gauge ; 40. Hydraulic system pressure gauge ; 41. Control box ; 42. Radiator flap control : 43. Compass.

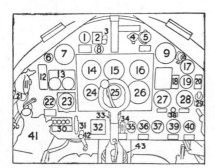

ment is at right angles to the direction in which we applied pressure to the end of the axle.

This strange feature of the gyroscope is used to govern the controls of an aircraft ; if the aeroplane tends to run off its set course, pressure is automatically applied to one or other side of the gyro axle, and immediately there is set up a movement which, suitably linked to the controls, operates the latter to correct the course. The rudder connexion is shown in page 42.

Now a word about the use of the gyro as a compass. Magnetic compasses have drawbacks which you can read about in our story of the Compass. That is why for many years inventors worked at the problem of a gyrocompass. The French scientist Léon Foucault (1818–68) pointed out that a gyroscope would naturally arrange itself with its axle parallel to the axis of rotation of the earth— at any place on or above the earth's surface except the N. and S. poles. Both these effects of the spinning gyro wheel are utilised in automatic controlling devices for aircraft. Here we have space only to

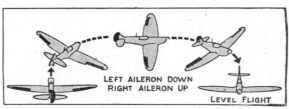

LEFT AILERON DOWN
RIGHT AILERON UP

LEVEL FLIGHT

MAKING A RIGHT TURN

When a pilot wishes to turn his aircraft to the right he moves his rudder to the right and depresses the left aileron, which at the same time raises the aileron on the right. This causes the aircraft to bank as well as turn.

mention the basic principles. Once the pilot has set his aircraft on the course he wishes to follow, he can switch on the automatic pilot, and this complicated mechanism will then guide and control the aeroplane, even though it is voyaging from America to Britain or the reverse. Moreover, in conjunction with radar-controlled landing devices, both on the ground and in the aircraft, automatic controls can bring down and land an aeroplane without the aircrew intervening.

Now we take up the thrilling story of the conquest of flight. Although the machine of bamboo and canvas in which the Wright brothers made their pioneer flight in 1903 was the first power-driven aeroplane capable of lifting a man and carrying him through the air, the problem of achieving human flight had for centuries tantalized the minds of men. Not surprisingly, most of them took birds as their models and tried to build flying machines with flapping

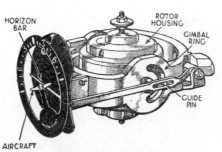

HORIZON BAR

ROTOR HOUSING

GIMBAL RING

GUIDE PIN

AIRCRAFT

ARTIFICIAL HORIZON

A tiny " aircraft " on the dial shows the pilot his position in relation to the horizon.

wings. One of the earliest of many inventors who endeavoured to achieve human flight by means of wings flapped by the arms and legs was Oliver of Malmesbury, an English monk who lived in the 11th century. The experiment failed, as did similar attempts by later inventors; for man is not built to fly under his own power. The human frame lacks the greatly developed sternum or breastbone of the bird, to which the wing muscles are attached; and the muscles of man's limbs are far weaker than the bird's wing muscles. Nonetheless, a considerable knowledge of the mechanism of flight was obtained by studying birds and winged insects, notably by Albertus Magnus (1193–1280) and Roger Bacon (1214–92).

Leonardo da Vinci (1452–1519) wrote various papers on the principles of flight which, by their grasp of essentials, have surprised modern aeroplane designers. By the end of the 17th century it was realized that the problem of human flight would not be solved by attempting to flap wings with the legs and arms, and a number of experiments were being made with gliders (q.v.). In 1660 Jules Allard, a Paris acrobat, managed to soar for a short distance, but was unable to control his movement through the air. In 1690 the possibility of power-driven flight was suggested by an Italian priest who designed an "aerial carriage" intended to be driven by the ignition of gunpowder rockets.

It was Sir George Cayley (1774–1857), a Yorkshire squire, whose practical and theoretical experiments entitled him to be called the father of modern aeronautics, who proved that the stability of a flying machine depended upon the angle at which the wings were set and upon the use of a rear fin and rudder. He made hundreds of experiments with propellers attached to gliders. Cayley said that a practical flying machine was impossible unless it had some source of mechanical power, but he still had the mistaken idea that such power must oscillate the wings of the machine as well as revolve a propeller.

The First Power-Driven Flight

The flapping wing fallacy died hard, but it was at last shown up by William Henson (1805–88), and John Stringfellow (1799–1883), who built a model aircraft which flew several yards. This was actually the first power-driven aeroplane to fly. The machine was a monoplane weighing 6½ lb. and had a wing surface of 18 square feet. It had two propellers, one on each side of the fuselage, driven in opposite directions by a rubber band from a centrally-placed steam engine. Steering and stability were provided for by a fan-shaped tail and a vertical rudder. The machine had a long fuselage below the wing, and was fitted with

Science Museum

EARLY 'BIRD-MAN'
An honoured place amongst the pioneers of flight belongs to the German, Otto Lilienthal, here seen in his glider in 1896, the year in which he was killed when his machine capsized.

landing wheels and a tail skid. Although the model made a number of short flights it was very unstable and erratic in flight.

Progress in this problem of stability was not advanced until 1870, when a Frenchman named Alphonse Pénaud (1850–80) succeeded in making a stable model aeroplane fitted with a twin-bladed propeller at the back driven by a length of twisted elastic. Careful shaping of the wings and tail kept the model remarkably steady in the air. On its first flight Pénaud's elastic-powered model flew a distance of 120 feet in 11 seconds. In 1879, another Frenchman, Jules Tatin, incorporated Pénaud's principles in a much larger model driven by compressed air. The machine weighed 4½ lb. and on its trial flight flew a distance of 200 feet at an altitude of 25 feet.

It is sometimes claimed that the first power-driven man-carrying aeroplane to leave the ground was the steam-engined machine named Avion, built and designed by Clement Ader (1841–1925) in 1890 and flown in France on October 9 of that year. But only one wheel of Ader's aeroplane left the ground. His machine was unstable and would have been quite incapable of any long flight.

Sir Hiram Maxim (1840–1916), better known as the inventor of a machine-gun, also devoted much attention to mechanical flight. In 1890 he completed a flying machine with a wing span of 100 feet, a height of 32 feet, and a length of 67 feet. With its 50 h.p. steam engine the Maxim aeroplane weighed 3½ tons. The inventor began experiments with his aeroplane running on two steel rails and with two timber guard-rails to prevent its rising more than two feet from the ground. On several occasions the machine lifted from the ground rails, but its behaviour proved that it was unstable, and its movement if it ever flew could not have been controlled. This brilliant inventor designed a remarkably light and efficient steam engine for his machine.

Further information essential to aeroplane stability was worked out by Otto Lilienthal (1848–96) who experimented with man-carrying gliders in 1891–95. He was the first man to obtain practical experience of the control of aircraft in free flight, and his work had far-reaching influence in aeroplane design.

About the same time, an American scientist, Samuel Pierpoint Langley (1834–1906), was carrying out flying experiments, and he built a model aeroplane in 1896. This had a wing span of 14 feet and was powered by a small steam engine. The aeroplane weighed 30 lb., including the engine, and on one occasion flew 4,200 feet at 30 m.p.h. Langley then turned his attention to the construction of a power-driven man-carrying aeroplane. This

aircraft, completed in 1903, was in shape and design an exact copy of the 1896 model. It weighed 800 lb. and was driven by a 52 h.p. petrol engine of the air-cooled radial type—the first application of the internal combustion engine to an aeroplane. On October 8, 1903, Langley's assistant took off from the

SUCCESS OF THE FIRST REAL AIRMEN

The Wright brothers, Wilbur and Orville, did not conquer the air in a day, or even in a year. Their success with an engine-driven machine on December 17, 1903, illustrated in the lower photograph, was the outcome of long experiments at Kitty Hawk, North Carolina, with gliders such as the 1902 type seen in the upper illustration.

U.S.A. The Wright machine, which achieved the distinction of being the first man-carrying aeroplane to fly under its own power, was a biplane with two propellers driven by a 8 h.p. petrol engine, and weighing 800 lb. Piloted by Orville Wright, the machine took off on the epoch-making flight and flew for a distance of 820 feet. For the next five years the Wright brothers continued their experiments. In September 1904 they made their first curved flight, and a month later flew a circular course of three miles in five minutes. By September 1905 they were able to fly a distance of 24 miles.

roof of a houseboat on the Potomac river; but before the machine became airborne it dived into the river. After that failure Langley ceased experimenting with aircraft.

On December 17, 1903, the first practical step in man's mastery of the air was taken by Wilbur Wright (1867–1912) and Orville Wright (1871–1948) on sandy hills near Kitty Hawk, North Carolina,

Although the Wright brothers' achievements created a sensation they received little public or official encouragement. Indeed, the American government refused to recognize their claim to have flown the first practical aeroplane.

Alberto Santos-Dumont (1873–1932), already well known as an airship pioneer, had made the first aeroplane flight in Europe on August 22, 1906. By 1908 aeroplane flying was really beginning to develop. In France, Voisin biplanes and Blériot and Antoinette monoplanes were flying regularly, while in Britain Alliott Verdon Roe (b. 1877) and Samuel Franklin Cody (1861–1913) were making experimental flights in machines of their own design and construction.

At that time, the farthest distance flown in Europe was the 12 miles by Henry Farman (b. 1874) in a Voisin biplane. In August 1909, however, Wilbur Wright brought a new biplane to France; and, on September 21 following, he flew a distance of 60 miles, remaining in the

" Daily Mirror "

CONQUEROR OF THE CHANNEL

This fragile-looking monoplane of his own design, with a 25-h.p. engine, took Louis Blériot, the Frenchman, on the first historic flight across the English Channel on July 25, 1909. His average speed was about 45 m.p.h.

AEROPLANE

air for 1½ hours. Aeroplane flying graduated from the experimental stage by 1909. In that year the first exhibition meetings took place in Europe, and pioneer airmen made a number of cross-country flights. On July 13, Louis Blériot (1872–1936) made the first place-to-place flight, on a triangular course of 33 miles from Etampes to Toury and Chevilly; 12 days later he flew the English Channel from Calais to Dover. Later in the year Henry Farman flew a distance of 118 miles in three hours and five minutes.

First Aero Meetings Near London

On February 27, 1909, J. T. C. Moore-Brabazon (b. 1884), later the first Baron Brabazon, flying a Voisin biplane at the Isle of Sheppey, Kent, made the first officially observed flight in Britain. On June 2, 1910, the Hon. Charles Stewart Rolls (1877–1910) flew the English Channel in both directions; and on December 18 of that year, Thomas Octave Murdoch Sopwith (b. 1888) piloting a British-made aeroplane of his own design, flew 169 miles from Eastchurch in Kent to Tirlemont in Belgium.

It was in 1910, too, that the British aircraft industry was established, when factories were opened by Hugh Oswald Short and his brothers, and by Frederick Handley Page (b. 1885). In the same year the first of many aero meetings was held at Hendon near London. In 1908 Geoffrey De Havilland, the founder of another famous aircraft firm, had made his first ascent in an aeroplane constructed by himself.

Not the least difficult problem to be overcome in developing practical aeroplane flight had been the evolution of a motor combining high power with low weight. The invention of the French Gnome rotary-engine was the first important step in that direction. In this engine the cylinders were arranged like the spokes of a wheel and revolved, while the crankshaft remained stationary. The propeller was fixed directly to the revolving crankcase, and the engine was cooled by the airflow created by its own rotation. Later, the "in-line" engine, with stationary cylinders of the motor-car type set in a row, was improved, and eventually excelled the Gnome in efficiency.

Rapid as had been its development in the 10 years since the Wrights' first flight, the aeroplane was still a comparatively flimsy and unreliable machine at the outbreak of the First World War in 1914. Its average speed was 80 m.p.h., its altitude 5,000–7,000 feet, and the maximum endurance (or time it could stay in the air) three hours. Under the tremendous impulse of war the aeroplane was to provide during the years 1914–18 the most remarkable advance ever achieved by any invention. At the beginning of hostilities there was little difference between civil and military aircraft, and the aeroplane was merely thought to be a useful aid for reconnaissance, artillery spotting or photographic work. The only weapons carried by many aircraft that went to France in 1914 were revolvers or rifles issued to pilots and observers. In a few "fighting biplanes" the observer had a machine-gun. Early in 1915 the Germans started armed reconnaissance flights over the British lines, and to defend its own aircraft the Royal Flying Corps (which later became the Royal Air Force) fitted a number of Bristol and Martinsyde scout aircraft with machine-guns. When the aeroplane had been armed, the logical step was to increase its speed so that it could chase and destroy enemy

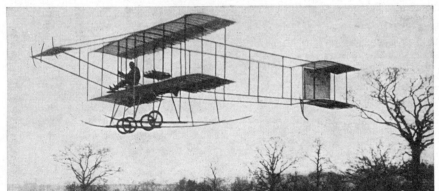

'Flight' and "Daily Mirror"

TWO FAMOUS PIONEERS OF BRITISH AVIATION

In the upper photograph is Claude Grahame-White flying a Henry Farman biplane. He made the first night flight in 1910, during a Manchester-London race. J. T. C. Moore-Brabazon, later Lord Brabazon, was the first Englishman to qualify for a pilot's certificate in England. In 1909, flying a Short-Wright biplane (lower), he won a prize for a circular flight.

Top photograph by courtesy of " Flight "

MODERN AIR LINER AND HISTORIC ATLANTIC FLYER

Vickers Viking air liners (top) are used by British European Airways. Fitted with two Bristol Hercules engines developing 1,675 h.p., the Viking cruises at 210 m.p.h., has a range of 1,700 miles and an all-up weight of 34,000 lb. This

Vickers-Vimy twin-engined converted bomber (lower) of the First World War was flown non-stop across the Atlantic in June 1919 by two British airmen, Captain J. Alcock and Lieut. A. Whitten Brown—the first direct crossing.

machines. By 1916, British, French and German fighters were flying at over 100 m.p.h., while engine power had risen from 80 to 200 h.p. When the war ended in 1918 there were fighters in service armed with four machine-guns and having single engines capable of developing 450 h.p. to give a maximum speed of 150 m.p.h.

The first bombers went into service late in 1916. They were converted " scouts " equipped with additional petrol tanks to increase their range, and fitted with external racks to carry a number of 20-lb. bombs. By the end of 1918 Britain possessed twin-engined 100 m.p.h. bombers defensively armed with two or more machine-guns, manned by a crew of five, and able to carry 2,000 lb. of bombs.

Equally rapid advances were made in the development of the seaplane. In 1914 a speed record of 86 m.p.h. had been set up with a seaplane, and during the war years of 1914–18 this type of aircraft was so improved that it could ride rough seas for hours if necessary and remain in the air for as long as 12 hours or more.

Along with the wartime development of the

aeroplane's structure, reliability and speed, there were steady advances in aids to safe and accurate flying. Aeroplanes were equipped with radio and with instruments for registering altitude, speed, angle of flight, drift, and so on. No less remarkable was the progress made in the engine. In 1914 the average aero engine weighed four pounds for each horse-power developed ; by 1918 this had been reduced to 1·8 lb. per horse-power.

When the First World War ended, nearly every country sought to apply military experience of aircraft use to commercial aviation. But as the aeroplane had been developed on military lines, the transport planes of the period just after the war were all conversions from military designs. The first London-Paris " ferry service " was made by a converted De Havilland bomber on August 25, 1919 ; the first direct Atlantic crossing by air was achieved on June 14–15, 1919, in a Vickers-Vimy bomber, as was the first England–Australia flight of November 11–December 10, 1919.

It was not long, however, before civil air transport demanded aircraft having greater flying

Fox

LONDON AIRPORT TERMINUS OF MANY SKYWAYS

Between Staines and Hayes in Middlesex, London Airport is situated on both sides of the Bath Road and when it was opened for civil aviation on January 1, 1946, it was the largest air terminal in Britain. It covers an area of 15,000 acres. The longest runway is 9,500 feet long, and all are surfaced with concrete a foot thick. Normally all long-distance passenger aeroplanes land at London Airport, and above a Lockheed Constellation is disembarking passengers.

comfort and lower petrol consumption than was possible in an aeroplane built for military purposes. Amongst the earliest of the purely civil aeroplanes was the British Pullman triplane of 1920. It was powered by four 410 h.p. engines, had a maximum speed of 120 m.p.h. and accommodated 14 passengers. One of the most striking advances in commercial aircraft design was the Handley-Page airliner of the Heracles type which Imperial Airways put into operation on the cross-Channel and main European routes in 1931. These machines were powered by four engines each developing 555 h.p. to give a cruising speed of 120 m.p.h. They carried a crew of four and 38 passengers. About the same time the Scipio flying boat was introduced on the Mediterranean links of the Empire air routes. It weighed 14 tons fully loaded, and carried 16 passengers and a crew of five. The four engines developed over 2,000 h.p. to give a maximum speed of 100 m.p.h.

Between the Two World Wars

Most of the foregoing aircraft were biplanes, mainly of wood construction ; but by 1934 the monoplane with retractable undercarriage had practically replaced the biplane for airline operation. An all-metal monoplane had been made by the German Junkers firm in 1918. In the next few years other countries adopted metal construction. One of the earliest of the all-metal monoplane air liners was the American Douglas D.C.2 Transport, known as the Flying Hotel. It was powered by two 710 h.p. engines, and carried 14 passengers and a crew of three at a top speed of 215 m.p.h. Within the next five years monoplane air liners were carrying passengers to India, Australia and New Zealand, and taking mails across the South Atlantic and to Canada and the United States.

Typical of the British air liner in service at the outbreak of the Second World War, in 1939, was the Armstrong Whitworth Ensign. This had accommodation for 40 passengers and a crew of five, and was powered by four 850 h.p. engines which gave the aircraft a maximum speed of 200 m.p.h. At the same time, flying boats had developed into such giants as the Short Empire. Powered by four 790 h.p. engines, this had a maximum speed of 200 m.p.h. and carried a crew of five, 17 passengers and two tons of mail.

Some idea of the advance in aircraft power and speed during the 25 years between the outbreak of the First World War and the start of the Second World War may be gained from the fact that whereas the fastest military aircraft in 1914 had an engine of 100 h.p. and a speed of 86 m.p.h., the British and German fighters of 1939 had engines of 1,000 h.p. and speeds of 340 m.p.h. By 1945, engine power of fighters had increased to 2,000 h.p. and speed to more than 500 m.p.h.

Great Technical Developments

During the course of the second great conflict, the fighter's armament of machine-guns was replaced by cannons and rocket projectors, while supercharging, special airscrews and pressurised cockpits enabled the aircraft to operate at altitudes of 50,000 feet. The largest bomber in service in 1918 had a top speed of 100 m.p.h. and a maximum bomb load of 2,000 lb. At the beginning of the Second World War the Royal Air Force had in service twin-engined bombers capable of flying 1,250 miles at a speed of 215 m.p.h., and carrying 4,000 lb. of bombs. By the end of the war four-engined bombers were carrying 20,000 lb. of bombs to a distance of 3,000 miles at a speed of 300 m.p.h. Amongst the principal technical developments incorporated in the bombers of the Second World War were the power-operated gun turrets, the bomb-aiming devices, and the radar and other aids to navigation.

Although the Second World War did not have such a revolutionary effect upon aeroplane design as had the conflict of 1914–18, it was responsible for two outstanding advances ; it made trans-

P.A.-Reuter

TAILLESS AEROPLANE WITH JET ENGINES

Constructed for research purposes, the jet-propelled A.W.52 made its first public flight on December 16, 1947. Its weight is 33,000 lb., and it is fitted with two Rolls-Royce Nene engines. The normal range is about 1,000 miles at a cruising speed of 280 m.p.h. There is less drag with tailless aircraft, and they weigh less than aeroplanes built with tails and having a similar performance. Behind the pilot's cockpit is a space for cargo or mail, with a capacity of two tons.

Atlantic flying a commonplace, and in the jet engine it provided the aeroplane with an entirely new kind of power unit.

In 1940 the Royal Air Force began flying American-built bombers to Britain. By the end of the war over 10,000 aircraft had flown the Atlantic, with a loss rate of only one per 1,000. Today the Atlantic air ferry is firmly established for the safe and regular transport of mails and passengers. Typical of the civil aircraft operating between England and the U.S.A. is the Boeing Stratocruiser, with four engines each developing 3,000 h.p. to give a cruising speed of 340 m.p.h.

Jet propulsion, which gave us aeroplanes that fly without propellers, was used by both the British and the German air forces for fighter aircraft in the last stages of the Second World War. The jet engine is more efficient at high altitudes than is the ordinary piston engine. In 1950 the de Havilland Comet, a civil airliner powered by four turbo-jet engines established a number of record flights from London to European and Near East countries. The Comet has accommodation for 48 passengers in a pressurised cabin, a cruising speed of 490 m.p.h. and a range of 3,400 miles. It has two auxiliary rocket motors to assist take-off. A jet-engined bomber, the Canberra, went into service with the Royal Air Force in 1951.

Because of their high speed, jet-engined fighters have replaced piston-engined fighters for first-line operational duties. The fastest British jet-fighter in service in 1950, the Meteor, had a speed of 585 m.p.h. with full fighting equipment. On June 19, 1947, a Lockheed jet-propelled Shooting Star set up a world speed record of 623·8 m.p.h.

Other Types of Aircraft

Aircraft is the name given to any kind of " flying machine," such as an airship, a balloon, or an aeroplane; as you will have read in the preceding pages, the aeroplane was the first to be brought to successful flight, so that for many years inventors concentrated upon it. But the Autogiro (q.v.) and the helicopter (q.v.) also are aircraft, distinguished by having one or more rotating members, or vertical airscrews. These rotors replace the ordinary aeroplane's propeller and fixed wings, but the Autogiro has also a horizontal airscrew. The glider is an aircraft without an engine.

Airships and balloons (both described under their own headings in other pages) are examples of lighter-than-air craft; they are supported in the

CONTRASTING POWER UNITS

Above is the Rolls-Royce Derwent turbo-jet engine, with which a Gloster Meteor put up a world record of 606 m.p.h. in 1945. The Rolls-Royce Eagle sleeve-valve engine (right) has twenty-four cylinders, is liquid-cooled and develops 3,500 h.p.

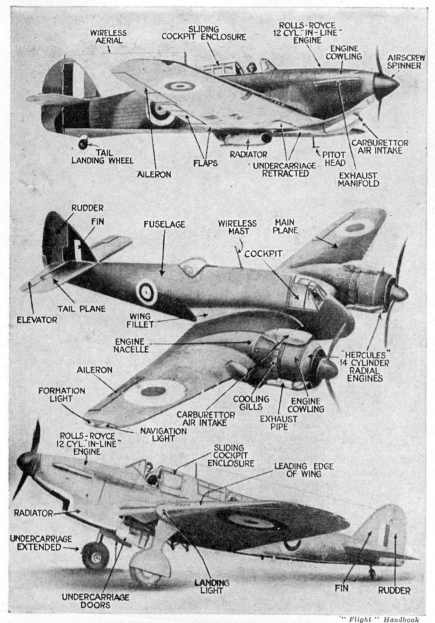

PARTS OF THREE SERVICE MACHINES

" Flight " Handbook

These photographs of three fighters famous in their day show the principal parts of the aircraft from above, beneath and grounded. Top, the Hawker Hurricane (1,260 h.p. Rolls-Royce engine.) Centre, the Bristol Beaufighter (two 1,400 h.p. Bristol Hercules engines). Bottom, the Fleet Air Arm Fairey Fulmar (Rolls-Royce 1,145 h.p. engine).

Gliders, as we have said, are aeroplanes without engines. A glider cannot take off under its own power ; it must be towed or launched into flight : Military gliders, towed by aeroplanes, are used to transport men and equipment of an airborne force. After they have been released, over the " target area," they can come to earth silently upon a clear or levelled area of ground, and do not require an aerodrome to land upon.

Powered heavier-than-air craft are of two principal types, the fixed wing (aeroplane) and the rotating "wing." The supporting surface of an aeroplane consists of fixed wings, but on some rotating-wing aircraft the revolving arms or rotors act as both supporting surface and lifters. In the helicopter the rotors or airscrews are kept revolving by an engine. The autogiro has a " free " rotor which acts like a windmill and is, in fact, normally turned by the air stream. In order to save a longer run at the take-off, there is an arrangement for driving the rotor from the engine, but after this the rotor is kept turning only by the wind caused by the autogiro's forward or other motion. When descending, the rotor acts like a parachute and slows the dropping motion, so that the autogiro can almost hover, like a flying insect. The helicopter can remain stationary a few feet, or many thousands, above the ground.

air by the buoyancy due to the light gas with which their flotation chambers are filled. All other kinds of flying machine are heavier-than-air craft, and will not leave the ground unless engine power is applied to drive them forward in the first place. How the aeroplane works has been explained earlier in this article ; as you will have read there, the airstream created by the forward movement of propeller-driven aircraft keeps the machine in the air. With jet-aircraft, gravity is defeated by the gas discharge to the rear, as in a rocket.

can really hover, and ary a few feet, or many ground.

Aeroplanes are generally classified by the number and arrangement of their wings ; a monoplane has a single wing, a biplane two superimposed wings. Most modern aeroplanes are monoplanes, of which there are three main types, high-wing, mid-wing and low-wing. Small aeroplanes are single-engined, while most long distance, large-carrying-capacity aeroplanes are four-engined.

Then there are jet-propelled aircraft, which do not require propellers but move through the air in much the same way as does a rocket.

The aeroplane may be again classified according to whether it is intended to take-off from or alight on land, water, or both. The first is called a land-plane and may have two landing-wheels and a tail skid; two landing-wheels and a tail-wheel; two landing-wheels fitted to the centre of the undercarriage and a third landing-wheel in the nose, an arrangement called a tricycle undercarriage; or it may have two pairs of central landing-wheels and a nose or tail-wheel.

Aeroplanes designed to take off or land on water are of two types, seaplanes and flying-boats. The seaplane has two floats in place of a pair of landing wheels, while the flying-boat has a fuselage shaped like a ship's hull which rests directly on the water when the aircraft is at anchor. An aeroplane able to operate from land or water is called an amphibian, and has a hull like that of a flying-boat, fitted with two landing-wheels which are retracted when the amphibian is on the water.

Passengers and Freight by Air

The first use of aeroplanes for commercial purposes was on September 9, 1911, when an air mail service was established between Hendon in Middlesex and Windsor in Berkshire, although the service lasted only a week. No further efforts were made to establish regular civil air transport until December 1918, when the R.A.F. formed a communications wing to carry government officials travelling between London and Paris. In March 1919 a second air mail service was set up to operate from Folkestone to Cologne, which was then headquarters of the British Army of occupation in Germany.

Between 1919 and 1920 a number of private companies were formed in Britain to carry passengers, freight and mail. By October 1922 British airlines were operating between London and Paris, Brussels, Cologne, Amsterdam, Cairo, Jerusalem and Baghdad. But it was realized that something better, on national lines, was needed, under government control. In April 1924, Imperial Airways was formed to take over a number of separate companies. Although maintaining services on a number of routes to the Continent, it was primarily concerned

"Flight"

SEAPLANE OF THE ROYAL NAVY
During the Second World War (1939-45) seaplanes were used by the Royal Navy for reconnaissance, amongst them being the Fairey Seafox. It had a 395-h.p. Napier Rapier engine, a speed of 120 m.p.h. with a range of 440 miles, and carried a crew of two. The Seafox was launched from its parent ship by catapult, and lifted on board by derricks at the end of its flight.

L.N.A.; Fox

OCEAN "PICK-A-BACK"
The idea of the Short-Mayo Composite aircraft was that a flying-boat (above) should take off with a long-range seaplane supported on a cradle on its back (right). The smaller machine was released at a safe height to continue its journey, and by this method was enabled to carry fuel for a much longer voyage. The seaplane had four engines of 395 h.p., a speed of 200 m.p.h., and a range of 3,500 miles. The Short flying-boat had four engines of 875 h.p.

Between 1925 and 1930 nearly every country in the world began operating air services. In some, as in Britain, air transport is a government monopoly ; in others, notably the United States, all air transport is in the hands of private companies. Air liners of 35 nations now provide services flying on regular time-tables to more than 200 countries, colonies and dependencies. Eight different nations maintain regular services

with developing services to the countries of the British Commonwealth. The first link in the chain of Imperial air communications, that between, Cairo and Basra, was established in January 1927 ; two years later the service was extended east and west to provide a regular air route between London and India. In February 1932, the London-Cape Town service began ; in July 1933, passengers and mail were carried by air from London to Calcutta, and at last, in 1933, a through air route was established between London and Australia.

Imperial Airways remained the sole operator of British overseas air services until the formation of British Airways in 1936. Three years later, Imperial Airways and British Airways were taken over by the government and amalgamated into the present British Overseas Airways Corporation. In 1945 all British European and internal air transport services were formed into a government-owned concern, British European Airways Corporation. British South American Airways, which had operated all British air services to South America, was absorbed by B.O.A.C. in 1949. The only private air transport concerns in Britain are the charter and air-taxi companies; they cater mainly for single journeys, but since 1950 have operated a few of the former B.E.A. services in the U.K.

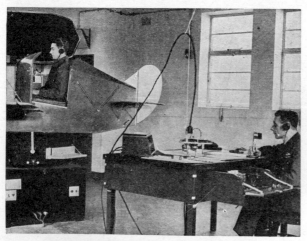

Miles Aircraft; Fox

GOODS LORRY OF THE SKY
This twin-engined Miles monoplane (top, in flight) can carry a ton of cargo 400 miles at 110 m.p.h. at a comparatively low cost for fuel and oil. It is called the Aerovan, can be loaded like a lorry (above), and will take nine passengers or a medium-sized car.

across the Atlantic at all seasons of the year. B.O.A.C. operate 66 return services weekly to different parts of the world, their aircraft flying 550,000 miles every week.

For its efficient operation, air transport require suitable airports. The largest civil airport in Britain is London Airport, at Heathrow, Middlesex (an illustration is printed in page 48). It has six concrete runways, the largest 9,500 feet long, on which the aeroplanes land or take off. Surrounding the runways is a perimeter along which the aircraft taxi preparatory to making their take-off run. Wherever possible, airports are built in an area free from obstructions. At night the tops of all buildings and masts, are marked with boundaries of the aerodrome, togther with the red lights; and usually there is a powerful red neon light which enables the approaching pilots to pick up the airport visually while still some distance away. There are also large wind-direction indicators, illuminated at night, and movable flood-lights to tell the pilot which runway he is to land on.

Other essential equipment are radio and radar direction finding transmitters; radio beacon approach and landing systems, which enable pilots to land safely even when they cannot see the ground; flash lighting for runways ; and a motor ambulance and fire service ready for any possible accidents.

Departure and arrival of air liners at an airport are controlled by signalling from a control tower overlooking the runways and under the supervision of an airport control officer. He lets the pilot know, either by visual signalling or by radio, when he can land or take off, tells him which runway to use and, when several aircraft wish to land at the same time, tells them in what order to come in. As is only to be expected,

LEARNING TO FLY ON THE GROUND
Pilots receive preliminary training on the ground in a Link trainer. The instructor (right) is connected by telephone with the pupil (left), and after giving him a course to fly checks this by instruments that show the course actually flown.

the kind of aeroplane and flying-boat used for carrying passengers and freight is rather different from that used in warfare. A steady speed, by no means as fast as that of the military aircraft, is aimed at. Comfort is well looked after, and safety is of course a primary requisite. Britain after the end of the Second World War (1939–45) looked to several new types of passenger aircraft on which to build up her oversea service. The Brabazon landplane, weighing 130 tons, was one of these. Flying boats have generally been replaced by land planes even for long sea crossings. The largest in service in 1950 was the Short Solent, powered by four piston-engines and having a speed of 200 m.p.h. She carried 78 passengers and a crew of five.

One of the latest aircraft developments is the flying wing, in which the aeroplane fuselage or body is merged into a single swept-back wing. Some are jet-propelled and others have engines driving airscrews. Among the former type is the British A.W.52 (*see page* 49), which is all wing and has no tail. It was built as an experiment and has two Rolls-Royce Nene jet engines which gave a top speed of 500 miles per hour; for cruising the speed was 280 m.p.h., and the aircraft could fly almost 1,000 miles at this speed. Behind the pilot's cockpit was a compartment for freight; up to nearly two tons of mail could be carried.

Since there was no tail, the fins and rudders were paired, and fitted at the wing-tips. One control surface fitted on each wing did duty for both elevator and aileron. The pilot's compartment was " pressurized "; this means that the air pressure was kept at about ordinary atmospheric pressure by means of pumps, regardless of the fact that the air pressure outside may be much lower as the aircraft flies higher.

In emergency, by operating a switch the pilot, on his seat, could be ejected right out of the aircraft in an instant; he was thrown clear of the machine, and could get his parachute into action. It is possible that the whole design of commercial aircraft may be altered in future years if the " flying wing " type proves a success.

Aeschylus (525–456 B.C.).

For rugged power, sublimity and grandeur, the plays of A e s c h y l u s (p r o n. ēs'-kil-*us*) stand without a peer. No modern dramatist could take any of his tragedies as a model, for the Father of Greek Tragedy wrote for the huge open-air theatre on the Acropolis at Athens, for the religious festival of the god Dionysus; thus it is that

AESCHYLUS
This bust in the Capitol at Rome well suggests a master of tragic drama.

his mighty conceptions cannot be confined within the limits of a closed modern theatre, or be properly seen by artificial light.

Aeschylus was born at Eleusis, near Athens, and no doubt he was influenced by the many religious processions and spectacles to be seen in this centre of Greek worship. He reached the prime of life when Greece was struggling for independence against Persia; he was present at the battles of Marathon—where he is said to have been wounded—and Salamis. He wrote 70 or more plays, of which unfortunately only seven have come down to us.

Many of his dramas were arranged as " trilogies," that is, groups of three related plays. The Oresteia (story of Orestes), consisting of the Agamemnon, Choephori and Eumenides, tells of the return of Agamemnon from Troy, and his murder at the hands of Clytemnestra, his unfaithful wife; the vengeance exacted by his son Orestes, who kills his mother and her lover; the pursuit of Orestes by the Furies and his absolution by the Areopagus at Athens presided over by the goddess Athena. The Persae is a song of triumph for the defeat of the Persians. The Prometheus Bound is a rendering of the legend of the superhuman benefactor who stole fire from heaven for men, and taught mankind the useful arts. (*See* Prometheus).

For some 16 years, between 484 and 468 B.C., Aeschylus carried off prize after prize, but in 468 his place as the favourite poet of Athens was taken by a man 30 years younger, namely Sophocles (*q.v.*). Shortly afterwards Aeschylus left Athens for Sicily and there, at Gela, he died.

Aesculapius.

(Pron. ēs-kū-lā'-pi-*us*). Although Homer speaks of him as a mortal, the classical mythology of Romans and

Alinari

AESCULAPIUS THE DIVINE PHYSICIAN
Aesculapius—known to the Greeks as Asclepios—was the Greek god of healing ; and in this sculptured panel, now in the National Museum at Athens, he is shown with his daughter Hygieia, goddess of health, receiving worshippers or patients in what might be called in modern parlance his " consulting room."

Greeks generally regarded Aesculapius (in Greek, Asclepios) as the god of medicine, son of Apollo. He was educated by the centaur Chiron. So profound was his knowledge of the healing art that he was able to restore the dead to life, and his power aroused the anger of the god Zeus, who, fearing that he might make all men immortal, killed him with a thunderbolt. As a token of the gratitude of mankind Aesculapius was raised to the rank of a god. In later times the chief seat of his worship was Epidaurus, on the coast of Laconia.

The temples of Aesculapius were usually placed in healthy situations outside cities, on hills or near springs; they served the purpose of hospitals. A cock was often sacrificed to the god by those who had been cured of their sickness. In 293 B.C. his worship was introduced into Rome, to avert a pestilence, the god being carried from Epidaurus in the form of a snake. A guild called the Asclepiadae, of which the famous Greek physician Hippocrates was a member, was formed of his supposed descendants. Homer speaks of Aesculapius as having two sons, one named Machaon and the other Podalirius. They were both skilled in the healing art, and attended the Greek army during the Trojan War in their professional capacity. In art Aesculapius is generally represented as bearded, with a Zeus-like head, the lower part of his body covered with a mantle. His symbol is a staff with a snake (the emblem of renewal) coiled round it. Down through the ages, it has been associated with medicine, and the rod of Aesculapius with a serpent entwined appears in the badge of the Royal Army Medical Corps.

Royal Army Medical Corps Badge.

AESOP

Though Aesop narrated his fables in Greece about 2,500 years ago, they are still universally regarded as the cleverest and most amusing of their kind.

Bust in Villa Albani, Rome

Aesop. (Pron. ē'sop). The frogs, according to the fable, were grieved because they had no king and sent ambassadors to Zeus, chief of the gods, to ask him for a ruler. Realizing that the frogs were very stupid, Zeus cast down a log into the pond. The frogs were terrified at the splash it made as it hit the water, and sought shelter at the bottom. When they noticed that the log did not move they grew to despise this lifeless ruler and climbed over the log and squatted upon it.

After some time they again sent messengers who requested the god to appoint another sovereign. This time Zeus sent an eel to the pond. He was an easy-going good-natured fellow, and the frogs thought that he too made a very poor king for them.

So they sent a third time to the god to ask for a different ruler. Zeus was now out of patience and sent them a stork, who each day ate up a frog or two until soon there was none left to croak and complain.

This story, which Aesop is said to have related to the citizens of Athens as a warning to them against attempting to replace the tyrant Peisistratus, is a very good example of the fables that have preserved Aesop's name.

Tradition says that Aesop, who lived from about 620 to 560 B.C., was originally a slave, ugly and deformed in person, but of brilliant mind. In his fables animals are made to act and talk as human beings, and moral lessons and pieces of wisdom are conveyed in such a forceful and delightful way that they have been popular with young and old ever since. Innumerable translations have been made of these stories in most languages, and Aesop is a favourite gift book for all occasions. Besides conveying practical moral lessons the tales are very witty—a character which even translation

HIS MASTER INTRODUCES AESOP TO THE FAMILY CIRCLE

In this painting by P. Glaize, Aesop, a slave of unusually ugly appearance, and quite unknown to fame, is being introduced into the household of Xanthus, his new master. The latter's family, who at first obviously thought little of their acquisition, were soon astonished by Aesop's brilliant wit. Actually, very little is definitely known of Aesop and his life, but his fables, translated into almost every language, remain as a perpetual memorial to his genius and wit.

AFGHANISTAN'S HILL-ENCIRCLED CAPITAL

Kabul lies on a plateau 7,000 feet above sea level and on every side are hills. The city itself is unimpressive, for most of the buildings, except the palace and one or two others, are old and dilapidated, and the streets are narrow and squalid. Kabul is the seat of Government. Although there are a Prime Minister, a Cabinet, a National Assembly, and a Senate, many of the tribes have little regard for law and order and pay tribute only when compelled to do so.

does not destroy. Aesop was freed by his master after a time, and gained such a reputation that he was invited to live at the court of Croesus, King of Lydia. His end came, it is said, when he was sent by Croesus to the temple of Apollo, at Delphi, where he so aroused the anger of the Delphians that he was thrown headlong from a precipice.

Aesop did not write out his fables, but recited them, and they were handed down from memory. Over two centuries later an Athenian wrote down the fables as they were then told, and still later a Greek named Babrius made another collection of them. For a thousand years they were lost to memory, until a copy of the collection made by Babrius was found in the monastery of Mt. Athos, in 1844. It is from this collection that later translations have been made.

Afghanistan.

There are but few roads by which the traveller may pass from the North - West Frontier Province of India (now a part of Pakistan) into the wild country of Afghanistan. Chief of these is the famous Khyber Pass, winding through the steep and barren Hindu Kush mountains from Peshawar to Kabul. Even today, at this grim gateway, the caravans may be attacked by fierce tribesmen for ever raiding along the whole of the frontier; until 1947 a strong British garrison was maintained at the head of the Pass always ready for action.

In every direction access to Afghanistan is difficult: northwards, a wall of mountains bars it from Russia; to west and south, barren deserts separate it from Iran (Persia) and Pakistan; in the east, mountains divide it from Pakistan. On all sides it is defended by a natural barrier.

Caravans going to Afghanistan start from Peshawar, the nearest railway centre of the Dominion of Pakistan. Occasionally a Hindu, perhaps a shopkeeper returning to Kabul, the capital of the country, is a traveller in this motley crowd ; and sometimes a white-faced European—but rarely. For a European must have a special permit before he is allowed to make his way into this forbidden country.

Into Pakistan the shuffling beasts of burden, ponies and camels, carry gorgeous embroideries and carpets from Turkistan and Iran, and cotton, wool, silk, dried fruits, madder, asafoetida, much liked by the peoples of India and Pakistan as a food seasoning, and hides. Back into their

MOUNTAINOUS AFGHANISTAN

This contour map shows the position of Afghanistan, set between Russia and the plains of the Dominion of Pakistan.

AFGHANISTAN

SHOPPING IN AFGHANISTAN
As in most Oriental countries, the equivalent of our shops are little stalls set in the roadway or jumbled together in the warren of lanes that form a bazaar. Above, tribesmen are turning over the goods in a clothier's store.

ment, enabled the British to control the foreign policy of Afghanistan for many years, but in 1919 (after the Third Afghan War) the country became wholly independent. In the Second Afghan War, Sir Frederick (later Earl) Roberts made a sensational march from Kabul to relieve a British force which was besieged at Kandahar.

In the First World War (1914-18), intrigue caused the murder of the reigning Amir, Habibullah, and then the determination of King Amanullah to westernize his country led to a revolution in 1928–29 and his abdication. The evacuation of the British residents of Kabul by the R.A.F. was a thrilling phase of the revolution. The throne eventually passed to Nadir Khan, who was assassinated in 1933. Mahommed Zahir succeeded him.

Afghanistan is a lofty plateau on which very high mountain ranges extend in a general south-westerly direction from the Hindu-Kush to the Persian boundary, sloping off into desert country in the south. A branch of the Russian Trans-caspian railway terminates about 75 miles north of Herat, at the boundary, and railways in Pakistan carry passengers to the head of the Khyber Pass and to other parts of the frontier. The Khyber Pass is fit for motor traffic, and trade routes with fairly good roads lead into Turkistan and Pakistan, and connect the principal cities of Afghanistan—Kabul, Mazar-i-Sharif, Kandahar, and Herat. The mineral resources of Afghanistan, mainly undeveloped, are gold and silver (in small quantities), coal, iron, antimony, lead, copper, sulphur, gypsum, and nitre. Much fruit is grown, and crops include wheat, millet, barley, and rice.

At Kabul are factories for the manufacture of matches, buttons, leather, boots and furniture, a wool factory at Kandahar and at Kabul, and a cotton factory at Jebal-us-Siraj. In 1946 Afghanistan embarked on a four-year programme of road-making, irrigation, bridge building and airfield construction. The area is about 250,000 square miles; population, approximately 10,000,000.

fastnesses they take cotton goods, tea and sugar. Four-fifths of the country's trade is with the merchants of Pakistan and India. The Afghans are primarily soldiers and farmers. The ruling tribe, the Durani, claims descent from the lost tribes of Israel, and has decidedly Jewish features.

Two costly wars (1839–42 and 1878–80), plus a constant subsidy from the Anglo-Indian govern-

ON THE ROAD FROM PAKISTAN TO KABUL
About thirty-three miles long and in parts only fifteen feet wide, the Khyber Pass connects Peshawar in Pakistan with Kabul, the capital of Afghanistan. Fierce fighting took place in the Pass during the Afghan Wars of 1839–42, 1878–80 and 1919. Through it runs the ancient caravan route from trade centres of Pakistan and India, and motor-vehicles have not completely replaced camels on this road. Its military importance today is as great as ever.

GLIMPSES OF AFRICAN LIFE IN VILLAGE TOWN & JUNGLE

Frits Henle

This young girl's home is in Tripoli, the principal city of Libya in North Africa, and her fine features are typical of her race. Her ornaments are those worn by the more prosperous Arab women—heavy metal bracelets, earrings scarcely less massive, and a necklace of metal charms and beads. She is standing against the background of a house whose white walls and tiny, window-like apertures are characteristic of the architecture of North Africa.

PAY-DAY IN THE AFRICAN BUSH

Though the greater part of Africa's vast expanse is left to Nature, the white man has succeeded in establishing many farms and plantations, particularly in the more temperate regions of the south. But even so, practically all the hard manual labour is performed by natives, for Europeans cannot stand many hours of exposure to the hot sun. Above we see a number of native labourers lined up to receive their well-earned wages, after clearing the bush.

BIG GAME 'SHOT' BY THE CAMERA

Paul L. Hoefler; Marcus Maxwell

South Africa was once the paradise of the big-game hunter, but in the 19th century the slaughter of its noble beasts went on so indiscriminately that now only the photographer is permitted to track them to their lairs without special permission. The lioness in the upper photograph gazes around her quite unaware that she is sitting for her portrait. Below, two rhinoceroses in East Africa who have also been unconsciously posing for the photographer.

SUSPICION AT THE WATER-HOLE

Great herds of elephants roam the jungles of Central Africa; but, except in the Belgian Congo, African elephants are not rounded up and used for beasts of draught or burden as are the Indian, for they are of a much fiercer disposition. Numbers of them, however, have been shot for their ivory tusks. This photograph shows a magnificent specimen of an African elephant that has come down to a pool in the evening for water.

ZULU BELLES AT THE VILLAGE POOL

Dorien Leigh

There are no water-taps in the African villages, and in the cool of the morning and again at sunset women walk perhaps several miles to obtain what water they require for domestic purposes—fortunately that is very little. This tramp, however, is no hardship to such women as the sturdy Zulus seen here carrying their primitive clay pots of native manufacture, for the time for drawing water is also the time for an enjoyable gossip.

UNHURRIED PLAY AND LEISURED BUSINESS

G.P.A.; Topical

Squatting in the open outside their living hut, the two young natives of Angola (Portuguese West Africa), seen in the upper photograph, are deeply engrossed in a variation of the game we know as chess. In the lower photograph, taken in the market-place of Bathurst, the fine seaport and capital of the British colony of Gambia (also in West Africa), an extraordinary assortment of clothes and knick-knacks is being offered for sale by the local ' shopwalkers.'

TRIBESMEN SKILLED IN SPORT AND DANCE

E.N.A.

About one third of the whole area of Africa is within the British Commonwealth. From the table-lands in the Northern Province of Nigeria, in West Africa, come the dancers seen at the top of this page. Far away, in Tanganyika, formerly part of German East Africa but now governed by Britain under United Nations Trusteeship, we find the native hunters seen below. Tanganyika abounds in antelopes, giraffes, lions and other big game.

SHOPPING IN AN AFRICAN BAZAAR

Fritz Henle

The arid country of Libya, which adjoins Egypt on the west, has been extensively developed and modernized in recent years. Native life in the ancient capital city of Tripoli is little changed, however, and, as seen in this photograph, merchants squatting on their rugs in the bazaar, partly shaded from the glare of the mid-day sun, offer choice wares to the occasional customer, always prepared to haggle earnestly and endlessly as to the price.

The HOMELAND of the NEGRO RACES

Second in size of the continents (Asia being the largest), Africa has a story as romantic as any in history. Land of ancient magic and mystery, its activities and peoples are becoming of increasing importance in world affairs.

Africa. Five thousand years ago Africa was the home of one of the world's earliest civilizations—Ancient Egypt. Yet the work of the Egyptians, great as it appears, was a mere scratch on the surface of the vast African continent. Farther west, Phoenician traders settled and laid the foundations of Carthage, which for a time challenged the supremacy of Rome. But only a few ruins of the Carthaginians are left to mark the scene of their flourishing culture of the 3rd century Before Christ.

One after another, Greeks, Romans, Vandals and Arabs occupied the Mediterranean fringe of the "Dark Continent." Great cities were built, prosperous states grew up, arts and letters flourished, Christianity was established and then succeeded by Mahomedanism. But none of these peoples ever measured its strength against the mysterious forces of the interior, or reached beyond a narrow strip along the northern sea. The roots of civilization remained planted in Europe and Asia. The faces of the settlers were always turned northward, while a hundred miles to the south the silent wilderness of desert or jungle watched night and day, ready to swallow up their work the instant their vigilance was relaxed.

Turn to the map of Africa as we know it today. From the tip of Cape Blanc in the Mediterranean to Cape Agulhas at the extreme south, the continent measures 5,000 miles. From Cape Verde in the west to Cape Guardafui in the east, the width is 4,600 miles. Between these four points lies a territory of 11,500,000 square miles, three times as large as Europe, nearly one and one-half times the size of North America, and more than one-fifth of all the land area in the world. But consider how compact this mass of land appears. Cut off by water from the rest of the world, except for the 80-mile strip of the Suez isthmus in the north-east, Africa's almost unbroken coast offered very few sheltering harbours,

Extent.—From Cape Blanc (37° 21′ N.) to Cape Agulhas (34° 51′ S.) ; and from Cape Verde (17° 33′ W.) to Cape Guardafui (51° 21′ E.). Length, 5,000 miles : breadth, 4,600 miles ; area, 11,500,000 sq. m.
Population.—About 125,000,000 blacks ; 30,000,000 light race.
Sahara Desert.—Area, 3,500,000 square miles, the largest desert in the world.
Chief Rivers.—Nile (3,500 miles) ; Congo (about 3,000 miles—greatest volume of water of any river in the world except the Amazon) ; Niger (2,600 miles) ; Zambezi (1,600 miles).
Highest Mountain.—Kilimanjaro (19,325 feet above the sea).
Largest Lakes.—Lake Victoria (26,828 sq. miles), next to Lake Superior the largest in the world. Lake Tanganyika, 12,700 sq. miles.
Greatest Cataract.—Victoria Falls on Zambezi River, between 370 and 400 feet high and one mile wide.

and early seafarers did not come often or stay very long on such inhospitable shores.

Consider next the structure of the land itself. In contrast with other continents, Africa has a very small area of low ground. Almost everywhere the walls of the great table-lands rise abruptly a short distance from the sea. The coastal strip between is usually barren and filled with brackish mangrove swamps. Early explorers found that the few great streams which succeed in breaking through these coast walls are almost invariably closed by sand-bars at their mouths, while their courses higher up are interrupted by rapids and cataracts, which rendered travel even in small boats next to impossible.

But these obstacles, forbidding as they appear, are only the defences of the outer gates. Turn your back to the Atlas Mountains in the north-west and to the site of ancient Carthage on the bay south-east of Cape Bon, or leave the ruins of the old Greek settlement of Cyrene on the promontory east of the Gulf of Sidra, and travel southward. Before many miles, the rocky hills smooth out into

Paul Hoefler

MASAI WOMEN OF EAST AFRICA
Most Masai live on a reservation in Kenya, though a few are still to be found in Tanganyika. With the women jewelry takes the form of metal rings usually worn as necklaces, but also on their arms and legs. The more rings a woman thus displays as personal adornment, the higher is her social position.

LIFE IN NORTH AFRICA'S DESERTS AND TOWNS

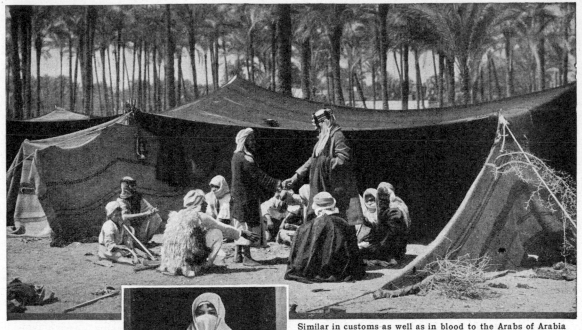

Veiled ladies in white, stepping out of doorways in Algiers (right), are part of the mysterious oriental charm of the city, with its Moslem ways.

Five cowrie shells in a row on the forehead of the Berber baby (below), protect him from the evil eye, so his mother believes.

Similar in customs as well as in blood to the Arabs of Arabia are these nomadic people whom we see above, camping in their haircloth tents in an oasis. Leisurely hospitality over the tall brass coffee pot is a gracious Arab custom.

Stone-lipped desert wells, like the one at the left, may be hidden by rims of blown sand. Yet the natives find them in the pathless Sahara with uncanny precision.

The streets of Tangiers resound to the music of wailing flute and throbbing drum now and then, when the begging Mohammedan dervishes are out to collect alms from the faithful.

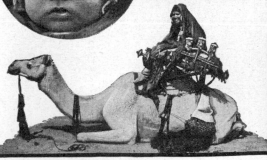

A contrast to the veiled women of the towns is this free, happy-looking girl above, riding across the Sahara in her gaudily adorned seat on the camel's back.

SOME OF AFRICA'S BLACK PEOPLES AT HOME

In some parts of the Belgian Congo the natives live in model villages like this, built under government supervision.

Conical "mushroom" huts made of reeds or rushes cluster together in this Mashona "kraal" or village in South Rhodesia.

Brass necklaces, wristlets, and armlets account for the smile of this Zulu belle in the doorway of her hut.

Little chaps, but mighty hunters, are the Congo pigmies called the Ituri. Full-grown men average only four and a half feet in height.

The Angola blacksmith (left, above) is hammering out a knife on a crude anvil, with a mate to fan his charcoal fire with a bellows. That fancy head-dress of the Natal rickshaw boy at the right is made of horns.

Gorgeous plumes and bedecked shield identify the Zulu prince at the left. The women are waving goat's-hair on sticks in the wedding dance. At the right is a Somali warrior in cotton dress, or "tobe."

rolling sand-dunes stretching endlessly toward the horizon. Trees and vegetation disappear. The heat grows intense, pouring down from above, then rising again in shimmering waves from the burning ground. This is the beginning of the great Sahara Desert, which for ages turned back the tide of civilization approaching from the north.

This ocean of sand and stone, spread out across the continent for 3,500,000 square miles, greater in size than the whole United States, is without a single river, from the Nile on the east to the Atlantic Ocean on the west. Here and there along the ancient caravan routes a traveller can find an oasis, a rare spot where a little water has forced its way to the surface, giving life to date palms, acacia bushes, and a patch of green herbage. Arabs moving south in winter and north in summer graze

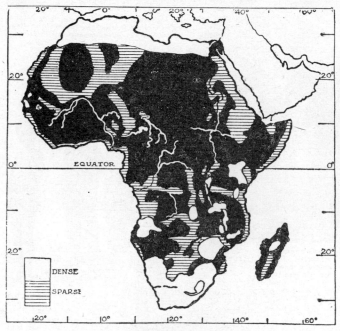

BLACK AND WHITE IN AFRICA

In this sketch map the portions of Africa most densely populated by people of the white races are indicated in white, those more sparsely populated (mainly by missionaries and a few traders) are lightly shaded. In the areas shown black all the people are of that colour.

their sheep, goats, and camels on the desert scrub. Now, across the face of this king of the world's deserts, motor-roads are slashed, and refuelling points mark man-made oases in what was untrodden sand. Aircraft cleave the skies : a passenger service from London Airport to Lagos in Nigeria does the trip in 24 hours.

The Lesser Atlas Mountains, with several peaks over 6,000 feet high, form the northern boundary of the Sahara from Morocco to Tunisia. On the southern boundary is Lake Chad, lying between French Equatorial Africa and Nigeria. When the Shari and Yo rivers bring their flood-waters from the south and west the lake is about 150 miles long and 20 to 25 feet deep; but it is slowly drying up, and it is only a matter of time before Lake Chad will have disappeared altogether. South of the Sahara lies that central plateau and forest region

which stood out to the last against the explorer, the scientist, the missionary and the soldier.

It would perhaps be better to enter this region from the west, in the footsteps of the first explorers, for the desert route is not the best way into the heart of Africa. Let us land, then, on the Guinea Coast, the Ivory Coast, the Gold Coast or the Congo Coast—those western shores whose romantic names conceal a history of cruelty, suffering, sacrifice, disease and death. It was here that the ranks of American slaves were recruited in their thousands. Here for nearly 100 years the fierce Negro warriors of the Ashanti kingdom successfully resisted the British, and here fever carried off so many victims that the lands of the west coast became known throughout the world as the " white man's grave." Two great rivers water this region, the Niger and the giant Congo. The latter is the largest river in Africa, and, next to the Amazon, the largest in the world if we count the volume of water that it pours into the ocean. The country drained by these rivers, crossed by the Equator, is marked by fierce heat and tremendous rains, which together produce for hundreds of miles a tangle of trees and vegetation so thick that it can be traversed only by way of the narrow footpaths beaten by the naked feet of savages for hundreds of years.

Dreaded Tsetse Fly

The elephant and the hippopotamus are able to force their way through this jungle, but few other large animals venture here. However, the giant trees, interlaced with huge creepers and vines, form the natural home of the chimpanzee and the great gorilla, who build their nests in the thick foliage. Countless varieties of monkeys chatter in the tree tops, and innumerable parrots and other birds of bright plumage dwell here, while insects find it a paradise. Africa, having comparatively few poisonous snakes, is said to have more varieties of scorpions, centipedes, spiders, ants, and other such creatures which bite and sting, than any other part of the globe. Worst of all is the tsetse fly, whose bite brings death to cattle, horses and dogs, and which spreads the " sleeping sickness " that kills thousands of men every year. This vast region of woods is inhabited by numberless tribes, often at war with each other, who live from 10 to 50 miles apart in clearings. There they grow the plantains, bananas, beans, tobacco, gourds, melons, etc., on which they live.

On the east coast we find different conditions. Although fever infests the coast line here also, the land rises to greater heights, usually affording quicker relief from the tropical heat. It is on the east side of Africa that the chief mountains of the continent are massed, running parallel to the coast line from the Red Sea in the north to the southern capes. In Tanganyika, about 200 miles from the coast and 200 miles south of the Equator, the peak of Kilimanjaro soars 19,325 feet, the highest mountain in Africa, on whose broad sides dwell

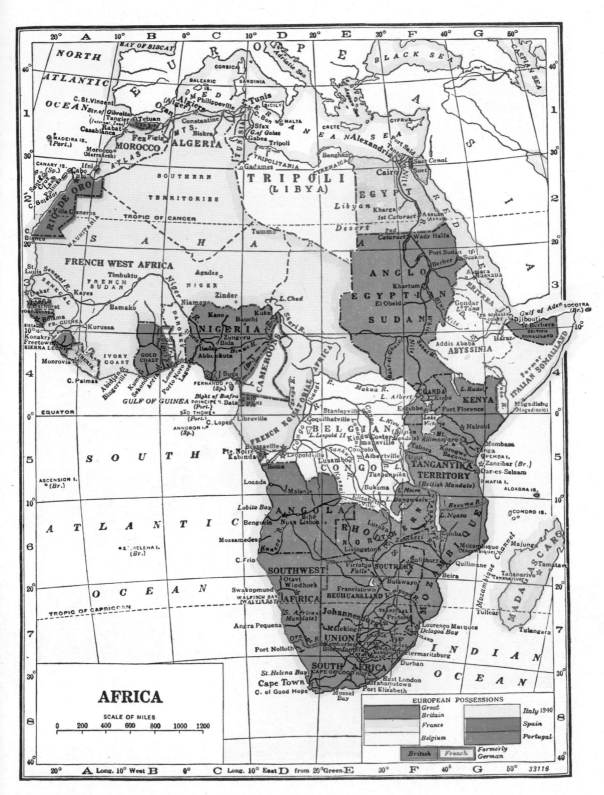

AFRICA

SCALE OF MILES

0   200   400   600   800   1000   1200

EUROPEAN POSSESSIONS

Great Britain		Italy 1940
France		Spain
Belgium		Portugal

British   French   Formerly German

33116

FACTS YOU SHOULD KNOW ABOUT AFRICA

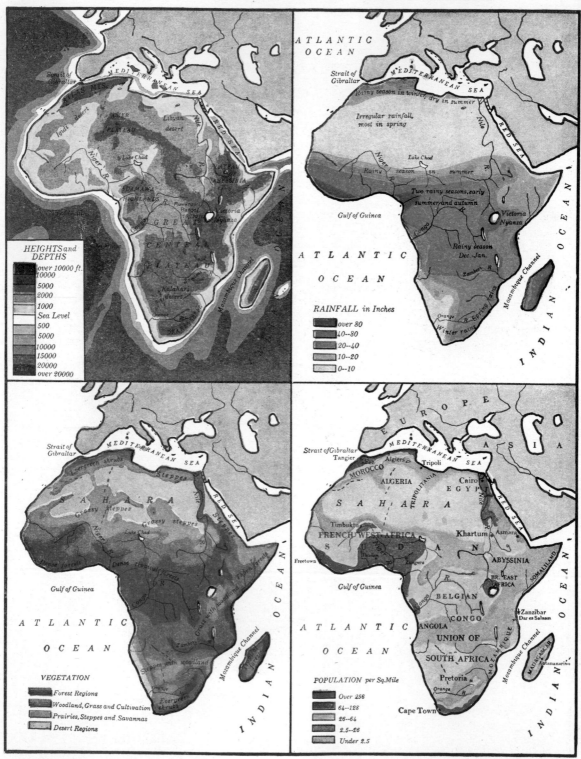

The development of every country is largely due to natural conditions. The most important of these natural conditions—physiography (physical features of the land) and rainfall—are shown in the first two of these four maps of the great continent of Africa. In the next two are presented, in the same clear, pictorial form, the facts with regard to vegetation and density of population, which are largely the result of the climate and physiography of the country.

To face page 69

more than 200 tribes. On these mountains, too, plants with which we are familiar in Britain grow to enormous dimensions. Thus, heather becomes a tree, while the groundsel, with us a lowly weed, is taller than a man.

Mountains in equatorial Africa rise suddenly out of the ground without many foothills. They do not run in great ranges, but seem to have been thrown up separately, while between them are wide stretches of high plateau land, called in Central Africa " savannas " and in the south the " veld." These lands are usually rocky, dotted with brush and tall grasses, and are the favourite home of several kinds of African big game.

Look again at the map. The African savanna region stretches from the Senegal river on the extreme west coast directly eastward to the headwaters of the Nile, including the Sudan and forming the northern boundary of the great forests and the southern boundary of the Sahara. It then turns southward, takes in the territory of the great lakes, then back to the west coast again, encircling the forests, while a broad spur stretches toward the south-east shores. Here dwell the lion, the leopard, the hyena, and its relative the aard-wolf or earth wolf, the rhinoceros, the buffalo, the zebra, the wild boar, the giraffe and its rare cousin the okapi, the ostrich, the hartebeest, and scores of other antelopes and gazelles; and in vast big-game reserves they can roam undisturbed by human hunters. Here also grow the gigantic baobab or monkey-bread tree, and elephant grass which grows to 10 feet in height.

The principal African lakes form a group running north and south along the " Great Rift Valley " formed by the east coast highlands. The greatest is Lake Victoria, or Victoria Nyanza (*nyanza* means " lake "), the principal feeder of the Nile; it measures 230 miles at the widest point and, next to Lake Superior, is the largest body of fresh water on the globe. The Kagera river, the ultimate headstream of the whole Nile system, flows into it. Lake Victoria in turn flows into Lake Albert to the north-west, a lake about 100 miles long and 20 broad, which receives also, through the Semliki river, the waters of Lake Edward, 100 miles farther south; the latter lake is about 40 miles in diameter. In between Lake Albert and Lake Edward, and east of the Semliki river, appear the snowclad peaks of Ruwenzori, the famous " Mountains of the Moon," where the ancient Egyptians believed the Nile had its source.

Directly to the south of Lake Edward the great Kirunga volcano with its mile-wide fiery crater divides the lakes which flow into the Nile from those which feed the Congo and Zambezi rivers. Greatest of these is Lake Tanganyika, the longest lake in the world, 400 miles in length, which at high water flows into the Congo through the Lukuga river.

Of the Zambezi lakes, Nyasa is the most noteworthy; 340 miles long, it reaches in places a depth of 2,600 feet. The Victoria Falls of the Zambezi are nearly 400 feet high and a mile wide.

Let us now approach South Africa by way of the sea. Herodotus, the Greek historian of the 5th century before Christ, relates that 100 years before his time Phoenician navigators sailed round Africa, hugging the coast from the Red Sea to the Mediterranean. If anything was learned on this early journey it was quickly forgotten: map makers for 2,000 years afterwards showed the continent ending at the romantically named " Mountains of the Moon."

A new era in exploration dawned, however, when early in the 15th century Prince Henry of Portugal, called " The Navigator," devoted him-

A. T. Schofield

UGANDA HUNTERS WITH A HATED ENEMY
Crocodiles are to be found in most of the rivers and lakes of tropical Africa, and in Uganda, as elsewhere, they are a menace to the women who fetch water from the streams. The hunters band together to kill these dangerous reptiles, which they try to surprise and spear while the creatures are asleep.

self to finding a sea route to the East round the African coasts. His untiring efforts, carried forward after his death by others, led at last to the rounding of the Cape of Good Hope by Bartholomew Diaz in 1488, and the successful voyage to India of Vasco da Gama in 1497-98. This achievement led a century and a half later to the Dutch settlement of Cape Town in 1652, the first permanent colony established by white men in South Africa.

Travelling northward from the Cape of Good Hope, we find the Nieuwveldt Mountains, the Great Karroo highlands, and farther to the east the Drakensberg range, rising abruptly from the coast to an altitude of from 2,000 to 10,000 feet. Passing through the high interior plateau or veld, we reach the Orange river, the only large stream in lower South Africa. Beyond the Orange river, and midway to the Zambezi, lies the Kalahari desert, 600 miles wide.

The animal inhabitants of the interior of South Africa do not differ greatly from those of the northern savannas. The native ostrich has been tamed to a large extent for the sake of its valuable feathers. The chief wealth of this region lies in its great diamond fields, centred at Kimberley, and its gold mines in the Johannesburg district, in the Orange Free State, and farther north in Southern Rhodesia. How these affected the history of this country is related elsewhere, see South Africa.

The warlike character of the natives long delayed a peaceful settlement. The Hottentots along the south-west coast were friendly enough, but the dwarf Bushmen beyond the mountains inspired terror in the later settlers, killing many with their poisoned arrows, and winning a reputation for great cruelty. But the most formidable obstacle was raised by the powerful and highly organized Zulu state to the north-east. It was not until the British had been defeated in several fierce encounters that the power of King Cetewayo of Zululand was finally broken by our forces in 1879.

Natives of Africa vary in colour from the white Berbers of Algeria to the almost blue-black West African Negro. Estimates of their numbers, which cannot be more than expert guesses, suggest that the blacks may number upwards of 125 million, while the lighter peoples of the north have been put at 30 million. Whites of European descent number about three million.

Africa's Four Races

Owing to constant intermingling of tribes and peoples the greatest confusion of races exists, but it is possible to distinguish broadly four elements : the *Bushman*, the *Negro*, the *Hamite*, and the *Semite*. The Bushman, found chiefly in the semi-desert north of the Orange river and in South-West Africa, has little relation to the Negro, although he is classed as a black. He is very short, and his skin is yellow. The shape of his skull and bones differs from that of his northern neighbours. The Hottentot of the South is believed to be a cross between the Bushman and other African races.

The Negroes who inhabit the great forests and the central and southern plateaus may be considered the true Africans in race and civilization. They fall into two great groups—the northern or Sudan Negroes (not to be confused with the Sudanese, natives of the Sudan), occupying a wide strip from the Guinea coast, sometimes called Senegambia, eastward to the sources of the Nile; and the Bantu tribes extending from the middle of the great forests downward, covering the southern horn of the continent.

The Sudan Negroes are mostly farmers, raising plantains, yams and manioc; they dwell in rectangular huts and wear bark-cloth or palm-fibre clothing. Until recent years they were often cannibals. They still indulge in scar tattooing, and file the teeth of the upper jaw into points. Their natural weapons are bows and arrows, and they carry wooden shields. Witchcraft and fetishism have a strong hold upon them.

SAMBO BRINGS THE WATER
This little African boy carries home the family's water supply in pitchers perched on his head after the manner adopted by many primitive peoples.

The Bantus, on the other hand, are cattle-breeders as well as farmers, and, as a natural consequence, are drinkers of milk, a beverage which is virtually unknown to the Negroes of the northern group. They build round huts and wear clothing of skin and leather. They know how to smelt iron ore and to fashion iron weapons. They usually carry spears and hide-covered shields. Cannibalism appears to have been rare among them. Some tribes file their teeth.

When we leave the pure Negro and go northward to the Mediterranean and eastward into the Nile valley and Abyssinia, the confusion grows, because almost everywhere the peoples called Hamites and Semites have mixed with each other, as well as with the Negroes whom they enslaved at an early date. The Hamites, however, predominate. They include the Berbers of the Atlas region, who are of pure white race ; the Kabyles and Tuaregs of the desert ; the Fellahin of Egypt; the Bisharin of the Red Sea coast; and the Gallas, Somalis, and Masai of East Africa. The Semites include the Arab tribes of North and North-West Africa and an important part of the inhabitants of Abyssinia. The vast majority of Hamites and Semites are closely bound together by the Mahomedan religion, which is the most powerful single influence in Northern Africa, see Mahomet.

The native peoples of Africa speak a great number of languages, perhaps as many as 1,800 or 2,000, but these may be divided into four main groups : Bantu, Sudanic, Hamitic, and Semitic. The Hamitic languages are spoken in the north and west, the regions around the Sahara; the Bantu in the centre and south; while Hamitic and Semitic speakers are found in the east, in and around Egypt and Abyssinia. The Bushmen and the pygmies have their own languages, but little is known of them. Those of the Bushmen and the Hottentots are notable for their use of clicks, or sounds made by the tongue.

Foreign Empires in Africa

In the year 1875 less than one-tenth of Africa was under European rule. Today huge tracts form part of the British Commonwealth ; Egypt has been an independent kingdom since 1922 ; Abyssinia, or Ethiopia, incorporated in the Italian Empire in 1936, regained its sovereignty in 1941; and Liberia on the west coast is an independent Negro republic, protected by the United States. The rest of Africa is included in the French, Belgian, Spanish and Portuguese empires, apart from the colonies taken from Germany after the First World War, now under United Nations trusteeship.

The slave trade and the barter for ivory and gold which followed the Portuguese discoveries of the 15th and 16th centuries had done little

STRANGE CREATURES OF THE AFRICAN WILD

The Oryx (1) is an antelope with a long, bushy tail, and a short mane. The Jerboa (2) is a tiny rat noted for the extraordinary distance it can jump. The bad-tempered Cape Buffalo (3) is extremely dangerous to Man. The Gnu or Wildebeest (4), another antelope, has a fringe of long hair dangling from its face. The rare Okapi (5) stands about as high as a big mule; the hind quarters of its blue-black body have white or yellow stripes. The African Hunting Dog (6) is about as large as a greyhound and a fast runner; each foot has only four toes. It hunts in packs, and can easily run down antelopes. The Eland (7), largest of the antelopes, may be six feet high at the shoulders; its horns (which are borne by both sexes) are twisted spirally. It is found in most parts of East Africa.

to encourage colonisation, and in the 18th century, Europe, engaged in constant warfare and busied with its own affairs, virtually forgot Africa. But in the course of the wars with Napoleon and his allies, Great Britain took possession of the Dutch colonies at the Cape of Good Hope, and the slow awakening began. By agreement of the powers, the slave trade was abolished by 1836, and the period of exploration opened.

James Bruce had discovered the source of the Blue Nile and traced the river to its meeting with the White Nile in 1772, and Mungo Park had explored the Niger between 1795 and 1805. But the real opening of Africa began with the missionary David Livingstone, who turned explorer and became a pioneer of trade and empire. In 1849 he crossed the Kalahari Desert from south to north, and began his famous series of travels which made known the great waterways of the upper Zambezi and the southern lakes. In 1862 J. H. Speke reached a stream in Central Africa which he followed through Egypt to the sea, being thus the first white man to read the riddle of the Nile. Paul du Chaillu, in 1865, found the pygmy races in the great forests. Six years before he had observed for the first time the giant gorilla, thus confirming the old Greek and Carthaginian legends about dwarf men and giant apes. The great hunter Frederick C. Selous began in 1872 his long series of travels, which did more than anything else to clear up the mysteries of South Africa.

But it remained for Sir Henry M. Stanley, the adventurous British explorer, to fire the European imagination with dreams of Africa. After a thrilling rescue of Livingstone in 1871, Stanley determined to explore the entire Congo region. Entering from the east coast in 1875, he reached the Lualaba, which had been mistaken by Livingstone for a branch of the Nile, and followed the river to the Atlantic Ocean on the west in 1877, proving it to be the main stream of the Congo.

Two events of the greatest importance to Africa's future had taken place in 1869. The Suez Canal had just been opened, and diamonds had been found in South Africa at the junction of the Vaal and Orange rivers. These events, coupled with Stanley's great achievement, whetted the appetites of the manufacturing and trading classes of Europe.

Scramble for African Territory

Leopold II, King of Belgium, a shrewd business man, started the race for Africa when he made known his personal project to form the Congo Free State and exploit the wealth of the great forest region. But he and the French clashed in the Congo. Germany blocked Britain in East Africa. Britain barred the way of France in the Sudan. Portugal obtained Britain's support for her claims at the mouth of the Congo, bringing a loud chorus of protests from France, Germany, and King Leopold. Italy seized the Red Sea coast of Abyssinia. Every nation involved was sending into the interior messengers armed with blank treaty forms, which they induced native chiefs to sign. Many chiefs signed cheerfully for every one who came along. Confusion soon reigned.

A conference of the powers (Austria-Hungary, Belgium, Denmark, France, Germany, Great Britain, Holland, Italy, Portugal, Russia, Spain, Sweden and Norway, Turkey and the United States of America) was called in Berlin, in 1884, which laid down rules under which annexations should be valid. It was agreed that each nation should notify the others of their projects for colonisation, outlining the territories for which they intended to be responsible.

The next 15 years saw most of Africa divided among six European nations. France obtained control of North-West Africa and the north bank of the Congo, as well as the island of Madagascar. Britain retained Egypt (where she had been forced to intervene in 1882), consolidated her possessions in South Africa, opened a large new colony in East Africa, and established herself at the mouth of the River Niger. Leopold took over the great Congo basin as the Congo Free State (transferred to Belgium as a colony in 1908). Portugal retained Angola in the west and Mozambique in the east. Italy, after a disastrous defeat by the Abyssinians, held a strip on the Red Sea and a large slice of Somaliland ; to these Tripoli was added after a war with Turkey in 1911–12.

Rail, Road and Air Routes

Great Britain was involved in a war with the Dutch settlers in South Africa between 1899 and 1902, as a result of which the Transvaal and Orange Free State were annexed. In 1910 the four South African provinces were united as the self-governing dominion of the Union of South Africa.

Germany succeeded for a time in defeating England's desire for an all-British strip from Cape Town to Cairo by thrusting in a broad wedge in East Africa. The Berlin government also obtained a large section of South-West Africa, north of the Orange River, a slice of the Congo region called Cameroons, and a thin strip on the Gold Coast named Togoland. After the World War of 1914–18, however, these possessions were taken over by the League of Nations, which appointed various countries to govern them on its behalf. In 1935–36 Italy conquered Abyssinia, which was liberated by British troops in 1941.

Communications inside Africa are steadily being improved. The big rivers are used for inland steamboat traffic, and steamers maintain services on the great lakes of East Africa. Railway communications are not good, and there are networks of connecting lines only in the south and in French North Africa. Elsewhere, isolated lines link seaports with inland trading centres. East African ports are connected by rail with Lake Victoria and Tanganyika. The South African railway system sends a line into the Belgian Congo, and reaches the east coast in Mozambique and the west in Angola. The Nile valley line extends to the south and west of Khartum, with branches leading to the Red Sea.

Because the cost of a metalled highway is less than that of a railway, road construction is going rapidly ahead. During the Second World War the Allies built two highways, more than 1,700 miles long, from ports on the Gulf of Guinea to the railway at Khartum ; and air routes, which already stretched from the Cape to Cairo and criss-crossed Central Africa, were extended. An air service, bringing war material, jumped the Atlantic Ocean from South America to West Africa, and then

AFTERNOON SCENE AT AN AFRICAN WATER-HOLE

THE picture divided across the next two pages shows a typical group of the animals which a naturalist or hunter might find at one of the water-holes in the big-game country of eastern or north-eastern Africa. The black spot on the accompanying map shows the region where the specimens were collected that form this great museum group. It is situated in Abyssinia (Ethiopia), but similar country is found in Kenya to the south and the Anglo-Egyptian Sudan to the west. It is a semi-desert —high, rolling, and spotted with outcroppings of rock, with here and there clumps of trees and bushes.

In this region streams are scarce. The animals must often travel great distances to find the infrequent water-holes. Here they gather in a more or less peaceful manner. Our picture shows a female rhinoceros in possession of one of these drinking places. She stands guard while her baby sips at the scanty patches of water lying in the hollows of the trodden mud. None of the other animals dares come to drink until the bearer of those two great horns moves away.

Behind the rhinoceros a herd of zebras waits. These striped runners have come from the sandy plain that stretches away toward the horizon at the right. Near by, a pair of guinea-fowl are watching for a chance to snatch a few beakfuls of water. They are standing in front of the double-towered nest of a colony of termites. Even these insects find the relatively moist soil of the place attractive.

(Continued on the back of the second plate)

Direct-colour photograph of habitat group in the Natural History Museum, Chicago. Specimens collected by White-Coats African Expedition (1929), prepared and arranged by C. J. Albrecht; background painted by Charles A. Corwin.

KEY PICTURE

1. GIRAFFE FAMILY
2. ABYSSINIAN ORYX
3. GRANT'S GAZELLE (MALE)
4. GAZELLE FAWN
5. WILD FIG TREE
6. YOUNG MALE GAZELLE
7. FEMALE GAZELLE
8. PAIR OF ELANDS

AFTERNOON SCENE AT
AN AFRICAN WATER-HOLE

KEY PICTURE

1. BLACK RHINOCEROS
2. BABY RHINOCEROS
3. GRANT'S ZEBRA
4. ACACIA TREE
5. NESTS OF TERMITES OR
   " WHITE ANTS "
6. GUINEA FOWL
7. AFRICAN CACTUS

(Continued from the back of the first plate)

Facing the rhinoceros and watching her with a mixture of curiosity and caution stands a great male giraffe surrounded by the members of his family. He is a giant of his kind, with a stretch of 16 feet between hoofs and horns. But those horns are ineffective weapons. He, too, will wait his turn.

The other beasts at the left are not impatient. They all belong to the antelope tribe and are used to going thirsty. The eland and the oryx, for example, have been known to live for weeks at a time in absolutely waterless country.

These gatherings of animals at water-holes provide the naturalist with a rare chance to study African wild life. When the Harold A. White-John Coats Expedition went to Abyssinia in 1929 to gather material for this group for the Natural History Museum, Chicago, its members spent much of their time watching these meeting places from near-by points of vantage. Sketches and photographs made on the spot by C. J. Albrecht, taxidermist of the expedition, were used later as guides in setting up and arranging the exhibit in the museum.

This exhibit is believed to be the largest of its kind in the world. It occupies a stage 45 feet wide and 22 feet deep. Each animal was collected and prepared specially for its particular role in this drama. The arrangement is of the diorama type. The foreground on which the animals are placed blends imperceptibly into the painted background. Mr. Albrecht spent nearly three years in carrying out the design, which is faithful to Nature even in those details that are invisible to the spectator who sees the group through its huge glass front.

While lions are to be found in the region depicted in this picture, it is not their favourite country. There is too little cover from which to spring upon their prey. They prefer the moister districts with more grass and underbrush. In any case, they hunt mostly by night and would rarely be found intruding on a scene like the one represented here.

Until the establishment of game preserves in the British portions of the big-game country, the habit of congregating at water-holes brought many species of African animals to the verge of extinction, since hunters could lie in wait there and get easy shots. Today, vast areas of this country are protected sanctuaries to which the animals flee from the neighbouring districts where they are molested. Thus, the reticulated giraffe (the variety shown in this group), which was once on the way to becoming as scarce as its South African relative, is now believed to be once more on the increase.

To face page 73

crossed the heart of the continent to the Middle East. France, Great Britain, and Belgium all maintain regular passenger services by air with their African territories.

The continent's immense mineral resources have never been fully surveyed. The rich gold mines of the Rand in the Transvaal are world-famous, and in 1946 an even richer gold reef was discovered in the Orange Free State. Most of the world's diamonds come from South Africa, the Belgian Congo, Angola, and Sierra Leone. Tremendous copper deposits exist in Rhodesia and in the southern Congo basin.

Tin, chromium, manganese, cobalt, mica, and asbestos are found in the central and southern areas of the great plateau, and the radio-active mineral uranium occurs in the Katanga district of the Belgian Congo. In many places, especially in Algeria, iron ore is abundant; but coal is generally scarce, although enough is mined in the Union of South Africa to meet local requirements. The Wankie coalfield in Southern Rhodesia has an area of 400 square miles. West Africa produces tin ; but petroleum is even scarcer than coal. Africa is rich in jungle products such as rubber, teak, ebony, mahogany, dyewoods and gum arabic ; cultivated crops include cotton, coffee, cocoa, palm nuts, ground nuts, maize, wheat and other cereals, rice, tobacco, sugar-cane, tea, sisal, fruits, spices, pyrethrum (for making disinfectants) and drug-yielding plants. Stock-raising is also important where the tsetse fly can be controlled. Skins, wool, and hides are exported. Africa is still one of the world's chief sources of ivory, though the elephant herds have been seriously reduced. Ostrich feathers are important, but the demand varies considerably with changing fashions.

Schools for Grown-up Natives

The Second World War, in which for the first time in history South African white and East and West African black troops fought overseas, brought great political changes to Africa. By 1941 the Italians had been driven from East Africa, and Abyssinia had been made independent again. When two years later the German and Italian armies in North Africa were defeated, nothing remained of the Italians' African empire.

The pressing needs of that war resulted in rapid development in South African industry. The giant Iscor steelworks, near Pretoria, which built armaments during the war, employs 10,000 Europeans and Africans and turns out nearly 400,000 tons of steel products every year. In East and West Africa, too, the natural resources were developed, especially cotton and ground nuts (used in making margarine) in the east, and rubber, tin, cocoa, and ground nuts in the western colonies.

In the British colonies, schools for native children range from simple mud huts in the bush to great institutions like Achimota College and Fourah Bay College in West Africa, and Makerere College in East Africa. The number of primary schools is increasing as more African teachers complete their college training and become qualified.

By means of mass adult education more natives are being taught to read and write, and instructed in improved methods of agriculture and standards of feeding and hygiene. The Emperor of Abys-sinia, Haile Selassie, anxious to introduce modern systems of education into his country, induced English teachers to go out there to work in new school-buildings designed by a British architect. In French North Africa there are Mahomedan as well as French schools, and well attended business and agricultural colleges.

At technical and trade centres in East and West Africa natives are trained as skilled artisans. New careers in teaching, law, engineering, medicine and journalism are open to Africans. Doctors and nurses trained at African hospitals can fill high posts in the medical services. Native law courts see that justice is carried out. And more and more Africans are occupying important positions of trust not only in the local but in the central governments of their territories.

Afrikaans. (Pron. af-ri-kahns'). On April 7, 1652, the Dutchman Jan van Riebeek landed at the Cape of Good Hope. His instructions were to establish a base for the ships of the Dutch East India Company on their voyages to and from the East, and he had no intention of founding a colony:

South African Railways

AFRIKAANS AND ENGLISH NAMES
The two official languages of South Africa are Afrikaans and English. At this railway station in Johannesburg the words " booking office " are displayed in both languages, side by side. Afrikaans closely resembles High Dutch.

but by degrees his countrymen were attracted to the fertile land, and within 150 years it became a flourishing Dutch settlement.

While the population was mainly Dutch, there were a number of Germans among them, as well as some French, Huguenots driven from their own country by religious persecution; at the end of the 18th century it was estimated that 53 per cent of the settlers were Dutch, 28 per cent German, and 15 per cent French. In 1795 the Cape of Good Hope was seized by a British force, and in 1806 it officially became a British colony. The discovery of diamonds and gold in the second half of the 19th century brought a new wave of colonists from Britain. Nevertheless, today nearly two-thirds of the white population of the Union of South Africa are of Dutch descent.

The original Dutch settlers used as their official language the same form of Dutch that was spoken in the Netherlands—High Dutch, as it is called; but among themselves they spoke a variety of dialects. Many of the Germans, too, spoke Low German, a dialect closely resembling Dutch. The fusion of these tongues, with the added French influence, gave rise to what was virtually a distinctive language. This was at first called Cape Dutch or simply " die Taal " (which means " the speech "); later it was given the name of Afrikaans.

Afrikaans is very like Dutch. Ninety per cent of the words in it are derived from the Dutch, though many have been adopted from French, English, and the South African native speeches. The pronunciation corresponds very closely to that of High Dutch, but spelling has been simplified. The grammar of Afrikaans is very much simpler than that of High Dutch.

The new language had reached something like its present form by the middle of the 18th century. Long after that, however, High Dutch was the official written language, and practically no examples of written Afrikaans occurred before 1860. In 1875 the Genootskap van Regte Afrikaners, or Society of True Afrikanders, was formed, to work for the establishment of a written Afrikaans and the production of an Afrikaans Bible. This society first used the name Afrikaans for the language.

Among the leading pioneers was S. J. du Toit, and he was followed in the 20th century by C. J. Langenhoven. It was due to Langenhoven's efforts that an act was passed in 1914 permitting Afrikaans to be taught instead of Dutch in elementary schools. In 1919 Afrikaans was given equal status with English as one of South Africa's two official languages, though Dutch was still used in Parliamentary documents. In 1925 this last restriction upon it was removed.

Afrikaans has a rich literature. Its true foundations were laid by a school of poets early in the 20th century, who included Eugène Marais, famous for his poem Die Winternag (The Winter Night); Jan Celliers, who published the brilliant poem Die Vlakte (The Plain) in 1906; and C. J. Langenhoven, the author of some fine poetry, novels, and short stories. Other novelists in Afrikaans were J. H. H. de Waal, D. F. Malherbe, J. van Bruggen, and Léon Maré. The Afrikaans Bible, Langenhoven's great ambition, did not appear until 1933, the year after he died. Of recent years many scientific and educational books have been written in Afrikaans, and an authoritative dictionary of the language was in preparation in 1947.

In South Africa today Afrikaans is principally the language of the country districts, while English predominates in the towns. Throughout the Union as a whole some two-thirds of the white population can speak both Afrikaans and English, while less than one-fifth can speak only English and less than one-sixth only Afrikaans. Applicants for government posts must be able to pass a test in both these languages.

Afrikander. The majority of the population of the South African provinces of the Transvaal and Orange Free State are of Dutch extraction and are known as Afrikanders, or Afrikaners. Their language, a variety of Dutch, is called Afrikaans (*q.v.*). To further the interests of the Dutch in South Africa and their language, a political association called the Afrikander Bond was formed in 1880, which aimed at the creation of an independent South African Republic, but favouring federation under the British Crown, it took part in the negotiations of 1910, which led to the formation of the Union of South Africa.

Agamemnon. Called by Homer the king of Men, Agamemnon, mythological King of Mycenae, was the leader of the Greek host that was

W. F. Mansell

AGAMEMNON WATCHED BY HIS SLAYERS
Painted by the French artist Guérin in 1817, this picture, now in the Luxembourg Palace, Paris, shows Agamemnon resting on his bed, while his wife, holding a dagger, and her lover Aegisthus, hesitate on the threshold of the bedchamber. In the story it is not made clear which of the two actually kills Agamemnon.

collected to sail to Troy. He was the brother of Menelaus, whose wife, Helen, had been carried off by Paris, and the army was going across the Aegean Sea to punish the Trojans—for Paris was the son of Priam, King of Troy—for this offence.

While the Greek ships were at Aulis ready to start they found that there was no wind and so they had to stay for some time in port. This delay, they said, had been caused by the goddess Artemis because Agamemnon had offended her by killing a stag which she regarded as sacred. The priest Calchas suggested that the king should offer a sacrifice to the goddess, selecting as the victim Agamemnon's daughter Iphigenia, but at the last moment, when everything was ready, the girl was carried away by the goddess in a cloud.

In the course of time the Greeks reached Troy and, while their ships lay drawn up on the shore, the heroes fought their battles, sometimes in single combat and sometimes in general engagements, on the plains of Troy. Agamemnon and Menelaus took the lead in these fights, and the warfare had been going on for ten years when Agamemnon quarrelled with the most famous of his followers, Achilles, about a maiden who had been made prisoner. Achilles sulked in his tent for a time, but later returned to the fight and killed Hector (*q.v.*).

Agamemnon returned home, only, however, to be murdered either by his wife, Clytemnestra, or by her lover Aegisthus. Later Agamemnon's son, Orestes, avenged this crime. The story of Agamemnon was much used by the Greek dramatists. Aeschylus wrote three of his greatest plays on the subject: The Agamemnon, which tells of the return and the murder; The Choephori ("Libation-bearers"), which tells of the revenge of Orestes; and The Eumenides, which tells how the Furies pursued Orestes.

Agassiz, LOUIS JEAN RODOLPHE (1807–1873). Few men have more fully realized an early ambition than this famous naturalist. When only 21 he wrote to his father: " I wish it may be said of Louis Agassiz that he was the first naturalist of his time, a good citizen, and a good son." All this and more came true. He became not only the greatest authority of his day on natural history and geology, but a great teacher and leader, who influenced later generations of nature students.

The son of a pastor, Louis Agassiz (pron. ag'-*a*-sē) was born in the Swiss village of Motier, near Lake Neuchâtel. He studied medicine in Zürich, Heidelberg and Munich, but his greatest enthusiasm was for zoology, and in 1829 he was invited to edit a work on Brazilian fishes. This

was followed by an extended investigation of European fishes, not only the living specimens but the fossil fishes preserved in the rocks; and this, in turn, led to an interest in geology. He spent a summer in a hut on the edge of a glacier, studying its actions ; and later put forward the theory, now universally accepted, that at different times the greater part of Europe was covered by these vast sheets of ice.

Agassiz was professor of natural history at Neuchâtel from 1832 until 1846, when he went to America to deliver a series of lectures in Boston. The following year he became professor of zoology and geology at Harvard University. In addition to teaching, he wrote widely, delivered popular scientific lectures and engaged in expeditions in the United States and Brazil. He was the founder of the Museum of Comparative Zoology at Harvard, often called the Agassiz Museum, and also established a summer school of science on the island of Penikese, off the south-east coast of Massachusetts. This was the first school for studying science directly from specimens and in really close contact with Nature.

Agassiz died at Cambridge, Mass., U.S.A., and on his grave were placed a boulder from the glacier where his hut once stood, and pine trees brought from his old home in Switzerland.

Though his ice-age theory has been very much expanded and we know that not one but several such ages existed, the value of Agassiz's work stands high. Another noteworthy service he rendered to science was his insistence that students should make first hand observations of Nature on the spot, and not merely study books and specimens.

Agave. (Pron. *a*-gā'-vi). It was once commonly believed that the American aloe (*Agave americana*), the best-known species of this remarkable and beautiful family of plants, bloomed only when it reached the age of 100 years, and in consequence it was called the century plant. As a matter of fact, the time of blooming depends

Dorien Leigh

AGAVE FLOWER-SPIKES

The agave, or American aloe, has one of the tallest flower-spikes of any plant. The leaves are used for fodder and fibre.

LOUIS AGASSIZ

This famous naturalist was born in Switzerland but for most of his life he was professor of zoology and geology at Harvard University, in the U.S.A.

entirely upon the vigour of the individual plant and the conditions under which it is grown. In warm countries, where the growth is rapid, flowers appear in a few years, while in colder climates the plant sometimes requires from 40 to 60 years or longer to reach maturity.

A native of Mexico, South and Central America, the century plant is cultivated in many gardens in England, and in Spain, Portugal and Italy is often used as a fence. The leaves—thick, fleshy and spiny-toothed—form a sort of rosette, from the centre of which springs, at the time of flowering, a tall branched stem with erect greenish-yellow clustered blossoms. This stem grows with amazing rapidity, and if the bud is cut out early in its development, a rush of sap comes forth which is

and resolved (as Shakespeare phrases it) " to busy giddy minds with foreign quarrels " by reviving the English claim to the French throne. Landing in Normandy, he found his way blocked by a great French army 20 miles north-east of Crécy—where King Edward III of England had defeated the French under Philip VI on August 26, 1346. The French knights, who were four times as numerous as the English—mainly foot soldiers—foolishly dismounted and proceeded to advance on foot, weighed down by their heavy armour, through the deep mud of the newly ploughed fields.

Three times they came on, in the narrow defile between two woods, and three times the clouds of arrows let fly by the skilled English archers forced them to retire. The defeat turned into a rout.

AGINCOURT BATTLE PRECEDED BY PRAYER

Dawn on October 25, 1415, found the English troops cold and weary after long marching and a rainy night. Yet when the French, vastly superior in numbers, launched their attack, they were met with such dauntless spirit that they broke in hopeless confusion. This painting by Sir John Gilbert shows the English at prayer before what was to prove one of the most glorious victories in the annals of the English race, largely owing to the longbowmen's skill.

More than 10,000 French were killed, including many princes and nobles, while the English lost only a few hundred. This decisive defeat of the French, together with the victory of Crécy and that at Poitiers on September 19, 1356, proved the superiority of the English longbowmen over the crossbowmen and paved the way for the overthrow of the dominance of the armoured knight, which was the military basis of the feudal system of the Middle Ages.

It is significant that while the French occupied the night before Agincourt in revelry, the English devoted the time to preparation. Henry V spent all the hours of darkness " walking from watch to watch, from tent to tent." At every stopping-place he

collected and fermented. The American aloe and numerous other species of agave are grown as a regular farm crop in Mexico. The sap when fermented produces the national beverage, *pulque*, and, distilled, it forms a spirit called *mescal*. The leaves are used as fodder, and rope, cord, bagging and matting are manufactured from their fibre. One variety yields the sisal hemp of commerce, and this is now cultivated in East Africa, especially Tanganyika. The juice of the leaves will lather in water, like soap, and is much used in washing.

Agincourt. (Fr. Pron. ah-zhan-koor′). One of the most famous battles in English history was fought on October 25, 1415, at the village of Agincourt in Northern France. It was the third great victory of the English over the French in the Hundred Years' War. The young king, Henry V, had recently succeeded his father, Henry IV, on the insecure Lancastrian throne of England,

spoke words of good cheer to the men, heartening them for the coming struggle. That he knew the fight would be a desperate one did not prevent him from showing the quiet confidence that is a host in itself. When the battle began many of the English archers were barefooted so that there might be less likelihood of slipping on the sodden ground. On being ordered to find out what he could about the position and number of the enemy, David Gam, the king's esquire, returned with the information that there were " enough to be killed, enough to be taken, and enough to run away." The morrow proved the truth of his witty report. The modern French village is called Azincourt. (*See* Hundred Years' War).

Agouti. (Pron. *a-gōō′-ti). A most troublesome pest to the sugar planters and banana growers in the West Indies and the northern parts of South America is the little rodent called the agouti. A

AGRA'S FORT BUILT BY THE EMPEROR AKBAR
Situated on the Jumna river in the midst of a great and fertile plain, Agra has for centuries occupied a prominent place
in the political and commercial history of India.   It is a centre of the Hindu religion and was the capital of the Mogul
emperors before Delhi assumed that position in 1658.   This photograph shows one of the gates of the Fort, built in 1566.

reddish-brown animal, it is rather like a rabbit,
but without the long ears.   Its average length is
about 18 inches.   The Latin name of the agouti is
Dasyprocta aguti.   Like many other small herbivorous
animals of this family, the agouti goes abroad
chiefly at night ; during the daytime it lies hidden
in the hollow trunks of trees or burrows into the
ground.   The animal feeds on roots, leaves, nuts,
etc., and is an excellent swimmer.

Agra.   One of the most famous buildings in
the world, the Taj Mahal (*q.v.*), lies just outside the
walls of the city of Agra.   That magnificent tomb
was built as a memorial to the dead wife of Shah
Jehan.   Agra is on the right bank of the river
Jumna, 138 miles from Delhi, with which it is
connected by rail.   It is one of the largest cities
in Uttar Pradesh (United Provinces) in the republic
of India.   Its population is over 284,000.

When the Mahomedans invaded India early in
the 16th century and set up the Mogul empire
they made Agra one of their chief towns.   In 1526
their leader, Babar, a word that means tiger, forced
his way into the city, where he found a good deal
of booty, including the Koh-i-Nur diamond which
in 1849 was presented to Queen Victoria.   Babar
chose Agra as the capital of his empire, and
here his grandson Akbar, called the Great, lived.
Akbar was really the founder of the city.   He built
the walls which surround it, the fort which
people still call Akbarabad after him, and the palace,
which is one of the most striking buildings in
India.   The walls are a mile and a half round and
70 feet in height.   In the city Akbar died and at
Sikandra, 5 miles away, he was buried.   His magnificent tomb can still be seen.

One of Akbar's successors was Shah Jehan,
who died in 1627.   He built not only the Taj Mahal,
the most beautiful tomb in the world, but also the
Pearl Mosque, which is one of the glories of Agra.

It is of white marble, and, like the Parthenon at
Athens, is famed for its beautiful proportions.
Agra remained the capital of the Mogul empire
until the reign of Aurungzebe, who transferred his
government to Delhi.

In 1803 Agra became a British possession, and
remained so until August 15, 1947, when India
was divided into the Dominions of India and Pakistan.   During the Indian Mutiny (1857) it withstood
a siege of several months by the mutineers.   Today
it is a manufacturing city, producing cotton,

AGOUTIS AGOG FOR FOOD
These little agoutis, members of the vast family of rodents,
are great pests in the West Indies, for they do extensive
damage to the sugar plantations.   Those you see here are
eager for their dinner in the London Zoo.

lace, shoes, carpets and mosaics ; and is a trading centre, as goods to it and from it can be carried not only along the Jumna and the railway lines, but also by the Agra canal. The British erected some fine modern buildings, including Government House, a medical school and several colleges.

Agricola, GNAEUS JULIUS (37–93). The duty of whole-hearted service to the state was instilled into Agricola (pron. a-grik'-ō-la) by his mother when he was a boy living in Massilia (Marseilles). " A Roman," she said, " must not spend his days in dreams, however noble they may be. He has practical work to do in the world. Remember that always, my son."

As a young man he served for a time in Britain, and after distinguished service elsewhere, returned in A.D. 78 as governor. First of all he completed the conquest of Wales, and after a campaign lasting some two years succeeded in establishing his rule over all the territory now known as England. He then penetrated into Caledonia (Scotland) as far as the Firth of Tay, and won a complete victory at the Mons Graupius, which by a false reading gave its name to the Grampian Hills, though it cannot be definitely identified. A chain of forts was erected between the Firths of Forth and Clyde.

Agricola governed well and justly. It is said that he was the first to prove that the country in which we live is an island by sending a fleet to sail round it. He returned to Rome in A.D. 84, and lived there for the rest of his life. He was father-in-law of the historian Tacitus who wrote his biography.

How the FARMER FEEDS the WORLD

Town-dwellers sometimes envy the tranquil life of those who grow food. But it is not always peaceful down on the farm. For today, scientific methods and high-speed machinery have supplanted the old unhurried ways.

Agriculture. The oldest of the world's industries is agriculture, and the farmer is the most important of the world's workers. To him we

HARVESTING OATS
Forerunner of the reaper-and-binder, this simple reaping machine is at work on an Ayrshire farm.

all look for our daily bread. If he were to lay down his burden, all other industries would stop and mankind would go back to primitive conditions.

Once upon a time, many thousands of years ago, there were no farmers. Men depended upon fruits and nuts, fish and game, and other foods they could get without cultivation. Famine was their most dreaded enemy, for the wild foods often failed. Men wandered from place to place in search of food, and fought with their neighbours for a share when it was found. There were no settled communities, and so there was little opportunity for progress of any kind. But when at last men learned to care for flocks and herds, and sow seeds, food became more abundant and life became easier. Communities sprang up in which some of the workers provided food for all, while the other workers applied themselves to various handicrafts, trades and arts. From such a division of labour, based on agriculture, have grown all the many activities that make up modern civilized life—the trade and commerce of the world, its arts and sciences, and the wonderful life of this 20th century.

But though agriculture has been practised since the late Stone Age, more progress has been made in the last two centuries than in all the thousands of years preceding. If a farmer of 200 years ago could visit an up-to-date farm of today, he would be astonished by the changes in farming methods wrought in the past two centuries.

With the wonderful labour-saving inventions at his command, the modern farmer can cultivate a thousand acres as easily as his forebear in the 1700s cultivated 50, or the primitive husbandman cultivated one. A stick was the first hand tool used to scratch the surface of the ground before sowing, and a forked stick, held in the ground by the ploughman while the oxen dragged it ahead, was the first plough. Improvement was very slow, and after thousands of years farmers were still using clumsy wooden hoes, wooden ploughs, and tools of similar crudeness. Not until the industrial revolution of the late 18th and early 19th centuries put better tools in the hands of the farmer was any great advance made in agricultural methods.

The Man with the Humble Hoe

But the period of greatest progress has been in the last 70 years, during which inventors have devised complicated machines for saving human labour in virtually every farm operation. What a contrast between the crooked stick with which the ancient Egyptians ploughed, and the modern plough, turning 10 to 20 furrows at a time, drawn by a powerful tractor ! And following the plough across our fields come wonderful cultivators and disk harrows and drills.

In the growing season the multiple hoes greatly lessen the work of the " man with the hoe." Later in the year, mowers, hay rakes, and elevators go to the hay fields. To the wheat fields go the reapers, binders, or harvesting machines, instead of an army of labourers with sickles or scythes. The threshing machine with a few men does in two or three days work which took all the winter on the threshing floor with the hand flail. To show what these astonishing machines mean to the farmer, experts have calculated that with modern appliances it takes only half an hour now to sow a quantity of grain that used to require ten hours. The **mowing**

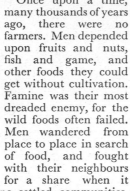

machine does more in one hour than the scythe would do in seven, and the potato planter multiplies the efficiency of a man with a hoe by eight.

Among other modern equipment for the farm may be mentioned the electric milker, cooler, and cream separator, the feed grinder, manure spreader, and a score of others. Many machines are operated by a petrol engine or a tractor at a great saving of time and labour. The first iron plough was made by James Small, a Scotsman, in the 18th century, although the share and mould board that turned its furrows probably originated in Holland some time before. Although not in general use in the United Kingdom, ploughs with revolving disks that break up a wide stretch of ground are common in Australia and the United States. Jethro Tull (1674–1741), an Oxfordshire farmer who ruined himself by his experiments, invented a machine for sowing in drills. His machine was improved by the Rev. James Cooke, a Lancashire clergyman, and others. In the second quarter of the 19th century, steam-drawn multiple ploughs were already in existence.

Such names as Boyce, Mears, and Plucknett are associated with the introduction of the reaping machine, while another clergyman, the Rev. Patrick Bell, minister of a parish in Forfarshire, Scotland, succeeded in making a reaper in 1826 which worked at the rate of an acre an hour, and deposited the grain at the side of the apparatus. Then came the mechanical reaper invented by an American, Cyrus H. McCormick, in 1831. Self-binders are now generally used, which cut the corn and neatly tie the sheaves. And there is the most remarkable machine of all—the combine-harvester, which cuts and threshes in one continuous operation. On the big farms of the western states of North America, and Australia, powerful tractors draw three or five harvesting machines and can cover 100 acres a day.

Not only the processes but even the plants and animals of the modern farm are different from those of early days. From a few wild grasses, plants and trees Man has obtained all his valuable cereals, vegetables and fruits ; and the taming of wild fowl and animals has given him flocks and herds. Cultivation and breeding, continued for many centuries, produced varieties of plants and animals very superior to their wild ancestors. But here, too, the researches of modern science have conferred

incalculable benefits on the farmer, teaching him how to develop new varieties and to improve the quality of plant and animal products in a comparatively short period of time.

Horses are bred, for example, either for speed or draft purposes. Many different breeds of cattle have been developed, some for better beef, others for greater milk production. Some sheep are bred especially for their mutton, others because of the quantity and quality of their wool. Much bigger supplies of bacon and eggs are produced by improved stocks. Scientific breeding and care have brought about many other wonderful changes, and no one can put a limit to the miraculous results still to come.

So too with plants. Careful selection of seed, breeding of new and improved varieties, and budding and grafting have done wonders. Potatoes, too,

RICE CULTURE IN THE ORIENT

About 100 million tons of rice are produced throughout the world every year in normal times, for it is the staple diet of most Eastern peoples. Rice grows best in swamps where, of course, motor-driven tractors cannot be used ; water buffaloes are employed to draw the wooden ploughs, as above. The upper photograph shows the primitive method by which rice is threshed on a farm in Ceylon.

in civilization. For example, some of the nations of antiquity were so advanced in the essentials of agriculture as to bear comparison with our farmers of fifty years ago, before agriculture enjoyed the advantages of modern chemistry, power-driven machinery and transportation facilities. The ancient Egyptians practised irrigation and crop rotation, and even the artificial incubation of poultry was not uncommon. The people of Assyria and Babylonia also raised vast

are likewise selected to produce good-sized, regular-shaped tubers with smooth skin, and to grow a larger number to the root. From the wild apple with its small sour fruit over 1,000 varieties have been developed with various qualities of size and flavour. In place of the tiny acid grapes full of seeds, we now have large and luscious fruit with few or no seeds. The yield of the grains has been increased, and special types have been developed, such as beardless barley. Even the constitution of the grain has been changed to produce larger proportions of protein, starch, fats or sugars, the better

Australian Trade Publicity

AGRICULTURE ON THE AUSTRALIAN PLAINS
The two photographs show scenes on a great wheat farm in Western Australia. At the top, four ploughs each drawn by a tractor are at work on a huge field. In the lower picture wheat is being sown by machines drawn by teams of eight horses abreast. Western Australia is a flat country and over 1,500,000 acres are under wheat.

to serve a particular purpose. Agricultural chemistry has been one of the chief factors in this progress. By its aid we learn what plant foods are present in a particular sort of soil and what fertilizers should be used in improving poor soils.

Veterinary science has greatly reduced the loss from disease among farm animals, and a study of plant diseases has cut down the loss from these and parasites attacking plant life. Entomology contributes its share by studying the life of insects to determine which are helpful or harmful to the farmer, and how best to encourage the helpers and curb the destructive pests.

Wherever husbandry has been held in highest esteem, there has been found a people advanced

cereal crops and cultivated the date palm by irrigation. Palestine afforded an early example of intensive farming, where small holdings were the rule. The limited farms, we learn from the Old Testament, produced abundantly, and their fertility was maintained by mixed husbandry and the application of manures. The ancient Romans were the foremost of their time in solving problems of irrigation, tillage and fertilization. Columella, Cato, Pliny and others taught many of the modern principles of scientific farming.

But after the break-up of the Roman Empire there followed 1,000 years of stagnation. Throughout the Middle Ages the most primitive practices prevailed. The upper classes devoted their energies

ROUND THE SEASONS ON THE FARM

Fox

Ponderous and slow is the movement of the patient horses as with click of tongue or well-worn phrase the ploughman coaxes his team up and down the field. Astonishingly straight furrows pay tribute to years of toil behind this skill. Here the main ploughing has been completed for some weeks past, and now farm-workers (seen in the background) are placing potato tubers at intervals in each furrow in advance of the ploughman who is guiding a special form of plough which splits the ridges so that the soil is turned, left and right, back into the planted furrows.

HARROWING IN THE SPRING SUNSHINE

Dorien Leigh

After the plough has cut its long straight furrows across a field, the next operation is performed by the harrow. This breaks up the ridges left by the plough, and makes the soil soft and smooth ready for the seed to be sown. The man who drives the harrow does not, as does the plough-man, walk behind, but, like this man harrowing a field in Kent, directs his team from the side. The harrow is as old as the plough, but originally it consisted only of branches of trees tied together; the iron harrow in use today is made in sections hinged together to give flexibility.

CUTTING THE CORN ON A SUMMER EVE

J. Dixon-Scott

Years ago corn was cut by men with sickles and was gathered together and bound into sheaves by hand. Then came reaping machines which at first only cut the corn but were gradually improved until they cut the corn and also bound it into sheaves. After the reaper and binder came the combine harvester which cuts and threshes in one operation, the grain being delivered into bags attached to the machine. Three horses draw the reaper and binder above, which is working on a farm at Shaldon Hill, in South Devon, famous for its crops and red cattle.

HARVEST HOME WHEN THE DAYS DRAW IN

Bernard Alfieri, Jnr.

If you walk in the country in August or September when the harvest is being got in you will see scenes like these on a farm where grain crops are grown. In the upper photograph, sheaves of corn are being piled on a wagon, which may be a hundred or more years old. In the lower picture a rick is being built. The straw is carried to the top of the rick on an elevator, a long trough with a travelling floor. The trough is raised as the rick grows higher. The straw used to be thrown up with forks, but with modern methods all that has to be done by hand is to spread it on the rick.

to hunting and warfare, and left the tilling of the soil entirely to the uneducated peasants. During all this period agriculture was bound fast in the deadly grip of the open or unfenced three-field system. The illustration in page 86 explains this old method of farming. The land under cultivation about each village was usually divided into three great fields without hedges or fences. Each of the fields was divided into long and narrow strips of about an acre apiece, and each peasant cultivated from 10 to 30 of these strips. Large stones or posts were used to mark ownership, and it was easy to move a "neighbour's landmark." The curious thing is that no man's

New Zealand Govt.

cultivation at all. All incentive and opportunity for progress was thus removed, and the yield was so poor that eight bushels of wheat to the acre was considered a good crop. Agriculture was at a low ebb.

This condition lasted in England until the Black Death, 1348-1357, which diminished the population by about one-half, led to scarcity of labour and caused a great advance in wages. To meet these conditions, some of the great landlords brought together and enclosed their domains and turned them into huge farms which could be more economically cultivated ; or else they pastured sheep upon them. The ensuing accumulation of capital presently made possible drainage, fertilization, and other improvement which could only be carried out on a large scale. Thus the medieval system of small intermixed holdings gave way to large enclosed farms.

TRACTORS INSTEAD OF HORSES

Heavy work on the farm has been made easier by the use of tractors, which also reduce cost of labour. In the upper photograph, taken in New Zealand, a tractor is drawing three appliances so that disking, harrowing and rolling are completed in one operation, saving three teams of horses and their drivers. Above, a tractor is hauling a mechanical seed-sower on an English farm.

land lay all together. The holdings were so intermixed that each man would have several separate strips in each of the three great fields, thus losing much time in going from one to another. This may have been due to the desire to divide the best and most favourably situated land equally amongst the cultivators ; or possibly additions, divided in strips amongst those who ploughed them in, were made from time to time to the cultivated area.

A rotation of crops was practised. All the holdings in one field would be planted one year with wheat or some other winter grain, the next year with spring grains such as oats or barley, and the third year they would be ploughed and left to lie fallow. Thus one-third of all the land was always idle, to say nothing of the immense tracts not under

Early in the 18th century came changes which practically amounted to a revolution in agriculture. The growing of root crops such as turnips was begun, and a root crop was introduced in the rotation plan in place of the fallow fields. This increased by practically one-third the production area in any year, and provided a surplus of feed for wintering stock. A four-crop rotation which has been followed more or less strictly to the present time is credited to the 2nd Viscount Townshend (1674-1738). About 1760 Robert Bakewell (1725-1795) established the principles of breeding by which all breeds of farm live-stock have since been improved by careful selection, mating and feeding. Then followed the great revolution in methods which accompanied the introduction of improved tools and

HOW FARMING WAS CARRIED ON IN THE MIDDLE AGES

A medieval village, with the lord's castle, the peasants' cottages, and the adjoining land divided on the "three-field system" of intermixed holdings are shown in this diagram. The house of a peasant (we will call him A) is shown, with his scattered "acre-strips," and the lord's strips, which his peasants tilled for him. Each year one of the three fields after being ploughed was allowed to lie fallow or unplanted, to let the soil recover its fertility. This wasteful system lasted in Europe for 1,000 years after the break-up of the Roman Empire in the 5th century.

machinery. Progress was rapid after the First World War. More and more mechanical power replaced human and animal labour. On large farms machines began to do such heavy work as ploughing, harrowing, cultivating and harvesting, formerly carried out with teams of horses. With one of the new power cultivators fitted for four-row use one man can cultivate 160 to 200 acres of corn in the time required for 30 to 50 acres with the horse-drawn one-row cultivator. Experts have calculated that the farmer of today can accomplish at least 15 times as much in his labour time as the farmer of 100 years ago. For example, with modern machinery an acre of wheat can be ploughed, seeded, harvested and threshed in under two and a half hours of actual working time, whereas it used to take more than 60 hours. Mowers, rakes and loaders speed up the harvesting of hay crops; mechanical elevators hoist the hay to the rick builders, and the completed rick may be roofed with machine-made thatch of straw. On poultry farms electricity operates incubators and brooders and lights the hen-house during the winter months, giving a longer day in which the hens may feed and lay.

Another tremendous impetus was given to British farming during the Second World War, when it became imperative that still more land should be made to produce every ounce of food of which it was capable. To this end farmers were guaranteed higher prices for their produce by the Government, who also set up Marketing Boards to buy from farmers direct.

In every county of England and Wales the Ministry of Agriculture and Fisheries (with headquarters in Whitehall, London) established County War Agricultural Executive Committees, consisting of farmers and agricultural experts, to deal with such problems as the amount of land to be ploughed and the crops to be grown in each area, and the supply of machinery and labour. Similar Committees were formed in Scotland (which has its own Department of Agriculture) and, as in England, farmers ploughed up much of their grassland to grow food crops; and in the Highlands deer were killed off and flocks of sheep introduced.

Shortage of farm workers was partly overcome by the Women's Land Army, whose first volunteers joined in 1938. Exempt from conscription to the women's auxiliary branches of the armed forces, paid by the farmers who employed them, they worked as tractor-drivers, or dairy farm hands: tackling, indeed, every farming task which needed to be done. Some of them even engaged in forestry when in 1942 the Women's Timber Corps became part of the uniformed Women's Land Army. This gearing-up of a truly essential industry proved to be a colossal task for all concerned. Faced with the fact that 48 million people of the British Isles depended on overseas sources for 60 per cent of their food, the 300,000 farms of this land were required to effect something approaching a miracle.

Every farm was surveyed and its condition reported upon and recorded. Much ground was in poor condition. It had to be improved, ploughed, sown or planted with all possible speed. Areas of farming districts were given a target of production. The national aim, in the first year of the Second World War, was to get an extra 2,000,000 acres of land promptly under cultivation.

New methods, new tools, had to be brought into action. Vast areas that never in living memory had carried a food crop were tackled. There were bold sweeps of the Sussex Downs that had borne their last food crops in Saxon days. Much ground had never, so far as history could tell, felt the touch of a plough. The Lower Pennines, and Devon moors, came into the food news. Bare Welsh hillside, and bog and fen, became noisy with intense activity. North, south, east and west this tremendous restlessness continued.

Farming by Artificial Lighting

Wheat and potatoes and other eatables sprang up as by magic in unaccustomed places—through sheer skill, and sweat of brow and chugging machinery and steady plod of burdened horse. That first winter of the war was one of the hardest in memory so far as Britain was concerned. For weeks on end the ground was in the iron grip of frost, and ploughs rusted in enforced idleness. And when the great thaw came, the ploughmen and all their kind strove valiantly to recover lost time.

Tractors and horses and workers had little rest whilst weather conditions were favourable. A seven-day week became commonplace. When nights were light, labour went on. When the moon failed, artificial lighting made toil possible in the ghostly fields. The only thing that could not be hurried was the growth of the crops: there, Nature persisted in her leisured way.

Tasks apparently far beyond their strength were accomplished by girls and women and men, with the aid of machines which many parts of the countryside had never before seen. Great clattering, lurching excavators, sometimes in the charge of girls, dug out and cleaned long-choked ditches to drain wet fields.

Bulldozers on caterpillar tracks forced a way through clogged undergrowth and smashed down trees, thus clearing a path for gyrotillers which, with revolving blades and big steel prongs, tore out tree-roots and rocks and made of many a forest stretch a cultivable field— that we might have essential bread, more milk, beet sugar, and all that vital table fare which war sought to deny to us.

W. H. AINSWORTH
The famous author of many historical novels that still live is here shown in a drawing by that great artist Daniel Maclise.

Ainsworth, WILLIAM HARRISON (1805–1882). In 1834, at a time when people were growing heartily tired of the "fashionable novel," Harrison Ainsworth published Rookwood, a novel based on the life of the famous highwayman Dick Turpin, which made him at a bound one of the most popular of novelists. Critics, to be sure, found fault with him for glorifying such sordid scoundrels as Turpin and Jack Sheppard, and subsequently he was more careful in choosing his heroes. Ainsworth wrote in all 39 novels, of which the best-known are, perhaps, The Tower of London (1840), Old St. Paul's (1841), Guy Fawkes (1841), Windsor Castle (1843), and The Lancashire Witches (1848). At first he was intended for the law, but he soon settled down as an historical novelist and magazine editor. Little concerned with analysing motives or with subtleties of character, he was content to give his large public a splendid series of brisk straightforward, thrilling, historical romances. It would be difficult to find a finer piece of descriptive writing than the wonderful account in Rookwood of Dick Turpin's ride to York. Harrison Ainsworth was born in Manchester, February 4, 1805, where he went to the Grammar School. He died at Reigate, Surrey, on January 3, 1882.

ANCIENT WAYS IN AGRICULTURE
Though on big farms tractors now do most of the work, there are places even in Europe where the earliest methods of agriculture still persist. This peasant farmer in the department of Haute Garonne, in the south of France, is ploughing his land with a wooden plough, such as the Romans used, drawn by a pair of oxen.

The INVISIBLE OCEAN in which WE LIVE

Says an old proverb, Man can live three weeks without food, three days without water, but only three minutes without air. Though the figures may not be accurate, they indicate air's supreme importance to us all.

Air. We live at the bottom of a gaseous ocean, the atmospheric air which covers the earth. Without air neither animals nor plants could live. Thus it is known that the moon has no life on its surface, because it has no atmosphere.

The climate which so affects the way in which we live—indeed often determines whether we can live—also depends upon the atmosphere and its movements. The cold winds from the north lower the temperature of a country, and the hot winds from the south raise the temperature. The winds also bring the clouds of water vapour over the land where it falls as rain, giving the moisture without which our food could not grow. The invention of the aeroplane has enabled us to use this invisible but very real substance to sustain heavier-than-air craft driven at high speeds. And so today we have girdled the globe with a vast net of air lines to supplement the ancient routes of land and water transportation.

And what is this marvellous substance, this air ? It is a mixture of a number of gases, principally of oxygen, nitrogen, and argon. It contains about 21 per cent of oxygen, about 78 per cent of nitrogen, and nearly one per cent of argon. Argon is a very peculiar gas in that it makes no chemical combinations. Though it makes up nearly one-hundredth part of the atmosphere, it was not discovered as a separate gas until 1894, by Lord Rayleigh and Sir William Ramsay.

Besides these three gases, air contains small quantities of carbon dioxide and hydrogen, and minute traces of four rare gases—helium, neon, xenon, and krypton. Very " impure " air, such as is found in poorly ventilated rooms, contains larger amounts of carbon dioxide. Free air also always contains water vapour. The amount of this water vapour naturally varies greatly from place to place and from day to day.

Why the Sky Sometimes Looks Blue

Oxygen is the life-giving element of the air. The nitrogen serves merely to dilute the oxygen to the point where living organisms can use it. The carbon dioxide in the air is produced by the action of the oxygen on the carbon which is an important part of all organic or living matter. Every breath we draw forms carbon dioxide ; every fire produces it. That is why the air in cities, where people are crowded together and where factory chimneys belch forth smoke, is less pure and healthful than country air.

This constant drain upon the atmosphere in the course of time would make the air unfit to breathe, if it were not for plant life. All green plants get their colour from a substance called chlorophyll which, under the influence of sunlight, seizes the carbon dioxide from the air, decomposes it, extracting the carbon for the use of the plant, and turns the oxygen back into the atmosphere.

While pure air may seem at first sight absolutely transparent, it is in reality not so. If it were so, the sky even in the daylight would look black, with the sharp bright spots of sun, moon and stars scattered over it. In fact, the tiny particles of dust and moisture in the air tend to scatter the sunlight. But the red rays are scattered very little, whereas the rest of the rays (which, without the red, have a bluish tinge) spread out through the atmosphere in all directions. That is why the sky overhead looks blue.

At sunset and sunrise, when the light must pass more horizontally through the heavy layer of air near the earth's surface, the bluish rays are virtually lost and only the reddish rays come through to us. This effect is increased by particles of dust and moisture which are floating in the air. The presence of dust particles in the air of a room can be seen when the room is darkened except where a narrow beam of sunlight comes in through a crack ; the dust particles can be seen dancing in the path of the light. The dust particles in the higher atmosphere are, in general, much smaller than those we see in a beam of light inside a house.

Where the Air Thins Out to Nothing

How much does air weigh? It varies with the heat and the pressure ; but at sea level, and at 62 degrees F., the ordinary temperature of a summer day, one cubic foot of air weighs about ·077 of a pound. That means that 14 cubic feet —or the air in a cube-shaped box of which each side measures a little less than 2 feet 5 inches— weighs a pound.

It is estimated that for all practical purposes the atmosphere stops 40 to 50 miles from the earth. In a highly rarefied form it undoubtedly extends much farther than that before the entirely airless space begins, but we shall speak of it within this limit. When a balloon rises, it finds the air growing thinner and lighter, so that the difference between the weight of the balloon and the weight of the air it displaces becomes less and less. When these two weights are equal, the balloon stops rising and floats at that level. If we decrease its weight by emptying sandbags overboard, it will rise to a higher level. If we decrease the amount of air it displaces by letting some of the gas out of the gas bag, the balloon will fall.

At very high levels the air does not contain enough oxygen to support human life. Men who rise to great heights in aeroplanes and balloons have to take tanks of oxygen for breathing. Passengers in balloons thus equipped have gone up about 14 miles ; small balloons carrying only instruments have risen more than 20 miles.

The weight of the air-belt around the earth produces at sea level a pressure of 14·7 pounds per square inch. This means that upon the skin of a medium-sized man there is a constant total pressure

GREATEST HEIGHTS AND GREATEST DEPTHS

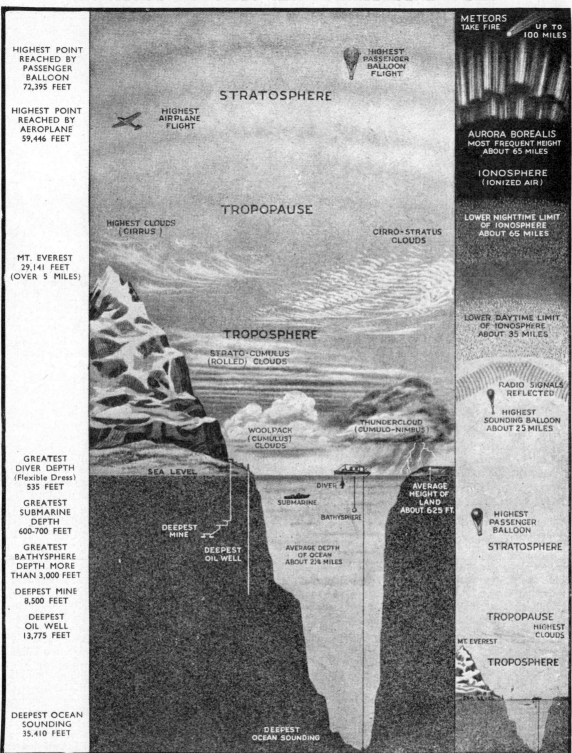

HIGHEST POINT REACHED BY PASSENGER BALLOON 72,395 FEET

HIGHEST POINT REACHED BY AEROPLANE 59,446 FEET

MT. EVEREST 29,141 FEET (OVER 5 MILES)

GREATEST DIVER DEPTH (Flexible Dress) 535 FEET

GREATEST SUBMARINE DEPTH 600-700 FEET

GREATEST BATHYSPHERE DEPTH MORE THAN 3,000 FEET

DEEPEST MINE 8,500 FEET

DEEPEST OIL WELL 13,775 FEET

DEEPEST OCEAN SOUNDING 35,410 FEET

METEORS TAKE FIRE UP TO 100 MILES

STRATOSPHERE

HIGHEST PASSENGER BALLOON FLIGHT

HIGHEST AIRPLANE FLIGHT

TROPOPAUSE

HIGHEST CLOUDS (CIRRUS)

CIRRO-STRATUS CLOUDS

TROPOSPHERE

STRATO-CUMULUS (ROLLED) CLOUDS

WOOLPACK (CUMULUS) CLOUDS

THUNDERCLOUD (CUMULO-NIMBUS)

SEA LEVEL

DIVER

SUBMARINE

BATHYSPHERE

DEEPEST MINE

DEEPEST OIL WELL

AVERAGE DEPTH OF OCEAN ABOUT 2¼ MILES

AVERAGE HEIGHT OF LAND ABOUT 625 FT.

DEEPEST OCEAN SOUNDING

AURORA BOREALIS MOST FREQUENT HEIGHT ABOUT 65 MILES

IONOSPHERE (IONIZED AIR)

LOWER NIGHTTIME LIMIT OF IONOSPHERE ABOUT 65 MILES

LOWER DAYTIME LIMIT OF IONOSPHERE ABOUT 35 MILES

RADIO SIGNALS REFLECTED

HIGHEST SOUNDING BALLOON ABOUT 25 MILES

HIGHEST PASSENGER BALLOON

STRATOSPHERE

TROPOPAUSE

HIGHEST CLOUDS

MT. EVEREST

TROPOSPHERE

The first layer in the atmosphere is the troposphere, in which are the clouds. In the tropopause, the next layer, the temperature is about 70° below zero (F). The stratosphere above is not colder at greater heights, but the air is too thin to support life. The higher regions of the air are shown on the right. It should be noted, however, that this column is not drawn on the same scale as the main illustration in the centre. Wireless signals are reflected by the ionosphere, which has a lower position in the daytime. The ionosphere is also the region of the northern lights or aurora borealis. The greatest heights and depths so far reached by Man are shown in the column on the left.

of about 25,000 pounds. The reason he is not crushed is because air pressure is transmitted equally in every direction. He is like an inflated toy balloon with pressure both outside and inside, so there is little strain on the delicate elastic tissue. When balloonists or aviators reach great heights, the outside pressure becomes so much less that blood often oozes from their ears, and they sometimes become unconscious because of this rush of blood to the head.

Besides varying in density as we go higher in the atmosphere, air alters in density also as the temperature changes, and as the weather alters. The barometer, which we usually regard as an instrument for foretelling the weather, is actually one for measuring the weight or pressure of the atmosphere; in the mercury instrument it tells us the length of a column of mercury which exactly, for the time being, counterbalances the weight of a column of air reaching high up into the sky. The barometer shows this length in

A LOAD WE CARRY BUT NEVER NOTICE

Not one of us could support the weight of three elephants in the manner shown above. Yet, as a matter of fact, an ordinary-sized man has distributed over his body air pressure equal to 25,000 lb., or about the weight of three elephants. The reason we are not crushed by this enormous burden is because air pressure is applied to our bodies inside and outside, equally in every direction.

inches, or in millimetres. An aneroid (portable) barometer uses a thin-walled box, almost emptied of air and sealed, instead of the mercury column. Air pressure outside compresses the box and moves an indicator over a scale; as pressure grows less, a spring returns the needle to its former place. Properly graduated, such a barometer can be used to measure heights, though today airmen use special instruments of different type.

Since air varies in weight and density, it naturally varies in its resistance to objects passing through it. At tremendously high speeds this resistance is so great that the friction creates fierce heat. Shooting stars or meteors are probably cold until they strike the atmosphere of the earth, but the heat of friction then becomes so intense that the rock or mineral of which meteors are composed catches fire and they usually burn up before they reach the ground. The height at which they start to burn is sometimes used to estimate the thickness of the earth's air belt.

But if the air resistance hinders our progress in one way, it is invaluable to us in another.

Without it, an aeroplane could not rise from the ground, for it is by driving the inclined planes against the dense atmosphere that the motor is able to force the weight of the machine upward. In a vacuum a feather and a ball of lead fall with equal speed, strange as it may seem at first thought

Another important fact about air is that it is compressible and is elastic; that is, when compressed it exerts an expansive force opposing the compression. Thus by means of a compression pump we blow up the tires of our bicycles and motor-cars, and the compressed air is even more elastic than rubber. By storing compressed air in tanks, the expansive force of the air can be used later for power, as in air brakes on railway trains, buses and trolley-buses, in rock drills and riveters, and in many other devices worked with compressed air.

We utilise the *weight* of the atmosphere in many machines and appliances: in the siphon and the pump for moving water and other liquids. Early steam engines used atmospheric pressure to drive the pistons in the cylinders, since all the steam did was to empty the cylinder of air. But most appliances worked by air depend on the *compression* of the air beforehand, so that when this pressure is released air can be made to do useful work. Rock drills, road drills, paving breakers and many other such tools are driven by compressed air fed to them by strong flexible tubes.

In factories, small hand tools such as drills, screwdrivers, nut-runners (for putting nuts rapidly on to bolts), and circular saws are driven by compressed air. Air (or rather the oxygen it contains) is *burnt* in internal combustion engines along with the oil or petrol. Aircraft engines and some car engines are " supercharged " with air—an extra supply being forced into the cylinders—to enable the engine to burn more fuel more quickly and so give out more power.

An ordinary " lift " pump sucks air out of the pump barrel, and then the atmospheric pressure on the surface of the liquid outside forces the liquid up into the pump. Since air can only exert pressure of about 14·7 pounds a square inch, it can only force up a corresponding weight of water. This limit is reached at a height of about 32 feet. Suction cannot draw water to a greater height. A " force " pump must be used to raise the lifted water higher. Often the two types are combined, in the " lift-and-force " pump (*see* Pump). Since liquid mercury is $13\frac{1}{2}$ times as heavy as water, atmospheric pressure will support only about a 30-inch column of mercury. This fact is most usefully applied in making a certain type of barometer.

A vacuum pump draws out air from a container; this kind of pump has to be very much more efficient than a pump for liquids, or else air will rush in at any tiny openings where there are joints or valves. Vacuum pumps are used in chemical and physical laboratories; also in refineries and works where synthetic chemicals or plastics are made. In industry such pumps have many applications: one is the drawing of air from electric lamp bulbs, radio valves, cathode ray tubes, X-ray tubes, and so on.

Vacuum pans are largely used in sugar refining, since the unwanted water contained in the syrup can be more easily evaporated away when the pressure inside the pan is lowered. At half an atmosphere —about 7·4 pounds to the square inch—the liquid in the pan will boil at as low a temperature as 178 degrees Fahrenheit; whereas we know that to boil water in an open vessel under ordinary atmospheric pressure we must raise the temperature to 212 degrees F. In preparing evaporated or "condensed" milk, if we boiled it at the ordinary temperature in an open pan we should spoil the taste and decompose it; by boiling the milk at a much lower temperature in a vacuum we are able to drive off as much water as we wish, and at the same time we can keep the flavour and other desirable qualities.

Air can be liquefied by compressing it and then lowering the temperature to about 312 degrees F. *below zero*, in a special cooler. When after this the air is allowed to escape through a very tiny opening in a valve, it expands enormously and becomes very cold, turning into a liquid which looks like cloudy water. If now poured on to a block of ice, the liquid air will "boil" and send off clouds of vapour. Cooling it still more—to 362 degrees below zero—will "freeze" it into a solid. Air is liquefied in order to obtain oxygen and nitrogen, and the rare gases which it also contains.

Air Force. The aircraft-of-war of a State, together with the men to operate them and keep them ready and efficient, constitute an air force. It has many and varied duties, sometimes acting independently and at others operating in close conjunction with an army or a navy force. It acts as the eyes of the navy or the army when it patrols, scouts and reconnoitres, reporting back to headquarters any enemy movements and concentrations.

For special purposes a "strategical" force may be organized, to hamper the war industries of an enemy country and to destroy factories, ports, railway marshalling yards and such installations. A "tactical" air force assists the armies in the field *directly*, by acting as the spear-head of an advance, crushing resistance beforehand by bombing, cannon fire, rocket fire or machine-gunning. It can operate, in fact, as a form of artillery—destroying vital roads and bridges, smashing down enemy defences, attacking tanks, guns, and so on.

Theorists sought to show that an air force could wage a successful war by itself, bombing cities and factories and railways and so terrorising the people of a country that they forced their government to seek a peace. The German air force attempted to carry out such a plan in 1940, but were defeated by

British Official

AIR FORCE OBJECTIVE BEING BOMBED
Among the targets of a strategic air force are the enemy's railway marshalling yards. Those seen here, with bombs descending, are at Hamm in Germany. This junction of main lines carried an enormous traffic in munitions during the Second World War, and under the stress of Allied bombings it was often out of action.

the "metropolitan" air force of Britain. Metropolitan was the term used loosely for that part of the Royal Air Force which was retained for the defence of Britain and normally did not go overseas to fight —an example of yet another kind of air force!

The first aircraft were of course balloons, and though they were used in war for observing the enemy we can hardly call them an air force. In Britain the first air force was constituted when an Air Battalion of the Royal Engineers was created (April 1, 1911). It had two companies, one dealing with aeroplanes and the other with airships. In April 1912 the battalion was absorbed into the Royal Flying Corps, having a naval wing and a military wing. Out of the former was created the Royal Naval Air Service, and then, in 1918, this was merged with the Royal Flying Corps to make the Royal Air Force (*q.v.*). So it was that Britain finally acquired her first air force so-called.

Dominion and Other Air Forces

Other countries developed air forces, and that of Germany was called the Luftwaffe, while the air force of Italy was named the Regia Aeronautica. During the Second World War (1939-45), there were the following national air forces operating with our own R.A.F.—trained in Britain or in the Dominions after their own lands had been seized by the Germans : Polish Air Force; Czechoslovak Air Force; Norwegian Air Force. The French had their Armée de l'Air, and when the Free French force was later formed it built up an "air arm." Among Dominion air forces were the Royal Australian, Royal Canadian, Royal New Zealand, Royal Indian and South African Air Forces. The United States of America had an Army Air Force, a Navy Air Force, and a Marine Corps Air Force, but after the end of the Second World War these separate forces were united into two—an air force independent of the army, and a naval one comprising the air arms of the Navy and Marine Corps.

WINGLESS CRUISERS *of the* SKIES

*D*auntless determination and great skill of those who pioneered in this branch
of air travel, seeking to solve the secret of controlled flight in lighter-than-air
craft, resulted at last in an airship that came very near to perfection.

Airship. An airship is an elongated balloon fitted with elevators and rudders and provided with one or more engines driving propellers, so that it can travel in any direction as it floats in the air. If you read the article on balloon, you will see that the controlled flight of a balloon is restricted to ascent or descent: it can be made to go up or down, but it can move horizontally only in whichever direction the wind is blowing.

Dorien Leigh

GRAF ZEPPELIN
Launched in 1928 this airship was in service for 10 years, making in all 148 Atlantic crossings with passengers.

Very early in the history of the balloon, inventors attempted to control its flight, and in 1785, only two years after Montgolfier constructed the first balloon to rise in the air, a French army officer named Meusnier prepared plans for an airship which, although never built, would have adopted some of the general principles employed in modern airships. Meusnier was the first to suggest the now familiar cigar shape for airships, and he proposed to have a car for passengers and crew, suspended from the gasbag by means of nets and rigging. He also proposed to drive the airship by means of a propeller connected to a crank and turned by the crew. But in any case a propeller turned by hand would not have been powerful enough. Other inventors built airships which they tried to propel with oars, or rigged them with sails like a ship.

All these early airships were " non-rigid." That is, the fabric envelope or gasbag was not stretched over a framework, but retained its shape by keeping the gas under a slight pressure. Henri Giffard (1825-1882), a French engineer, was the first to build and fly a practical airship able to travel in any direction the navigators desired. The airship was 144 feet long and 40 feet in diameter, and held 88,000 cubic feet of gas. The car containing the engine and passengers was slung from a long wooden pole attached to the envelope by rigging. An airship with a pole or keel fixed to the bottom of the envelope is called " semi-rigid," and Giffard was the first to adopt a method of construction which later was to become quite common. Giffard's airship was propelled by a three-bladed airscrew 15 feet in diameter, driven by a 3 h.p. steam engine. Steering was by means of a triangular sail which was stretched over a bamboo framework and hinged to the keel below the envelope.

On September 24, 1852, Giffard made the first flight in his airship and attained a speed of three miles an hour. He was able to fly on a straight course and proved that his aircraft could progress against the wind. But the airship's speed was slow, and it could not fly on a circular course owing to its low power and clumsy rudder. Giffard later built a larger airship, but was unable to increase the power of his engine without making it too heavy for the gasbag to lift. In 1855 lack of money compelled him to abandon his work on airships.

Electric Motor Driven by Batteries

No further experiments were made with mechanically-propelled airships until 1883, when two Frenchmen, the brothers Albert (1839-1906) and Gaston (1843-1899) Tissandier attempted to use electrical power to drive a propeller. Their airship was in the form of a tube 92 feet long and 32 feet in diameter, with a gas capacity of 37,500 cubic feet. The car, which was made of bamboo and accommodated three persons in addition to the electric cells and motor, was suspended by rigging from a jacket or large tarpaulin which partially covered the gasbag. A single propeller was driven by a 1·5-h.p. electric motor taking its power from 24 bichromate batteries weighing a total of 500 lb. On its first flight at Auteuil on October 8, 1883, the Tissandier airship attained a maximum speed of seven miles an hour in still air, but it was unable to make any progress against the wind. The weight of the power unit (over 400 lb. per horse power) was too great.

Another electrically-propelled airship was La France, designed and constructed by Captains Krebs and Renard of the French army and successfully flown in 1884 and 1885. The envelope of La France was 165 feet long and 27 feet in diameter. The propeller was driven by a 9-h.p. electric motor running off batteries. Inside the gasbag was a ballonet or air bag, to allow for the expansion or shrinkage of the gas. On its trials La France achieved a maximum speed of 14 miles an hour, and was capable of steady flight under control, but its range was short as the batteries soon ran down.

Envelope of Aluminium Plates

All these early airships were either non-rigid or semi-rigid, and it was not until 1897 that the first "rigid" airship was built by a German experimenter named Schwarz. A rigid airship is one in which the envelope has an internal framework, and keeps its shape whether or not it is filled with gas. Instead of a fabric gasbag, Schwarz's airship had an envelope built up of aluminium plates 8/1,000ths of an inch thick and stiffened internally by a framework of aluminium tubes. In using a metal skin he was thirty years ahead of his times. The airship, which was the first to be driven by an internal combustion engine, was lost in its trial flight, as the aluminium envelope was not sufficiently gas-tight.

With the development of the internal combustion engine, which proved to be the only suitable power unit for aircraft, the building of airships proceeded

apace. On October 19, 1901,
Alberto Santos Dumont (1873–
1932) navigated a semi-rigid
airship around the Eiffel Tower,
Paris, at a speed of 19 miles an
hour. It was 108 feet long, 20
feet in diameter, and powered
by a petrol engine. Santos
Dumont followed this up with
a number of successful cross-
country flights, and built several
more airships, all of the semi-
rigid type.

In Germany, at about the
same period, Count Ferdinand
von Zeppelin (1838–1917) was
experimenting with rigid airships. The German government
encouraged their construction
for military purposes. Zeppelin
completed his first airship in
June 1900, and it set the pattern
for almost all later rigid airships

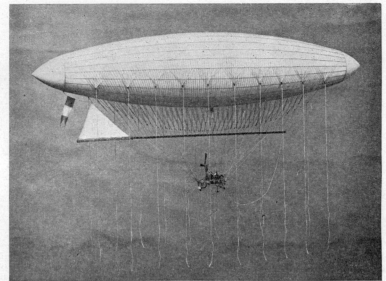

Science Museum

FRENCH DEVELOPMENT OF THE AIRSHIP

In 1852 the first real airship—that is, a dirigible (steerable) balloon—was constructed by a Frenchman, Henri Giffard. A model (top) of this machine is in the Science Museum at South
Kensington, London, and shows the fragile nature of its construction. It was powered by a small
steam engine. A famous airship 60 years later was the Adjudant Vincenot (lower), which was
attached to the French Army from 1911 to 1916 to make reconnaissances.

"Zeppelin," as
these airships came
to be called, trav-
elled 250 miles in
eleven hours, but
was later wrecked
in a storm.

At the outbreak
of the First World
War in 1914, Ger-
many had a fleet
of 25 military
Zeppelins, a num-
ber which was
eventually in-
creased to 88. The
largest was 700 feet
long and 75 feet
in diameter, and
had a framework
of duralumin, an
alloy of aluminium,
copper, and nickel.
The framework
was made up of
girders running its

length and supported at intervals by cross girders in
the form of rings. Thus the framework of the hull
consisted of 16 or more bays, each of these bays
containing a gasbag filled with hydrogen.

Eight engines, each driving a propeller, were
distributed amongst cars attached to the front,
centre, and rear of the keel. The forward car also
contained the navigating instruments and the airship controls. Inside the framework were the
petrol tanks, crew's quarters, and store-rooms. On
top of the airship were gun positions fore and aft
for defence against hostile aircraft. With a speed
of 70 miles an hour, the wartime Zeppelin cruised
at an average height of 16,000 feet. It had a lifting
power of 30 tons in addition to its own weight
of 30 tons—a big load in those days.

Although Zeppelins carried out a number of
bombing raids over Belgium, France, and Britain,

to be built in Germany and in other countries.
Realizing that a long, unsupported gasbag tended
to buckle when driven against the wind, Zeppelin
constructed a rigid framework of aluminium,
covered with varnished silk and containing a
number of separate, drum-shaped gasbags. The
engines and propellers were attached directly to
the framework instead of, as in earlier instances, to
a car slung beneath the envelope.

Zeppelin introduced a system of elevators (or
horizontal rudders) to enable his airship to increase
or decrease its altitude, or height above the ground.
Hitherto, the practice had been to throw sand or
water ballast overboard when it was desired to
make the airship rise higher, or to release gas from
the envelope when it became necessary to descend.
On its trial flight Zeppelin's first airship attained a
speed of 18 miles an hour. In 1908, another

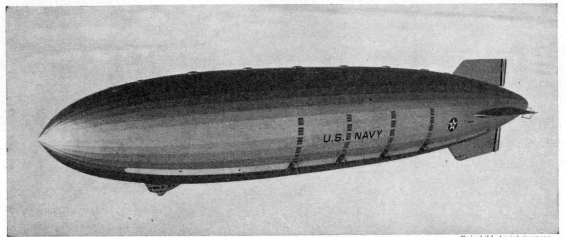

Fairchild Aerial Surveys

GIANT AIRSHIP OF THE UNITED STATES NAVY

At the time of launching in 1931 the American naval airship Akron was the largest in the world. It was 785 feet long and had a speed of 83 m.p.h. After two years' service, it crashed into the sea in April 1933. The U.S. Navy lost two other big dirigibles—the Shenandoah in 1925 and the Macon in 1935, with a total of 90 killed. After this, only small non-rigid airships were built ; many of this type served with the U.S. Navy during the Second World War.

these great airships proved a disappointment to Germany. Their huge bulk and comparatively slow speed made them easy targets for aeroplanes, and they ceased to be used for raids after 1917.

Although the success of the first Zeppelin led to a number of rigid airships being built in Britain for the Navy, little use was made of them ; but before and during the war of 1914–18 the British made progress in building and operating non-rigid airships popularly called " blimps." The largest of these were 267 feet long, had a diameter of 60 feet and a gas capacity of 360,000 cubic feet. Two engines each of 240 h.p. gave the airship a speed of 57 m.p.h. and the vessel could lift nearly 11 tons, including its own weight. Throughout the First World War (1914–18), British blimps flew some 2½ million miles over the English Channel and North Sea, chiefly on anti-submarine patrols and convoying ships through danger zones.

British Airships Which Met Disaster

In 1916, the Zeppelin L.33 was brought down in England almost intact and from her design the British government built the R.34. The letter R meant rigid, and was the prefix given to all British rigid airships. The R.34 was 643 feet long, with a diameter of 79 feet, and was driven by five 250 h.p. engines at a maximum speed of 62 m.p.h. In July 1919 she flew from East Fortune, Scotland, to Long Island, U.S.A., and back—being the first aircraft in the world to make the double crossing. The R.34 was wrecked in 1931 as the result of an accident over the North Sea. A slightly larger British airship, the R.38, which had been built by Britain for the United States, broke her back over the Humber, 45 lives being lost.

After these disasters Great Britain abandoned the rigid airship for military purposes, but in 1924 the Air Ministry ordered construction of two airships for empire air routes. These were the R.100 and the R.101, which carried out trials in 1929 and 1930. The R.101 was 777 feet long, with a diameter of 131 feet and a gas capacity of 5,500,000 cubic feet. R.100 successfully flew to Canada and back ; R.101 was lost over France in October 1930, while on a maiden voyage to India. The R.100 was then sold for scrap and broken up, and no more airships were built in Britain.

When the ban on German airships was lifted in 1926 the famous Graf Zeppelin was laid down, and was completed in 1928. She was 772 feet long, with a diameter of 100 feet, and her five engines developed a total of 2,650 h.p. to give a maximum speed of 80 m.p.h. The Graf Zeppelin, which was in continuous service until June 1937, made 148 ocean crossings, carrying a total of 13,000 passengers. In March 1936 a larger Zeppelin, the Hindenburg, was commissioned. She was 810 feet long, 135 feet in diameter, and inflated with 6,720,000 cubic feet of gas. She was driven by four diesel engines each developing 1,100 h.p. to give a speed of 78 m.p.h. She had a range of 8,000 miles and could carry 75 passengers and two tons of mail. The Hindenburg was destroyed by fire at Lakehurst, New Jersey, on May 6, 1937, and the Graf Zeppelin was withdrawn from service.

America built three large airships on Zeppelin lines : the Shenandoah was launched in 1923 ; she broke her back and crashed in a thunderstorm in 1925. The Akron, launched in 1931, was lost at sea two years later. The Macon, launched in 1933, was lost at sea in 1935. The Akron and Macon had a range of 8,000 miles and a speed of 70 m.p.h., and were equipped to carry four aeroplanes.

After the loss of the Hindenburg no rigid

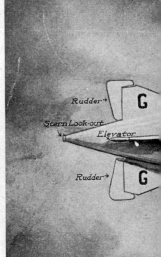

airship was put into service, and the advent of the multi-engined passenger aeroplane spelt the doom of these huge " gasbags." Unless they are inflated with helium (q.v.) there is always the danger of their catching fire, while they are at the mercy of a storm. Then, too, the airship is too slow to compete with the aeroplane. Although she gave up building large rigid airships, the United States for a time continued the development of non-rigids, both as civil and military transports. Until America entered the Second World War in 1941 United States non-rigid civil airships had carried some 400,000 passengers and flown over 4,000,000 miles without mishap. During this war, the U.S. Navy had 150 of such airships in service, and they played an important part in the campaign against German submarines operating in American waters. Two were flown across the Atlantic. For an account of the way in which airships and balloons are supported in the air, see the article on Balloon.

Ajax. (Pron. ā'jax). Among the Greek warriors of legend next in strength and bravery to Achilles was Ajax, the son of Telamon, known as Ajax the Great. He led the men of Salamis in 12 ships against Troy. Homer in the Iliad describes him as of gigantic stature, " shaking his far-shadowing spear " and bearing his " tower-like shield of bronze, overlaid with sevenfold oxhide." He was the " bulwark of the Greeks " and struck terror into the hearts of the Trojans. At the death of Achilles, Ajax as the bravest of the Greeks claimed

Daily Mirror

FAMOUS BRITISH AIRSHIPS OF THE PAST

In July 1919 the R34 (above) achieved the first Transatlantic flight by airship, flying from East Fortune, Scotland, to Long Island, U.S.A. and back to Pulham, Norfolk. Her design was based on that of the Zeppelin L33 shot down in England in 1916. Above the R34 is a non-rigid North Sea " blimp." The R101, launched in 1929, differed considerably from the R34, being 134 feet longer and 52 feet wider in diameter; its main features are shown below.

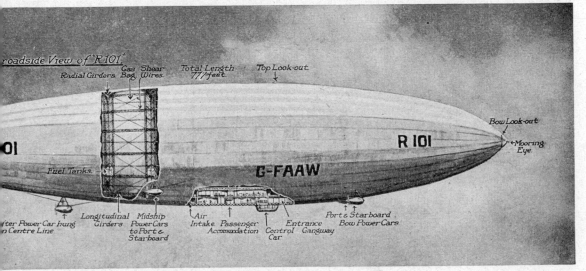

the hero's armour, but he was forced to contend for it with Odysseus (Ulysses), and the latter won the prize. So enraged was Ajax at this decision that he went mad and killed himself.

Another Greek hero who bore the name of Ajax was the son of Oïleus, king of Locris. He was known as the " lesser " Ajax. He was small of stature, but was brave and skilled in throwing the spear, and was next to Achilles in swiftness of foot. He was boastful and arrogant, however, and was punished for defying the gods by being wrecked and drowned on the return voyage from Troy. Like his namesake, the other Ajax, he was the enemy of Odysseus.

Alabama. The "Cotton State," as Alabama is sometimes called, is one of the most important of the United States, lying in the heart of the industrial south between Mississippi and Georgia. The great cotton-growing belt, which has exceptionally rich soil, lies in the south-east, where the descendants of the Negro slaves still toil in the plantations. Of the other crops, maize is the most important. Cotton, cereals, linseed, sugar, tobacco, timber and cattle are exported, and oil is produced. Coal and iron are mined in large quantities, particularly in the district around Birmingham (the largest town, population about 267,000). Other towns are Montgomery, the capital (about 78,000), and Mobile, the chief seaport (about 79,000). Population of Alabama state is 2,833,000 ; its area is about 52,000 square miles.

Alanbrooke, ALAN FRANCIS BROOKE, 1ST VISCOUNT (b. 1883). During the Second World War, while the British generals were fighting their great battles overseas, there was another general at the War Office without whose brilliant planning victory might never have been possible—the Chief of the Imperial General Staff, General Sir Alan Brooke, later Field-Marshal Lord Alanbrooke.

"Wizard " Brooke they called him, from the seemingly magic extent of his military knowledge. The fifth son of Sir Victor Brooke, Bart., he was born at Bagnères de Bigorre, in France, and educated abroad. After passing through the Royal Military Academy at Woolwich he became an officer in the Royal Field Artillery, and in 1909 was posted to the Royal Horse Artillery. The First World War found him in India, and he went to France with the Secunderabad Cavalry Brigade. During that war he won the D.S.O. and bar.

In the period between the two World Wars he earned a reputation as the army's leading gunnery expert. From 1929 to 1932 he was Commandant of the School of Artillery, commanded the 8th Infantry Brigade from 1934 to 1935, and in 1937 was promoted Major-General and given command of the Mobile Division, which later became Britain's first armoured division. In 1939 he was General

Topical
VISCOUNT ALANBROOKE
As Chief of the Imperial General Staff, 1941-1946, Field-Marshal Lord Alanbrooke was one of the most brilliant of the Allied war leaders in the Second World War.

Officer Commanding in Chief of the Anti-Aircraft Command, and later of Southern Command.

When the Second World War came General Brooke was sent to France in command of the 2nd Corps, and took part in the withdrawal from Dunkirk (q.v.) in June 1940. The following month he was appointed commander-in-chief of the Home Forces, which meant that if the Germans attempted an invasion as they were expected to do, he would have been in charge of the armies opposing them. But no invasion came, and in November 1941 General Brooke was made Chief of the Imperial General Staff, a post he held until his retirement in 1946. In June 1944 he was made a Field-Marshal, and in August 1945 was created a Baron.

Advanced to the rank of Viscount in the New Year's Honours of 1946, he was awarded the Order of Merit in June of the same year. In that summer he retired. On the death of Field-Marshal Lord Wavell he became Constable of the Tower of London in July 1950.

Alaric (370?–410). No foreign conqueror had entered Rome for 800 years when in A.D. 410 the mighty hordes of Alaric (al'aric), the Visigoth, flushed with 15 years of plundering, came thundering at the gates of the imperial capital. Honorius, the feeble Emperor of the West, had shut himself within his marshy fastness of Ravenna. Stilicho, Rome's ablest general, though himself of barbarian blood, had twice checked the invader, once in the heart of Greece and again six years later on the banks of the Po in northern Italy. But Stilicho was now done to death by the cowardly Emperor's orders, and Italy was defenceless.

The people of Rome, facing starvation within their walls, tried to buy the German leader off. The ransom he demanded was so high that they said they could not pay it, and they threatened the Goth with their numbers. " The thicker the hay," said Alaric grimly, " the easier it is mowed." They persuaded him to reduce his demands to 5,000 pounds of gold, 30,000 pieces of silver, together with gifts of pepper, scarlet skins, and silken tunics; and the siege of the city was ended. When the Emperor, safe in his swamp-protected retreat, failed to pay the promised treasure, Alaric again besieged Rome. Treacherous to the last, Honorius employed a barbarian chieftain to attempt a surprise attack on the Goths. This failed, and Alaric entered and sacked the Eternal City.

Alaric, who was of the royal race of the Visigoths, or West Goths, died in southern Italy. According to the legend, his followers turned the river Busento from its course and forced captives to dig a grave in its bed wherein Alaric was buried. That no man might discover the tomb the river was returned to its channel and the captives who had been compelled to dig the grave were killed.

TREASURE CHEST *of the* FAR NORTH

*B*etween Canada and Asia lies a vast territory which late in the 19th century was
despised as a worthless waste. Now, however, every year that goes by reveals
more and more of its varied store of natural riches.

Alaska. The purchase of Alaska by the United States from Russia for a sum equivalent to about £1,450,000 aroused at the time a storm of indignation and ridicule. Nothing could be more foolish, it was argued, than to pay good gold for a mass of useless glaciers and frozen waste, as Alaska was then generally thought to be.

The Americans called Alaska " Seward's Folly," " Walrussia," " Polaria," and a " giant icebox." But William Henry Seward (1801-72), Secretary of State, who sponsored its purchase in 1867, believed he had made a rare bargain.

Seward was right. His critics first realized this in the 90s of last century when the discovery of gold changed the " icebox " into a treasure chest. Since then Man has dug from this chest riches worth nearly 100 times the purchase price. Gold alone has yielded 50 times the cost of Alaska. In some years the value of the copper output exceeds that of gold. Since 1900 copper worth more than £50,000,000 has been dug. Present production of coal and petroleum but hints at the vast resources untapped. There are also deposits of silver, lead, tin, gypsum, antimony, bismuth, tungsten and platinum. Marble and limestone are quarried from the rock-ribbed hills. Wealth lurks in Alaska's icy waters. Plump salmon (tinned for export), succulent halibut, and shellfish, fur-bearing seals, and many other prizes of the sea provide a money yield of millions of pounds each year.

Could Feed Ten Million People

In the forests, towering hemlocks, Sitka spruce, and scattered red and Alaska cedars bend over plunging streams that will some day supply power to crush them into pulp for paper. Animals of forest and tundra (flat, marshy plains) provide fortunes for fur dealers and give food and clothing to Indians and Eskimos. Giant moose, white mountain sheep, brown and black bears and their Polar cousins, caribou deer, mountain goats, wolves, coyotes, foxes and their smaller furry kin—all these are more or less plentiful. Fur farms add to the rich take of pelts. A few reindeer brought specially from Siberia between the years 1892 and 1902 to give a livelihood to natives have grown to herds of nearly a million.

The promised wealth of fertile valleys awaits the settlers whose pioneer spirit bids them face the

ALASKAN TOTEM
That the Indians of Alaska have artistic ability is shown by this wonderfully carved totem pole.

dangers and seize the opportunities of this " last frontier "—the last undeveloped region of the United States. Alaska's farmland can feed 10 million people, experts tell us. Yet only 90,000 people were living there in 1947—one to almost six and a half square miles. Some 65,000 square miles of arable land lie undeveloped, for the plough has touched but a few hundred square miles. This great storehouse of wealth has an area of 586,400 square miles—one-fifth that of the United States. The coast is 26,000 miles long and its westernmost point on Bering Strait is less than 50 miles from the mainland of Asia. The great mass of Alaska lies in about the same latitude as Norway and Sweden.

Alaska's gaunt beauty charms the traveller, and its strange wild nature allures the scientist. Tourists sailing northward from Seattle along the " inside passage " between the south-eastern mainland and the fringing islands of the Alexander Archipelago stare in astonishment at those terrific mountains which rise abruptly, almost with menace, from the sea. Ice and water gleam like steel ; plumy green forests, softened in blue haze, cover the fierce rocky mountain sides. So close are the coast walls in southern Alaska that some of the towns have to clamber up their rugged sides. Four great mountain chains lift their white ridges in the Pacific coast section—the Coast Range, the St. Elias Range, the Alaska Range and the Aleutian Range, including many peaks over 15,000 feet high. The crown of the Alaska Range is Mt. McKinley, the highest peak in North America, soaring 20,464 feet ; this is now enclosed in one of the U.S.A.'s National Parks. Many volcanoes, among them Mt. Wrangell, are situated in the coastal ranges, and here, too, vast glaciers cover more land than the whole of Switzerland. Malaspina is the greatest glacier in the whole of North America, and the beautiful Muir Glacier is a national monument.

Vast Glacial Streams Pour Down

Like the United States and Canada, Alaska has a central plateau of rolling country, drained by the Yukon and Kuskokwim rivers. North and east of the plateau sweeps a broad cordillera, an arm of the Rocky Mountains. Great plains descend from these mountains to the Arctic shore, a vast wind-bitten slope situated within the grip of the Arctic Circle. Nearly three-fourths of the country, however, lies

ALASKAN SUMMER FLOWERS AND A GLACIER

About a third of Alaska lies within the Arctic Circle, and all the natural phenomena of a country in which the temperature is for many months of the year below zero are to be observed there. The Mendenhall Glacier (above), near Juneau, is over a mile wide and 100 feet in height, and during the short hot summer it is fringed by wild flowers, which spring up in abundance and almost overnight.

and its tributaries contain thousands of square miles of land well suited for ranching and farming with a climate at least as favourable as that of Finland. By the time the winds reach the Arctic slope they are so dry that less snow falls in this desolate region than on the Atlantic seaboard of the United States.

Myriad islands spangle the seas that wash Alaska's shores— from the thousand and more isles of the Alexander Archipelago to ice-encrusted rocks in Bering Strait. Kodiak Island, south-east of the Alaska Peninsula, harbours in its fastnesses Alaska's great Kodiak brown bear, named from its island home. The 80 Aleutians are strewn for over 1,200 miles like stepping stones across the North Pacific from Alaska almost to the coast of Asia. Of these, Unimak Island, 65 miles long and 25 miles wide, is the largest. During the Second World War the Japanese tried to use the Aleutians as stepping-stones for an invasion of North America ; their troops landed on Kiska and Attu in June 1942, but by May 1943 the islands had been retaken by United States forces.

In Bering Sea, the five rocky islets of the Pribilof group welcome a million fur seals, which in the springtime seek these boulder-strewn shores as their breeding place. Coastguard cutters escort these prized travellers from their winter resort in

in the north temperate zone, although much of it is more violent than temperate in its ways. At Fairbanks the summer sun circles about the sky until the people long for the restful dark. Hardy grains, berries and vegetables fairly leap out of the rich soil, spurred on by the long sunlight hours. Yet when the deep night of winter closes down, frost bites far below the surface with a hold so tight that in many places the ground thaws only two feet deep even in midsummer. Only along the Pacific coast, where the warm Japan Current passes, is the climate mild. The Japan Current is the Gulf Stream of the North Pacific Ocean ; its warm water flows north-east from Japan to the Aleutian Islands, then turns south-east along the west coast of Alaska. The moist warm air accompanying this current meeting the chill Alaskan air causes heavy downpours of rain.

Snow also falls thickly, masking the tall mountain crests and pouring vast glacial streams down the valleys into fiordheads, where broken chunks float off as icebergs. The snowfall on the high peaks exhausts the moisture of the winds, leaving the interior semi-arid, with temperature extremes of 100 degrees Fahrenheit in summer and 76 degrees F. below zero in winter. Yet, despite such variations, the vast valleys of the Yukon

Dorien Leigh

ALASKA'S GOLD-RUSH CAPITAL

The capital of Alaska is Juneau, founded after gold had been discovered in the territory in 1876. For a time the town flourished, but after the First World War the low grade ores of the Alaskan goldfields could no longer be worked profitably, and the population dropped from about 8,000 in 1920 to about 6,000 in 1940.

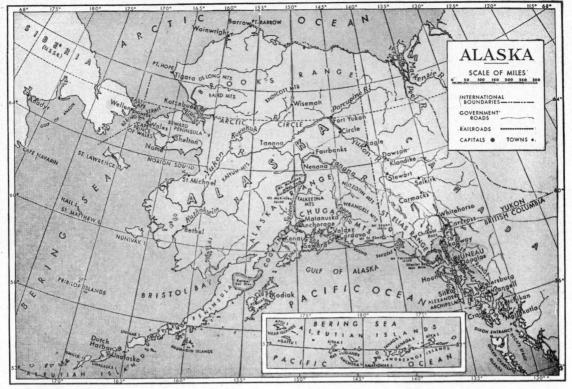

ALASKA, AMERICAN NEIGHBOUR OF ASIA

Separated by the narrow Bering Strait from Asiatic Russia, Alaska is an outpost of the United States' defences ; air and naval bases, aerodromes, radio and weather stations were established there both during and after the Second World War (1939–45). There are many harbours on the Pacific. The Aleutian Islands extend 1,200 miles across the North Pacific.

southern waters, to protect them from being hunted at sea. A small settlement of natives with white overseers on the Pribilofs slaughter the selected seals and cure their glossy pelts. They also prepare fluffy furs from the rare blue foxes of the island fur farm. On mossy, treeless St. Lawrence Island, patient diggers have found fossil foliage, cones, and wood from sequoia trees, like the living redwoods of California and the fossilized remains in Greenland, Siberia, and northern Europe. These fossils help to confirm the belief of scientists that an ancient land bridge, or isthmus, once stretched from Asia to North America, carrying life from one continent to another, and accounting for the likeness between Asiatic and American plants and animals.

The native people of Alaska are the Eskimo or Innuit hunters of the Arctic slopes ; the Aleuts in their island chain ; the Tlinkits on the Panhandle's shores ; the Haidas or Kaigani on rocky Prince of Wales Island ; and the Athabascans or Tinneh in the interior. All but the Eskimos are thought to be offshoots of North American Indian tribes.

The capital of Alaska is Juneau (population about 6,000), in the Panhandle, with wooded mountains rising almost perpendicularly behind. It reaches to the water, and as the rock formation on which it stands is irregular, many of the houses are on stilts, thus overcoming the necessity of blasting to make level foundations.

An example of the development being carried out by the United States Government (which is represented by a resident Governor) is the University of Alaska at Fairbanks—northernmost seat of higher education in the whole world.

Alaskan history has four important dates: 1741, 1867, 1898, and 1903. It was in 1741 that the country was first explored by the Danish navigator Bering, who was in the service of the Tsar, and it was settled by the Russians three years later. They looked for gold and silver, but failed to find them. In 1867, as we have seen, Russia sold the land to the United States. In 1898 the Klondike district, partly in Canada and partly in Alaska, became the goal of seekers for quick wealth. Nome, Fairbanks and other places were soon on everybody's tongue. In 1903 the Alaskan Boundary Commission settled a dispute which had arisen between Great Britain and the United States in regard to the boundary line separating Alaska and Canada.

Mail Planes Over Frozen Wastes

Communications are not easy in mountainous, frozen Alaska. The Alaska Railroad runs from Seward to Fairbanks ; another line connects Skagway, near Juneau, with Whitehorse in the Canadian Yukon. The Northwest Highway, constructed in 1942 (during the Second World War) to provide overland communication between Alaska and the United States, links a road which runs from the U.S. to Dawson Creek in British Columbia with Fairbanks in Alaska, part of the highway passing through Alberta, Canada. It is 1,630 miles long and 24 feet wide.

Air travel has been found the best way of covering the difficult country and Alaska makes more use of the aeroplane than any other territory of like population. Mail planes wing swiftly over frozen wastes where straining dog teams once took weeks for a winter trip. Wireless and cable stations dot the land far into the Arctic Circle, bringing news of the world to places that were once ice-locked for many weary months of the year.

The Second World War brought a small boom to Alaska. Its population rose by some 20,000 in four years. Anchorage, in 1940 a town of 3,500 inhabitants, grew to 14,000, and the population of Fairbanks increased from 3,400 to 7,500.

Alban, St. (died about 305).

The story goes that a priest who was being pursued by persecutors was rescued in the nick of time by a man named Alban, who hid him in his own house and exchanged clothes. The earnest piety of the priest made such an impression on his newly-made friend that he was converted to Christianity and fearlessly confessed his faith. He was martyred outside the Roman city of Verulamium, now St. Albans (q.v.). According to another legend Alban was a Roman soldier who was converted to Christianity in Rome. It is said that the abbey of St. Albans was built on the spot where he died. The pavement round the shrine of the saint is worn deeply by the feet of countless pilgrims who once worshipped there.

Albania. (Pron. al-bā′-ni-a).

Picture a small, wild, mountainous country—a country so backward that many of its rivers are unbridged and the natives swim across supported by inflated sheepskins, or make their laborious way in dugout skiffs. Picture never-ending hills separating many tribes into semi-independent and often hostile groups. That is Albania, even in the 20th century.

The rough roads in the mountain districts are travelled chiefly by primitive ox-carts and pack-horses. No effort to link Albanian cities with railways was made until 1940, when work was started on a short line between Elbasan and the port of Durazzo, to which Tirana, the capital (population about 30,000) is linked by a road suitable for motor traffic. By way of contrast the country has excellent air transportation, since this is far easier to establish in so rugged a country.

With an area of only 10,629 square miles, stretching along the east coast of the Adriatic Sea between Yugoslavia and Greece, Albania has been called the " stepchild of Europe," for it has been a bone of contention among the neighbouring nations ever since the fall of the Roman Empire. Within its borders it shows all the differences of mountain and valley, of racial and religious animosity, which characterize the Balkans as a whole. Partly owing to the deplorable economic backwardness of the country, but largely because of their fierce love of independence, the Albanians have achieved national unity only in quite recent years. Tribe has been perpetually at war with tribe, with the code of the feud as the supreme law. About two-thirds of the population of 1,003,000 are Mahomedans, and the rest are Christians of the Roman Catholic and Greek Orthodox Churches.

The history of this little country dates back to before the days of the Roman Empire, for the Albanians are descendants of the oldest race in Europe, namely the ancient Illyrians and Epirotes, with an intermixture of Slavic and Turkish blood brought in over long periods by wave upon wave of barbarian invasions.

The Albanians' great national hero is George Kasiriota, nicknamed Scanderbeg (1403-1467), who maintained a guerrilla warfare against the Turkish invaders for nearly 25 years. His nickname is a corruption of the title Iskender Bey (Prince Alexander) bestowed on him by the Turks. Handed over in his youth as a hostage to the Mahomedans, he was promoted to high military command ; but when opportunity came he revolted and gathered the Albanian clansmen around him in their mountain fastnesses. But the unity he created perished with him, and soon after his death Albania fell under Turkish dominion. The Turkish yoke was not shaken off until 1912, when Albania was recognized as an independent state. A few months later a German prince, William of Wied, was made ruler, but was forced by his subjects to flee in 1914. War and anarchy followed. In 1917 independence was again proclaimed, and in 1928 Ahmed Zogu, who had been president since 1925, was made king as Zog I. On April 7, 1939, his country was attacked by Italy, who conquered and annexed it. When Italy capitulated to the Allies in September 1943, German forces took over the occupation of Albania but were driven out by

ALBANIAN HILL-TOWN OF SHKODRA
Architecture is primitive in Albania, and this street scene in Shkodra, formerly Scutari, is typical of most of the poorer quarters of the towns. Shkodra is situated to the south-east of Lake Scutari, about 12 miles from the Adriatic Sea. Overlooking the town is the 15th century citadel, built by the Venetians.

ALBATROSS WIDE-WINGED IN FLIGHT
Always surrounded with mystery, the albatross is one of the most remarkable of all birds, for it can follow ships for hundreds of miles without ever alighting on the water or coming to land. A master of gliding, it seldom even flaps its wings, which may have a span of fifteen feet or more. It is the largest of all sea-birds, and a native of the south tropic seas.

of the South Pacific Ocean, and to Tristan da Cunha in the South Atlantic, where the mother bird lays her egg, a large whitish one with brown spots, on the bare rock. There are about 16 species of the albatross, and all live in the tropic seas, except one which is found as far north as Alaska.

the end of 1944, and Albania once more became free. King Zog, however, did not return (he had fled to Egypt in 1939), and in January 1946 the country was declared a republic under the leadership of General Enver Hodja.

Albatross. Sailors of old believed that the great wandering albatross of the southern seas, which followed a ship for days at a time with seemingly motionless wings, possessed an unnatural power, and few sailors were so bold as to harm one of them. It was about this old maritime superstition that Samuel Taylor Coleridge constructed his well-known poem entitled The Ancient Mariner.

The albatross (*Diomedea exulans*) is the largest of all the sea-birds. Its wings measure 10 to 14 feet from tip to tip, and sometimes as much as 17 feet. Its body, however, weighs only about 18 pounds. The feathers covering the body are white with wavy black or brown lines, and they are very thick. The wing feathers are dark, and, at the tips, quite black. The male and female birds dress exactly alike.

The albatross lives almost entirely on the wing. It alights on the water only to snatch a fish or a bit of refuse from a ship. When it wishes to rise again it lifts its great wings and runs along the top of the water for 70 or 80 yards before it can acquire sufficient impetus to do so. Once in the air the albatross makes use of air-currents to gain speed and height in the same manner as a man controlling a glider or sailplane. In the nesting season these birds go to rocks and islands

Albert, PRINCE CONSORT (1819–1861). Younger son of a German duke, Albert of Saxe-Coburg and Gotha married our Queen Victoria on February 10, 1840.

" To sink his own individual existence in that of his wife—to aim at no power by himself or for himself—to shun all ostentation—to assume no separate responsibility before the public—to make his position entirely a part of hers—to fill up every gap which, as a woman, she would naturally leave in the exercise of her regal functions—continually and anxiously to watch every part of the public business, in order to be able to advise and assist her at any moment in any of the multifarious and difficult questions brought before her, political, social or personal—to place all his time and powers at her command as the natural head of her family, superintendent of her household, manager of her private affairs, her sole confidential adviser in politics, and only assistant in her communications with the officers of the government, her private secretary, and permanent minister."

This very long sentence is in Albert's own words, from a letter he wrote to the Duke of Wellington, and well describes what he considered was expected of him and what he set himself to carry out during the 21 years of his married life with Queen Victoria.

The Prince interested himself not only in politics but in music, painting, literature, science (more especially in its relation to industry) and social improvements, thus finding scope for his immense fund of energy, wide knowledge and many-sided talents. Seldom did any man work harder or more conscientiously. As his biographer, Sir Theodore Martin, wrote of him: "While yet young in years he had

ALBERT AND VICTORIA
This painting at Windsor Castle by Sir Edwin Landseer shows Albert, the Prince Consort, displaying to his wife, Queen Victoria, the results of his day's shooting in Windsor Park.

done the work of a long life." But the continual strain undermined the Prince's constitution, never very strong, and he died of typhoid fever on December 14, 1861.

Perhaps Albert's crowning achievement was his organization of the Great Exhibition of 1851. For six months before its removal to Sydenham, the Crystal Palace (burned down in 1936), designed as the Exhibition building, stood in London's Hyde Park, and was thronged with over six million visitors; and it was to the proceeds of that exhibition that we owe the Victoria and Albert Museum at Kensington, London. The Prince also bought Balmoral Castle, which has been a favourite summer residence of the royal family ever since. (*See also* Victoria, Queen).

Albert I, KING OF THE BELGIANS (1875–1934). In the front line in Flanders during the First World War, a tall figure in mud-caked uniform might often be seen, walking with a slight limp— the result of a wound—along the duckboards at the bottom of the trenches.

On November 22, 1918, when the war was won, that same figure rode proudly at the head of his armies down the flower-decked streets of Brussels; and the throngs of joyous Belgians cried out, " Here comes the King!"

King Albert, the hero-king of the Belgians, came into his own at a time when the kings and kaisers of the Central Powers were scurrying like frightened rabbits to safe hiding-places. And in Belgium the men who fought in the war of 1914–18 tell their children and grandchildren how they saw their king in a soiled uniform, eating the warmed-up soup of the regular rations, sharing his match with a soldier from whom he had just received a cigarette, or helping to render first aid to the wounded.

When Prince Albert first learned that he was to succeed his uncle Leopold II as king of the Belgians, he decided that he needed more knowledge for his future task. He thought he could obtain this more readily if people did not know who he was. So, disguised as a newspaper reporter, he went to the principal seaports of Europe to study shipping and shipbuilding. Later—in 1898—he visited the United States to investigate the railways; and he went to Africa to observe at first hand conditions prevailing in the Belgian Congo.

When he became king in 1909 he began to apply the knowledge he had gained. He improved the mercantile marine of the country, and brought about better conditions in the Congo ; but his plan to reorganize the army was only half completed when, on August 2, 1914, Germany demanded a passage through Belgium in order to attack France. This King Albert refused, and war followed. The king at once hurried from Brussels to join his army, and he never left it except when it was necessary for him to cross into France or to go over to England for the purpose of conferring with heads of the other armies. Though all but a few square miles of his country was occupied by the enemy this leader never failed his people. Not far from the king in all the four years of that war, working in the hospitals just behind the lines, was his wife, Queen Elisabeth, caring for the wounded and feeding the hungry, except for brief trips to England to visit her children who had been sent there for safety.

King Albert was accidentally killed while climbing in the Ardennes, on February 16, 1934. He was succeeded by his elder son, the Duke of Brabant, as Leopold III. (*See* Leopold, Belgian Kings).

Alberta, CANADA. Much of the wealth of Canada is derived from the three prairie provinces, the most westerly of which, Alberta, lies at the foot of the Rockies. This vast region has an area of nearly 256,000 square miles—more than twice the size of Great Britain and Ireland. Its average elevation is considerably higher than that of its eastern neighbour Saskatchewan, and its scenery is much more varied. Of the 85 million acres which is the surveyed area of the province approximately 70 million acres can be profitably used for farming.

More than 16,000 square miles are mined for their valuable coal, and the coal reserves amount to 87 per cent of those of the entire Dominion. Natural gas is found in large supplies, chiefly in the Medicine Hat district, which is rapidly becoming an important manufacturing centre because of the advantages afforded by this cheap fuel. The province is the second largest producer of oil in the British Commonwealth. Turner Valley is the richest oil region. Development of a new oil-field 20 miles south-west of Edmonton began in 1946. Extending along the Athabasca river in the Murray district are some 30,000 square miles of oil-soaked sand. There are also vast salt deposits ; one beneath the town of Waterways is about 200 feet thick.

There are three natural divisions of the province. Southern Alberta is open prairie, except for the foothill country. This region was at one time given over to ranching, but it is now chiefly devoted to

KING ALBERT AND KING GEORGE V
During the First World War, Albert, King of the Belgians, and (on his right) King George V formed a firm friendship. They had in common the simple tastes of home-loving men, and had frequent meetings behind the lines. They are here seen at La Panne, Belgium, on August 13, 1916.

grain farming. Here the winters are tempered by warm dry winds, which frequently melt the winter snows and raise the temperature from below zero to spring-like warmth within a few hours, making it possible for cattle and horses to graze in the fields all the winter. This natural advantage is partially counterbalanced by the fact that these warm winds make it necessary in some parts to practise irrigation and dry farming. The latter is carried out by leaving stones on top of the soil to conserve moisture by protecting the top soil from the sun and drying winds.

Central Alberta, the country lying north of Calgary, with Edmonton (the capital, population about 93,800) as its centre,

Canadian Official

ALBERTA'S BANFF NATIONAL PARK
One of Canada's oldest and largest playgrounds, situated in the heart of the Rocky Mountains, Banff National Park has an area of 2,585 square miles. It is preserved in its natural state and forms a sanctuary for wild animals. In the centre above is the Banff Springs Hotel, magnificently situated in the Park on the banks of the Bow river.

is the most thickly settled part of the province. In the north it has considerable timber, principally poplar and other softwood trees. The rich black soil, on account of its moisture-holding qualities, is better than that of Southern Alberta. Central Alberta is the great mixed farming, dairying and pure-bred stock-raising part of the province. It produces heavy crops of grains, hay and roots.

Northern Alberta, so far as development is concerned, is the Peace River Valley. This part of the province is attracting settlement to a greater extent than any other part of Canada. The timber resources of Northern Alberta are large. The foothill country abounds in game—Rocky Mountain sheep, goats, moose, caribou, and useful game birds such as grouse, partridge, geese and ducks. Fur-bearing animals such as bear, beaver, marten, otter, muskrat, and prairie timber wolf furnish an output valued at many hundreds of thousands of pounds. The lakes and rivers abound with fish. There are several reservations in Alberta, the most notable being Banff National Park (the oldest Canadian park) and Buffalo Park, at Wainwright, where thousands of bison and a number of elk (or wapiti) are preserved on a tract of land of more than 100,000 acres in extent.

Since its organization as a province in 1905, Alberta has had a government similar to that of the other provinces of the Dominion. Good provision is made for education by a system of public, secondary and college institutions. The University of Alberta was founded at Edmonton in 1908. There are technical schools in the cities and a system of secondary agricultural schools in small towns for farm boys and girls. The growth of the province has been remarkable, the present population of about 796,000 being more than ten times the population at the beginning of this century.

Alcohol. This is "spirit of wine," produced when a sugary liquid is fermented. If yeast is added to fruit juice, grain mash, or other liquid containing sugar, bubbles soon begin to rise. The yeast has split the sugar into alcohol and carbon dioxide, and the carbon dioxide gas rises in bubbles.

Home-made wines such as parsnip or elderberry wine contain alcohol, the amount depending on the degree to which fermentation is allowed to go on. Cider (from apples) or perry (from pears) also contain alcohol, though the quantity generally is small in these wholesome beverages and hence they are often ranked as "teetotal" drinks. Beer, ale and stout contain a bigger proportion of alcohol, in ordinary times up to about 9 per cent in the stronger types. They are made by fermenting malted barley or other cereal grain.

Wines made from the grape may contain up to about 14 per cent. Spirits, such as brandy, whisky, rum and gin are made by distilling previously fermented liquors—brandy from wine; rum from sugar cane; whisky from grain; gin from grain (flavoured with juniper berries).

Yeast produces one of those strange substances known as enzymes (described under their own heading), which have the power to change sugary liquids by fermentation. Another kind of enzyme is produced when barley grains are allowed to germinate and sprout; this enzyme acts upon the starch in the barley grain, and converts it into malt-sugar and into dextrin. A mash made of the malted grain and water is then allowed to ferment.

When spirits are to be made from grain, the fermented mash is boiled in a closed vessel and the steam thus evaporated is led through a long coiled pipe immersed in water; the steam turns into liquid, or condenses as it is termed, and the alcohol is thus separated off from the rest of the substances which were in the mash. Alcohol for industrial purposes is made from potatoes or other suitable starchy vegetable, and can be produced from a variety of natural substances, including wood waste. Glucose, fermented by yeast, is another source.

An Aid in Illness or Emergency

Alcoholic beverages taken in moderation have a stimulating effect, and some people find them an aid to appetite and digestion. But the amount of alcohol which the body can tolerate without harmful effects is quite small. Alcohol is a food which is almost immediately burned up in the body and turned into energy, so that in illness or emergency it may be a valuable aid; but a person accustomed to frequent drinking would not experience this benefit in time of need when most wanted.

In excessive amounts—and what is safe for one person may be too much for another—alcohol has a stupefying effect upon the nervous system. A small quantity reduces sensitivity to mild pain, produces a feeling of well-being, and may easily cause over-confidence which will soon shade off into recklessness. Motorists and other people in control of powerful machinery, or those whose powers of observation and quick reaction to emergency are essential, should be especially sparing in the use of alcohol. A larger quantity hinders control of muscular movements, causes disorders of vision and speech, and loosens self-control. Still larger quantities cause stupor, delirium and even death.

One of the worst dangers of drinking alcohol is that in some persons an almost or entirely uncontrollable craving for drink may develop, with the bad results that everyone knows. That is why in most countries the sale of alcoholic beverages has been brought under strict control, by more or less heavy taxation and the regulation of the hours during which such drinks may be sold.

For Preparing Drugs and Medicines

Industrial alcohol, for use in manufacturing and processing, is free from these restrictions and is taxed at a much lower rate. But it is "denatured" by adding to it a proportion of methyl alcohol, and it is sold only to firms or persons using it for proper purposes. Methylated spirit is a similar denatured alcohol, but contains also pyridine to give it an acrid, nauseous taste and prevent drinking. It is coloured violet (by the addition of methyl violet) to distinguish it. Despite these precautions, foolish people do sometimes drink methylated spirit, with dreadful results; the state of intoxication lasts for days, and besides the effects of severe poisoning, even partial or complete blindness may occur.

Chemists use the name alcohol for a large class of compounds. Methyl alcohol or wood alcohol used to be made mainly by distilling wood in retorts ; as we have said, it is used to denature industrial and methylated spirit ; but its main use today is as a solvent of resins for making varnishes and similar preparations. Ethyl alcohol is the kind

produced by the fermentation of sugary liquids or of starchy vegetable substances. As thus obtained the alcohol is weak, so it has to be fractionally distilled, or " rectified," to extract yet more of the water. The name rectified spirit denotes that the liquid contains 90 per cent by volume, or 85·68 per cent by weight, of alcohol. It is used in preparing drugs and medicines.

" Proof spirit " contains 56·8 per cent by volume, or 49·25 per cent by weight, of alcohol. This term is used in measuring the alcoholic strength of brandy. whisky and other spirituous liquors, which are specified as so many degrees under proof, and so on. " Absolute alcohol," containing 95·5 per cent alcohol, is the strongest made commercially. It is used in chemical laboratories, where the greatest purity is required. On account of its very low freezing point, alcohol is used as the liquid in thermometers, coloured to make it more distinguishable. The freezing point of ethyl alcohol is − 200 degrees F. ; it boils at 153 degrees F.

Alder. This common tree, *Alnus glutinosa*, grows on the banks of streams or ponds and other

ALDER OR SCOTS MAHOGANY
All over Britain the alder is to be found growing near water. In Scotland it is called Scots mahogany because the wood turns red when cut. Being durable under water, the wood is used for the foundations of piers and bridges.

marshy places. You may recognize it easily at different seasons by various signs, apart from its stiff uprightness. In spring, before the leaves come, its branches are decorated with a large number of graceful catkins. These are reddish-brown, and by this you may distinguish them from the similar catkins of the hazel, which are yellowish-green.

After the catkins have withered the leaves appear, and these are so unlike those of any other tree that once you have seen them you cannot fail to know

ALDER DETAILS
Above are the long reddish-brown catkins of the male flower, and next to them are the little green cone-shaped seed cases. These cases usually fall into the water, and float until they come to rest in the mud. On the right is a spray of leaves.

them again. They are more or less heart-shaped, but they look as if they had grown the wrong way round. The point of the heart is at the stalk and the two rounded lobes are at the extremity, and the notch between them falls just where other leaves have a pointed tip. After the leaves have fallen you may know the alder by its cone-like seed cases.

Besides these the twigs bear three kinds of bud; namely, leaf buds, which grow singly; buds of the female catkins, which are similar but grow in little clusters; and buds of the male catkins which are like tiny fingers. But at any time you may recognize an alder by its buds, for each has a small stalk. When an alder is cut its wood becomes red, and on this account it is sometimes called Scots mahogany, for it is a common tree in Scotland. The Highlanders make red dye from its bark, and also a green and a brown dye from its flowers and twigs. Its wood makes durable piles for piers, foundations of bridges, and is used for the soles of clogs.

Inside the seed of the alder there are air-tight compartments. So when it ripens and falls into water, as it usually does, it floats and is carried along by wind, wave or current until it is washed up on the mud, where the seed may germinate.

WORLD-CONQUEROR at TWENTY-THREE

The man famed in history as Alexander the Great conquered the known world of his day when he was hardly out of his 'teens. But, as you will read here, he has many other claims than this to remembrance.

Alexander the Great, KING OF MACEDON (356-323 B.C.). A boy whose name has been remembered through the ages as that of a great explorer and conqueror once said: " My father will leave nothing for me to do! " That boy was Alexander, son of Philip, king of Macedon. But though Philip had made himself master over nearly all of the Greek states, the rest of the civilized world remained as a vast field for Alexander's conquests—a field not too great for his boundless ambition and his far-reaching genius both as a soldier and a statesman.

During the 13 years of his reign, 336-323 B.C., Alexander wrote his name large on the history of four civilizations—the Greek, Semitic, Egyptian and Persian (Iranian)— and made himself a place with the few men like Caesar, Charlemagne and Napoleon, who have decisively changed the current of world history by their mighty deeds.

Born at Pella, the capital of Macedon, and carefully educated by the great Aristotle, he early gave evidence of his remarkable gifts. When only 16 he took command of the army in his father's absence. A year later he showed such courage in the battle of Chaeronea, where the Macedonians defeated the Greek forces, that his father, embracing him, said: " My son, ask for thyself another kingdom, for that which I leave is too small for thee."

At Philip's death, Alexander, not yet 20 years old, ascended the throne and prepared to finish the conquests which his father had begun. When Thebes revolted, he struck terror into all Greece by razing the city to the ground, sparing amid the general ruin and desolation only the temples and the house where the poet Pindar had lived. With all Greece at his feet, Alexander was now

free to realize the almost incredibly bold design of conquering the Persian Empire—an empire 50 times as large as all Greece and with 20 times as many people. For centuries the life of Greek civilization had been menaced by Persia, which had pushed westward to the Aegean Sea. The danger was ever present of some sudden powerful stroke which should crush the culture of the West and plunge the entire world into Eastern semi-barbarism. Already the softening influence of Oriental life and superstition was beginning to sap away the strength of Hellenism (Greek culture).

Cutting the Famous Gordian Knot

Alexander's mission was first to free the Greek cities of Asia Minor—one-third of the Greek world; then to sweep Persian power from the rest of the eastern Mediterranean; and finally to crush Persia itself so thoroughly that centuries were to elapse before the East should ever again seriously menace the West. By extending Greek civilization over all the shores of the Mediterranean and into interior Asia, Alexander unwittingly paved the way for the spread of Christianity three centuries later.

Crossing the Hellespont (Dardanelles). Alexander invaded Asia Minor in 334, and defeated the Persians in a number of battles, overthrowing with his own lance the son-in-law of the king. The cities of Asia opened their gates to the conqueror as he marched to meet the great king Darius himself. On the way he came upon the famous Gordian knot, with which a Phrygian king had bound his chariot yoke so tightly and so intricately that no one had been able to untie it. An oracle foretold that whoever should untie that knot should become master of all Asia. Alexander resolved the

ALEXANDER THE GREAT AT A LION HUNT

In this spirited representation of a lion hunt, Alexander is supposed to be the figure on the left. Part of a panel on a royal sarcophagus or stone coffin found at Sidon on the Syrian coast, the carving was done soon after Alexander's death and may be considered to be accurate. The coffin was made to hold the remains of a ruler of Sidon.

From Hamdy Bey et Reinach, ' Une Nécropole royale à Sidon '

problem characteristically: drawing his sword, with one stroke he cut through the knot. From that day the expression " cutting the Gordian knot " has been used to describe the solution of difficulties by sudden, bold strokes.

Alexander met the Persian king Darius III in the great battle of Issus, between the mountains and the sea at the north-eastern corner of the Mediterranean. Here the irresistible Macedonian phalanx utterly routed the disorderly masses of the Persians (333 B.C.). The Persian monarch offered all Asia, as far as the Euphrates, for peace; but his conqueror refused.

Onward he swept, reducing the enemy's strongholds one after another. Egypt easily fell into his hands, and there he built one of the 70 cities he is said to have founded—Alexandria (*q.v.*), destined to be in a few decades the metropolis of Egypt.

With the Mediterranean world in his grasp, Alexander now thrust at the heart of Persia itself. He met Darius again in the spring of 331 at the battle of Arbela, near the River Tigris. The Persians greatly outnumbered the Macedonians, but their army was easily crushed. Darius, utterly vanquished, fled, and not long afterwards was stabbed to death by a band of traitors.

ALEXANDER THE GREAT
This bust of Alexander the Great gives a striking portrayal of the fine features and head of the man who was one of the world's great soldiers and statesmen.

Alexander entered in triumph Babylon and Susa, the storehouse of the treasures of the East, and Persepolis, the capital of Persia. Continuing eastwards and northward, he conquered the Scythians on the banks of the Jaxartes River. He then turned southward, planning to conquer India. But when he had reached the Sutlej, the eastern boundary of the Punjab, his soldiers, wearied with nearly eight years of fighting, refused to follow him farther.

On his way to Babylon he had been met by ambassadors from all parts of the world waiting to pay him homage. Not satisfied with this homage, and perhaps moved by the fact that the eastern peoples he had conquered would not permanently acknowledge the sway of any except a king who claimed divine descent, Alexander had for some years demanded that his subjects should worship him as a god. In a passion he had even killed his friend Clitus, who mocked at his pretensions to divinity. Like many another conqueror, Alexander was himself partly conquered by the life and ideals of the people he had overcome.

It was Alexander's settled policy to rule Asia in Asiatic fashion, and to graft Greek culture upon Persian civilization as far as he could. He married two Persian princesses, and assigned to many of his followers Asiatic wives. He wore Persian costume and adopted the ceremonies of the Persian court, to the indignation of his sturdy Macedonian followers. He kept the ancient Persian system of government for the most part; but he put three officials of equal rank at the head of each province, instead of the one all-powerful satrap (governor) of the Persian system, thus affording better protection to the central government and the people.

Alexander vigorously promoted enterprises for the benefit of his subjects and in the pursuit of knowledge. Thus he erected many great public buildings, ordered the restoration of the canal system of Babylonia, and set on foot many other public works. He never ceased to take a deep interest in learning. Even on his great campaigns he collected hundreds of natural history specimens and sent them to his old teacher Aristotle, in Athens. He sent an exploring expedition up the Nile to ascertain the causes of the annual overflow of the river, one of the earliest scientific expeditions of which we have record.

But with the greatness of Alexander's character there were mingled elements of weakness. He gave way at times to dissipation, and it was perhaps as a result of a drunken debauch that he contracted the fever of which he died at Babylon. His body was taken to Alexandria for burial.

Alexander I, King of Yugoslavia (1888–1934). The prince who became the first king of Yugoslavia was born on December 17, 1888. His father was Peter, king of Serbia, and when his elder brother, George, renounced his rights to the throne, Alexander became the heir-apparent. He commanded divisions of the Serbian army in the wars of 1912–13 against Turkey and Bulgaria and acted as commander-in-chief during the First World War. In 1914 he was made regent and in 1921, after Serbia had been regained from its German and Austrian conquerors, he became king of the new state of Yugoslavia. In 1929 he made himself dictator of the country, but five years later, on October 9, 1934, he was murdered at Marseilles by one of his Croat subjects ; M. Barthou, the Foreign Minister of France, being murdered at the same time. Alexander married Marie, daughter of Ferdinand, king of Rumania, and was succeeded as king of Yugoslavia by his young son, Peter.

Alexander, Harold Rupert Leofric George, 1st Viscount (b. 1891). When in August 1942 the German and Italian armies had advanced

LAST DRIVE OF ALEXANDER I
King Alexander of Yugoslavia was assassinated at Marseilles on October 9, 1934. He is seen with M. Barthou, French Foreign Minister, who was mortally wounded.

to the very gates of Alexandria in Egypt, General Sir Harold Alexander was appointed British commander-in-chief in the Middle East. " A specialist in retreats," commented one Italian newspaper, " just in time to lead another." But within two months it was the Italians and Germans who were retreating, and Alexander's forces pursued them into Tunisia and there wiped them out.

Alexander certainly had led two great retreats. In May 1940 he took over command of the British Expeditionary Force from Lord Gort and organized the epic evacuation from Dunkirk (q.v.). And in February 1942 he led hopelessly outnumbered British armies in Burma on a long and arduous withdrawal to the Indian border, and there held the Japanese at bay.

Alexander, third son of the 4th Earl of Caledon, was born at Caledon Castle, County Tyrone, Northern Ireland, on December 10, 1891. From Harrow School he went to Sandhurst, and in 1911 became an officer in the Irish Guards. He served in France in the First World War: a battalion commander at 25, he won the D.S.O. and M.C., was five times mentioned in dispatches, and twice wounded.

He became a major-general in 1938, taking over the 1st Division, which he led against

VISCOUNT ALEXANDER
This great British soldier, seen showing a Lueger pistol to his younger son Brian, received the surrender of the Germans in Italy in April 1945 and was made a Viscount in 1946.

Topical

ALEXANDRA THE WELL-BELOVED
As the Consort of King Edward VII, Queen Alexandra won the affection of the British people. Here she is seen with her two daughters, Princess Victoria (left) and Princess Maud (right), who became Queen of Norway in 1905.

in April 1945, forced the Germans to surrender. With effect from June 4, 1944, the date of the fall of Rome, General Alexander was made a Field-Marshal. In August 1945 he was named Governor-General of Canada, and in the New Year's Honours of 1946 he became a Viscount. In memory of his great victories he chose the title of Viscount Alexander of Tunis.

Alexandra, QUEEN (1844-1925). A remarkable tribute to a beloved Queen is paid in Great Britain once a year, in June, when women and girls are seen in the streets selling artificial wild roses. They do this to raise money for hospitals and other charities. A day in June is chosen, since it was in this month, in 1862, that Princess Alexandra first landed in England. The wild rose was adopted as the emblem because it was her favourite flower.

Alexandra Caroline Marie Charlotte Louise Julie was the eldest of the three daughters of Christian, Prince of Schleswig-Holstein, and his wife, Louise, who in 1863 became king and queen of Denmark. She was born December 1, 1844, and brought up in Copenhagen. Of her two brothers, one succeeded his father as king of Denmark, and the other became king of Greece. Her two sisters married Alexander III, Tsar of Russia, and the Duke of Cumberland.

When the future queen was only 16 or 17 years of age she was mentioned as a possible bride for the Prince of Wales, three years her senior. But it was not until 1862 that they were engaged. Albert Edward and Alexandra were married in St. George's Chapel, Windsor, on March 10, 1863, and between 1864 and 1871 six children were born to them.

In 1871 she nursed her husband in his serious illness, and the next 30 years, since Queen Victoria was living in retirement, she took a leading part as Princess of Wales in social activities. Very beautiful, she became extremely popular with the people. In January 1901 Queen Victoria died and the Prince of Wales became king as Edward VII. He and the Queen were crowned in Westminster Abbey, on August 9, 1902. The queen paid regular

the Germans in Belgium and France in 1940. Shortly before the evacuation from Dunkirk he was promoted to command the 1st Corps. Alexander went to Dunkirk on May 31, 1940, where he met Admiral Abrial, the French commander, who told him to hold a line from Bergues to Les Moeres, and thence to the sea. Alexander thought the line was so close to the beach and to Dunkirk that the Germans might soon stop the evacuation by short range artillery fire. However, he arranged to hold the line indicated until midnight on June 1-2, in order to cover Dunkirk and so enable the French to evacuate as many of their troops as possible.

The Germans did not make an all-out assault on the exhausted Allied troops, and on June 2 Alexander withdrew his forces to the outskirts of the town. The dive-bombing and shelling of the beaches and shipping was continuous throughout the evacuation, but Alexander's coolness cheered and sustained his men.

By midnight on June 2-3 all the remaining British troops had been embarked. Alexander refused to leave until he had gone along the beaches in a motor-boat to see if any British soldiers had been overlooked.

He reached Burma in February 1942, and in August, his task there completed, went to the Middle East to direct operations against the Italians and the German Afrika Korps. He drove them out of Egypt, out of Libya, out of Tunisia (where he was deputy to the American General Eisenhower); then as commander of the 15th Army Group he planned the landings in Sicily in July 1943 and in Italy the following September.

His British and American forces, with contingents from New Zealand, Canada, South Africa, India, Poland and France, fought their way through Italy and at last,

FIRST ALEXANDRA ROSE DAY
Until within two years of her death Queen Alexandra drove through the streets of London on every Rose Day, and many of those who lined the route threw roses into her carriage. She is seen here on the first Rose Day (in 1912) driving with her daughter, Princess Victoria.

ALEXANDRIA SEEN FROM THE AIR

Sir Alan Cobham

This photograph shows Alexandria, Egypt's great port on the Mediterranean, with the vast docks through which most of the country's trade passes. Alexandria is a place where East meets West, and its quays and streets are thronged with folk of every race and nation.

gigantic Pharos—the first of lighthouses and one of the Seven Wonders of the ancient world.

Within the city, and ringing a wide semi-circle of blue sea, were great palaces and towers surrounded by beautiful parks and gardens adorned with tropical trees, lakes, fountains and sculptured monuments. And here, in the midst of this natural beauty, gathered the most celebrated intellects of the world. For Alexandria had then become not only the greatest commercial centre of the Mediterranean, but also the most famous seat of the art, philosophy, science and religion of the known world.

visits to her family and friends in Copenhagen, but most of her time was passed in Great Britain. When Edward VII died in May 1910, Queen Alexandra took up residence at Marlborough House, her former home, and was officially known as the Queen-Mother. Troubled by increasing deafness, she lived largely in retirement until her death at Sandringham on November 20, 1925. She was buried in St. George's Chapel, Windsor.

Alexandria, EGYPT. For 2,000 years

Alexandria has been a famous city and port. Founded by Alexander the Great, it once even rivalled "the glory that was Greece and the grandeur that was Rome."

Let us picture Alexandria in the early centuries of the Christian era. Over the blue waters of the harbour glided Roman war galleys, with dazzling sails and flashing oars. At the docks were moored big grain ships loading for Rome, their tall sides towering above the buildings along the shore. Near by were ships that had braved the Atlantic storms along the coast of Spain, and oriental craft which had passed through the Nile canal from the Red Sea and Indian Ocean, bringing rich goods from other eastern lands.

On the noisy quays gathered a motley crowd—Jews, Greeks, Romans, Egyptians and Negro slaves from Nubia—mingling all dialects and all manner of costumes. Heaps of native wheat, bars of tin from the British Isles, silk from China and cotton fabrics from India littered the wharves. And above the whole picturesque scene towered the

D. McLeish

'POMPEY'S PILLAR'

One of the few remains of the Greco-Roman city of Alexandria is Pompey's Pillar, 90 feet high and erected in A.D. 302 as a landmark for sailors. Apparently it was originally an Egyptian obelisk.

In Alexandria flourished the famous Hellenistic or later Greek civilization. Its great museum contained a library of over 400,000 manuscripts, and was founded by the first Ptolemy, when he became king of Egypt at the death of Alexander the Great in 323 B.C. Among those priceless documents generations of writers, scientists and philosophers, including Euclid the father of geometry, Theocritus the Greek poet, and later Ptolemy the geographer, had held grave discussions. And since the dawn of Christianity, the problems of the new religion were fought out in bitter controversies, culminating in the great split between Athanasius, the bishop of Alexandria, and the priest Arius, founder of the Arian heresy.

The old temples, where once the pagan gods were worshipped with extravagant splendour, were thronged with monks at their devotions. Through the gardens and airy colonnades wandered bronzed and ragged hermits from the desert—men whose fierce religious zeal showed in their wild eyes, their limbs wasted with long fasts and torn with self-inflicted wounds. They had left their cells in the wilderness to denounce the sinful luxury of the great city.

Their prophecies of approaching decline were fulfilled. When in the 7th century A.D. the Arab succeeded the Greek and Roman, and perhaps destroyed her wonderful library, a long night of Egyptian darkness set in. Only in the 19th century, with the cutting of the Suez Canal and the British occupation of Egypt, did Alexandria regain something approaching her ancient greatness.

Alexandria was founded by Alexander the Great in 332 B.C. It originally lay on the island of Pharos, connected with the mainland by a mole nearly a mile long which separated the two harbours. It soon spread over a large area on the mainland. The city was divided into three parts, the Jews' quarter, that of the Egyptians, and the royal or Greek quarter. Among the principal buildings of that day were the palace of the Ptolemies and the temple of the Caesars, beside which stood the two obelisks, afterwards known as " Cleopatra's needles." One of these obelisks is standing today in the heart of London (*see* Cleopatra's Needle).

ALFRED'S JEWEL

This piece of jewelry once belonged to the great Saxon king and may perhaps bear his portrait.

Among the very few architectural glories of ancient Alexandria still standing in position is Pompey's Pillar, a sailor's landmark rising to a height of 90 feet, erected in A.D. 302.

Alexandria played a prominent part in Napoleon's Egyptian campaign of 1798, and was bombarded by the British in 1882 at the time of Arabi Pasha's rebellion against the Khedive. During the Second World War, Alexandria became chief British naval base in the Middle East ; the city was raided several times by German and Italian aircraft but no serious damage was done. The barracks and military installations were handed over by the British to the Egyptian army in February 1947 in accordance with a promise made by the British Government to withdraw its military forces from Egypt.

Modern Alexandria shows few traces of the ancient city. The mole has become silted up and forms a neck of land on which live most of the Mahomedan inhabitants. There is an Arab quarter with oriental bazaars, a large European quarter, and an industrial district with asphalt works, and oil, rice and paper mills; the chief industries are cotton spinning and weaving. The city is connected by canal with the river Nile and Cairo, and is linked by a network of railway and telegraph lines with other towns of Egypt. A first-class motor road leads to Cairo. The harbour is not only used by the shipping of all nations, but is a commercial airport of considerable importance. The chief exports are raw cotton, grain, rice and sugar. The value of these exports is about £40,000,000 for a normal year ; the imports handled amount to about as much. Alexandria is now, as in the days of old, one of the most cosmopolitan cities of the world,

British Museum

ALFRED'S PENNY

This penny, both sides of which are shown, was struck by King Alfred to commemorate his recapture of London in 885.

and with the founding of a university in 1939 it became once more a seat of learning. Population is about 686,000.

Alfalfa. (Pron. al'fal'fa). A valuable plant for feeding cattle, alfalfa (Arabic, *al-fasfasah*, meaning good food) is the Spanish name for a member of the pea, bean and clover tribe. The scientific name is *Medicago sativa*. In Britain it is known as Lucerne.

Alfonso, KINGS OF SPAIN. There have been 13 kings of Spain with the Christian name of Alfonso. The last of them was born in 1886, a few months after the death of his father, Alfonso XII, so that Alfonso XIII was king from his birth, though until he was 20 years of age his mother acted as regent. In 1906 he married Princess Victoria Eugénie (Ena), daughter of Prince and Princess Henry of Battenberg and a granddaughter of Queen Victoria. His married life began inauspiciously, for on his wedding day an attempt was made to assassinate him and his bride. His 25 years of personal rule were marked by many political troubles. They reached a crisis in April 1931, when the elections showed that very many people wanted a republican form of State. Alfonso decided to leave the country rather than plunge it into civil war; but he refused to renounce the throne and declared his belief that he had conscientiously served his country. A man of quick intelligence, high courage and intense patriotism, he had striven for peace and progress, but the rivalries of political parties and the economic backwardness of the country created at length a situation with which he and his military advisers were unable to cope. In exile he lived mostly in Italy, dying in Rome in 1941. Of his four sons, the eldest two renounced their rights to the throne. Six weeks before his death, Alfonso proclaimed his third and only surviving son, Don Juan, " King of all the Spaniards when Spain considers the time has come."

Alfred the Great, KING OF THE WEST SAXONS (848–901). When the Danes, or Northmen, had mastered the northern kingdom and East Anglia, they began in 870 an attack on Wessex, in south-western England. Here King Alfred had taken refuge from the invaders who had for years been over-running the country. One day, so the story goes, Alfred was sheltering in a herdsman's hut and the housewife bade her guest watch the cakes baking before the fire while she went out. This Alfred promised to do, but his mind soon began to may subtract the same number (4) from each side of the equation and get another equation. (In order to help you to picture this algebraic sum our artist has drawn the three diagrams in the opposite column.)

By means of the equation and the use of letters to represent unknowns, we can shorten and simplify the labour that is often necessary in arithmetic. This method of solving problems is called algebraic and every educated person should be able to use it.

Algebra has had a long and interesting history. It had its beginnings in ancient Egypt, about 2000 B.C., when some unknown mathematical writer discovered the principle of the equation. In the treatise which he wrote on the subject he used the Egyptian word *hau* (literally "heap") instead of the letter x to denote the unknown quantity.

Certain Dark or Mysterious Things

In the days of Alexander the Great a certain learned man is said to have written a work on algebra which he called by a Syriac title meaning "the book of dark or mysterious things." Seven hundred years later (about A.D. 350), Diophantus, a Greek who taught in Alexandria, Egypt, earned the title "Father of Algebra" by his systematic attempts to work out the science. The name of the science was derived from the word *aljebr* (Arabic, meaning "binding together") in the title of a famous work written by Mohammed ben Musa, a mathematician of Baghdad, about the year 800. An Italian merchant named Leonardo Bonaccio acquired a knowledge of the science while travelling in the east about 1200, and introduced it among his countrymen. Algebra did not assume its present form until the 16th century. Even since that time many interesting and valuable improvements have been made, so that now a boy or girl in the fourth form of the secondary school can get a broader view of algebra than the most learned men were able to obtain in the old days.

In some respects algebra is very much like arithmetic. In arithmetic, for example, we learn how to add, subtract, multiply, and divide with numbers represented by the digits 1, 2, 3, 4, etc. In algebra we continue to study how to use the processes of addition, subtraction, multiplication and division with numbers, but the numbers are regularly represented by letters, such as is sometimes the case in arithmetic. Thus, e.g. the interest rule often used in arithmetic, *the interest for a given time equals the principal times the rate multiplied by the time*, is in algebra work always translated into the statement $I = PRT$, that is, Interest = Principal × Rate × Time. Such a use of letters enables us to write statements of some length in very concise forms.

The signs $+$, $-$, $\times$, $\div$, $=$, and $\sqrt{}$ have the same meaning in algebra as in arithmetic. But in algebra ab means a times b without the use of the multiplication sign; a dot is also used at times instead of the sign $\times$ to indicate multiplication; thus $a \cdot b$ is read a times b.

When a group of letters is to be multiplied or divided as a whole by some other letter, we enclose

Here is a sim... we want to ... scale, and w... The 10-poun... begin by ca... al...

We now ... sugar the ... just like a ... one side o... the other. ... as follows... sugar add...

An equ... if the ... at once... equatio... cancel... answe... one si...

turn to affairs of state and to plans for defeating the Danes, and when the woman returned she found her cakes burned to a cinder.

Another story tells how Afred went into the Danish camp disguised as a minstrel or wandering singer, in order to spy out the strength of the enemy. The Danes were so pleased with his singing that he had difficulty in getting away again. He then summoned his warriors from their homes, to which they had scattered at the end of the preceding campaign to care for their families and prepare their crops. With this newly-formed army he defeated the Danes in battle and drove them back into their fortified camp, where he besieged them for 14 days. Since they were now separated from their ships and cut off from supplies, the Danish leader Guthrum made a treaty in which he agreed to leave Alfred's kingdom and to accept Christianity. Later a new treaty was made which fixed the Thames and the old Roman road called Watling Street as the boundary between Alfred's kingdom and the Danish lands north of it.

This treaty brought peace to the land and allowed Alfred to turn his attention to other pursuits than war. One of the things in which he was greatly interested was the encouragement of learning. After Alfred had become king in 871 he invited learned men from other countries to his kingdom to instruct his people. He established a school similar to the Palace School of Charlemagne, and he translated a number of books from Latin into English, so that the people might read them. Under the King's direction was begun, also, the Anglo-Saxon Chronicle. This is a record of events, year by year, kept by the monks, and from it we get most of our knowledge of those days.

W. F. Taylor

ALFRED'S STATUE IN HIS CAPITAL

Winchester was the capital of Wessex, and this fine statue by Hamo Thornycroft is the city's tribute to the greatest of the old English kings. Alfred died at Winchester in A.D. 901 but no traces of his grave remain.

ALGAE INCLUDE SEAWEEDS

These seaweeds, or algae as the scientist calls them, are among the simplest of all forms of plant life. Both types seen here have the characteristic swellings, which act as buoys to keep them up in the water ; and the one on the left has an additional growth of the feathery Polysiphonia, or sea-fir.

But not all of Alfred's time was devoted to books. He rebuilt London, which had been partially destroyed by the Danes. He improved the army so that his kingdom might never again suffer as it had from those Northmen. He saw that England needed a navy as well as an army, and so he began to build ships ; for this he is known as the "father of the English navy." He encouraged industries of all kinds, and he collected and revised the old laws of the kingdom.

His aim was expressed in his own words: "To sum up all," he said, "it has ever been my desire to live worthily while I was alive, and after my death to leave to those that should come after me my memory in good works." That he succeeded in this is proved by the fact that the English cherished his memory as "protector of the poor," and now we call him "Alfred the Great."

In the Ashmolean Museum, Oxford, is an ornament of gold on which is a crude portrait in enamel, with words that mean "Alfred had me wrought." It is known as the Alfred jewel. It is quite likely that the portrait is that of Alfred the Great, particularly as the jewel was found at Athelney, Somersetshire, where the king was at one time in hiding from the Danes.

Algae. (Pron. al'-gē). The most lowly organized of the green plants are called algae, Latin for seaweeds. The first little plants were sailors. As they floated about in the water, the living drop of jelly-like material that we call protoplasm took in food through the thin walls of the cells. One cell budded from another and broke away to start a new family, or clung to the parent cells to form a bead-like string, or a knot. Sometimes they budded all round the sides and formed what may be likened to mats and flat networks of cells.

Some of these nets and mats floated on rocks in quiet places where the motion of the water

was not strong enough to float them off again.
As the rocks sheltered them, the plants were not
so easily torn apart. The cells that lay on the rocks
could not gather so much food, so they learned to
cling, while the floating cells gathered food, and
budded and spread into feathery leaf-like fronds.

So, by and by, they divided the work just as
people do in a village. It was the business of
some plants or cells to cling to the rocks. Others
waved in the water and gathered food. Certain
cells now began to collect budding material in
little raised dots on the fronds. When these dots
ripened they were washed off. These bud dots were
spores. They were not seeds, they were just the
hints of seeds ; and the cells that clung to the rocks
were hints of roots ; and the cells that spread out
and floated were hints of leaves. All together they
formed—seaweeds. And seaweeds belong to the
plant family called Algae.

How Algae Help in Industry

All algae contain a green colouring matter
called *chlorophyll*, which is the housekeeper in a
plant cell. By the process called osmosis, raw
materials like carbon, hydrogen, nitrogen and
magnesium are brought in from the air and water.
Whenever the sun shines, the housekeeper becomes
energetic and manufactures food for the plant ou
of these raw materials. Such work is called *photo
synthesis*. (*See* under that heading).

The seaweeds occupy an important stage in th
compounding of vitamin D, sometimes called th
" sunshine " vitamin. This food factor preven
and cures rickets. It is found in the fresh liver oi
of members of the cod family, which obtain it fro

How PROBLEMS ar

A nyone who takes the trouble reall
fascinating " magic " called Alge
to a host of problems th

Algebra. People sometimes think that alge
is only a form of arithmetic which uses let
instead of figures, and they wonder why pu
should be required to spend their time in maste
what seems a useless subject. Perhaps we
best see how mistaken this view is if we
with a very necessary algebraic idea, that o
equation, and see how useful it may turn out t

In order to find the weight of a pair of balanced s
is placed on one pan of a 4-pound weight, bal
The flour, together with a 4-pound weight, bal
10 pounds of weights on the other pan.
it is a well-known principle of balanced
that if one takes the same amount from each
the balance is not disturbed. Hence, if we su
the balance is taken from each pa
that a 4-pound weight is taken from each pa
seen that the flour will be balanced by 6 p

This solves the problem; but let us ana
a little farther. The important fact in the p
is that an unknown number of pounds c
plus 4 pounds in one pan balances 10 pou
the other pan. Suppose we let x repres
unknown number of pounds in the bag
and use the sign of equality to represent the
balance of the scales. we can express the

Algebraic Solution

Let x = number of feet in the shorter part.
Then $4x$ = number of feet in the longer part.
and $x + 4x$, or $5x$ = length of the pole.
Then

$$5x = 20$$
$$x = 4$$
$$4x = 16$$

Hence the parts are 4 ft. and 16 ft. long respectively.

The statement $5x = 20$ is called an *equation*.
The " literal " (letter) number x is called the
unknown. The equation is said to be solved when
the correct value of the unknown is found. Thus
$x = 4$ is the solution of the equation $5x = 20$.
Such a value is called a *root* of the equation.
Thus 4 is a root of the equation $5x = 20$, because
when 4 is put in place of x the equation is true.
This process is called *checking* the solution.

There are four fundamental laws used in solving
equations : the addition law, subtraction law,
multiplication law, and division law.

Addition Law.—" If the same number be added
to both sides of an equation, another equation is
obtained." *E.g.* in the equation $4x - 2 = 10$,
if we add 2 to each side of the equation, the result
is $4x = 12$. We can find $x = 3$ by dividing both
sides of the equation, $4x = 12$, by 4.

Division Law.—This says, " If both sides of
an equation be divided by the same number
(excluding division by zero), another equation is
obtained." Thus, if $4x = 12$, then $x = 3$, because
both sides are divisible by 4.

Subtraction Law.—" If the same number be subtracted from both sides of an equation, another
equation is obtained." *E.g.* in the equation
$3x + 4 = 16$, if we subtract 4 from both sides of
the equation, we get $3x = 12$, whence, by the
division law, $x = 4$.

Multiplication Law.—" If both sides of an equation
be multiplied by the same number, another
equation is obtained." *E.g.* in the equation
$\dfrac{x}{3} = 5$, if we multiply both sides of the equation
by 3, then $x = 15$.

Kinds of Equation and Their Use

Equations are of two kinds, *identical* and *conditional*. An identical equation, or an identity, is
an equation that has no letters in it, or that is
true for all values of the letters. Thus $2 + 4 = 6$
and $7x = 10x - 3x$ are identities. The identity
states that the two sides of the equation are the
same except for form. A conditional equation is
an equation which is true only for certain values
of the unknown. Thus $5x + 2 = 12$ only on the
condition that $x = 2$. The conditional equation
always asks for what values of the unknown the
equation will be true. The equation is indispensable in solving *verbal* or *thought* problems
like the one in which it is required to find the
two parts of a pole 20 feet long. As a rule it is
not difficult to solve the equation once the correct
equation is obtained, but often one may make a
mistake in interpreting the conditions of the
problem. The following steps in the algebraic
solution of verbal problems may be helpful:

(a) In every problem certain facts are given as known
and one or more as unknown and to be determined.
Read the problem so as to get these facts clearly in mind.

(b) In solving the problem denote one of the unknown
numbers by some symbol, as *x*.

(c) Express all given facts in algebraic language.

(d) Find two different expressions which denote the
same number and equate them. Join by the sign of
equality (=).

(e) Solve the equation for the value of the unknown
number.

(f) Check the result by re-reading the problem, sub-
stituting the result in the conditions of the problem to
see if these are satisfied. Note that it is not sufficient to
check the equation, for you may have written the wrong
equation to represent the conditions of the problem.

Arithmetic Instead of Algebra

Many arithmetical problems may be solved
with much greater ease by using algebraic formulae.
For instance, in a problem on areas we might
wish to find the difference between the squares of
two numbers. To do this arithmetically we should
have to square each number separately and then
subtract the products. By using an algebraic
formula, however, $(a^2 - b^2) = (a + b)(a - b)$,
we find that the same result can be arrived at by
adding the two numbers together, subtracting
the two numbers and multiplying their products.
When the numbers are long and very near each
other, this method saves considerable time.

For instance, to find
$(593)^2 - (591)^2$. Let $a = 593$ and $b = 591$.
Then $(593)^2 - (591)^2 = (593 + 591)(593 - 591)$
$= 1184 \times 2 = 2368$.

If the only difference between arithmetic and
algebra lay in the fact that letters are used to
represent numbers instead of the ordinary digits,
we should have merely literal arithmetic. But
when the study of algebra is begun new kinds of
numbers are introduced called *relative* numbers
or *signed* numbers. In arithmetic the addition of
two numbers is always possible, but it is not always
possible to subtract. If the subtrahend is larger
than the minuend we cannot subtract in arithmetic
—the problem would have no meaning. In algebra,
however, subtraction is always possible because of
signed numbers. *Signed numbers* are numbers which
are given two opposite senses or directions These
two opposite senses or directions are distinguished
by calling one number *positive* and the other *negative*.
Either may be called the positive number, but the
number which has the opposite sense is always
negative. Thus, if a distance to the right of some
starting point (called the zero point) is positive,
then the distance to the left of the zero point is
negative. All real numbers are usually represented
on a line called the number line and extending
from the zero point in two opposite directions. A
positive number is denoted by $+$, and a negative
by $-$. If no sign is given it is understood that the
number is a positive one.

The fundamental operations of addition, subtraction, multiplication and division (except by
zero) are always possible with positive and negative
numbers. The four laws are as follows :

Addition Law.—If the two numbers to be added are
positive, the sum is clearly positive; if negative, the
sum is negative. Therefore, *to add two algebraic numbers
of like sign, find the sum of the two numbers arithmetically
and prefix to the sum their common sign.* Thus, the sum
of $+5$ and $+10$ is $+15$; of -7 and -5 is -12. If
the two numbers to be added have opposite signs,
find the difference of the numbers arithmetically and
prefix the sign of the larger number. Thus, the sum
of $+15$ and -8 is $+7$.

Algeria.

France, which [...]
across the Medite[...]
is one of the n[...]
France here has [...]
the intelligent n[...]
themselves as fa[...]

Algeria is no[...]
a part of Franc[...]
ments—Oran, [...]
which sends on[...]
to the French [...]
have their own [...]
the supreme a[...]
general, and sin[...]
French are ad[...]
decree of 1944,[...]
Algerian Mosle[...]
Moslems. In [...]
granted Algeri[...]
principal reform[...]
Assembly to c[...]
administration [...]

Algeria lies [...]
Tunis on the e[...]
daries extend [...]
desert districts [...]
400 miles farth[...]
the great Atlas [...]
a comparativel[...]
district along [...]
well watered b[...]
plains and valle[...]
raise wheat, b[...]
tobacco, espart[...]
warmer lowla[...]
producing da[...]
bananas, pom[...]

ALGE[...]
TUNIS[...]
and MOR[...]
SCALE OF [...]
0   50   1[...]
1 inch   about 245[...]
CAPITAL ⊛ HIGH [...]
INT'L BOUNDARY[...]

North-West Af[...]
Atlas Mountair[...]
to East. Betw[...]
Tell district, an[...]

Subtraction Law.—In subtraction we are always concerned in finding a number called the difference which when added to the subtrahend will give the minuend. Thus, -4 subtracted from 6 equals 10 because $-4+10 = 6$; and -12 subtracted from $-17 = -5$ because the sum of -12 and -5 equals -17. The result of subtracting any number, say b, is the same as adding $-b$. Therefore, *to subtract one algebraic number from another change the sign of the subtrahend and add.*

Multiplication Law.—There are four possible cases of the multiplication of positive and negative numbers. Illustrations will make the law clear. Since multiplication is a short process of addition, $(+4)(+3) = (+4) + (+4) + (+4) = +12$. Likewise $(-4)(+3) = (-4) + (-4) + (-4) = -12$. Then if we assume that positive and negative numbers follow the law for arithmetic numbers, and since we know in arithmetic that $3 \times 4 = 4 \times 3$, then $(+4)(-3) = (-3)(+4) = -12$. If in multiplying (-4) by (-3) the -3 were $+3$, we should get -12 as a product, but since the multiplier is -3 we get $(-4)(-3) = +12$. These examples illustrate the law of signs for multiplication which is as follows: *The product of two algebraic numbers of like signs is always positive. The product of two algebraic numbers of unlike signs is invariably negative.*

Division Law.—Since in division we are concerned with finding one of two numbers called the quotient which when multiplied by another number called the divisor will give the dividend, it is clear that

(1) $(+8) \div (+2) = +4$, because $(+2)(+4) = +8$.
(2) $(+8) \div (-2) = -4$, because $(-2)(-4) = +8$.
(3) $(-8) \div (+2) = -4$, because $(+2)(-4) = -8$.
(4) $(-8) \div (-2) = +4$, because $(-2)(+4) = -8$.

Therefore the law of signs for division is as follows: *The quotient or number resulting from the division of two algebraic numbers of like signs is positive. The quotient of two algebraic numbers of unlike signs is negative.*

Adding and Subtracting Polynomials

A one-termed number is called a *monomial*, a two-termed number a *binomial*, a three-termed number a *trinomial*, and so on. A *polynomial* is an expression containing two or more terms. Thus $3x^2$ is a monomial, $2a+3b^2c$ is a binomial, $3x^2+4x+6$ is a trinomial. Monomials may be added by adding as the first operation the positive terms and the negative terms and then finding the sum of these results. Thus, $27x + (-14x) + (-11x) + (21x) = +23x$.

The method of adding polynomials is illustrated in the calculation below.

$$\begin{array}{r} 9x+3y+2z \\ 5x-4y+6z \\ -3x-8y-5z \\ \hline 11x-9y+3z \end{array}$$

In the monomial $2x^3y^4$ the 2 is called the *coefficient* of the term, and the 3 and 4 are called *exponents.* The exponent indicates how many times the letter is to be used as a factor. The degree of a monomial is indicated by the sum of all the exponents in the monomial, and the degree of a polynomial is given by the term of highest degree in the polynomial. Thus, $x^5+x^3+x^2+1$ is of the fifth degree in x, while $x-2xy^2+y^3$ is of the third degree in y and first degree in x. The subtraction of one polynomial from another is shown in the example below.

$$\begin{array}{r} 4x^2-3xy+6y^2 \\ 3x^2-5xy-7y^2 \\ \hline x^2+2xy+13y^2 \end{array}$$

One of the simplest products is that of multiplying a polynomial by a monomial. Before this

type can be fully understood one must know that when two numbers with exponents are multiplied together (say $a^3 . a^5$), the product is the number with an exponent equal to the sum of the original exponents. Thus, $a^3 . a^5 = a^8$.

If we multiply $a^2-2ab+3b^2$ by $3a$, each term of the polynomial must be multiplied by the monomial and the resulting products added. For example, $3a(a^2-2ab+3b^2) = 3a^3-6a^2b+9ab^2$. The product of two polynomials is found by multiplying every term of one polynomial by each term of the other polynomial and adding these products. Thus $(x^2+2xy+y^2)(x+y) = x^3+3x^2y+3xy^2+y^3$.

The actual work appears as follows:

$$\begin{array}{r} x^2+2xy+y^2 \\ x+y \\ \hline x^3+2x^2y+xy^2 \\ +\ x^2y+2xy^2+y^3 \\ \hline x^3+3x^2y+3xy^2+y^3 \end{array}$$

Multiplication of Binomials

There are certain type products that one should study carefully because this enables one later to see the factors of certain expressions more readily. The first of these is the product of multiplying a polynomial by a monomial. If one knows clearly that $2a(3x^2+4y+6bz) = 6ax^2+8ay+12abz$, one can more easily find the two factors of $6ax^2+8ay+12abz$. The terms of $6ax^2+8ay+12abz$ are said to be *similar* terms because they each contain the factor $2a$. In trying to reduce to factors any algebraic expression one should therefore first look for a monomial factor which is common to all of the terms of the expression.

The second type product with which one should be familiar is the product obtained by multiplying two binomials together. The following examples will illustrate the method:

1. $(2x+3)(4x+5)$.

   Solution: $$\begin{array}{r} 2x+3 \\ 4x+5 \\ \hline 8x^2+12x \\ +10x+15 \\ \hline 8x^2+22x+15 \end{array}$$

2. $(3a+5)(2a-8)$.

   Solution: $$\begin{array}{r} 3a+5 \\ 2a-8 \\ \hline 6a^2+10a \\ -24a-40 \\ \hline 6a^2-14a-40 \end{array}$$

3. $(5y+4)(5y-4)$.

   Solution: $$\begin{array}{r} 5y+4 \\ 5y-4 \\ \hline 25y^2+20y \\ -20y-16 \\ \hline 25y^2\qquad-16 \end{array}$$

4. $(2x+3)(2x+3)$.

   Solution: $$\begin{array}{r} 2x+3 \\ 2x+3 \\ \hline 4x^2+6x \\ +6x+9 \\ \hline 4x^2+12x+9 \end{array}$$

If we agree to use the binomials $ax+b$ and $cx+d$ to represent any two binomials where a, b, c, and d are known numbers like those in the products above, then it is possible for us to discover a short cut in multiplying $ax+b$ by $cx+d$. By way of an

example :
$(cx+d)$.

The arr
products w
seen that *t*
first term of
t'e last tern
the sum of t

Product
easily by
" cut and

The m
correct pa
and then
factors to
the follow

Factori

SOLUTIO
shown bel
$2x+1$
$x+$

It is c
since the

It is v
factors o
are called
to remem
not facto
numbers
are not f

One c
importan
(1) T
(2) F

(3) C
The p
by anot
metic.
If we
of polyi
of the fc
(i) A

(ii)
6.1
6.1

blocks of concrete. In the suburbs there are many beautiful villas and splendid hotels.

In Algeria is the headquarters of the famous Foreign Legion of France, recruited from adventurous spirits from all parts of the world.

Split up into small warring tribes, the native Berbers of Algeria were for centuries an easy prey for invaders—Phoenicians, Carthaginians, Romans, Vandals and Arabs. Under the lax rule of the Turks, who conquered the country in 1518, the Algerians became dreaded pirates. For three centuries corsairs (pirates) from Algeria and the other Barbary States (Morocco, Tunisia and Libya) preyed on the Mediterranean commerce of every nation, in spite of expeditions sent against them by European powers and the Americans. Christians were still eking out a living death in the filthy dungeons of Algiers, Tunis and Tripoli in 1816 when Lord Exmouth, with a small British and Dutch squadron, shattered the defences of Algiers and liberated the wretched slaves.

The French seizure of Algeria originated as the result of a dispute over a debt between France and the Algerian government, when the ruler, Dey Hussein, struck the French consul with a "fly-swatter." War resulted, and in 1830 Algiers surrendered; Algeria became a part of France in 1842.

ALGIERS, FORMER FASTNESS OF BARBARY PIRATES
This is no European port, but Algiers, the one-time fastness of pirate Moors, and for the last hundred years the chief centre of French influence on the Barbary Coast. Through it passes a stream of traffic between France and her African colonies.

Algeria and Algiers assumed great importance in the Second World War, both politically and militarily. After the surrender of France to the Germans in June 1940 Algeria was ruled by the pro-German Vichy Government of Marshal Pétain, and many of the officials and troops were not in sympathy with the Allies. Bad feeling was caused by the " melancholy action " (as Mr. Winston Churchill described it) which took place on July 3, 1940, off Oran. There lay a French fleet, including four battleships, and to prevent their falling into the hands of the Germans or Italians an ultimatum to join the British or sink his ships was sent by the Allies to the French commander. When he ignored this, a British battle squadron attacked and almost destroyed the French fleet. The French battleship Dunkerque was badly damaged and had to be beached, while its sister ship, the Strasbourg, was hit by a torpedo. It was able, however, to slip out of Oran at night and reached Toulon in France.

At dawn on November 8, 1942, a great Anglo-American force made surprise landings in French North Africa, going ashore at various points in Algeria and Morocco. Admiral Darlan, the Vichy Minister of Defence, was in Algiers at the time and he ordered the French forces, who had at first resisted the Allies, to cease fire. Algiers was occupied on November 9 and became

British Official

ALGERIA VISITED BY KING GEORGE VI
During the Second World War, Algeria was visited by King George VI, and here he is seen in June 1943 inspecting members of the Black Watch at Maison Blanche aerodrome outside Algiers. Several of the airfields constructed by the Allied air forces in Algeria for heavy bombers are now used by civil air lines.

Metallurgists, working first in their laboratories, have given the world thousands of alloys, mixing metals of different kinds so that they were able to produce an alloy with almost any required group of properties—stainlessness with hardness and the ability to hold a keen edge in cutlery; lightness, toughness and great strength in sheet metal used to build aircraft, and so on.

By far the most important group of alloys is that in which iron plays the leading part—the so-called "ferrous" alloys, from "ferrum," the Latin name for iron. The iron group of course includes the steels, which are alloys of iron with certain proportions of carbon. Generally iron ore contains the carbon already, and some of it has to be taken away in the process of smelting the ore or treating it afterwards when molten. The distinction between irons and steels is not a clear one.

Stainless and Other Steels

Wrought iron (made by refining pig iron) is workable by the smith, whereas cast iron (made by pouring molten pig iron into suitably shaped moulds) is brittle and will not stand hammering; wrought iron contains very little carbon—about one-tenth of 1 per cent; cast iron contains 2½ per cent or more carbon. Between these two come the carbon steels, with differing amounts of carbon, according to the purpose for which the metal is to be used. Mild steel, used for all sorts of purposes, is the metal for enamelled pots and pans, corrugated "iron," and a thousand other products. It will not serve for tools, since it cannot be hardened and tempered; it contains about a quarter of 1 per cent of carbon; steel for tools which need great hardness contains five times as much carbon as mild steel.

There is an old saying that a good tool-steel must be able to get hot without losing its temper. Ordinary carbon steels used as cutters in machine tools such as lathes or milling machines get overheated at the tool edge unless the cutting is done fairly slowly. In 1868 Robert Mushet, an English metallurgist, discovered that a tool made of steel containing a proportion of tungsten kept its edge even though the tool got red-hot from friction with the work. From this discovery developed the "high-speed" steels commonly used today, which allow work to be done more quickly, and permit deeper cuts to be made by the tools. Other metals are now alloyed with the steel, which will contain about 20 per cent tungsten, 5 per cent chromium and small amounts of cobalt, vanadium, or other elements.

Speaking of chromium, it was a chance discovery which led to its use in stainless steels. A Sheffield experimenter named Brearley was trying out alloys for gun barrels, among these mixtures being a steel with 14 per cent chromium; the test piece was thrown away along with others which Brearley thought unsuitable for his gun barrels. Some months later he saw these throw-outs on the scrap heap and noticed that one had remained bright while most of the others had rusted. The bright piece was the one made of steel with 14 per cent

ALLOYS IN T...
Alloys are used increasingly ...
and fittings. This stainless ...
very little trouble. The tap ...
cabinet doors and handles ...

chromium. La...
proportion of ...
steel improved ...
stainless steels ...
parts and spec...

Manganese ...
Hadfield in 1 ...
tough as we ...
per cent of m...
and was int...
tramcar whe...
rails, manga...
carbon steel ...
or so. Ano...
during the ...

An...
The alloy ...
under the ...
say someth...
in alumini...
ium is a v...
soft. But ...
zinc and ...
weight fo...
ores, and ...
became ...
incendia...
the meta...
its melti...
intense ...

ALGERIAN OASIS *Dorien Leigh*
Though the coastland of Algeria is fertile enough, behind lies a great expanse of arid mountains and desert. Here men would be unable to exist were it not for the oases (such as the one above) where palm branches sway above whitewashed homes or the tomb of some holy man.

the Anglo-U.S. headquarters. General Eisenhower, Allied Commander-in-Chief, at first nominated the French General Giraud to be head of the new French Government in Algeria. Giraud had been landed for a few hours in Algeria from a British submarine before the Allied invasion, and his secret negotiations with certain French officials had materially assisted the Allies.

However, when Darlan declared himself willing to cooperate with the Allies he was nominated in Giraud's place on December 1. He established an imperial council at Algiers which included General Giraud and representatives of the pro-Allied Fighting French. Darlan's appointment was very unpopular with the Fighting French and certain of the Allies, especially the British. On December 24, 1942, Darlan was assassinated in Algiers, and General Giraud was chosen by the imperial council as his successor.

At the end of May 1943 General de Gaulle, the leader of the Fighting French who had come to England from France in 1940 to continue the struggle against the Germans, met Giraud in Algiers. They discussed the establishing of a French Government to represent all Frenchmen who were opposed to the Vichy Government and as a result of their meeting the French Committee of National Liberation was formed on June 3, 1943.

With the conclusion of the campaign in North Africa in May 1943 Algeria became a huge Allied naval and military base, where preparations were made for the invasion of Sicily and Italy. Many distinguished people visited the naval and military establishments, including King George VI.

On June 2, 1944, the French Committee of National Liberation changed its title to that of the French Provisional Government, but it remained in Algiers directing the French war effort and upholding the rights of France. Algiers was regarded as the capital of unoccupied France until the liberation of Paris in August 1944, the government moving to that city on August 31. Algeria retained its military importance to the Allies until the end of the campaign in Italy in April 1945.

An Arab movement for further measures of self-government caused disturbances in the Constantine area in 1946, but these were suppressed by the French authorities without much difficulty.

Alhambra. (Pron. al-ham′-bra).

Undoubtedly the most wonderful relic of the Moorish occupation of Spain is the Alhambra. This marvellously beautiful palace and fortress of the former Moorish rulers of Granada is situated on a hill overlooking that city. In the park are a number of English elms presented by the great Duke of Wellington in 1812 in acknowledgment of an estate conferred on him by Ferdinand VII. In Arabic the name means (al) the (hamra) red, and was given to the vast building doubtless because the solid outer walls are made of brick of that colour.

Begun in 1248, it was not completed until about 1354—over a century later. Today, only

ALHAMBRA'S MAIN GATEWAY
The main entrance to the famous palace of the Moorish kings at Granada was known as the Gate of Judgement (above). In the massive square tower which surmounts the gateway the Moors of old used to hold an informal court of justice, from which the gate derives its name.

are slow and difficult. Its chief food is fish, but it is also fond of small reptiles, and devours dogs and other quadrupeds when it can get them. During the winter months the alligator buries itself in the mud, but with warm weather it reappears. It may then be seen basking in the sun, and at times the loud roar of the male echoes like thunder.

The female alligator lays a great number of eggs, with hard shells, which in size and general appearance resemble fowls' eggs. The nests are built in a curious manner. Along the bank is spread a layer of mud and grass or leaves; on this is placed a layer of eggs, then another layer of mud and grass about seven or eight inches in thickness, then another layer of eggs carefully covered, and so on, until often 30 or more eggs are deposited. Although the eggs are hatched by the heat of the sun and of the decaying vegetable matter, the mother alligator watches the nest carefully. As soon as the young, which are helpless little creatures, are hatched, she

leads them to the w
duck does her brood
enough to defend
yelping of the you
about resembles th

Alligators have
and for their hides
that their number
horny scales cann
bullet of a high-
wounded behind t
the winter month
dition, they are of
Another reason
the little ones are
and even by lat
guard. In Flori
aside for them,
basis on alligato
common alligato

New METALS GIVEN US

*Thousands of years ago the primitive metal-workers
hardening copper by mixing it with tin, but most
our civilization possible are the creations of q*

Alloys. Until a few years ago this word meant a mixture of metals, or of a metal and a non-metal combined by melting. But today there is the comparatively new science and art of powder metallurgy, by which powdered metals are mixed and then compacted under very heavy pressure without melting. Intricately shaped machine parts which otherwise would have to be cast from molten metal, and then shaped in lathes and other machines, can be moulded direct in steel dies filled with the powdered alloy.

An American motor-car works which during the World War of 1939-45 had to produce parts for gun mountings was able to save 5,000,000 man-hours in a single year by using powder metallurgy — turning out 20,000 sets of parts, each set comprising 90 different parts. The pressure under which the powder is moulded may range from 100 to 500 tons per square inch. Sometimes the powdered metal is heated; for the softer metals it can be moulded cold.

Now let us look at some of the earliest alloys known to Man—those of copper and tin. Pure copper is a soft, weak metal and tin is even weaker and softer. But an alloy may have very different properties ; if we mix nine parts of copper with

one of tin we
hard and stro
progressed fr
implements;
proportions
most import
account of i

From earl
works of an

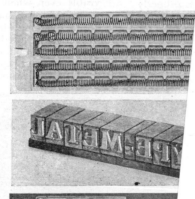

ALLOYS IN EVERYD
The heating element (top) of an ele
of nickel and chromium. Type
composed of lead, antimony and
studs (lower), are used to mar
122

---

used for building aircraft. An alloy of nine-tenths copper and one-tenth aluminium (technically known as a bronze) is as strong as mild steel.

A German metallurgist discovered by accident that an alloy of aluminium with about 3·5 per cent copper and 0·5 per cent magnesium grew stronger and harder in the course of a few days after making. This increase in strength with time is called age-hardening. The new alloy became known as duralumin, and was used by the Germans for their Zeppelin airships and for aircraft parts. It proved to be the forerunner of a long line of aluminium alloys with great strength. In America, metallurgists sought to counteract a defect of such alloys, which were easily corroded ; as a result a "sandwich" of sheet metal was produced which was named alclad. This consisted of a sheet of duralumin or similar alloy, protected from corrosion by a thin layer of pure aluminium sheet on either face.

At the other end of the scale are the soft alloys which are used as bearing metals, to line the bearings in which machinery shafts and spindles turn. One of the earliest, and still the most common, is Babbitt metal, composed mainly of tin, copper and antimony. It melts fairly easily, and can thus be poured round the shaft in its bearing and take the close fit needed. If too much friction develops in the bearing when the machine is running, causing great heat, the Babbitt metal melts before the high temperature can injure the shaft or its support.

The antimony in the mixture is most important: it causes the molten metal to expand as it cools, so filling the space in the mould. Antimony is used for this property in type-metal, stereo metal and other alloys used for die-casting. If John Gutenberg or Peter Schoeffer had not stumbled upon this valuable property of antimony, we might have had to wait many long years for a metal which would cast type faces sharply and thus allow letters to be designed with pleasant thick and thin strokes, and hair lines. The type metal for the Monotype from which this book was set up consists of lead, antimony and tin in the proportions 76, 16 and 18 per cent respectively.

Almond. (Pron. ah'mond). Although the almond tree has long been cultivated on account of its beautiful flowers and delicious nuts, we never see it in a wild state. Even so far back as Biblical times it was grown and highly prized in Syria and Palestine. It probably originated in this region or somewhere along the Mediterranean, and, strange as it may seem, it belongs to the great rose family, which includes most of the fruit trees, and is a close relative of the plum.

The almond tree is of moderate size, reaching a height of from 20 to 30 feet. The delicate white or pink flowers appear early in the spring and are followed by

THE WOOLLY ALPACA
From the hair of this curious animal is made alpaca wool, introduced into use for light-weight cloth by Sir Titus Salt in 1836.
124

R. Malby

ALMOND'S EARLY BLOSSOMS
To the town-dweller one of the welcome signs of spring is the almond blossom, which you see here. The leaves appear later. The lovely white or pink blossom makes the dullest of city streets charmingly gay.

the leaves, which are oval, pointed and notched at the edges. The fruit consists of a leathery husk enclosing the very hard and wrinkled shell, within which is the seed or kernel.

The tree which has white blossoms produces bitter almonds; the one with pink blossoms bears sweet almonds. Bitter almonds are used in the manufacture of flavouring extract and various drugs used in medicine. Sweet almonds are highly valued as a food. The long variety known as the Jordan almond comes from Malaga; it is believed to owe its name to an old corruption of the French word *jardin* (garden). The Valencia almond is broader than the Jordan.

Almonds are grown extensively in Western Asia, in the Mediterranean countries of Europe, and in California. Even where, owing to climatic conditions, the almond does not bear fruit, it is often planted for ornamental purposes. An additional advantage in this connexion is that the almond tree stands a smoky atmosphere well and is therefore suitable for planting in cities. The dwarf almond, which is a native of Russia, is employed in many countries for this purpose. The scientific name of the almond tree is *Prunus amygdalus*.

Alpaca. (Pron. al-pak'-a). The traveller who climbs 16,000 dizzy feet above the sea to the lofty table-lands of Chile, Ecuador or Peru, finds few other living creatures to share his solitude. But look! Do you see those grey and tan "mice" over there against the background of giant cliffs? As they come nearer they turn into woolly animals the size of deer, and it almost takes your breath away to watch them scamper sure-footedly over boulders, up steep crags, and a.ong yawning gorges.

These are the alpacas, semi-domesticated animals related to the camel and the llama, millions of pounds of whose strong, silky elastic wool, clipped every year or two by the native Indians, are shipped to Europe and N. America. They are reared solely for their wool, and are never used as pack animals as are their cousins the llamas.

The long warm coat—the hair is 7 to 15 inches in length—enables the hardy alpaca to endure the snow-storms and icy winds of his lofty home. He is extremely active and alert, and Nature helps him to overcome many difficulties. His cushioned feet with their hard curved toe-nails help him to climb steep crags with safety; his long flexible camel-like neck and pointed muzzle enable him to reach herbage growing on high ledges; and his strong teeth help him to chew the tough leaves and stalks; while his queerly constructed stomach, with its reservoir for fluids, makes it possible for him to endure hunger and thirst for considerable periods. All this fits him to live in comfort at an altitude that would make us ill.

The *vicuña* is a wild variety of the same group, smaller than the llama but larger than the alpaca. It is trapped in herds on mountain heights by the Indians for its wool, which is one of the lightest and warmest known. Another wild species, related to the llama as the vicuña is to the alpaca, is the *guanaco* which ranges from Peru to Patagonia.

Genuine alpaca cloth is very firm, strong and lustrous, closely resembling mohair. Most of the cloth sold under the name of alpaca, however, contains little or no alpaca wool, being a mixture of cotton and wool with a hard shining surface. So-called vicuña cloth is mostly a very soft fabric of wool and cotton. The scientific name of the alpaca is *Lama huanaco* or *paca*.

Alphabet.

We all know our A B C. But do you know its wonderful history? Do you know that A was once the picture of an eagle, and B of a crane (some say a house)? That N was the water's waves, and D a hand? That R was a man's mouth, and O his eye?

Do you know, moreover, why it is that so many people can read in lands where English, French or German is spoken, and so few in China? Indeed, it is not because European peoples prize education more highly than do the Chinese, for nowhere in the world is a scholar more honoured than in that mysterious land. The reason is that a Chinese must know about 3,000 different signs to read even an ordinary Chinese book, and really learned Chinese must know over 40,000. Every *thing* or *idea* in Chinese writing has its separate sign. In Europe and America, on the other hand, we need to learn only the 26 letters or so that make up our alphabets according to the language we speak. This great advantage of the alphabet—the word, by the way, is derived from the first two letters of the Greek alphabet, *alpha* and *beta*—arises from the fact that its letters now represent not things but

| Values | EGYPTIAN | | SEMITIC | LATER EQUIVALENTS | | |
	Hieroglyphic	Hieratic	Phoenician	Greek	Roman	Hebrew
a	eagle			A	A	א
b	crane			B	B	ב
k (g)	throne			Γ	C	ג
l (d)	hand			Δ	D	ד
h	meander			E	E	ה
f	cerastes			Y	F	ו
z	duck			I	Z	ז
x (kh)	sieve			H	H	ח
θ (th)	tongs			Θ	...	ט
ı	parallels			I	I	י
k	bowl			K	K	כ
l	lioness			Λ	L	ל
m	owl			M	M	מ
n	water			N	N	נ
s	chairback			Ξ	X	ס
a	....			O	O	ע
p	shutter			Π	P	פ
(ts)	snake			...	...	צ
q	angle			...	Q	ק
r	mouth			P	R	ר
(sh)	inundated garden			Σ	S	ש
t	lasso			X	T	ת

HOW WE GOT OUR A B C

This table shows plainly how we have derived our alphabet from the Egyptians, by way of the Phoenicians, the Greeks and the Romans. "A," for example, was first of all the picture of an eagle or ibis. This was gradually simplified until it took the form we know today.

sounds; by combining these signs for sounds in various ways we are able to form syllables and words.

Alphabetic writing was developed from *syllabic* writing, which in turn grew out of *ideographic* or *picture* writing, such as the Chinese still use. It has been stated that the Egyptians were the first to invent an alphabet, but perhaps it would be more correct to say that they had certain one-letter words with which they used to spell. From inscriptions discovered in Sinai about 1915 it would appear that the Semites were responsible. Some of these were written in Egyptian hieroglyphs, but did not make sense. Scholars, however, have been able to interpret them, and it is thought that the Semites had chosen certain pictures, about 25 in number, from the Egyptian characters and made these into an alphabet.

The ancient Aegean people of the island of Crete also possessed an alphabet at an early date, but it was the Phoenician traders of Tyre and Sidon first, and the Aramaean merchants of Damascus later, who spread the knowledge of alphabetic writing east and west, in Europe and in Asia. Today the use of alphabetic writing is general throughout the whole of the world outside of China.

Altogether there have been some 400 different alphabets since the days of the Phoenicians; and at the present time there are about 50, not counting slight variations due to dialects. None of these alphabets is perfect. "The ideal alphabet," as one authority puts it, "would indicate one sound by one symbol, and not more than one sound by the same symbol." As all our English vowels have several sounds, while some of our consonants have two sounds that are duplicated by other letters, and a few have the sound values of diphthongs, the English alphabet falls far short of this ideal.

All the alphabets of Europe were derived, either directly or through the Latin, from the Greek, which in turn had its source in the Phoenician. The Phoenician alphabet had 21 or 22 letters, all of which represented consonant sounds. The vowels *a, e, i* and *o* were present, but were used merely as " aspirates " similar to our *h*. Centuries were required to bring this imperfect alphabet up to the requirements of the classic period of Greek literature. The aspirates were converted into true vowels, superfluous sounds were dropped, and the letters *q* and *x* replaced diphthong combinations. In its final form the Greek alphabet of ancient Athens comprised 24 letters.

British Official

ALPHABET OF THE BURMESE

In the East the alphabet is written in many ways. This Burmese girl is pointing to a letter which represents our G. Many schools in Burma were destroyed in the Second World War, so classes were held out of doors.

The Latin or Roman alphabet, which came into use in Italy about the 6th or 5th century B.C., became the medium for the classical literature of Rome. The oldest Roman inscriptions show the original Greek letters in simplified forms, but some of the Greek letters disappeared except in borrowed Greek words, and others were altered. In Julius Caesar's time (50 B.C.) the Latin alphabet had 23 letters. Our modern English alphabet was completed by the differentiation of *i* and *j*, of *u* and *v*, and by the introduction of the letter *w*. The German alphabet also comes from the Latin, but the letters long retained the queer Gothic shapes of the Middle Ages.

The Russian alphabet, which today has 32 characters, was derived indirectly from the Greek, through the ancient " Cyrillic " alphabet, invented by the missionary saint Cyril in the 9th century A.D. in order to translate the Gospels into the language of the Slavs of Bulgaria and Moravia. There are also separate alphabets for Hebrew, Arabic, Sanskrit, and many of the Asiatic languages.

As trade and travel bring the nations of the Earth into close relations, there is a growing tendency to adopt the Roman alphabet. Turkey now uses it in place of the Arabic, and the Japanese have begun to use it for commercial purposes.

The GIANT MOUNTAINS of EUROPE

Centred in Switzerland but stretching rocky tentacles into all the surrounding lands is Europe's greatest mountain mass. Here Man is dwarfed by the majestic peaks, and yet here, too, Man has one of his favourite playgrounds.

Alps. Most of the great mountain ranges of the world lift their eternal peaks in a solitude little troubled by Man. But in the Alps a population of sturdy, freedom-loving men clusters in the valleys, and their tiny chalets with wide-projecting eaves, like dolls' houses, are to be seen clinging to the steep mountain slopes.

The Alps with towering snow-clad peaks are often covered and swathed in veils and bands of soft mist that shift and change colour in the changing light. Only rarely do the peaks emerge, visible in their entirety. This means that the quantity of rain and snowfall in the Alps is heavy. Indeed, the Alps are a reservoir from which four great river systems—the Rhine, the Rhône, the Danube and the Po—are fed perpetually, even during the

driest season. The sharp slopes and the unfailing water in the streams furnish the abundant hydroelectric power used by Swiss railways.

On the high peaks more snow falls each year than is melted on the spot; and this snow accumulates in valleys and is gradually formed into ice, which descends the slopes of the mountains in the form of glaciers and feeds these rivers. There are more than 1,000 of these glaciers, most of them very small. Few of them are as much as three miles long, and the great majority are less than one. One of the largest, and perhaps the most beautiful, is the Mer de Glace (" Sea of Ice "), which is on the northern slope of Mont Blanc.

The Alps extend over parts of no fewer than five countries. The Republic of Switzerland includes the centre of the Alps, but they thrust their spurs and sentinel peaks into France, Italy, Austria and Germany. The higher peaks, of which there are a large number, rise out of a series of lower chains and foothills to great heights —Mont Blanc, the "monarch of mountains" as Lord Byron calls it, being 15,782 feet high. On the Italian side the Alps fall more steeply than on the other side.

Although the peaks of the Alps are crowded together, no other mountains of such a height are so easily crossed. Winding

Swiss Federal Railways

ALPINE BEAUTY
Beyond a little village church is the beautiful peak of the Jungfrau, surrounded by steep precipices. Those who do not wish to climb can reach the summit by mountain railway.

roads lead up through deep-cut valleys to many passes (Mont Cenis, Great St. Bernard, St. Gotthard, Brenner, etc.). The Romans knew a number of the passes well, and often made use of them. Through the passes the northern barbarians descended on the Roman Empire from the forests of Germany, and through them Hannibal and Napoleon led their conquering armies. Now the St. Gotthard, Simplon, Mont Cenis and other passes are pierced by railway tunnels.

The Alps, particularly the Swiss Alps and the Austrian Tirol, have an irresistible attraction for tourists from all over the world. Indeed, the tourist trade, lasting almost throughout the year, was one of Switzerland's main sources of income before the Second World War, and her railways, hotels and stores depended largely upon it ; many thousands of people each year used to go to Lucerne, to Interlaken—where the Jungfrau ("Maiden") mountain pierces the clouds in virgin purity—to Chamonix, below Mont Blanc, and to dozens of other beautiful places. And each year enthusiastic mountaineers, many of them members of the famous Alpine Club, with alpenstocks, ropes and native guides. made the difficult ascent of the Matterhorn and other peaks.

Serious mountaineering in the Alps began in the 18th century. The summit of Mont Blanc was first reached by Dr. M. Paccard and his guide Jacques Balmat,

ALPS TOWERING ABOVE CHAMONIX
Dividing France from Switzerland is the Mont Blanc range (above) of the Alps, the rounded summit being Mont Blanc itself, Europe's highest mountain (15,782 feet). In the valley at the foot of the mountain mass is Chamonix, a French tourist resort, in the department of Haute-Savoie.

LIFE-SAVING DOGS OF ST. BERNARD

Many tales are told of the heroism of the monks of St. Bernard, whose monastery at the summit of the pass between Valais in Switzerland and Piedmont in Italy, 8,000 feet above sea-level, has existed since about Anno Domini 962. The monastery provides accommodation for travellers crossing the Alps, and the famous St. Bernard dogs have proved their mettle many times in finding travellers whose lives were endangered.

century. During every storm the big heroic St. Bernard dogs go forth among the mountains to rescue travellers who have had the misfortune to lose their way in the snow. There was also a school at the hospice, but the pupils and a number of the monks were withdrawn in 1947. Under the terms of the Italian peace treaty of that year the monastery on the Little St. Bernard Pass, which is about 15 miles south-west of the Great St. Bernard, went to the French. These passes are not wholly in any one country : the Little St. Bernard leads from France into Italy, the Great St. Bernard from Switzerland into Italy.

on August 8, 1786. The Jungfrau, however, was not conquered until 1811, and the ascent of the Wetterhorn made by Sir Alfred Wills in 1854 marks the real beginning of the organized " sport " of mountaineering. The Matterhorn was first climbed in 1865, by a party including Edward Whymper.

Many pleasure resorts with enormous hotels have been built, especially near the gem-like lakes, rimmed by mountain and forest. Lakes Geneva, Lucerne, Como, Garda and Maggiore are famous for their beauty, and smaller lakes nestle in the valleys. For tourists who prefer to motor over the passes instead of going by train, roads that are marvels of engineering have been blasted out of the rock, bridges thrown across torrents, and long walls built to stop avalanches and guard precipices.

High on the slope at the Great St. Bernard Pass the monks of St. Bernard pass their days in their famous monastery, which was founded in the 10th

Possibly you will want to know how the monastery, the pass, and the dogs came by their name. St. Bernard was the son of Richard de Menthon, a baron of Savoy. Although a lover of peace, he felt compelled to resort to the sword when the hated Mahomedans tried to settle in the valley of Aosta.

Dorien Leigh

ALPINE PASS CROSSED BY A MOTOR ROAD

One of the highest motor roads in Europe, this masterpiece of roadmaking zigzags over the Stelvio Pass, reaching a height of over 9,000 feet. The pass is in Italy, close to the Austro-Italian frontier, and over it goes the main road between Innsbruck in Austria and Milan in Italy. The road was built by the Austrians, 1820–1824, and has since been improved greatly.

IN THE ALPINE WONDERLAND OF ICE AND SNOW

Dorien Leigh

At all seasons of the year the Alps are surpassingly beautiful and at every mile the traveller is struck by some new and glorious prospect. Thus, as seen here, on a perfect day in early spring not a ripple disturbs the clear waters of the lake and the towering, snow-clad peaks of the Alps are reflected as in a mirror. This photograph was taken near Kufstein in the Austrian Tirol, where the River Inn turns north on its way to the Bavarian high plateau in Germany.

SPRINGTIME IDYLL ON AN ALPINE SLOPE

When spring comes to Switzerland there are glorious vistas of lovely colour. Some of the valleys are carpeted with crocuses, and the sight of millions of these tiny blooms, with snow-clad peaks for a background, is never to be forgotten. This photograph was taken in the Engadine, a valley in the canton of Grisons. Some sixty miles long and up to one and a half miles broad, between two chains of the Rhætian Alps, this lovely valley is a health resort.

IT'S ALWAYS WINTER ON THE MATTERHORN

Ilford Ltd. (Selo Film)

The sharp peak of the Matterhorn makes it easily distinguishable among the Alpine heights. It lies six miles south-west of Zermatt, and rises to a height of 14,782 feet. Here two men on skis are approaching the summit, but they will not get much nearer, for on the precipitous slopes of the peak itself there is no deep layer of snow to give a grip. The long narrow skis have cut right through the surface snow, and the track is bordered by the marks of ski-sticks.

TWO MONARCHS OF THE SWISS ALPS

The Finsteraarhorn lies between the cantons of Berne and Valais, and rises to a height of 14,025 feet. It was first climbed in 1812. Seen in the centre of this photograph is the curve of a glacier creeping slowly down the mountain side.

Swiss National Tourist Office

This mountaineer has made a fine climb, for he is taking a rest on the Jungfrau (German for 'maiden'), one of the peaks of the Bernese Oberland, over 13,000 feet high. In his hand is an ice-pick used to cut a foothold in glaciers, while the life-line, a thin strong rope by which mountaineers are strung together lest one should slip is seen behind him. He is far above the cloud level, and beyond and below the array of snow-clad peaks a sea of fleecy clouds is visible.

He aroused the enthusiasm of the inhabitants and bade them hurl back the tide of invasion which threatened to engulf the Christian faith. St. Bernard triumphed, but unfortunately his enemies destroyed the hospice on the pass, and he knew that by this act alone they would continue their vengeance, for it stood on the route of the faithful making pilgrimages to Rome and Jerusalem. So he rebuilt the hospice, and from that day the monks and their faithful four-legged friends have carried on their work whenever snow reigns supreme in the pass.

As many stories tell, in winter the big St. Bernard dogs used to be sent out alone, with little kegs of cordial hanging from their collars, to search for lost wayfarers. This is no longer done, for now the monastery is connected by telephone to the villages at the foot of the pass, and the monks receive warning when travellers are setting out on the perilous journey. If these do not arrive at the expected time the canons of the hospice themselves conduct a search. The dogs accompany them, being at once their guides and the advance party of rescuers. They are trained to lead the way in snowstorms and to track down wanderers buried in the snow, and they even help in rendering first-aid—by licking the victim's face to restore circulation.

Guides have to go through a very stiff examination before they are allowed to take parties up the mountains. One of the tests is the ascent of a lofty summit and making the return journey by any route that the examiners may think fit to select. It was the British who first discovered the fascination of the Alps in winter. There are rinks for skaters and curlers, and runs for those who love the thrills of the bobsleigh and the luge, which resemble the more humble toboggan. Ski-ing, which was imported from Norway, is another favourite pastime, although the long wooden runners are a little difficult to manage at first. The rare mountain air has healing qualities for those with weak chests and lungs, and many an invalid has returned with renewed health and vigour. The Alps are usually divided by geographers into seven divisions: the Maritime, the Cottian, the Graian, the Pennine, the Lepontine, the Rhaetian and the Noric Alps.

Alsace-Lorraine, (Pron. al-sas-lo-rān'), FRANCE.

France and Germany long contested for the possession of Alsace-Lorraine, a land which is so often spoken of as a single territory, but is in reality composed of two regions quite distinct in geography and history.

Alsace after a stormy history marked by many wars, became definitely a part of France in the 17th century during the reign of Louis XIV. It was left in French hands after the Napoleonic Wars, but in 1871 it was wrested from France by Germany as part of the price of defeat. After the First World War (1914–1918), it was returned to France, together with the portion of Lorraine annexed with it by the Germans in 1871. During the Second World War it again became German after France was overrun in 1940, but in 1945 the territory was once more restored to

France after the Germans had been driven back over the Rhine by the victorious Allied armies.

Lying in the trough of the River Rhine, between the steep scarp of the Vosges to the west and the Black Forest to the east, its plain forms a natural highway between France and Germany. It is a generally fertile land, and rich in timber. Its oil-field at Pechelbronn and its potash deposits west of Muelhausen are of great economic importance. Although the language of the people in the country districts is a dialect of German, their sentiments have been decidedly French since before the days of Napoleon Bonaparte.

Lorraine has been French in language and in spirit since the 12th century. The province extends from the Vosges to Champagne. The part seized by Germany in 1871 was about a third of the whole, but included the chief city of Metz, which was strongly fortified, and a large part of the rich iron-ore deposits of Briey, between Metz and Longwy. These and the coal deposits in the Saar Valley form the chief wealth of this region. Cereal crops, however, grow in abundance and many factories flourish. The population of Alsace-

ALPINE WINDING RAILWAY
Up the Engadine Valley runs the winding Albula railway, one of the most wonderful narrow-gauge tracks in the world. A train is seen crossing the stone viaduct over the Landwasser, a tributary of the Upper Rhine. Inside the mountain on the left are two loop tunnels —their position indicated, above, in faint outline.

ALSATIANS IN GALA ATTIRE
On special occasions the people of Alsace-Lorraine still wear their traditional costumes (above). In Strasbourg, the chief city of Alsace-Lorraine, is a fine medieval house (below) where Johann Gutenberg, the inventor of printing, lived in the 15th century.

of shipping in normal times. The population of Strasbourg is about 175,000.

Aluminium.
Though this metal is very plentiful in the earth's surface it is never found in the metallic state. For this reason it was very scarce and expensive until about 30 years ago, and at one time was even used for jewelry! Today we know it or its many alloys as the metal from which kitchen-ware and utensils are made, and as the sheathing metal for aircraft bodies or motor vehicle parts; it is familiar also in a thousand other uses.

Why has aluminium become so general in use? For the same reason that certain other metals are valued: it resists corrosion and is not seriously affected by the acids and alkalis in food. Like tin, it does not

Lorraine is about 1,700,000, and the territory has an area of some 5,605 square miles.

After 1918, although eager to return to French rule, the people of the recovered provinces desired to retain their own languages and institutions. The French government wanted to assimilate them with the rest of France as speedily as possible. Hence there were serious conflicts over questions of religion, education and administration. A well-organized minority, composed largely of Germans who had been made French citizens by the change in government, vigorously demanded home rule, with their own laws and institutions, administered by their own officials. Even the moderate element felt that France should be less abrupt in its attempts to reshape the ancient ways of the people. The discontent was quieted somewhat by various concessions, among them the establishment of an Alsace-Lorraine Government Department in Paris. France, meanwhile, built up a system of defences against Germany. The old German forts at Metz and Thionville in Lorraine, and at Strasbourg in Alsace, were turned round to repel attack from north or east and incorporated in the immense chain of defences along part of France's eastern frontier called, after its architect, the Maginot Line.

The city of Strasbourg contains a cathedral which is a fine example of Gothic architecture. Built in the 13th and 14th centuries, it possesses a famous clock, 30 feet high, with many automatic moving figures. The University was founded in 1567. Lying as it does on the main roads of travel between France, Germany and Switzerland, Strasbourg has been of military and commercial importance ever since Roman legions made it their headquarters. A great river port, it handles an immense amount

rust, and keeps its white colour. It is light in weight. Until cheaper means of separating it from its natural compounds were discovered it remained scarce and dear. C. M. Hall in America, and P. Héroult in France, found out that aluminium could be separated from its oxide (alumina) by passing an electric current through it. Both these inventors were born in 1863 and died in 1914. Their important discovery was made independently about the year 1886.

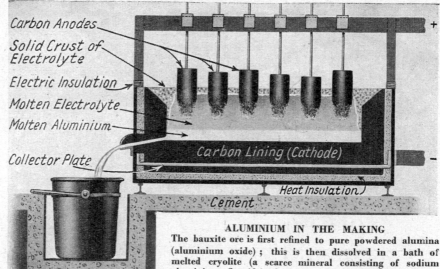

Labels on diagram: Carbon Anodes, Solid Crust of Electrolyte, Electric Insulation, Molten Electrolyte, Molten Aluminium, Collector Plate, Carbon Lining (Cathode), Heat Insulation, Cement, +, −

ALUMINIUM IN THE MAKING
The bauxite ore is first refined to pure powdered alumina (aluminium oxide) ; this is then dissolved in a bath of melted cryolite (a scarce mineral consisting of sodium aluminium fluoride), forming the electrolyte. A heavy electric current passes from the insulated metal bar down through the carbon anodes to the carbon lining (cathode). In going through the electrolyte, the current splits the alumina into aluminium and oxygen. The metal settles to the bottom; the oxygen combines with the carbon of the anodes to form gases, which pass off into the air.

Aluminium ore, of which bauxite is the commonest form, cannot be smelted like iron and other metals ; it needs a temperature of 2,000 deg. C. to liquefy it, and it can be split up into oxygen and aluminium only when dissolved in certain other substances. Cryolite, a strange mineral found mainly in Greenland, is used for this purpose; it is chemically a sodium-aluminium fluoride. Bauxite is first refined into a pure form of alumina, and then alumina is dissolved in red-hot cryolite—about one part of alumina to 10 parts of cryolite.

How Metallic Aluminium is Prepared

This mixture will melt at about half the temperature which would be necessary to melt alumina alone. The melting and separation are done in an electric arc furnace (*see* diagram). A very heavy direct current passes through the furnace, and breaks up the alumina into metallic aluminium and the gas oxygen. The metal settles towards the bottom of the furnace and is drawn off. The oxygen, after combining with the carbon of the carbon anodes (or " entering " electrodes) to form other gases, passes out to the air. The cryolite is not consumed during this operation.

Progress in separating aluminium would have been impossible if it had not chanced that plentiful supplies of electricity were becoming available. In America the falls of Niagara were harnessed to produce electric energy (1890); in other parts of the world also water power was used to generate light and power. In producing 1 lb. of the metal, 12 kilowatt-hours of electricity are used up— sufficient to light 120 electric lamps of 100-watt rating for an hour ! Or the same amount of current would operate 12 two-bar electric fires (the type used in many homes) for an hour.

During the Second World War aluminium became one of the vital metals. By the year 1940 Germany and her satellite countries were producing about half as much again as the United States of America, or about half the world's output of aluminium. The winning of the war meant first the winning of the battle for production, and aluminium was in the forefront of this battle. From a world output of fewer than a million tons in 1939 this figure was gradually increased to between three and four million tons by 1944.

Most of the metal was used in the form of alloys, and in our story of alloys we tell a few of the outstanding facts about these wonder-working substances. Much pure aluminium is made into electric cables, since for its weight the metal conducts current better than any other metal. Duralumin, one of the earliest aluminium alloys, was developed in Germany from 1906 onwards for making the frames and skeletons of airships ; it came to be used later for aircraft, and surprised metallurgists because it showed the property called age-hardening—it gradually became stronger and harder after manufacture, during four or five days.

Why Aluminium Resists Corrosion

Other alloys of this type were produced in many countries, some of them as strong as or stronger than steel, weight for weight. Some alloys develop strength when they are " worked " ; others are made stronger and harder by heat-treatment. Among metals alloyed with aluminium to give certain desired properties are magnesium, silicon, nickel, copper, iron and titanium, which are used mostly in quite small proportion.

The reason why aluminium resists corrosion is that its surface becomes coated with a thin layer of oxide which stops attack by chemicals. Aluminium melts at 659 degrees C., as compared with pure iron melting at 1,533 degrees C. A cubic foot of aluminium weighs about 170 lb., as compared with about 500 lb. for iron. Among other forms of aluminium oxide we must mention corundum, and its impure form emery, which are only a little less hard than the diamond and are used as grinding agents. The gem-stones ruby and sapphire are

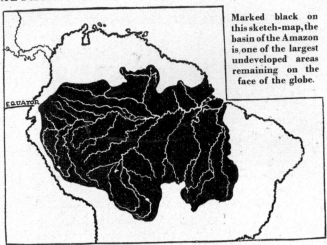

Marked black on this sketch-map, the basin of the Amazon is one of the largest undeveloped areas remaining on the face of the globe.

THE GREAT BASIN OF THE AMAZON

crystallised forms of the oxide. By melting aluminium oxide in the electric furnace, the artificial abrasive called alundum is produced, widely used for grinding-wheels and powders today. The chemist's symbol for aluminium is Al. The atomic weight of the element is 26·96 ; its specific gravity is 2·7.

Amazon. (Pron. am-a-zon). The greatest river of South America sends such a vast flood of water into the Atlantic that the sea-water is said to be fresh for 50 or even 100 miles from the shore.

The Amazon, indeed, is not so much a river as a gigantic water reservoir, extending in the rainy season from the sea to the base of the Andes and varying in width from five to 400 miles. It is thus the largest river on the globe, and if it is not the longest also it is still very long. The Marañon, as its upper course is called, rises in the Andes of Peru, within 60 miles of the Pacific Ocean. From here it flows eastwards through Brazil until its mouths empty into the Atlantic, just at the Equator. Its extreme length from source to mouth is about 3,350 miles. The width of the main stream at its mouth is 60 miles, and the tides travel up it 400 miles. Two thousand miles from the sea it is still more than a mile wide, and the depth for 750 miles is nowhere less than 175 feet.

The Amazon with its branches is navigable for small steamboats for approximately 16,000 miles. There are more than 200 branches and lesser tributaries forming main trunk, and the drainage area includes about one-third of South America. There is scarcely a perceptible fall in the river from the Andes to the mouth, and there is good reason for thinking that the whole region was once a vast gulf, now filled by the rising of the land and the silt carried down from the interior by the river's current.

The greater part of this great basin is a " sea of vegetation," extending, as a traveller says, " in an unbroken evergreen circle of 1,100 miles' diameter."

AMAZON JUNGLE OF VAST TROPIC PROFUSION

Nowhere in the world does vegetation grow more luxuriantly than on the banks of the mighty Amazon. As the traveller pushes his way through the tangled undergrowth his nostrils are assailed by the scent of tropic flowers and his eyes dazzled by the brilliant colours of birds and butterflies, while all the time he is oppressed by a sense of his own insignificance in this vast waste in which Nature holds undisputed sway. Most of the region is still largely unexplored.

The extensive forests are truly tropical, being so dark and thick, so twisted and matted and interlaced with trees, vines and shrubs as to present an almost impassable barrier. There are probably not 25 square miles cleared and under cultivation, except in the almost inaccessible mountain regions of its source. A few hundred thousand scattered Indians, engaged in hunting, raising cacao (shrub from whose beans cocoa and chocolate are made), and collecting rubber and Brazil nuts, make up the greater part of the population of an area which is equal to five-sixths of the whole United States.

In all this vast area there are practically no roads and but a few miles of railway. Travel is mostly by water, and very largely in the long black native canoes which the Indians pole upstream at the river's edge or through the innumerable channels which parallel and intersect the main stream. On the banks of reddish clay we see broad-leafed magnolias and oaks. In sheltered coves and lagoons grow innumerable pond lilies, one species of which has leaves turned up all round the edge and measuring three to five feet across. And everywhere clambers the cypress vine with its slender leaves and starlike blossoms. On sunlit slopes along the banks great lazy alligators sleep; and at the slightest unusual sound hundreds of timid forest creatures scamper noisily away through the dense undergrowth. The monkeys are endless in number—small, grey, long-tailed creatures chattering angrily in the tree tops, seemingly unafraid, but disappearing as if by magic at the first attempt to capture them. Birds are few, and these of brilliant colours, but with harsh and ugly voices.

Here and there are the few little villages, built of mud and logs in clearings on the steep banks, or on piles driven into the river's bed. Even the plantation owners usually build their houses in this manner over the river, as a means of escaping the mosquitoes and other insects, which swarm in the forest. One scarcely ever sees a dog, and horses and cows are practically unknown.

There is some doubt as to the origin of the word "Amazon." According to some, the word is derived from the women warriors ("Amazons"—*see* the following article) encountered in the 16th century by the Spanish explorer Francisco de Orellana, the first European to navigate the

E.N.A.

AMAZON INDIANS AT HOME
Deep in the dense and humid jungle of the Amazon basin live tribes of half-savage Indians, whose customs are primitive in the extreme. These Waiwai natives, found and photographed by a white men's expedition, are resting in the family "benab," a temporary shelter made of branches and leaves, with a framework of poles.

whole length of the Amazon. Others maintain that the name comes from the Indian word *amassona* ("boat-destroyer"), applied to the "bore" at the mouth of the river. (*See* Brazil.)

Amazons. Of all the mighty hosts described as fighting in the siege of Troy, the Amazons were the strangest. They were a mythical nation of female warriors, ruled alike in peace and war entirely by women. It was said that their country bordered on the Black Sea, and that no man might dwell therein. Even the boy babies were sent to their fathers, who dwelt outside the borders. The girl babies were kept and brought up by their mothers, and trained to agriculture, hunting and the art of war. The arms of the Amazons were the bow, spear, axe and a shield shaped like a crescent. In sculptures the skirt is often worn high; in vase pictures they wear Persian trousers. Usually they fought on horseback, and they were most formidable warriors. Greek legends tell of the adventures of Hercules and Theseus in the land of the Amazons; and it was said that Achilles slew their queen in a fierce battle under the walls of Troy. Many Greek works of art portray these female warriors, along with the centaurs. In historical times they are heard of in the age of Alexander the Great, and even as late as the 1st century B.C.

In out-of-the-way places on the globe geographers have found strange people among whom the rights of the mother are stronger than the rights of the father, and societies in which women have an importance and

AMAZON OF AFRICA
In West Africa the kings of Dahomey had regiments of Amazons, like the warrior above, until the French conquest in 1894.

perform many duties which elsewhere belong to men. It is thought that the Greek stories of the Amazons arose from such travellers' tales.

History records many instances of women warriors. In modern times the King of Dahomey, in western Africa, had an army of women; and in the Russian Revolution of 1917 there was a women's " Battalion of Death." Women also fought with the Russian army and air force and Yugoslav patriot forces during the Second World War (1939–1945). According to one view, the River Amazon, in South America, received its name from the fact that the Spaniard, Francisco de Orellana, one of the earlier explorers, was there attacked by a tribe of savages, among whom the women fought valiantly alongside the men, so reminding him of the Amazons.

AMBER'S PRISONERS
Imprisoned in amber when it was liquid resin, these insects have been preserved for thousands of years in exactly the same state as when they died.

Ambassador. Practically every country in the world has a representative in foreign capitals. Thus Great Britain sends an ambassador to France, the United States, Spain and so on, and they send ambassadors to us. Less important countries are represented by ministers, or *chargés d'affaires*. Ambassadors are called ordinary when their post is permanent, and extraordinary when they are sent on a special mission. It was not until the middle of the 17th century that permanent ambassadors were generally employed. An ambassador has a right to see the monarch or head of the state personally, although in practice he is always accompanied by a minister, usually the Foreign Secretary. His duties are to watch the interests of the country which he represents and to smooth over difficulties that may arise from time to time. The residence of an ambassador is regarded as standing on the soil of the country which he represents. He is therefore free from rates and taxes, and he and his staff and attendants enjoy diplomatic immunity, which means that they cannot be sued for any breach of the civil law or be prosecuted for breaches of the criminal law that they may commit.

Amber. Countless ages ago clear pitch or resin exuded from pine trees, and great heaps of it were covered up by various layers of soil. In the course of time these buried resins became hardened and changed in substance; they became amber.

Amber is a brittle yellow translucent substance, hard enough to be cut into beads and ornaments, but not hard as compared with marble or glass. The ancient Phoenicians, Greeks and Romans valued amber highly, and attributed mysterious powers to it, because it becomes electrified when it is rubbed and attracts light bodies. The Greeks called it *elektron*, from which we get our word electricity. Occasionally insects of species now extinct are found in amber, having been caught when it was resin. The variety of pine which produced amber grew chiefly on the site now occupied by the Baltic Sea and the North Sea. This part of the earth's crust gradually became submerged. When these waters are disturbed by violent storms, pieces of amber are frequently cast up on the shores. The ancients got all their amber by picking up these fragments, but today most of our supply is obtained by mining. Amber is usually found in small pieces, but some lumps weighing up to 15 and 18 lb. have also been obtained. Small quantities are found in Great Britain, Sicily, Siberia, Greenland and the United States, but the chief source is along the shores of the Baltic, expecially in that part of Poland and the U.S.S.R. which was formerly East Prussia.

Amber is used chiefly for the mouthpieces of pipes, for cigar- and cigarette-holders, for the handles of umbrellas, and for ornaments, though in recent years its place has largely been taken in these uses by plastics.

Ambergris. The scent as of flowers in a bottle of perfume is sometimes distilled, not from jasmine or violets or lilies of the valley, but from a substance called ambergris, formed in the intestines of the spermaceti whale. This substance, which is black or dark grey with a marbled appearance due to the veins in it, is found floating in great masses, sometimes more than 200 pounds in weight, on the waters of the Atlantic Ocean, and washed up on the coasts of Brazil, Madagascar and parts of Africa, and many countries in the Far East ; supplies for England come mainly from the Bahamas. In its natural state ambergris has a sweetish, rather unpleasant smell. It is dissolved in alcohol and volatile oils and used in small quantities in perfumery, and in Eastern countries traces of it are put into food as a flavouring.

Ambrose, St. (c. 340–397). The author of the familiar proverb, " When in Rome do as Rome does," was Ambrose, the patron saint of Milan. Although a layman Ambrose was appointed to the see of Milan in 374, and his early study of the law proved very useful to him in various religious disputes. Fearing none, he gave a severe reproof to the emperor Theodosius for permitting the massacre of 7,000 people in Thessalonica. He introduced the so-called Ambrosian Chant from the East and composed many hymns. The Ambrosian library in Milan, damaged during the 1939–45 war, was named after him.

Amen. When in church we say " Amen " after a prayer, psalm or hymn, we are making use of an old Hebrew word meaning verily, or so be it. The early Christians used to *shout* it after the consecration of the bread and wine in the Lord's Supper. The word may be heard, too, in Jewish synagogues and in Moslem mosques. The Mahomedans also repeat Amen thrice as a charm.

How the NEW WORLD *was* DISCOVERED

*So great is the part played by the American countries in the modern world
that it is difficult to realize that only five centuries ago men who suggested
that there might be lands beyond the Atlantic were laughed at as mere fools.*

America: ITS DISCOVERY. Columbus was not really the first discoverer of America, for in about 1000 Leif Ericsson, setting forth from Norway, reached Greenland, and then sailed westwards until he came to the coast of North America—a new land, abounding with grape vines and " self-sown wheat." This he called Vinland. But Leif Ericsson's discovery of America bore no fruit, for it did not become generally known and was soon forgotten.

When in the 11th century Europe began to emerge from the Dark Ages, it was eastwards that her eyes were turned. The products of the East transformed European life. Near the close of the 13th century the great Italian traveller Marco Polo returned to Venice after a long stay in China, and the tales he told of the fabulous riches of the Orient cast an enduring spell over the European mind. Commerce and learning combined to advance the science of navigation, and little by little it became safer for ships to venture into unknown seas.

In 1400 the continents of North and South America and Australia, as well as most of Africa, and the Atlantic and Pacific Oceans, were still a closed book to Europe. They came to be revealed largely because the nations that were gaining power in Western Europe desired a share of the very profitable trade with the Far East.

During the Middle Ages the kings of Western Europe and their feudal nobles were fighting for supremacy. The merchants generally sided with the king and supplied him with money in return for the privileges and the security which he gave them. Under the king's protection they were able to develop manufacturing and commerce. Soon they were prepared to fit out ships for the mariners voyaging in quest of a new route to the Orient. They usually secured the king's promise that he would defend their claims to lands discovered. The king, in return, would claim a share of any valuables found, such as gold and silver.

The Italian cities did not take part, for they enjoyed a monopoly of the old route. The Scandinavian countries were far removed from the central paths of Europe's commerce. Germany, split into many small states, lacked resources. The work of discovery, therefore, fell to Portugal, Spain, England and France. Portugal took the lead with a long series of discoveries during the 15th century along the western coast of Africa; the commerce of the Orient flowed into Portuguese ports, and their wealth became the envy of the Western World.

About the year 1473 there appeared in Portugal an adventurous Genoese mariner—one Christopher Columbus. He had conceived the idea of sailing straight across the Atlantic. Long years passed before his plans were finally accepted in 1492 by Queen Isabella of Castille, who provided most of the money for the voyage. He sighted one of the Bahama Islands on October 12, 1492. Then he discovered Cuba and Haiti (Santo Domingo). Although he made three later voyages, finding the mainland of Central and South America, he died believing that these lands were all part of Asia.

Amerigo Vespucci's Claim and Fame

When Columbus first returned to Spain the Portuguese asserted that he had merely visited a part of their dominion of Guinea in Africa. Pope Alexander VI decided the dispute by drawing a line running north and south across the Atlantic Ocean. If Spain discovered lands to the west of this line she was to have them if they were not already owned by a Christian ruler. In 1494 the line was made to run through a point 370 leagues (931 sea-miles) west of the Cape Verde Islands. A few years later (1500) a Portuguese mariner, Cabral, sailing along Africa on the way to India, was carried by a storm to the coast of Brazil. He accordingly claimed the land for Portugal.

When the news of Cabral's discovery came to Portugal, the king Emmanuel in 1501 sent out an expedition which sailed hundreds of miles along the coast of South America. An Italian merchant, Amerigo Vespucci, who asserted that he was a member of the party, wrote an alluring letter telling of the lands, animals and people he had seen. A German scholar included this letter in a popular geography and suggested that the new land be called America, or the land of Americus (Amerigo). The name caught the fancy of Europe and stuck. Vespucci was not a navigator and in all likelihood

COLUMBUS DISCOVERS AMERICA

The drawing on the right, supposed to have been made by Christopher Columbus, shows the ship of the ocean-going fleet (Oceanica Classis) with which he discovered Santo Domingo (Hispaniola, ' Insula hyspana,' or Spanish island). The wood-cut on the left, from a contemporary pamphlet, illustrates his landing on the island.

RED INDIANS WATCH THE ARRIVAL OF THE WHITE MAN

When the first ships approached the coast of North America they were viewed with mingled curiosity and fear by the aboriginal inhabitants of the continent. In this illustration the artist has depicted Red Indians watching ships of the time of Cabot (1450–98) approaching the shore. Though the ships were mere cockle-shells according to modern ideas, the natives, who had seen nothing afloat larger than their own canoes of birch-bark, regarded them as apparitions.

he had not seen any part of the mainland of America before Columbus. Chance brought him an honour he did not deserve.

By 1510 it was realized that the territory discovered by Columbus was not the part of the Orient he had sought. But it was still thought that China and India were close at hand. In 1513 Balboa, a Spanish adventurer from Haiti, crossed the Isthmus of Darien, and, first among Europeans, beheld the shining waters of the Pacific.

First to Sail Around the World

Spain by this time claimed that the Papal line of 1494 extended round the globe. But where it fell in the Eastern Hemisphere was not known. A Portuguese seaman, Ferdinand Magellan, believed that there might be an opening in the New World that would lead to the Orient. He convinced the king of Spain that the wealthiest parts of the Far East would lie within the region reserved for Spain by the Papal line. Accordingly he was commissioned to find a new route to the East, keeping in Spanish waters all the way.

Magellan sailed from Spain in 1519 to Brazil, whence he proceeded south until he entered the straits that now bear his name and rounded the continent into the ocean which he called the Pacific. Magellan was killed in the Philippine Islands, but one of his vessels went on to India and returned to Spain in 1522 by way of the Indian Ocean and the Cape of Good Hope. For the first time the globe was circumnavigated, and the enormous extent of the Pacific Ocean was revealed. No longer could the American lands be regarded as being outlying parts of the continent of Asia.

Both Spain and Portugal now claimed that the rich Spice Islands of the East lay within its particular territory. But Spain's new westward route was so much longer than Portugal's eastward route round Africa that Spain could not profitably use hers for trade. Consequently, in 1529 she surrendered to Portugal her claims to the most valuable lands of Asia, receiving the Philippine Islands as her own. Magellan's great voyage, therefore, failed to break down Portugal's supremacy in the Oriental trade.

Meanwhile Spanish adventurers continued the exploration of the eastern coast of North America. There were pearls and gold to be found and Indian slaves to be captured and sold. Ambitious leaders were allowed to govern newly-conquered lands. Missionaries brought a new faith to peoples worshipping strange gods. The Indians who resisted were pursued with fire and sword, and the dread of Spanish arms spread far and wide. One adventurer, Ponce de Leon, sailed in 1513 from Porto (now Puerto) Rico to a new land which he called Florida.

He was interested in slave-raiding and exploration; also he hoped to find a fabled island said to contain a wonderful fountain whose waters made men perpetually young. He returned to Florida in 1521 to build a settlement, but lost his life instead in a fight with the Indians.

About the same time Spain's vision of wealth was realized when Hernando Cortes conquered the Aztecs, who inhabited the rich kingdom of Mexico. Other adventurers turned north to the lands now forming the southern part of the United States. In 1539 Hernando de Soto came from Spain by way of Cuba to the eastern coast of Florida. Thence he toiled overland to the banks of the Mississippi, wandered in Arkansas and Oklahoma, and later floated down the river Arkansas to its mouth. Francisco Vasquez Coronado searched for the seven fabled cities of Cibola. Indian traditions and stories of Spanish wanderers told that somewhere north of Mexico the golden towers of these cities glistened in the sun. He penetrated to the heart of the northern continent, but found only poor Indian towns (pueblos), destitute of gold, and returned to Mexico in 1542 defeated. Although he

HOW THE EXPLORERS VOYAGED TO AMERICA

We say that Columbus "discovered" America in 1492; but it took 300 years to discover merely the outline—the shape—of the Americas, and it took a great many bold navigators to do it. As you can see by McClure's route, up in the icy seas of the North, it was not until the beginning of the latter half of the 19th century that the work was completed by the discovery of the North-West Passage, which so many explorers had vainly struggled to find. First came Columbus in 1492; then his second voyage in 1493, and his third and fourth in 1498 and 1502. Meanwhile, in 1497, John Cabot, sailing on behalf of England, was the first (except the Norsemen, whose names are not included among the explorers because we know next to nothing of the route they took) to touch the Continent of North America.

had penetrated as far as the heart of the northern continent, the Spaniards did not care to conquer the disappointing lands which he had seen. Earlier, in 1524–25, a Portuguese mariner, Estevan Gomez, serving the king of Spain, explored the coast of North America from Maine to New Jersey. His descriptions of this region led the Spaniards to consider it far less valuable than the lands they were occupying to the south, and they ignored the greater part of the North American coast.

The Portuguese made one important discovery in this northern region, when, in 1501, Gaspar Corte-Real reached the shores of Newfoundland. His voyages were not followed up, for all the resources of Portugal were soon needed for developing her East Indian empire and her colony in Brazil.

England's first centre of western seafaring was Bristol. Its merchants hoped that if a new route to the Orient should lead directly west from Europe, their city would become the principal centre for eastern trade. In 1497 they sent John Cabot, a Genoese mariner, in search of a new passage across the Atlantic. Having touched land between Newfoundland and Nova Scotia, Cabot came back believing that he had visited the outlying parts of Asia. This voyage gave England her later claim to North America.

Rich Plunder on the High Seas

After it was realized that Cabot had not reached Asia, England attempted to open the "Northeast Passage" to the Orient round northern Europe. But in 1576 Sir Humphrey Gilbert argued in his book Discourse that a water route led round North America to Asia—the "Northwest Passage." He later lost his life on a voyage to establish a base at Newfoundland for prosecuting this search. Martin Frobisher and John Davis each made three voyages between 1575 and 1589 to the network of inlets and straits north of the St. Lawrence river, but neither could find a way through to the Pacific Ocean.

Then Queen Elizabeth chartered the East India Company in 1600 to give England a foothold in the Far Eastern trade. In 1602 the Company sent George Weymouth to find a passage through America to the Pacific Ocean, but he did not sail beyond Labrador. Another expedition of this year under Bartholomew Gosnold explored the coast of New England from Massachusetts to New Hampshire. When Virginia Colony was founded in 1607, one of the main motives of Capt. John Smith and the first settlers was the hope of finding a water passage by which to travel across the country to the western ocean and so to the back door of India.

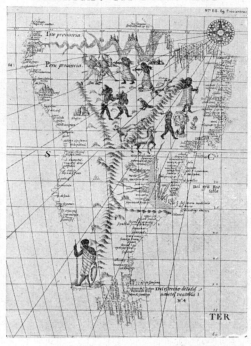

EARLY MAP OF SOUTH AMERICA

Sebastian Cabot led an expedition to South America in 1516, and this is part of his own map of the world. Like most cartographers of his time, he enlivened his maps with sketches of people and animals.

England's mariners had another motive for taking to the sea; they wanted to weaken Spain as a European power. Spain wished to restore the Pope's authority over England. A great part of the wealth which supported the Spanish armies, navies and diplomatic schemes came from the silver mines in Mexico and Peru. Another source of revenue was the high duty levied on the Spanish traders who had a monopoly of the importation of Negro slaves into the Spanish colonies.

John Hawkins, an English sea-rover, began to smuggle Negroes to the Spanish West Indies, and made three voyages for this purpose between 1562 and 1569, winning handsome profits. On his third voyage Hawkins was defeated by a Spanish fleet and lost all his vessels but two. Hawkins escaped, and with him his cousin, Francis Drake. It struck Drake that there was more for the English to gain by seizing Spanish treasure in the West Indies than by illegal trade in slaves. He went to the Caribbean on a raiding expedition in 1572, but found the Spaniards there so well protected that he obtained but little spoil. Now he planned a bolder stroke. Knowing that the Spanish vessels and ports on the Pacific were totally unprotected, he sailed from England in 1577, passed through the Strait of Magellan, and found the Spaniards in Chile and Peru everywhere at his mercy. He took so much plunder that his vessel became ballasted with silver. Then he went north seeking a passage east across America through which he might return to England. Failing in this, he sailed across the Pacific and followed the route of Magellan's party from Asia to Europe. These and other raids helped to plunge England and Spain into open war. In 1588 the great Spanish Armada preparing to invade England was completely crushed. Spain's sea-power rapidly declined in consequence, and with it went her means of excluding England from the New World.

Frobisher and Raleigh Seek Gold

The riches of Spanish America induced many Englishmen to look for gold in regions which Spain had not occupied. In 1576 Martin Frobisher brought home samples of ore believed to consist chiefly of gold, and for a time it was thought that England's dream had come true. Sir Walter Raleigh, the prince of gold-hunters, sent out parties between 1584 and 1587 to explore and colonize the southern part of North America, which was named Virginia, but his ventures failed.

While the Spanish conquerors were busy in Central America, Spain and France were at war in Europe. Francis I, king of France, wanted a share of the trade with the Orient to provide money for his armies. Accordingly, he commissioned a Florentine navigator, Giovanni da Verrazano, to find a passage to Asia. Verrazano in 1524 touched the American coast at North Carolina, and then sailed north to Newfoundland. His report to the king contained the first description of the north-eastern shore of the United States, and gave France her claim to North America.

The next explorer from France was Jacques Cartier, who made three voyages between 1534 and 1541 in quest of the new route to China, ascending the River St. Lawrence as far as the site of Montreal. After Cartier's voyages France was prevented from sending out other exploring parties by a long series of religious wars at home. Attempts were made, however, to establish two colonies as places of refuge for the Huguenots, or French Protestants. One colony in Brazil (1555–58) was destroyed by the Portuguese; the other in Florida (1562–65) was wiped out by the Spaniards. Meanwhile, French fishermen, chiefly from Brittany, visited Newfoundland each year after 1540.

When France was again united and at peace under Henry IV (1553–1610) she once more sent her mariners in search of the undiscovered strait to the Pacific. Samuel de Champlain sailed to Quebec in 1608 and there began the first permanent French colony in America. Then he explored the interior, always hoping the river St. Lawrence would lead to the western ocean. Jean Nicolet in 1634 carried the French flag across Lake Michigan to the Fox River in Wisconsin. Then, in 1673, Louis Joliet, a fur trader, and Père Marquette, a Jesuit missionary, discovered the Mississippi, following its course towards the sea until they were convinced that it did not empty into the Pacific.

Strange Animals and Inhabitants

René Robert Cavelier, Sieur de la Salle, was now inspired by stories of this noble stream. He believed it might become the centre of a vast empire that would eventually swallow the English settlements on the Atlantic coast. For 12 years he held to his plans, and in 1682 reached the mouth of the Mississippi on the Gulf of Mexico and claimed its great valley, which he called Louisiana, in the name of Louis XIV of France.

The early history of the Dutch is the story of a long war for independence from Spain. While this struggle was at its height, Spain in 1580 annexed Portugal, and thereby secured control of the Oriental trade. The Dutch, already renowned as a seafaring people, realized that Spain might be weakened by striking at her trade with America and the Orient. Accordingly they formed the Dutch East India Company, and dispatched

Prima ego velivolis ambiui Cursibus Orbem
Magellane novo te duce ducta freto
Ambiui, meritoq; vocor VICTORIA: sum mi
Vela, alæ, præciu, gloria, pugna, mare.

ONE OF MAGELLAN'S SHIPS

Four ships accompanied Magellan in 1519, and one of them, the Victoria, of only 85 tons, seen above, was (as stated in the Latin inscription) the first ship to complete the voyage round the world. The picture is from A Collection of Voyages, printed in 1602.

Conveniunt rebus nomina sæpe suis.

Henry Hudson, an English navigator, to find a short cut to the Orient. He entered the Hudson river in 1609, and ascended it as far as the present Albany. About 14 years later the Dutch established their first colony, this being on Manhattan Island.

The strange animals and inhabitants of the New World amazed the early explorers. The copper-coloured inhabitants whom they called "Indians" proved quite unlike the natives of the real Indies in Asia. The American Indians lived chiefly in tribes, and they were in various stages of civilization. There were the wandering tribes of the north, who lived by hunting and fishing and whose weapons were made of stone. Farther south were the cliff dwellers and the Pueblo Indians. In Mexico and Peru the Aztecs and Incas had developed permanent dwellings grouped in cities. But even they were far behind the civilizations of Europe and Asia.

There was another difficulty. The New World was seriously handicapped in developing a civilization of its own by the lack of any large animals capable of domestication. The ox, horse and ass were all lacking in the Western hemisphere ; Man was unable to tame the bison, and the llama was too weak to be of much use.

So, because of their inferior culture, the aborigines of America were conquered and crowded out by European settlers. In time the two continents came under the sway of Old World nations. England eventually held the greater portion of North America, while Spain possessed Mexico, Central America and all of South America except Brazil, which was in the hands of Portugal. But, beginning in 1776, with the revolt of the 13 colonies which founded the United States, the colonies started to break away from the Old World dominion. Today practically the only possessions held by European nations in either of the two continents are the Guianas in South America (divided between Great Britain, France and Holland), British Honduras in Central America, and the British colony of Newfoundland ; the self-governing Dominion of Canada is a member of the British Commonwealth.

The islands of the West Indies are usually considered part of the two continents of America, and they include the Bahamas, Barbados, Jamaica, the Windward Islands, the Leeward Islands, Trinidad and Tobago, all belonging to Great Britain ; Guadaloupe and Martinique are both French islands; Curaçao is Dutch; Puerto Rico and the Virgin Islands are possessions of the U.S.A. ; and there are the republics of Cuba, Haiti and Santo Domingo.

For an account of the geographical features of America, *see* the articles on North America, South America and Central America.

The BIRTH of a MIGHTY NATION

How different might have been the course of history if Britain's colonies in America had not broken away from the Mother Country. Perhaps by now the centre of the Commonwealth would have been on the other side of the Atlantic!

American Independence.

There have been in the course of history two British Empires. There is the one which exists today as the Commonwealth of which we are all proud to be citizens. There was an earlier one which was lost to Britain because of misunderstandings that led up to a bitter and disastrous conflict between men of the same race, language, and traditions. This empire comprised 13 Atlantic states of what is now the United States of America.

Emigrants from England settled in what became Virginia in 1607, and in 1620 the "Pilgrim Fathers" went out in the Mayflower to what was later Massachusetts. During the troubled years of the 17th century many other persons, discontented with religious and political conditions at home, sought a haven in America, and so Connecticut, Rhode Island and the other "New England" states were established. Later, Penn founded Pennsylvania, and the Carolinas and Georgia came into being. By the middle of the 18th century the British colonies in America stretched from French Canada to Spanish Florida. Behind them was the vast, largely unexplored and unpeopled French territory of Louisiana, and in the wars with France—known in English history as the War of the Austrian Succession (1741–48) and the Seven Years' War (1756–63) — the colonists gave considerable assistance to the British troops engaged in fighting the French in America. As a result of the latter war the British possessions were increased by the conquest of Canada and the acquisition of the territory between the Allegheny Mountains and the Mississippi river. But the long struggle had left Britain staggering beneath a heavy load of debt, and so, to help meet the expenses, incurred largely in the defence of the colonies the British Government decided to raise money in the colonies.

Various taxes and duties were proposed, but roused such opposition that in the end all were withdrawn save the duty on tea. This, however, was particularly obnoxious because the colonists were forced to buy the surplus tea of the British East India Company. So tea which the company sent to Boston was thrown into the harbour by men disguised as Indians (the "Boston Tea Party," 1773). The British Parliament replied by passing with great majorities the Coercive Acts which closed the port of Boston, remodelled the government of Massachusetts, quartered British troops on the inhabitants, and permitted men to be taken to England for trial in certain cases. To meet this emergency the first Continental Congress was assembled at Philadelphia on September 5, 1774. Shortly afterwards armed conflict began with the battles of Lexington and Concord, both in Massachusetts, hostilities continuing till 1783.

The struggle upon which the colonists had embarked was in a sense a civil war. Thousands of the colonists at first hoped for reconciliation with the Mother Country; but after several fruitless attempts at a peaceful settlement they were forced either to side with the "rebels" or with those who continued to uphold England. The latter called themselves "Loyalists," although to their exasperated neighbours they were always "Tories." But if there were Loyalists in the colonies, there were also many in England who rejoiced with William Pitt, Earl of Chatham, that America had resisted, and felt that "three millions of people so dead to all feelings of liberty as voluntarily to submit to be slaves would have been fit instruments to make slaves of all the rest."

On June 15, 1775, George Washington was appointed commander-in-chief of the colonists' army, and two days later the battle of Bunker Hill

COLONIZATION OF NORTH AMERICA
This map shows the early European settlements on the Atlantic coast of North America. English colonization began in 1607 in Virginia, and by 1732 the whole coast between Spanish Florida and French Canada was in British hands.

was fought. Although this resulted in the defeat of the colonists, it proved that their hastily-levied volunteers were a worthy match for regular troops. In 1776 the British, under General Howe, prepared a fresh plan of campaign which at first promised to be successful. Washington and his army were forced to retreat, with Howe harassing them continually. Things looked dark for the Americans. Many of Washington's men had enlisted for three months only, and when their time of service was over they returned home. General Howe also offered pardon to all who would voluntarily come forward and take the oath of allegiance to the Mother Country, and hundreds of people promptly accepted these terms. Then the general trend of events changed. On the night of December 25, 1776, Washington and

AMERICA DECLARES HER INDEPENDENCE
By the Declaration of Independence the thirteen states of America broke all political ties with Great Britain. Though the Declaration was read in Congress on July 4, 1776, and Independence Day is celebrated on July 4, it was not until July 19 that the Declaration was ordered to be written out and signed. This illustration from a painting by Trumbull shows the final scene.

his tattered troops crossed the Delaware in the teeth of a raging snow-storm and surprised and captured a number of Hessian troops, hired by the British Government from a petty German prince. A week later they gained a brilliant victory over the British forces at Princeton, and went into winter quarters in the neighbourhood of Morristown. The 13 states had declared their independence on July 4, 1776, Princeton ending the first campaign fought on this issue.

In the following spring the British prepared to carry out their plan of campaign of the previous year, and General Burgoyne started out from Canada to conquer the state of New York. But disaster upon disaster overtook him; his enemies outnumbered him;

BIRTH CERTIFICATE OF THE UNITED STATES
In nobility of sentiment and dignity of phrasing the American Declaration of Independence ranks high among the great state documents in the English language. Above is a facsimile of part of Thomas Jefferson's draft of that epoch-making document, adopted by the Continental Congress on July 4, 1776. The additions are in the handwriting of Benjamin Franklin and John Adams.

and on October 17 he and his whole army had to surrender at Saratoga. The British, however, still held the city of New York and had captured Philadelphia on September 26, 1777. Despite this victory at Saratoga the winter of 1777–78, spent by Washington at Valley Forge, was for the colonists the darkest period of the war. The British, comfortably housed in Philadelphia and New York, were able to purchase abundant supplies from the farmers because they could pay with gold; while the colonist who would supply food to Washington's starving men must accept " continental " paper money, which was so worthless that the expression " not worth a continental " is sometimes still heard in the United States to describe a thing that has no value.

Treaty of Peace Signed in Paris

But the crisis of the war had really passed with the surrender of Burgoyne. When the news was carried to France by Paul Jones, that country decided to come openly to the aid of America. Up to this time numbers of French soldiers, the most prominent of whom was Lafayette, had joined the American army, and the French government had secretly supplied money and munitions to help in the cause. Now she made an open alliance with the United States (1778), agreeing to continue the fight until victory. Spain entered the war in 1779 in a vain attempt to win back Gibraltar; and, in addition, Holland declared war against Great Britain for trade reasons.

In this way it came about that the war which originally had been merely a colonial struggle was transformed into a world conflict. To this, as much as to their own fighting ability, the colonists owed their ultimate success. Even now, however, the British had hopes of winning, until they suffered another disaster. Shut up at Yorktown by the Americans under Washington and the French fleet under Admiral De Grasse, General Cornwallis, after a 20 days' siege, was compelled to surrender with his army of 7,000 men (October 19, 1781).

This victory at Yorktown was decisive. " The play is over," wrote Lafayette; and when the news

reached Lord North, the head of the British Ministry since 1770, he too cried, " It is all over." A new ministry, more favourable to the colonists, then took the place of North's cabinet. It was nearly two years, however, before the treaty of peace was signed in Paris (September 3, 1783). It recognized the independence of the 13 colonies and granted them all the land east of the Mississippi except Florida, which was returned to Spain to compensate her for her failure to recover Gibraltar. Favourable terms were also granted the United States concerning the fisheries off Newfoundland.

Ammonia. You may be surprised to learn that you probably have never seen ammonia. The pungent liquid that goes under that name as a household cleanser is a solution in water of the true ammonia, which at ordinary temperatures and pressures is an invisible gas, a compound of one nitrogen atom and three hydrogen atoms (NH_3).

This gas is one of the most important chemicals of industry. It is widely used in refrigerating plants (see Refrigeration), and in the manufacture of nitric acid. By combination with acids it yields several valuable ammonium salts. Ammonium chloride is the " sal ammoniac " employed in the manufacture of dry batteries (see Battery) and also as a deoxidizer in soldering, to remove a coating of oxide from the surface of the joint. Ammonium sulphate is used as a fertilizer ; ammonium nitrate in making certain explosives ; ammonium carbonate is used for smelling salts. In these compounds the gas unites with a fourth atom of hydrogen, forming within the larger combination one of those specially close unions called " radicals " which behave in many respects as if they were simple elementary substances. In this case the ammonium radical (NH_4) acts like a metal of the alkali family (see Alkali Metals). Ammonia plays an important part in various methods of nitrogen fixation, through which the nitrogen of the atmosphere is artificially combined into fertilizers and other essential chemicals. (See Nitrogen).

Ammonia can be formed by the dry distillation of proteins, and its old name " spirit of hartshorn " goes back to the days when it was produced from hoofs, hides, and horns of animals. Much ammonia is still obtained from protein derivatives in coal in the process of gas making. By being subjected to cold and pressure, it is easily liquefied.

Ammonite. Many millions of years ago there lived snail-like animals that were first cousins to the beautiful pearly nautilus which inhabits the Pacific and Indian oceans. Their fossils are frequently found, and vary in size from that of a pea to 10 feet in diameter. The shell was curved like a coiled snake, and contained many chambers, only the first of which was occupied by the animal. All types of ammonite are now extinct. The name is derived from a fancied resemblance of the fossils to the ram's horns of the ancient Egyptian god Ammon.

AMMONITE FOSSIL ENCASED IN ROCK
One of the most familiar of all fossils is that shown here—an ammonite, easy to recognize by its spiral coils. In this specimen you see both the actual fossil (right) and the imprint it has left in the block of rock (left). It is many millions of years since any ammonite was alive.

In former times larger specimens were mistaken for petrified snakes, the absence of heads being accounted for by a legend of a saint decapitating the snakes.

Amsterdam. Though The Hague is the seat of the government of the Netherlands, the city of Amsterdam is the commercial capital. Like Venice, it is cut up by canals into some 90 islands, and like Venice it is a city made great by its commerce. Houses are built on piles driven into the low-lying soil, and the first step necessary in the erection of a building is to pump the site dry. Great blocks of flats and huge modern offices in concrete have arisen amid the picturesque red-brick houses of the past.

Amsterdam is the largest city in Holland. Founded in 1240 when a dam was built across the River Amstel—from which the city took its name—Amsterdam had become by the 17th century the foremost commercial centre of the world, at a time when the Dutch were the greatest maritime nation. Since that date its importance has declined, but it still has extensive commerce and holds first place in the diamond-cutting industry. It has also sugar refineries, and factories for making aeroplanes, silk, ropes, dyes, chemicals, and gold and silver plate. Other industries include shipbuilding and printing; glass, paper, cocoa and chocolate are manufactured. The Bank of the Netherlands is one of the leading financial institutions of Europe.

In order to increase the city's sea-borne trade, two canals were cut, one west to the North Sea at Ymuiden, completed in 1876, the other south to the Rhine in 1892. From the city's airport at Schipol, which is situated six miles to the south-west, air services operate all over Europe, and to the Netherlands East Indies and Australia.

The Dam—a large square that owes its name to the fact that it is the eastern boundary of the original dam across the river—is the axis around which Amsterdam is built. From it radiate in a semicircle the principal streets of the city, and every tramcar in the city starts from the Dam. Near it stands the Royal Palace. In the Ryks or State

Museum are displayed paintings by Rembrandt, the most noted of Amsterdam's sons. Although Amsterdam was bombed by the German and the Allied air forces during the Second World War it suffered no extensive damage, but the dock installations and locks were wrecked by the Germans in September 1944 in case of a hurried evacuation. Occupied by German forces on May 10, 1940, the city was liberated by Canadian troops on May 7, 1945. The population is 814,000.

Amundsen, ROALD (1872–1928). The distinction of being the first man to reach the

South Pole, the first to circumnavigate the globe through the icebound waters of the Arctic regions, the first to fly over the North Pole in an airship, belonged to Roald Amundsen (pron. ah'moon-sεn).

The son of a Norwegian shipowner, he was born at Borge, Smaalenene, Norway. He was educated at the University of Christiania (now Oslo), where he studied medicine for two years. Then he entered the naval service. At 25 years of age he was chosen, because of his strength and skill and knowledge of the sea, as member of an important expedition to the Antarctic. Over six feet tall, he had the powerful build and the dauntless spirit of the adventurous Norse vikings of olden times.

The more Amundsen saw of sea and land, the more he was fired with ambition to penetrate

AMSTERDAMS ANCIENT AND MODERN
Dorien Leigh; Netherlands Bureau
Standing sentinel over the Oude Schans canal, where it nears the Prins Hendrik Kade (Quay) and Amsterdam's East Dock, is Montalbaans Tower (top), a landmark of the old city. Contrast is provided by enormous blocks of modern flats in New Amsterdam (lower). In the background are low-lying fields under cultivation.

deeper into the mysteries of the Arctic and Antarctic Circles. In 1903 he set sail in the ship Gjöa for the purpose of locating the magnetic North Pole. For 19 months he remained at King William Land in the north-eastern part of Greenland making observations, and as a result was able to show that the magnetic pole probably has no stationary position but is in continual movement. On this expedition, too, he traversed what navigators of many nations had been seeking for hundreds of years—the North-West Passage from the Atlantic to the Pacific. This completed the first part of what was to be his Arctic journey round the world.

Returning to Norway, he made plans for an expedition in Dr. Nansen's ship, the Fram. This time he intended to drift right across the North Polar Sea. Then came the news that the American explorer Peary had discovered the North Pole, so Amundsen decided to make for the South Pole instead. He left Norway, in the Fram, in 1910. The story of how he and his men wintered at the edge of the Great Ice Barrier on the Bay of Whales, and how they made their dash over mountains and perilous glaciers to the South Pole, is told elsewhere in this work (*see* Polar Exploration). Honours were heaped upon Amundsen, and he lectured in most of the countries of Europe and North America, and in Australia. His book The South Pole was translated into almost every language. In 1914 he was making preparations for another expedition, but this he was forced to postpone on account of the First World War.

At last, in the summer of 1918, Amundsen's plans were complete, and he was able to set sail for the North Polar regions in his ship Maud. His plan was to drive his ship as far northward as he could, then to lodge it in the ice, and allow it to be dragged along with the enormous floes. He expected that it would take him near the North Pole. His purpose, however, was not primarily to reach the Pole but to make scientific observations in the far north. For 19 months he was not heard from. Then he arrived at Anadyr, a trading post on the Bering Sea in eastern Siberia, in April 1920, having left his ship and companions fast in the ice and travelled some hundreds of miles by sledge to seek supplies and news of the civilized world. In July he was in Nome, Alaska, on the opposite side of Bering Strait. He had sailed from the Atlantic to the Pacific across the seas bordering northern Europe and Asia, thus completing the second part of his journey round the Polar Circle.

AMUNDSEN IN THE ARCTIC
Roald Amundsen (left) was the first man in history to reach both the South Pole and the North Pole. For the latter achievement the great explorer used the airship Norge, which arrived at its Spitsbergen base, King's Bay (seen in the photograph above), on May 7, 1926.

Amundsen next proposed to fly by aeroplane from Alaska to Spitsbergen across the Polar basin and over the North Pole, a distance of 2,614 miles. A trial flight was made in 1923, but the project was abandoned. After a plucky attempt in 1925 he failed to reach the Pole by 220 miles. The following spring Amundsen tried again, using an Italian-built dirigible piloted by General Umberto Nobile of the Italian air service. Leaving Spitsbergen on May 11, 1926, the airship flew to the Pole and thence to Teller, in Alaska—a distance of 2,700 miles—in 71 hours.

Two years later came his last and greatest adventure. He set out from Norway to fly to the relief of Nobile, who had met disaster in another exploring trip, and his aeroplane vanished in the Arctic mists. Months later a bit of floating wreckage from the plane told the tragic story of his end.

Anaesthesia.   (Pron. an-ēs-thē'-zi-*a*).

This word comes from the Greek and means loss of the power of feeling. An anaesthetic is some drug, or the vapours of drugs, used to produce insensibility of one's surroundings and, above all, of pain. Attempts to produce anaesthesia are as old as civilized man. The myrrh with vinegar offered to Christ on the cross was not, as is often supposed, meant to distress Him, but to ease His pain.

Homer, the Greek poet, knew of the anaesthetic properties of opium, our great pain-relieving drug of the present day ; concoctions of hemp, which produced intoxication, were used by the Chinese; and in more modern times to make the patient dead-drunk with alcohol was the most efficient anaesthetic then known.

It is amazing to reflect that just as the steam engine is only some hundred years old and yet the modern railways have revolutionised travel, aeroplanes have only been known some 50 years and yet they have revolutionised transport and warfare, so anaesthetics, in the sense in which we understand the word, are but some hundred years old and their effects on surgery are hardly to be measured. Before the everyday use of anaesthetics great speed on the part of the surgeon was absolutely necessary to avoid pain to the patient and to avoid shock, and the surgeon was considered great in proportion as he was quick. These values are now entirely altered by careful preparation of the patient before the anaesthetic, by the choice of a suitable anaesthetic, and by skilled treatment of the patient after the operation. The surgeon can have all the time that he wants for detailed careful work without damaging the patient's chance of recovery ; and in fact this slowness makes recovery more sure. In olden days the operation was a thing to be dreaded ; in our times we do not think of the operation as such, and most of us merely dislike the thought of the anaesthetic.

General and Local Anaesthetics

The real and practical beginning of modern anaesthesia was in 1844 when Dr. Horace Wells, a dentist in Connecticut, had a tooth removed under nitrous oxide (called " laughing gas " because the patient often laughs when inhaling it), the gas which even now is often used when we have a tooth removed at the dentist's. Another American dentist, about the same time, employed a vapour of sulphuric ether as a " general " anaesthetic when removing teeth. Soon the good news spread to the British dentists and surgeons, and thence to the Continent. (A general anaesthetic is one which takes away consciousness ; a local anaesthetic merely affects the nerves of the part of the body which is to be operated on, by temporarily depriving that part of all feeling.)

Then Sir James Simpson, of Edinburgh, began to use ether to allay pain at childbirth, going on in time to use chloroform. This drug had just been discovered, and is still the drug of choice for this purpose in England, although ether is preferred in America. Ethyl chloride is another popular substance of which the gas, when inhaled, gives a period of anaesthesia for short operations ; or it may be used to induce unconsciousness, which will be maintained by giving ether.

Anaesthetics is a highly specialised branch of medicine. The men who practise it are known as anaesthetists, and they have many complicated forms of apparatus and methods for keeping the patient unconscious and completely safe. If the patient is not breathing well and deeply the modern anaesthetist often gives him CO_2 (carbonic acid gas). This seems a strange thing to do when the patient is obviously short of oxygen, but now we know that the natural stimulus to breathing

is a high content of CO_2 round the breathing centre in the brain ; and by raising this content artificially, by giving CO_2, the patient can soon be induced to breathe deeply and naturally.

Anaesthetics are not necessarily given as a gas or vapour. Some are given by the mouth, or are introduced into the body in other suitable ways. Thus, avertin may be given by the rectum, though in a long operation some sort of inhalation method is needed as well, in order to prolong unconsciousness. This last is also true of some wonderful new anaesthetics, such as pentothal, which are injected into a vein. Morphine and a substance called scopolamine, when injected together, blur pain and are especially useful in blotting out the memory of pain, which aids the patient's recovery.

How a general anaesthetic works is not completely understood. It is believed that the brain cells work by reason of the activity of their tiny and complicated ferments (rather like the chemical agents which cause fermentation in wine or in anything going sour), and that anaesthetics stop the activity of these intricate substances and so cause mental processes to stand still, putting the cells of the brain temporarily out of action.

Injections into the Spinal Cord

While the main use of an anaesthetic is to stop pain it can also be used to relieve severe spasms, such as occur in lockjaw, in strychnine poisoning, and in some sorts of fit. Also, it is often very difficult to examine a patient in pain and find out what is wrong with him, because he unconsciously tightens up his muscles to protect the painful parts; under an anaesthetic he relaxes.

Local anaesthetics are those which cause insensitivity over a small area. Some are painted on, and some are injected ; others, like cocaine, act by their very nature ; while some, like adrenalin and freezing sprays, drive away the blood supply from the part. The injection of a cocaine preparation into a main nerve can anaesthetize, if need be, a whole limb. Moreover in modern anaesthesia suitable substances are injected into the spinal cord, making various areas of the body insensitive according to the level at which they are introduced. It is very interesting to observe a patient having, for example, his appendix removed and watching the operation in a mirror, while at the same time he is completely unaware of the touch of the surgeon. The discovery of anaesthesia belongs to the most outstanding achievements of medicine for the relief of the distress of Man— and of course of his lesser brothers, the domesticated animals. In this same class of beneficent discovery comes asepsis and, perhaps, the use of morphia to relieve pain.

ANAESTHESIA UNKNOWN
At one time a barber was not only a hairdresser but also something of a surgeon, specializing in blood-letting and teeth extractions without the use of anaesthetics to dull the pain. The barber's pole (above) is a relic of those days, the stripes representing a bandaged and bleeding arm.

What LIES HID BENEATH the SKIN?

The branch of anatomy called Histology examines the cells which build up the body. Embryology treats of the development of the unborn animal; Physiology, how the body works; Pathology, the sick cell and the sick organ.

Anatomy. The word anatomy comes from a Greek one meaning to cut up, and it is by carefully dissecting, by teasing out with knife and nippers, all the tissues of the body that the student learns exactly of their position and what their function is. While such examination of the dead body has been made since history began, the ignorance and superstition of people foiled scientific workers throughout the Middle Ages. The Belgian, Vesalius, is held to be the founder of modern anatomy; and in the same 16th century Fallopius, an Italian, did work which helped all later researchers.

Until recent centuries bodies were often stolen from graves to give physicians and surgeons material to examine and from which to teach their students. Even in the 19th century Burke and Hare, professional murderers, were supplying the bodies of their victims to a certain Dr. Knox, of Edinburgh, for

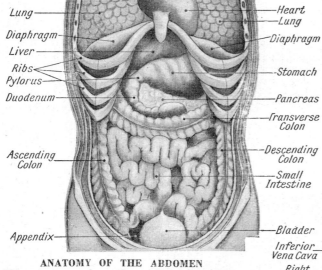

Lung — Diaphragm — Liver — Ribs — Pylorus — Duodenum — Ascending Colon — Appendix

Heart — Lung — Diaphragm — Stomach — Pancreas — Transverse Colon — Descending Colon — Small Intestine — Bladder

ANATOMY OF THE ABDOMEN
The organs are here shown diagrammatically. Actually, the pancreas is more behind the stomach and, with the duodenum, is covered by the transverse colon, which is higher than shown here.

experiment. To this day you may see, in some old London churchyards, the watch-houses where men stayed during the night to foil the body-snatchers. Happily in our time people take a more enlightened view of dissection after death; quite a number, who may be suffering from rare diseases, leave their bodies to be investigated, in the hope of helping scientific knowledge in the cure of ills.

The functioning of the body is looked after by various systems or groups of organs. Thus the digestive system—a chain of tubes and organs running from the mouth to the anus—deals with the mastication of food and its preparation for absorption to meet the needs of the

living animal. The respiratory system comprises the lungs and the air passages which deal with the exchange of oxygen and carbon dioxide gases—the combustion or burning up of food which is associated with all animal life. The circulatory system is built up of a strong muscular pump, the heart, which forces blood through artery, capillary and vein to reach all the body tissues; the blood conveys oxygen to the tissues, and removes carbon dioxide.

The bony skeleton of the body supports and carries the whole structure; to the bones are attached by tendons the muscles which allow of movement and progression. The nervous system is responsible for our senses, such as sight, hearing, taste, touch, smell. The brain, protected by the dense bony cap of the skull, is the site of higher mental life, such as memory and reason, as well as the other type of unconscious mental control which looks after various physical functions (such as breathing and the beating of the heart), without the direct action of our will.

The study of the structure of our body by dissecting it is called practical anatomy; it is the essential basis of the surgeon's skill and, in a lesser degree, of the physician's also. Comparative anatomy studies the structure of animals other than Man, to establish their relationship to one another. In the 18th century the French anatomist Cuvier began to classify animals not by their looks but by their internal formation. In the next century our own Charles Darwin showed how certain animal groups were somewhat alike in structure because they had a more or less common descent from earlier forms of animal.

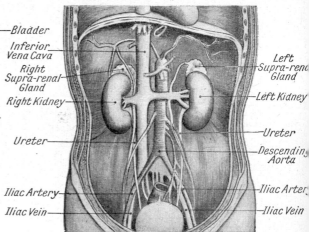

Inferior Vena Cava — Right Supra-renal Gland — Right Kidney — Ureter — Iliac Artery — Iliac Vein

Left Supra-renal Gland — Left Kidney — Ureter — Descending Aorta — Iliac Artery — Iliac Vein

ABDOMEN AND SOME ORGANS
Further still within the abdomen are shown the structures on the rear abdominal wall. The left kidney is somewhat higher than the right. In both diagrams the bladder is represented filled; when empty it lies behind the pubic bones.

Functional anatomy deals with the working of the various parts of the body; and in this branch an outstanding name is that of the Englishman William Harvey, who proved the circulation of the blood in 1628. He had studied at Padua under the influence of the work done there by Vesalius and Fallopius; before Harvey's discovery the queerest ideas of blood movement prevailed, and it was even thought that it ebbed and flowed backward and forward, but did not go round in a circuit.

Artistic anatomy is yet another subdivision of this wide subject : the artist and sculptor must be familiar with the internal reasons for the external appearance of the body before he can successfully reproduce this in his chosen medium of colour or stone.

In reading about anatomy (perhaps you may do this when learning first aid) you may be bothered by the many foreign names which are used for parts of the body. Most of these names are Latin, though as the earliest anatomy books were written in Greek, there are plenty of Greek forms also. People often ask why the terms cannot be put into English. They could, of course, but one advantage of Latin is that it allows brief and precise names to be given.

Another point is that the descriptive language of the physician and the surgeon ought to be an international one, so that not only English speaking people but those of other lands could use the same names for the same things. Most of the sciences have come to use words which have been derived from Latin and Greek for this sort of reason.

Many parts are named after famous anatomists who first described them. Thus we have the veins of Galen (*c.* A.D. 130–200), in the skull; the fissure of Sylvius (1614–72) in the brain; the ligament of Poupart (1661–1709), in the groin; Hunter's canal, down the inside of the thigh—after John Hunter (1728–93). Galen was a Greek who practised in Rome. Sylvius was a Dutch professor at Leyden university, and Poupart was a French anatomist. John Hunter was born in Lanarkshire; his father died when the boy was only ten years of age, and so John was apprenticed to a step-brother who was a cabinet-maker. His master failed in business when John was nearly twenty, so the young man wrote to a brother, William Hunter, who was a lecturer on anatomy in London. William invited John to come to London, and here he worked for a time as an assistant in the dissecting room.

In less than a year young John had acquired so much knowledge of anatomy that he was given a class of students; later, after surgical studies at Chelsea and St. Bartholomew's hospital, he was appointed surgeon at a hospital. He made rapid progress in the profession he had thus entered so strangely, winning honour and respect. He spent much of his money in building up a collection of specimens for the study of comparative anatomy. After Hunter's death, at the age of 65, his great

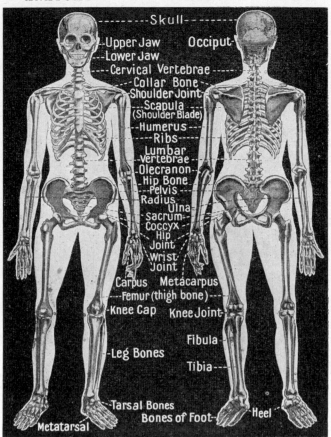

A KEY-DIAGRAM TO HUMAN ANATOMY

The detailed anatomy of a human being is exceedingly complex, but the skeleton itself is fairly simple to understand. This drawing shows the principal bones and joints of the human frame as seen from in front and from behind. It is, of course, the muscles attached to these bones and joints that give the power of movement.

collection was purchased by the British government for £15,000 and was handed over to the Royal College of Surgeons. It is housed in their headquarters, at Lincoln's Inn Fields, London. Hunter was the greatest pathologist of his time, besides being an outstanding genius in anatomy.

The stories of the French anatomist Cuvier, of Charles Darwin, and of William Harvey are told under their own headings in other pages. A few particulars about Gabriello Fallopius (1523–62) and Andreas Vesalius (1524–64) will complete our story. Fallopius was born at Modena in Italy and became professor of anatomy at Ferrara. Later he taught anatomy, surgery and botany at the university of Padua. His book entitled Observations on Anatomy was published in 1561.

Vesalius was born in Brussels. He, too, went to the famed university of Padua to teach anatomy and surgery; afterwards he taught at other Italian universities, and at the Swiss one of Basle. Appointed physician to Charles V of Germany, he was forced to leave the court because he insisted on dissecting human bodies in order to obtain anatomical knowledge. In 1543 he published his most important book, a treatise on the heart and its valves.

Andersen, HANS CHRISTIAN (1805-1875).

There is a famous fairy story of an ugly duckling that grew up to be a beautiful swan. It is really a story of the author's own life ; for little Hans Andersen was an ungainly, awkward boy, as odd in his ways as in his looks, and no one who knew him in his boyhood could have guessed that some day he would become world-famous.

In Odense, a little town in Denmark, he lived in one small room, which served also as a workshop for his father, a cobbler. When Hans was 11 years old the father died, his mother had to go out washing, and the little boy was left to himself. He played with a toy theatre, read plays, and invented stories. People laughed at him and wondered what would become of him; at school he dreamed away his time and learned very little.

At 14 he went to Copenhagen to try his fortune. Failing to earn a living as an actor or opera singer he determined to write plays. In this he failed, too, at first; but a friend, seeing that he had talent, induced the king to help towards Andersen's education. At last he produced a novel entitled The Improvisatore, that brought him popularity. His financial troubles were now at an end.

HANS ANDERSEN
The king among tellers of fairy stories was Hans Andersen, a Dane, whose life-like statue at Copenhagen is an object of hero-worship for children of all ages and nations.

From his boyhood Hans had made up fairy tales, and one day someone suggested that he should put some of them in a book. He laughed at the idea, but decided to try it; and in 1835 the first volume of his immortal Fairy Tales appeared. He quickly became the idol of his own country and of all Europe.

The ugly duckling had proved to be a swan. He was still awkward, to be sure, and dressed in odd old-fashioned clothes, but children forgot about his queer appearance when they listened to his wonderful stories. When he wrote the story of his life, he called it a " wonder story." " How beautiful the world is ! " he said, when he was dying. " How happy I am ! " His statue stands in one of the public gardens of Copenhagen. Children play about it and look up into the face of the great writer, who sits in his chair, book in hand and finger uplifted, as if calling on them to listen to the story of The Wild Swans, or The Tinderbox, or The Little Mermaid.

Besides his fairy tales, Andersen's chief works were : The Improvisatore (1835); Only a Fiddler (1837); Picture-Book Without Pictures (1840); Story of My Life (English translation, 1927); and a travel-book, In Spain, published in 1863.

SOUTH AMERICA'S MOUNTAIN BACKBONE

Separating the forests and pampas of South America from the waters of the Pacific Ocean there stretches a vast wall of tremendous mountains—an eternal challenge thrown down by Nature to mortal engineers.

Andes. There is a great " world ridge " of mountains which nearly encircles the Pacific Ocean passing from the tip of South America, through Alaska, Japan and the Philippines, to New Zealand. The Andes portion of this world ridge forms the longest mountain system, for it extends from the Isthmus of Panama to Tierra del Fuego, a distance of 4,500 miles.

Ranging from the tropic heat of the northern coast to the frigid temperatures of the glaciers of Patagonia and of the snow-clad cones which rise under the equatorial sun, the Andes present a variation of climate that is unique. North of Chile the snow-line has an elevation of some 15,000 feet, and the broad plateaus below have the climate and products of temperate-zone valleys. These regions were thickly populated by advanced tribes of Indians when the Spanish explorers conquered them 400 years ago, and they are today the chief centres of population.

In the northern part of the continent the winds blow westward from the Atlantic, and give up their moisture as they rise over the mountains. As a result the eastern slopes of the Andes are deluged with tropical rains. Thus the Amazon is supplied with the greatest flood of waters that any river system pours into the ocean ; while just across the mountains on the Pacific slope lie the arid deserts of Peru and northern Chile. In the south, westerly winds prevail, and the coastal plain and central valley of southern Chile are well watered, while east of the Andes in the same latitude are the dry plains of western Argentina.

Except in the extreme south, the Andes are all but uncrossable. The high passes are mere gorge-like channels of mountain streams, with paths for pack-mules and llamas winding along the overhanging slopes. At the summit of the Cumbre Pass, between Chile and Argentina, at a height of 12,000 feet above sea-level, stands a bronze figure of Christ 26 feet high. It was erected in 1904 to commemorate the settlement of a boundary dispute between the two countries and as a token of lasting peace. Only at three points do railways cross the Andes. By awe-inspiring feats of engineering, by trestles across fearful chasms, and by bridges suspended at dizzy heights above abysses, the Trans-Andean railway connecting Valparaiso (Chile) with Buenos Aires (Argentina) was completed in 1910. The line from Buenos Aires to La Paz, Bolivia, at one point in Bolivia reaches a height of over 13,000 feet. Another trans-continental line, from Salta in northern Argentina to the Chilean port of Antofagasta, was opened in 1948. Elsewhere pack animals are used.

Fabulously rich mines of gold, silver and copper were worked by the Incas and their Spanish conquerors. Deposits of lead, iron, platinum, quicksilver and tin also exist. Indeed, the Andes are so rich in minerals that their name is from the

Peru northward the mass widens to 400 miles and is lifted to extensive plateaux bounded and crossed by lofty ranges and peaks. From Ecuador and Colombia, the Andes descend toward the low isthmus and throw out eastward a great spur along the coast of Venezuela.

The plateaux and passes of the Andes are as elevated as the highest summits of the Alps, and peaks towering up to 23,000 feet overtop everything on earth except the summits of the Himalayas. Chimborazo (20,517 feet), Sorata (21,484 feet), Illimani (21,024 feet), and Aconcagua (22,860 feet) are among the highest peaks. Cotopaxi (19,580 feet) is the highest active volcano in the whole world. The entire Andean system is subject to violent earthquakes.

The populated regions of the Andes are divided into three sections—an almost unpopulated district extending north from Patagonia to the Puna de Atacama in southern Chile ; a dry central area from the Puna de Atacama to northern Peru, where mining is the chief industry ; and a damp zone in the north, where agriculture is the principal occupation.

In the Puna de Atacama there are a few shepherds and a small number of people who collect salt from deposits in the mountains. From there north to the Caribbean Sea the greater part of the population on the west coast and of the Caribbean republics, and, with few exceptions, the chief cities, are to be found in the Andes. The southern and drier portion of this region is a mining area, and the railways which penetrate the ranges from the Pacific coast were constructed specially to transport the products of the mines to the nearest ports.

In the damper mountains of Ecuador, Colombia, and Venezuela the chief industry is agriculture. Everywhere the muleteers, who carry so much of the products from the mountains to the coastal plains, form an important section of the population.

Indian word *anta*, which means copper, or metals in general. But these mountain fastnesses are so inaccessible that the greater part of their wealth still awaits development.

The Spanish name for the Andes is Cordilleras, from an old word meaning a cord or rope. At their narrow southern end the Andes form only one distinct range, which descends to Cape Horn in foothills and rises again in glaciated volcanic cones on Tierra del Fuego (" the land of fire "). In Chile a low coast range and high rocky ridges called *sierras* enclose a wide central valley. From

Ewing Galloway; G. M. Dyott

ANDEAN PEAKS PERPETUALLY SNOW-CLAD

Winding amid towering crests of the Andes in Peru is the highest broad-gauge railway (upper photo) in the world, climbing to over 15,000 feet, and equally remarkable for the dazzling views it affords the passengers and for the engineering skill that brought it into being. In the lower photograph a rider is silhouetted against the Pasco Knot, a section of the Andes on the Peruvian-Bolivian border, whose great glaciers, melting in the sun, feed the river Amazon.

Andrée, SALOMON AUGUST (1854–1897). After completing his studies at the technical college at Stockholm, Andrée became interested in aeronautics, and he decided it would be possible to reach the North Pole by balloon. On July 11, 1897, accompanied by two friends, Strindberg and Fraenkel, he made an ascent from Dane Island, Spitsbergen. The three men were never seen alive again.

Four days later a carrier pigeon, shot by the crew of a sealing vessel, was found to be carrying a message which had been written by Andrée two days after leaving Dane Island. The message gave the position of the party as being 145 miles north and 45 miles east of the starting-point.

No further news was received, and in 1898 and 1899 parties searched the north Asiatic coast, the New Siberian Islands in the Arctic Ocean, and Eastern Greenland. None was successful, and only scanty information was obtained from the discovery of buoys, containing messages, which the balloonists had arranged to drop periodically.

In the summer of 1930 a party of Norwegian scientists came by accident on the bodies of three men on the ice at White Island near Franz Josef Land. The mystery of the fate of Andrée, Strindberg and Fraenkel was solved. With the bodies of

ANDRÉE'S BALLOON ON THE ICE

In 1897 Salomon Andrée, a Swede, left Spitsbergen in a balloon with two companions in an attempt to reach the North Pole. Little more was heard until 33 years had elapsed. The discovery of the explorers' bodies on Franz Josef Land in 1930 solved the mystery of their fate ; among the other finds was the negative of this photograph of the balloon's landing.

the Swedish aeronauts were logs and diaries recording the balloon's progress and its descent on the ice, and also photographs which were successfully developed. A further relic of this ill-fated expedition came to light in September 1937, when a globe of copper which had been thrown from the balloon was found on Bastion Island, to the north-west of Spitsbergen ; it contained a report on the progress of the ill-fated flight.

Anemone. (Pron *a*-nem'-*o*-ni). The anemone, sometimes called "wind flower," belongs to the buttercup family, and grows in temperate climates. The name anemone comes from the Greek word for "wind." Two varieties are found growing wild in Britain, the white-blossomed wood anemone (*Anemone nemorosa*), which is a beautiful spring flower found in woodlands and pastures, and the purple-blossomed pasque-flower (*A. pulsatilla*), which grows on chalky pastures in the southern and eastern counties of England. Other varieties grow in Asia, North America, and Europe. Several are cultivated in Britain, including the poppy anemone and Japanese anemone.

The dainty blossoms of the wood anemone nod and sway on their slender stems, which bend but never break in the strong blasts of early spring ; at night or during a rainstorm the petals curl up. Some of the other varieties, particularly the cultivated ones, have firmer stems, while the blossoms occur in many beautiful colours.

Some of the anemones are greatly prized by the Chinese, who use them in their funeral rites. According to a Greek myth the flower sprang from the tears shed by the goddess Aphrodite over the death of Adonis. The Greeks believed, too, that only the wind could open its petals.

M. H. Crawford

ANEMONE OF THE WOODS

Britain's only widely distributed wild anemone, the wood anemone or wind flower, is one of the prettiest of all our spring blossoms. Often it is so common as to carpet the woodland and pastures with its delicate white flowers, mingling with the primroses and bluebells.

Anglesey. Also sometimes spelt Anglesea, this is an island county of North Wales. It is separated from the mainland at Caernarvonshire by the Menai Strait, across which are two famous bridges: the suspension structure constructed by Telford carrying the roadway, and Stephenson's tubular bridge which carries the railway to its terminus at Holyhead. This seaport, on the smaller island of Holy Island within the county, has a regular service of steamers to Dun Laoghaire (Kingstown) in Eire. Beaumaris (pop. 1,800) is the county town, but Holyhead is more important. Also on Anglesey (area 275 square miles; pop. 49,000), at Penmon, near Beaumaris, is a local transmitter of the B.B.C.— and Llanfairpwllgwyngyllgogcerchwyrndrobwlltysiliogogogoch

ANGUS HOME OF QUEEN ELIZABETH
At Glamis Castle, ancestral Scottish seat of the Earls of Strathmore, Queen Elizabeth, consort of King George VI, spent three months during each year of her childhood. The castle dates mainly from the 17th century, but parts of the original 11th century walls survive from the days of Macbeth, "thane of Glamis."

(usually shortened for convenience' sake to Llanfair p.g.), the village with the longest name in Britain.

Anglesey was known as the isle of Mona to the Romans who conquered it in Anno Domini 61 and again in A.D. 78. There are remains of a Roman camp at Holyhead. In 1272 the island was seized by the English under Edward I, who built Beaumaris Castle in the year 1293.

Angus. This Scottish county, bordered by Aberdeenshire and Kincardine to the north, Perthshire to the west, the North Sea to the east, and the Firth of Tay to the south, was known from the 16th century until 1928 as Forfarshire. The name of Angus is derived either from a legendary chieftain or the hill of Angus which is situated in the county. The northern part of Angus is in the Highlands,

and reaches over 2,000 feet in several places. Farther south is the great vale of Strathmore, in which is Glamis Castle, home of the Strathmore family, from which came Queen Elizabeth, consort of George VI. Strathmore is one of the most fertile plains in Scotland. On the Perthshire boundary are the Sidlaw Hills. The North and South Esk are the most important rivers.

Agriculture is the chief industry of the county. Jute and flax manufacture is carried on, the centre of the industry being at Dundee (q.v.). Other towns are Forfar (the county town; pop. 9,000), Arbroath, Brechin and Montrose. Kirriemuir was the birthplace of Sir James Barrie and is the "Thrums" of his world-famous novels. The area of Angus is 873 square miles, and its population 273,000.

ANGLESEY AND ITS TWO LINKS WITH WALES
Connecting the island of Anglesey with the mainland of Wales are two bridges over the Menai Strait. The Menai road suspension bridge (left) was opened in 1826. The Britannia tubular bridge (right), completed in 1850, carries the main railway line to Holyhead, whence there is a regular steamship service to Dun Laoghaire, Eire. Anglesey, in the foreground, was a stronghold of the Druids and was conquered by the Romans in A.D. 61 and 78.

The VARIED WEB of ANIMAL LIFE

How amazing are the variations of structure and habit included in the Animal Kingdom! There are nearly a million known living species of animals, differing enormously in size, form, colour, and mode of life.

Animal Kingdom. A noted scientist once said that " the difference between plants and animals is that plants are animals that have made a busine·s of standing still." That is a good, rough-and-ready dis·inction, but it will not fit all cases, for there are a few animals like sponges and corals that remain fixed in one place nearly all their lives. It is easy enough to tell one of the higher animals from one of the higher plants, but it is not so easy when we get down to very primitive types of life like the sea-anemone. In fact, there are certain very low forms of life—especially those minute one-celled organisms from which scientists believe all higher forms have developed—which even learned men do not know how to classify.

One of the simpler schemes of classification, in which the animal kingdom is divided into eight branches, is as follows:

1. *Protozoa.* The simplest animals, microscopic and composed usually of a single cell such as the amoeba or the malarial germ; if of several cells, these are all of one kind. (All the remaining groups are many-celled and are collectively called *Metazoa*.)

2. *Porifera.* Sponges.

3. *Coelenterata.* Jelly-fishes, sea-anemones, coral animals, etc.

4. *Vermes.* Worms, a very large group, often separated into several branches; includes jointed worms, smooth worms, shelled worms, tape-worms, etc.

5. *Mollusca.* Mussels, snails slugs, oysters, clams, devil-fishes, cuttle-fishes and squids.

6. *Echinodermata.* Animals with spiny skeletons like starfishes, sea-urchins, sea-cucumbers, etc.

7. *Arthropoda.* Lobsters, crabs, crayfish, spiders, centipedes, bees, ants, butterflies, beetles, etc. There are some 400,000 known species in this branch, more than all the known species in all the other branches combined.

8. *Vertebrata.*
   (a) *Fishes.* (b) *Amphibians.* Frogs, toads and newts. (c) *Reptiles.* Snakes, lizards, alligators, turtles. (d) *Birds.* (e) *Mammals.* Animals that nurse their young, including Man.

As we go up the scale of life, moreover, we find one fairly clear distinction, in addition to the fact that nearly all animals move and have special organs for moving, while most plants do not. That distinction is this: nearly all plants get their food from gases in the air and chemical substances in the soil and water, while animals live by eating plants or other animals or both.

The struggle for existence in the animal world, therefore, seems fiercer and more cruel than among the plants. The three great things in an animal's life are to eat, to avoid being eaten, and to propagate its kind. Throughout the animal kingdom we find the most marvellous adaptations to carry out these purposes. Thus the lion and the tiger are provided with long claws and sharp teeth for captur-ing their prey. The porcupine has sharp bristles to drive away an enemy ; the skunk drives off his pursuers by throwing off a disgusting odour; and the flying fish actually leaps out of the water and escapes danger by the use of its wing-like fins.

Still another example of adaptation is the bright plumage of birds, which is their show dress during the mating period. There are also butterflies whose wings so perfectly imitate the blossoms or leaves of plants that when they are motionless only the keenest eye can pick them out.

Enormous Numbers Fail to Grow Up

Animals that are not well adapted to the struggle for life soon die off and disappear. As it is, Nature produces millions of animals which survive only for a brief period; in the great struggle for existence enormous numbers die when young, or are killed and eaten by other animals. If this were not the case a single species would soon overrun the entire earth. The turbot, for example, is said to lay 8,500,000 eggs. It is estimated that if each egg grew to maturity, and reproduction continued at the same rate, every ocean and sea would be full of these fish in 10 years.

The length of life of an animal seems to be con-nected in some way with its size and the rate at which it multiplies. The largest animals, which have few young, such as the whale with a span of life believed to be 70 years or more, and the elephant which sometimes reaches the age of 100, seem to live the longest. On the other hand, certain flies which multiply very rapidly live only a few hours.. Some animals, such as tortoises, crocodiles and many snakes, live to a surprisingly great age, apparently because they lead such sluggish lives.

From Primitive Type to Higher One

After thousands of years of study scientists have been able to trace out the general design of this great family tree. They have learned that all the animals, from the tiny one-celled amoeba to Man himself, are related to one another ; and they have classified all the various kinds of animals— more than 950,000 of them—showing how they are related. At the head of the animal world they place Man, who is closely related in structure to the monkeys, the man-like apes and the other animals that nurse their young, and differs from them more in the development of his intelligence than in his bodily structure.

In evolution it is always the more primitive types, not the more specialized, that evolve into higher types. Crabs, for instance, could not be used to evolve vertebrate animals. But while primitive types have evolved into new and higher types, some of their relatives have remained at pretty much the same level, and with only slight evolution. For instance, while the many forms of higher mammals have evolved from primitive mammals, some of the latter have changed but little relatively

Naturalists recognize six great Haunts of Life, each with characteristic inhabitants. At the bottom is the Deep Sea, home of the angler fish, the pelican fish, the gurnard, the sea-urchin, the hedgehog-mouth, and the giant squid. Fixed to the sea floor are animals that look like plants—sea-pens, sea-lilies, sponges and corals. In the Shore Haunt are other sponge and coral forms, sea-cucumbers, starfish, crabs, lobsters, crocodiles, and sea-lizards. Next, the Open Sea, with whales, sharks, flying-fish, turtles, food fishes and sea birds. The other Haunts are the Fresh Waters, Dry Land, and Air. The creatures shown are not proportionate in size.

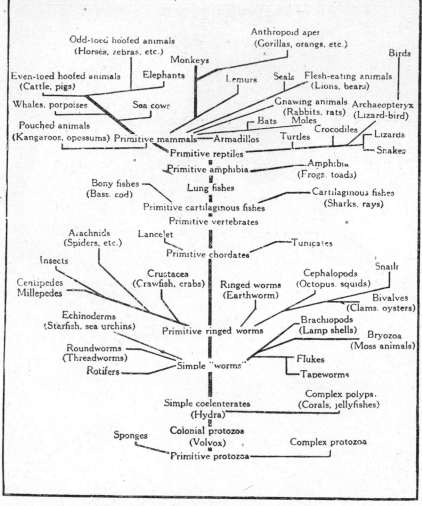

together as "worms." These "simple worms" were not worms as you usually know them, but probably very small, perhaps swimming and crawling and not jointed.

One of the most obscure points in the evolution of life is the origin of vertebrates, or backboned animals from invertebrates. Somewhere there came in a new type, with the nervous system at the back and other new characters, which scientists call "chordates," but still without a jointed "backbone." This undiscovered type gave rise to several very lowly relatives of the vertebrates as well as to real vertebrates, with a jointed backbone. The fishes possessed of only a gristly or cartilaginous skeleton gave rise to fishes with bony skeletons, as well as to fishes with both lungs and gills ; and these, through amphibia and perhaps reptiles, to the highest animals.

Another illustration is afforded by the lizards. Living lizards are nearest to the primitive reptiles. But the lizards have given rise to the more specialized reptiles as well as to birds— a very uniform group.

In classifying animals it is important to have a precise and invariable system of designating each kind and each group. Since the popular names of animals vary from country to country, scientists have adopted a universal system of nomenclature (naming) which uses Latin or latinized terms. The system is fully explained in the chapter on Biology, but we may indicate here its method of arrangement. Each species is designated by two names, one for the genus to which it belongs, and one for the species, just as people have a surname and a Christian name. Thus the domestic cat is called *Felis domesticus*, the wild cat *Felis sylvestris*, the lion *Felis leo*, and the tiger *Felis tigris*.

The cat and its closest relations together make up the genus *Felis*. This genus is grouped with other closely-related groups (lynxes, cheetahs, etc.) in the family *Felidae*, which with other families of flesh-eaters constitute; the order *Carnivora*. Orders are grouped in sub-classes and classes, and finally in primary divisions or phyla (singular, phylum).

FAMILY TREE OF THE ANIMAL KINGDOM

Here in diagrammatic form is the way in which the animal kingdom has evolved in the course of many millions of years. From the smallest, simplest protozoa to the most highly developed of the vertebrates, the anthropoid apes, and above them, to Man, the evolution of the animals has been roughly in a direct line—the stem of which, however, has been broken in many places where links have been lost in far-back ages of the earth's history.

and are still found in our day as the lowly mammals known as marsupials or pouched animals.

Let us try to trace some of the main events in the evolution of animal life. Primitive life gave rise to the simplest single-celled plants and animals, which were the points of departure for the evolution of the plant and animal worlds. The simplest protozoa were to give rise to the thousands of kinds of protozoa of great variety, as well as to the colonies of protozoa—colonies of cells—and these to forms similar to the hydra, a genus of freshwater polyps which multiply when divided. The hydra-like animals give rise to the more specialized polyps and jelly-fishes, as well as to higher animals.

One of the most interesting types which we assume existed was a form more complex than the hydra, which became the point for the evolution not only of the higher forms of life, but also of the large number of diverse types often classified

Is it INSTINCT or INTELLIGENCE?

What makes animals act in the clever way in which we often see them do? We may say " Instinct," but such examples of animal behaviour as are given here may well suggest the possession of some form of intelligence.

Animals, BEHAVIOUR OF. In the spider, one of the simplest living creatures we know, we find a sort of mind. As we think of the animal kingdom it is hard to resist the feeling that animals have learned some of our mottoes. They seem at first sight to act every day as if they had taken thought for the morrow. They take the line of least resistance. They look before they leap. They know that in union there is strength. They save for a rainy day. They seem to understand quite well that a stitch in time saves nine and that for everything there is a time and for everything, too, there is or should be a place.

Think of the spider and its web. The web seems as well thought-out as a new arterial road. The spider builds as if it had studied stress and strain like an engineer. It makes one kind of road for itself and another for its victims; it anticipates danger. Go to the tiny ant. How many know the wonderful things these creatures do? They will capture the aphids that infest our roses, make them prisoners, "milk" them, and protect their eggs to insure a continued supply. These, and many other so-called instincts of lower life, make us wonder if a limited but ordered intelligence may be at work.

A Home and Storehouse for Winter

Long before the days when men had built the first bridge, the beaver had built his dam; long before men had thought it all out, the beaver had arched his dam against the stream and made very effective little sluices. The beaver builds a lodge at his dam and a storehouse for winter. Frozen-in by ice, he seeks and finds a free water gate through which he can receive supplies. The bees have established a civilization that excites our wonder. They toil and build and store; they obey laws and punish those who break them; they live and move and have their being impelled by a patriotism of the hive beyond the dreams of men.

We think of this wonderful behaviour of animals and call it instinct. But what is instinct but a sort of unchangeable mind, fixed by natural law? A man is lost; he works his way home by the stars, and we call

it mind at work. A dog is lost and it finds its way home across miles of country by exercising what we call instinct. We must not deceive ourselves by the words we make. Probably the spider, the ant, the beaver, the bee, and the dog do not *reason* as we people do; but if intelligence consists in the individual's ability to profit by his own experience, as well as the racial experience which constitutes instinct, we cannot deny intelligent behaviour even to what we call the lowest creatures in the scale of animal life.

Wonderful Sense of Direction

A crocodile emerging from its egg will find its way towards a stream; a frog taken away from water will go straight back to the nearest water on being set free. A young eel, unable to develop in the sea, leaves the tidal river and goes far up the inland waters; and when the time comes it returns to the sea to lay its eggs. The life-history of the eel is, indeed, one of the most fascinating stories in the whole of natural history. Only recently were biologists able to fix with certainty the Atlantic spawning grounds of the eel.

The little shellfish called a limpet has no eyes, but every limpet knows its spot on a rock. It moves about at high tide and feeds, and it finds its way back infallibly to its dwelling-place. The nightingale born in an English thicket flies to Africa; it goes to the right place at the right time, moved by some innermost understanding. It is not driven by hunger, for if it stayed till hunger came it would arrive too late. A homing pigeon will bring a general his dispatches; one was known to fly all the way from Rome back to its loft in an English town. It took a month to complete the journey, flew 1,000 miles, and crossed a range of mountains and 20 miles of sea guided by its instinct.

A horse will take a lost man home on a dark night; a horse has taken its dead driver home through the busy streets of a great city. A cat, taken 100 miles in a box, will find its way back to the old fireside. A St. Bernard dog in the Alps will find a traveller buried in the snow, dig him out, and go for

SPIDER AND ITS GOSSAMER WEB
Sheer mechanical efficiency such as that of the spider is really instinctive, though this is sometimes hard to believe. Every thread of this web, when completed, will have its function, and there is no more efficient way of doing the job than that which the spider has evolved on its own.

help. There was in Pelorus Sound, New Zealand, for 20 years a dolphin, protected by the government, that piloted ships through this dangerous strait. As a ship approached, Pelorus Jack would dart from his hiding-place and swim ahead, going steadily until he reached French Pass, where he disappeared. He never went beyond, but up to that point no human pilot was ever more reliable than he. There are cormorants that catch fish for us, cheetahs that catch deer, captive elephants that catch and help to tame wild elephants. They will do these things for their employers as unfailingly as workmen.

There was a frog that answered to its name when called by Professor Romanes. There were fishes that would answer a bell rung by Sir Joseph Banks. There was a tortoise in Gilbert White's village of Selborne in Hampshire which would hobble every morning to meet the old lady who fed it. A crocodile has been known to have an affection for a cat. A snake, so it is recorded, has pined on being separated from its owner, and wriggled with delight when he returned. Friendships between horses and dogs are quite common.

Everywhere the wisdom of life is manifest in the animal kingdom, and the student of evolution finds himself confronted with facts such as those

F. G. Korth

BEAVER, FIRST-CLASS ENGINEER

As an example of an animal whose efficiency can rival if not exceed that of Man, consider the beaver. The one above is helping to make a dam, which will create a little lake in which several families will build their lodge. The beavers have felled the trees and hauled the logs ; and mud, stones and grass will be piled on by the animals to weight the dam down if the water is deep.

concerning South African buffaloes in Matabeleland. They used to feed by day, now they come out by night. They have changed their habits since plague destroyed nearly the whole of their race, and it is not impossible that these dumb creatures may have discovered that the tsetse fly which carries the plague germ does not fly by night. There would be nothing incredible in that discovery. Animals act consistently as if they knew.

Could anything be more wonderful than the preciseness of the knowledge of the fairy-fly (*Mymaridae*), the tiniest of insects, sometimes so small that five can walk abreast through a pinhole! The mother finds a larger insect, and lays her eggs in its body *exactly when and exactly where the egg of the larger insect is forming*. The larger egg is formed with the fairy-fly's egg inside it, and the fairy-fly's egg produces a grub, which lives by eating the larger egg and then emerges, a complete, winged, little insect.

But the examples are beyond all counting. We find them in thousands among horses and dogs. Who has not heard of the bear that will stir the water to bring a piece of bread towards him, or deftly scoop a fish out of the water with his paw? Who put into the head of the eagle the idea of driving

Fox

BLIND—BUT HE IS SAFE WITH HIS DOG

While the instinctive behaviour of animals is remarkable, the things creatures will do with training are more marvellous still. Here you see a ' guide dog,' trained successfully to lead a blind man across the street, knowing when and where and how to cross in safety. Few animals display such high intelligence as this.

DOG AND BIRD HAVE THEIR WITS ABOUT THEM

Have you ever come across in your garden a stone surrounded by shattered snail-shells ? The upper photograph here shows how they came to be there, for the song-thrush is clever enough to use a stone as an ' anvil ' on which to hammer the snails to bits, so as to get at and gobble up the soft body inside each shell. Among dogs, of course, we are accustomed to clever tricks, but even so the skill with which the sheep-dog (lower) collects the sheep and eventually herds them into a narrow pen shows him to be an animal possessing a high degree of intelligence.

out one deer from a herd and frightening it towards a precipice? Who will deny the power of a sort of reasoning to the crow that fetched a companion to help to battle with a dog for its dinner-bone?

We see everywhere a deliberate preparation for the morrow. It illustrates, better than words, the theory of the " survival of the fittest." The butcher-bird impales his prey on thorns, and leaves it till he wants it. Squirrels and jays and woodpeckers, like rats and mice and men, lay up stores for the future. Even the rattlesnakes gather into companies for warmth in the long winter sleep, and separate when the need for food comes. They know there is warmth and comfort in company, but that too many rattlesnakes together will impoverish food supplies when they awake. They mobilize at the right time for the right purpose, on the principle which drives many groups in the animal world to defend their own herds against animals that hunt in packs as a matter of course.

Dorien Leigh

ANKARA IS TURKEY'S CAPITAL IN ASIA MINOR
In the heart of the plains of Asia Minor, Kemal Ataturk, Dictator-President of Turkey from 1923 to 1938, built a new capital, called Ankara, to replace Istanbul (Constantinople). Before the town became the capital on October 13, 1923, it was generally known as Angora. Yenishehr (above), the modern quarter of the city, was designed by German architects.

If we could speak of affection in the animal kingdom we should hardly expect to find it in wasps and crocodiles; yet allied to their instinct is something touched with the glow of emotion. The crocodile buries its eggs in the hot sand, and when the young cry out at hatching-time it scrapes the sand away and liberates its new-born family. The solitary wasp, as though deliberately providing for the future of the race, stores up before it dies food for the unborn that it will never see.

A chapter of natural history tells of the gallantry of the stickleback and the devotion of the whale in defence of their young. There is the wonder of the emperor penguins and their eggs; they stand for weeks during the long Antarctic night with the egg between their feet, keeping it warm; and the parents share the patient task between them.

Many students of animal behaviour seek to account for some such instances as these on purely mechanical or even chemical grounds. In the lower organisms especially, they find the explanation in what are called various " tropisms," or the tendency of living matter to respond definitely to such external stimuli as light, heat, touch, and the like. Thus it is they explain the behaviour of the moth when it flies to certain death in the candle's flame as a reponse to the stimulus of light.

Animals. CRIES OF. Babies " crow," children chatter, grown-ups talk. What do animals do?

Here is a list of some of the more important and generally recognized animal cries.

Bees hum or drone	Lambs baa or bleat
Bitterns boom	Lions roar
Bulls bellow	Mice squeak
Cats mew and purr	Monkeys chatter or gibber
Cattle low	Mosquitoes " ping "
Cocks crow	Nightingales warble
Cows moo	Owls hoot or screech
Dogs bark	Parrots screech
Donkeys bray	Peacocks scream
Doves coo	Pigs grunt or squeal
Ducks quack	Ravens croak
Eagles scream	Rooks caw
Elephants trumpet	Sheep bleat
Flies buzz	Snakes hiss
Frogs croak	Sparrows chirp
Geese cackle	Swallows twitter
Hens cluck	Tigers growl
Horses neigh or whinny	Turkeys gobble
Hyenas laugh	Wolves howl

Ankara, (ANGORA), TURKEY. Planned as the capital of the new Turkey on the most modern lines, the new part of Ankara is utterly unlike the old Oriental quarter. The latter is notorious for its ill-built houses and narrow streets, its almost total lack of the amenities of civilization.

It was in 1923 that Kemal Ataturk, the "strong man " of Turkey after the First World War, decided to move his Republican Government from Istanbul (Constantinople) to Ankara, then a sleepy provincial town in the barren plains of Asia Minor. Kemal chose it as the stronghold of the Turkish Nationalists largely because of its inaccessibility to his enemies. The new city, set beneath the citadel of old Angora, is an astonishing sight in

Dorien Leigh

ANKARA'S FINE STREETS AND BUILDINGS

Many of the houses, and blocks of government offices, in Turkey's capital are typically European in design. The Sergieva building (above) is used for exhibitions. Traffic in this broad street is controlled by a policeman protected by an awning from the weather. Traffic in Turkey keeps to the right of the road, not to the left as in Great Britain.

this unusual environment, and the modernity of the many embassies, government buildings and villas betrays the hand of the German architects who assisted in their construction. There are many fine boulevards and parks. The older part of Ankara is interesting historically, with remains of Roman and Byzantine occupation. In 1402 the town saw the defeat of the Turks by the conquering Tartar hosts.

Ankara stands on the river of the same name, and is an important station in the centre of the Anatolian railway system, being connected directly with Istanbul (215 miles away) and other cities. Air transport has still further reduced its original remoteness. Agriculture, especially the breeding of the famous Angora goats, has long flourished in the district. The population in 1945 was over 227,500.

Anne, QUEEN OF ENGLAND (1665–1714). What pictures of stately, dignified, quick-witted womanhood the word "Queen" brings to mind! Unfortunately Anne, who was the last of the Stuart rulers of England, falls far short of our pictured ideal.

She was so dull, slow and obstinate that it has been said that there was "only one person in the kingdom more stupid than she—and that was her husband, Prince George of Denmark." Queen Anne was, however, pious and good-hearted; she served the state to the best of her ability and undoubtedly deserves the title of "Good Queen Anne." But she had strong prejudices and was easily influenced by her friends. John Churchill, who rose to be Duke of Marlborough and commanded the English armies at Blenheim and on many another glorious field, and his beautiful but imperious wife, Sarah Jennings, were foremost among Anne's intimate advisers during the first years of her reign.

Anne was the daughter of James II, against whom she supported William of Orange when he came to the throne of England as a result of the

Langfier

QUEEN ANNE AND HOUSES OF HER TIME

Some of the buildings and furniture which have come down to us from Queen Anne's reign (1702–14) are so distinctive in design that they have been named after her. Typical examples of the architecture of her time are the houses (above) in Queen Anne's Gate, London, with a statue of the Queen on the left. Studied proportion gives these houses, with their deep sash windows, grace and beauty.

ANNE, QUEEN OF ENGLAND 1702-1714
One of the most perfect and lifelike of the wax effigies of
English kings and queens preserved in Westminster Abbey
is that of Queen Anne (above). It is clothed in robes
which the queen actually wore. The jewels are artificial.

" Glorious Revolution " of 1688. She succeeded
her brother-in-law William in 1702. Her reign
(1702-1714) was marked by the War of the Spanish
Succession, which brought an important increase
in British sea-power, by the Parliamentary union
of England and Scotland (1707), and by the activities of such brilliant writers as Addison, Pope,
Dryden, Swift, Steele and Defoe. A most vivid
picture of life in Queen Anne's time is given in
Thackeray's famous novel entitled Henry Esmond.

Anne was a devout Protestant, while her exiled
father and his son the Pretender were Catholics.
Just before her accession a law was passed providing
that the crown of England, after her death without
direct heirs, should pass to the nearest Protestant
branch of the Stuart family. It was this Act of
Settlement which brought King George I of the
Hanoverian line to the British throne in 1714.

Various suggestions have been offered as to
why we say " Queen Anne is dead " when any-
body tells us a piece of stale news. It has been
explained as follows. Formerly barristers wore
parti-coloured robes, but for a year after the death
of a monarch they wore black. For some reason
or other they did not go back to their parti-coloured
robes a year after the death of Queen Anne;
indeed, they are still in mourning for that sovereign!
No doubt many people asked why the black robes
continued to be worn, and the reply would always
be " Queen Anne is dead."

Anning, MARY (1799-1847). One morning
in 1811 twelve-year-old Mary Anning scanned
the cliffs at Lyme Regis, Dorset, in search of the
fossils by the sale of which she had lived for a year
since her father's death. Her curiosity was aroused
by some bones protruding from the rock; with her
geologist's hammer she traced the extent of the
fossilized beast, and within a few days, with the aid
of hired diggers, she had uncovered the skeleton.
This fearsome object, 30 feet long, with enormous
jaws and eyes as big as saucers, was the first specimen of that great fish-like reptile, the *Ichthyosaurus*.

The girl had often been taken by her father in
search of fossils, shells or other objects that might
find a sale, and from him she must have acquired
a keen interest in such studies, for it was not by luck
alone that she was enabled to make her discovery.

Mary Anning became famous. While for years
eminent scientists discussed the nature of the animal
she received hosts of visitors, distinguished in the
realms of both science and society. In great pain
from cancer, which ultimately proved fatal, she
resorted to opium, and was consequently regarded
as a drug addict. But the scientists were truly grateful for her work, and she was ultimately awarded
a Government grant.

Her discoveries did not end with the first
Ichthyosaurus; she found other specimens of that
creature, as well as the remains of the first *Plesio-
saurus* and of the first *Pterodactyl* found in England.
Her name was soon forgotten—her only memorials
some of her finds of skeletons, now in the Natural
History Museum, South Kensington, London.

Natural History Museum
MARY ANNING, GEOLOGIST
Few girls have achieved fame in such an original way as Mary
Anning, of Lyme Regis, Dorset. In 1811, when only 12
years old, she discovered there the first fossil Ichthyosaurus
and, later, fossil remains of other extinct creatures.

The MARVELS HIDDEN in AN ANT-HILL

The more we study the ways of the ants, the more we are amazed by the quality of their achievements. They are the most advanced of the social insects, and the inexorable law of their life is : Work or perish.

Ant. So wonderful is the way in which ants live together in colonies, so intelligent seem their methods of building their homes, obtaining food, dividing their labours, and conducting their wars, that some observers have thought that these insects actually are able to reason. Lord Avebury (Sir John Lubbock), a great scientist who spent many years studying the ants, said: " It is difficult to altogether deny them the gift of reason. Their mental powers differ from those of men not so much in kind as in degree."

There are more than 6,000 species of these amazing little insects, of which 49 are found in Great Britain. The most common are the *red ants* and *black ants* which you so often see—slender-waisted little creatures with six legs, and two long slender antennae which are constantly waving to and fro as the ants move about. Their bodies are divided into three very distinct regions: head, thorax and abdomen. The head bears the antennae, or feelers, by which the ant recognizes and communicates with other ants, and finds its food. It also bears powerful jaws for biting and carrying objects, and eyes sufficiently developed to recognize light and darkness, and to find its way about, although some ants are blind. Some ants also have stings from which they eject a powerful poison called formic acid.

How an Ant Colony Starts

All ants are social insects, that is, they live together in large groups—sometimes hundreds of thousands—like the honey bees. These communities are much like little nations, with their queens, their winged males and females, and their wingless workers and nurses. In some colonies the workers are divided into large and small workers and soldiers. The soldiers have large heads and more powerful jaws, and their task in life is to protect the colony against its foes.

An ant colony is commenced by a single female; she leaves the parent community at the swarming time to meet a male, winged like herself, from some other nest; after mating, she returns to earth and lays her eggs, which hatch into tiny maggots or larvae. She feeds the young larvae from her own body until they spin their cocoons and pass into the *pupa* stage, from which they emerge after several weeks. These worker ants now take over the duties of the colony and wait on the queen, so that she can spend all her time in egg-laying. Since this first brood has been very poorly fed, the ants comprising it are smaller

than those of the later broods, which are abundantly fed and tended by their small elder brothers and sisters. If you watch an ant-nest carefully you can often see the workers carrying the tiny maggot-like larvae and the cocoons in which are the pupae out into the sun to hasten their growth, and then back to the underground chambers.

After the queen ant has produced a large number of workers, she at last lays eggs which hatch into a brood of males and females with wings. These are tended and fed by the workers, until they are ready for the marriage flight some sultry day.

After the wedding flight, the females enter the ground to make new nests and form new colonies, except those who are captured by the workers and dragged back to their old homes to replenish the

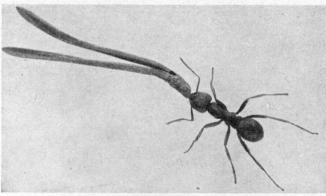

H. Bastin; A. E. Smith

ANTS AT WORK AND AT WAR

For its size the ant is extraordinarily strong, as you can see from this one (top) carrying a pine-needle much larger than itself. When two of these creatures are matched together, as in the lower photograph, there is a tremendous struggle, although often the combatants appear little damaged at the finish of the encounter.

parent colony. Having no more use for their wings, the females pluck them off, and spend the remainder of their life—which in the case of a queen may be as long as 15 years—underground.

But the unfortunate winged males have no such long life ahead of them. Their work is done, and the industrious workers have no more use for them. They are not allowed to return to the parent colony, from which they emerged for their few brief hours of glory, and soon fall a prey to birds or perish in some other way. The law of ant life is inexorable: Work or perish. In some colonies it is the custom to kill the old members as soon as they become too feeble to be useful.

Snug Dormitories and Nurseries

For their nests, or formicaries, as they are called, many kinds of ants build marvellously complicated structures. Most nests are many-storeyed labyrinths of galleries and chambers, extending for several feet or even yards underground. The mound-building ants, such as the big wood-ants common in Britain, rear great structures sometimes three feet high and 12 feet in diameter. Other ants are carpenters, cutting long tunnels and galleries in dead trees, while some pile up great heaps of leaves and twigs to build their homes. Some of the chambers in these colonies are used for sleeping during the winter, others as nurseries for the larvae, and as store rooms for food and stables for their " cows "— the wonderful little aphids. (*See* Aphis).

Ants eat many kinds of animal and vegetable food, but they like nothing better than the " honey-dew " produced by the aphids. Since the aphids are soft, defenceless little creatures, an easy prey for other insects, the shrewd ants take various measures to protect them. Sometimes they carry the aphids into their colonies and feed them there on the food they like best. More often the ants guard small groups of the aphids, protecting them from their foes, carrying them from withered plants to fresh vigorous plants, and from one sort of plant to another kind more favourable for " honey-making."

Their Stores of Grain and Honey

Some American species of ants form " mushroom gardens " in their chambers below the ground, cutting and carrying to these special quarters large quantities of leaves. These leaves soon become a fertile field for a mould or fungus which the ants then make their only food. Others collect large stores of grains. Some species gather nectar from flowers, which is preserved in a remarkable fashion ; some of the workers remain within the nest, suspended by their feet from the roof of the chamber, while other workers forage for nectar and pour it into the mouths of these living " honey-pots." From time to time the " nurse " workers draw out from them the supplies to feed the young.

In some hot countries, like the central parts of Africa, South America and Southern Asia, there are species of ants which are flesh-eating, which capture live creatures for food. In West Africa these ants are called *driver ants*. Such ants are very much feared, for they hunt in long columns of millions of individuals and are as savage as tigers. The largest and fiercest animals are helpless before them, and are driven frantic by the millions of bites unless they can flee to water and drown their tormentors. Animals confined in pens will be killed and

PARASOL ANTS ON THE MARCH
These parasol ants, found in South America, are carrying fragments of leaves to their underground ' mushroom gardens,' where the leaves will be worked into a pulp to grow the mould or fungus on which the ants feed. Several other species of leaf-cutting ants of similar habits are found in North and South America.

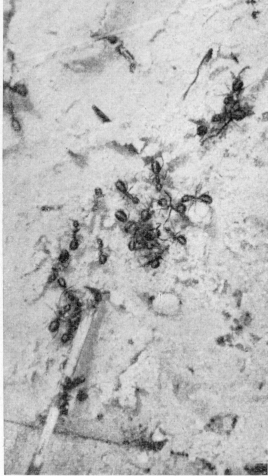

Pathé Pictures, Ltd.

These four photographs are part of a cinematograph film which depicted a war between two ant cities. A single scout (top left) has encountered a patrol from the rival city. Fierce fighting (top right) has broken out, and casualties are already littering the field of combat. The invaders make an attack on the queen (lower left) of the city, the queen being the large ant in the centre. The defenders must have been vanquished, because (lower right) pieces of the city are being carried away by the victors. Battles are frequent when large nests are close together.

ANT

devoured in a few hours. In Africa, when a swarm is seen approaching, the people leave their houses temporarily and let the ants clear out any insects they may find there, as well as rats and mice.

The so-called " white ants," which are so much dreaded in hot countries for their ravages, are not true ants and are rarely white, and should be called by their proper name, *termites*. They build enormous domed mud dwellings, sometimes 25 feet high, as described in our story of the Termites.

Some kinds of ants, even common English species, actually keep slaves. They go out in great armies on expeditions against smaller kinds of ants, drive them out of their nests, and carry off their eggs and larvae and pupae to their own nests, as well as their stores of food. The captured eggs, larvae and pupae are carefully tended, and when

A. B. Beattie

WOOD-ANTS' TEEMING CASTLE
From the outside, the nest of a community of wood-ants appears to be just a rough pile of pine needles and twigs. These nests may be four feet above ground and reach a similar distance below the surface. Hidden away is an intricate system of galleries and chambers.

they develop into ants they are made to work for their captors. Some of the robber-ant communities do no work at all for themselves and live wholly on the food captured from other colonies and collected by their slaves. They thus become so helpless that if their slaves are taken away they perish miserably. In a robber-ant community the soldiers are of two sorts, large and small. On the march the small soldiers are drawn up in a long narrow column, while some of the large soldiers appear to act as scouts and others as officers.

Besides these creatures deliberately enslaved by the ants, there are others, found in many ant-nests, which live there of their own free will and which are termed " ant-guests." These are for the most part beetles, though some are degenerate forms of other types of insects. Some pass their whole lives in the ants' nests, others only a part of it; some actually live on the ants, eating them or their young and surviving only because they are clever enough to keep out of the ants' way ; others are valued by the ants for the honey-dew they excrete, which the ants greedily devour, and in exchange for which they get food; some live by stealing food from the ants, intercepting it actually as one worker gives it to another! These ant-guests have been much studied, but the why and the how of their behaviour is still a problem for entomologists.

A wonderful example of such a guest is provided by the Large Blue butterfly and related species. The caterpillar of this insect, which is found in many parts of the world, including the British Isles, spends the greater part of its life (six months or more) in the nest of a species of ant, being tended by the ants and being carefully looked after by them. Like the aphids, these caterpillars provide the ants with honey-dew—which comes from their bodies when the ants stroke them. In return for this food, the ants allow the caterpillars to feed on the aphids in the nest.

Any one who wishes to study the fascinating habits of ants may do so with little trouble at home. Take a round jar made of clear glass, fill it three-quarters full of moist earth gathered from a field or garden. Make a cylinder of thick dark paper which will fit snugly round the outside of the jar to the height of the earth inside and will slide easily up and down. Next find an ant colony and capture as many ants as possible, taking care not to injure them. Dig out their nest and get their grubs and cocoons, and, if possible, a queen ant, easily recognized by her greater size.

Carry your prisoners home and put them in the jar with the earth ; the top should be covered with paper, in which small holes have been pricked with a pin to let in the air. If the jar is left undisturbed, then the ants will at once start building a new home, tunnelling particularly along the sides of the jar. From time to time food should be placed in the jar—a little sugar, small bits of cooked meat, dead flies, etc.—and a few drops of water should be sprinkled over the earth occasionally. After a week or so, draw off the cylinder; you will see a network of tunnels, alongside the glass, through which ants are hurrying in orderly fashion about their work.

Ants (*Formicidae*) belong to the order *Hymenoptera*, which also includes the bees and the wasps. The common black ant of our gardens is *Acanthomyops nigra;* the red ant, which builds the ant-hills in the woods, is *Formica rufa* ; also common in woods is the small black negro ant, *Formica fusca.*

The FROZEN LAN...

*At the southernmost tip of the u...
and lashed by blizzards. Th...
below zero, none but the h...*

Antarctica. At the beginnin...
20th century maps of the world show...
blank around the South Pole. Nation...
territory elsewhere, had neglected this...
it appeared to promise nothing of an...
Exploration seemed next to impossib...
gales buffeted any ship that approa...
bound shores of Antarctica ; nearer...
made difficult by vast fields of drif...

The earliest discoveries were ma...
ning of the 19th century aroun...
60° W. William Smith in 1819...
Shetland Islands. A year later F...
R.N., with Smith as pilot, sigh...
the northern part of the Graha...
Apart from the expeditions of S...
of the total number of expec...
Antarctic since 1820 there...
Norwegian, 24 American, 19...
three Argentine, and two...
countries, for example Jap...
expeditions to the region.

The known coast of Ant...
laden rampart of capes...
rocky rim the land slopes...
that surrounds the Sout...
tion of this plateau is...
above sea-level. On th...
however, the surface...
breaking the contour...
twice as large as th...
taken out of the c...
nent. This forms the...
Sea. Another bite t...
South America for...
Weddell Sea.

Great mountain...
with peaks e x c...
15,000 feet guar...
terior, while the...
volcanoes on...
—Erebus, over...
and Terror—...
cons pointing...
A great ic...
nearly all...
Antarctica...
Polar pla...
probably...
and 8,00...
the area...
about...
miles—...
the Un...
of Cana...
fossilized tre...
plants and leaves have...
been discovered within...
180 miles of the Pole,
showing that the climate
of the continent was

were in...
The huge size o...
fact that Cape Horn (nea...
statute miles from tn...

Safely anchored on the edge of the vast ice-sheets of the
Antarctic, the exploring ship Terra Nova looks small
enough compared with the great iceberg in the foreground
of this photograph. From the berg long, slender icicles
hang down, reminding us that even in these regions of

H. G. Ponting, British Antarctic Expedition, 1910-13; copyright, Paul Popper

perpetual cold, ice may melt and freeze again as it flows.
The ship, equipped for sail as well as for steam, is typical of
those whose names—Erebus, Terror, Endurance, Discovery
—figure as prominently in the epic story of Antarctic exploration as do those of the gallant men who manned them.

169

3 S I

zone, Admiral Byrd recorded a temperature of 80° F. below zero. Although this does not break the Arctic record of —93° (125 degrees of frost), established in February 1892 at Verkhoyansk, Siberia, the winter average throughout Antarctica is lower than that in any part of the Arctic zone.

Since the moisture of the region is kept perpetually frozen, rain is unknown except on the more northern seaboards, and even the snowfall is light. High winds prevent accurate measure of the snowfall; but when a food depot buried by Scott in 1903 was visited six years later it was covered by 8 feet 2 inches of snow. This is equivalent to about 7½ inches of rainfall a year. The winds increase the bitterness of the climate. Sir Douglas Mawson, the Australian explorer, said that during 1912 in Adélie Land the average wind velocity was 50 miles an hour. Winds of tremendous violence— over 100 miles an hour—are common.

A few specimens of flowering plants have been found in Graham Land, but the only vegetation in Antarctica proper consists of algae, mosses and lichens. The latter have been seen as far south as the Thorne glacier. The only form of life so far discovered at any great distance from the sea are mites, microscopic rotifers, and a few tiny wingless insects such as springtails (" snow-fleas "). They are found in sunny pools or moss in midsummer. During the rest of the year they lie dormant.

The ocean around Antarctica, however, teems with life, and water-feeding birds and mammals swarm on the shores. At the bottom of the scale are the microscopic plants called diatoms that exist in the sea in such quantities that they stain the waters yellow and colour the icebergs with brownish streaks. Upon the diatoms and other tiny organisms feed great schools of shrimp-like creatures, the whole mass of this living food, called plankton, forming the main food supply of fishes.

Plankton is also the principal food of the baleen, or " whalebone," whales. The toothed whales of the region, such as the sperm whale, the bottle-nose and the porpoise, feed upon squid and fish ; while the large dolphin called the " killer whale " eats seals and penguins. The whaling industry has taken catches worth over £4,000,000 from Antarctic waters in a single year.

Antarctic seals lack the fur undercoat which makes commercial sealskin. The commonest seal is called the crab-eater. These seals float about on ice floes and dive for their food. The fish-eating Weddell seal is next in numbers; its hide yields a fair leather, and explorers value its meat and oil. This seal cuts holes through the ice in winter, to crawl out on the surface to sleep. The seven-foot Ross seal is seen about Graham Land and the Weddell Sea. Huge sea elephants breed on the sub-Antarctic islands, while the dangerous sea leopard is common on the northernmost parts of the continent.

As there are no land animals proper such as Polar bears or men, the habits of seals are entirely different from those in the Arctic. In the south a seal will climb out on to an ice floe or the shore and sleep for days. If woken up by an explorer and frightened, the seal will go farther from the water where he only knows of danger from killer whales. In the Arctic a seal sleeps for not more than 30 seconds at a time, then he puts his head up to look for danger from Polar bears or men; if he is suspicious he returns immediately to the water where he is comparatively safe.

The most interesting birds in the region are the penguins. Most of the penguin species rear their

Paul Popper

VOLCANIC FIRE AMIDST ANTARCTIC ICE

On Ross Island, off South Victoria Land in Antarctica, the explorer sees the strange spectacle of a volcano—Mt. Erebus—sending up clouds of smoke from its internal fires above a land of ice and snow. Mt. Erebus was discovered by Captain James Ross in 1841, and he named it after one of the two ships of his expedition. It is the most southerly active volcano in the world.

Paul Popper

ANTARCTIC SEALS AT REST ON FLOATING ICE

After the seals called crab-eaters, Weddell seals (above) are the most numerous in Antarctica. They are sometimes hunted by explorers for their meat and oil. Principal food of the Weddell seals is fish, and while they are in the water feeding they themselves are often preyed upon by the ferocious killer whales, actually large dolphins, reaching a length of 20 feet.

young during the short Antarctic summer; but the hardy emperor penguins defiantly raise their chicks in the winter. The albatross ranges the southern seas, and occupies islands north of the continent for its breeding season. Five species of petrel have been noted—the fulmar, the Antarctic, the giant, the snowy, and Wilson's stormy petrel. Skua gulls are abundant, as are also shags.

Why should men risk their lives to explore these regions ? The reason is that they are seeking answers to scientific questions. Studies of the Antarctic ice-cap may help to explain the many "ice ages" which other parts of the earth experienced in the past. Another question is whether the ice-cap is breaking up and melting at the edges faster than it is being restored through snowfall. If so, the oceans of the world will continue to rise. If the entire ice-cap should melt, distant coastal cities would be deep under water. Antarctica may have been linked to other continents in the past, and scientists would like to learn if it served as a " land-bridge " for the passage of animals and plants. Meteors, the earth's magnetism, and cosmic rays, can be studied to great advantage in the Antarctic.

Until recent times governments applied maritime law in governing their citizens who visited Antarctica. Then a desire to regulate whaling led several governments to assert sovereignty over various Antarctic regions. Such claims also would give control over any minerals found. In 1908 British letters-patent named the governor of the Falkland Islands as governor of the Falkland Islands Dependencies, which include South Georgia

(a permanent whaling station), the South Orkney Islands, the South Shetlands and Graham Land.

The Ross Dependency, which includes the Ross Sea and the route to the Pole, was established under the governor of New Zealand in 1923, and the Antarctic Territories were placed under the authority of Australia by an Order in Council of February 7, 1933. This order recognized the French claim to Adélie Land. In 1928 the British waived claims to Bouvet Island in favour of Norway, whose claim to Queen Maud Land was recognized in 1939. The United States declared in 1946 that no claims were made or recognized by them in the Antarctic. In the same year, and again in 1948, Chile and Argentina together disputed the possession by Great Britain of certain territories in the Falkland Islands Dependencies, including Graham Land.

In 1943 the British Government made arrangements to resume scientific and survey work in the Falkland Islands Dependencies as part of a long-term investigation of the land areas which would supplement the oceanographical work carried out over a number of years by the Discovery Committee of the Colonial Office. Two permanent bases were set up in 1944 at Port Lockroy and Deception Island. The following year the expedition was considerably reinforced and a total of six bases in Graham Land are now permanently manned where intensive meteorological investigations are carried out. In 1948 Australia and South Africa set up permanent scientific stations, and France renewed her interest in Adélie Land. (*See* Arctic Regions ; Polar Exploration).

Anteater. A number of different animals are known by this name, the one point they all have in common being their habit of eating ants and other insects. The long flexible tongue, covered with sticky saliva, is protruded among the insects and suddenly withdrawn when a number have collected upon it. One species, the aardvark (*q.v.*), is found only in South Africa. The great anteater of tropical S. America has a large plumelike tail. The spiny anteater of Australia is related to the duck-billed platypus.

Antelope. On the deserts of Central Asia antelopes have been known to attain a speed estimated at 60 miles an hour. Besides being the most beautiful, these widely distributed animals are the fleetest of beasts, excepting the cheetah. They belong, like deer, to a group between cattle and goats. Their long, curved horns, unlike those of the deer family, are ringed and hollow and are not renewed annually.

The different types vary greatly in size, the pygmy antelopes of South Africa being only eight or nine inches in height, while the largest kinds are from five to six feet. Antelopes are found in Europe, Asia and Africa, as well as America.

The common antelope (*Antilope cervicapra*), found in India and Eastern Asia, is about two-and-a-half feet high at the shoulders, with erect diverging horns bent in a spiral form. It is so swift that greyhounds cannot catch it, and it leaps easily a height of 10

ANTEATER ERECT

This curious little creature comes from South America. His strong claws dig out the ants, and the long tongue shoots out beyond his snout and licks them up in an instant.

or 12 feet, while the length of its bound is often 10 or 12 yards. The Chinese antelope is found in the deserts of Central Asia; its flesh is very much prized. The gazelle (*Gazella dorcas*) of North Africa was known to the ancients, its beautiful black eyes being often mentioned by Arabian poets.

In the Alps we find the chamois and in South Africa the eland, the largest of all antelopes. The springbok or springbuck, a species found in Africa, gets its name from the great leaps that it makes. Other members of the antelope family are the gnu, with its curiously curved horns, the reedbuck, the waterbuck, the steinbok, all natives of Africa, and the Indian nilgai.

Peculiar to North America is the Rocky Mountain goat (*Oreamnos americanus*). As a rule it is found in the mountains just above the timberline, in high inaccessible spots where only the boldest hunter can follow. In appearance it is clumsy, but it is remarkably agile and is an expert in climbing rocks and icy steeps. It is probably not a true antelope, but comes in a little group showing resemblance to both antelopes and goats.

Antimony. (Pron. an'-ti-m*o*-ni). For the clear, sharp print of your newspaper you may thank antimony, a metal which expands when it passes from the melted to the solid state. This helps to sharpen the type letters by forcing the alloy into every corner of the mould. It also hardens the lead and tin with which it is mixed, so that thousands of copies

Gambier Bolton

ANTELOPES BROWSING IN THE SOUTH AFRICAN BUSH

Few creatures are as swift as the antelopes, and though those you see here are standing still, their whole expression is one of alertness and they are ready to be off at the slightest alarm. They are sable antelopes, characterized by their strong, sharp horns and dark coats; and they are typical representatives of their group in South Africa. Though some species are rare or almost extinct, the sable antelope survives in numbers as an ornament to the African scene.

of newspaper or book can be printed before the type, or the metal of the stereotype plates, becomes worn. As a hardening agent, antimony is mixed with lead for battery grids, shrapnel bullets, solder, and cable covers ; or with tin and copper to make Babbitt metal for bearings and to make Britannia metal for tableware. (*See* Alloys).

Compounds of antimony enter into many products. Its sulphides are used as paint pigments and in making matches and fireworks. A sulphide, called antimony red, is used in tinting and vulcanizing rubber. Oxides of antimony serve as bases for white enamels. Another of its compounds, known as tartar emetic, is used in medicines and as a mordant in dyeing leather and textiles.

Antimony ore, usually a black sulphide called stibnite, is mined chiefly in China, Mexico, and Bolivia. It is mined also in Germany, Algeria, and the United States. Pure antimony is brittle and silver white. With a specific gravity of 6·70, it is almost as heavy as iron. On Mohs's scale, antimony has a hardness of 3, about the same as copper. Chemical symbol Sb. Atomic number, 51. Valency, 3 and 5. It forms poisonous salts.

Antioch, TURKEY. The name of the famous city of Antioch has been changed by the Turks to Antakiyeh. It lies on the left bank of the River Orontes in the district of Hatay, in Turkey, 20 miles from the Mediterranean, and was handed over to Turkey by Syria in 1939 under the terms of the Franco-Turkish agreement for mutual assistance, Syria then being under French control. It does not even remotely suggest the splendours of ancient Antioch, the " Queen of the East," and at one time one of the greatest cities in the Roman Empire.

The old city was founded about 300 B.C. by one of the generals of Alexander the Great, and became the capital of the Seleucid kings of Syria. It drew great wealth from the caravan trade to India, and grew into a centre of Greek culture. Just beyond its 70-foot walls lay the famous and beautiful grove of Daphne, filled with magnificent temples which attracted pagan pilgrims from all parts of the civilized world of those days.

The proverbially abandoned luxury of Antioch, even after it had passed under Roman rule, attracted the reforming spirit of the Apostles, especially St. Barnabas and St. Paul—and perhaps St. Peter—who are said to have sowed the seed of Christianity which eventually converted half of the 200,000 population. It was here that the name " Christian " was first used (Acts xi, 26). The most famous " saint " of the region was Simeon Stylites, who spent 30 years doing extremely uncomfortable penance on top of a high pillar.

After suffering severely from earthquakes, Antioch was sacked in A.D. 538 by the Persian king Chosroes, and it never recovered its former glory. It was taken from the Seljuk Turks by the Crusaders after a nine months' siege in 1098. For nearly two centuries it remained a Christian principality, then fell again to the Mahomedans in 1268, after great destruction and slaughter. This last blow ended ancient Antioch. Little remains of the old city except a few ruins of the great aqueducts and parts of the walls.

The Antakiyeh of today is a trade centre for tobacco, corn, cotton and silk, grown in the sur-

H. J. Shepstone

ANTIOCH'S MOSQUES AND MINARETS
Little remains of the ancient city of Antioch, which was founded about 300 B.C. and sacked by the Persians in A.D. 538. The modern town, which is called Antakiyeh by the Turks, is a trade centre for the district of Hatay, which was handed over to Turkey by Syria in 1939.

rounding regions, and it exports considerable quantities of liquorice. But the city is shabby and poor in appearance, and still suffers from its ancient foe—earthquakes. Population is about 28,000.

Antiseptics and Asepsis. Both these words are from the Greek. Anti means " against," septic comes from a word meaning " putrefaction." Sepsis means the presence of germs, while asepsis means their absence.

An antiseptic, then, is something which opposes sepsis or putrefaction—*counteracts* the growth of germs. We should be clear right at the start about the distinction between an antiseptic and a disinfectant, though if we use a strong antiseptic it will *destroy* germs, and will then be acting as a disinfectant. But we use a disinfectant to destroy germs outside the body, and most disinfectants would harm the patient if used for internal treatment.

It was because surgeons found out that some antiseptics were too strong, and so damaged the tissues, that the method of asepsis was developed. Instead of using something to hinder or prevent the growth of disease germs which had made their way into a wound (antiseptic treatment), the surgeon and his nurses did everything they could to exclude germs altogether : this is aseptic procedure.

The story covers roughly a century of research and experiment. Along with the story of anaesthesia (*q.v.*), it is one of the great epics of medicine and surgery. In order that you may understand the immensity of the problem which had to be solved, we must say a few words here about bacteria; you can read more about them under their own heading.

Bacteria are minute organisms visible only under the microscope. They are of many shapes and sizes and many thousands can lie in a speck of dust. Associated as they are in our modern minds with the causing of disease and fevers it may seem strange that these minute creatures, many of them standing half-way between the animal and vegetable kingdom, are most helpful and beneficent to mankind. In the presence of moisture and some degree of warmth they attack all matter which is dead or unable to resist their onslaught.

The Age-Old Problem of Decay

So it is they change all matter back into its simple chemical origin ; so it is they change a dead animal body back to its component parts, enabling us to repay our debt to Nature who had given us the loan of the structure, allowing her to use the material again to build other forms of life or other types of matter in the universe. Again, it is to the presence of bacteria in the soil that we owe its power to hold down substances such as nitrogen which are necessary to the growth of certain crops used for food.

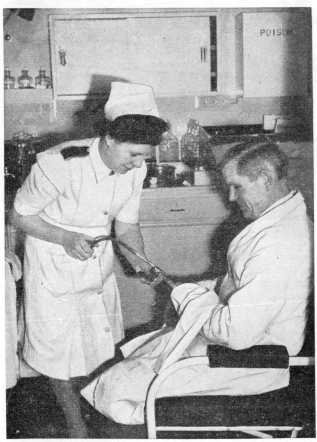

ANTISEPTICS IN MOBILE DRESSING STATION
The nurse is blowing penicillin powder on to a patient's injured finger with a powder spray, or insufflator. The powerful and efficient new drugs which chemotherapy has given us are particularly useful in emergency dressing of wounds and other injuries, as here.

Throughout the ages this problem of decay and its mechanism had occupied the minds and speculations of learned men. Even though with the help of the newly invented microscope they had observed the process, they could not explain it fully.

The problem solved itself from different angles and directions. In civilized countries women had their babies safely enough. But too often after being well for a few days after the birth, the mother fell ill with fever and died. In Vienna, Semmelweiss, the chief of its great maternity hospital, was much perplexed by this. In 1847 he jumped to the cause and its cure. The cause had something to do with dirt—with the coats worn by the nursing and medical staff and their unwashed hands ; the cure was great cleanliness of linen and hands on the part of the attendants. Down came the death rate. Indeed, this was a step forward, though a step taken in the dark.

The essential answer was found by the great French scientist Pasteur in 1865 while he was conducting researches into the fermenting of wines and the souring of milk. Micro-organisms were at work, and it was they which wrought the change in the milk and the wine. It was Pasteur who worked out the relation of micro-organisms to disease. Year after year surgery, even without anaesthetics, had been learning new methods, inventing new instruments, but the simplest operation was a menace. The operation might be perfectly done, but in a few days inflammation would set in and the patient, comfortable enough till then, would flare into fever and die.

Lister, a young Edinburgh surgeon, read of the researches of Pasteur. His scientific imagination saw to the heart of the matter. The formation of pus and the onset of fever were due to the invasion of the wounds by microorganisms. He was laughed to scorn by his fellows but he fought on. Everything in his operating theatre was boiled, for most germs are killed by the heat of boiling. White gowns which had been baked had to be worn by all present at the operation. A solution of carbolic acid, an antiseptic, was sprayed over everything. And even after serious operations patients made a perfect recovery. The reign of sepsis in surgery was over. Asepsis and antisepsis had come into their own.

Sunlight a Means of Germ Control

Quite often it has turned out that in using remedies or applying treatments we have copied Nature, or have made it easier for her to work her own wonders. Thus, sunlight is one of Nature's own means of germ control, as shown by the death of the tubercle bacillus in sunshine ; modern medicine uses the same principle when ultra-violet light treatment is given in cases of skin infection such as boils or acne. (Ultra-violet means " beyond the violet," in the full spectrum of rays comprised in sunlight ; at the opposite end of the band or spectrum are the infra-red —beyond the red—rays. We can see only the rays from red to violet; those beyond at both ends are invisible to the unaided eye.)

It had long been known that exclusion of air keeps matter free from germs; so tinned meat and fruit are preserved. Low temperature is also unfriendly to germs, and so foodstuff is stored in a refrigerator. Boiling and baking are common methods of killing germs. As moisture is one of the principal factors aiding decay, dryness is naturally a preservative state.

Some of the earliest antiseptics were solutions of chemicals. Thus Lister, as we have seen, used carbolic acid in large quantities to spray over everything. But with chemical antiseptics the difficulty is that such substances which kill the germs also tend to injure living tissues. Our great firms of manufacturing chemists are always experimenting with new material, producing under different trade names disinfectants which destroy germs but do not hurt the body of the user. Many of these are now on the market. Among disinfectants known to us all are the safe and gentle boracic acid; and hydrogen peroxide, which kills germs by stealing from them their oxygen content (as a stealer of oxygen it is used to bleach hair, because thus the colouring matter of hair is destroyed). Iodine is a household word ; and so is permanganate of potash (generally used too strong as a gargle—the solution should be a very pale pink at most). Alcohol, carbolic acid, and sulphur are among antiseptics of well-tried value.

Chemicals which kill insects and other small pests —flies, lice, fleas, bugs—write an interesting chapter in the study of antiseptics. Insects carry disease; the common house fly, going from filth to food, carries germs on its feet and by its feeding habits; lice carry typhus; fleas are a medium for plague; the mosquito carries malaria from man to man, acting as host to an intermediate stage of the malarial parasite. A successful method of attack on the mosquito is to spoil its breeding grounds by running oil on to the surface of the tropical waters where the larvae or immature young of the insect float at one stage of their development. This film of oil alters the surface tension of the water, and the larvae cannot maintain their precarious balance.

A universal method, very successful against fleas, was to sprinkle them with very fine powder made from pyrethrum. This is the basis of some well-known insect powders. It kills the insects by blocking the breathing holes which are arranged down their sides. It is not possible to drown a flea or an insect of similar type because under water they can get enough oxygen from the water to maintain life.

The Second World War (1939–45) stimulated research which produced a master remedy against all insect pests. D.D.T. is an abbreviation for the very long chemical name—dichlordiphenyl-trichlorethane. It was perfected because Japan controlled the pyrethrum supplies of the world. This is an outstanding example of how war for some side-reason tends to an increase in scientific knowledge. A Man-

STERILIZING BY BOILING WATER
The boiling of hospital utensils in water is an old method of sterilization. Modern science allows it to be used successfully in even mobile dressing stations like this one. The nurse is seen lifting metal trays from the boiler by means of tongs. Her hands must not touch the trays.

chester firm of dyestuff manufacturers began a search for some chemical which would discourage the attack of moths. These chemists also were looking out for a general insect-killer, and by 1937 they had produced D.D.T. For its full tests it had to wait until wartime. In 1943 typhus broke out in Naples on a large scale; more than a million and a quarter persons were treated with the new preparation, which kills insects by contact; in a few weeks the plague had been brought under control. After this the clothing of Allied troops embarking for the war zones was impregnated with D.D.T. in order to protect the wearers against lice (which carry typhus).

Drugs that Check Bacteria Growth

Allied with this group of subjects is the entrancing chemotherapy. (It derives obviously from the same root as chemistry, and from the word therapy—healing.) Here the main findings belong to our own generation, and here again they were beaten out on the iron anvil of the Second World War. The term chemotherapy covers mainly the sulpha group of drugs, penicillin and streptomycin—substances which, when introduced into the blood-stream of an animal, check the growth of bacteria, each drug according to its kind.

The sulpha group is often described in English medicine by the letters " M & B." These are the initials of the firm of manufacturing chemists which first made them available. But the parent substance was really come upon by Gerhard Domagk, a chemist experimenting with prontosil, an aniline dye, for the big German combine, I. G. Farben, in 1935. Mice, which he was using in his work, were cured of a pneumonia-like condition by the prontosil he injected into them. His small daughter was at that very moment dangerously ill with pneumonia. He treated her with it on the offchance, and like the mice she recovered past all reasonable expectation. So was born the sulpha group. A large number of germs are susceptible to its action. It seems to ally itself with the protective mechanisms of the body, spoiling the chemistry of the germs so that they cannot breed.

Penicillin is the second magic name in this story. The existence of such a substance had long been suspected. There was a broken window in a laboratory of St. Mary's Hospital, London, where Mr. Alexander Fleming was a senior worker. He was watching in a shallow dish a growing culture of staphylococcus, the germ which causes boils, among other things. Something must have fallen on the dish, he argued, for around a certain area the germs for no obvious reason lay dead. Investigation showed that indeed a mould, actually a yeast, had developed. Penicillin, named after the mould family to which it belonged, was very successful in the treatment of wounds and disease during the Second World War. Modern chemistry can now make the vital principle of penicillin at the laboratory bench. Where the sulpha group does not yield results against germs penicillin often does so. Streptomycin, also formed from a mould and another of the several " antibiotics," as they are called, attacks the tubercle bacillus.

Antitoxin. This term means a serum given to a patient in treatment of a toxin; toxin, another name for a poison, is specially applied to the poisons produced in the body by germs which have gained entrance. The word antitoxin is derived from two Greek ones meaning " against " and " arrow-poison." It is a key word in the subject of " immunity," and it is simplest to consider the term in relation to the whole picture. Immunity means resistance of the animal to the attack of bacteria, or to the effects of poison. Immunity may be *natural*. Where a disease is always in evidence some inborn resistance to it comes down through the generations; where it is not in evidence, resistance is poor; thus a Negro does not easily get yellow fever, and a child in an English village would probably get but a mild attack of measles. Reverse the situation and both patients would probably be acutely ill. Pigeons are not poisoned by morphia, and rabbits eat deadly nightshade without harm. This goes to show that different species of animal give quite different reactions to certain substances.

Then there is *acquired* immunity. It may result from recovery from a certain disease, and lasts for a variable time. For example, measles and mumps generally confer lifelong protection on the patient who has recovered from the one attack. Influenza and pneumonia give a very short period of protection. The white cells of the blood, which are among the main protective mechanisms of the body, keep their power to devour the enemy bacteria as long as these bacteria are deluged by the serum of the victor animal. Then some chemical " conditioning," caused by the reaction of the body cells, or by the serum of the blood, seems to leave behind it a " memory " of past success in fighting the invading germs; thus the cells or the serum continue to repel the same invader.

Next we come to *artificial* immunity, which has two sub-divisions, active and passive. Active

immunity to poison is seen in the bee-keeper who does not suffer ill effects from the stings of his bees because his tissues have learnt gradually to accept the acid, which is the toxic principle of the bee sting. Then there is the alcohol addict, who drinks at a gulp, without apparent effect on his behaviour, an amount that would spell disaster to a teetotaller.

White Cells of the Blood Stream

Active immunity is much used in modern medicine. The underlying idea is to kill some bacteria of the particular disease, and then to inject into the animal to be protected the dead bacteria or toxic material retrieved from the bodies of the dead germs. This toxic material, given in graduated doses, excites more and more the animal's own protective mechanism; this mechanism cannot tell whether the germ attack is a real one or a faked one, but the result is the same. The white cells of the blood stream, the main fighting defence force of the animal, increase in numbers. They sharpen their lances and form into attacking squadrons against an enemy that does not as yet exist. Then, when the real germ later on appears, it is met by an unexpected resistance and is repelled with heavy slaughter.

The vaccine against the common cold, antityphoid vaccine, and so on, are examples of this acquired immunity; so is Pasteur's famous treatment against hydrophobia, in which disease the long incubation period allows of the building up of resistance by injection in suitable doses of the poisonous principle itself, before the signs and symptoms of the disease appear. Another example of this method of giving artificial active immunity to a person is vaccination against small-pox; here the patient is given an attack of cow-pox, a mild " cousin " of dreaded small-pox. The modern method of protecting persons against diphtheria by " immunisation " is a further instance.

The Fight Against Diphtheria

Passive immunity is that form of artificial immunity lent to one sick animal by another animal which has recovered from the disease, or has itself been rendered highly immune by increasing doses of the toxin. An outstanding example is the rescue of the diphtheria patient who is making a bad fight by introducing into his veins the serum of a horse which has been caused to acquire this high degree of immunity against the diphtheria toxin. Again, we have the rescue of the patient ill with tetanus or lock-jaw, by using the serum of a horse after this animal has been given resistance to the specific poison of tetanus.

You will have noticed that we said " a high degree of immunity " above. Science has not yet arrived at the stage where a treatment can be guaranteed to cure. Persons are all so very different in make-up, and so the doctor can but try his best with proved remedies. In less serious cases serum treatment is likely to become more useful as time goes on. For example, while measles may cause little concern in the case of a normal strong child, it may be quite another matter for the delicate boy or girl. But a delicate child exposed to the contagion of measles can be given an injection of the serum from a convalescent patient, and may then escape an attack; failing this happy result, the resulting attack will be a mild one.

Ant-lion. This name is especially applied to the young or *larva* of the insect, which itself somewhat resembles a dragonfly, but is smaller. The adult fly lays its eggs on sandy soil, and when the larva hatches it digs into the sand, using its head as a shovel, and forms a funnel-shaped pit, about two inches deep, with steep sides. At the bottom it lies —a short humpbacked creature, with a large head and strong curved jaws, which work from side to side.

With its body buried in the sand, leaving only its curved jaws projecting, it lies motionless until some unwary ant or other small insect falls over the edge of the pit. If the victim seems likely to escape, the ant-lion casts up a shower of sand, and thus hastens the descent of the struggler. The scientific name of the European species is *Myrmeleon formicarius*.

H. Bastin

Antrim. The Irish county of Antrim (whose capital town bears the same name) is situated at the extreme north-east corner of the island, and may be considered the keystone of Northern Ireland. In it are the metropolis of Belfast (*q.v.*) and the broad expanse of Lough Neagh, which is the largest lake in the British Isles (150 square miles). It is the centre of the famous Irish linen industry. Antrim town (pop. 2,000) has ancient relics, and at Lisburn there is a broadcasting station.

County Antrim is hard to beat for beauty. North from historic Carrickfergus runs the magnificent Coast Road, flanked on one side by the Nine Glens and on the other by the cliffs and the Irish Sea. On the northern coast of the county are the basalt rocks called the Giant's Causeway (*q.v.*); Portrush, famed for its golf-links; and Dunluce Castle, scene of thrilling episodes in Irish history.

Between Antrim and the neighbouring county of Londonderry is the River Bann; the Lagan, on

H. Main

ANT-LION
Larva of a fly-like insect, the ant-lion (left) lurks in a burrow at the bottom of a shelving pit (above), dug by itself.

which Belfast stands, forms the boundary with County Down in the south. Most of the inhabitants, apart from those engaged in textile and other manufactures, grow potatoes, flax and cereals. The population, excluding Belfast, is 197,000, and the area is 1,176 square miles.

Antwerp, BELGIUM. Besides being one of the greatest ports in Europe, Antwerp, on account of its situation, has long played an important part in history. Situated 55 miles from the open sea, on the right bank of the River Scheldt, which is here 2,200 feet wide, Antwerp possesses one of the finest harbours in the world, through which passes a huge volume of imports and exports. Besides its commerce Antwerp is important for its diamond-cutting, sugar-refining, brewing and distilling, and its extensive manufacture of textiles.

The city was founded some time in the 8th century and by the middle of the 16th century Antwerp had become one of the most prosperous cities in Europe and the world's chief money-market. But in 1576 it was pillaged and burned for three days during the "Spanish Fury," because it had taken part in the revolt against Spain, which then ruled the Netherlands. The city suffered a further disaster in 1585, when the Duke of Parma captured it and ordered all Protestants to leave.

Not until the days of Napoleon did it start again on the upward road, when it fell into the hands of France. Napoleon began the improvement of its harbour to make Antwerp a rival to London and a "pistol held at the heart of England." With this impetus Antwerp continued to grow even after the downfall of Napoleon's empire in 1814. Its commerce received another set-back in 1830 when Belgium separated from Holland, for the latter country controlled both banks of the lower Scheldt and imposed heavy tolls on all vessels ascending or descending the river. This obstacle was not removed until 1863.

Antwerp suffered another heavy blow at the opening of the First World War in

Dixon-Scott

ANTRIM VILLAGE BETWEEN SEA AND HILLS
Here we have a typical Northern Ireland village, with its one street of whitewashed houses, sheltered by the misty mountains behind. It is the village of Waterfoot, on the Glenariff river, at the head of Red Bay. In this part of the county are the 'Nine Glens of Antrim,' of which Glenariff is the most beautiful. Its Gaelic name means Arable Glen.

1914. Its fortifications had been strengthened after the Franco-Prussian War of 1870–71, but it took the Germans only 10 days to drive out the Belgian army. On October 8, 1914, the invaders occupied the town, until their withdrawal from Belgium in 1918. In the Second World War the Germans seized the port in May 1940 and later in that year used it to concentrate barges intended for the invasion of England. It was liberated by British troops in September 1944, and the port was reopened to shipping by the end of November. During the winter of 1944–45 the Germans bombarded it heavily with flying-bombs and rockets, and about half the houses in the city were destroyed.

Wide World; Belgian Rlys.

ANTWERP'S SOARING TOWERS AND SPIRES

In the great port of Antwerp, ancient and modern, American and medieval, are often cheek by jowl. The top photograph shows the first skyscraper ever built in Antwerp ; its 24 storeys tower above the Meir, one of Antwerp's oldest streets. Above is the magnificent cathedral of Notre Dame, with the Scheldt in the background.

until 1867—over three centuries. It was the finest printing house in the world. One of the most famous works produced by the Plantin Press was a Bible in several languages that filled eight volumes. The types, presses and other apparatus of this old printer are still preserved. The population of the city of Antwerp is about 254,000 and that of the province to which the city gives its name is 1,250,000.

Ape. The tailless semi-erect apes—the chimpanzee, orang-utan, gorilla and gibbon—which inhabit tropical Asia and Africa, are the animals that most closely resemble Man.

Some of them show many traces of an almost man-like intelligence ; but a popular error should be corrected—their progress is not towards humanity, but towards a more perfect ape-like character. Here it may be stated that the theory of evolution does not teach that any existing ape is in the direct line of Man's ancestry, but that the simian (or monkey) line and the human line branch off from a line of remote ancestors common to both. This diversion took place many long ages ago.

In spite of all these many disasters there still stand in Antwerp some of the old buildings. The most famous is the cathedral of Notre Dame, which was started in the 14th century. With its lofty tower it is the most conspicuous building in the city, and in it are three of Rubens' great paintings, The Descent from the Cross, The Elevation of the Cross, and The Assumption. Other important buildings are the richly decorated 16th century town hall, and the gallery containing a priceless collection of Rubens' and Van Dyck's paintings. Boulevards now mark the site of the old walls.

Not far from the cathedral stands the shop and nome of Christophe Plantin, " the king of printers." He set up his establishment in 1549, and the business was continued after his death by his descendants

In 1891 a Dutch doctor in the island of Java, while watching native workmen digging in a river bank, saw them unearth some very old fossil bones —teeth and part of a skull; and a year later near that same spot he came across a thigh bone that had evidently belonged to this same prehistoric skeleton. Studying these remains he decided that what he had found was a specimen of the long sought " missing link," the supposed ancestor alike of Man and the higher apes. He named his discovery *Pithecanthropus erectus* (" erect ape-man "), and soon the

Here you see four main types of anthropoid apes, our nearest relatives among the animals. The gorilla (top left), famed for its strength and size, has a comically human expression, at least when it is young, like the one shown here. The very name of the orang-utan (top right) means 'man-of-the-woods.' Everyone knows the chimpanzee (bottom left), since the way in which it can imitate almost any action of its audience or keeper has made it a tremendous favourite in zoological gardens all the world over. The silver gibbon (bottom right), despite its long arms, is as closely related to Man as are any of the anthropoids; it walks on its hind legs without difficulty.

world rang with discussions as to its meaning. Scientists now hold that the creature was not the earliest of the apes, but the earliest of men of whom we have found material traces.

In the structure of their bodies apes approach Man very nearly, and the bodily distinctions are no greater than those which separate the various species from one another. The main differences between the brain structure of the apes and the lowest of mankind are chiefly in size, in convolutions, and microscopic structure. The convolution or ridge containing the brain cells that preside over speech (called the convolution of Broca) is lacking in the apes, and there are other very important distinctions.

Apes live chiefly on fruits and other vegetable food. The gorilla is as large as, and heavier than, Man. All apes can walk erect as men do, though they are more at home on all-fours, or climbing trees, as is shown by the hand-like character of their feet; they have no tails and no cheek-pouches. Apes have great strength and intelligence. The gorilla, especially the male, is among the most dangerous of wild animals when disturbed. The orang-utan is less savage. The chimpanzee and,

APES AND THEIR COUSIN MAN
These skeletons show the bodily relationship which exists between Man and his fellow primates—the anthropoid apes. Left to right are the gibbon, orang-utan, chimpanzee, gorilla, and Man himself. All five walk more or less upright, but the structure of Man alone is completely specialised for this habit.

especially, the gibbon are timid creatures.

A very peculiar alteration takes place in the gorilla as it begins to grow old, when whatever resemblance it may have had to Man —at best only a caricature—almost entirely disappears. Then, to use the words of a famous naturalist, the head becomes "something between the muzzle of the baboon, the bear, and the boar." Even the skeleton undergoes marked change. "The skull of an aged gorilla," adds Dr. R. Hartmann, "grows more projecting at the muzzle, and the canine teeth have almost attained the length of those of lions and tigers. On the upper part of the skull, which is rounded in youth, great bony crests are developed on the crown of the head and on the hind part of the skull. The arches above the eye-socket are covered with wrinkled skin, and the already savage and revolting appearance of the old gorilla is thereby increased."

Although there are the same number of teeth as in Man, the tusk-like canines already mentioned are certainly not characteristic of ourselves, and the teeth are arranged differently in the mouth. None of the Man-like apes has a duplicate of the human ear, and our skeleton is far more delicate. Whereas Man can live in any part of the world, and endure the extremes of burning sun and Arctic cold, the apes live only in the hottest parts of Africa and Asia. The apes form the family *Simiidae* of the Primates, highest order of mammals, which includes lemurs, monkeys and Man. (*See also* Chimpanzee; Gibbon; Gorilla; Orang-utan).

Apennines.
The great Apennine range which forms the backbone of the Italian peninsula, covering about two-thirds of its area, may be described as a vast dreary mountain wall with parts of its surface bare, and a few projecting peaks to break the dull monotony of the scene. It extends from Savona, near the head of the Gulf of Genoa, as far

Dorien Leigh

APENNINE VALLEY AND SNOWY PEAKS
Forming the backbone of the Italian peninsula the Apennines reach their highest point in the Abruzzi, Mount Corno rising to 9,560 feet. The Abruzzi is a department of Central Italy traversed by the range. Snow lies on the highest peaks throughout winter, though in the valleys the climate is mild. South of the Po valley the rivers of Italy rise in the Apennines, those on the Adriatic side, where the mountains are close to the sea, being torrential streams.

as Reggio in the toe of the boot that Italy resembles. The general shape of the range is that of a bow, 800 miles long and from 25 to 85 miles in width,

Only in the Abruzzi in the centre of the peninsula, and in the marble mountains of Carrara and Serravezza, do the bold and magnificent forms of the Alps appear. Here the mountains parallel the eastern coast so closely that in many places there is hardly room for more than a narrow road between the abrupt mountain sides and the Adriatic. The highest summit of the Apennines, Mt. Corno (9,560 feet), lies in this part of the range. Few of the peaks are more than 6,500 feet high. The famous Mt. Vesuvius (*q.v.*), an active volcano which in ancient days destroyed with its ashes and lava the Roman cities of Pompeii and Herculaneum, lies in a smaller chain to the west, sometimes called the Lower Apennines.

The wide-spreading uplands and slopes furnish excellent pasturage where there is water, and the lower flanks are in many places covered with groves of orange, lemon, olive and even palm trees. Along the western base are found many pleasant valleys, much wider than the valleys of the Alps, covered with a varied vegetation and sheltering famous cities and picturesque villages. There is little mineral wealth, and lack of coal and iron is a great drawback to Italy. The want of coal, however, is largely compensated for by the development of hydro-electric power. The swift streams of the Apennines are harnessed, and in the winter, during the rainy season when the streams are swollen, surplus power is carried over power lines into the frozen Alpine country. In exchange for this, the hydro-electric plants in the Alps send power into the Apennines during the dry Apennine summers.

The fumaroles (natural steam springs) of Tuscany provide another source of power—" volcano power" it has been called. The fumaroles discharge steam, sometimes rising to a temperature of 350° F., heated volcanically, and this natural steam is carried by means of pipes to adjacent electrical generating stations.

In some parts you may meet wolves and wild boars, and occasionally bears are to be seen. Several of the principal passes owe their origin to the tireless energy and engineering ability of the Romans. All the rivers of Italy south of the Po valley rise in the Apennines. Those on the Adriatic side, where the mountains approach nearest the coast, are mere mountain torrents. On the west there is room for larger streams to develop ; of these the Arno and the Tiber are best known.

Aphis. (Pron. af´is). On the stems, leaves and blossoms of plants one often notices tiny green or black insects with soft, rounded balloon-shaped bodies ; usually they are in dense colonies. These are aphids (strictly, the plural is *aphides*; singular, *aphis*) or plant lice; well-known kinds are the "greenfly" or "blackfly" of our gardens. They belong to the order *Hemiptera*, family *Aphididae*.

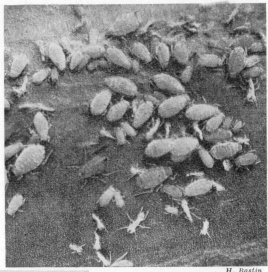

H. Bastin

HARMFUL APHIDS
Above you see (about 15 times life-size) a mass of the little ' greenfly,' or aphids, which are responsible for so much damage to garden roses. The picture on the left shows galls made by the Chermes aphids on spruce shoots.

There are many different kinds of these insects, the smallest measuring only about one-twentieth of an inch when fully grown, and the largest about one-fifth of an inch. Nearly every kind of plant has its aphid pests at some time or other of its growth, and usually each different kind of plant has its own species of aphid which feeds upon it exclusively.

With their sharp beaks aphids pierce plant tissues and suck up the sap as food, often causing serious damage to the plant. Some of the sap thus drunk up is transformed within the body of the aphis into a thick liquid, called honeydew, and dropped from little openings at the posterior end of the body. Shiny, sticky drops of this honeydew often appear on foliage, at times so abundantly as to form a sugary crust when they dry.

Honeydew is sought after and eaten by numerous kinds of insects, but it is the ants which especially relish it as food (*see* Ant). Some aphids live underground and feed upon root juices ; others are taken into the ants' nests and cared for by ants.

Some aphids multiply by laying eggs, but among most forms the females bring forth the young alive, in certain generations without mating between the sexes—this is called parthenogenesis or virgin birth.

These young are mostly females. The first adults in each year are always wingless females, reproducing their own sex parthenogenetically, many of the young being winged forms when adult. These winged females also reproduce in the same manner, but when the summer is well advanced, males and females, both winged and of normal form, are produced. These mate in the normal insect fashion, the females of this generation then laying eggs. The eggs serve to bridge the winter period, and in the spring they hatch into the wingless form with which this interesting cycle started.

In many cases the winged generations feed on different plants from those used by the wingless, and sometimes there are two regular hosts. Aphids in which this occurs are naturally worse pests than those in which there is only one host-plant, for control must be exercised over both types. Some very serious pests of timber trees, such as the aphis (*Chermes*) which lives alternately on the spruce and the larch, belong to this type. Other notorious aphids are the woolly aphis or " American blight " of fruit trees ; rose aphis (" greenfly "); and bean aphis (" blackfly ") of our gardens.

Aphids increase with such rapidity that if unchecked they would soon kill the greater part of all plant life. But their natural enemies keep them down. These enemies are birds, and lady-birds and various other insects. Many are killed by cold weather and rains. They may be artificially controlled by spraying or dusting at intervals with various kinds of insecticide.

Aphrodite. (Pron. af-rō-dī'tē). The Greeks recounted that far back in the dawn of creation, the goddess Aphrodite sprang full-grown from the sea, where its waters had been dyed a rosy red with the blood of one of the gods, wounded in a

and a company of beautiful maidens appeared to receive her. They decked her with garments of immortal fabric, placing a crown of gold on her brow, a glittering chain about her neck, and precious rings in the lobes of her ears.

They escorted the new-born goddess, thus arrayed, to the summit of Mount Olympus, where the other gods had their dwelling. At the sight of such surpassing beauty the gods were entranced and each desired her for his wife, but the proud Aphrodite rejected them all. So, to punish her, Zeus, the king of gods and men, gave her to be the bride of Hephaestus (Vulcan), the lame and awkward but good-natured and skilful god of fire. He gave her a palace in the island of Cyprus, built of white marble, with towers and ornaments of gold and silver. In it were golden harps which made music all day long, and singing golden birds.

The name Aphrodite means " born of the sea-foam." Aphrodite is often represented as accompanied by her son Eros (Cupid), a lovely child with a bow and a quiver of love-compelling arrows. The worship of Aphrodite was widespread. Her connexion with the sea endeared her to sailors, and on land many temples were built in her honour. Sacred to her were the swan and dolphin, the dove and sparrow. As goddess of flowers and fruitfulness she loved especially the rose, the poppy and the myrtle. As goddess of love she ruled the hearts of men, and even the gods were often unable to resist her powers.

The Romans identified their goddess Venus with the Greek Aphrodite. One of the most beautiful statues that have come down to us from antiquity is the famous Venus de Milo, found buried amid ruins in the Greek island of Melos (Milo) in 1820, and now in the museum of the Louvre in Paris. Another famous statue is the so-called Medici Venus in the Uffizi Gallery at Florence, where also is the picture on the left.

W. F. Mansell

APHRODITE ' RISES FROM OUT THE WAVE '
The goddess of love—Aphrodite to the Greeks and Venus to the Romans—has been for ages a favourite subject with painters and sculptors. One of the most famous of the artistic productions in which she is represented is Botticelli's picture reproduced here. The original of the lovely painting is in the Uffizi Gallery in Florence, Italy.

quarrel with his son. From the tossing foam arose the radiant Aphrodite, goddess of love and beauty, the fairest creature of heaven or earth. A huge sea-shell floated near by, as it chanced. Lightly the goddess sprang upon it, and as she stood there the glistening drops of water rolled from her shining limbs and tresses and fell into the shell as pearls.

Entranced with her loveliness, Zephyrus, the god of the west wind, breathed upon the shell and wafted it to the island of Cyprus. At the touch of her feet on the dry sand, grass sprang up and flowers burst into bloom. Verdure clothed the whole island to greet the new-born queen of love,

Apollo. (Pron. *a*-pol'ō). Ancient Greece had twelve great gods, of whom the most widely worshipped and many-sided was Apollo. He was the god of light and of youth and manly beauty ; and as he was the god of prophecy the priestess of the oracle at Delphi was his servant.

One of the earliest deeds of the young Apollo was the slaying of the deadly serpent Python, born of slime and stagnant waters, which infested the slopes near Delphi. No man dared to approach the monster, and the terrified people cried out with uplifted hands : " O Apollo! Save us from this plague of suffering and death! "

APOLLO DANCING WITH THE NINE MUSES

As god of music, Apollo is frequently represented as the leader of the choir of the Muses, the goddesses of the liberal arts. In this reproduction of a painting by Giulio Romano, a pupil of Raphael, the names of the nine Muses are given in Greek. Apollo is in the centre with his quiver of golden arrows. The Muses, reading the scroll from right to left, are Urania (the muse of astronomy), Thalia (comedy and pastoral poetry), Euterpe (lyric poetry), Polyhymnia (religious music), Terpsichore (dancing), Melpomene (tragedy), Erato (love poetry), Clio (history), and Calliope (epic poetry).

Then the young god, beautiful as the morning and the enemy of all things ugly or evil, came down from Olympus with his shining bow in his hand and a quiver upon his back. Twang! sang the bowstring and away sped a golden arrow. And soon the writhing monster had ceased to send forth his poisonous breath. In memory of this conquest Apollo instituted the Pythian games, held every four years in ancient Greece, in which the victor in feats of strength, swiftness of foot, or the chariot race, was crowned with a wreath of laurel leaves. Apollo was also the god of song and music, and charmed the gods with his playing at the banquets held in their palaces on Mount Olympus. It was said among the later Greeks that he it was who invented the flute.

Once a vain and boastful satyr named Marsyas found a flute which the goddess Athena had thrown away because playing it distorted her features. When Marsyas discovered that of its own accord it gave forth the most delightful strains, he became so conceited that he challenged Apollo to a musical contest. The nine Muses—goddesses of the liberal arts—were chosen as judges. Marsyas was first called upon to play, and charmed all by his melodious strains. The Muses bestowed upon him much praise, and then bade Apollo surpass his rival if he could. The god seized his lyre and brought forth the most wonderful melodies. A second time they strove, and on this occasion Apollo sang to the accompaniment of his lyre. He was hailed by all as the conqueror; and Marsyas forfeited not only the contest but his life, for according to the agreement the one who lost was to be flayed alive.

Apollo was the son of Zeus and twin brother of Artemis (Diana); he was born on the island of Delos in the Aegean Sea, his mother being the goddess Leto (Latona). Later, through confusion

GREEK CONCEPTIONS OF APOLLO

The Greek sculptors loved to carve representations of the god Apollo, and here we have two fine statues. The one at the left is in the British Museum, in London, and the one above is the Apollo Belvedere at Rome.

with Helios, he came to be considered especially as the sun-god. The Greeks connected him with agriculture, and called him " the protector of the grain," "the sender of fertilizing dew," " the preventer of blight," " destroyer of locusts," and " destroyer of mice." They considered him also the guardian of flocks and herds and in general, a health-giving god. He was hailed as the "god of the silver bow," and also, in wartime, as " the helper " and " god of the war-cry."

At Delphi, in western Greece, near the foot of Mount Parnassus—which was sacred to Apollo and the Muses—was the oracle of Apollo. Here his priestess, seated on a tripod, told the future of all who consulted her, giving guidance in matters of sickness, war and peace, and in the building-up of colonies. As the symbol of the god of prophecy, the tripod was held to be sacred to Apollo.

Apollo was represented more frequently than any other deity in ancient art. Sculptors delighted in portraying him as a beautiful youth with flowing hair tied in a knot above his forehead, which was bound with a wreath of laurel, and bearing his lyre or bow. The most famous statue of him is the Apollo Belvedere, so called because it is in the Belvedere Gallery in the Vatican palace, at Rome. This ancient masterpiece in marble represents him at the moment of his conquest over the Python.

Apostle.

" He went into the mountains to pray, and continued all night in prayer to God. And when it was day he called his disciples, and he chose from them twelve men whom he also named apostles." In these few words the New Testament tells us of the choosing by Jesus of the twelve men whom He selected to be near Him for continuous instruction and later to spread abroad His message.

The word *apostle* (from Greek words meaning " from " and " to send ") signifies a messenger and teacher. These men were Simon (called Peter), Andrew his brother, James the Elder (son of Zebedee), John his brother, Philip of Bethsaida, Bartholomew, Matthew, Thomas, James the Younger (son of Alpheus), Simon (called Zelotes), Jude (called Thaddeus, the brother of James the Younger), and Judas Iscariot (who betrayed Jesus to the high priests and then, overcome with remorse, committed suicide). The number 12 was symbolical, signifying the 12 tribes of Israel. Matthias was chosen by the drawing or casting of lots to supply the place left vacant by Judas Iscariot. Simon Peter and Andrew,

and John and James the Elder, were fishermen, and Matthew was a " publican " or tax-gatherer.

Save for the meagre accounts in the New Testament, there is no certain knowledge of the lives of the Apostles. It is natural, therefore, that a great mass of tradition should have sprung up around the names of these enthusiastic leaders who established the Christian Church.

Peter, apparently, was the leader of the Apostles, and was present at most of the incidents in the life of Jesus recorded in the New Testament. He, with the sons of Zebedee (James and John), formed a little inner circle within the 12, and this favoured group was present at the raising of the daughter of Jairus, the Transfiguration on the mount, and the scene in the Garden of Gethsemane. Although Andrew, brother of Peter, is mentioned only a few times, he, too, seems to have been later included in this little inner circle; for when the Greeks asked Philip if they might see Jesus, he consulted Andrew before laying the matter before the Master. A widespread tradition concerning Peter holds that he went to Rome and suffered martyrdom there by crucifixion. (*See* Peter, Saint).

Andrew, it is said, suffered martyrdom in Greece, on a cross shaped like a letter **X**, whence comes our " St. Andrew's cross."

John, " the beloved disciple," is represented throughout the Gospels as fiery-natured. After the Crucifixion John was with Peter and the other Apostles at Jerusalem, and he is, after Peter, the most prominent of those who bear witness to Christ's resurrection. There has been much controversy as to the authorship of the Gospel, the Epistles and the book of Revelation named in his honour.

His brother, James the Elder or the greater, must have been very prominent in the early Church. He was the first of the Apostles to be martyred, being slain by King Herod in Jerusalem (Acts xii, 1, 2). Some authorities believe that John also was slain at that time, although tradition has given him a long life of missionary service.

Thomas, sometimes called "doubting Thomas," because he would not believe in the Resurrection until he could see and touch the Master, is yet a character of singular charm and interest. When Jesus, despite imminent danger at the hands of the Jews, declared his intention to go to Bethany to heal Lazarus, Thomas alone supported the Master against the other disciples, who sought to dissuade him, and said, "Let us also go, that we may die

EMBLEMS OF THE APOSTLES
The two illustrations above, taken from an old manuscript, show the twelve Apostles with their distinctive emblems. They are, from left to right, top : Peter, Andrew, James the Elder, John, Thomas, James the Younger. Lower, Philip, Bartholomew, Matthew, Jude, Simon, and Matthias.

THE APOSTLES GATHERED WITH JESUS AT THE LAST SUPPER

In this, the supreme masterpiece of Leonardo da Vinci, one of the world's greatest painters, we are shown the scene at the Last Supper, at the moment when Our Lord has just told the Apostles that one of them will betray Him. This impressive work—a fresco on the wall of the refectory of the Dominican convent church of Santa Maria delle Grazie in Milan, Italy—was painted in 1494. It was slowly fading until it was placed in an airtight, glass-fronted case in 1947. The figure on Our Lord's right hand is St. John, and on his left, beckoning with his finger, is Judas Iscariot.

with him " (John xi, 8-16). Tradition says that Thomas went to India after the crucifixion. The name " Christians of St. Thomas " is often applied to the members of the ancient Christian churches of south India, which claim him as their founder.

Of Philip, Bartholomew, Matthew (the reputed author of the First Gospel), Simon Zelotes, Jude, and James the Younger, we learn little from the New Testament. Bartholomew is said to have gone on a missionary trip to India, a very wide designation in those days. Tradition says that he was flayed alive and crucified head downwards in Armenia or Cilicia. In works of art he is generally represented with a large knife, the instrument of his martyrdom, and in Michelangelo's Last Judgement he appears with his skin hanging over his arm. Early authorities state that Matthew died a natural death, but by other writers he is said to have suffered martyrdom in Ethiopia. James the Younger, it is said, was either stoned to death or killed by a blow from a fuller's pole.

The Youth Who Fled from the Garden

The name " apostle " was later applied to Paul and to Barnabas, who accompanied Paul on his travels (see Paul, Saint). It is also given at times to such apostolic assistants as Luke " the beloved physician," the traditional writer of the third Gospel and the Book of the Acts. It will be noted that only two of the four Gospels bear the names of real Apostles. Mark, to whom the Second Gospel is ascribed, is believed to have been the unnamed youth who fled from the Garden when Jesus was made prisoner. Later he was Peter's constant companion in his missionary travels. The Gospel which bears his name, and which critics generally agree that he wrote, was the first to be written and was based on his recollections of Peter's teachings.

The symbols of the Apostles are usually given thus, with their traditional explanations. Andrew, a cross, because he was crucified; St. Andrew's cross is shaped like the letter **X**. Bartholomew, a knife, because tradition says he was flayed alive. James the Elder, a scallop-shell or pilgrim's staff, because he is the patron saint of pilgrims. James the Younger, a fuller's pole, because he is said to have been killed by a blow on the head with a pole by Simeon the Fuller. John, a cup, with a winged serpent coming out of it, in allusion to a tradition concerning a priest of Diana who challenged him to drink a cup of poison; John made the sign of the cross over the cup and Satan flew out of it. Judas Iscariot, a bag, because he " had the bag, and bare what was put therein " (John xii, 6). Jude or Judas (Thaddeus), some say a club, because he was martyred with one, though traditions are conflicting. Matthew, a hatchet or halberd, because he was killed with one. Matthias, a battle-axe, because he was beheaded with one. Simon (Peter), a bunch of keys, because he has " the keys of the kingdom of Heaven "; also a cock, because he wept when he heard the cock crow. Paul, a sword, because he was beheaded. Philip, a staff surmounted by a cross, from the legend that he was hanged on a tall pillar. Simon (Zelotes), a saw, from the manner of his death. Thomas, a lance, because he was pierced by one.

The symbols of the four Evangelists are as follows: Matthew, a man holding a pen, with a scroll before him, looking over his left shoulder at an angel; Mark, a seated man writing, with a winged lion lying beside him; Luke, a man with a pen, poring over a scroll, with an ox or cow chewing the cud; John, a young man with an eagle behind him.

Earlier symbols of the four were: Matthew, a man's face; Mark, a lion; Luke, an ox; John, a flying eagle, from the four beasts round the throne of God (Rev. iv, 7). According to St. Irenaeus " the lion signifies the royalty of Christ; the calf His sacerdotal office; the man's face His incarnation; the eagle the grace of the Holy Ghost."

Appalachians. (Pron. ap-*a*-lach'i-*anz*).

For long this vast range of mountains in North America and its bewildering number of forest-clad ridges kept the English colonists from extending their settlements westward; but today, at a dozen or more points, by means of tunnels, cuts and zigzag climbs, the railways surmount the natural barrier, so that the sleeping traveller in his Pullman scarcely realizes that the obstacles ever existed. Then, too, broad well-paved highways run through the gaps where the rivers have been quietly cutting their way to the ocean for ages. This mountain system extends from Newfoundland and New Brunswick south-westwards for 1,500 miles to Central Alabama, in two ridges roughly parallel with the Atlantic coast. Between the western ridge, the Allegheny Mountains including the Catskills at the north end, and the eastern ridge, called the Blue Ridge, lies the Great Appalachian Valley. The mountain sides and summits are covered with forests. The ridges generally have round-topped summits rising to roughly uniform heights.

In the spring, when the laurel, rhododendron and azalea are in bloom, the slopes and valleys of the southern Appalachians are a maze of riotous colour. White pine is found in the north; the maple, white birch, ash and beech also grow on the northern mountains; and the oak, cherry, white poplar and yellow pine farther south. On the poorer lands evergreens flourish, and their dark foliage, covering the summits of the Black Mountains of North Carolina, gives this range its name. Bears, mountain lions (puma) and wild cats (lynx) haunt the more remote fastnesses. Foxes are numerous, deer are found in some districts, and moose in the extreme north. Wild turkeys and smaller game birds are plentiful on the southern ranges. American state and national governments are preserving the wild beauty of the Appalachians by creating forest reserves and national parks.

To speak of anything several million years old as " young " seems odd to anyone but a geologist. But in the history of mountains a million years is merely the tick of a watch. If it were possible to cut North America in halves it would bring into sharp contrast the difference between the old, worn-down Appalachians and the comparatively young and still sharply outlined Rockies. Mount Whitney, in the latter range, is nearly three miles high, while Mount Mitchell, less than half as high, is the loftiest of the Appalachians. Centuries of battle with the winds and storms and frosts and running water wear down the loftiest of mountains.

The highest peaks are found in the Black Mountains of North Carolina, the loftiest of which, Mount Mitchell, reaches an altitude of 6,711 feet. In the north, Mount Washington, in the White Mountains of New Hampshire, is the topmost peak, rising to the height of 6,293 feet.

Apple. Of all fruits the apple is the best-

known, and it has been cultivated since the earliest times of which we have any knowledge. Charred remains of apples have been found in ruins of prehistoric lake-dwellings, and rude pictures of this fruit were carved long ago by the Stone Age men. References to it are common in the literature of almost all countries and all ages, and fairy-tale and folk-lore abound with stories connected with apple-trees and golden apples.

The apple is mentioned in the Bible many times, and popular tradition always supposed that an apple was the fruit with which Eve tempted Adam. In Scandinavian mythology Idun, goddess of youth and spring, was keeper of the golden apples by which the gods preserved their youth. The winter god stole her and her apples, and the gods began to grow old. In the spring she regained her freedom, and the gods grew young again. The Greeks loved to tell of the three apples of Atalanta (*q.v.*), and of the golden apples of the Hesperides which Hercules (*q.v.*) managed to obtain with the help of Atlas. Then there was the " apple of discord " offered by Eris, goddess of discord, to the most beautiful of the three goddesses, Hera, Athena

Dorien Leigh

APPALACHIAN PEAKS THROUGH A SEA OF CLOUDS
Here is a scene high up in the Appalachian Mountains, one of the most important ranges of the North American continent. The photograph was taken at a great height, looking over a sea of clouds, and the peaks that stand out above them are clad with firs, a growth typical of North American mountains. They are sometimes found at a height of as much as 4,000 feet.

and Aphrodite, the judgement between whom by Paris has inspired many a fine painting.

Pliny the Elder, a learned writer of ancient Rome, tells of 22 varieties of apples common in his day. The fruit was probably introduced into England by the Romans during the three centuries of their rule.

It seems curious to find that the apple belongs to the great rose family, *Rosaceae*, as do also the peach, cherry, plum, raspberry and many other fruits ; its own Latin name is *Pyrus malus*. We can see a resemblance between the exquisite pink-and white blossoms of the apple-tree and the wild roses which bloom in such profusion along our country roads. It was probably as a hybrid of two species of small wild crab-apples that the apple as we know it in history first appeared in Asia Minor.

Apples are among the most delicious as well as the most wholesome of fruits. They can be stored and kept many months, eaten raw, or cooked in any number of ways. Cider (*q.v.*) is made by pressing out the juice of the apple, and from this juice also the best vinegar is made.

No fruit can be cultivated over so wide an area of the globe, and none is grown so far north. In Europe there are apple orchards in Scandinavia, and as far south as the mountain regions of Spain. The tree thrives best, however, in the middle temperate climates.

Adam's apple—the projection of the larynx in the front of the throat—is said to have got its name from the old belief that it marks where a piece of the apple given to Adam by Eve stuck in his throat.

Apricot. (Pron. ā′pri-kot). As soon as the first warm breath of spring moderates the winter's chill the fruit buds of the apricot trees begin to stir. The dainty shell-pink blossoms beautify the bare twigs of the mother tree long before most other fruits have heard the gentle call to waken. Although closely related to the peach and plum, the apricot does not survive in the colder regions as do its cousins ; this, no doubt, is mainly because of its early-blooming habit.

Tiny leaves appear soon after the flowers, and when the petals have fallen away the tree is covered with luxuriant light green foliage. The small green fruits grow very slowly until the stone is formed, but after this has developed they fill out rapidly and ripen, as a rule, in the latter part of July and in August. Indeed, the name apricot comes from Arabic and late Greek words meaning " early ripening."

The fruit resembles both the peach and the plum. The tree is plum-like in leaf and habit, and peach-like in bark. Each tree bears a large quantity of fruit, which makes excellent jam. The apricot, of which there are three species, is a native of China. It was introduced into Europe in the days of Alexander the Great. The scientific name of this tree is *Prunus armeniaca*.

April Fool's Day. No one can say for certain when the custom of playing tricks on April 1 first began, but the practice is found not only in Britain but in nearly all the countries of

APRICOTS ON A SUNNY WALL
In England apricots are ripened without difficulty when the trees are trained against a sheltered wall facing south, such as the one above at Aynho, near Banbury, Oxfordshire. The apricot was introduced into Europe in the days of Alexander the Great, 356–323 B.C.

Fox

Europe and also in the Dominions, North America and the sub-continent of India. Amongst the Scots an " April fool " is called a gowk—the word for " cuckoo." The victim may be told that he (or she) has a muddy face and when he looks in the glass is at once greeted with derisory laughter ; or he is asked to keep an appointment which is not to be kept or to phone somebody with a non-existent number. In France the April fool is known as *poisson d'avril*, perhaps because a fish (poisson) caught in April would be young and so inexperienced as to snap quite readily at the hook.

As for the origin of the custom generally, it may be a relic of the festivities once held at the vernal equinox, which used to finish on April the first.

Apteryx. In New Zealand there lives a bird with a very long beak, but otherwise about the size of the domestic chicken. It is called by scientists the apteryx, a name derived from the Greek and meaning " wingless "; but it is more commonly known as the kiwi, a name given it by the natives because its cry resembles the sound of that word.

The wings are so small that they are quite useless for flying, but its legs are stout and strong. The feathers are so long and simple in construction that they give the bird the appearance of being covered with hair. The apteryx is the only member of the feathered world that has the nostrils at the tip of the beak, and when hunting for worms, beetles and berries it seems to be always sniffing. as though guided by smell as well as by sight. Another of its funny little ways is that the male bird sits on the one or occasionally two eggs that are laid during the course of a year ; these eggs are larger, in proportion to the size of their parents, than those of any other bird. The apteryx does not trouble to build a nest, but instead scoops a hole in the earth.

These birds are nocturnal. sleeping by day and hunting for food during the night. Although

detail, every strange shape, every vivid colour is clear to you. The angel fish floats among the fronds of seaweed with fins of pearl ; trout swim to and fro in their speckled suits; conger eels wriggle over the rocky bottom; and soles, plaice, codling, and fish of amazing beauty of form and colour bring the wonders of the ocean depths before your eyes.

Behind the exhibition halls machinery is running night and day, pumping, filtering, aerating, and heating or refrigerating water to suit the needs of the varied forms of life. The sea fish live in sea water brought from the coast. Each species, salt water or fresh, must be supplied with appropriate food, tended in health, and nursed in sickness.

World-famous aquariums are maintained in the Zoological Gardens, London, at Naples, Monaco. Antwerp, New York, and Chicago.

Any boy or girl can have, on a smaller scale, a successful fresh water aquarium. The most practical is a " balanced " aquarium, a type based on the law of nature that green plants remove carbon dioxide from the water and give off oxygen, while animal life uses the oxygen and exhales carbon dioxide. By stocking the aquarium with growing plants to provide oxygen for the fish, the demands of both plant and animal life are satisfied. If the animals are overcrowded, or if the water is allowed to get too warm or foul, or if too few plants are provided to furnish the necessary oxygen, a few hours will convert a thriving aquarium into a " water cemetery." by killing the occupants.

It is necessary that the aquarium be in a light place, as darkness promotes the growth of parasites harmful to fish life, and plants give off oxygen only under the influence of light. The tank must, however, not be in the direct rays of the sun, for direct sunlight overheats the water and thus kills the animal life. Many a collection of goldfish in the

Gambier Bolton

APTERYX, WINGLESS BIRD
Surely no other bird is so strange-looking as the apteryx—or kiwi, as it is frequently called. It has no wings, and its long beak is very sensitive, helping it to find worms deep in the mud. It is not found outside New Zealand.

very timid, they sleep so soundly that even if tapped with a stick they rarely do more than flutter their feathers. The Maoris—New Zealand aborigines—regarded the kiwi as a delicate dish, but the birds have become so scarce that they are protected by government decree and may no longer be killed.

Aquarium. To put on a diver's helmet, sink beneath the waves, and watch the strange ocean world whose dwellers wander at will among the tree tops of their watery forests or dart over jagged mountains of painted coral as easily as we cross a room—this is an experience very few of us can have. But almost as marvellous is a visit to a great public aquarium. Once inside the darkened halls, you might easily imagine yourself to be taking a trip aboard a huge submarine, looking out through great windows into the very heart of the ocean. Concealed lights shine down from above into the tanks that flank the walls, so that every

AQUARIUM AND ITS NIMBLE OCCUPANTS
It will be noticed that this well-stocked aquarium has a sheet of glass above it to exclude dust—an important precaution. The glass is raised a little to admit air. The gaily coloured fish make a fascinating picture as they swim amidst the water-plants, which are rooted in sand at the bottom. Normally there would be fewer fish in an aquarium of this size : overcrowding leads to disease and other troubles.

See text overleaf

A COMPOSITION IN 'WATER COLOURS'

KEY TO COLOUR PLATE

QUICKER than a blink, as giant flashlamps flared, the colour camera caught in mid-motion the group of tropical aquarium fishes shown in the previous page. This successful fraction of a second came only after hours of patient waiting and several failures, for it is a rare feat of colour photography to take a close-up showing so many of these twisting, darting water midgets in an artistically effective " composition."

The key-picture here on the left helps to identify the camera's " catch." The red Helleri (1) is a hybrid product of the fish fancier's art, a cross between a Mexican swordtail (*see below*) and a red moonfish or "platy." The ancestors of *Betta splendens* (2) were famous fighting fish of Siam. If another male of his species were near by, those drooping greenish fins would change colour and be spread out like blood-red sails. Three members of the Gourami tribe got into the picture—the thick-lipped Gourami (3), the Dwarf (4), and the Three-spot (5), all originally from the Malay Peninsula. *Pterophyllum scalare* (6), from the Amazon river, is commonly called an angel fish. The Mexican swordtail (7) gets its name from the long projection of its tail fin, only a part of which is visible here.

The display of small tropical aquariums in stores, hotels, restaurants, and homes has become widespread in recent years. Lighted at top and sides with electric lamps which are shielded from the front view, they make lively colourful decorations. Sometimes the whole equipment is set flush into the wall of a room, with access to it through a door on the other side of the wall. The lamps provide enough light for the plants which in turn supply the fish with oxygen. The lamps may also be adjusted to keep the water at the right temperature to suit the fishy population.

To face page 193

Fox; Alfieri; " The Times "

FISH OF MANY SORTS IN THE ZOO AQUARIUM

One of the most fascinating features of the London Zoo is the Aquarium, opened in 1924. Here, in a darkened building, are big, brilliantly-lit tanks, where almost every kind of fish lives and swims, as far as possible, in its natural surroundings. The lower picture is of a shoal of perch in their freshwater tank ; top left, a visitor watches the movements of various sea fish ; and, right, a close-up of two quaintly shaped and beautifully marked angel-fish from the tropics.

usual round glass globe has been killed in a few hours by exposure to sunlight. The curved glass focuses the rays of the sun and soon scalds the fish to death. Sufficient room must be provided. Each fish three inches long needs about a gallon of water.

The sides of the best aquariums are of plate glass, so that the fish may be seen from all sides as well as from the top. The frame may be of metal and the bottom of metal, slate or marble, covered with perfectly clean sand and pebbles.

The most convenient size for a home aquarium is one holding from three to eight gallons. A five-gallon tank will provide room enough for three or four fish not more than three inches long, four or five of the acrobatic little water newts, three or four small tadpoles, and six or eight snails.

To stock it you may need to make a couple of visits to some near-by pond. Get your plants the first time and leave the fish for another trip. The most useful plants are duckweed, American pond-weed (common in Britain), *Vallisneria spiralis*, water crowfoot, the Aponogetons, and water starwort.

Now put about two inches of coarse gravel in the bottom of the tank. Wash it well, so that it will not make the water muddy. A few bits of rock may be put in. When you have filled the tank with water, anchor the roots of the plants in the gravel by tying to the base of each plant a stone sufficient to weight it down. Three or four vigorous plants are enough. Leave them to get used to their new home before putting in the animals. When the plants are established you will see bubbles of air occasionally rising from them. Be sure to include a few of the water-snails found among dead leaves in the shallows of ponds and ditches, choosing those of smaller size. These will clear your aquarium of the dead leaves of water plants, and will keep the sides and surface free from scum. Sticklebacks are interesting little fish to keep, but you had better put in only a single pair, because they are quarrelsome, especially with their

own species. Goldfish and minnows are also good aquarium fish.

Bits of meat make good food for tadpoles, and the fish will eat breadcrumbs and insects, and the so-called "ants' eggs," which are the pupae of ants. If pieces of food accumulate on the bottom, remove them by lowering into the tank a glass tube, pressing your thumb over one end until it is immediately over the object. Lift the thumb, and the water with the refuse will rise in the tube and can be lifted out by pressing your thumb over the end again. Keep the level of the water constant, and if you have the right balance between fish and plants it will rarely need to be changed.

Aqueduct. (Pron. ak'-wē-duct). Amongst the most striking engineering achievements of the Ancient Romans were the giant aqueducts built by them to bring water to their cities.

The city of Rome had 11 such aqueducts, built at different times, some with several channels, one above another, and ranging in length from a few miles to more than 60 miles. The conduits were built for the most part of masonry lined with Roman cement, and some of the aqueducts are still in use. Since the water flowed entirely by gravitation, the grades were carefully surveyed. Here an aqueduct winds gracefully round the side of a hill, there another pierces boldly through by means of a tunnel, while across the low plains near the city itself stalk giant arches holding aloft the channel for the precious water high in the air. At Nîmes in France and Segovia in Spain such aqueducts are still to be seen intact, with double or triple rows of arches, one row on top of another, to lead the water channel across a river or deep valley.

The one near Nîmes—the Pont du Gard, it is called—is 880 feet long and 160 feet high. When the French philosopher Rousseau first saw it as a

Aerofilms Ltd.

AQUEDUCTS THE ROMANS BUILT MORE THAN 1800 YEARS AGO

Some of the most remarkable relics of Roman civilization are aqueducts by which water supplies were carried to the old cities. They were mostly underground, but where a valley or a river had to be crossed the aqueduct was carried on such graceful arched structures as the two pictured here. The great aqueduct of Segovia (top), in Spain, crosses the roadway at a height of 130 feet; it dates from about A.D. 100. The Pont du Gard (lower), which was built about 18 B.C., carries the aqueduct that supplies Nîmes across the valley of the River Gard in the south of France.

boy he is said to have murmured with awe : " Oh, that I had been born a Roman! "

At Segovia is an aqueduct which runs from the Sierra Guadarrama, 10 miles distant, and is carried on granite arches varying from 23 feet to 94 feet in height.

Roman aqueducts follow a uniform slope throughout, the water flowing by gravity. After the fall of the Roman Empire, it was not until the middle of the 18th century that aqueduct-building was resumed to any great extent. One of the chief differences between ancient and modern structures is that the engineer of today, with high explosives and modern machinery, usually finds it quicker and more economical to build a tunnel for his water conduit. Pipe lines, the application of the principle of the siphon, and the use of great pumping engines, free him also of such complete dependence on gravitation to bring the water to the city.

Los Angeles, in California, is supplied with water by an aqueduct 240 miles long—one of the longest in the world—which brings water from the Owens river in the heart of the Sierra Madre Mountains.

BUILDING AN AQUEDUCT OF MODERN TYPE
Usually the term aqueduct is applied to bridges of stone carrying channels for water across a valley. Here we see another type, under construction. It is a 14-foot tunnel at Drumjohn, in Galloway, Scotland, with a pipe-line to carry across country the water for an electric power plant.

It supplies more than the city needs, so the surplus is used for irrigation, and the great fall in its course serves to supply water-power.

The word aqueduct comes from the Latin *aqua* meaning "water," and *ducere* meaning "to lead."

ISLAM'S CRADLE *in the* ARID WASTE

Here we have the story of the peninsula of Arabia—that vast region of rocky desert which was the homeland of Mahomet and of the race of fighters whom his religion inspired to far-flung conquest in the 7th and 8th centuries.

Arabia AND THE ARABS. The Beduin Arab remains among the few unchanged figures of the world. For centuries he has swayed on camel-back across the billowy dunes. For centuries he has prayed as the Prophet taught him. With a handful of dates he can satisfy his hunger for days, and in rags of filthy cotton and rough camel's hair he can defy desert sun or bitter chill. He is a mystic, and an aristocrat. For good or ill, the Arabs are what Arabia has made them, and to understand these people we must know something about their rather gaunt homeland.

Geographically, Arabia is a loose term which includes not only the nations within the peninsula but Palestine, Syria, Iraq, and Transjordan. Politically the name is generally taken as signifying the whole of the peninsula south of the borders of Transjordan and Iraq, containing the states of Saudi Arabia, Yemen, Aden, the Hadhramaut, Oman, and Kuwait, with several smaller territories.

This corner of Asia is the largest peninsula in the world, its area being approximately 1,000,000 square miles, or nearly five times that of France. The population of the peninsula has never been accurately ascertained. Estimates vary widely, but 10 million is probably near the correct figure. Of these, about half are Beduin who roam the arid regions with their flocks and herds, seeking pasture and water, as did their fathers in the days of Abraham.

Arabia is shaped like a boot. Along the " back seam," up and down the Red Sea coast, runs a ridge of mountains. The whole peninsula slopes down from the ridge toward the Persian Gulf, except for the high mountains of Oman, which are on the very toe of the boot.

At the top of the boot is the Syrian Desert, of dark flint and gravel slopes with hidden spring pools and caked salt marshes in the Sirhan valley. The " shin bone " of Arabia is Nejd—the heart of the country, geographically and politically. Mountainous and solid, it is nearly surrounded by sandy desert—on the north by the Great Nefud Desert with its billowy red dunes, on the east by the white sands of the Dahna, and on the south by the frightful Ruba-el-Khali, or " empty quarter." This vast ocean of well-nigh lifeless sand was never crossed by a European until the winter of 1930-31, when an Englishman, Bertram Thomas, wazir to the sultan of Muscat, made the remarkable 900-mile journey in 58 days. He found oyster shells and sea-fossils 100 miles inland from the Hadhramaut coast, showing where sea waters once covered the land, a salt lake below sea-level seven miles long, dunes of " singing sand," and caravan tracks made by travellers of ancient times. The desert was again crossed by H. St. John Philby, in 1932. He was the first European to visit the hidden city of Shabwa. This is said to have been the capital of the

ARABIA

Queen of Sheba, mentioned in the Bible as having paid a visit to King Solomon; and a British mission in 1937 saw signs of an ancient civilization in the foundations of great buildings, while mounds indicated a buried city. Numerous ancient caravan tracks were observed, substantiating the tradition that dealers in frankincense and myrrh passed through Shabwa on their way from Darfur in the Anglo-Egyptian Sudan to Palestine.

Before the rise to power of Ibn Saud, the King of Saudi Arabia, the desert province of Nejd was mainly inhabited by roaming Beduin tribes. Now, however, the Arabs are being persuaded to settle in towns, which from isolated oases are growing into sizeable centres of population. Riyadh, the capital of Nejd, has about 60,000 inhabitants, and Hufuf and Taif about 30,000 each. The produce of Nejd includes dates, grain, wool and hides, besides livestock such as camels, horses, donkeys, sheep and goats. Oil is worked.

Of the more bounteous coastal regions, Oman, an independent sultanate with an area of 82,000 square miles and a population estimated at 500,000, is the orchard of Arabia, where oleanders and acacias bloom, and the farmers raise grain, sugar cane, cotton, vegetables, alfalfa, indigo, dates, grapes, apricots, peaches, oranges, lemons, mulberries, mangoes and melons. Muscat, the capital, with a population of 4,200, was once the head-quarters of pirates and slave traders. Hence the people have to a large degree the blood of Negro and Baluchi slaves, and in Muscat and the neighbouring city of Matrah, with a population of 8,500, there are hardly any Arabs. Since the time of the 1914–18 war Oman has been a British protectorate.

The coast along the " sole " of the Arabian boot is considerably less of an earthly paradise than Oman. In the " instep " lies the Hadhramaut province, with about 150,000 inhabitants, ruled by tribal chiefs who jealously exclude all European visitors, though it is included in the Eastern Aden Protectorate under the control of the governor of Aden. It has one fertile valley, a few oases which produce dates, wheat, millet, indigo and tobacco, and some of its mountains have been famous since Bible times for trees producing myrrh and frankincense.

Aden, the heel of the boot, is a British colony. The city of Aden bakes in the crater of an extinct volcano—rocky, almost waterless, and perhaps hotter than any other city in the world, as told in our article on Aden.

Rounding the heel and moving up the Red Sea coast, we find Yemen, fertile in its mountain valleys, hot and sterile along the coast. It has an area of some 75,000 square miles and a population estimated at 3,500,000. Its coast city of Mocha was once the centre of a large coffee trade. Imam Yahya was acknowledged king by a treaty with Great

Air Force Official

ARABIA'S SKYSCRAPER CITY OF SHIBAM

One of the most interesting cities of Arabia is Shibam, which lies in the Hadhramaut district in the south. It had never been visited by a European until 1931, when Hans Helfritz, a German traveller, visited this and other Arabian cities. It is a city of skyscrapers built of clay bricks, and some houses rise to as many as ten storeys. This photograph was taken during an air survey of the Hadhramaut valley by a squadron of the Royal Air Force. Shibam is a very primitive city, and life there is much the same as it was 11 centuries ago, in the time of the Arabian Nights.

Britain and India signed in 1934. Sana, his capital, has something over 20,000 inhabitants.

Asir, north of Yemen, and Hejaz, comprising the remainder of the Red Sea coast, have been included with Nejd. The capital of the Hejaz is the Mahomedans' holy city of Mecca, with a population of 120,000. The port of Jeddah and the city of Medina have each about 30,000 inhabitants; the rest of the population of the Hejaz, about 3,500,000 in all, are mostly Beduin. The Hejaz railway, running north from Medina to Transjordan and Syria, has not operated south of the Transjordan border since 1925. Saudi Arabia also includes the Hasa district, which Ibn Saud seized from the Turks in 1914. El Hasa produces the delicious Khalas dates, a special breed of big white donkeys, fine camel's hair mantles, and leather work. To the north of the Hasa is the small independent sheikhdom of Kuwait, the "Paris of Arabia," which Ibn Saud often tried to snatch from British protection. And both Ibn Saud and the Persians have had an eye on Bahrein, the rich island of the pearl-divers. It is now ruled by a native sheikh under British protection. It has a population of 120,000. Oil was discovered in Bahrein in 1932, and an oil refinery established. British Overseas Airways Corporation have a landing ground on Muharra Island, to the north-east of Bahrein.

Now we have skirted the coast of Arabia, where the wealth is, and we return to the vast inland, desert Arabia, where the power is. It is a power which seems to come up out of the desert silence, both to mould and to crumble the Beduin Arab. The hard desert life has made him thin and steely strong, scornful of luxury or comfort. Rough and ready justice the desert demands. A sheikh is chosen for his power to rule; the Beduin obey him blindly, giving him power of life and death. Death is always near on the burning sands. Therefore, the tribesmen must share the brackish water in sheepskin bags, help the weak, and behave like brothers. A stranger must always be fed and sheltered in their black goat-hair tents. To be sure, when the guest departs, his hosts may follow and rob him after four days—the time which they believe is required for the last of the host's salt to leave the guest's body. Raiding, or going on "gazu," ranks between a sport and a business. Material goods belong to anyone who can capture them. The owner is thereby lucky. He has no rightful claim to his possessions in Beduin eyes.

But while the guest is in the tent, he is given the best his host can afford. For a great feast, the meal may appear in a huge brass or enamelled pan two yards wide, with a wall of rice, and perhaps leaves of thin, hard bread all around, a whole sheep served in chunks in the centre, with the head at

ARABIA, PENINSULA OF DESERT AND MOUNTAIN

Although the boundaries of some of the border states are not definitely fixed, Arabia as a whole is a compact country, forming a great peninsula bounded on three sides by the Red Sea, the Persian Gulf and the Gulf of Oman, and the Arabian Sea. For many years it was divided into petty states, but much of it has been united in the 20th century under King Ibn Saud to form Saudi Arabia.

Carl Raswan

ARABS ENCAMPED ABOUT A DESERT SPRING

Though some motor roads now run across the deserts of Arabia the chief means of transport for the Beduin are camels and horses. Such transport is only made possible in this arid land by water-holes such as that seen above, where in the cool of the evening man and beast refresh themselves in the springs that bubble to the surface.

The walls of his house are of two tones of plaster, one cut out over the other like lace work. His door is blue, yellow or green. His coffee hearth in the living-room is an oblong 10 inches deep in the floor, round which life centres. In the heat of the summer the Arab of Iraq may take to a cellar to which lead air shafts, while the Arab of the Arabian coast seeks his roof in the evening for cool air.

It is not only in the Arabian peninsula that the Arabs dwell. The race has spread and travelled to and from the far corners of the earth. They are numerous throughout Syria, Palestine, and Egypt. They dominate the population of Libya, Tunisia,

the top, whole chickens, vegetables swimming in gravy and butter. Rice and meat are kneaded tidily into a ball with two fingers and a thumb, then popped into the mouth with a flick of the thumb. Slaves roast the coffee in a long iron spoon over the camel-dung fire, pound it musically in a great brass mortar, season it (if in Nejd, with cinnamon or cardamom seeds) and offer it in tiny cups containing the three sips required by politeness. After the meal, slaves pour water over the guest's hand, offer him soap, perhaps perfume, or drop a bit of aromatic wood on the fire. In the poorest tents, however, everyone merely wipes his hands on a greasy tent flap. When no guests

D. McLeish

WELCOME WATER FOR THE WAYFARER

In the cities of Arabia there is no regular water supply, but in the sun-baked streets there are wandering vendors of water, who bring into the city camels laden with pitchers from which the passer-by may take a drink for a trifling sum. The pitchers of native pottery have remained unchanged in shape for centuries and, being porous, keep the water cool.

are present, dates, camel's milk, and hard bread ground up with butter and sugar, are the common fare, except in the homes of the rich town Arabs.

The "town Arab," so much scorned by his Beduin brother, wears, if he can afford it, clothes of fine silk or velvet, with gold embroideries.

Algeria, and Morocco. Inter-married with the Berbers, they produced the once powerful Moorish stock. Arab traders were criss-crossing equatorial Africa from Cape Guardafui to the Gold Coast and from Timbuktu to Zanzibar long before any European knew what lay south of the Sahara. Arab

ARAB HOMES IN TOWN AND TENT

Hans Helfritz; Carl Raswan

Though we usually think of the Arabs as nomads living in tents in the desert there are cities in Arabia with skyscraper-like dwellings, such as Seyun (top) in the south. The Arabs of the desert, who live in tents (lower), generally despise the town-dweller as one unable to endure hardships. The tents are divided into two sections, one for the men and the other for the women. The men's quarters are larger than the women's, because in them male guests are entertained and tribal gatherings held. The women do the cooking, but remain hidden when strangers are present. The riders on the camels skilfully control their mounts by a single piece of thin rope attached to a wooden bobbin fixed in the camel's nose. On command the beasts kneel down, to allow their masters to mount or dismount.

Carl Raswan

ARAB HOSPITALITY, ROUGH BUT GENEROUS

In their goatskin tents in the desert the Arabs have none of the conveniences of civilization, even a sheikh's home (top) being simply furnished. Coffee pot and cups await the arrival of the three horsemen, and beside the low table is a pipe of the type used in the East. Below, Arabs are taking a meal of rice and meat. Knives and forks are not needed, because all feed themselves with their fingers from a large tray placed within reach of all.

a great civilization flourished in Arabia. Then the lamp of progress grew dim, as it did in Europe after the decline of Rome, only to be relighted seven centuries later by Mahomet. Yet the power which Mahomet set up declined again rapidly. Arabia broke up into petty tribal domains, sank into filth, poverty and ignorance. To-day there are signs that the Arab nations of the Middle East, free now from foreign domination, may again play an important part in the affairs of the world. The Arab League, which was formed in 1945, unites the seven independent states of Syria, the Lebanon, Iraq, Transjordan, Saudi Arabia, Yemen and Egypt.

A penetrating observation about the Arabs was made by Col. T. E. Lawrence ("Lawrence of Arabia"), who led an army of them against Turkey in the First World War. "Arabs could be swung on an idea as on a cord," he wrote. "None of them would escape the bond till success had come, and with it responsibility and duty and engagements. Then the idea was gone and the work ended—in ruins . . . Their mind was strange and dark, full of depressions and exaltations, lacking in rule but with more of ardour and more fertile in belief than any other in the world. They were people of starts, for whom the abstract was the strongest motive, the process of infinite courage, and the end nothing."

seamen and Arab settlements were also found in the East Indies already engaged in the spice trade, by the first Portuguese, Dutch and English explorers. Yet it is surprising how the race has preserved its traits wherever found. The rich Arab of Algiers in white silk, low-voiced, courteous and suave, and the noisy Beduin, striding about in a brown "aba" (cloak), over a soiled white robe, his red-checked head-cloth held on by a ropy "ighal," are both Mahomedans, believing that their fate is inevitably fixed by the will of Allah. The Arabic language is spoken, in varying forms, from Morocco to Kuwait and Syria.

The rise and fall of this race is one of the world's great mysteries. They have not only had their "day," but their several "days," and a new one may be dawning. For ten centuries before Christ

Against this slack-twisted Arab spirit, which can achieve anything and hold on to nothing, was opposed, after the First World War (1914–18), the powerful will of Abdul Aziz Ibn Saud. This dominating ruler, as a young man of 24 in the year 1900, was living without land or power under the protection of the sheikh of Kuwait. His family had once ruled in Riyadh, capital of Nejd. One starlit night in 1901 he led 20 of his followers on camel-back and seized Riyadh from the Rashid family. This was the beginning of Ibn Saud's rise to power. During the First World War he gave little aid to the British, but damaged the Turks when he could and refrained from smiting his old enemy, Husein, who actively assisted the Allies and adopted the title of King of the Hejaz, repudiating Turkish authority. In 1919 Ibn

Saud's banner was unfurled against his enemies. He conquered the Jebel Shammar province in 1921 and finished the Rashids. Mecca fell in December 1924; Medina in January 1925; Jeddah in February.

Husein had abdicated in 1924 and his son and successor, Ali, fled from the country in consequence of the victories of Ibn Saud who, in 1926, made himself ruler of the kingdom of the Hejaz. With Nejd, which he already ruled, and Asir, he formed his possessions into a kingdom which was now called Saudi Arabia, comprising almost all the peninsula.

By a treaty signed at Jeddah on May 27, 1927, Great Britain recognized Ibn Saud as an independent ruler, and most of the other powers followed suit. By a decree of September 22, 1932, the unification of the territories was effected. Separate administrations for Nejd and Hejaz are maintained, and after the unification King Ibn Saud appointed his eldest son Viceroy of Nejd and his second son president of the council of Ministers in the Hejaz. Each state has its own capital. The boundaries of Saudi Arabia are not very exact, and the annexation to Transjordan of the northern province of Aqaba-Ma'an has never been recognized by Ibn Saud. How was this ruler able to mass such

Carl Raswan

ARAB HORSEMEN AND YOUNG CAMELS

Arabs consider the camel to be one of the most useful animals in the world and they take very great care of the young ones, which are sufficiently 'grown up' when about a year old to feed on the desert scrub (top). The men are magnificent horsemen (lower), and their mounts are a famous breed, noted specially for great speed and endurance in the desert.

power in the Arabs? He " swung them on an idea," that of religious and national unity. He united them, as Mahomet had done, in a " holy war " against unbelievers—including Moslems of other sects. He was of the Wahabi sect, the Puritans of the Moslem world, and his men were the Ikhwan, or brothers—brothers of fierce intolerance. The Ikhwan refuse to smoke, drink, sing, smile, to wear silk or jewels, to use perfume, to walk with a swagger, to laugh, or to lend money. They kill trees, flowers and grass in their cemeteries, smash tombs of saints venerated by other Moslems. They even wrecked Mahomet's birthplace when they swept into Mecca before Ibn Saud could stop them. They feared that the Prophet might come to be worshipped instead of Allah. Yet with these wry-lipped brothers Ibn

Saud established law and order in Arabia. The hand that stole was ruthlessly cut off.

Caravans could now move unmolested. Each year thousands of pilgrims to Mecca from Arabia, Egypt, Turkey, Syria, West Africa, India, Java and the Philippines rode safely to their holy city. Many of them who came by ship to Jeddah, Arabia's chief port, went on by motor bus. They were no longer robbed, cheated or endangered by the scum of Mecca. Ibn Saud installed wireless stations in Mecca and Riyadh, and electric lights were permitted in the mosque at Medina. He cleaned up towns, built roads, and sped over them with his harem and retinue in a fleet of aluminium-topped motor-cars. In 1936 he forbade the im-

ARABIAN SPORT AND FASHION

He finds his recreation in hawking, this Arab with the falcon—a bird skilled in the sport—perched on his wrist. At rest, as here, the trained falcon is hooded. The womenfolk when they appear in public wear a yashmak, a veil that covers the face below the eyes, as in the top photograph.

portation of slaves into his country unless they had been slaves in the country of their origin, and he also improved the conditions of freed slaves and enforced the better treatment of existing slaves.

To civilize his nomads he offered gold to any man who would sell his camels and settle down to cultivate the soil. Many an Arab has done so—built a house, dug irrigation ditches, planted crops, and then, with the true Arab hostility to success, has turned his back on his labours, refused to reap, and returned empty-handed and free to the lonely desert. Can Ibn Saud sift the fatalism out of the Arabian heart, or will the Arab always spin only a rope of sand? Time alone can answer.

Typical animals of Arabia are the edible lizards (ighourt), dromedaries, gazelles, hares, foxes, conies, monkeys, wolves, hyenas, panthers, ibex, a large antelope (*Oryx beatrix*); quail, bustard, doves, pigeons, ostriches; scorpions, centipedes, and locusts. Plant life comprises the date, and many cultivated fruits, including the banana and fig.

Arabian Nights. A Persian king was in the habit of taking a new wife every day

and putting her to death the following morning. To stop this cruel practice Scheherazade (she-hā-rā-zah'de), a clever princess, becomes the king's bride. She is a gifted narrator of stories and during the marriage night tells a story, and breaks off her tale at so interesting a point that the king spares her life until the next night, in order that he may hear the story's end. So it continues for a thousand nights. Meanwhile Scheherazade bears the king a son. Presenting him to her lord, she tells him of the craft she has used, and the king, who has grown to love his wise and beautiful bride as well as to look forward to her stories, happily spares her life.

This, in a few words, is the framework of The Arabian Nights' Entertainments, or Thousand and One Nights, the most famous book in Arabian literature. It has been translated into many languages, and has probably been read more than any other book of tales ever written. The stories of Aladdin and his Wonderful Lamp, of Ali Baba and the Forty Thieves, of Sinbad the Sailor and the Old Man of the Sea, with their incidents of adventure, of magic, and boundless treasure, are among the most prized possessions of literature.

The basis of the collection was translations of tales from the Persian through Arabic. To those were added many other stories originating in Baghdad and in Egypt. Many of the tales deal with the times of the great Caliph Haroun-al-Raschid (763 809), the contemporary of Charlemagne. They all throw valuable light upon Arabian civilization at its highest point.

The world owes its knowledge of The Arabian Nights to a Frenchman, Antoine Galland, who began life as a poor boy, and by pluck and hard work rose to be Professor of Arabic at the College of France and antiquary to the king. His first edition appeared in Paris in 1704, and the stories filled no less than 12 volumes. Whether he heard the tales during his wanderings in the East or discovered them in one of the French libraries is still a matter of dispute.

For hundreds of years the romances were handed down by word of mouth, repeated in the bazaars of Baghdad, passed from father to son as they sat in their tents in the desert, told on the boats on the way down the Tigris, and in a myriad other places. They form a gorgeous pageant of Oriental folk-lore, history and religion.

Aral Sea.

The largest body of water in Asia with the exception of the Caspian Sea is the Sea of Aral (in the Kazak Republic of the U.S.S.R.). Indeed, it is the fourth largest inland body of water in the world, its area being about 26,000 square miles. Geographers believe that it was much larger at one time, and was connected with the Caspian; and even now it is still becoming smaller, owing to evaporation. The water is slightly salt, but the fish belong to freshwater species. Its two tributaries are the ancient Jaxartes (Syr-Daria) and Oxus (Amu). The shores are practically uninhabited, owing to the fact that the sea is almost surrounded by steppes, rocky plateaux and swamps. In spite of its comparative shallowness, navigation is made dangerous by violent storms. Seals and sturgeon are caught in the Sea of Aral.

Arbitration.

About a century ago two nations—the United States and Mexico—quarrelled over the boundary between their lands. The United States claimed that the dividing line was the Rio Grande, while Mexico contended that it was the Nueces river, some hundred miles to the eastward. Bitter messages followed, and finally in 1846 the two nations engaged in a war which cost hundreds of precious lives and much treasure to determine where the boundary lay.

About 50 years later two nations—this time Great Britain and Venezuela—were involved in a quarrel over the dividing line between Venezuela and British Guiana. Each side meant to take the territory it claimed, but just when war seemed inevitable, Great Britain, acting upon the suggestion of the United States, offered to let an impartial commission made up of men from different countries decide where the boundary line should be. The claims of both countries were heard, and in 1899 the dispute was settled peacefully instead of by war. This method of settling disputes is called arbitration; it may be applied to almost all political and social relationships.

A great number of disputes between nations have been settled in friendly fashion by arbitration. Several of these cases have been between Great Britain and the United States, and they include the settlement by arbitration of the northeast boundary of the United States, the boundary in the inlet to Puget Sound on the Pacific Coast, the conflicting interests of the two countries in the Newfoundland fisheries and the

sealing in Bering Sea, and—an historic case—the claim concerning the steam cruiser Alabama, during the American Civil War. In all these cases a solution equitable to both parties was quickly achieved without any resort to force.

The Alabama, built in an English shipyard, was allowed through an oversight of the British government to put to sea (July 29, 1862) in spite of warnings by the American minister, Charles Francis Adams, that it would be used as a warship by the Confederate (Southern) government. For two years the Alabama ranged the oceans, destroying Northern merchantmen, until it was finally sunk by the Federal cruiser Kearsage, on June 19, 1864. After prolonged discussions the British government agreed to submit to arbitration the claims to damages arising out of the Alabama case. The five arbitrators met at Geneva, Switzerland, in December 1871. After hearing evidence they decided that Great Britain had not exercised " due diligence " in permitting the Alabama to escape, and awarded to the United States £3,100,000 damages. This ended a dispute which threatened to disturb the friendly relations between the two countries. It was also a great victory for the principle of the peaceable settlement of international disputes by arbitration.

It is said that altogether there were only six cases of arbitration in the 18th century, but as many as 471 in the 19th century.

The cause of international peace was further advanced by The Hague Court of Arbitration in Holland established by The Hague Peace Conferences of 1899 and 1907. But this could act only when both parties to a dispute agreed to refer it to

Dorien Leigh

ARBITRATION PALACE AT THE HAGUE
When the League of Nations ceased to exist on April 18, 1946, its work of arbitration in international disputes was continued by the International Court of Justice of the United Nations. The Court sits in the Palace of Peace (above) at The Hague, in the Netherlands. The cost of the building, which had also been used by the Arbitration Court of the League of Nations, was defrayed by a Scotsman, Andrew Carnegie.

that tribunal. A more important step was the formation in 1919 of the League of Nations (*q.v.*) with a constitution providing that the nations which became members must settle their quarrels by arbitration or other peaceful means before resorting to war. The League of Nations ceased to exist on April 18, 1946, but its work of arbitration in international disputes was continued by the United Nations (*q.v.*).

Where property is compulsorily purchased by the government — for the construction of railways, and in the nationalization of certain industries — the price to be paid is settled by arbitration. It is just as useful in settling disputes between employer and employee; its use has prevented or settled many bitter strikes and saved large sums of money to employers and men, and untold suffering to the wives and children of the latter.

ARBUTUS 'STRAWBERRIES'
The arbutus, or strawberry tree, has the flowers of one year and the ripened fruits of the previous year on show at the same time. Here they are, together with sprays of the tough, leathery, green leaves.

Arbutus. (Pron. ar-bū'-*tus*). Belonging to the same genus as heather is the order of evergreen shrubs known as arbutus. It has only a few species, some of which are American, while others are native to the Mediterranean region. One, *Arbutus unedo*, the strawberry tree, grows wild near the lakes of Killarney and in one or two other places in Ireland, but is not found in Great Britain except in gardens. Though it grows under favourable conditions to a height of some 20 or 30 feet, the arbutus is a big bush rather than a tree.

In September it sends forth clusters of little cream-coloured bell-shaped flowers, and these give rise to round, red berries with a rough surface. The berries are not ripe till more than a year after the flowers have withered. So you may see a

strawberry tree bearing fruit of one season and blossom of another, or fruit of two seasons at the same time. The fruit looks like the cultivated strawberry, but has an unpleasant taste. The real strawberry belongs to an entirely different family. Several foreign species of Arbutus are sometimes grown in our gardens. The tree has reddish bark which peels off in long pieces ; the tough evergreen leaves have short hairy stalks, toothed edges and a shiny upper surface. The bell-shaped flowers are supported by a calyx of five sepals and there are 10 stamens and one pistil.

Arcadia. (Pron. ar-kā-'di-a). A great many medieval romances were written about the beautiful land of Arcadia or Arcady, where light-hearted shepherds and shepherdesses spent all their days in joyous dance or wandering through green meadows beneath the fairest of skies. Nowhere is there any misery or wickedness, and all are young and fair. For centuries poets have delighted to picture such a land, peopled by a race—

With nature pleased, content with present case,
Free of proud fears, brave beggary, smiling strife
Of climb-fall court, the envy-hatching place.

Arcadia in this sense is a wholly imaginary country. But in Greece, on the central plateau of the Peloponnesus, there is a real Arcadia, from which this fabled land of romance received its name. Shut off from the coast on all sides by high mountains, its people in ancient days lived simple pastoral lives quite untouched by the progress that marked the rest of Greece. There was no immigration, and customs and dialect remained for centuries unchanged. The name Arcadia thus came to be a symbol of ideal simplicity and happiness. Today the population remains sparse, although the district now extends to the Gulf of Nauplia and has a sea-coast of about 40 miles. Much of it is covered with forest and the soil is mostly unproductive.

Arch. Why are brick and stone bridges, and some concrete ones, built with a curved surface ? Why do we build arches over windows or door openings ? The answers are, because the arch is one of the strongest means of bridging an opening and supporting weight above.

An arch, whether built in brick or in stone, consists of a number of wedge-shaped units arranged about a curve. Or the units may be rectangular, but the joints between them will then be wedge-shaped. Many brick arches are built in the last-mentioned fashion, where there is no need for a nice appearance, and the surface will be covered by plaster. (Such an arch is shown in the next page.) In better brickwork the sides of the bricks are cut to a wedge shape, and this sort of work is called gauged brickwork. In the rough

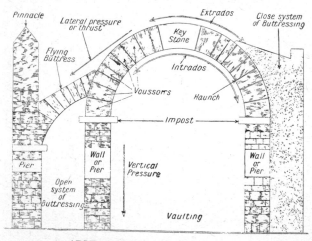

ARCH SUPPORTING A WALL
The wedge-shaped bricks or stones are locked by the ' key ' stone or brick ; the weight above the arch is transferred sideways and downwards on to the arch piers, which are prevented from overturning by the abutments. More side support is given by buttresses.

brick arches, it is the mass of mortar between the joints which is wedge-shaped.

Stone arches are almost always built of wedge-shaped stone blocks, closely fitted together, and with one central block at the top or crown of the arch, called the keystone. The mortar joints are thin. The arch need not even be curved, and many " flat " arches are used. But in these also there is the principle of the curved form, and we must imagine a curve running through the arch from the springing line (where the arch starts) on one side to the springing line on the other side.

In constructing an arch, a timber frame called a " centre " is built below the line of the arch, and the bricks or stones are then laid in position upon the woodwork ; after the brickwork or masonry has become firm, the wood framework is " struck," or taken down. What is it that prevents the stones or bricks from falling down ? Of course there is the mortar, but this would not be sufficient alone; it is the weight of the stones or bricks, in conjunction with the wedge shape, which binds the whole structure together. The keystone, or the bricks which serve the same purpose in a brick arch, locks the units in position. The weight of the arch, and that of anything built above, such as a roadway, or the wall of a building, exercises what engineers call a " thrust " against the supports and the abutments. So that in a properly designed and built arch the pressure is mainly sideways and not downwards through the arch ring. This means that the pressure is directed through the arch stones sideways and then on to the piers or the parts of the adjoining walls on which the lower ends of the arch abut. Of course the piers or the walls must be firm and massive, or they would be overturned by the thrust from the masonry above the arch. When a pier stands separately, as in our first diagram (left-hand side), it may be sustained against sideways thrust by a flying buttress. On the right-hand side of this same diagram (in page 204) we see another method —close buttressing—in which the buttress is a solid mass of concrete built close up to the arch pier. These methods are used in churches and similar big buildings.

SEMI-CIRCULAR ROUGH BRICK ARCH
In building this arch, a wooden ' centre ' of the same shape at the top surface is fixed first, then the two rings of brickwork are laid. You can see that it is really the mortar in the joints which, when set hard, locks the bricks in position.

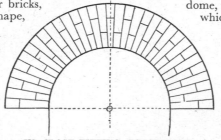

IN CLOSE-FITTING BRICKWORK
Here the bricks are ' gauged '—that is, accurately sawn to the proper wedge shapes. They are softer, better quality bricks than those in the top diagram.

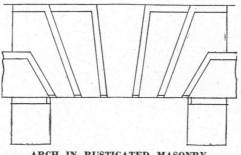

ARCH IN RUSTICATED MASONRY
Rusticated is the name for the simple form of ornamentation. Although this arch is ' flat,' we have to imagine a curve running through it, and the lines of the joints radiating from a common centre below.

invert, and its purpose is to withstand *upwards* thrust of the ground due to heavy masses or brickwork, etc. at the sides.

The Romans first used the arch in conjunction with columns. Before this, a beam called a lintol had been placed on top of the pair of columns, spanning the opening, in the timber construction which preceded the use of stone for building. By adopting the arch the Roman builders gained freedom to use higher and wider openings ; eventually the arch developed into the vault, or deeper space covered with arching ; and into the dome, or spherical form of roof (of which a better name is the cupola).

In the story of Architecture you can read how later builders than the Romans made many experiments with arches, until we got the elaborate and beautiful arches of the Gothic style.

In modern architecture, though the constructional need for arches has become less important, with the use of steel and reinforced concrete " framed " buildings, the arch is still used for its decorative value. And of course we still see it employed in churches and other important public buildings.

Galileo pointed out centuries ago that a suitable curve for an arch could be obtained by hanging a chain of short links between two supports; the chain, in equilibrium and acted upon only by the force of gravity, takes a natural curve called a catenary (from the Latin word for chain). Of course the curve here is inverted, but this identical shape is used for the supporting chains or ropes of suspension bridges. Further, when engineers build dams today they use the catenary form, but it is as if the arch is laid down on its side, with the convex or bulging face towards the face of the dam where immense pressure is exerted by the water.

Some of the arches used in ordinary domestic building are shown in other of our diagrams. You must remember, as we said earlier, that though the appearance may differ, the principle is the same in all real arches. Sometimes dummy arches are used for the look of the thing. There is a strange form of arch which is built with the curve *downwards* and is found in tunnels or in some railway cuttings. This is called an

DIGGING UP *the Long-buried* PAST

Mounds of earth and great heaps of rubbish—what could be more depressingly dull? Yet when the archaeologist gets busy with his spade, what wonders of bygone ages are revealed, what light thrown upon ancient ways!

Archaeology. (Pron. ar-ki-ol'-o-ji). The scene is a valley near Thebes, in Upper Egypt. It is the late summer of 1922. A party of Englishmen descend a short flight of steps cut in the rocky cliff, pass along a descending entrance gallery to an open doorway, and enter an underground chamber which no human foot has trod for 3,250 years.

This is the tomb of the ancient pharaoh Tutankhamen, discovered by the archaeologist Howard Carter. He allows nothing to be touched ; everything stands precisely as it was left by the pharaoh's relatives. Along the rear wall of the chamber are three enormous couches covered in gold, and on the floor beneath them beautiful caskets containing the wardrobe and the personal ornaments of the young king, including a very lovely group of staffs and walking-sticks, many of them adorned with gold.

In the wall behind the left-hand couch there is a hole at floor level, through which it is possible to thrust a flashlight and see another chamber similarly filled with beautiful things. The hole was made by ancient tomb robbers shortly after the burial of the king, and they were caught carrying away the treasures of gold, silver, and gems.

At the other end of the chamber are two life-size statues of the king, of dark wood adorned with gold. They seem like sentinels guarding a doorway, traces of which could be seen on the wall between them. The doorway was entirely filled up and plastered, and the soft plaster bears over

Planet News

ROMAN PAVEMENT COMES TO LIGHT
After they had dug down through the debris accumulated during some 1,500 years the archaeologists at the old Roman city of Verulamium, near St. Albans, Hertfordshire, laid bare this beautiful mosaic pavement.

150 impressions from eight different royal seals. Under Mr. Carter's direction the seals were copied and deciphered, and disclosed the fact that, behind this doorway, the body of King Tutankhamen still lay in its burial chamber!

The work of making such discoveries as this is called archaeology. The word is derived from two ancient Greek words, the first meaning " old," or " old things," and the other, " science," or " knowledge." The " science of old things," is the simplest meaning of the word archaeology. This science is very young, for its most important researches began early in the 19th century. Napoleon's campaign in Egypt, just before 1800, and the reports of scholars who accompanied him did much to arouse interest in the fascinating study.

Few of us realize what an enormous number of works of earlier men have survived to our own time. Archaeological research has shown that the surface of the earth, especially in the Old World, is strewn with evidence of the life of Man in ages far remote. Thus a schoolboy in England may pick up a Roman coin 1,800 years old, lying among the fallen walls of an old Roman building, or may see a Roman mosaic flooring which has been uncovered by the spade of some archaeologist. It is especially in the lands surrounding the

The Times

ARCHAEOLOGISTS AT WORK
One of the most remarkable ' finds ' ever made by archaeologists was the tomb at Luxor in Egypt of the young Pharaoh Tutankhamen, who died in 1353 B.C. When, in 1923, Mr. Howard Carter (left) reached the inner chamber, there were revealed treasures of almost unbelievable splendour, just as they were left at the time of burial.

LYNX-EYED ARCHAEOLOGISTS
Little escapes the notice of archaeologists when excavations are being made. Here they are examining the soil of the great earthworks of Maiden Castle, in Dorset. Even the dust is passed through a fine sieve.

Mediterranean, that is, in Italy and Greece, and in the region which we call the "Near East," that evidences of the ancient life of Man are very plentiful. Archaeological excavations in China and India, only recently begun, are important and interesting, but they are not in the historical line of our own civilization. If the objects discovered come out of a tomb like that of Tutankhamen, where they have been protected from the weather and from the destructive effect of moisture, almost anything may survive the lapse of a long period of time. In the case of this young pharaoh, we find that his friends had put into his tomb almost every kind of thing that he had used during his life. The Egyptian custom of equipping the dead in this elaborate manner, combined with most favourable conditions for preservation in a dry climate, has resulted in the survival of a very large variety of objects that filled the life of royalty over 3,000 years ago.

Such conditions, however, are not to be found everywhere. If we turn to other countries like those of Western Asia, where there is a rainy climate, almost nothing buried in the earth will survive except pottery, metals, especially coins, and some few other materials, such as glass, bone, ivory, and various kinds of costly stone. Besides such small and portable objects there are large monuments of sculpture and architecture, such as tombs, public buildings, and city walls, canals, bridges and harbours. If we were to visit leading archaeological museums in different countries of the world we should find that probably the majority of the exhibits in these museums have come from ancient tombs and cemeteries. A cemetery has necessarily always been in close proximity to a city; and even after it has been laid in ruins for thousands of years, a city of the living always contains remains of the life of the people who were once its inhabitants.

Two ancient cities have been preserved by a catastrophe of Nature. An eruption of Vesuvius in A.D. 79 overwhelmed Pompeii and Herculaneum, in Southern Italy. Modern excavation has cleared Pompeii, so that one may walk through the streets and enter the houses and see the furniture; and Herculaneum is also largely uncovered. In the cities of the ancient world the buildings have mostly disappeared, or are covered by modern towns. In the Near East, however, a forsaken site may be a treasury of bygone human life.

We recall the parable of Jesus about the man whose house fell down. Such an occurrence was a common experience, because the houses were of sun-baked brick, and in course of time yielded to the rains and fell. The owner built his new house on top of the levelled ruins. As this experience was repeated all over the town for centuries, the town rose until it stood on a mound. Eventually it might be forsaken because of famine or war, and fall into ruins. Archaeologists may cut down through it, the lowermost layer, perhaps, being thousands of years old. The excavator gives each level a number, and is thus able to note the level at which every object he uncovers is found. And so his records give him a picture of the successive stages of life. Powerful rulers would erect large buildings, sometimes of stone. The wreckage of many contain pieces of sculpture or wall paintings and show us the stages by which architecture developed.

The service of archaeology to written history goes further. Ancient Hittite, ancient Babylonian and Assyrian, the language of ancient Egypt and of ancient Crete, have long ceased to be spoken. Archaeological excavation has uncovered many monuments and documents bearing written examples of these lost languages. By their use it has

AS THEY WERE IN ANCIENT DUST
Excavations at Ur (the Biblical Ur of the Chaldees) have resulted in the discovery of many small objects as well as great ruins. Three lyres unearthed there are seen above. Though they were partly decayed, archaeologists salved them in such a condition as to make restoration possible.

ARCHAEOLOGY

Department of Antiquities, Government of Iraq

RUINS OF ERIDU, MOST ANCIENT OF CITIES

After nearly 6,000 years the Temple of Enki (above) at Eridu was excavated in 1947. In the right foreground is the stone table at which worshippers made offerings to the 'God of the Deep' before 3500 B.C. At the right centre, back, is a rectangular altar, and at the left centre is a stone staircase. The site of ancient Eridu is 14 miles south of Ur, in Iraq.

The earliest implements of Man are preserved in geological deposits. Ice long covered Northern Europe and part of North America, and retreated for the last time over 8,000 years ago. Stone weapons of prehistoric hunters of the Glacial Age have been found. In the ancient bed of the Nile, formed at about the beginning of the Ice Age in Europe, or possibly a little earlier, archaeologists found stone weapons shaped by early North-East African hunters perhaps a million years ago. Thus archaeology discloses the rise of civilization in the ancient Near East, and its gradual movement westward to Europe.

Egyptology—that is, the study of the life and work of the ancient Egyptians—is, by its very nature, largely concerned with archaeology. Indeed, perhaps

been possible to decipher all the ancient languages mentioned above, except that of ancient Crete.

At Boghaz Keui, in Central Asia Minor, in 1906, Hugo Winckler kicked up with his boot-heel some cuneiform tablets, forming part of the royal archives of the Hittite emperors. A study of them made possible the deciphering of the several ancient Hittite languages. Similarly, our present-day knowledge of the history of the ancient Babylonians was made possible by the excavations of archaeologists—notably Sir Leonard Woolley.

Writing, however, is less than 6,000 years old. Man had been living ages before, making stone weapons and implements (called artifacts) during all that time. Thus for a study of Man's life preceding writing we are exclusively dependent on archaeology. In prehistoric cemeteries the later graves may contain painted pottery bearing a signature. In earlier graves such examples of writing may be lacking, and knowledge must be drawn entirely from a study of articles buried with the deceased. The earliest known implement of metal is a copper pin found in an Egyptian tomb which must date before 5000 B.C.

Beyond this stage of human advance lies one of several hundred thousand years. The later stages of the Stone Age are revealed in remains of prehistoric towns and settlements, especially the so-called Lake Dwellings in Switzerland. Evidences of a still earlier age are disclosed by the stone implements found in European caverns, where men made their homes for long periods. Some contain wall-paintings. (*See also* Cave-dwellers; Stone Age).

the greatest of all modern Egyptologists, Sir Flinders Petrie (died 1942), was famous as a practical archaeologist; it is interesting to note, too, that he wrote a treatise on Britain's most important antiquity, Stonehenge (*q.v.*). Archaeological research has been greatly aided in recent years by the use of photography, and air survey in England has brought to light many interesting traces of Roman and Saxon times.

At Knossos, on the isle of Crete, Sir Arthur Evans unearthed extensive relics of the early Aegean civilization, and in the Holy Land of Palestine an expedition was led by Professor John Garstang to Jericho in 1935.

In 1947 excavations at Atchana-Alakakh, the ancient Hittite capital in the Hatay province of Turkey, disclosed the ruins of a king's chapel, dating back to about 2000 B.C. Remains of Roman London were laid bare by German bombs during the Second World War, and other relics were discovered when mounds of rubble were cleared away; digging on the bombed site of the Saddlers' Hall in Gutter Lane, north of Cheapside, revealed continuous occupation from the first century A.D. to late medieval times and onwards.

One of the most amazing discoveries of 1947 was made in the Mexican state of Chiapas at the base of the Yucatan Peninsula. There an American expedition was guided by pure descendants of the Mayas to the ancient capital of Bonampak. Forty-eight building sites were located, some of them perfectly preserved. The finds included huge carved stone pillars, two altars and at least

1,200 square feet of brilliantly coloured frescoes, painted more than 1,200 years ago by Maya artists.

Another sensational discovery made after the end of the Second World War was that of the remains of the ancient Mesopotamian city of Eridu, the centre of the civilization which preceded the Sumerian (Babylonian) culture. Buildings and temples still in excellent preservation after nearly 6,000 years testify to the great skill and craftsmanship of the prehistoric builders. Eridu, some 14 miles south of Ur at a place now known as Tell Abu Shahrain, is generally believed to be the most ancient city in Mesopotamia. (*See also* Aegean; Architecture; Babylonia; Egypt, etc.).

Archery. There is magic in the words " bow and arrow." At their mere mention one can almost hear the twang of the bowstring and the whirr of the arrow as it speeds through the air. One thinks of Robin Hood, who used a Norman king's deer to perfect his marksmanship with the bow and arrow; and William Tell, the famous Swiss crossbowman, who drew his bow with such sure aim; and the " godlike " Teucer, as Homer called him, who was the master archer of the Greeks at the siege of Troy.

The bow and arrow were among Man's earliest weapons, going back to the Stone Age. Archery was a serious business with our early ancestors, since they depended upon the bow and arrow for their food and clothing, and for protection against enemies. The bow and arrow have been found in practically every country of the world except Australia. Pictures of archers have been discovered scratched on the rocky walls of the caverns in France and Spain inhabited by the cavemen of long ago; archers are depicted in Assyrian sculptures, in ancient rock carvings in Sweden, in Roman carvings in stone, in Egyptian hieroglyphics and in paintings by medieval artists. Primitive men in all ages seem to have turned instinctively to the bow, and even today it is used by most uncivilized tribes who lack firearms.

Various sizes and weights of bows have been used, from frail ones less than three feet long and weighing only a few pounds to heavy ones more than six feet long, weighing 100 pounds or more. By the " weight " of a bow we mean the weight or force required to draw back the string of a braced or " strung " bow the length of the arrow used. Bows simply constructed of a single piece of wood are called *self* bows; those made of two kinds of wood, or of wood and some other material such as raw-hide, are *backed* bows.

Two of the most popular bows for war and the chase have been the *crossbow* and the *longbow*. The crossbow was used by medieval warriors. It was made by placing a bow across a stock which had a groove or barrel to guide the missile, either an arrow or a bolt. The string of the bent bow was

A BASTION OF HISTORIC LONDON WALL
During the Second World War, 1939–45, hundreds of acres of London were laid in ruins by German bombs. Archaeologists seized the opportunity to dig down beneath the rubble in search of Roman London. At Cripplegate a bastion (above) of old London Wall was exposed. The top of the structure is medieval, but the stonework at the lowest level is Roman.

ARCHERY IN THE 20TH CENTURY
As a recreation the ancient sport is still popular in Britain, where the Royal Toxophilite Society is the governing body of archery. These schoolboys are gaining prowess in the handling of their bows and arrows. A bullseye in the straw-and-paper target counts nine.

Fox

At another time, it is said, Archimedes (pron· a r - k i - m ĕ′ - d ē z) ran naked through the streets of his native city (Syracuse, in Sicily), crying, "Eureka! Eureka!"—which is Greek for, "I have found it, I have found it!" The ruler of that city had ordered a goldsmith to make a crown of pure gold, and suspecting that the goldsmith had cheated him by dishonestly adding alloy (a cheaper and lighter metal, which would make the crown of greater "volume" than a crown formed of pure gold), he handed the crown to Archimedes with instructions to find out if indeed it were of pure gold.

This problem worried Archimedes. One day he had gone to the baths, and noticed that as he got into the tub the water rose higher up the sides. The amount of water displaced or pushed aside by his body was an index to the volume of that part of his body which was submerged. If he were to immerse the crown into a vessel previously filled with water, some of the water would be pushed out over the brim; if then he were to immerse in water, in a vessel of the same size as the first one, a mass of pure gold which weighed the same as the disputed crown, the amount of water pushed out should be the same as in the first experiment—*if* the crown were of pure gold.

But the story goes that the real gold pushed out *less* water, which showed that the jeweller had cheated the king. For a crown made with some base metal mixed in would have more volume than one of pure gold. It was the realization of this fact which caused Archimedes to run home, as the story tells, without waiting to dress after his bathe.

held in place by a notch and released by a trigger. The longbow, more ancient in origin and probably developed by the Scandinavian races, came to be the more practical weapon in war, and in time entirely supplanted the more cumbersome cross-bow. It was in the Battle of Hastings that its great usefulness was demonstrated by William the Conqueror. During the Hundred Years' War the English longbowmen, with their overwhelming successes at the battles of Crécy, Poitiers, and Agincourt, became the most celebrated archers of Europe. The longbow, usually made of yew, is held in the hand and shoots a long feathered arrow. It is generally five feet or more in length.

After the 15th century firearms replaced the bow and arrow among civilized nations as a means of warfare. But archery has always remained a popular recreation, particularly in the form of target shooting. The standard four-foot circular target, as set up at each end of the ground, was adopted in 1844. It is generally made of straw and covered with a fabric or paper face painted in rings around a golden bull's-eye. A bull's-eye counts 9; red, 7; blue, 5; black, 3; and white, 1. The governing body of archery in Britain is the Royal Toxophilite Society, so called from the Greek word "toxon" meaning bow.

Archimedes. (287–212 B.C.) "Give
me a place to stand and to rest my lever on," said this ancient Greek mathematician and inventor, "and I will move the earth." If you do not grasp the shrewd truth behind the philosopher's claim, look up the principle of the lever in our story of Mechanics.

ARCHIMEDES DESIGNED THIS SCREW
By using the Archimedean screw, water may be made to flow upwards. When a gimlet is driven into a piece of wood, the sawdust is forced up the winding thread and ejected at the top. The Archimedean screw employs this principle to raise water and is still used in Egypt.

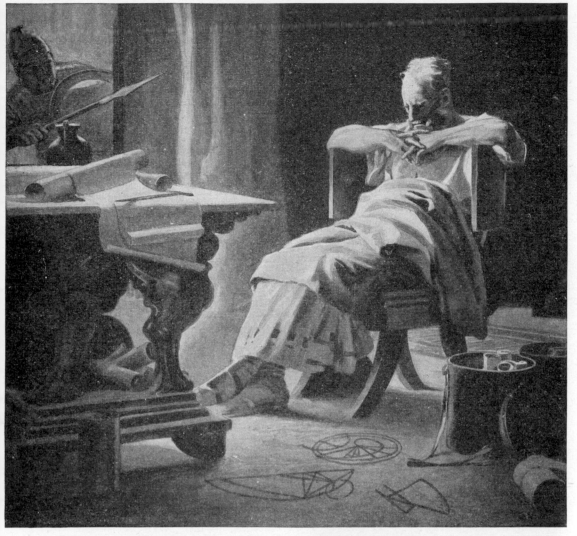

ARCHIMEDES: 'DON'T DISTURB MY CIRCLES!'

Illustrated books were unknown when Cicero and Livy wrote about the death of the great Archimedes. Since they said that the invading Roman soldier killed the scholar because he would not leave off studying geometric figures he had drawn in the dust or sand, later historians and painters imagined the scene as pictured above. Then archaeologists found in the ruins of Pompeii an early Roman mosaic showing the scientist studying circles drawn on his counting board on the table instead of on the floor. Thus archaeology has clarified historical detail, without taking from us the inspiration of a man who could say to the soldier about to kill him: "Don't disturb my circles!"

Archimedes proved this law of hydrostatics : "That a body immersed in fluid loses as much weight as the weight of the volume of fluid which it displaces." We can put this in another way : the support given to a floating body by the water in which it rests is equal to the weight of the water displaced by the under-water portion of the body. The "displacement tonnage" of a ship is the weight of the vessel and her contents when loaded, and is calculated from the volume of that part of the ship which is under water. There are thousands of other practical applications of this law which the great Archimedes first perceived.

Not only was Archimedes the greatest mathematician and writer on the science of mechanics among the ancients ; he was their greatest inventor.

He was the first to realize the enormous power that can be exerted by means of a lever. He also invented the compound pulley ; and a spiral screw for raising water and other substances, which is still widely used and is called the Archimedean screw. Another example of this last principle is found in the winding thread of a carpenter's auger. When a hole is being bored, this thread conveys to the surface and out of the way the shavings taken off by the cutters at the point.

When Syracuse was besieged by the Romans he invented new war engines for its defence, and is said to have suggested a method for using burning glasses to set fire to the besieging ships. The Romans took the city, but only after three years. Archimedes was slain in the ensuing massacre.

HISTORY TOLD *in* CHAPTERS *of* STONE

There is a history written in books and another, quite as interesting when you know how to read it, to be learnt from our buildings of stone and brick, concrete and steel. Here we are given the key to its understanding.

Architecture. In their first attempts at building, men sought merely shelter. Later they developed a feeling for beauty which showed itself in improved workmanship and the use of decoration. A cave becomes more than a mere shelter when men decorate its walls with drawings or carvings—though no doubt these embellishments at first had to do with religion rather than a sense of beauty. A hut becomes a work of art when it is made to please the eye through its proportions, its materials, and its careful workmanship. This blending of the useful with the beautiful in building is called architecture—one of the fine arts.

Our story begins among the ruins of ancient Egypt and Babylonia, for the Egyptians and the Babylonians were the first races known to have developed a great architecture. The chief end of Egyptian architecture was to provide everlasting tombs for kings, and temples for gods. In comparison with these, dwellings for the living were of little account. The remains of the tombs and the temples tell us of many hundreds of thousands of people hewing great masses of granite and sandstone in distant quarries, or transporting them many

ANCIENT EGYPTIAN TEMPLE
Built more than 5,000 years ago, the ruined temple (above) which lies close beside the Step Pyramid of Pharaoh Zeser at Sakkara, south of Cairo, is a wonderful testimony to the architectural skill of the Egyptians in those far off days.

The Times

miles with the most primitive means, or carving and polishing them by hand, into columns, gigantic obelisks, and great building blocks.

Today we are lost in wonder at the vast conceptions of the architects and the accuracy and skill of the workmen with the few and rather primitive tools they used. We admire the decorations of their buildings, chiefly painted patterns in vivid but harmonious colours. We wonder at the prodigious size and the massive construction of their temples and their pyramids, built to house the mummified remains of kings to the end of time ; but there is little of delicate beauty or intricate design in Egyptian architecture. All is massive, and the architecture bears the characteristic stamp of hewn masses of stone.

Material Dictated the Sort of Shape

Ancient Babylonia presents a picture with one great difference. No stone quarries were to be found along the Tigris and Euphrates rivers, so the Babylonians had to do their building with baked or sun-dried bricks. But they, too, constructed temples and palaces on a huge scale, the temples in the shape of great tapering towers rising from the flat plains, the palaces usually in the form of fortresses. The material dictated the sort of shape; if we wish to build a wall of earth or mud or of the sun-dried brick of the Babylonians, we must make it thick at the base, and taper it upwards gradually.

Since bricks were much smaller and more " flexible " units, and could be laid in more varied shapes than the great stone slabs or blocks of the Egyptians, we find more curved and broken lines in Babylonian buildings. They made great use of the arch, which the architects of the Nile seldom employed in their larger structures. Arch construction made necessary another notable feature of Babylonian architecture, the huge abutments— heavy masses of material, placed against the sides of an arch to sustain the sideways pressure or " thrust."

The Assyrians, to the north of the Babylonians, copied the architecture of the latter on an even larger scale, and introduced stone. They learned to decorate their walls with designs of glazed brick in varied colours—an art invented by the Egyptians. Their skill, in turn, was passed on to the Chaldeans, or later Babylonians. These, under the Chaldean king, Nebuchadrezzar, developed some magnificent buildings ; and Babylon, with its temples, palaces and hanging gardens, was reckoned one of the wonders of the ancient world.

The Persians, who conquered Assyria and Babylonia and later invaded Egypt, combined the architectural arts of all three. They built huge palaces of brick and stone in which they used round columns as well as square pillars, and added elaborate decorations of their own, but few remains of these have come down to us.

During these same early centuries a greater and more fruitful art was being developed on the coasts

THE PARTHENON AS IT IS AND AS IT WAS

With the great crags of Mount Lycabettus and distant Pentelicus as a background the Acropolis commands the entire city of Athens. Its crown is the Parthenon, temple to Athens' patron goddess, the architectural wonder of the classical world. In front of it lie shattered stones, every one of which perhaps could tell us some thrilling tale of the Greek city's ancient greatness and stirring history.

From this reconstruction we may gain some faint conception of the majestic beauty of the Parthenon as it appeared in the days of its perfection, five centuries before Christ. In its proportions and design it reveals the high architectural attainments of its builders, while its sculptured statues and friezes were amongst the supreme glories of ancient Greek art and have had many imitators.

To face page 212

AN ARCHITECTURAL GEM OF ANCIENT GREECE: POSEIDON'S TEMPLE AT PAESTUM

This is a reconstruction of the Doric temple of Poseidon (Neptune), the centre of religious life in the Sybarite colony of Poseidonia. One of the noblest examples of Greek architecture, it rivalled the Parthenon in grandeur. Built of travertine (white limestone), it was formerly overlaid with white stucco on which blue and gold and red decorations were lavished.

and islands of the Aegean Sea, and reached its height on the island of Crete. Nearly 2,000 years before the Christian era began, the Cretan builder had learned how to plan a structure so that it would "come out right." The ruins of the great palace at Knossos show with what skill the architects of Crete could bring together, in beautiful and regular arrangement under one roof, a large number of rooms, halls, and long passage-ways. Egyptian architecture reached its highest expression in tombs and monuments to the gods; Cretan architecture was more alive to the needs and comforts of living men.

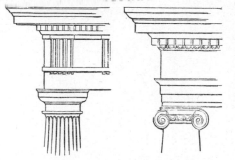

HOW ROMAN BUILDERS ADAPTED GREEK STYLES
Here are the Roman versions of the Doric and Ionic orders (left and centre), also the new order they produced, Composite (right, from Trajan's forum). They made the Doric more slender than the Greek original ; with Ionic they were less happy. The Composite is somewhat like Ionic, but with a necking of acanthus leaves.

Out of this earliest European civilization grew the culture of Greece. The Greeks were clear and logical thinkers. If a pillar or a column had to support a heavy weight, that pillar should be strong and also *look* strong; if it were to support only a light weight, then it should be slender and *look* so. They avoided tricks of decoration, and the sham of idle stonework. Greek architecture depended for its beauty very much upon good balance and proportion.

Greek architecture, like that of most early peoples, developed from tomb building and, later, the construction of temples. Tombs had to be heavy and massive to keep out wild beasts and robbers. Outside the inner chamber wherein the body was immured they might be lighter in construction, and be decorated. Then, too, early buildings were often of wood: a framework of stout square or cylindrical posts, on top of which were laid long beams horizontally to support the roof beams—early structures were mainly of one storey —and the ends of the roof beams projected and made a pleasing pattern under the ornamental cornice. When later builders began to use stone instead of timber, they naturally followed in their constructions the styles and methods of the wooden structures they knew so well.

Greek architecture followed three main styles, generally distinguished as *Doric, Ionic* and *Corinthian* (*see* page 215). These can be recognized by the design of the capital or top of the column, and by the entablature, which is the name given to that part of the building directly above the column. The Doric was the simplest of the three and was the most sturdy and massive. It is found in the buildings of the most artistic period; the Parthenon was a Doric temple. The Ionic, with ram's horn curls, is more delicate and graceful, though it retains much of the Doric simplicity. The elaborate scroll and carving of the Corinthian, with its capital modelled on the acanthus plant, marks the beginning of the decay of Greek art under Eastern influence. Of the three orders, the Doric was the most used, and the Corinthian the least.

The Romans borrowed the forms of Greek architecture but changed the details to suit their own taste (*see* illus. above). It was in their version of the Corinthian order that the Roman architects were most successful. As altered, it suited the more ornate manner of their buildings. We must mention two orders which the Romans made up for themselves: the

BYZANTINE ARCHITECTURE'S FINEST CHURCH
Whenever you see a great dome, you have a reminder that it is to the period of the Byzantine Empire at Constantinople that we owe its introduction into Europe. Here you see the finest of the many superb churches built in that style, the cathedral of Santa Sophia in Constantinople (Istanbul). For many years a Mahomedan mosque, it is now an art museum.

Tuscan, which was a heavier type of Doric ; and the *Composite,* in which some Corinthian details were added to the Ionic, notably the use of acanthus leaf decoration. The effect is seen in our picture (p. 213) of a fragment from the forum of Trajan.

The Romans were far greater engineers than the Greeks, and they took the arch and made it the most useful of all building devices. While they were borrowing their ornaments from Greece, they were inventing many structural forms all their own. With the arch the Roman engineers bridged wide valleys and built aqueducts to bring water from distant hills to Rome. They constructed sewers, triumphal arches, tombs, temples, and circuses, all on much the same principle. They had invented a strong cement made from lime and sand, which they used for uniting brick and stone. Then they went on to use "concrete," in which broken stone or rock was mixed with lime, sand and water. This set into a strong, hard mass, and eventually became their favourite building material.

ROMANESQUE ARCH
It is lightened in appearance by being recessed— 'set back in orders,' it is termed.

From the old Etruscan civilization the Romans had inherited the semi-circular or tunnel vault. They discovered that when two arched tunnels cross each other, a square vault is formed with ridges running to the four corners. Because of these ridges such a vault is called a groined vault. By gradually increasing the size of this vaulting they could roof over large square rooms without breaking up the floor space with columns or other supports.

Then, by applying their knowledge of the arch principle to the dome, they were able to develop this last form of roof (which had been used on a small scale in eastern countries), into a covering for huge circular compartments. The Pantheon in Rome is an excellent example of the mixture of Greek ornament and Roman engineering construction. The front or portico is modelled after the Greek temples, but behind rises the typical Roman dome. While the exterior of this dome is in no way beautiful, the interior which it covers is impressive in its magnificent size and because of the clear, uniform lighting which is accomplished

VAULTING IN THREE STYLES
The aisles of Romsey Abbey, Hampshire, display the original Norman vaulting, also instances where this was later replaced by Romanesque and Gothic vaulting.

through a great circular opening in the crown of the dome. The use of the arch and dome tended against lightness of style. To overcome the sideways thrust of the arches, the Romans built their walls thick and with few openings.

When the emperor Constantine in the year 330 made Byzantium the new capital of the Roman Empire (giving it the name Constantinople), the way was prepared for a new and vigorous style of architecture. Constantine protected the Christians, and these people were now free to build churches instead of worshipping secretly in caves and odd places. In the West the Church followed the pattern of the Roman basilica, an oblong building with an apse and colonnades, used as a law court. For many years after, this shape was usual for churches.

The Greeks had devoted their best efforts to making the outside of their buildings pleasing to the eye. The Byzantine builders turned their attention to the inside. They used the dome as the main element of their greatest structures. Our picture (p. 213) of the interior of the famous church of Santa Sophia—the " Holy Wisdom of God "— in Constantinople (now Istanbul) shows how they obtained their effects of vastness and grandeur. The great central dome rests upon half-domes at each end, which in turn are supported by still smaller half-domes, creating a huge enclosure, with an unequalled sweep of open floor-space.

The Romans had learned how to construct a dome over a circular compartment, but the Byzantine architects invented a way of putting a dome over a *square* room. It was done by filling up the corners with a mass of masonry which continued the curve of the dome until it tapered off to a point at the lower end. This device is called a pendentive.

Byzantine architecture was later copied to some extent in Italy, notably in the great domed cathedral of St. Mark in Venice. But in the main it continued to be a thing of the East, travelling northward into Russia, and furnishing inspiration for the Mahomedan architecture which filled the Orient with graceful domes and minarets.

Meanwhile, in Western Europe architecture declined after the downfall of the old Roman Empire. When the Christians set to building churches, they modelled them, as we have seen, after the basilicas of Rome. No great improvements were made until after Charlemagne, in the 8th century of our era, had succeeded in reviving in Western Europe the memories of Rome's ancient greatness, and had kindled the hope that Christendom might be united for ever in a Holy Roman Empire.

This brought a revival of architecture based on Roman forms, out of which was born a new style which came to be

THE THREE ORDERS OF GREEK ARCHITECTURE

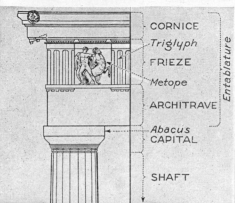

The remarkable genius of the Greeks produced the three famous orders of Greek architecture—Doric, Ionic and Corinthian. Above we see the simple severe Doric in the Temple of Neptune, or Poseidon, at Paestum, Italy. Note how the columns taper, and how cleverly they are spaced, closer together at the corners, farther apart toward the centre. Another subtle effect is the feeling of combined stability and 'live' gracefulness conveyed by the columns.

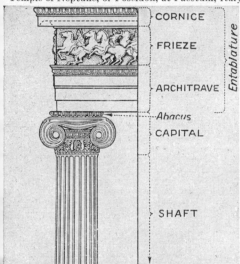

The graceful Ionic style was never used by the Greeks in a large building, but the Romans used it in the big Temple of Saturn in the Roman Forum (right). Alongside each photograph on this page are detailed drawings of the various styles. The capitals determine the style, and each had its characteristic cornice and frieze. Note how these columns, while graceful and soaring, do not seem as reassuringly 'solid' and stable as those of the Doric style.

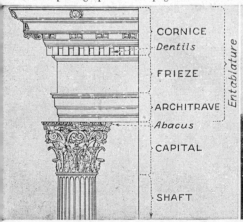

Most ornate of the three Greek styles is the Corinthian, with ferny leaves spraying up around the capital. The dentils shown in the sketch at left are reminiscences in stone of the ends of beams used when temples were of wood. The church of the Madeleine in Paris, at the right, is the best known modern example of the use of the Corinthian column. In the 19th century the Corinthian style was much in favour because of its elaborate magnificence.

HOW HISTORY IS WRITTEN IN LETTERS OF STONE:

The story of great buildings begins with these Egyptian slaves, nearly 5,000 years ago, pulling and prising along the huge blocks of stone out of which the pyramid in the background is being built. Next we see the descendants of these same slaves working on the great Karnak Temple, 1,500 years later. The building art has improved, and wheeled carts are used to haul the stone. In the next step we cross the Mediterranean from Egypt to Greece and find the free Athenian citizens of the 5th century B.C. busy on a corner of the famous Parthenon. Next we find a colonnade going up on the Campus Martius in the days of Imperial Rome. These men were great engineers, showing their skill especially in the construction of the arch.

called *Romanesque*. It started in Italy and spread rapidly across the rest of Europe. The outstanding feature of this style was the development of the old groined vault of the Romans. Having no concrete, with which the Romans reinforced their work, and being obliged to economize in weight and building materials, architects now had to find a simple method for strengthening these vaults. To achieve this, they developed the groins or ridges at the four angles into independent ribs of stone, which met in the centre of the vault.

Resting upon the corner supports of the vault the ribs took the form of two diagonal arches, crossing each other in the middle something like the ribs of an open umbrella. Upon them the roof of the vault, made now of light stone, was laid. The four side arches leading into the vault also became independent stone ribs, the latter supporting the sides of the roof.

Since each of these rib arches was a perfect half-circle, those spanning the vault diagonally had to be wider, and were naturally higher, than those spanning the sides. When the roof was laid, therefore, it had to be domed up from the side arches over the taller centre arches. Having learned from the early Christian basilicas that round columns could be trusted to support arches, the Romanesque builders used them to hold up the new style of vault. In this way they found they could put many equal-sized vaults end to end, roofing over a long enclosure. This enclosure would then be flanked on each side by a colonnade, as a row of columns is called.

The nave, or central part of the church between the colonnades, was a high clear space from the entrance at one end to the altar at the other. The altar usually stood in a semi-circular projection,

covered with a half-dome, which was called the apse and had been used in the basilicas, and which closed that end of the structure, supporting the outward thrust of the last vault.

To the right and left of the nave were the aisles, covered by a lower roof composed of smaller vaults. The outer arches of these smaller vaults were filled in, forming the exterior walls of the church. Small arched windows pierced these walls and lighted the aisles. Sometimes the aisle space was divided into two storeys, each of which looked out upon the nave through rows of smaller columns and arches built between the big main columns. In front of the altar, and cutting the aisles and nave at right angles, there was usually a more open space like the arms of a cross. This was called the transept, and is symbolic of the Christian Church.

Usually the nave rose to a considerable height above the roofing of the aisles, leaving a clear wall space through which windows were cut, these thus admitting light directly into the upper part of the nave itself. This device, known to us as the clerestory (pron. clēr'stŏri), was used by the Egyptians in their temples.

Then there was born in northern France a new architecture and a new art. It was the style we call "Gothic," though it had nothing to do with the

Goths, and merely meant that the architecture was not "classical," or derived from that of Greece or Rome. In Britain the Norman Conquest had brought over many skilled workers from Northern France, with their native ideas of building construction. The monks who had accompanied the Conqueror included architects imbued with the new ideas. Many English cathedrals and other large churches today show Norman work, and you can see a typical example in our picture of part of Waltham Abbey in page 219. Note the massive rounded arches, on equally sturdy columns.

A natural thing for architects in all ages to do was to try to lighten the construction without losing strength, gaining experience as time went on. Influenced by

When the Roman court moved to Constantinople, Byzantine architecture developed, marked by Oriental love of decoration. We see (top) two men inlaying the mosaic of an angel on the wall of the great church of Santa Sophia, completed in A.D. 537.

In the bottom picture on the left, a priest is directing French townsmen in the building of a 13th century Gothic cathedral. Like the Greeks, these men are engaged in a labour of love. Religious zeal and civic pride, fostered by the guilds of skilled craftsmen, are their motives.

The top centre picture shows an Elizabethan mansion, typical of 16th century England. Brick was now used again—the first since Roman days —and dignity and comfort were combined. In the lower central picture is a bit of the interior of St. Peter's at Rome, showing how the Renaissance architects went back to the round vaults and arches of Roman times. Finally, at the extreme right, we come to the steel-ribbed skyscraper of our own time. Here we find embodied usefulness and efficiency, with Man's complete mastery over the new materials now available. Huge as they seem, lightness is the outstanding structural quality of such buildings as this, which are examples of "functional" architecture.

elaborate scheme of decoration. You notice, too—for this is a key to the whole new style—the great lofty window spaces filled with glowing coloured glass. Finally you gaze at the bewildering exterior, with its system of slender arched props springing from the tops of the solid buttresses, and curving like long thin fingers to the clerestory walls, where they resist the enormous outward pressure of the heavy vaulted stone roof. These are the flying buttresses, without which the structural miracle of the Gothic cathedral would be impossible.

These results of greater height and more window area were obtained by bold engineering. The architects gathered the entire weight of the great vaulted roof on a network of ribs springing from piers of clustered columns. Thus much of the burden of the roof was removed from the walls, and the builders were free to fill in the spaces

something of this sort, the Romanesque builders began to set back the arch rings in steps (*see* diagram in page 214) giving that recessed effect known as "set back in orders." This simplified the construction, for the wooden "centre," or temporary ring on which the arch stones were laid, need now be only as wide as the lowermost arch ring. The other steps were supported by those beneath them, which they partly overlapped.

Then, too, the Romanesque builders improved details of groining and vaulting, and made way for the pointed arches which became the hall mark of Gothic architecture. The picture in page 214 shows Norman vaulting at Romsey Abbey, Hants, along with Romanesque and Gothic vaulting which later replaced some of the Norman work.

Great social changes swept over Europe, and particularly over France, during the 12th and 13th centuries. The religious zeal fanned by the monks had set on foot the great Crusades. While knights and princes were fighting for Christianity in the East, a new feeling of independence and power was born among the townsmen at home. With the new freedom came intense city pride, fostered by the guilds of skilled workmen. Men turned their energies to building cathedrals, as the churches of bishops were called, and each city sought to outdo its neighbours.

In scores of towns of France and Germany one glorious Gothic cathedral after another sprang into being. By looking at the cathedrals of Amiens and Notre Dame of Paris you can pick out the most important points in which they differ from the Romanesque structures. You notice the increased height of the interior, the lightness and delicacy of the clustered pillars, and you observe that the pointed arch has very largely taken the place of the round arch throughout the amazingly

H. Felton

MOATED CASTLE AND TIMBERED HALL
Our countryside is studded with glorious examples of domestic as well as ecclesiastical architecture, and here you see two of them. At the top is Hurstmonceux Castle, Sussex, a stone-built stronghold of the 15th century. Lower, in Moreton Old Hall, Cheshire, we have a 'black-and-white' timbered manor house of about the same period.

between the columns with enormous window openings. The side thrusts were carried by deep but narrow buttresses braced against the exterior walls, and by the flying buttresses.

The great wall spaces which the Italians had filled with paintings gave way to exquisite creations in stained glass, telling Biblical stories and Christian legends. The art of the sculptor was brought in to adorn the whole fabric with a myriad of images of men, animals and plants.

From France the Gothic style spread to Germany, Spain and England, taking on subtle differences that mirrored national character. In England there arose a tendency to emphasize straight lines,

PRINCIPAL STYLES OF CHURCH ARCHITECTURE

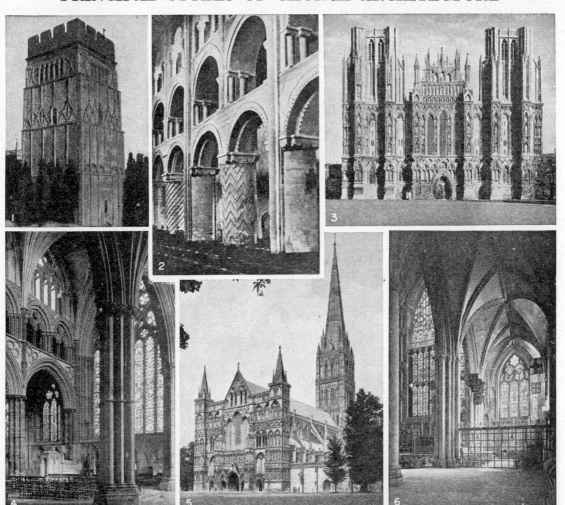

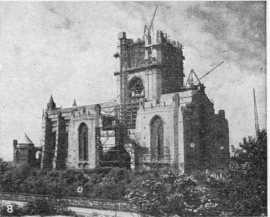

H. Felton, Miss Hawthorn, B. C. Clayton, Will F. Taylor, Donald McLeish, A. F. Kersting, Stewart Bale

Visits to our cathedrals and churches can be much more interesting if we know how to identify their style of architecture. Above are examples to serve as 'keys': (1) Earls Barton church, Northants, showing the fine Saxon tower; (2) Waltham Abbey, with Norman round arches and chevron ornament; (3) Wells Cathedral west front, a fine example of Early English or Pointed Style; (4) Lincoln Cathedral, the Angel Choir, in the Decorated style; (5) Salisbury Cathedral, Early English, with tower and spire in the Decorated style; (6) York Minster: left, the Late Decorated East Window of the Lady Chapel, and right, All Saints' Chapel in Early Perpendicular; (7) St. Paul's Cathedral, London, Late Renaissance period; and (8) the new Anglican Liverpool Cathedral.

especially in the mullions and bars of the enormous windows. This tendency led to the formation of a definite style known as the Perpendicular.

At the same time, the ribs holding up the vaulting were multiplied and cross ribs were added, dividing the surface into elaborate patterns of delicacy and complexity. Instead of this " fan vaulting," magnificent open timber work, such as that in many Oxford and Cambridge colleges, was often used to support the roof. Church towers and spires reached a high development in Gothic times. At first built separate from the churches, like the campaniles (pron. kam-p*a*-ne'-le) or bell towers of Italy, in Romanesque times they became parts of the church itself.

The knowledge of engineering acquired in building Romanesque and Gothic churches made possible also those great castles of the Middle Ages, erected by kings and nobles for military purposes. Indeed, the whole story of those stirring days is summed up in a way by those two types of building —the castles and cathedrals on the one hand, and the town halls and guild halls on the other.

Architecture of the Renaissance

But the reign of Gothic art was comparatively short. With the Renaissance came a revival of the old Greek and Roman styles. Men became enslaved for a time by the worship of antiquity, declaring that there was no art to compare with that of Rome and Athens. In the 15th century,

under the influence of the revival of classical learning and art, the pointed arch again yielded to the round arch of the Romans. The old classical columns, capitals, and other details were again employed, together with the many forms of ornament of the Graeco-Roman patterns.

At the same time there came a vast improvement in the comfort of domestic arrangements. With the introduction of window-glass, in the last part of the 16th century, builders began to construct elaborately decorated and furnished residences. This taste for comfort gradually found expression in such palatial mansions as the Pitti Palace in Florence, and Hampton Court in England. In England the reign of Queen Elizabeth was marked by the building of scores of noble residences—the Elizabethan manor houses, many of which still stand as among the greatest achievements of English architecture. The Romans had brought brickmaking to Britain in the 5th century, but it fell into disuse until the time of the Tudors. Its re-discovery provided the architects of this period with a plentiful, convenient and adaptable material.

But it was not long before men's tastes ran to elaborate decorations and florid styles, called *Baroque* and *Rococo*. No great new principles of building were invented, and in many large public buildings the greatest mixture of styles prevailed, with a bewildering and often tasteless intermingling of straight lines and curves, arches and pillars, scroll work and sculpture.

In this period architecture as the expression of a national spirit waned. Instead, there grew up scores of " schools," founded by successful architects, each following its own tastes. While the results were not always happy in the larger public enterprises, there was steady progress in giving to private homes more beauty and comfort and individuality. Merely to quote the names of leading architects of those days is to conjure up visions of stately and noble buildings they designed: Inigo Jones (1573–1652); Christopher Wren (1632–1723); John Vanbrugh (1672–1726); James Gibbs (1674–1754); William Kent (1684–1748); Robert Adam (1728–92); and his brother William; William Chambers (1726–96); John Soane (1753–1837); John Nash (1752–1835). This brings us to the dawn of the 19th century, in which much in architecture was to change—materials, styles, and resources.

But it was not until steel and reinforced concrete construction began that any vitally new architecture arose. This style finds its highest expression in the modern business building. Crowded together as these structures are in many cities, it is difficult to appreciate their full and vigorous beauty, when handled by a master architect.

Now things began to move so swiftly that we must skip much that is interesting. As the century wore on, machinery took the place of much hand labour, both in preparing and working materials, and in handling them. Wrought and cast iron, and then steel, took a larger place. "Reinforced"

W. F. Taylor

GEORGIAN HOUSE AT SALISBURY
For dignity and straightforward appearance, no style can compare with early Georgian architecture, of which the house above, in the Close at Salisbury, is a fine example. Characteristics of this period in domestic architecture are often introduced into modern houses.

BATTERSEA POWER STATION: FUNCTIONAL ARCHITECTURE

Fitness for purpose dominated the design for this great electricity generating station. Built alongside ' London river,' the Thames permits the delivery of the enormous quantities of coal needed for fuelling the boilers ; its waters furnish the cooling liquid by which the spent steam from the giant turbines is lowered in temperature and condensed. The building was still incomplete when this photograph was taken and a fourth chimney was to go up.

concrete, strengthened with steel rods, came into use. Steel skeletons and frames held a building together ; the walls no longer bore most of the weight, but were mainly a screen or filling between the steel or concrete columns or stanchions and the horizontal framing members.

But alongside this severely utilitarian trend there developed, strangely enough, a revival of Gothic architecture—not the Gothic we have described but a " modern " Gothic, of which the Royal Courts of Justice in the Strand, London, are a good example. This building, designed by George Edmund Street, was the last really big attempt to bring back the Gothic tradition. Before Street, Augustus Pugin (1811-52) had tried to re-kindle the flame of Gothic in Britain, and succeeded so well that the new Houses of Parliament were designed to be built in modern Gothic. The architect was Charles Barry (1795-1860), and Pugin assisted him. Some few other big buildings (including a great railway terminal office-block and hotel at St. Pancras, London) were built in this style, and quite a number of churches.

Now to return to the more prosaic kind of building, for blocks of offices, concert halls, theatres, railway stations, factories, and so on. Steel and concrete enabled these to be built with much more freedom. As we have said, the weight was no longer borne by brick or stone walls, but this did not prevent architects clothing the steel or concrete framework in those homely materials, with their pleasing brown or reddish or creamy shades. Fine,

dignified brick buildings, in which the best traditions of the Elizabethan or Georgian architects were observed, were so arranged as to give ample room inside for modern uses, and with plentiful natural light. Brick came into new uses in making admirable patterns on the face of the structure, in conjunction with what architects term " fenestration," or the window arrangement. Stone facings lent grace and dignity to steel framed or concrete structures, so that the best of the old and also of the new methods was retained.

Domestic houses of the smaller kind, in the early part of the 19th century, were drab and dull as a rule. Builders sought to place as many as possible in a given area, and many were built in terraces. In the outer regions of a big city, where people of more leisure lived who could afford to drive to town in a carriage, bigger and more elaborate houses were put up in large numbers, but there was little of interest even about most of them. A favourite treatment was to clothe the brick with stucco, a form of plaster, and to shape this into cornices, ornamental mouldings and other ornaments. A porch with brick columns, encased in stucco, became quite popular.

At the end of the 19th century and in the early years of the 20th, roads had become better, and mechanical transport came in. Well-to-do people could come to town in motor-cars, while others could ride in by motor-bus or fast and frequent trains from the suburbs. People by the hundred thousand moved out farther from the cities, and

SKYSCRAPER ARCHITECTURE
The Empire State Building, in New York City, has 102 storeys and is 1250 feet high. Skyscrapers belong to sites where ground space does not allow expansion sideways ; for light and air the builders must go up and up and up.

houses had to be built for them. Very many of these dwellings were as dull and uninspiring as those built nearer the cities three-quarters of a century earlier. But this was to some extent unavoidable, for a builder could not have a thousand different styles to please the whims of his clients. The cost would have been far too heavy.

We must not be too hard on people who wanted their houses to look " different," or desired them to have " Tudor " features, or a half-timbered appearance. Individuality is a most valuable quality, and ours would be a very humdrum world if everyone in a suburb lived in the same sort of house. What many do not realize is that the charming old cottages we meet with in country villages are seldom as convenient as they are pretty. The very qualities that make them look interesting are those which produce small rooms, low ceilings, and so on. The architect of today strives to give us ample light and air, in a labour-saving house that is convenient to run. If we insist, he may import into the design some of the " old-world " features we fancy, but the result is not always satisfying or convincing.

In between the two World Wars a good deal of experimenting with new materials and new styles for domestic houses went on. For example, concrete came into use, with very pleasing results in many cases. Almost the entire front of the house, on ground floor and top floor, was filled in with windows—in metal frames which allowed thinner dividing bars between the panes of glass, and narrower vertical bars between one frame and another. This produced a veritable " sun-trap," excellent in sunny localities or sunny aspects.

Under pressure of the big demand after the Second World War of 1939-45, all-steel and even aluminium houses were built, but brick and stone still hold their own for small houses.

Why Skyscrapers Came Into Being

In American cities where ground space did not allow expansion sideways, enormous many-storeyed blocks of buildings were thrust up into the air. The style was imitated elsewhere in places where conditions did not make it necessary, probably out of a mere desire for bigness. The full realization of the architectural possibilities of the " skyscraper " did not take place until the 1920s. Like huge stalagmites, unbroken crags of steel, stone and glass push upward as if in answer to the challenge of a new age. In this geometrical simplicity of clean lines, shorn of all artificiality and scorning all known styles of decoration, we have a revolution in architecture. Twentieth-century skyscraper style has been achieved rather through the efforts of the engineers than of the architects, for its beauty lies in its fitness for its task and in its sound mechanical proportions.

The skyscraper is an extreme example of the kind of architecture described as " functional." Its forms are primarily dictated by the purpose which the building has to fulfil. The functional building does not pretend to be what it is not ; the functionalist architect will have nothing to do with the idea of making an electricity generating station look like a Gothic cathedral, though many would urge him to do something of this sort. An outstanding example of a design dictated by fitness for purpose, and which presents a magnificent picture despite its stark simplicity, is the enormous generating station at Battersea, on the south bank of the River Thames (see page 221).

Giant Thames-side Generating Station

The generating station was built by the riverside in order that the very large quantities of coal needed for fuel might be brought up and unloaded speedily right at the site. Then, too, enormous quantities of cold water are needed for condensing the spent steam from the turbines; it is taken from the river. Vast quantities of ash from the furnaces have to be loaded into lighters for a journey down the Thames. The photograph on page 221 shows some of the giant cranes which do this work of loading and unloading.

Three towering chimney shafts provide the draught for the furnaces where steam is raised to drive the turbines, which are coupled to the electrical generators. As first built, there were only two chimney shafts; the third was added later, and the complete building will have four. But, looking at our illustration, we can easily visualise the fourth shaft, and can appreciate what a fine piece of architecture is this great edifice—with a beauty derived from its fitness for its functions.

What IT'S LIKE on TOP of the WORLD

Once thought to be ice-covered land of perpetual snow, where only the hardiest of mankind could survive, there are Arctic meadows gay with flowers where the thermometer may soar to 100 degrees Fahrenheit.

Arctic Regions. In the map in this page you are looking down on the "top of the world." That dotted line of the Arctic Circle, 3,300 miles in diameter, marks off the region around the North Pole, where at least on one day in every year the sun does not rise above the horizon. As you get nearer the Pole the number of sunless days per year increases, until at the Pole itself there are six months of darkness. Of course, for every day when the sun does not rise there is a corresponding day six months from then when the sun does not sink below the horizon.

This phenomenon is due to the fact that the Earth's axis is not perpendicular to the plane of its rotation around the sun ; so that the Pole sometimes is leaning towards the sun and sometimes away from it. This "lean" amounts to about 23° 27'. Since the Pole is 90° north of the Equator, the Arctic Circle is 66° 33' N.

For about four-fifths of its circuit the Arctic Circle passes over land, cutting off fringes from Europe, Asia and America. The remainder of the Arctic regions—a vast tract of more than 8,000,000 square miles, half as large as all of North and South America—consists of the Arctic Ocean, 9,000 feet deep at the Pole, and the many islands it contains. The Arctic Ocean itself has an area of approximately 5,400,000 square miles.

Apart from the continental fringes of Europe, Asia and America, the greatest land mass of this region is Greenland.

It is a peculiar island; except for a coastal fringe of high mountains, the country is covered by a vast ice sheet from which glaciers force their way down valleys to the sea to give birth to the icebergs which are eventually a menace to North Atlantic shipping. This ice sheet rises in the centre to about 10,000 feet, and the thickness is about 1,000 feet less than the total height above sea level; thus Greenland is

like a rectangular saucer, the bowl containing the ice. About 1,600 miles long and nearly 800 miles wide at its greatest width, it is the largest island in the world and belongs to Denmark. Other islands important for their size are Baffin Island, Banks Island, Victoria Island, and Grant Land, lying north of Canada ; the Svalbard group (including Spitsbergen), Novaya Zemlya and Fridtjof Nansen Land, lying north of Europe; and New Siberia and Lenin Land, lying north of Asia. These are for the most part uninhabited, and visited only in the summer-time by hunters, fishermen and ivory-miners—seeking the tusks of mammoths that roamed the region ages ago.

Cryolite, a rare and valuable mineral used in aluminium production, is mined at Ivigtut in S. Greenland. Coal mining is carried on in Spitsbergen. Iron ore is mined in Lapland. On Victoria Island there is copper ; oil companies are reserving fields for development in the far north.

The Arctic regions, being reasonably accessible to Europe, were early explored. The Viking called

ARCTIC ROUTES AND LOCATIONS
This is a map-story of the Pole that the explorer Peary found and that others have visited by air. The Magnetic Pole and the North Geographical Pole are far apart : special flights carried out by the Royal Air Force in 1945 established the Magnetic Pole to be in Bathurst Island, 300 miles N.N.W. of its supposed position (as indicated above) in the Boothia Peninsula.

Erik the Red, outlawed from Iceland, founded a colony in S.W. Greenland in A.D. 983. During its most flourishing time this Norse colony numbered about 2,000 people. Sixteen churches were built, of which some of the remains may be seen today. Those hardy Vikings also visited Baffin Island and Labrador, and were thus the first Europeans to reach the American continent.

During the 14th century, probably owing to the Black Death in Europe, communication with Europe became more and more irregular until it finally ceased. Cut off from Norway and essential supplies, the people died or were absorbed by the Eskimos; and the first period of Arctic colonisation ended in mystery. Greenland remained unknown until the Norwegian missionary Hans Egede, in 1721, once more began to colonise the West Coast and to Christianise the Eskimos. The East Coast was not revisited until 1884, when the Dane, Gustav Holm, travelled up the coast by rowing boat from Julianehaab and found a settlement of Eskimos at Angmagssalik.

Contented Eskimos of Greenland

Greenland is a closed country, which means that no one is allowed to go there without permission from the Danish Government; and this permission is given only to approved explorers. Thus the culture of the Eskimos has been preserved and their lives largely safeguarded from the temptations and dangers of civilization. The Greenland Eskimos are probably the most contented people in the world in consequence.

The Eskimos who inhabit the North American shore and off-lying islands speak the same language as those in Greenland, though there are many different forms of dialect. The administration of the Canadian Eskimos is largely undertaken by the Hudson's Bay Company and the North-West Mounted Police. But, unlike Greenland, travellers and missionaries of all denominations are allowed to mix with the Eskimos, who have thus lost much of their way of life.

In summer, Eskimos live in tents made of seal or caribou skin, spending their time in fishing and in hunting seals, walrus, narwhal, in their kayaks. The latter is a one-man canoe about 19 feet long, very fast and easily upset. Some Eskimos are able to roll their kayaks right round and right themselves again, so that if upset accidentally they will not drown; in spite of which, however, 70 per cent of the male deaths are due to kayak accidents. During a summer an Eskimo will move his camp several times, packing his tent, dogs and all his possessions, into a " umiak," a big open boat about 50 feet long which, like the kayak, is made of seal-skin stretched over a wooden frame. The umiak is always rowed by women.

When autumn comes several Eskimo families will get together and build a house of turf and stone. As many as 20 families may live in the same house, which is really one big room with a sleeping bench along one wall. The bench is divided by low skin screens, thus making a compartment for each family. In North Greenland and in the far Northern Canadian Arctic instead of a stone house the Eskimos build snow houses, known to us as igloos. Only in regions where the temperature can be relied upon to remain below

Planet News

FIRST AEROPLANE PARTY LANDED AT THE NORTH POLE

The Arctic regions have a great effect on the climate of Europe, and in 1937 a party of Russian scientists flew to the North Pole to find out all they could about weather conditions there. It was the first expedition to be landed on the ice at the Pole and to be supplied by air. Their camp (above) was on floating ice, and their nine-months' drift of some 1,500 miles towards the east coast of Greenland was one of the most valuable results of the expedition.

Once a vast inland sea, with only a few of the highest points here and there emerging as islands, the pampas today still resemble a sea — but a boundless sea of waving grass, at times so high as to hide a man on horseback. The soil is almost invariably fertile where Nature or irrigation provides sufficient moisture. Only along the banks of the few rivers and streams are there native trees, but settlers have begun to plant the eucalyptus and fruit orchards. Roads are generally mere tracks of dust or mud, but national roads, built since 1932 and suitable for motor traffic, link up the provinces.

The prairie is divided into vast cattle and grain ranches, some containing a hundred square miles of land, and the average being about six square miles. A comparatively few wealthy owners were allowed by the government to take up those great *estancias*, thus bringing about conditions the reverse of those in North America, where the land is in the hands of many settlers. Argentina may be said to be still in a state of agricultural feudalism, which has been one of the retarding features in its development.

The rural population of the country is divided into two sharply contrasted classes, the wealthy landowners and their impoverished and ignorant labourers and tenants. Because of the vast distances, and because of the gulf fixed between the rich and the poor, Argentina has no such rural life to offer as our own land, with its many schools and churches and social advantages. Of recent years laws have been passed with the idea of breaking up the great estates and creating smaller holdings.

Argentina's prosperity dates only from 1880. Before that time it did not produce cereals enough

Paul Popper

ARCTIC FISH FOR THE ESKIMO'S LARDER

Part of the Canadian mainland lies within the Arctic Circle and winters are very severe. To fish, the Eskimo has had to cut a hole in the thick ice of the Coppermine river, in the North-West Territories, and he must remove his catch quickly before it freezes to the net. Eskimos, in the far north of Canada, live by hunting and fishing.

zero Fahrenheit is it possible to live in snow houses. If it is really cold outside, then the inside can be kept warm without fear of the structure melting. For heating and light the Eskimo uses a blubber stove. Without the seal Eskimos could not live, as it provides food, fuel and clothes.

The Lapps are an Arctic people inhabiting Northern Norway and Sweden, and engaged entirely in herding reindeer. The Samoyeds in Russia proper live on the shores of the Arctic Ocean, hunting and fishing like the Eskimos; while the American Indians are found in Alaska and Canada, but these hunt inland and do not venture out to sea.

We of the temperate zones once thought of our Arctic cousins as living in an ice-covered land of perpetual snow. It was thought that only the hardiest of races, those accustomed to long periods of extreme cold, could support themselves in this climate. But famous explorers, particularly Stefansson, have told of Arctic meadows gay with flowers, where plants grow under a blazing sun that never sets for many days in summer and the thermometer may touch the 100° F. mark. More than 2,000 species of plant life have been discovered—flowering plants, ferns, mosses and lichens, and willows, junipers and birches stunted by dry winter winds.

Stefansson predicted that these vast prairies would become the future source of the world's meat supply, with millions of reindeer and musk-oxen fattening on the coarse grasses. These hardy animals need no shelter or grain-feeding in winter. They can outlive the fiercest blizzard, finding their food by digging through the snow to reach young

roots and mosses germinating in the soil below. Reindeer and dog have been tamed to help Man in his conquest of the Arctic. He hunts other animals for food and furs—musk-ox, caribou, polar bear, wolf, fox, hare, lemming and ermine. With the exception of the blue fox and the brownish-black musk-ox, all these grow winter coats that are white or nearly white. This colour is most economical in conserving bodily heat, and it hides them against their snowy background, against which dark colours would be easily detected by the beasts' human or animal enemies.

Thirty-five species of birds migrate to the Arctic —some to within 400 miles of the Pole—but only the raven and the Arctic owl stay through the winter's darkness. Mosquitoes breed in vast numbers in pools that form when the top soil thaws in summer. The Polar waters teem with life. Countless numbers of microscopic plants furnish food for the myriad fish. The fish, in turn, are eaten by whales, seals and walruses. The fisheries of the North are increasing in importance as the world comes to need their resources.

Soviet Russia is opening up the Arctic region of Siberia to shipping and aircraft, and several townships have arisen along these barren coasts. In 1937 Soviet airmen flew non-stop from Moscow to California across the Arctic Circle, a distance of 6,305 miles, and during the Second World War the Arctic air route was much used between America and Great Britain. Experts are agreed that in the near future the main inter-continental air lines will run N.-S. across the Arctic, saving thousands of miles on the old E.-W. routes. Great

ARCTIC'S SU...
One of the most surprising thin...
which, in the few weeks of summ...
up and clothes the ground. He...
plant. A brigh...

possibilities of developm...
Arctic were opened by th...
ment of " Exercise Musk ...
journey in 1946 from C...
Edmonton, Alberta. An ...
America was founded at N...
to act as a co-ordinating ce...
(*See also* Antarctica ; Pola...

ARGENTI...

Although ther...
vast plains...

Argentina. (Pron...
ar-jen-tē'-na). The firs...
Spanish settlers in Sout...
America held the fla...
monotonous plains ...
Argentina in little esteer...
This south-eastern pa...
of the South Americ...
continent lacked t...
rugged picturesq...
scenery of the An...
regions, with their sto...
of precious metals, ...
well as the vast ...
mysterious forests of ...
Amazon. Yet in ...
enormous fortunes ...
uninviting prairies, ...
is now the leading c...
One-sixth of the ...
consists of these imm...
which occupy the ce...
from the Atlantic s...
Andes. To the nor...
low plain, largely un...
and swamps, inhabi...
As the continent na...
pass into the cold ...
This little-known...

'CHRIST OF THE ANDES' *G.P.A.*
Marking the boundary between the Argentine and Chile this great statue, placed above the Transandine railway tunnel, marks the end of a controversy which caused bad blood between the two lands from 1847 to 1902. It stands amidst desolate mountains, 12,000 feet above sea-level.

for even its own use, and its meat exports were confined to Brazil and Cuba. Today the long-horned cattle of the early years have given place to Aberdeen-Angus and Beef Shorthorn pedigree stock, just as the native *gauchos*, or cowboys, are disappearing with the advent of more scientific farming. A census in 1945 showed that the country possessed 34 million head of cattle and 56 million sheep. Argentina leads the world in exports of maize and flax seed. It also produces and exports vast quantities of wheat. Enormous quantities of frozen and tinned meats, of hides and wool, are sent every year to Great Britain and other countries.

In railway development the Argentine Republic leads all South American states, with more than 26,000 miles. Lines radiate inland in all directions from Buenos Aires to the great wheat and cattle districts, and to Chile. River transportation is also available for many parts of the country, chiefly on the three great rivers, the Uruguay, the Paraná and the Paraguay, which unite to form the estuary of La Plata—one of the greatest among the river systems of the world. Airways connect Argentina with other South American countries and with the U.S.A. and Europe. Argentina has 55 broadcasting stations, and wireless telephony is in use between Argentina, Chile, the U.S.A., and Europe.

Nearly one-fifth of the population is concentrated in the magnificent capital Buenos Aires, the foremost city of Latin America. Through the great

estuary of La Plata at its door ploughs a steady stream of liners from every quarter of the world, in normal times bringing swarms of immigrants and imports and taking away vast stores of meat and wheat. The remaining part of this huge country has only about six inhabitants to the square mile.

It is not likely that Argentina will ever become a great manufacturing centre. So far as is known it contains little coal and iron, though abundant supplies of oil are being developed. On account of the difficulties of mining operations and transportation in the Andes, the mining industry has been neglected, though there are a few rich deposits of silver, gold, copper, and other minerals.

Argentina more than any other Latin-American country is a white man's land, for the Indian population numbers only about 20,000 and the half-breed element well under 100,000. The white population is chiefly from Italy and Spain, the remainder being mainly of Russian, German, British, French, Turkish, and Uruguayan origin. Language and customs are almost entirely Spanish.

Captain Juan de Solis (1515) and Sebastian Cabot (1526) were among the first Europeans to visit the region of the Plata River. In 1535 Don Pedro de Mendoza founded a settlement where the Argentine capital now stands, but it was soon destroyed by Indians. Seven horses and five mares escaped to the plain at that time and became the ancestors of the immense herds of wild horses that once roamed the pampas. In 1580 Buenos Aires was refounded and Spanish settlers began spreading over the country.

Argentina became the seat of a vigorous revolutionary movement against Spanish rule in South America as early as 1810. Desultory fighting went on for six years, until (in 1816) a revolutionary congress assembled and declared Argentina's independence. England and the United States were

ARGENTINE GAUCHO *Dorien Leigh*
On his small, thick-set mount, the gaucho of the Argentine looks, and is, as fine a horseman as may be found anywhere in the world. Notice the simple reins and trappings, and the sheep-skin saddle cloth. The lasso is hung behind.

Plataea the next year. When m
states decided to form an allia
Persia (the Delian Confederacy), v
at their head, Aristides, because
known honesty and fairness, wa
make the arrangements and to
expenses of the war on the diffe
Yet when he died, about the year
was so poor that he was buried a
cost. The Athenian government
recognized the statesman's many
Athens, and gave his daughters c
his son an estate.

Aristophanes. (c. 44!

The entertainments " put on " b
Athenian comic dramatist were
what we now call revue. They
a mirth-provoking central id
some task to be carried out by
which, having been expounded
formed by the actors, was foll
series of colourful topical episod
the results of the hero's labou
with fine poetic passages and l
and concluding with the triu
hero.

Little is known of Aristopha
a-ris-tof'-a-nēz) private life. A
above, the years of his birth—v
ably took place in the island c
and death are both uncertain.
doubtful whether he was a
citizen. He was intensely con
his views; for him the beginnin
century, the Athens of the Persia
the golden age ; the newer
distasteful to him. He ridicu
learning, in the person of So
savagely lashes Euripides, wh
the inquiring attitude that he
Socialism, women's rights, the fo
citizens for serving on juries nov
been raised—these and other

ARISTOPHANES
The choruses of the old Greek com
grotesquely garbed so as to represent
we see how a Greek potter orname
Aristophanes's early p

the first to recognize the new republic. Soon after, a patriotic army under General San Martin crossed the Andes—one of the greatest feats in military history—and helped Chile and Peru to shake off the Spanish yoke. Despite his military success, San Martin refused to accept civil office and withdrew to Europe.

A period of civil wars followed in Argentina which ended only in 1852 with the fall of General Rosas. In 1853 the republic adopted a constitution closely modelled on that of the United States. For a time (1865-70) there was a fierce war against Paraguay, in which Argentina, Uruguay, and Brazil were allied.

ARGENTINE PAMPAS ROUND-UP
The vast herds of cattle which range the plains of the Argentine rival wheat as the country's chief source of wealth. There are over 34,000,000 head of cattle in the republic, and here is a scene on an Argentine ranch where a herd has been rounded up on the grazing land and driven into pens by horsemen called gauchos.

To commemorate the arbitration which ended troublesome boundary disputes with Chile in 1902, the two nations united in setting up the famous peace statue, " The Christ of the Andes "—a colossal bronze figure which stands above the principal mountain pass leading from the one country to the other. In the Second World War (1939-45), Argentina remained neutral until March 27, 1945, when she declared war on Germany and Japan, and she became one of the original members (totalling 51) of the United Nations.

The government of Argentina is a federal republic. The President is elected for six years. Congress consists of a Senate and a House of Deputies. Provinces have their own local governments and retain full authority in local matters.

Argonauts.

(Pron. ar'gō-nawts). The ancient Greeks believed that in Colchis on the distant shores of the Black Sea there was once the fleece or skin of a wondrous ram, all of pure gold, which was hung on a tree in a sacred grove. It was guarded by a sleepless dragon, and despite its value no mortal had ever braved this danger to win it.

At last an adventurous youth named Jason, heir to the throne of Iolcus in Thessaly, made a vow to perform this dangerous task. With the aid of the gods he built an enchanted ship called the Argo, and, accompanied by the noblest heroes of Greece —Castor and Pollux, Heracles (Hercules),

Dorien Leigh
ARGENTINE OXEN DRAG HOME THE WOOL
Sheep are even more numerous than cattle in the Argentine—it is estimated, indeed, there are over 56,000,000 head. This photo shows rolling plains over which oxen drag heavy carts loaded with the results of a day's shearing. The hides of the cattle and the wool of the sheep bring in nearly as much wealth as the great meat-packing industry.

ARGONAUTS
Having taken the Golden Fleece
fellow Argonauts set sail from C
the Bradford Art Gallery, we see
so that her father's ship woul

Orpheus, and others—he se
journey was long and peri
Argonauts at last reached

The king of Colchis pror
Fleece if he would yoke to
breathing bulls presented to
(Vulcan), and plough a fi
Ares (Mars), and sow it
From these, armed warri
seek to slay Jason. When t
posed of he must still fight w

With the aid of the kin
powerful sorceress who ha
Jason, the latter success
dangerous labours. A m
him from the fiery breath of
were made to attack and
dragon was put into a pro
potion, and Jason was ena
cut off its frightful head.
Golden Fleece, Jason fled
and sailed back to Iolcus.

Jason, alas, proved untr
her magic she made for
wondrous beauty, but of s
it burned like fire and p
When the frantic Jason r
sorceress, she disappeared
drawn by dragons through
the ship and a Greek w
gave the Argonauts their
mollusc called the argon
(Argonauta argo). Its beau
to the animal's body, and i

Argyllshire. O
Scottish counties, with an a
miles, Argyll includes seve
long, indented coast-line.
group known as the Inner
Jura, Tiree and the rest.

ARISTOTLE THE THINKER
Aristotle was first the pupil and then the rival of Plato, and
his intellect was one of the greatest of all time. In pose
and in facial expression this statue (now in the Spada
Palace, Rome) is the personification of intellectual power.

to finish his schooling under the great Plato, whose
fame had reached to the far corners of the earth.
When his father died leaving him a fortune, the
youth journeyed to Athens. But when in 367 B.C. he
arrived at the grove of the *Academia* (Academy),
where Plato taught, he learned that the philosopher
was abroad, and would be gone for three years.

Meanwhile, Athens lay before him. The political power of the city had been broken in wars with
Sparta and Thebes, and already the menacing
greatness of Macedon was looming in the north.
But Athens still reflected the glory of the " golden
age of Pericles." Idle luxury and youthful gaiety
were arrayed on one hand; the best of learning
on the other. The young man chose the serious life.
He bought a house and began collecting a library.

Laying Foundation of New Learning

During those three years of waiting for Plato,
Aristotle became a man of the world. Witty, logical, independent, he soon disposed of scoffers. When
Plato returned the master recognized the overpowering genius of his new pupil, a genius which
was to shatter the Platonic doctrines themselves, to
lay the foundation of new learning in the world,
and to win for the lad from Stagira (his birthplace
in Macedon) the proud distinction of being the
greatest thinker of those days.

Aristotle remained 20 years in Athens, until the
death of Plato in 347 B.C. Then he was called by
Philip of Macedon to instruct his son Alexander, soon
to become known as " the Great." For 12 years

the philosopher remained with the future conqueror
of the world, first as teacher, then as adviser and
friend. During this time, while Demosthenes
was thundering his " Philippics," warning Athens
against the power of Macedon, Aristotle was
sowing the seed of culture in the Macedonian
mind : influence that really saved Athenian civilization when the inevitable conquests came.

When Alexander set forth on his campaigns in
Asia, Aristotle returned to Athens and established
there a school called the Lyceum, from its nearness
to the temple of Apollo Lyceius. In this school
was a promenade, called " peripatos " in Greek,
and from the master's habit of walking here as he
talked to his pupils, his teaching came to be known
as the peripatetic (walking about) philosophy.

After the death of Alexander the Athenians
revolted, and although Aristotle had taken no part
in politics, his early associations with Macedon
were seized upon by his enemies. He was accused
of impiety, the same charge upon which Socrates
had been put to death 76 years before. Aristotle
fled to Chalcis in the island of Euboea, in 323 B.C.,
where he died the following year.

Called " Master of Those Who Know "

The life of Aristotle was not a sensational one.
He was above all a student. His amazing brain
grasped at the whole field of knowledge. He was
not only a deep thinker, but a careful observer,
" a philosopher of facts," an organizer and systematizer of knowledge, whose greatest service was to
establish science and philosophy on a substantial
basis. By defining and classifying the various
branches of knowledge—as Physics, Metaphysics,
Psychology, Ethics, Politics, Rhetoric, Poetics, and
Logic—he laid the foundation of all the sciences
and philosophies of today.

" To my father," said Alexander the Great,
" I owe my life; to Aristotle the knowledge how
to live worthily." Two thousand years later
Goethe, the famous poet, confessed, " If now in
my quiet days I had youthful faculties at my command, I should devote myself to Greek. Nature
and Aristotle should be my sole study. It is beyond
all conception what that man espied, saw, perceived, remarked, observed." There was a time
when the old philosopher was neglected, followed
by another period in which he was regarded as the
final authority on all scientific matters—the
" master of those who know," as Dante said—but
today we recognize him as one of the world's
greatest teachers and students, whose life was filled
with the love of truth. He spared neither himself
nor his helpers the tiring task of gathering facts,
and was the pioneer of what is known as the
" scientific method."

Many of Aristotle's writings have disappeared
and others have been ascribed to him which he
probably never wrote. Among the lost books are
letters, speeches, poems, philosophical dialogues,
treatises on national festivals and dramatic contests,
and manuals of natural history and rhetoric—
works upon which his reputation was founded. Of
those that remain some of the best-known are
treatises on Logic (known as the Organon);
Rhetoric ; Poetics ; History of Animals ; Metaphysics ; Physics ; De Anima (Psychology) ; Ethics ;
Politics ; and Constitution of Athens.

FASCINATING SCIENCE *of* NUMBERS

Schoolboy or girl, housewife, city man, scientist : whatever our occupation, a knowledge of arithmetic is as necessary to us as the ability to read and write. In many spheres of life it is quite indispensable.

Arithmetic. The boy scoring at a cricket match, the mother making out her shopping list, the business man buying and selling stocks and shares, the sailor or airman plotting a course, the scientist working on his latest theory, all of these in their own way depend on their knowledge of arithmetic. For arithmetic is the foundation of every kind of calculation.

To some people, as accountants and statisticians, the rapid and accurate solution of mathematical problems is so important that machines have been invented for the purpose (*see* Calculating Machines). But no machine can take the place of a thorough grounding in arithmetic. Moreover, arithmetic is itself a valuable training; it develops the power to think clearly, it teaches accuracy, and instils concentration and perseverance. It is the most widely used, and to most people the most generally helpful, division of mathematics, which may be defined as the whole body of calculating lore, the methods used and the principles governing these methods. Running through all mathematics and giving all its calculations definite meaning in specific problems is the idea of number. Arithmetic may be called the science of numbers.

From Fingers to Notched Sticks

The word itself comes from the Greek *arithmos*, which means number, and for thousands of years men in all parts of the world have been performing simple sums in arithmetic. At first, we may well believe, they counted their sheep and oxen on the fingers of their hands. The word digit, which means any single figure from 0 to 9 inclusive, reminds us of this, for " finger " in Latin is *digitus*. Then they came to making notches on sticks. Up to the year 1826 the Government accounts in England were recorded by means of notched sticks, or tallies as they were called. The next step was to invent a suitable notation—that is, a system of signs and symbols by means of which each number might be recorded. The ancient Greeks used the letters of their alphabet for the purpose: the letter A stood for 1, B for 2, I for 10, K for 20, P for 100, and so on. Then a thousand was represented by A with a tick underneath it, 2,000 by B under-ticked, and so on.

The Romans dropped most of the letters of the ordinary alphabet and instead made seven letters— I, L, D, V, X, C and M—do all the work, as is explained under the heading Numerals.

These " Letter Systems " were employed in *writing* sums. Generally, however, calculations were performed by the aid of an abacus (Latin, from Greek *abax*, " board for reckoning on "), a frame with a number of parallel, vertical or horizontal wires stretched across it, with beads or counters strung on each wire. In the vertical abacus, the tops of the wires were open ; the right-hand wire stood for units ; the next tens ; the next hundreds, and so on. Thus 18 was represented by

1 bead on the tens wire and 8 beads on the units wire ; 118 would be the same, with the addition of 1 bead on the hundreds wire. Later came the closed abacus, with horizontal wires and 10 beads on each ; the wires were long enough to allow the counted beads to be moved to one side. The units wire was then the bottom one, and so on.

Strangely enough, the ancients never invented a letter or symbol for 0, though on the abacus 0 was indicated by the absence of a bead.

It was left to the Arabs to introduce the notation which we use nowadays; this, as we all know, has a different symbol for each digit (1, 2, 3, 4, 5, 6, 7, 8, 9), has a separate sign for nought or zero (0), and, moreover, makes use of the principle of " place value." Whereas in the Greek alphabet system one letter stands for 8, another for 80, and a third for 800, under the Arabic system the same sign 8 is used each time but in a different position (alone, before one nought, and before two noughts).

When the Arabic numbers and the use of a 0 to indicate " place value " (as in distinguishing 13 from 1030) came to Europe, the idea was so startling that the very words for 0 acquired new meanings. Since " 0 " meant " no quantity in this place " (as in the " tens " place in 101) the Arabs called it *sifr,* a word meaning " empty." This word came into Italian as " zero," and into medieval Latin as *cifra.* Later, people took " cipher," the English form of cifra, to mean any number, and also, as a verb, " to calculate." To avoid confusion, mathematicians called 0 by the Italian word " zero."

The great improvements mentioned above were introduced into Europe by the Arabs in the Middle Ages, but they were really invented by the Hindus

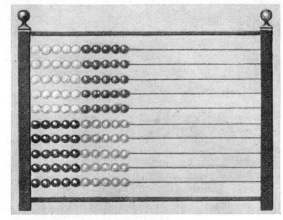

ABACUS IN SIMPLE FORM
The oldest of calculating contrivances, the abacus was commonly used for counting, by people of all ages, in ancient Greece. It survives in the Orient for commercial reckoning ; and lingers in Britain as a device on which young children learn to count. The abacus has several forms.

of an armistice does not in itself end a war, and in theory hostilities may be resumed if peace terms are not definitely agreed.

From 1919 to 1938 Armistice Day was observed all over Britain and the Empire by religious services and a two minutes' silence. In London the chief service, attended whenever possible by the King and the members of the Royal Family, was held at the Cenotaph in Whitehall. Artificial poppies were sold in the streets to raise money for Earl Haig's British Legion Appeal Fund.

In 1946 it was decided to replace Armistice Day with a new Remembrance Day, for the fallen in both the First and the Second World Wars, this to be observed on the Sunday preceding November 11, unless November 11 or 12 fell on a Sunday.

From ARMOURED KNIGHT to BATTLE TANK

The defeat of armoured knights by warriors of the bow, and by matchlock and gunpowder, was the beginning of the struggle between armour and specialised weapons which has continued into battles of modern times.

Armour. On a September day in the year 1356 the little army of the Black Prince of England met and conquered the vast hosts of the French king at Poitiers. The camp had been astir from dawn. The last council of the captains had been held, and the Prince himself was being arrayed for battle. Over his head was drawn the shirt of chain mail, reinforced with breastplate and backplate and shoulder- and arm-guards of burnished steel plates. Next he donned waist-piece and loin-guard, and thigh-pieces, knee-guards, greaves and shoes of jointed mail. Then the great visored helmet was placed over his head, with a coif of flexible mail to protect the neck ; and iron gauntlets were drawn upon his hands.

Piece by piece the jointed plates were fixed to shoulder, elbow, hip, knee and instep, so as to permit of the greatest freedom of motion possible; and all was securely made fast with buckles, locks and rivets. Then the sword was girt about the Prince's waist and on his left arm he took his shield.

Such armour as this was the result of centuries of progress in warfare. The earliest protection consisted of only a shield, to ward off blows from club, axe, sling-stone, javelin, sword or arrow—such as the shields of the ancient Egyptians, Assyrians, Etruscans, Greeks and Romans. As the need for greater protection was felt. the helmet was adopted to save the head. Then came the breast-plate, and then greaves or sheaths of metal or other material for the legs from knee to ankle.

Eventually, to protect the whole body, small plates of metal, or metal rings, were sewn closely together upon a tunic of leather or stout cloth, and worn to supplement other defences. The Greeks and Romans were equipped with all these devices. A similar garment, which hung from neck to knee and eventually acquired sleeves—known as a coat-of-

fence or hauberk—was commonly worn by the followers of William the Conqueror.

As time went on the pieces of metal were sewn closer, until they overlapped, so giving rise to scale armour. Chain mail, in which the rings were woven together, was often to be seen at the time of the Crusaders, and until the 14th century.

Bit by bit, meanwhile, the coat of mail was reinforced with plates of wrought iron or steel. For 200 years this gradual change went on.

The practice of wearing heraldic figures on shield and surcoat became necessary as a means of identifying the wearer when his face and body were completely covered with armour.

Such complete equipment of knight and horse in plate armour was mainly used in tournaments and joustings. Already the English longbow and the crossbow, even before the coming of firearms, had put the armoured knight at a disadvantage on the actual field of battle, especially if he could be unhorsed. But the breastplate and other forms of half-armour were used until the 18th century.

When ships began to be built of iron instead of wood the idea of armour was revived and applied to the protection of big battle-craft. The battle of the Monitor and the Merrimac in the American Civil War was the first demonstration of armoured ships in actual combat. The Monitor gave its name to a class of armour-clad warships (really floating gun-platforms).

At first armour-plate was of cast iron or wrought iron. Then steel came into its own, first as the outer slice of a " sandwich " with wrought iron beneath. As tough alloy-steels were invented, the best were used for armour plate. As the power of guns increased, improved armour was devised, and so the race has continued between the resisting power of armour-plate and the armour-piercing

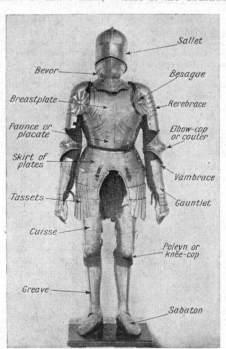

FULL SUIT OF ARMOUR
This armour with the principal parts named, was made about 1470. One of the most skilled trades of the Middle Ages was that of the armourer, the craftsmanship being superb.

Labels on the image: Sallet, Bevor, Besague, Breastplate, Rerebrace, Paunce or placate, Elbow-cap or couter, Skirt of plates, Vambrace, Tassets, Gauntlet, Cuisse, Poleyn or knee-cap, Greave, Sabaton

TWENTY CENTURIES OF MEN IN ARMOUR

Greek
Hoplite
4th Century B.C.

Norman
Warrior
11th Century

English
Knight
12th Century

Roman
Legionary
1st Century
B.C.

Chain
Mail
14th
Century

Full Plate
Armour
16th Century

The heavy-armed Greek foot-soldier, or 'hoplite,' wore a visorless helmet, corslet of metal plates, greaves for the legs, and carried a round shield. His arms were the sword and spear. The Roman legionary had much the same arms and armour, except that he lacked the greaves.

Duke William's Normans who conquered England were only a little more advanced in armour. The 'hauberk' or 'byrnie' might be of metal rings sewed on leather or cloth, or of overlapping scales as shown here. In the next century the hauberk was longer, and of interwoven metal rings or small overlapping scales, covering the neck and terminating in a steel cap or 'basinet.'

The two mounted figures show the knight with his steed, in later days fully armoured like his master. Plate defences for the shoulders, upper arms, elbows, breast, knees, shins, and feet were common by the 14th century. Such full plate armour as that shown for the 16th century knight was used chiefly in tournaments.

If the long-dead warriors could revisit the earth they would look much as you see them here. We begin with the Greek 'hoplite' who defeated the Persians. Then follows the Roman, with short sword. Then, after a period of a thousand years, we see the Norman man-at-arms; next the mail-clad knight on foot; after that the mounted warrior of the 14th century in chain mail, and finally the knight in full plate armour, mounted on his armoured steed.

has made the armoured car too vulnerable to be used as a weapon of assault, and it is principally used now for long-range reconnaissance.

British armoured cars in the Second World War carried a crew of three, protected by armour 14 millimetres thick; the Humber and the Guy had one 15-millimetre and one 7·9-millimetre Besa gun mounted parallel with one another ; the Daimlers which replaced them mounted a 2-pounder anti-tank gun, and had a range of 200 miles with a top speed of 60 m.p.h.

For short-distance scouting and inter-communication the British forces used the Daimler scout car, a kind of miniature armoured car with no turret and armed only with a Bren gun and an anti-tank rifle. The armour was 30 millimetres thick in front and 14 millimetres at the sides ; the engine was at the back, and the steering-wheel was mounted at an angle to enable the car to be driven at high speeds in reverse when necessary.

The Bren carrier was not classified as an armoured fighting vehicle ; it was open at the top and only very lightly armoured. There was a carrier platoon in every infantry battalion, and their rôle was to bring fire to bear at short notice when there was not time enough to bring up an infantry section. The vehicle was never used as a tank, but was parked " hull down"—on the horizon out of sight—while the crew dismounted to go into action. The Bren carrier was low-built, fast, and good across country; from it a vehicle was developed called the universal carrier, which could be used for bringing up supplies or ammunition, scouting for armoured units, or as an observation post for artillery.

Other types of armoured fighting vehicle included the infantry carriers such as the Kangaroo, a tracked vehicle with light armour and room for a section of infantry with its weapons ; and the flame-throwers, the large types on tank and the smaller on carrier chassis. The armoured command vehicle was an armour-plated office on wheels, unarmed but equipped with radio. Bulldozers, used for clearing the way for lorries or tanks, were sometimes fitted with light armour.

In a separate class were the various amphibious armoured vehicles, both wheeled and with caterpillar tracks instead of wheels. Since the whole success of the invasion of the Continent in 1944 depended on the Allies' landing on the French coast, particular attention had been given to the design of land-and-water vehicles. Most of them, however, were unarmoured, and it was from the unarmoured Alligator that the most successful armoured amphibious vehicle, the L.V.T. (A.) or Landing Vehicle Tracked (Armoured), otherwise called the Buffalo, was developed. (*See* illus. p. 247)

The Buffalo could plunge straight from a cross-country run into a river, float across it driven by its tracks, and climb out on to all but the steepest banks on the other side. It could carry a section of infantry or a six-pounder gun with its crew ; later models were fitted with a rotating turret mounting an anti-tank gun. (*See also* Army ; Artillery ; Navy ; Tanks.)

SPECIALISTS *of the* MODERN ARMY

Concentrated training is given, not only to those who actually handle the ingenious weapons and devices of modern high-speed war, but also to others who specialise in rendering essential service to the users.

Army. Upset a big jig-saw puzzle on the floor, and it may take you quite a long time to collect all the scattered pieces and fit them together again. That, or something like it, is what happened to our Army organization when the British Expeditionary Force had to be evacuated from Dunkirk, France, in the first year of the Second World War. It was in June 1940, when our French Allies could not stand up to the German onslaught, and the valorous remnants of our Army, after great rearguard actions, had to leave the Continent—abandoning guns and equipment—and return to England to be re-formed.

A brand-new jig-saw had then to be prepared, at top speed, to represent a very different picture. The war, when resumed, was to be one of swift movement, with many tanks and large numbers of " carried " infantry swooping down on the enemy. No more trench warfare. No more standing still for months on end. It was to be an army mostly fighting on wheels, with the R.A.F. and the Royal Navy backing it up in "combined operations." And so our Army was reborn ; its backbone the "plain" soldier, styled private, gunner, trooper, fusilier, guardsman, rifleman, driver, sapper or craftsman according to his arm of Service.

All the wonderful mechanization did not change the age-old function of the infantry—of holding ground captured from the enemy. Tanks alone cannot do that, nor the artillery. It is the infantry's job. And so they still bear the heaviest burdens and suffer the greatest losses. Their rifles and bayonets are supplemented by automatic weapons, mortars, light flame-throwers, grenades and anti-tank guns. They may reach the battlefield in troop-carrying vehicles of the Royal Army Service Corps, or armoured carriers may take them almost to their objective ; or they parachute to battle out of the skies, or arrive in gliders towed by planes.

All the Army Airborne units are in the Army Air Corps formed in February 1942. The Glider Pilot Regiment was formed in December 1941, a little later than the Parachute Regiment which provides men for the Parachute Brigades and the Independent (Pathfinder) Companies within the

HORSEGUARDSMAN
Royal Horseguardsman in Whitehall, London, in full ceremonial dress.

ARMY BADGES OF RANK

Some badges of ranks below that of commissioned officer are shown in the two upper rows (left). 1.—Regimental Sergeant-Major. 2, 3, 4.—Master Gunner, Class I, II and III respectively. 5.—Warrant Officer, Class I. 6.—Company Sergeant-Major, superseding 7, the old badge. 8.—Staff Sergeant or Company Quarter-Master Sergeant. 9.—Sergeant. 10.—Corporal. 11.—Lance-Corporal. 12.—Bandmaster. Officers' badges are given in the two lower rows. 1.—Field-Marshal, without the cypher of the reigning sovereign. 2.—General. 3.—Lieutenant-General. 4.—Major-General. 5.—Brigadier. 6.—Colonel. 7.—Lieutenant-Colonel. 8.—Major. 9.—Captain. 10.—Lieutenant. 11.—Second-Lieutenant.

Certain units of the R.A.F. (which until 1918 was called the Royal Flying Corps and formed a part of the Army), with the title of Army Co-operation Squadrons, act as the eyes of the ground troops, scout behind the enemy's lines, provide rapid means of communication and direct artillery fire. Fighter squadrons also help the infantry by knocking out tanks and strong-points and attacking enemy troops and transport columns, with machine-gun and cannon fire. The Royal Air Force Regiment, though it has often fought with the Army, is a part of the R.A.F.

The Royal Regiment of Artillery (" the Gunners ") mans the Army's field, medium, heavy and coastal artillery and also some anti-tank and anti-aircraft batteries, and operates self-propelled guns (guns built on to, or into, a motored chassis) which are attached to all armoured divisions and fight with the Royal Armoured Corps. Gunners also operate searchlights in anti-aircraft defence systems. Guns are now drawn by tractors, the

Airborne Divisions. The Pathfinders (not to be confused with the Pathfinders of the R.A.F.) land before the main body of airborne troops to find the pre-arranged areas in which the force is to assemble ; they scout along routes or mark places at which other parachutists or gliders are to land.

The Glider Pilot Regiment provides pilots and co-pilots for the gliders of an airborne force. After the gliders have landed and discharged their loads the pilots come into action on the ground and for this purpose are formed into squadrons. So they are trained (by the R.A.F.) to pilot the towed gliders and (by the Army) to fight as infantry. Airborne divisions, striking behind the enemy's lines, performed great deeds of heroism during the Second World War, especially in Normandy, and at Arnhem in the Netherlands. Landing by parachutes or from gliders, the infantry are accompanied by airborne units of Royal Artillery, Royal Armoured Corps, Royal Engineers, Royal Army Service Corps, Royal Army Medical Corps, etc.

In 1940 special formations of infantry, called Commandos, were trained to carry out raids in enemy-occupied territory, and they were often the first troops to land on enemy-held beaches. Though the formations were disbanded after the war, commando-training continued to be carried out by the Royal Marines, controlled by the Admiralty.

GRENADIERS FOR THE KING'S GUARD

Fox

The ceremony of mounting the Guard at Buckingham Palace or St. James's Palace is one of the most popular sights in London. Before the Second World War scarlet tunics and bearskins were worn, as above. The Guard consists of four officers and 49 men of one of the regiments of Foot Guards, with the King's Colour. Grenadier Guards are here seen marching out of Wellington Barracks, Birdcage Walk, to perform this duty.

1.—Tank landing craft m[...] 2.—An infantry landing [...] its occupants. 3.—Li[...] through surf. About [...] craft carried machine-g[...] beaches during the Se[...] were used chiefly by [...]

troop-carriers which may accompany assaulting tanks. R.A.S.C. drivers may also be seen at the wheel of ambulances and staff cars. The R.A.S.C. operates its own fleet for the coastwise distribution of military stores, target-towing and other military purposes. Most of the clerks at brigade and higher headquarters and at the War Office are R.A.S.C. personnel. With all its responsibilities it is not surprising that the R.A.S.C. accounts for one-eighth of the whole strength of the British Army.

The Royal Army Ordnance Corps sees that the soldier gets his clothing, weapons, vehicles, ammunition and equipment, and is responsible for supplying all spare parts and components for equip-

teams of horses havi... disappeared before t... Second World War, e... cept for a few batter... overseas for service... mountainous regions.

The cavalry also had... part with their belo... horses, though they k... their old badges and... traditions, and beca... regiments in the R... Armoured Corps. T... and armoured cars... placed the horses,... with these the new ca... act partly as a scree... and scouting force,... partly as assault t... with the armoured... sions. Only in pea... are the Royal... Guards and the... Guards — the Hou... Cavalry—mounted... vide spectacular... for the Sovereign o... monial occasions... do sentry-duty... Horse Guards Pa... London's Whiteh... April 1939 units... Royal Tank Cor... into The Royal... the title of the... 1916, was change...

To the Royal... and clearing ene... points, laying... barracks, bridge... systems. Assault... private of the R... a name derived... of constructing... by which soldie... the enemy's def... infantry and th... active service a...

ment and for its maintenance. The Royal Electrical and Mechanical Engineers (R.E.M.E.), formed in 1942, maintain and repair the technical equipment in use in the Army, ranging from tanks and artillery to watches ; nearly all its men are experts at some craft, so the R.E.M.E. private is given the title of craftsman.

Formed in October 1939 as the Auxiliary Military Pioneer Corps, the Royal Pioneer Corps undertakes bridge-building, road, railway and dock construction ; special companies work as dockers and stevedores ; others operate generators that throw out smoke screens to hide the Army's movements from enemy eyes.

The modern army must heal and restore to the fighting line as many casualties as possible ; and disease must be prevented or dealt with, in the main, by the Royal Army Medical Corps. The Army's teeth are cared for by the Royal Army Dental Corps. The Royal Army Chaplains Department looks after morale and spiritual welfare. The Royal Army Educational Corps strives to improve the standard of education in the Army and to prepare men for re-entry into civilian life when at last they leave the Service.

The Royal Army Pay Corps keeps the accounts of officers and men, and makes payments to families and dependants. On active service, units of the R.A.P.C. accompany forces in the field to deal with the exchange of foreign money and the provision of money for paying the troops. The Army Catering Corps, formed in 1941, provides trained cooks at home and abroad.

The Royal Army Veterinary Corps takes care of all the army's sick or wounded animals and provides remounts. Hundreds of dogs employed as guards at supply depots in Europe and the Middle East are tended by the R.A.V.C. which also

Imperial War Museum; British Official

BRITAIN'S ARMY IN TWO WORLD WARS

Infantry of the First World War (1914–18) are seen in the top photograph passing a battery of field guns ; in the distance, on the left, is a tank, and in the centre background are cavalrymen. During the Second World War (1939–45) infantry sometimes rode into battle on tanks (lower), which replaced the cavalry of the First World War.

breeds and fattens cattle, sheep, goats, pigs and rabbits to provide fresh meat for our overseas forces.

The Royal Corps of Military Police (known as "Red Caps," because they wear a red cover over the top of the headdress) have a history as long as that of any regiment or corps in the British Army. They control traffic, reconnoitre routes, guard military stores, and search and guard prisoners of war. Military Police were among the leading troops through the mine-fields of El Alamein and on the beaches of North Africa, Sicily, Italy and Normandy in the Second World War.

The Army Fire Service was developed during the Second World War from fire-fighting units normally attached to barracks, permanent camps and supply depots. Equipped with vehicles and fire-floats, the A.F.S. safeguard vast quantities of fuel, ammunition, stores and shipping at home and overseas. And there are camou-flage experts, who so disguise guns and men and fortifications as to render them almost invisible.

In February 1948 a new forma-tion joined the British Army—the Gurkha Regiment. It consisted of the four regiments of Gurkha

ARMY TRAINING IN PEACETIME
British Official
Bren carriers (top) are lightly-armoured tracked vehicles that can go almost anywhere. The soldier in the circle is learning to handle a sub-machine gun. Anti-tank gunners (lower) manhandle their gun in difficult country.

Gurkhas to serve in the British Army, and young Gurkhas can go to the Royal Military Academy at Sandhurst, Berkshire, to obtain commissions.

Realistic preparation for battle is the lot of every soldier after he has joined his unit or corps from the General Service Corps depot. Having survived various ordeals he takes part in a " battle " in which real bullets whistle around him, real shells burst ahead, real mines explode (at a safe distance) and aeroplanes drop bombs and fire machine-guns and cannons. He may then go for training in Combined Operations, learning to fight with the Navy and R.A.F. as a team. The sailors and airmen carry out preliminary bom-bardments of an " enemy-held " beach ; the Navy puts him ashore ; the R.A.F. puts an " umbrella " of aeroplanes above him and engages enemy de-fences ahead of him—but he, the soldier, has to drive the enemy from the field of battle itself.

The composition of an army varies according to its task, but it usually consists of two corps and a certain number of Army troops. The latter are not allotted to any particular corps or division but are held as a reserve under the Army commander.

The famous British 8th Army, commanded by General Montgomery at the Battle of El Alamein (in Egypt), October 23 – November 5, 1942, had three corps—X, XIII and XXX. It is not possible to group divisions under their corps, because several of them changed their corps as the battle developed. The order of divisions from north to south of the 40-miles front was : 9th Australian, 1st South African, 4th Indian and 50th (Northum-brian) Divisions, with some Fighting French and Greek units. Close behind the front line were the 51st (Highland), the 44th (Home Counties) and the 7th Armoured Divisions, acting as the tactical

Rifles—the 2nd, 6th, 7th and 10th—which had elected to be transferred to the British service when the old Indian Army was divided between the Dominions of India and Pakistan in 1947.

The Gurkha Regiment was intended to provide the Gurkha element of the British Gurkha Division stationed in the Far East. The brigades were each to consist of two Gurkha and one British battalion; the 7th Gurkha Rifles providing the divisional artillery, plus a British element. The Government of Nepal (the home of the Gurkhas) allows 10,400

British Official

ROYAL ENGINEERS ERECT A BAILEY BRIDGE

Bridge-building is one of the most important tasks of the Royal Engineers. A retreating enemy seeks to halt his pursuers by destroying bridges, so the faster new ones are built the brighter become the chances of overtaking the enemy. Bailey bridges were extensively used by the Allies in the Second World War (1939–45). This quickly erected bridge—a British invention—consists of interlocking latticed panels of steel, which can be used with or without supports.

reserve. Somewhat farther back still was the Xth Corps, composed of the 1st and 10th Armoured Divisions and the 2nd New Zealand Division. Also, the Army commander had at his disposal more than 800 guns.

Opposing the 8th Army were the Germans and Italians under the German Field-Marshal Rommel. The German 15th Panzer and Italian Littorio Armoured Divisions were near the coast, and the 21st Panzer and Italian Ariete Armoured Divisions were facing the 4th Indian Division. In all, the battle cost Rommel some 75,000 men, 500 tanks and 1,000 guns—against the 13,500 casualties suffered by the 8th Army. In addition, the Germans and Italians lost several thousand transport vehicles.

At the outbreak of the First World War (1914–18) the British army was composed wholly of volunteers, but on January 24, 1916, all single men between the ages of 18 and 41 became liable for service with the armed forces, and Great Britain had a national conscript army for the first time; with the end of that war the army reverted to the voluntary system, but conscription was brought back with the international crisis of 1939 preceding the Second World War.

Until then the most important of our " non-regular " defences was the Territorial Army. A woman's corps known as the Auxiliary Territorial

Service (A.T.S.) was formed in September 1938, and became a part of the regular forces when women were conscripted for national service. The Territorial Army was reorganized in 1947 to include an airborne and two armoured divisions. The manning of the general defences of Great Britain — principally A.A. batteries to which

British Official

ARMY SIGNALS IN OPERATION

To provide communications at all times and in all circumstances is the task of the Royal Corps of Signals. They fix up telephone exchanges (above) in forward areas as well as with the higher commands. Besides providing communications the Corps maintains all signal equipment.

members of the A.T.S. (in 1948 they were re-named the Women's Royal Army Corps) may also belong—is entrusted to the Territorials, as it was in 1939.

On January 3, 1947, the Royal Military Academy, Woolwich, and the Royal Military College, Sandhurst, combined to form (at Sandhurst, in Berkshire) the Royal Military Academy, through which officers for all arms of the service now pass. The War Office, in Whitehall, London, is the government department responsible for the army.

In contrast to all this, the army of ancient Egypt consisted chiefly of archers, and archers continued to be the mainstay of armies until Agincourt and even later. The Egyptians also had cavalry and chariots. The Israelites built up an army of infantry, horsemen and chariots, as did the rulers of Babylon and Assyria.

The Persians had a military organization superior to all their predecessors, consisting of cavalry and infantry. The Greeks were almost entirely foot-soldiers, armed with a long lance, a sword and a shield, while their light infantry were armed with a short spear and a small shield or with javelins, bows and arrows, or slings, and no shield.

The armies of ancient Rome, which conquered the greater part of the then known world, were irresistible chiefly owing to the perfection of their military organization. The legions of Rome

Keystone

AIRBORNE TROOPS

Parachutists (top) hold parachutes on their knees preparatory to making a practice jump. The nose of a glider (lower) is raised and out drives a jeep ready to go into action.

consisted not merely of armed men, but carefully trained and drilled soldiers. They were mainly infantry, although every legion had its cavalry. The Roman infantry were protected by shields and helmets, and armed with swords, lances, or javelins.

In the Middle Ages the strength of an army was chiefly determined by its mounted men-at-arms, with their chain-mail and steel armour. The invention in the 14th century of gunpowder completely changed the course of military history.

The modern army may be said to date from the time of Gustavus Adolphus. During the Thirty Years' War (1618–48) he originated the army of professional or mercenary soldiers, developing the idea from the bands of *condottieri* in Italy who used to sell their services to the highest bidder. His example was soon followed by Louis XIV of France and most of the other crowned heads of Europe. A great revolution was brought about in 1798, when France revived universal service or conscription which had been used by Sparta and Rome of old. (*See* Armour; Artillery; Tanks).

Artemis. (Pron. ar'-tem-is). After a long and exciting chase the huntress goddess and her nymphs had stopped to bathe in a mossy pool in the wood. Hearing the girlish shouts of laughter, a rash mortal named Actaeon, who also hunted in that forest, drew near, and as he gazed entranced the virgin goddess saw him. A dash of water from her palm into his presumptuous face turned him into a stag with spreading antlers; and he was torn to pieces by his own hounds. Greek myth tells us that this goddess of the

British Official

PARATROOPS WITH MOTOR-SCOOTERS

Amongst the equipment dropped to men of Airborne Divisions during the Second World War were folding motor-scooters which were released from aircraft in parachute containers. One man could lift them easily and they were strong enough to be ridden over rough country. They were used chiefly by scouts and messengers.

ARTEMIS TAKES REVENGE ON ACTAEON

Actaeon, the hunter, one day spied upon Artemis bathing in a stream. As a punishment the goddess, who is usually represented as a huntress, changed him into a stag, whereupon he was hunted by his own dogs, urged on by Artemis and her nymphs. This painting by the French artist, Le Sueur (1616–1655), depicts the scene. It is in the museum of Le Mans.

bow and quiver, whom the Greeks called Artemis and the Romans Diana, was the daughter of Zeus and the twin sister of Apollo. The Greeks worshipped her as the guardian of youths and maidens. Artemis came also to be looked upon as the moon goddess, just as Apollo was viewed as the sun god. But, most of all, the Greeks loved to think of her roaming the wilds as the protector of the beasts of the field. Her favourite animal was the deer, though bear, lion, and others were sacred to her.

Artemis is usually represented as a huntress, tall and fair, slender and light of foot. Her hair is bound in a knot at the back of her head, and her dress is girt high for speed. On her shoulder she bears her bow and quiver, and by her side is a dog or deer. The finest statue of her is that found in a villa of the Roman Emperor Hadrian, and now in the Louvre in Paris.

At Ephesus, in Asia Minor, a goddess was worshipped under the name of Artemis or Diana, but she differed in many respects from the true Artemis. This Asiatic goddess is noteworthy for her great temple at Ephesus, one of the Seven Wonders of the World, and because of the allusion to her in the Epistle of St. Paul to the Ephesians.

Artesian Wells AND BOREHOLES.

These are wells in which the water rises up by gravity and does not have to be pumped. Many hundreds of years ago in the French province of Artois it happened that a well was sunk so deep that it passed through the water-tight strata to layers of porous rock and gravel where the water was confined under heavy pressure. At once the water gushed forth, overflowing the curbing; and the name " artesian well " (from Artesium, the Roman name of the province) is still given to such flowing wells.

As you know, most of the water which falls to the earth sinks into the soil or porous rock beneath the surface, and flows out again at some point lower down, forming an ordinary spring. If there is a dip in the pervious layer of rock, and at some other place this layer comes up to the surface, rain falling on this surface will soak through and collect at the dip. The water at the dip is pressed down by the weight of the water in the upward sloping parts of the layer, but cannot, of course, rise upwards until we bore a well-hole at the dipping part of the layer. The diagram opposite shows an imaginary slice through part of the London region: on top, at the centre, is the layer of " London clay " which is impervious, or not able to be penetrated very much by rain. (Clay, in fact, is often used to make a watertight lining to a reservoir or pond.) Beyond this clay layer is the great chalk bed which comes up to the surface in the Chiltern Hills and the North Downs.

Water collects in the pervious strata to a certain depth, depending on the season and the amount of rainfall; it rises up to a level called the plane of saturation. (Now look at the smaller diagram, which shows what happens when the pervious layer dips so much that the plane of saturation is above ground level at the well-head.) If we bore a well towards the middle of the dip, water will spout up under pressure until it rises nearly to the level of the saturation point; on the flanks of the dipping layer of chalk this point is well *below* ground, but at the centre of the dip the horizontal level of the saturation plane is a considerable height *above* ground. So the water spouts up into the air.

Many factories and large buildings in which much water is used draw their supplies from artesian wells. The great depth from which the water is drawn makes it impossible that it should be contaminated, and therefore no elaborate process of filtration, such as must be employed when water is drawn from rivers or lakes, is necessary.

Although water rises up in an artesian bore, it often has to be pumped to the surface, and it is only in some such wells that water is forced up naturally above the ground. The pumping of water from deep below ground has always been a problem for engineers. Savery's engine, and that of Newcomen, were the earliest to be used for steam pumping. It was the crying need for good pumping machinery for mines which spurred on James Watt to improve on Newcomen's idea and produce an efficient steam engine. Then there was the Cornish pumping engine, which did not turn any wheels but merely moved an enormously long pump rod up and down. The long rods made all such machinery heavy and extravagant in consuming power. Today engineers often use a submersible motor pump.

In this kind of pump the motor itself is suspended deep down in the borehole, under water ; electric current is taken down in cables enclosed in a watertight casing; water is pumped up through a pipe connected to the top of the pump. The machine is so efficient that pump and motor can be fitted into a case which will go down a borehole as small in diameter as eight inches. Enough lubricant is packed around the motor bearings to keep them oiled for 250 days and nights of constant running.

How Boreholes are Drilled

After prospectors, following a study of the geology of the proposed site, have decided on the position for boring, a derrick is erected. This is a steel or wooden framework to support the drilling rig over the hole. Slung from the derrick is the drilling machine, which is similar in principle to the drill used for making holes in wood or metal; it is furnished with a tubular cutter of hard steel (for very hard rock it may be necessary to use a cutter which has "teeth" of diamonds), and is

HOW AN ARTESIAN WELL WORKS

This is an imaginary cut through a dip in pervious layers. Rain falling on the outcrop (where the layer comes to the surface) soaks down and fills the dip up to the saturation level. If the well-head is below the plane of saturation, water (which always finds its own level) will gush up the bore into the air.

twisted to cause it to enter the ground or rock, being thrust down by its own weight. Above the drill shaft is attached some sort of driving motor—steam, electric or compressed air—to turn the drill. But there is an important difference between this drill and the ordinary rotating drill : the rock drill not only twists, but is urged down by percussion.

You may have seen a workman making a hole in a brick wall for the insertion of a wood or fibre plug; he strikes the head of the drill or chisel with a hammer, and gives the drill a half-turn at each hammer-blow. That is what is meant by rotary-percussion, and the borehole drill operates in the same way. But it is a tubular drill, not a solid one, and so cuts out a cylindrical core of soil or rock, from about eight inches to 18 inches in diameter, according to the size of the bore.

As the drill tube gets down lower, new sections are coupled on at the top to lengthen it, and the cores cut out are extracted. The depth required to reach a plentiful supply of water may vary a good deal; by boring down 175 feet deep in Sherborne, Dorset, with a 12-inch hole, a well giving 30,000 gallons per hour was established. Near Northwich in Cheshire a bore had to be taken down more than 1,150 feet to strike water.

In the London area water is obtained by bores of 450–400 feet in depth. As an example, let us see what kinds of soil were encountered in boring at Tottenham. First came 11 feet of ballast, below the top eight feet of soil; then about 70 feet of clay, followed by 20 feet of greensand and 18 of sandy clay. Next a shallow layer of sand and pebbles was reached, followed by about 20 feet of grey sand. Then came the water-bearing layers, of chalk, or chalk and flints, totalling about 260 feet.

After this the bore had disclosed a layer of silver sand one foot thick, with nine feet of flints. At the

LONDON'S FOUNDATIONS PIERCED BY ARTESIAN WELLS

London gets most of its water supply from the vast artificial reservoirs of the Metropolitan Water Board, which are fed by the Thames and the New River. Owing to the geological formation beneath the metropolis in the 'London Basin' it has also its own underground 'lake' from which many public and private buildings draw their water supply by means of artesian wells. Some of the most important details of that geological formation are shown in this diagram.

ARTHUR'S APPEAL TO HUBERT
There is a pathetic scene in Shakespeare's play King John, when
the young Prince Arthur pleads with Hubert not to burn out his eyes with
a hot iron, as the king had ordered him to. There seems to be no proof
that the incident actually took place, but W. F. Yeames, a famous Royal
Academician of the 19th century, has given this vivid reconstruction.

1841 that water was reached and began
to gush out plenteously, at a depth of
about 1,800 feet. An elaborate fountain
was built, and the jets reached a height
of 100 feet. Twenty-five years later a
well was dug at Passy, near Boulogne-
sur-Seine; but meanwhile engineering
science had developed, and a steam-
driven apparatus could be employed.

Eventually the well-sinkers attained
their object. But—and this exemplifies
what often occurs—the flow from the
Grenelle well now fell off a good deal,
proving that both wells were drawing
their water from one and the same
subterranean reservoir! The same thing
has been happening in the London
Basin, where the water level in the
ground has dropped by several hundred
feet in recent years, owing in some
measure to the sinking of more and
more artesian bores. Only about a
tenth of the water consumed in the
London and suburban area comes now
from artesian wells.

Arthur, DUKE OF BRITTANY (1187–
1203). When Richard I died the barons
of England and of Normandy gave their
support to John as his successor, although
Arthur of Brittany, the son of the late
king's brother Geoffrey, certainly had a
claim to the throne. Brittany, Anjou
and Maine declared for the boy, and
with the help of his devoted mother,
Constance, he hastened to seek the aid
of Philip of France, with the result that
the young heir was made lord of the
three provinces. But Philip was merely
thinking of himself, and in less than 12
months he acknowledged the English
monarch as overlord of Brittany.

Unfortunately for himself John
offended Philip, who made a treaty with
Arthur, which gave him Anjou, and
offered him the services of his knights
to conquer it. Arthur's first military operation was
an attempt to capture his grandmother, Queen
Eleanor, who held Aquitaine for her son, and had
shut herself up in the castle of Mirebeau. John
was some 80 miles away, but within two days he
and his army had made a forced march of amazing
rapidity and taken the besiegers completely by
surprise. Some 200 of Philip's knights, and
many others, were captured, in addition to Arthur.

The unlucky young prince was first imprisoned
at Falaise, and afterwards at Rouen, where he died.
Ugly rumours soon spread that Arthur had been
murdered, whereupon John gave it out that the
captive had fallen from the battlements of the castle
in making an attempt to escape.

In his play King John, Shakespeare makes
Arthur a pathetic and appealing character. He
is put in charge of Hubert, who is ordered to burn
out his eyes. As the captive pleads the iron grows
cold, and the gaoler's heart is melted to compassion.

The actual sequel to Arthur's death was that
Normandy, Brittany, Maine and Anjou were lost
by John and so ceased to be connected with
England, as they had been since 1066.

very bottom was a stratum of chalk and flints,
between 50 and 60 feet thick. To anyone with
some knowledge of geology this list tells a fascinating
story of the past history of the London Basin.

It has been said that the Chinese were the first to
bore deep wells, using some form of percussion drill.
In France there are the ancient wells of Artois,
from which, as we have said, we get the term
Artesian. Many such wells were made in France
later, and it was the fashion to employ them to
furnish gushing water for ornamental fountains
on the great pleasure gardens which became a
feature of country houses. Well-sinking was done
in those days by *real* horse power: ropes were coiled
around large drums set horizontally on a vertical
shaft; horses harnessed to the lower end of the
shaft walked round in a circle all day long to turn
the drill, or to hoist up the soil which was dug out.

In digging a well at Grenelle, near Paris, in 1833-
35, it took nearly two years to get down to 1,400 feet.
Then a heavy iron cylinder belonging to the apparatus fell down the well, and had to be broken in
pieces with hammer and chisel to retrieve it, a task
occupying more than a year. So it was not until

The FOUNDER of the 'TABLE ROUND'

*In legends that have grown up concerning King Arthur and the Knights of the
Round Table since those colourful early days of the British race is enshrined
a wonderful spirit of knightly chivalry and valour.*

Arthur, KING. All the ideal virtues of knighthood are illustrated in the literature that has grown up around the figure of this prince of the ancient Britons. But of the historical truth of the stories told about him we can only say, in the words of one of the old writers, that they are " nor all a lie, nor all true, nor all fable, nor all known—so much have the story-tellers told and the fabler fabled, in order to embellish their tales, that they have made all seem fable."

The real Arthur seems to have lived in the 5th or 6th century and to have gained fame as a leader of his people after the Romans, who had ruled the island of Britain for three centuries, abandoned it to the rising power of the barbarians. He carried on war successfully against the heathen Saxon invaders, but was finally defeated. The conquered Britons, who fled to the mountains of Wales and to Brittany in France, began to tell wonderful stories of Arthur's valour and goodness, and fancied that he had not really died but would one day come again to give them victory over their enemies.

Later, the knights and poets of chivalry, because Arthur had been a Christian fighting against heathen, fancied him a knight like themselves, and about his name there began to cluster a cycle of tales in which many other knights appeared. These were said to be members of King Arthur's Order of the Round Table, about which all sat as equals under their liege lord.

In these stories Arthur appears as the son of King Uther Pendragon and the husband of Guinevere, the fairest princess in the land. He maintains his court at Camelot, Cornwall. Percival, Tristram, Galahad, Lancelot and the enchanter Merlin are among the members of his circle. One set of legends tells of the search for the Holy Grail, a cup used by Christ at the Last Supper, which only the pure in heart and deed might gaze upon.

Arthur is said to have gained no fewer than 12 victories over his enemies. Marching toward York he wins a battle outside the walls and then besieges those who sought refuge within. Help comes to the latter, but the army is surprised by a sudden attack and compelled to leave the field. Then 600 ships crowded with German warriors arrive, and Arthur retires to London. Messengers are sent by him to King Hoel of Armorica (Brittany), who lands at Southampton with 15,000 men. After a terrible battle at Lincoln, those of the enemy who are not dead on the field escape to a forest, only to be starved out. Promising to return to Germany, they break faith and march on Bath. The king hurries to the city and relieves it, and a final victory is won by the Duke of Cornwall in Thanet.

In the end Arthur is killed in battle by his nephew, Modred, who has revolted against his rule. Arthur's body is mysteriously carried to the island of Avalon to be healed of its wounds, whence he is expected to return in after ages to restore the rule of right.

The stories of King Arthur were written down by Geoffrey of Monmouth about the year 1136, and by various French writers at a slightly later date. Sir Thomas Malory, an Englishman who lived about 300 years later, translated the stories of the old French writers and published them in one of the first English printed books, entitled Morte d'Arthur (The Death of Arthur). It is from this source that modern writers, including Tennyson, for his Idylls of the King, have drawn their wonderful tales concerning Arthur and his splendid band of heroes. One of the best-known of the old legends about him tells how young Arthur won his crown.

Long, long ago, according to this story, Prince Arthur was the goodliest youth in the whole of Britain. Handsome, brave, true-hearted and gentle-mannered, he had grown up in the old castle of Sir Hector, and had always thought of himself as the son of that good knight, and younger brother to Sir Tor and Sir Kay. One day they all rode up to London. King Uther had long been dead, and the Archbishop had commanded the nobles to meet in the great church and choose a new ruler. Sir Kay, who had just been knighted, forgot his sword, and asked Arthur to go back for it. But the drawbridge was up, and the warden was deaf.

Unable to get into the castle Arthur stopped at the churchyard and drew forth a splendid sword that he saw fixed upright in an iron anvil. When

KING ARTHUR AND THE HOLY GRAIL
The Holy Grail is the name given to the cup used by Jesus at the Last Supper. According to an old legend, a vision of the Holy Grail was seen by Arthur and his knights as they sat at the Round Table. Thereafter the knights searched for the Sacred Cup. This illustration is from a 14th century French manuscript in the Bibliothèque Nationale in Paris

he told Sir Hector where he had found the sword, the old knight dropped on his knees and kissed Arthur's hand.

"Sire," he said, "it is your own. That was the sword of your father, King Uther. No one but his true heir could have drawn it from the anvil." Then Arthur learned that when King Uther died the wise magician, Merlin, had taken him, the infant prince, to Sir Hector. To hide him from enemies who would have killed him, the good knight had brought him up as his own son. Merlin had told the holy archbishop so to fix the royal sword in the anvil that only King Uther's son could, in the fullness of time, draw it forth.

At Christmas, Twelfth Day, Candlemas and Easter, Arthur was called upon to prove his right to the throne. The greatest

Tate Gallery

ARTHUR, THE HERO-KING, IS DYING

The legend of Arthur tells that as the King lay dying he was attended by four Queens waiting to bear him to Avalon—in Celtic mythology a place of rest and reward equivalent to the Valhalla of the Norsemen. In this picture of the last scene, by James Archer, we see the vessel in readiness, and in the foliage on the right an angel carrying the Holy Grail.

nobles and knights in the land were unable to move the sword when it was replaced in the anvil, but when Arthur touched the golden jewelled hilt the blade came free. So Arthur was crowned King, and as a sign that he dedicated himself to God, he laid the royal sword on the altar.

Artichoke. Three forms of vegetables are known as artichokes. The globe artichoke, *Cynara scolymus*, somewhat resembles a large thistle, and the edible portion is the unopened flower-head. It originated in Asia, but grows wild in the south of France, and is often called French artichoke.

The Jerusalem artichoke, *Helianthus tuberosus*, grown in Europe and America, is named from a corruption of the Italian *girasole* (sunflower). Its tubers, which cluster underground like potatoes, are excellent food for human beings and for cattle. The plant contains a sugar called laevulose, which is used to sweeten foods for diabetics. Both the foregoing belong to the family Compositae.

The Chinese artichoke, *Stachys tubifera*, grows not more than about a foot in height, and its small, edible tubers are spiral in shape. It is of Japanese origin, and belongs to the family Labiatae.

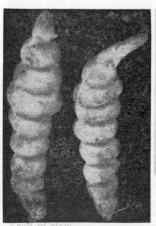

Carter's Seeds Ltd

ARTICHOKES OF THREE KINDS

The strangely shaped tubers at the left are those of the Chinese artichoke. Jerusalem artichoke tubers are seen in the centre. The part of the globe artichoke that is eaten is the fleshy scales of the unopened flower-head (right).

DEADLY GUNS *of* LAND *and* AIR WAR

The guns used by land forces are called artillery, from the French 'artillerie,' denoting the early engines of war. Naval guns differ from those of the land forces and are described under the heading Navy.

Artillery. A speeding speck in the sky, an aeroplane is hit by a shell from an anti-aircraft gun. Gunner's luck ? Partly—and partly " black magic." That anti-aircraft gun, which automatically held its aim on the swift target, following every move of the pilot to dodge the shells, was aimed by a predictor, an elaborate calculating instrument that predicts, or foretells, the point where the shell from the gun and the enemy aeroplane should meet.

If the gun were fired direct at the distant aeroplane, the target would have travelled forward some distance by the time the shell arrived—and the shell would be wasted. To find out the exact meeting-place, the predictor juggles with such details as height, bearing, course and speed of the target (some of which it receives by electrical transmission from radar sets), and strength and direction of wind.

Electric cables connect the predictor with the guns ; and when the meeting-place problem has been worked out by the predictor, electrically operated pointers show the answer at the guns, which are moved sideways or elevated accordingly by the gun-layers—or sometimes by electrical transmission from the predictor. The fuse required for any one shell is also adjusted automatically.

Radar helps the predictor to be more accurate than was possible when readings from height-finders and other instruments had to be " set into " the predictor by means of hand-wheels. Radar has also made it possible to fire at unseen targets, such as aircraft in clouds, and to aim accurately at night without searchlights. In the case of a 4·5-inch battery of four guns, the detection by radar of a bomber squadron could result in the squadron meeting a barrage of thirty-six 55-lb. shells a minute.

Anti-aircraft (A.A.) guns used in the British Army during the Second World War included the 40 mm. (about 1½ inches, the diameter of the shell) Bofors, a quick-firer using 2-lb. shells which could be automatically fed into the gun's breech one after the other from clips, each clip holding four shells. This gun was widely employed in the defence of small targets and against low-flying enemy aircraft. The heavier weapons such as the 3·7-inch (whose shell can go up more than 30,000 feet), the 4·5-inch and 5·25 inch, were placed around towns, etc.

Rockets for use against enemy aircraft were fired, in multiples of two, off rails mounted on projectors which could be raised or lowered and moved sideways. The rockets, lying on the rails, were fired electrically by a switch fixed to the side of the projector. Not having any " spin," as a shell has, they lacked accuracy in flight. But that was made up for by using them in large numbers : 64 projectors, each mounting two rockets, fired at the same time, putting up a barrage of 128 rockets. A similar rocket barrage was used as medium artillery in the field.

The standard weapon in the field artillery of the British Army is the 25-pounder (weight of shell) with a range of about 13,000 yards. This weapon, like nearly all the others, is really a gun-howitzer. A howitzer does not throw its shell very fast or far; the shell goes up in a steep curve, then falls to earth almost perpendicularly. The gun (as distinct from a howitzer) hurls its shell faster and farther, and the missile follows a much straighter path.

The 3·7-inch howitzer was an old design ; it could be taken to pieces and was used by mountain batteries with mule transport, and it came into use again when a weapon was needed which could be carried in gliders or other aircraft. It fires a 20-lb. shell a distance of 6,000 yards and is very accurate. Other field types range from the 4·5 and 5·5-inch gun-howitzers to the giant 9·2-inch.

Artillery was for the most part drawn by four-wheeled motor tractors during the Second World War, but for special rôles self-propelled (S.P.) guns were introduced. These were mounted on tank chassis, the crew sitting in a sort of armoured pulpit,

British Official

ARTILLERY FOR THE ARMOURED CORPS
During the Second World War (1939–45) guns were given greater mobility by mounting them on tracked chassis. They were known as S.P., or self-propelled, guns, and the sides of the compartment behind the gun were armoured to give protection to the crew. These guns acted as artillery with the armoured divisions.

and could go across the country like a tank. The guns used in this manner ranged from the 17-pounder to the 105 mm. (about 4 inches diameter), and the 7-inch gun with which the Russians were experimenting at the end of the war. The Americans produced an 8-inch giant, weighing about 31 tons, which fired a 240 lb. shell 20 miles.

A gun weighing 1,500 tons and capable of firing a 7½ ton shell up to a range of 28 miles was used by the Germans during the Second World War. It was emplaced on railway tracks and served by 1,500 men, and one of its giant shells was eventually displayed at the Imperial War Museum, London.

In British coastal artillery the 6-inch gun, mounted on a turntable, has for many years been a standard weapon. Its working parts and the gun-crew are enclosed in a steel box shield, the limit of range is about 26,000 yards, and its 100 lb. shell can sink a destroyer or damage a large warship. Heavier weapons such as the 9·2-inch, the 12 and 18-inch guns, are also used for coast defence. The big guns of forts can throw shells each weighing more than a ton a distance of 20 miles at a speed of approximately 900 miles an hour.

Some types of gun are used for more than one purpose. The mobile 3·7-inch anti-aircraft gun makes a useful field gun and has been employed against shipping. The high angle to which the barrel can be elevated has on occasions enabled it to reach targets inaccessible to other guns. The 25-pounder was used as an anti-tank weapon during the Second World War, especially in North Africa.

The German 88-mm. was a very successful weapon, being able to engage aircraft, or tanks or other ground targets, according to its mounting.

The Bofors 40-mm. was sometimes employed as a super-heavy machine-gun and was most effective against small vessels. In the desert these guns periodically fired rounds of tracer over the heads of their own advancing infantry to indicate the limits of their sectors and the direction of their objective during night-fighting. Rocket guns fired anti-aircraft barrages, covered troops landing on invasion beaches and engaged tanks and strong points. Coastal artillery are normally given land targets which they can fire upon in event of a land raid or invasion. Naturally, targets at sea are their primary objective. They have also been used against minelaying aircraft, operating over harbours.

Most artillery shells are steel cylinders fitted with a pointed head, and all have a fuse. The purpose of a fuse is to enable a shell to be exploded at any desired moment, and it is the most delicate part of the shell. The fuse may be of a type which explodes when it strikes a solid object, or it may be a time fuse which can be set to explode the projectile at any desired moment during its flight, or it may be a combination of both. The "self-destroying" fuse, used in anti-aircraft gunnery, explodes the shell if it misses the target, thereby preventing it from falling to the ground and causing unintended damage and casualties.

Positively uncanny is the radio proximity fuse, consisting of a tiny radio transmitter and receiver,

Fox

ROCKET PROJECTORS FIRE AN ANTI-AIRCRAFT BARRAGE

Rockets are very effective against many different targets, especially as an anti-aircraft weapon. They are fired off rails mounted on projectors, which can be raised or lowered or moved sideways. The rockets are ignited electrically by means of a switch fixed to the side of the projector. They lack the accuracy of the gun-fired shell, but that can be made up for by using them in large numbers. Tanks and assault craft are also equipped with rocket projectors.

BRITISH GUNS OF PROVEN WORTH IN BATTLE

1.—The 4·5-inch gun throws a 55-lb. shell 20,000 yards. 2.—A 6-pdr. anti-tank gun awaits a target in a narrow lane. 3.—The 25-pdr. is a very accurate weapon and the finest gun of its type in the world. It has an extreme range of about 13,000 yards and can be brought into action very quickly. 4.—The 7·2-inch howitzer fires a 200-lb. shell 16,000 yards; the ramp behind takes the recoil. 5.—An 18-inch gun for coastal defence with a range of 21 miles. 6.—A barrage of British guns illuminates the sky south of Caen, in Normandy, in 1944. Enormous quantities of ammunition are expended in a short space of time when a large number of guns is firing a barrage.

complete with battery and aerial, the whole being fitted in the nose of a shell of 3.7-inch calibre or bigger. While the shell is in flight the tiny transmitter sends out electromagnetic (radio) waves, and when the shell gets within 70 feet of an aircraft or other target the waves are echoed back and picked up by the receiver, which operates a switch, causing the electric detonator to explode the charge. The shell then bursts, and wrecks the target. Many of the German flying bombs, or "doodle-bugs," shot down in 1944–45 were destroyed by shells fitted with this fuse.

The common shell is filled with high explosive, and does its damage by blast and splinters. The armour-piercing anti-tank projectile is solid. A fragmentation shell has its case partly cut through so that it breaks up into sharp flying fragments when the charge explodes. In other shells a small bursting charge releases smoke or gas. A star shell throws out a flare which illuminates the ground or water as it descends slowly, suspended from a parachute. Small guns use "fixed" ammunition like huge rifle cartridges; but the larger ones load their shell and the explosive separately.

Cannons were first used in European warfare in the 14th century, probably at the battle of Crécy in 1346. Begin-

Planet News

RADAR-CONTROLLED ANTI-AIRCRAFT GUN
This 3·7-inch gun is aimed by a Radar set, which transmits electrically the height, course and speed of the target to the predictor. Radar has made it possible to fire accurately at unseen targets, such as aircraft in the clouds. The 3·7-inch gun shoots a shell more than 30,000 feet.

ning as small metal tubes fastened to crude supports, they grew in size until such a huge weapon as the great bombard of Ghent appeared in 1382. This huge piece weighed 13 tons, was more than 16 feet long and fired a 25-inch granite ball weighing about 700 lb. By the middle of the 16th century artillery mounted on wheels had become an important part of military equipment; and cast iron balls, either solid or hollow, replaced stones. The hollow balls when filled with powder became the first shells.

The old muzzle-loading, smooth-bore guns were inaccurate except at point-blank range. It was the custom of rifling (grooving) the inside of the barrel, introduced in the middle of the 19th century, that made artillery much more powerful: spiral grooves cut inside the barrel give a spinning motion to the shell and so enable guns to fire tapering projectiles which will not turn somersaults in flight. And the introduction of gas-tight breech blocks did away with the muzzle-loader.

The tremendous "kick" of firing made it necessary to re-aim the piece after each shot, until a buffer system was invented to absorb the shock of the recoil, thus increasing the rate of fire. The discovery of more powerful explosives than gun-

powder increased the range, and rendered the cannon made from one solid piece of cast or forged metal useless. Modern high explosives would burst such guns like paper. Now a method known as "building up" is used to give the necessary strength. A solid piece of steel is bored out to form the inside tube, then a second tube or sleeve is made which when cold is too small to fit over the first tube, but when expanded by heat will just fit—and after it has cooled it grips the inner lining like a vice. A third or even a fourth sleeve may be put on in the same way. Some guns are wound between the sleeves with miles of the strongest wire.

One of the greatest problems in artillery is the on-the-spot ammunition supply. Whilst opposing armies at Waterloo (1815) exchanged not more than 37 tons of shells throughout the entire battle (so it is said), a single modern 25-pounder firing five rounds a minute can use a ton of ammunition in 20 minutes, and hundreds of guns may be firing at this rate in one sector alone.

Long and intensive training is required to make an efficient gunner. The School of Artillery, at Larkhill on Salisbury Plain, is the instructional centre for handling of artillery for the British Army.

Aryan. (Pron. ār′-i-an). English as well as most of the languages of Europe are included in the Aryan or Indo-European group. Persian, Armenian and Sanskrit (a language of ancient India) also belong to this family. Formerly the term Aryan was applied not only to this group of languages but also to the peoples who spoke them. Most scholars today prefer to restrict the use of Aryan as a race-name to the eastern branch of the Indo-European peoples, which includes the ancient inhabitants of Persia and northern India and their modern descendants.

The Aryans are supposed to have reached India from the highlands of Central Asia in about 2500 B.C. They were nomad tribesmen, possessed of wheeled carts. The invention of the latter may have been the impetus to their wanderings, and so they pushed on through the grassland and forest, laboriously carving a path through the wilderness. Their settlement in India seems to have been a long process, and it was perhaps to avoid their intermarrying with the numerous conquered peoples and so losing their racial characteristics that they devised the caste system of B r a h m i n s (priests), Kshatriyas (fighting men) and V a i s y a s (cultivators and artisans), with the natives as Sudras or slaves in the lowest caste. This caste system was condemned by Mahatma Gandhi (1869–1948), the great Indian leader, but it still retains its hold on the mass of the people, whose lives from birth to death are governed by rigid caste rules which prevent them from changing their occupation or marrying whom they wish.

Asbestos. This is the name given to various minerals containing silicates of magnesium and found in fibrous forms. The material, after crushing, cleaning and separation, can be woven into fabric, or mixed with cement and other binders to produce sheets or blocks. Asbestos is incombustible, and little affected by acids. Protective clothing for fire fighters, fire-resisting curtains for theatres, stove mats to prevent saucepans burning, pads on which to rest smoothing irons—these are some of the uses for this mineral. Light but strong flue pipes for geysers and gas fires; and the baffles or down-draught preventers of such apparatus, are commonly made of "asbestos-cement." Thus roofing tiles, roofing sheets, and wallboards for lining the inside or outside of buildings are formed from asbestos fibre mixed with cement and cast or rolled into the desired form. Another type of use for asbestos is in lining the brake bands of vehicles. Yet another is in insulating hot water or steam pipes against loss of heat.

Asbestos is quarried in Canada, Rhodesia, South Africa, Cyprus and Russia. Its name comes, through

Topical

ASBESTOS SUIT PROTECTS FIRE-FIGHTER
Wrecks of crashed aircraft usually blaze fiercely, because the petrol may catch fire almost at once. Fire-fighters in the Royal Air Force are equipped with asbestos suits to help them in dealing with such emergencies. Thus clad they are able to approach close to the flames and drench them with a special foam mixture sprayed from a cone-shaped nozzle.

Latin, from a Greek word meaning unquenchable. Three-quarters of the world's asbestos comes from Canada, mainly from mines near Quebec which have been worked since about 1880. The deposits of this unique mineral had been observed as long before as 1847, but nothing further was done until prospectors began to get interested in 1876. The form of asbestos found here is that called " chrysotile," which has long fibres and is thus more valuable. It occurs in narrow veins of the rock known as serpentine, the fibres running across the veins, so that the width of the vein governs roughly the length of the asbestos fibre. But the veins are often split by a narrow seam of iron ore, and usually the fibres themselves are not more than about an inch in length.

Originally the mineral was obtained by open quarrying, huge pits being dug, deep and wide, to reach the veins. Today, however, shafts are sunk as in other mining. Since the presence of wood splinters or fragments among the asbestos won from the excavations would spoil the mineral, and destroy its intrinsic value as a fire resister, all the props for the shafts, and all other similar members, even to the sleepers of the railway along which the loaded wagons are hauled, are made of metal or concrete instead of timber.

After the rock is brought up to the surface it is dried, crushed and screened (sifted) repeatedly to free the fibrous asbestos. This material, being so light, is sucked away from the waste rock by air. Fans create the suction for this part of the process. More screening follows, to clean the asbestos and to sort the fibres according to length, since the longer stuff fetches the best price. Much of the

Canadian asbestos goes into the United States for manufacturing, and finished asbestos products to the value of about £500,000 are shipped back to Canada every year. The output of asbestos from Canada is valued at about £4,000,000 annually.

It is only the longer fibre which can be spun into yarn for weaving into fabrics—made into firemen's protective clothing, etc. Yarn is also made into other products for sealing joints in steam pipes or in other jobs where resistance to heat is essential. Mineral with shorter fibres is combined with magnesia and other materials in making the laggings placed around pipes to keep in heat. Such short-fibre asbestos is used also for moulding into brake-linings, or into the filtering pads through which acids are filtered. Another of the principal uses for the mineral is, of course, in making the hundred-and-one parts and articles moulded from asbestos-cement, mentioned above. Though asbestos-cement is brittle and cannot withstand blows or shocks, there are very many uses where these drawbacks are of little account.

Ash. The wood of this tree has few rivals in the manufacture of carriage shafts and wheels, ladders, handles of agricultural tools and other articles needing lightness, pliability, and toughness.

The tree is tall and slender, often reaching a height of 80 to 100 feet with a trunk about three feet in diameter. During winter the flattened, stout, greyish twigs with their black buds are easily recognized. In the early spring small flowers appear on the slender branches, the broad, pinnate leaves opening much later than those of other common trees. The seeds, called " keys," are conspicuous in great bunches in the autumn. Each has a twisted wing by which it whirls away when falling.

There are several species of ash, thriving in many countries; the familiar English one is *Fraxinus excelsior*. It is a rapid grower and beautiful and graceful as a shade tree.

The so-called "mountain ash " or rowan tree, whose berries of orange red are so conspicuous in autumn, is not a true ash. The mountain ash or rowan belongs to the family *Rosaceae*, which includes apples and pears, and its scientific name is *Pyrus Aucuparia*. It is plentiful in Britain, especially in the Scottish Highlands, and in many parts of continental Europe. It is one of the most ornamental trees in British woodlands.

ASH TREE AND ITS FLOWERS
One of the commonest of British trees, the ash may be readily distinguished by its open, drooping head of branches. Its leaves are pinnate, i.e. several leaflets are attached on each side of the leaf stalk. Some of these are shown at the top left. At the lower left are the flowers, which appear before the leaves, springing from the bare branches.

LARGEST *of all the* CONTINENTS

Turning the pages of this chapter, what a vision is ours of strange peoples having their homes in lands as strange! Not only in size but also in population does Asia stand supreme amongst the continents.

Asia. This great continent stretches from the frozen plains of the Arctic Circle to tropical forests of the Malay Peninsula, and from Europe and Africa to within nearly 50 miles of North America, and includes nearly one-third of the dry land of the globe. It is so much the largest of the six continents that you could put all Europe and Africa upon it and have nearly 2,000,000 square miles to spare. Asia contains the highest lands of the world and the lowest, the wettest and the driest, and regions where the variations between heat and cold are most extreme. It is the cradle of the human race, of all religion, wisdom and civilization. With vast resources and more than half the population of the whole world, it perhaps contains the future of civilization as well as its past.

There are people in Asia who will tell you that they pasture their flocks on " the roof of the world," as they call the Great Pamir region in Russian Turkistan. Its valleys are 10,000 to 17,000 feet above sea-level, higher than the tallest peaks of the Alps, and its mountains rise to another 10,000 feet. In fact this whole region with its area of 30,000 square miles lies so far in the cold upper air that it has only three weeks of real summer. Spring and autumn last two months each, and for the rest of the year the lakes are frozen as solid as stone. Nothing has time to grow except the patches of grass that furnish such fine pasture for the sheep of the Kara Kirghiz nomads.

The Great Pamir is not really the roof of the world, but only a gable of the roof. Just east lies the mysterious country of Tibet, the highest inhabited place on the globe. Tibet lies at altitudes of from 12,000 to 17,000 feet.

The roof has other gables as well. One of these is the basin of the Koko-Nor or Blue Lake at the edge of Tibet, lying at an altitude of about 9,000 feet; another the Iranian plateau, including Afghanistan, Baluchistan and Persia (Iran); another, Turkey-in-Asia (Asia Minor), and a fourth, the Deccan, covering the V of the peninsula of India south of the Vendhya range and having an average height of from 1,500 to 2,000 feet.

Extent.—North to south, 5,300 miles; east to west, 6,700 miles; area, about 17,000,000 square miles.

Population.—About 1,155,000,000, more than all the rest of the world together; chiefly of the yellow race (Chinese, Japanese, etc.), with other races of all colours from the white Slavs of Siberia to the negroid peoples of southern India and Ceylon.

Mountains.—Himalayan system, with four highest peaks in the world, including Mount Everest, 29,141 feet, and Kanchanjanga, 28,146 feet. Continuations: Hindu-Kush through Afghanistan to Elburz range (Persia) south of Caspian Sea, highest peak Mount Demavend, 18,600 feet, to Mount Ararat, 17,160 feet; mountains of Armenia, Caucasus, Taurus in Asia Minor; Tien Shan to north-east Altai and Sajansk ranges; Ural Mountains between Asia and Europe.

Plateaux and Deserts.—Tibet, highest plateau in the world, height 12,000 to 17,000 feet; plateau of Iran, including Afghanistan, Baluchistan and Persia; Armenian plateau; plateau of Asia Minor; Pamir plateau, valleys 10,000 to 17,000 feet above sea-level; Deccan plateau in India; Arabian desert; Gobi desert; Takla Makan desert; Kirghiz, and Siberian steppes.

Principal Rivers and Lakes.—In Siberia, Yenisei, Ob, Lena Rivers; in China, Amur, Yangtze, Hwang, Tarim; in the Dominion of Pakistan and the Republic of India, Ganges, Brahmaputra, Indus; in western Asia, Tigris, Euphrates, Caspian Sea, Dead Sea, Aral Sea, Lake Balkash; and in eastern Asia, Lake Baikal.

Chief Countries.—China, U.S.S.R. (part), the Republic of India and the Dominion of Pakistan, Japan, Siam or Thailand, Afghanistan, Burma, Persia or Iran, Turkey, Arabia, Indo-China (French), Indonesia, Malayan Federation (British).

You might say that Asia contained the cellar as well as the roof of the world. The Dead Sea to the north of the Arabian peninsula lies 1,300 feet below sea-level, and is the deepest hollow in the lands of the world. The Great Pamir itself sheers off into the lowlands about the Caspian Sea, which is 85 feet below sea-level.

However, more than one-twelfth of the surface of Asia has an elevation of over 10,000 feet, so that even with the lowlands its mean level is three times as high as that of Europe. The four mountain systems that radiate from the Sarikol range in the Great Pamir—the Hindu-Kush to the west, the Himalayas to the south-east, the Kuenlun to the east, and the Tien Shan to the north-east—are the loftiest in the world. Everest (*see* page 1243) in the Himalayas, with a height of 29,141 feet, is the highest peak in the world, while three other Himalayan peaks look down upon all other mountains. In these "abodes of eternal snow" (that is what the name Himalaya means) rise the great rivers of India and China.

The northernmost point of Asia is Cape Chelyuskin in Siberia, lying within 12 degrees (about 800 statute miles) of the North Pole. If you should travel from there as far as the southernmost point, which is Cape Romania at the tip of the Malay Peninsula, within a degree and a half of the equator, you would have covered a distance of 5,300 miles as the crow flies. Along the northern shores you would see the tundras or frozen plains stretching down to the frozen Arctic Sea. Here a sun shining day and night at mid-summer only thaws the ground deep enough to give root to a few berries and to the moss on which feed the reindeer.

The few people here live in skin tents, dress in furs, and lead a wandering or nomadic life. The reindeer furnish them meat and milk and skins for their tents, and draw their sledges. In this Arctic region is Verkhoyansk, the coldest inhabited place on the globe, where a winter temperature of 93 degrees below zero has been recorded.

Far to the south you would find a people for whom life is as easy as it is hard for the tundra people. The tribes of the Malay Peninsula need only to hunt the animals or eat the fruits of the tropical forests, grow rice in the wet jungles, or prepare sago by one month's work to have their food for the year assured.

In travelling from the west of Asia to the east you would make a longer journey still. It is about 6,500 miles from Cape Baba on the Mediterranean, the westernmost point, to Bering Strait.

On the west, Asia touches Europe at the Ural Mountains and the Caucasus, which forms the parting line between the animal and vegetable kingdoms of Europe and Asia as well as between the continents themselves. It nearly touches again at the two ends of the Sea of Marmara, the Bosporus and the Dardanelles. Because of this close connexion between Europe and Asia, geographers sometimes refer to the two continents jointly as Eurasia. From Africa, Asia is separated only by the Red Sea, ending in the Suez Canal to the north, where only a man-made waterway divides the two continents, and in the narrow Strait of Bab el Mandeb to the south. On the east there is one point at which Asia almost touches North America, for Bering Strait at its narrowest is less than 50 miles wide.

Asia's Coastline and Islands

Three of the boundaries of Asia are oceans, the Arctic, the Pacific and the Indian. Since the coast line is broken by peninsulas and hemmed in by islands, these great bodies of water are divided up into a series of seas, gulfs and bays. The most important of these, from north to south, are Bering Sea, the Sea of Okhotsk, the Japan Sea, the Yellow Sea—so called from the yellow mud of the Yangtze River that colours it for 100 miles from the shore—and the China Sea; and then the Gulf of Siam (Thailand), the Bay of Bengal, the Arabian Sea, the Persian Gulf, and the Gulf of Aden.

The shape of Asia may remind you a little of Europe, magnified of course to many times the size. The Arabian peninsula would be Spain, the Indian peninsula Italy and the Indo-Chinese peninsula would be Greece, with the eastern archipelago taking the place of the Aegean Islands. Then you might think of Japan as balancing the British Isles.

Notice, however, that the eastern coast of Asia has not one set of islands but a whole fringe of them. This fringe extends from the very north to the south, so far that you cannot be quite sure at first where the islands of Asia end and the islands of Australasia begin. Science has, however, drawn a line of demarcation—the Wallace line, named after the naturalist who first indicated it—at the Strait of Macassar, between Borneo and Celebes, where the Australian flowers and animals begin to predominate. The Philippine Islands are a part of the Asiatic fringe, lying across the China Sea.

In Asia you will find more than half of the people of the whole world. In 1940 its total population was estimated at 1,155 million people, of whom the yellow races of China and Japan make up some 600 million, and the Indians nearly 400 million.

At first as you look at the map it seems strange that Asia should support so large a population. Most of the continent consists of places where no one can live at all, or where people can only hunt, or graze sheep or reindeer. Even in China, which contains more people than any other country in the world, there are vast tracts of waste land.

Most of Mongolia consists of the Gobi desert. This is one of the most desolate regions in the world. It is still so little known that story writers feel safe in making it the scene of amazing adventures along the route of the camel trains that brave the stinging sand- and dust-storms to trade between China and Siberia. But recent explorations have gone to show that it may be here, during millions of years, that the animal life of the whole earth was centred, and here, too, the animals of our own time were first evolved.

The sands are now covering the countries round about the Gobi. In the Lob Nor (*nor* means "lake") basin to the west, sand has choked up a whole inland sea until it is now merely a series of marshy lakes in which the once great river Tarim loses itself. Dunes as high as hills are threatening the river, and explorers have found in the region known as the Takla Makan desert ruins of great old cities buried in the sand. This country, merging into the Gobi and called Chinese Turkistan, is almost as dreary and barren as the desert itself.

Here and there, however, you will see little oasis settlements surrounded by fields of grain and scant patches of beans and melons, and shaded by dusty-looking walnut and mulberry trees. Here, too, are large cities, important trading centres for the merchants from China, the countries of India and Pakistan, Russian Turkistan, and Russia. In the bazaars of Yark and Kashgar and Khotan you will see people exchanging bags of musk for cheap tea moistened and compressed into blocks, similar in shape to small bricks, which often serve as money, or haggling for bright-coloured silks and cottons, while water carriers and jugglers move about among a crowd exhibiting all the varied costumes of Asia.

Large Inland Ocean Disappearing

These Chinese desert lands, including part of fertile Manchuria (Manchukuo) to the north, are only one section of a broad belt of desert that extends across Asia to the Sahara in Africa. Russian Turkistan (now known as Soviet Central Asia), beginning at the Pamirs and the Tien Shan mountains, is a desert country like Chinese Turkistan. The sands are drying up the Oxus River, or Amu as it is called today. Its outlet, the Aral Sea, all that is left of a large inland ocean, is disappearing rapidly, but contains a variety of fish.

In this desert of Central Asia are the shrunken modern remnants of great cities of old time. Merv lies in a fertile oasis of nearly 100 square miles, and 20 or 30 square miles of it are ruins. It was here that the traders of China came with silks and spices and pearls to meet European traders in the days before history, and here that Alexander destroyed one great city and built another. Other old oasis cities are Tashkent, Samarkand—which was the capital of the Mongol conqueror Tamerlane—Bokhara and Khiva. Afghanistan and Baluchistan are also a part of this desert, and a considerable tract east of the Indus River.

The central part of Persia (Iran) is also a desert. You can see the sands creeping up and drifting in upon the city of Yezd, dooming it as the cities of Chinese Turkistan were doomed. The river system, choked with sand, is a network of water-courses running nowhere, and no longer makes fertile a land which once blossomed like the rose. The westernmost peninsula, Arabia, is all desert except

ASIA —
at the time of the
SECOND WORLD WAR

As the vast continent of Asia was still in 1949 so unsettled politically, we have preferred for the present to leave the map as it was at the time of the outbreak of the Second World War. It is of great value for the student in recording the natural geographical features, the national and racial divisions, and the dependencies of foreign powers. It is thus a cartographical record of the end of a great historic era and the uneasy birth of a new epoch. On the reverse we print a list of the alterations in the names of states, countries, and dependencies in Asia, which have been recognized since 1939 until going to press with this Edition of THE NEW BOOK OF KNOWLEDGE.

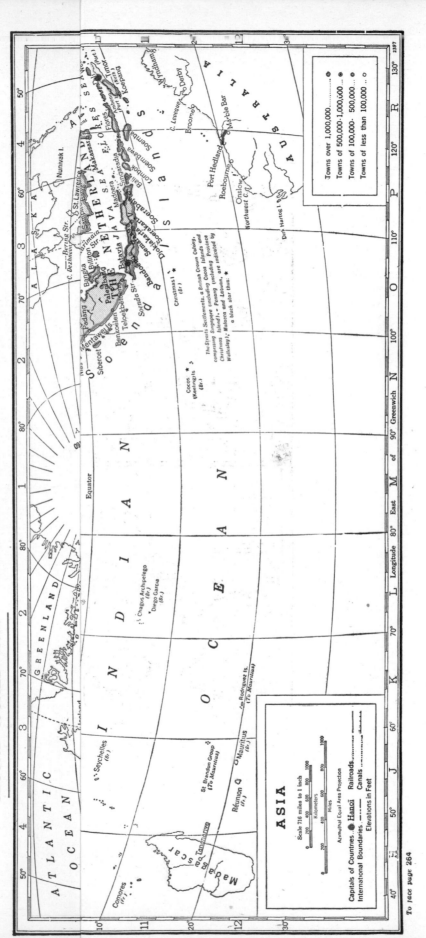

Note

CHANGES IN THE MAP OF ASIA

ughout Asia.

To face page 265

BRITISH MALAYA became the FEDERATION OF MALAYA on February 1, 1948. It consists of the nine Malay states of Perak, Selangor, Negri Sembilan, Pahang, Johore, Kedah, Kelantan, Trengganu and Perlis, and the British settlements of Penang and Malacca. Singapore forms a separate crown colony. NORTH BORNEO became a crown colony on July 15, 1946. SARAWAK became a crown colony on July 1, 1946. BRUNEI remained a British protected area.

BURMA, a part of the British Commonwealth up to January 4, 1948, became an independent republic on that date.

CEYLON, a British Crown Colony since 1802, became a self-governing Dominion within the British Commonwealth on February 4, 1948.

CHOSEN readopted its former name of KOREA after the surrender of Japan to the Allies on August 15, 1945, when it ceased to be a part of the Japanese Empire. It was sub-divided along the line of the 38th parallel of latitude into NORTH KOREA and SOUTH KOREA.

FRENCH INDO-CHINA now comprises the Republic of VIET-NAM, established on September 17, 1946, and the kingdoms of CAMBODIA and LAOS, all within the French Union. Viet-Nam consists of the former protectorates of Annam, Tongking, and Cochin-China.

INDIA. On August 15, 1947, the sub-continent of India was divided into the Dominions of INDIA and PAKISTAN. In January 1950 the former became a republic within the British Commonwealth.

IRAN in October 1949 officially resumed the name PERSIA.

MANCHUKUO, a Japanese-controlled state formed out of Chinese territory and established on March 25, 1932, was returned to China in August 1945 after the defeat of Japan by the Allies, and was renamed MANCHURIA.

NETHERLANDS EAST INDIES in 1949 became the UNITED STATES (in 1950, REPUBLIC) OF INDONESIA.

PALESTINE, held as British mandated territory until May 14, 1948, was claimed both by the new Jewish state of ISRAEL and by Arab states, particularly the former TRANSJORDAN. Boundaries were still unsettled in 1950.

PHILIPPINE ISLANDS. The Commonwealth of the Philip-pines was proclaimed an independent republic on July 4, 1946.

SAKHALIN ISLAND, which had previously belonged partly to the U.S.S.R. and partly to Japan, became wholly Russian after the surrender of Japan in 1945.

SYRIA and LEBANON became two independent republics on January 1, 1944.

TAIWAN (FORMOSA), which was taken from China by Japan in 1895, was restored to that country in 1945, and retained by Chinese Nationalists after the Chinese mainland had come under Communist domination.

TRANSJORDAN, previously held under British mandate, was proclaimed an independent state on June 17, 1946. In June 1949 it changed its name to the Hashimite Kingdom of the JORDAN.

the very rim; and Iraq, with the exception of the once fertile Tigris-Euphrates valley, is also mostly desert. Across its burning sands caravans patiently make the 60-day journey from Damascus to Mecca, or traverse the ancient route to Baghdad.

Nor are the deserts and mountains the only places where few people can live. On the rim of the deserts are waving plains of grass, which the Russians call steppes. The Asiatic steppes, extending from Manchuria across Mongolia, Turkistan, southern Siberia, Asia Minor, Persia and Arabia, cover an area far greater than the whole of Europe. These grasslands, too dry for agriculture, either because they lie too high or because they are too far inland to receive rainfall, furnish rich pasture. Scattered nomad tribes wander from pasturage to pasturage during the season when the grass springs up. When the sun has dried the last of it to a reddish-brown mass the wandering peoples return to some oasis to wait for the next growth.

In Arabia these nomads are called Beduins. They live in prosperity, dependent only on their flocks and herds for meat, skins, milk and wool. They are, however, very warlike and exact toll from caravans and oasis cities.

Similar people are the Kirghiz of Siberia. The Siberian steppes have vast grasslands and limitless opportunities for agricultural development.

Lonely Fur-Hunters and Fishermen

There are still other vast regions in Asia that support few people. The Siberian forest stretches nearly across the continent in a belt 5,000 miles east to west, and 1,000 to 2,000 miles broad. In some places its dark recesses have hardly been penetrated by Man. It is visited chiefly by the hunter seeking rich skins—wolf, bear, fox, sable and squirrel, for in these cold forest depths the animals grow fur of surprising thickness and lustre—and by migratory tribes from the tundra or frozen plain who come here to fish in the dark forest streams. Here and there you will find a clearing with a few log huts clustered together, but scarcely a town and never a city, for hunters and fishermen are not city dwellers nor do their simple life and limited wants support more than a trading post. In the jungles of the Ganges valley in the Republic of India, the elephants, monkeys, rhinoceroses, tigers, buffaloes, wild boars and wolves are scarcely asked to share their territory with human inhabitants. The same scarcity of population characterizes the dense tropical forests covering much of the Malay Peninsula.

What then is the secret of the vast population of Asia when so large a part of the land is desert, grassland, forests, and mountain peaks? If you could visit the great river valleys of China and India you would see. China has more than one-third the people of Asia, or more than the population of Europe. India contains almost as many as North America, South America and Africa together.

The Yangtze in China is the most densely populated river valley in the world. The river is navigable for 2,000 miles or more, and all along its banks are little farms. Here for thousands of years people have grown crops and kept their soil fresh by the use of river mud and fertilizers. People live even on the river itself, in little boats called sampans, whose matting roofs are the shape of half a barrel. These river dwellers keep shop and even grow things on their boats. In the valley of the Amur to the north there is a smaller population, but people fairly swarm along the fertile Hwang River valley. More than 12 centuries ago China constructed what is practically a fourth great river, the Grand Canal, 850 miles long. Following this and countless smaller canals are more of the tiny close-packed farms and flooded rice-fields. Where mulberry groves are planted for the silkworm, crops are grown between the rows.

In the Republic of India and the Dominion of Pakistan there are populous river valleys, particularly the Ganges, and the fertile valley between the Ganges and the Brahmaputra. The Indus valley is less productive, owing to the Indian desert just east of it. In all, the sub-continent of India has a population of just under 400 million.

The three great rivers of Siberia, the Ob, the Yenisei and the Lena, of course do not support such great populations. They are broad and deep enough to be navigable, and the soil is fertile, but they are frozen during the greater part of the year. The great rivers of western Asia, the Tigris and the Euphrates, water a valley which was fruitful 5,000 years ago, but is little developed.

Other countries where a great many people live are those which are blessed by rain-laden ocean winds breaking against mountains. Thus Japan, which for all its hundreds of islands has a comparatively small habitable area (about 263,000 square miles), has a population of about 100 million. On the other hand, the Asiatic territories of the U.S.S.R., totalling nearly 8 million square miles, support a population of only about 60 million.

To make up for its many dry places, Asia contains the wettest region in the world. This is Assam, south of the eastern Himalayas. It has a recorded rainfall of 400 inches as against the less than 10 of northern Siberia, Arabia, Persia, and Gobi desert. This warm wet climate, with enough of a slope to drain the water from the roots of the plant, is just what is needed for tea-growing, which is the industry of Assam as it is of Ceylon.

First Abode of Civilized Man

Asia has been called the cradle of the human race, and some scientists have pointed to definite regions such as the Caucasus or Asia Minor as the first abode of civilized Man, the place from which he migrated to Europe and southern Asia.

However this may be, Asia can show remains of the oldest known civilization in the world except Egypt. At Troy in Asia Minor, the peninsula lying between the Mediterranean and the Black Sea, the heroes of Homer's epics were fighting 3,000 years or more ago, and archaeologists have found on the same site still older cities. In Caucasia, the broad isthmus between the Black Sea and the Caspian, lay Colchis, the rich and fertile land whither Jason went in search of the Golden Fleece.

Scientific men tell us that here the stone-fruit trees, such as the peach, the apricot and cherry, first developed from the same wild ancestor. Here, too, are the ruins of the great old cities of Armenia, and here rises the peak of Mount Ararat, where, according to tradition, the Ark came to rest.

Palestine along the Mediterranean coast of the Arabian peninsula is the scene of the Bible story

OLD WAYS STILL HAMPER ASIA'S ADVANCE

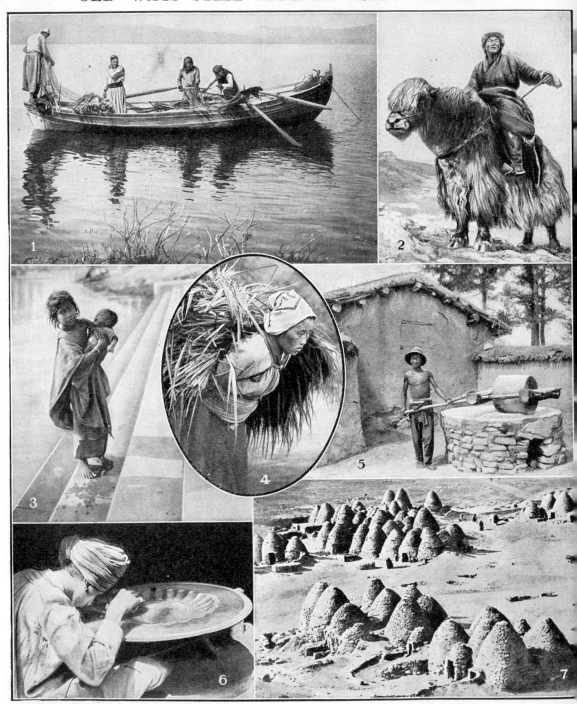

In spite of much progress in the cities, most Asiatics cling to the ways of their fathers. 1. In the Sea of Galilee the fishermen cast their nets with much the same equipment as in the time of Christ. 2. The yak is as useful a creature to the Tibetans and Mongolians as the camel is to the Arabs. Ridiculous as it looks, the creature serves as a mount, and furnishes butter, leather, wool cloth, and meat. 3. All too primitive are some of the notions of the people of the sub-continent of India, where little girls like this one coming up from a bath in Benares may be the mother of a baby while she herself is little more than a child. 4. This Japanese peasant woman carrying grass for fuel would welcome the motor lorry. 5. An old way of grinding grain is that of the Chinese lad patiently operating this crude mill. Such backwardness keeps China poor, starving, sick torn with civil war. 6. But there is another side to ' the old ways,' the aspect of fine craftsmanship, such as we see in the hands of this skilled Hindu brass worker. 7. The once important town of Harran, about 100 miles north-east of Aleppo, is today but a Turkish village of mud huts, shaped like old-fashioned beehives. Aleppo, an important town of northern Syria, is about 50 miles south of the Turkish frontier.

CONTRASTING CUSTOMS IN HOMES OF ASIA

In the daily life of the people of Asia, the visitor is struck with its many elaborate ceremonies on the one hand and its utter simplicity on the other. 1. The coming-of-age ceremony of the girls in some parts of the sub-continent of India is a gorgeous affair, with a splendid throne and a real débutante party. 2. Simple details of life are carried on with charming ceremonies in Japan. How decorous and orderly is the prim luncheon of these Japanese ladies! The Japanese, like the Chinese, eat with two chopsticks, instead of knives, forks and spoons. 3. A picturesque way of reeling cotton has this woman of India, who will probably weave up her homespun thread into a very beautiful fabric. 4. A curse of most Asiatic countries has been the seclusion of women. Persia, where this veiled lady walks, was one of the last oriental countries to cling to this Mahomedan practice. 5. See the smiles of these Bakhtiari women of Russian Turkistan, freed from veils and seclusion by the Soviet government. 6. The girls of Java spend many hours each day dying fabrics by hand in intricate patterns by the batik method, where parts of the material which are not to be dyed are coated with hot wax. 7. This baby of Ceylon is being given a primitive open-air bath in the garden. Here such a bath is a pleasure as the climate is warm all the year round.

and of the development of the ancient Hebrew civilization. Persia as a political power dates back to 559 B.C. when Cyrus made his sweeping conquest. And oldest of all civilizations in the world except Egypt is that of Mesopotamia—now called Iraq—in the Tigris-Euphrates valley, where there were great cities as early as 3000 B.C., followed by the empires of Babylonia and Assyria.

In the two other fertile flood plains besides Mesopotamia there were early civilizations, though nobody knows how old. In China there are definite records as far back as 1100 B.C. In India the princes rode on elephants and lived in splendid palaces at the time of Alexander the Great's campaign to the Indus in the 4th century B.C.

For thousands of years, however, the civilization of Asia stood still. The Indians of Alexander's time were skilled in all the arts they ever possessed down to the time of the British occupation. The Chinese preceded Europe in the invention of printing, paper-making, porcelain, guns, gunpowder, fine weaving, and perhaps the compass. But having found a good way of writing, governing, making cloth, and tilling the soil 3,000 years ago, they simply stopped searching for new ways.

The Arabs, sweeping over the feeble remnants of Greek and Roman civilization in the early Christian centuries, absorbed and developed the learning they fell heir to. Throughout the Middle Ages they led the world in agriculture, building, weaving, metal working and mathematical science. But until recently their culture remained at the same stage, while that of the West went ahead.

Asia has been the cradle of the great religions. From Mesopotamia came the seeds that developed into the three systems that now hold the western world. The first was Judaism, which developed very early in Palestine. From Judaism sprang the other two—Christianity and, in A.D. 622, Mahomedanism. The latter, from small beginnings at Medina in the Arabian desert, became one of the most widely followed religions of the world. Its followers are believed to number over 200 million in Asia and Africa alone.

World-Famed Places of Pilgrimage

From the Aryan group in Asia as well as from the Semitic have come other great religions. The Persians developed Zoroastrianism, based upon the principle of the conflict between good and evil; and the Hindus originated Brahminism and its outgrowth, Buddhism, which between them now total perhaps 380 million followers in Asia. From the land of the yellow man has sprung the great moral code originated by Confucius (d. 478 B.C.), which has been the religion of most of the Chinese ever since.

As a result, Asia contains places of pilgrimage for the whole world. Palestine has been visited by Christians since long before those medieval military pilgrimages, the Crusades. Every year hundreds of thousands of Mahomedans go to Mecca and Medina in the Arabian desert. For Buddhists Tibet is a holy land. For the Chinese, the tomb of Confucius is a place of pilgrimage.

The name Asia is believed to come from a Hebrew root which means, like the Latin root of the word *orient*, " the east " or " the rising sun." And Asia contains the whole so-called Orient—

Near East and Far East alike. For thousands of years the riches of Asia have poured into Europe —spices, incense, rubies, pearls, silks and muslins. Until 500 years ago these precious things from China, India and southern Arabia came by way of the camel trains that spent months, sometimes years, making their way through the deserts of Turkistan, Persia and Arabia, to Asia Minor.

After Vasco da Gama discovered the ocean route round Africa to India in 1497–98, part of the traffic was carried by sailing vessels. Within 50 years the Portuguese navigators had pushed still farther, to China and Japan, and had established a line of trading posts which amounted to a coastal empire. In the first years of the 17th century Holland, England and France had also their commercial companies in the Far East. Just before the middle of the 18th century there began a 40-years' duel between England and France for supremacy in southern Asia, England at length coming out victorious. In the meantime Russia had started across Siberia in 1580, and within 80 years had obtained a slice of Asia to the Pacific Ocean and the Amur River.

The Envied Wealth of all Asia

In the 18th and 19th centuries American clipper ships did a flourishing trade in tea, coffee, ivory, spices and fine fabrics ; and it was an American, Commodore Perry, who opened the doors of Japan, in 1854, after they had been closed to the western world for a century and a half. A war between China and Japan in 1894–95 resulted in the cession of Formosa, or Taiwan as the Japanese call it, and Pescadores to Japan ; and the Russo-Japanese War brought the cession of the southern half of the island of Sakhalin to Japan in 1905, while Korea was annexed to the island empire in 1910. After their defeat by the Allied nations in the Second World War, the Japanese withdrew from Korea and restored Southern Sakhalin to the Russians. The Philippines had been transferred to the United States at the close of the Spanish-American War in 1898 ; their independence was granted by the U.S.A. in 1946.

In the last decade of the 19th century various attempts were made to shorten the distance between Europe and Asia. The Suez Canal was dug, connecting the Mediterranean with the Red Sea so that ships could go through to the Indian Ocean without rounding Africa, while Russia built railways across Siberia and Central Asia.

The wealth of Asia tempted the modern world to conquest. A keen rivalry sprang up between Russia and Britain for influence in Asia, mainly from a fear lest one or the other should gain an advantage in territory or in military strength. India and her neighbouring lands were the bone of contention between Western powers for many years (*see* India). Western merchants established trading posts in many parts of Asia, and then looked to their own governments to protect them.

Some European lands sent out colonists who did much to develop and civilize the regions where they made their homes *e.g.* British India, as it was until 1947, and the former Netherlands East Indies.

After the Bolshevik revolution of 1917 the new rulers of Russia imposed the Soviet system upon

WORLD'S GREAT RELIGIONS DAWNED IN ASIA

In the Orient have arisen the world's religions, Christianity, Buddhism, Mahomedanism, Shintoism, Confucianism, the religion of the Jews, Hinduism in all its branches, and the lama worship of the Tibetans. 1. A temple like a palace is mirrored in a pool in Calcutta to celebrate the religion of the Jain sect. 2. Buddha's smile greets his worshippers in a grotto in western Tibet. 3. Temple dancers go through a mystic ritual to Brahma on the Island of Bali. 4. To the elephant god, Ganapati or Ganesha, this Hindu child says a prayer. 5. On Mt. Sinai, made famous by the Biblical story of the Ten Commandments, rises a Christian cross over a monastery built in A.D. 527. 6. A Beduin Arab washes his hands at Mary's Well in Nazareth. 7. The Buddhist lama of Peking prays before an incense-burner. 8. The Mosque of Omar, in Jerusalem, is sacred to Moslems, Jews and Christians. On the rock below, Abraham prepared to sacrifice Isaac; here stood Solomon's temple, and in another temple Christ conversed with the doctors.

THE ORIENT'S PAST AND PRESENT SPLENDOUR

1. This modern palace of the Maharajah of Mysore glitters with electric lights by night. 2. When a Siamese boy or girl is about 12 the childhood top-knot of hair is cut off, in a three-day festival. 3. Cambodian dancers repeat in costume and posture dancers carved on the walls of Angkor Vat (picture 6). 4. These Indian elephants, attired in silk or velvet, bright with paint and gold and jewels, are pulling a rajah's car on a state occasion. 5. Oriental rulers, such as this former Emperor of Annam, wear gorgeous attire of the past. 6. Mysterious and magnificent is the temple of Angkor Vat, built in Indo-China in medieval times, and used first for Hindu, then for Buddhist worship.

more than a third of the 17 million square miles of Asia. In the former Russian Turkistan five self-governing Soviet Socialist Republics were established—Kazakh, Uzbek, Turkoman, Tajik and Kirghiz—and in other ways a communist rule from Moscow was fastened more securely upon Siberia and Central Asia. These developments did nothing to allay the old antagonism between Russia and Japan who, by creating the state of Manchukuo in 1932 at the expense of China, strengthened her own power on the mainland.

Japan had for many years been irked by her own lack of a share in Asia outside her own islands. In 1941, when she seized large territories which had been hitherto administered by Britain and the U.S.A., her declared object was to create a "Greater East Asia Co-Prosperity Sphere," which she would control. Her defeat in the war ended this dream.

Elsewhere, too, Asiatic countries showed a desire for greater independence, sometimes from European interference and sometimes from their own ruling caste. Thus Persia, in 1925, deposed its shah, and created a new ruling dynasty by setting up the prime minister in his place.

Arabia, too, passed to a new master, when in 1925 the sultan of Nejd drove out the king of the Hejaz and established his authority over the greater part of the peninsula. In 1927 he secured from Great Britain a recognition of his country's complete independence. In 1932 a parliamentary form of government was established in Thailand (Siam) reducing the powers of the king under the new constitution.

The most far-reaching changes, as we have seen, came after the Second World War. In 1947 Britain granted self-government to India (which was divided into the two Dominions of India and Pakistan) and complete independence to Burma. Malaya was formed into the Mayalan Federation, in preparation for its achievement of self-government within the British Commonwealth. Ceylon became a Dominion in 1948. The Netherlands East Indies as the United States (later Republic) of Indonesia was granted self-government in union with the Netherlands in 1949. France granted self-government within the French Union to Viet-Nam, Laos, and Cambodia, in Indo-China.

The Japanese overseas empire ceased to exist.

Asia Minor.
Since the 5th century B.C. the name of Asia Minor has been applied to that great peninsula which juts westward from the main continental mass of Asia, separating the Black Sea from the Mediterranean and facing Europe across the Dardanelles, the Sea of Marmara, and the Bosporus. On the east it is bordered by Iraq and the Soviet Union. In modern times the name Anatolia, meaning " the East or Sunrise " has been given to this great region. Its area is about 200,000 square miles, and its population about 16,300,000. Today nearly all the peninsula forms part of the republic of Turkey, and in it is the Turkish capital, Angora, now called Ankara. The chief ports are Izmir (Smyrna) on the Aegean Sea and Trabzon (Trebizond) on the Black Sea.

Asia Minor consists mostly of a high, barren central plateau, fringed on all sides by rugged mountains, including the great Taurus range to the south. Only on the slopes between the mountains and the sea do we find forests and green fields, though in ancient days, before it was stripped of its trees, the land was fertile.

This country has been the battle ground of warring nations since the days of ancient Troy, which stood near its extreme western tip. It was the home of the Hittites of the kingdoms of Phrygia and Lydia, and of important Greek colonies along the coast. It saw the victorious armies of Croesus and of the Persian kings, the famous " March of the Ten Thousand " described by Xenophon, and the conquests of Alexander the Great and of Rome. Finally, beginning in the 11th century, it passed gradually into the hands of the Turks.

Asia Minor possesses tremendous undeveloped mineral wealth, extensive forests and many fertile valleys. Grapes, wine, tobacco, cotton and olives are grown, and the peasants keep immense herds of sheep and goats, the latter chiefly for their hair. The Anatolian Railway is the chief means of inland transport. The main line extends from the Bosporus via Konya and Aleppo (Syria), continuing into Iraq to Baghdad. (*See* Turkey).

Asparagus.
The tall, plume-like growths of the cultivated asparagus (*Asparagus officinalis*) are, when they are allowed to mature, as beautiful as a delicate fern, with numerous bright red berries. And what table vegetable is more palatable and healthful than these same luscious shoots, if cut when they first poke their purplish-white caps through the rich bed in which they grow? Yet the wild asparagus, as it grows on the southern coast of England, is an insignificant plant, with growths only a foot high and thin stems On the plains of Rnssia the wild varieties are so plentiful that cattle feed upon them.

For 2,000 years asparagus has been cultivated for the table. It is a perennial plant and early in the spring sends up its thick tender stalks, which are ready for cooking when six or eight inches high. The plants are grown in rows, and beds take several years to establish, though after they bear for years.

Of the 150 species of asparagus widely distributed in tropical and temperate countries, many are cultivated only for ornamental purposes, some reaching a height of 15 feet.

Carters Seeds Ltd

ASPARAGUS SHOOTS
Asparagus, even in the season, from April to June, is an expensive luxury, for after the seed is sown five years must elapse before the stalks can be cut. Evesham, in Worcestershire, is a centre for growing asparagus.

ASPHALT DISCOVERED BY SIR WALTER RALEIGH
During a voyage to the West Indies, Raleigh landed on the island of Trinidad at a spot where some of the pitch from the asphalt lake had trickled down to the beach. He used it to caulk his ships, and he tells us that he found it to be ' most excellent and good and it melteth not with the sunne as the pitch of Norway.'

be remade and freshened up with new material for use again.

Lake asphalt comes mainly from the famous " pitch lake " in Trinidad. It is said that although you dig out a train-load the hole fills up again and the supply appears never to diminish. This form of asphalt contains about half bitumen. In use for roads, etc., it is mixed with crushed stone; lake asphalt is mixed, too, with rock asphalt. One very important use for these materials is in laying a damp-proof course in the lower part of a brick or stone wall, to prevent damp rising from the ground into the building. Basements, water tanks, and such places are waterproofed with asphalt; protective paints are made from it; it is used for " expansion joints " in concrete roads, and there are many other uses for this gift from Nature.

Synthetic asphalts are made from mixtures of suitable rock and one or other of the petroleum or gas-tar products, which are

Asphalt.

Natural asphalt consists of lime-stone rock which has become impregnated with bitumen. Bitumen is one of the class of chemical compounds called hydrocarbons, composed of hydrogen and carbon. It is thought that the slime pits mentioned in Genesis were natural deposits of bitumen, and Moses s mother is said to have daubed the basket of bulrushes with slime and pitch.

The ancients undoubtedly used some bituminous mixture for caulking the seams of boats, and for other such purposes. Another name for asphalt is pitch, but this is applied also to many other substances.

Rock asphalt is found in France, Switzerland and Germany. After quarrying, the blocks are crushed and powdered; then, when the asphalt has been heated, it is laid down as a surface for roads, or as a top layer over flat roofs to repel water. So " lively " is this material that even after it has stood the traffic for a long while, and the road or pavement has to be broken up and relaid, the worn asphalt can

forms of bitumen. Thus pitch or coal-tar can be used with crushed natural rock, the mixture being heated until it is semi-liquid in consistency, and then laid and pressed.

Many natural petroleums are said to have an asphalt base. which means that the residue after refining contains a product which has many of the characteristics of liquid asphalt. By heating this

Keystone

ASPHALT LAKE ON TRINIDAD ISLAND
The famous asphalt ' lake ' of the British island of Trinidad, just off the mouth of the Orinoco river in South America, has supplied material for paving the streets of many great cities. Negro labourers dig up the asphalt and carry it away in baskets, but the supply remains undiminished because as soon as any quantity is removed some more oozes up to fill the hole.

substance with sulphur, the process whereby the natural solid asphalt was formed by Nature, artificial solid asphalt is obtained.

Ass. The patient ass is a far older friend of Man than the horse, for it was captured in the deserts of Egypt and western Asia and domesticated long before the horse had been first subdued in his northern grasslands. Wild asses still flourish in the Nubian deserts, Sudan and Somaliland, and the arid interior of Asia. Travellers tell us that those who have seen the donkey only in its civilized state have no conception of its wild ancestor. For the latter is one of the fleetest of animals, the

Keystone

FROM ASPHALT LAKE TO CITY STREET
Before it is used for repairing the surface of a road the asphalt is crushed and freed from any impurities, such as earth. The powder is then heated on the site, laid on the road, and smoothed and rolled with heated irons to render it impervious to water. Liquid asphalt is used to form a damp-proof layer in brick or stone walls, and to make a waterproof finish on top of a flat roof.

perfection of activity and courage. The domestic ass or donkey (*Equus asinus*) is descended from the African ass of Abyssinia. It is smaller in size than the horse, and its colour is usually grey.

The reputation of the ass for stupidity is very old. Even the Egyptians represented an ignorant person by the head and ears of an ass. In the Middle Ages the boy who was last to enter the school on St. Thomas's Day was called the "ass Thomas." In northern France the "Feast of the Ass" commemorated the Flight of Mary and the infant Jesus into Egypt; Balaam's ass also appeared and uttered prophecies. The festival degenerated into a vulgar farce and was suppressed in the 15th century. In southern Europe the ass has been carefully bred

and thus greatly improved, but it is seen at its best in Syria and Egypt. Its milk is used for food.

Assam. A state in the extreme northeast of the Republic of India, between the Himalayas and the Burmese mountains, Assam is known all over the world for its tea plantations. It is bounded on the north by Bhutan and Tibet, on the east by Burma and on the west by Bengal, to which presidency it was attached politically until 1912. When India was divided into the two dominions of India and Pakistan in 1947 the Sylhet region of Assam was added to E. Bengal, becoming a part of Pakistan. Assam has an area of 55,043 square miles and its many valleys are watered by the Brahmaputra and its tributaries. The population

Carl Raswan

WILD ASSES AT HOME IN THE ARABIAN DESERT
These wild asses grouped on the skyline, are watching the photographer with interest mingled with suspicion There are several types of wild ass, and those shown here are the Arabian species. As you can see, Arabian asses are considerably more graceful than the 'donkeys' of Britain. Another difference is the absence of the stripe which crosses the back of our own asses. Their long ears and short necks are enough to distinguish them from any type of wild horse

ASSASSINS IN THEIR CASTLE

The word assassin is derived from the word hashish, for Indian hemp. In Persia in the 11th century there was a sect known to Europeans as Assassins who, under their founder, Hassan Ibn Sabbah, committed many murders, nerving themselves by taking hashish beforehand. This illustration from a 14th century book shows Hassan Ibn Sabbah giving this stimulant to his followers.

numbers about 8,500,000, of whom nearly 90 per cent are engaged in agriculture. Although a considerable quantity of rice is grown, it is not sufficient to feed the people, and a great deal has to be imported.

The principal industry of Assam is the cultivation of tea. The area of the tea plantations is over 400,000 acres and the yield more than 288 million lb. Assam is well served by railways. The capital is Shillong, on the Brahmaputra, which has a population of about 17,000, and other important towns are Manipur (Imphal), Dibrugarh and Aijal in the east and Gauhati in the west.

During the Second World War, 1939–45, Japanese armies drove British forces out of Burma in the course of a campaign lasting from December 1941 to May 1942. The British took up positions along the Assam-Burma border to resist a Japanese invasion of India, and in April 1944 the Japanese launched an attack towards the Imphal-Kohima road, but their advance was halted by the British defence of Imphal. In May another Japanese force attacked Kohima, but after long and heavy fighting the invaders were driven out of Assam, and by the end of August 1944 the British 14th Army was pursuing them southwards into Burma.

Assassins. Near the end of the 11th century a Mahomedan named Hassan Ibn Sabbah established himself in a mountain fortress of Persia. This

became the headquarters of a secret Mahomedan sect, which for two centuries spread the terror of its name from India to Egypt. Instead of fighting his enemies in battle Hassan resorted to secret murders, planned and carried out with great skill by his numerous followers.

The head of the sect was known as the " Old Man of the Mountains," and from a certain group of uninitiated followers called the " devoted ones " Hassan demanded blind obedience. This he obtained in a strange way. He maintained beautiful and luxurious gardens, carefully guarded, into which he introduced the young men, after giving them a heavy dose of a dream-producing drug called hashish, made of Indian hemp. The next day they were told that the magnificent visions which they could faintly remember were a foretaste of the heaven which awaited them if they obeyed their leader. They were then sent forth on their murderous missions. This use

Carter's; C. W. Teager

ASTERS OF DIFFERENT KINDS

Popular in British gardens are two kinds of plant known as aster but not bearing much resemblance. The China asters (above) die after flowering. The true asters, or Michaelmas daisies (top), live on from year to year.

of hashish won for the members of the sect the name of *Hashishins* or " Assassins," a name later applied to all political murderers.

Assyria. The second of the three great Semitic empires that grew up in the Tigris-Euphrates valley in ancient times was that of the Assyrians, who dwelt about Nineveh. The history of Assyria is closely intertwined with that of Babylonia. (*See* article Babylonia).

Aster. Two kinds of plant are grown in British gardens as aster. The true aster is familiarly known as Michaelmas daisy, from its habit of flowering in the autumn round about Michaelmas Day (September 29). These Michaelmas daisies, of the genus *Aster* (Greek, meaning star), are perennials : the tops die each year but growth starts again from the base the following spring. They are natives of N. America and Europe ; many species and varieties are now cultivated, and the height varies up to about four feet. Two species are found wild in Great Britain : the purplish flowered sea aster (*Aster tripolium*), occurring in salt marshes around our coasts ; and the rare *Aster linosyris*, with bright yellow flowers, confined to a few limestone cliffs.

The familiar China aster of our gardens is an annual: it dies completely after flowering. Native to China, it belongs to the genus *Callistephus*. Under cultivation the China asters have assumed diverse forms of flower and colouring and range in height up to about two feet.

Both Michaelmas daisy and China aster belong to the family *Compositae*.

ASTRAKHAN AS HEADGEAR

In Western Europe astrakhan, the soft fleece of newly-born Persian lambs, is used chiefly for ladies' coats, though sometimes men's overcoats have astrakhan collars. Further East men's hats are often made of the fleece. The Georgian boy (left) from the Caucasus is wearing an astrakhan cap. The boy in the centre has a sheepskin headdress.

Astrakhan. (Pron. as-tra-kan'). The beautiful curly glossy-black fur called " astrakhan " is the skin of new-born Persian lambs, and it gets its name from the city of Astrakhan, an important commercial centre near the Caspian Sea. The city, which has a population of 254,000, is a picturesque but dirty semi-oriental town, built on an island in the Volga River, 50 miles from where it empties into the Caspian Sea. For centuries it has been one of the important distributing centres for the products of Europe and Asia. Through it pass every year gold, silks, embroideries, spices, drugs and grain, which the nations of Central Asia exchange at Astrakhan for cotton,

leather, salt, sugar and other products. Among its most important exports also are petroleum from the great near-by wells of Baku, and fish, principally sturgeon and salmon, from the Volga, the longest river in Europe. A university was established there in 1919.

The government of Astrakhan, of which this city was the capital, was the fourth political division in point of size of the old Russian Empire, with an area of 91,042 square miles. After the formation of the Russian Soviet Federal Socialist Republic in 1918 the old divisions of the country were abolished, and the town became a commercial centre in the Stalingrad region of the R.S.F.S.R.

The WONDROUS SCIENCE of the STARS

How wonderful are the heavens, whose glory sparkles above us in the silent night ! In this article just a suggestion is given of the amazing knowledge which the patient research of the astronomers has built up.

Astronomy. Even prehistoric Man or the simplest savage could not escape some thought about things in Nature, the earth under his feet and the heavens above his head. The ordered movements of the ever-changing sky did not escape the gaze of the early shepherds on the hills, of the primitive mariner or hunter who guided his course by the stars, and of the farmer who sowed and planted and harvested at the will of sun and moon.

Everything in life about primitive Man seemed in some mysterious way to change with the shifting stars and moon and the sinking and rising sun. Is it any wonder then that the study of astronomy goes back to the earliest times of human history ?

The ancient Greeks, without telescopes or modern instruments, obtained a surprising knowledge of the heavens; but they owed a great debt to still earlier peoples, the Chaldeans and Egyptians who lived in the valleys of the Euphrates and the Nile. It is told of the early Greek astronomers that they used to go to Egypt, where the science

of the stars was jealously guarded by the priests, in order to learn the secret of determining the number of days in a year.

Without a considerable knowledge of the heavens, our remote ancestors could not devise the simplest calendar to foretell the seasons. And what was more important still, they could not navigate the seas. It is to the science of astronomy that we owe the first voyage of the Phoenicians, and to astronomy in later times we are indebted for the discovery of America and Australia.

More than a century before the Christian era the Greeks were familiar with the apparent uniform motion of the fixed stars and the variable motions of the planets, and with the idea that the earth was a sphere. They knew how to measure latitude and longitude, and how to foretell eclipses; they had determined the fact and effect of the precession of the equinoxes, a discovery that is the more remarkable when we realize that the so-called " precession " alters the time of the equinoxes (roughly, the beginning of spring and autumn) by only a few minutes each year. One of the greatest early observers was Ptolemy, the Greek astronomer and geographer, whose books were the standard sources of information for over 1400 years. His chief astronomical error was in believing that the earth was the centre of the heavens, and that the sun, planets and fixed stars revolved round it.

Quite a goodly number of people have had the invention of the telescope fathered on them. It has even been suggested that Democritus, the Greek thinker and traveller, who died 350 B.C., used some kind of instrument "that brought things nearer," because he gave it as his opinion that the Milky Way consisted of countless stars. The Laughing Philosopher, as he was called, was certainly in advance of the times, but it is not likely that so important a discovery would have died with him.

Roger Bacon is another name mentioned in this connexion. Writing in 1260 he mentions that "from an incredible distance we may read the smallest letters," adding that "a small army may appear a very great one, and, though very far off, a very near one. And thus also the sun, moon and stars may be made to descend hither in appearance, and to be visible over the heads of our enemies." This, like so many other statements made by Roger Bacon, seems rather of the nature of an astonishing prophecy than of an accomplished fact.

MADE BY GALILEO
These telescopes were made by Galileo, and preserved in the Arcetri observatory at Florence. Though small, they enabled him to discover the phases of the planet Venus.

Thomas Digges, who gained fame as mustermaster-general of the army which Queen Elizabeth sent to aid the Netherlanders in 1586, and also as the author of several treatises on astronomical problems, boldly states that his father had glasses which enabled him to see "what hath been done in private places at a distance of seven miles." However this may be, it was only a comparatively short time after the death of Digges that John Lippershey, of Middelburg, actually made a telescope, which he presented to Count Maurice of Nassau. This was in 1608, and in the same year another Dutchman, named Jacob Andrianzoon, also produced a similar apparatus.

News of the discovery spread quickly, and among those who heard of it was Galileo. Its importance was at once recognized by this professor of mathematics, who with infinite patience and skill set about constructing an instrument for himself. He made his first telescope with a piece of organ-pipe, placing a lens at each end. It magnified only three times, but later he made a telescope that magnified 30 times. With this he saw the mountains on the moon's surface, found that the Milky Way was a mass of very faint stars, and discovered the four large satellites of the planet Jupiter. He also noted the peculiar appearance of Saturn, which was later shown to be due to a great ring, or a series of rings, surrounding that p'anet.

His discovery that Venus shows phases like the Moon's converted him to Copernicus's view that the earth rotates on its axis and revolves round the sun, and his ardent support of this idea was the cause of difficulties with the Church. There is a story that, as he rose from his knees after having withdrawn his views before the Inquisition, he whispered defiantly, "Nevertheless it does move"—referring, of course, to the earth; but this story is a fiction invented at a later date.

The modern science of astronomy begins with Copernicus (1473–1543), who first saw that it is the sun, and not the earth, that is the centre of what we now call the solar system. Other observers confirmed this theory. The next great advances were due to improvements in the range of the telescope and, in addition, to the discovery of the law of gravitation by Sir Isaac Newton. The telescope immensely increased our powers of observation. But the progress of the science would be slow if observation were not coupled with a corresponding effort to discover and apply, by means of interpretation, the underlying laws of the heavens. Newton's discovery was, undoubtedly one of the greatest triumphs of interpretation.

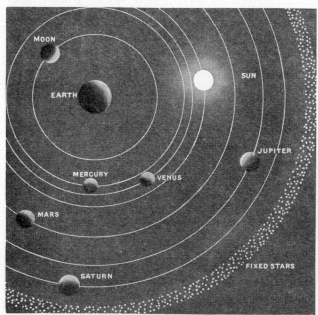

AN EARLY ASTRONOMER'S ERROR
For fourteen centuries it was believed that the earth was the centre of what we now call the solar system and that the sun and planets revolved round it. This theory is called the Ptolemaic theory after Claudius Ptolemaeus, who lived at Alexandria in the 2nd century A.D. The illustration shows a Ptolemaic conception of the universe.

Galileo first found the satellites of Jupiter, but he did not know why they revolved round that planet instead of flying off into space; Newton supplied the explanation. But a knowledge of laws does more than merely explain

MARVELS OF ASTRONOMY & SOME OF ITS USES

SATURN a planet having 9 moons

SUN Only one of millions of similar suns. Composed of hydrogen, oxygen, helium copper, iron, silver, lead, and other substances

FIXED STAR so far distant from the earth that, though it moves with terrific speed, it appears stationary

DOUBLE STARS revolve around each other and appear as one

NEBULAE stars in early stages of development. Composed of gases

METEOR (Shooting Star) a small heavenly body made white hot by its flight through the earth's atmosphere

EARTH a sphere

MOON a dead satellite of the earth

The measurement of time, without which modern business would be impossible

Galileo the father of telescopic astronomy

The discovering and charting of strange lands

Navigators could not steer a true course on the seas unless they knew the motions of the heavenly bodies

Knowing latitude and longitude enables us to find the exact location of sinking ships

The crossed rays of light below mark the mirror supports of the reflecting telescope through which this photograph was made.

Astronomy reveals the immensity of space. The arrows point to Pluto, ninth and farthest of planets. It is 4,000 million miles from Earth. The nearest fixed star is 6,400 times as far away.

It enables us to figure, centuries in advance, the exact moment of future eclipses and other heavenly phenomena

We see here how much Astronomy has to do with the affairs of men: the discovery and charting of new worlds, the measurement of time, navigation upon the world's wide waters, and the rescue of ships. In the centre is a picture of Galileo, seated by two telescopes; the larger of the two is about as big as the instrument with which he discovered four of the moons of Jupiter. The nebulae shown below Saturn (top left) are an island universe of millions of stars.

THE MILKY WAY AS IT MIGHT APPEAR FROM OUTER SPACE

STAR CLUSTER IN WHICH
OUR EARTH IS HIDDEN

A

SUN

A NEARER VIEW OF CLUSTER "A"

STARS HIDING OUR EARTH
Even the closer view of cluster A does not show us the position of the Earth ; all we can see is innumerable stars.

OUR WORLD IN STELLAR SPACE
We look up at night at the Milky Way, which is all that our eyes can see of the Universe. But this illustration shows the Milky Way as it might appear seen from outer space with the world occupying an insignificant place in a star cluster, a nearer view of which is given on the left below.

what has already been observed. It enables the astronomer to make new discoveries and to predict the changes in the heavens thousands of years in advance. As a result of astronomical discoveries our conception of the universe is vastly different from that of our ancestors. We live on our little earth, which is part of the solar system, but we realize now that beyond the solar system are immensities of space entirely above conception.

We take our solar system—the system revolving round our sun—and even here the facts are staggering beyond all understanding ; but the truth is that in the boundless universe the solar system is like a grain of sand upon the seashore. The sun is about 866,000 miles across, with a mass about 333,000 times that of the earth, and it is over 93 million miles away from us. Round it swing nine planets—

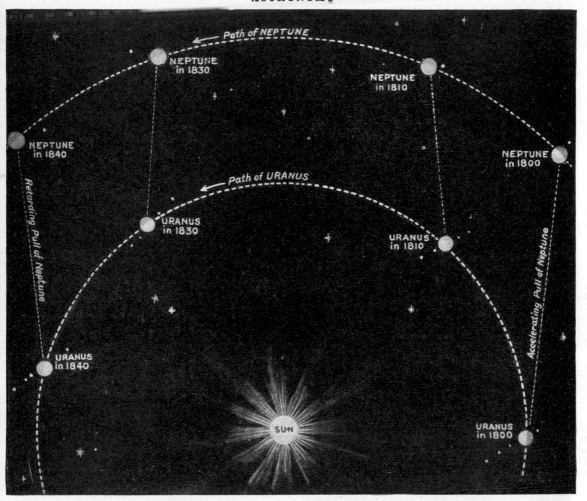

HOW THE PLANET NEPTUNE INTERFERED WITH URANUS

This diagram explains how Neptune could hurry Uranus forward in one part of its path through the sky and hold it back in another. In one part of the orbits of the two planets Neptune is pulling forward. The result is that between 1800 and 1810 Uranus moved along much faster than usual, while between 1830 and 1840 conditions were reversed. By 1840 Neptune was pulling almost straight back on Uranus, which was trying to go on its regular round. It was this swerving by Uranus that caused astronomers to believe that an unknown world was pulling it and so led to the amazing simultaneous prediction, by Adams and Leverrier, that a new planet would be found in a certain place in the sky.

the earth and the smaller planets, Mercury, Mars and Venus; and Jupiter, Saturn, Uranus, Neptune and Pluto, larger than the earth. The distances of these planets from the sun vary from 36 million miles for Mercury to 3,680 million miles for Pluto.

It was not so very long ago that Saturn was the farthest thing we knew anything about in space——Saturn, only 886 million miles from the sun. But then in 1781 Uranus was discovered, nearly 1,000 million miles beyond it; and in 1846 men turned their eyes on Neptune, 1,000 million miles beyond Uranus. In January 1930 came the discovery that another planet, now named Pluto, exists almost 1,000 million miles farther still. That is how the map of the solar system has widened since the telescope revealed the heavens to us; and beyond the bounds of the solar system the same thing has been happening. Outside this system lie millions upon millons of mighty suns, sweeping through space, some, perhaps, with attendant

planets; and the more our knowledge grows, the more the wonder of the universe grows too.

We look up at the stars which are whirling about at tremendous speeds, dazzling space with their light for thousands of millions of miles. Compared to their average speed of 72,000 miles an hour, our fastest aeroplanes travel at a snail's pace. One small star among them is a laggard, creeping through space at 43,000 miles an hour, and attending on its round is a tiny globe a million times smaller, lit up with the light of the laggard star. That laggard is the sun, and the little globe is the earth!

How vividly this makes us realize that the affairs of the whole earth itself are like the flickering of a candle in the vast immensity of all those boundless worlds. So great is distance in the heavens that we do not measure it in miles; we count it, instead, according to the distance light travels in a year. A ray of light will travel in one year just over 5,878,000,000,000 miles, and that is the distance we

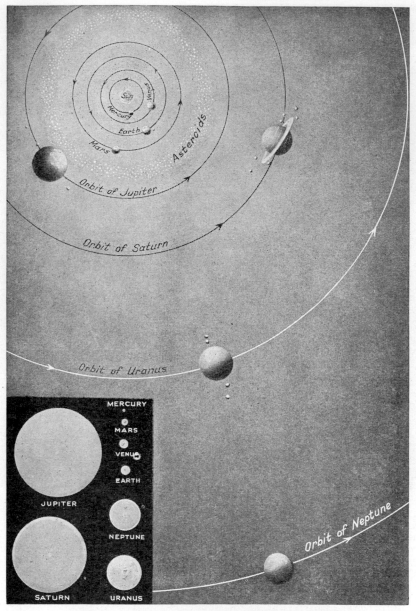

THE EARTH'S PLACE IN THE SOLAR SYSTEM

A contrast to Ptolemy's conception of the importance of the earth (p.276) is afforded by this diagram of the solar system as it really is. The orbits of the planets are given, showing their relative positions. Inset is a diagram showing the comparative size of the planets. Neither orbits nor sun are drawn to scale, for even with the sun no bigger than it is shown here the earth should be 20 inches, and Pluto (not shown) 22 yards, away.

star on one side of it takes 300 years to cross to the other side!

If we could travel out into space at the same speed as light (186,273 miles a second), we should reach Pluto, the farthest planet, in about six hours. But to reach the nearest fixed star, Alpha Centauri, would require more than four years. From some of the most remote, light rays may now be reaching us that started 100,000 years ago. This gives some idea of the enormous distances which separate our solar system from the stars we see in the heavens. (*See* Constellations; Planets; Sun and Solar System; Stars).

How many stars are there in the Milky Way? The most recent calculations of astronomers estimate the total number to be as high as 200,000 millions—about 100 times as many stars in the heavens as there are people on earth. Many of the stars that look like one to the unaided eye or through a small telescope are really double or binary stars; that is, they consist of twin bodies revolving around a common centre of gravity.

Of special importance to students interested in the evolution of the stars and the origin of the solar system are numerous faint objects, each of which has the appearance through the telescope of a small diffuse cloud or patch of light. Such a body is called a nebula, from the Latin word meaning a "small cloud." Nebulae fall into two distinct classes. The galactic nebulae (*e.g.* the Great Nebula in Orion) are clouds of gas that are caused to shine by the stars embedded in them. As members of our galactic system they are relatively close objects. The extragalactic nebulae (*e.g.* the Andromeda nebula) are huge assemblies of stars which are held together, often in spiral form, by mutual gravitational attraction. These are incomparably farther off than the galactic nebulae, and form "island universes." (*See* Nebulae).

mean every time we speak of a "light-year." Well, we now believe that if there is any boundary to the universe, it must be *hundreds of millions* of light-years away. The telescope has reached out to stars beyond the Milky Way, even to outlying spiral nebulae, some of them so far distant that the light that now reaches our eyes came into being 250 million years ago.

Of one great cluster of stars alone, the cluster in Hercules, we can photograph the light today which left the stars 36,000 years ago, when most of Europe was under ice; and a ray of light from a

Another class of heavenly bodies comprises what are known as comets (from the Greek word meaning "hair," for the reason that they resemble a star

COLOURFUL ASPECT OF THE 'RED PLANET'

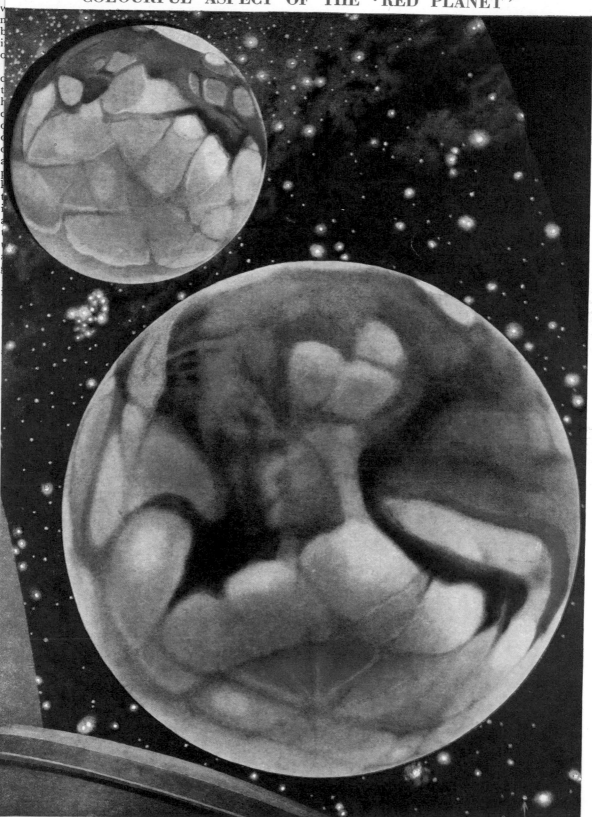

ese two views of Mars, prepared by S. W. Clatsworthy, show variety of coloration on the planet at different periods of year. The smaller disk shows (at the top) part of the ge polar snow-cap, the green vegetation and the bluish waters of the planet in spring, whereas in the larger we see the brown and purplish vegetation of autumn and the dark waters which will re-form the polar snow-cap of winter. Certain straight, dark lines have been called 'canals' by some astronomers.

this vast area with its hundreds of millions of suns has all the romance and excitement of an expedition to the North Pole, or to the source of the Amazon. (*See also* Observatory ; Telescope, and articles on the great astronomers, Galileo, Kepler, etc.).

'As You Like It.'

According to this delightful comedy of Shakespeare, there lived in a greenwood forest a banished Duke together with many loyal courtiers who had followed him into exile. Thither a little later came this banished Duke's lovely daughter Rosalind, also banished, and disguised as a page. Her lover, Orlando, fleeing from a cruel brother, came likewise to the happy Forest of Arden, where there was " no enemy but winter and rough weather."

Unrecognized in her disguise by either her father or her lover, Rosalind played many a merry caper with both before revealing who she was. Her wit, the clownish humour of the faithful fool Touchstone, the acid wisdom of the melancholy courtier Jaques, and the Duke's calm philosophy in misfortune, make " As You Like It " still a favourite play of the stage, and lines from it are frequently quoted, *e.g.*, the Duke's description of the charm of life " under the greenwood tree ":

> And this our life, exempt from public haunt,
> Finds tongues in trees, books in the running brooks,
> Sermons in stones, and good in everything.

Atalanta.

One of the loveliest maidens of all the lands of Greece, and one of the fleetest-

HOW TO FIND YOUR WAY BY THE STARS

High or low in the sky of the northern hemisphere on clear nights is always to be seen a certain group of bright stars. There are seven stars in this group, and they form a big 'plough.' Four of the stars make the ploughshare (blade). The other three stars, at the top, are the handle. Fix your eyes on the two stars that form the outer line of the blade and imagine a straight line drawn from the lower to the upper star and extend the line upwards in the same direction until it runs into another bright star. That is the north or Pole star, and when you face towards it you will be looking almost due north. For hundreds of years sailors guided vessels by the pole star, before the compass or the movements of the heavenly bodies were understood.

footed, according to Greek myths, was a king's daughter named Atalanta. When this princess was born, her father—disappointed to see a daughter instead of the longed-for son—left her on a mountain to the mercy of wild beasts and the elements. She was nursed by a she-bear, and was saved by some hunters who carried her to their home.

When at last Atalanta was restored to her father's court, the king, having no other heir, entreated her to marry. Many youths came seeking to win her hand. But Atalanta declared that she would wed only the youth who should outrun her in a foot race, and further that all who entered the race and were unsuccessful must forfeit their lives.

At last there came a youth who had obtained the protection of the goddess Aphrodite (Venus), and carried concealed beneath his garment her gift of three golden apples. When the race began, Atalanta, as usual, easily passed her rival ; but as she sped onward, an apple of gold rolled past her feet. For a moment she hesitated, then turned aside to pick up the precious fruit. Her adversary thus gained the lead, but soon Atalanta again passed him. A second apple tempted her from her course, but she recovered her lead, and had all but won the race when the youth tossed

J. W. Debenham

'AS YOU LIKE IT' IN A SYLVAN SETTING

Shakespeare's woodland comedy, 'As You Like it,' finds an appropriate setting in the Open-Air Theatre in Regent's Park, London. This scene is from Act 1, and shows the wrestling match between Charles, the Duke's wrestler, and Orlando, the hero of the play. On the left, sitting on the white seat, are Rosalind, whom Orlando loves, and Celia, her cousin.

ATALANTA LOSING HER RACE WITH MILANION

Atalanta, princess of Arcadia, offered to marry the first man who could outrun her, but this no man could do. Aphrodite, in return for a suitable sacrifice, gave a youth named Milanion three golden apples and told him to throw them in the path of Atalanta during the race. Atalanta stopped to pick them up one by one, and so lost. True to her promise, she married Milanion. The picture is Sir Edward J. Poynter's (1836–1919) famous 'Atalanta's Race.'

the third apple in her path. As she paused to pick it up, he passed her and reached the goal.

True to her promise, Atalanta married the youth—his name is given as Milanion—who had outrun her. Unhappily, the bride and bridegroom unknowingly profaned a sanctuary, and they were both turned into lions.

Athena. (Pron. *a-thē-na*). Next to Zeus himself, his daughter Athena was the wisest of all the Greek deities. She was especially the "goddess of wisdom," and old myths told the strange story of her birth—how she had sprung fully armed from the head of Zeus and startled heaven and earth with her battle-cry.

Athena was the patroness of all the heroes who fought against evil men and monsters. Thus she was the constant companion of Hercules in his toilsome adventures; she helped the Argonauts in their quest of the Golden Fleece; she was the guide of Odysseus (Ulysses) in his many wanderings. On her shield was the head of the snaky-haired Gorgon, Medusa, slain by the hero Perseus through her aid, which had the power of turning to stone those who gazed upon it. In the long war about the walls of mighty Troy, she was ever the friend and counsellor of the Greek chieftains.

But Athena loved peace more than war, for she was the goddess of spinning and weaving, agriculture, and all the useful arts. The invention of the plough and the loom was ascribed to her. She was the protector of towns, and her city of Athens was especially sacred to her. How this city came to bear her name is explained by one of the old legends. Zeus had decreed that the city should be awarded to that one of the gods who should create the most useful gift for its inhabitants. Poseidon created the horse, but Athena, with superior wisdom, created the olive tree, the sign of peace and source of prosperity, and the prize was given to her.

Athena was very proud of her skill as a weaver, and this once led her to an act of great injustice. A girl named Arachne had rashly boasted that she could weave as well as the goddess Athena herself. Athena heard this boast and challenged Arachne to prove her word.

The two stood at looms side by side and wove cloth covered with wonderful pictures, and

ATHENA MOURNS THE NOBLE DEAD

This bas-relief of Athena in the Acropolis Museum, Athens, shows the goddess, weighed down by sorrow, leaning on her spear. It symbolizes the grief of Athens for her slain.

when the goddess discovered that she could find no fault with Arachne's work, she became terribly angry. She struck Arachne and tore the cloth on her loom.

Arachne was so frightened that she tried to hang herself. Athena then became sorry for her and saved her life by changing the rope into a cobweb and the girl into a spider. So Arachne (the Greek word for spider) lives to this day, and still weaves wonderful webs upon the grasses and bushes by the roadside.

Athena was a virgin goddess—strong, pure, just, and wise. She is often called "Pallas Athena" or simply "Pallas." To her as the maiden (*parthenos*) goddess was dedicated the

Parthenon, the beautiful temple on the Acropolis of Athens, the most perfect building the world has ever seen (*see* Acropolis). Every year at the festival of the *Panathenaea*, a robe, or *peplos*, woven by Greek maidens, was carried in procession through the streets of the city and presented to the image of the goddess. The huge gold and ivory statue of Athena in this temple, wrought by Pheidias, greatest of Greek sculptors, represented her as a grave, majestic woman, helmet on head, in her right hand a winged figure of Nike, goddess of victory, in her left a spear.

The Roman goddess Minerva, who occupied a similar place in the Roman mythology, came to be identified with the Greek Athena.

ANCIENT CITY *of the* VIOLET CROWN

When we think of Athens, it is usually not the modern city but that of Pericles and Plato that we have in mind. It is interesting to compare the flourishing commercial city of today with the ancient centre of classical culture.

Athens, GREECE. From the deck of a ship entering the harbour of Piraeus, the port of Athens, the traveller sees in the distance—

Temple of Olympian Zeus

Radiant, violet-crowned, by minstrels sung, Bulwark of Hellas, Athens illustrious.

Rising afar and almost encircling the Attic plain, Mt. Parnes on the north, Mt. Pentelicus on the north-east, and Mt. Hymettus on the east, wrapped in purple mist, still give to the "queen of cities" her violet crown, and after 2,500 years her glory is not faded. Landing at Piraeus, we take a train for Athens, five miles away. The railway follows almost the same course as the famous "long walls" built by Themistocles in the 5th century B.C. to connect Athens with Piraeus and thus ensure to the sea-trading Athenians access to the sea even though the city was besieged.

Modern Athens, lying to the north-east of the ancient city, is "a city of whiteness and brightness." The buildings are nearly all of marble or limestone, or else of stucco made of powdered marble; and, seen against the brilliant blue of the clear sky, the effect is dazzling. The streets are lined with graceful pepper-trees, bright green in summer, blazing with red berries in the autumn, and everywhere are squares and gardens filled with fragrant orange-trees, date-palms, and rose-hued oleanders. Rising above the modern city and still dominating it as in ancient days is the hill of the Acropolis, "its noble temples seeming fairly to hang in the air like a vision disclosed of Paradise."

No one, it is said, can live in the presence of noble and beautiful things without being influ-

enced by them. Perhaps this accounts for the spirit of culture that still pervades Athenian life. The Athenians of today, like those of 20 centuries ago, love outdoor life. The restaurants which do not have adjoining gardens set their tables on the pavement. The most popular theatres are those roofed only by the sky. A stadium in which games and sports are held as in the ancient days was erected in 1895 for the first of the modern Olympic Games, occupying the site of the old stadium of Athens. Crowds gather in the streets to celebrate the great festivals—New Year's Eve, the Carnival before Lent, and Easter; and at all times the priests of the Greek Orthodox Church are familiar figures in their long black robes and tall hats.

The royal palace in Constitution Square is a rather plain building of limestone and marble set in a luxuriant garden. Few of the more modern buildings in the city are of any real architectural note. The newer quarters are mostly at the base of Mt. Lycabettus, to the north-east.

From this modern city we easily step back into the world of the past. The Arch of Hadrian and the great ruined temple of Olympian Zeus are the chief remains from the period of Roman rule. Of the 104 elaborately carved Corinthian columns of the temple, each 56 feet in height and more than five feet in diameter, only 15 remain erect. At their base little tables are set where fashionable men and women gather to gossip and enjoy their coffee and *loukoumi*, or Turkish delight.

From the great period of Athens's independence we have the Theseum, so called because it was once believed to be the Temple of Theseus—the best preserved of all Greek temples. It has suffered somewhat from earthquakes, and its marble facing was long ago burned to make lime, but its 34 Doric columns still support the roof and indicate its majestic proportions (*see* illus. in page 286).

Passing by the ruins of the Theatre of Dionysus, where the ancient Athenians listened to the masterpieces of Aeschylus, Sophocles and Euripides, we ascend to the Acropolis. On this rocky plateau, which rises 200 feet above the level of the city,

ATHENS AND THE RUINS OF HER ANCIENT GLORY

Crowding up to the base of Mount Lycabettus lie the newer sections of Athens. This district has grown rapidly since 1922, when Greek refugees came pouring in from Asia Minor. We are looking at Lycabettus from the summit of the immortal hill of the Acropolis. The first three pictures below show some of the famous structures of the Acropolis itself.

On the right is the exquisite Ionic Temple of Athena Nike. Its parapet once was carved with Winged Victories.

Doric majesty in the Parthenon, below, reminds us that culture culminated in Athens, Athens in the Acropolis, the Acropolis in the Parthenon.

Towering Corinthian pillars 55 feet high and over six feet thick in the Temple of Zeus, below, built by the Roman Emperor Hadrian about A.D. 129, show how the grandiose taste of Rome affected the pure Greek style.

A public clock was the Tower of the Winds, below, which stands in the old Agora or Market-place. Its eight sides face the points of the compass and bear reliefs symbolic of the winds. Before the door once stood a sun-dial. A water-clock within told time in cloudy weather, and a bronze Triton rode the roof as weathervane. It was an early structure of the Graeco-Roman period.

The stately Porch of the Maidens, above, which is a part of the Erechtheum, is the supreme example of the successful use of the human figure as a supporting column.

A Greek soldier of today stands before an ancient fluted column

ARCHITECTURAL GEM OF ATHENS

The Theseum, which stands on the west of the old Athenian market-place, is regarded as the most perfect relic of ancient Athens. Though it is commonly called the Temple of Theseus, archaeologists declare that it is actually the sanctuary of Hephaestus (Vulcan). It owes its good state of preservation to the fact that in the Middle Ages it was a Christian church.

quered her, in spite of the efforts of Demosthenes, but this conquest itself became the means of spreading Athenian art and literature to the remote corners of Egypt and Asia through the world-empire of Philip's son Alexander. In Roman times Athens was still the great intellectual centre. Cicero and other famous men went there to study.

In the Middle Ages the Goths and other barbarians harried Athens as they did Rome. From 1204 to 1458, as a result of the Fourth Crusade, the city was ruled by feudal lords from western Europe. Then the Turks conquered Athens. During a Venetian campaign against Turkey in the 17th century, the Parthenon was used as a powder magazine by the Turks and suffered damage from bombardment.

The Greek war of independence (1821–29) made Greece free once more and established Athens as

we come into the midst of the magnificent structures which have been the inspiration of all the world. The Parthenon as it exists today, shattered, defaced, almost entirely roofless, robbed of its statues and wonderful friezes, is still awe-inspiring in its beauty. Time has faded the brilliant painting and gilding with which the ancients decorated the pure white marble of their noblest temples, but it has given to the marble a wonderful colour of amber-gold. Someone has remarked that the stone seems not to have been taken from the earth, but to have been quarried from the golden light of the Athenian sunsets. (*See* Acropolis).

From the Acropolis we look out upon several lesser hills. To the west is the Pnyx, where the popular assemblies were held; and north of that we see the Areopagus—the Hill of Ares (or Mars)—which was the seat of the council of nobles called the venerable court of the Areopagus. Here the Apostle Paul addressed his famous words to the Athenians, beginning: "Ye men of Athens, I perceive that in all things ye are too superstitious."

When we recall that only a little more than a century ago Athens, except for the ruined monuments of her ancient greatness, was but a squalid Turkish village, the growth of the modern city may be regarded as remarkable.

The beginnings of Athens are lost in myth and legend. It is said to have been founded by Theseus and named in honour of the goddess Athena. When the Persians at the beginning of the 5th century B.C. sought to conquer Greece, Athens played a leading part in resisting the invader. Under the great statesman Pericles Athens reached its peak of power and splendour, and those fine works of architecture and sculpture were produced which made this the Golden Age of Greece.

But Athens had built up its greatness largely at the expense of its allies in the Delian Confederacy, and many of them, dissatisfied with this policy, turned to its rival, Sparta. The long-drawn-out war which followed, known as the Peloponnesian War, put an end to Athens's imperial greatness.

As a centre of culture Athens was important for centuries more. Philip of Macedon con-

YOUNG ATHENS ON PARADE

These youths of Athens, in a procession on a State holiday, are wearing the national costume of the men of Greece, including a cap with tassel, white linen skirt or fustanella, embroidered jacket, long stockings and tufted shoes.

the capital. The city fell into the hands of the Germans and Italians in 1941 during the Second World War, but was liberated in October 1944. Later, insurrectionists occupied a part of Athens and their artillery caused more damage than had that of the enemy during the war. Fighting ceased in January 1945 when an agreement was arrived at between the Government and the left-wing rebel leaders.

In addition to a flourishing university, there are in Athens foreign schools of classical archaeology for advanced students from France, Great Britain and the United States. Athens is the financial and governing centre of Greece, but its industries, chief of which are cotton, silk and leather manufactures, are located in the flourishing port of Piraeus. The port, which was very badly damaged during the Second World War, is five miles from the capital, with which it is connected by railway. Other lines from Athens extend to the

ATHENIAN ATHLETES' ANCIENT STADIUM
A Roman governor built a stadium in the amphitheatre beside the Ilissus stream at Athens in the second century A.D. Excavated in the 19th century, this was restored and used for the first modern Olympic Games, which were held in 1896. Sports meetings are still held on this ancient site.

Peloponnese, south-east to Laurium, and north to Salonika and central Europe. The population of Athens and Piraeus together is estimated to be over 1,000,000 ; that of the city alone is 400,000.

ACHIEVING FITNESS *through* ATHLETICS

The word athletics covers a variety of physical activities. Those we glimpse here—running and jumping, throwing the discus and the javelin, pole-vaulting and putting the weight—are amongst the most important.

Athletics. For a long period the keen desire of every normal boy to excel in athletic sports—to run faster, jump higher, or play games with more skill and vigour than his companions—was only half tolerated, and time spent in athletic pursuits was often regarded as time lost. But the energetic spirit of youth finally conquered the old-fashioned prejudices, and men came to realize that athletics form just as essential a part of education as books.

We have rediscovered a truth which was clearly recognized by the ancient Greeks, among whom the cultivation of athletics went hand in hand with that of science and art, and their great achievements may be credited to the emphasis they placed on training all the faculties, physical as well as mental.

There is no need, nowadays, to point out the advantage in every occupation or profession which the strong, vigorous, clean-cut man, the athletic man, possesses. A moderate amount of athletic recreation taken all the year round is far more beneficial than short and strenuous indulgence in a particular sport. In recent years girls and women have come to take an increasing interest in athletics. Almost all men's games are played by them, and statistics gathered in schools and girls' colleges show improved physical conditions as the result, though here especially the dangers of over-exertion must be guarded against.

The term athletics usually excludes gymnastic exercises, physical training and such organized sports as football, cricket, hockey, lawn-tennis, netball and so on. The contests commonly grouped as track and field events, which include walking, running, jumping, hurdling, putting the weight, and throwing the hammer, the javelin and the discus, are those which are nowadays generally regarded as coming within the scope of athletics. In modern times athletics, using the word in the narrow sense, have become one of the most scientific of all forms of sport, especially in the sprint races, in which a fifth of a second may make the difference between winning or losing a championship. Athletes aiming at national or international distinction, therefore, are at pains to have slow-motion films taken of themselves in action, so that every movement may be studied, compared with that of their rivals, and used to improve their own style.

A wasteful lift of the leg, too much arm-swing— these are the points for which to watch in order to gain that fraction of a second. But in spite of the way in which athletics are approached, there is still room for a diversity of styles and for further improvement. This is well shown by the high jump. Formerly, the athlete simply leapt, with all his force, as high as he could over the bar, often having a long run to give himself impetus. His feet cleared the bar, his body was crouched above them, his head perhaps going three feet higher than his feet.

But then someone realized that here was wasted effort. Why lift your head three feet higher than your feet, when you might be using that energy to get your whole body a little higher? So a new system, or rather, a series of styles, was evolved, in which the jumper now "rolls" over the bar, his whole body parallel with it, and not even his head clearing it by more than very little. And the world's high jump record goes on rising. In just the same way, study of every movement has been applied to every event. The long jumper gives an extra kick in mid-air, the hurdler must keep to an exact number of strides through all but the end of his race, the discus thrower and the javelin thrower go through the most precise movements like pieces of machinery: and in every event, it is no longer the strongest man, but the man who can combine exactness of style with his strength who wins. That is why the greatest athletes, the men who win Olympic championships, keep in training every day of their lives.

Running, which makes up half of modern athletics, is dealt with under its own heading. An important event which combines speed on the flat with exactness and jumping ability is hurdling. The hurdler, whether he runs the 120 yard "high hurdles," or the 440 "low" race, must above all maintain an even rhythm. Between each flight of hurdles he takes an exact number of steps, and his take-off and his alighting are as regular as clockwork. As little energy as possible is wasted in the actual clearing of a hurdle, for the run-in after the last obstacle is taken at sprinting speed, and on it as often as not depends the race. Time and again you may see a whole batch of hurdlers clearing every obstacle as one man, one of the most inspiring of all sights in Athletics; yet one man may shoot away at the finish and win the race by several yards.

The javelin and discus-throwing, which have come down to us from ancient Greece, have become popular in Britain only during the present century. Each requires its own training, its own rigorous rhythm if success is to be attained. This, too, applies to jumping. Whether you go in for the high jump or the long jump, you must pay almost as much attention to your run and take-off as to the actual jump. Even for the long jump the trained expert takes an exact number of strides for his run, starting slowly, increasing his speed until he finishes as fast as a sprinter. With the high jump you need accuracy and a smooth, powerful take-off rather than tremendous speed. And for the pole-vault, most difficult of all jumping events, the same applies, though for that great height—over 12 feet if you are to be first-class—you need more speed.

Two events in which brawn is bound to count more than anything are the weight-put, and throwing the hammer, and until you have left school you will probably be well advised not to take the former too seriously—at least with a full-size "weight"—and the latter will probably be beyond you. To watch the champions in action at these events is to witness trained strength at its most impressive.

Amateur athletes may not take payment for their services, and in only comparatively few sports—chief among them cricket and golf—do paid and unpaid athletes compete with and against each other. In Britain the controlling body of athletics is the Amateur Athletic Association, who use the White City stadium at Shepherds Bush, London, as their headquarters for meetings.

Who the first athletes were no one knows quite knows. There were records of the victors of the Olympic Games from 776 B.C., but the contests were held regularly long before that date. It is believed that the Greeks copied some of the forms of exercise common amongst the Egyptians. One of the earliest sports meetings to be organized in the British Isles was the Tailtin Games in Ireland, which are said to be between 2,000 and 3,000 years old. The origin of the Highland Games is also lost in the past, but they are undoubtedly very old. Allied to them are the Westmorland and Cumberland sports.

In London during the time of Henry II (1133–89), young citizens amused themselves by jumping, wrestling and casting the stone. Later, sports became popular amongst the nobility, and Henry VIII (1491–1547) was famed for throwing the hammer, or casting the bar as it was then called. During the reign of Elizabeth (1558–1603) it was mostly the humbler people who indulged in these sports.

Running became popular in the time of the Stuarts, when the noblemen kept running footmen and matched them against one another. Pepys, the famous diarist, describes a match between one of these footmen and a professional runner in London's Hyde Park on August 10, 1660. One of the first athletic meetings was that organized by a Major Mason in 1807, in connexion with an athletic society at Necton, Norfolk. The various events included wrestling, jumping in sacks, and foot races. Exeter College, Oxford, instituted annual athletic meetings at that University, the first being held in 1850. Cambridge University did not follow suit until 1857. Athletics have now become so popular that nearly every public school, university and institution has its annual meeting.

ATHLETIC ACTION

Here is a contestant in the Long Jump at the Amateur Athletic Championships, which are held annually at the White City Stadium, London. Notice how he still appears to be running while in the air and the perfect balance of his body.

CHAMPION ATHLETES DISPLAY THEIR PROWESS

Athletes are never satisfied with their own style and are always striving after improvement. Here is demonstrated the right way to perform several athletic activities. Top left, about to throw the discus. The weight of the discus, which is of wood with a leaden centre, is 4½ lb., and experts hurl it over 150 feet. Top right, a javelin thrower. At the centre, left, a weight-putter is about to spring forward and cast the weight. At the centre, right, a Negro high-jumper is rolling over the bar close on six feet high. At lower left, runners are taking 3½-foot hurdles in their stride. Lower right, a pole-vaulter is about to heave himself over the bar; he leaves the pole behind him and lands on loose sand. As the more expert of these athletes clear 12 feet or more, the fall is considerable.

Atlantic Ocean. Four hundred years ago the Atlantic Ocean seemed a boundless expanse of water, as terrifying as it was vast, but today it furnishes us with a great highway of traffic between the Old World and the New, while wireless telegraphy and the submarine cable give almost instant communication from one side to the other. And aircraft have mastered the vast barrier.

Of the three great oceans of the world, the Atlantic is first in commercial importance and second in size. It considerably exceeds the Indian Ocean in area, but it is only about half as large as the Pacific.

If by some means the water could be drawn off from the Atlantic basin, we should see a broad undulating plain, broken here and there by volcanic peaks, mountain ranges, and plateaux. On the average the ocean is between two and three miles deep, but near Porto Rico, in the West Indies, a sounding of 27,962 feet has been made.

A striking feature of the Atlantic floor is an S-shaped ridge running from north to south throughout very nearly its entire length. The ocean depth above this ridge averages from 9,000 to 10,000 feet but on each side the floor of the Atlantic sinks into valleys 15,000 to 17,000 feet below the surface. The highest peaks of this submarine mountain range project above the water, forming the Azores islands as well as St. Paul, Ascension, and Tristan da Cunha.

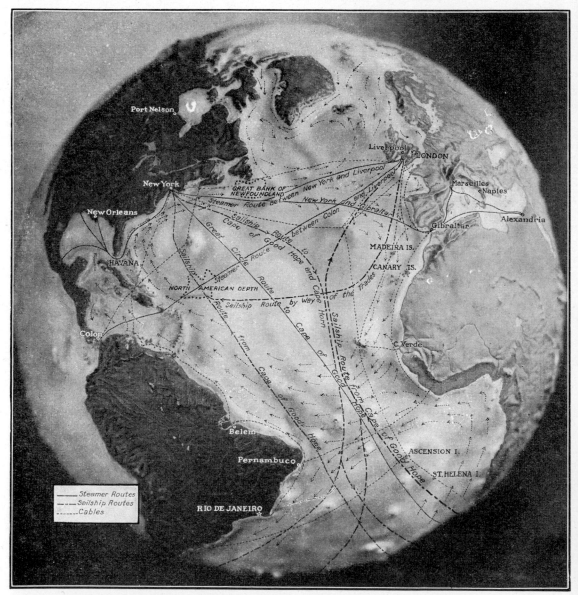

ATLANTIC OCEAN CABLES AND SHIPPING ROUTES

Every day is a busy day on the great Atlantic. Can you doubt it, looking at that web of traffic lanes and cables? Vividly the importance of these most-travelled of ocean waterways is brought home to us by the lines showing the routes of steamships and sailing vessels, and the cables. Arrows indicate the direction of the ocean currents. The spot marked 'North American Depth' contains the deepest known place in the Atlantic, over five miles deep.

In the history of submarine cables, the Telegraph Plateau, lying between Newfoundland and Ireland, will always occupy an important place, for without this comparatively shallow bottom the laying of the first ocean cables would have been almost impossible. Twenty-one cables now cross the Atlantic. In the intermediate depths—that is, from 500 to 1,500 feet—the Atlantic Ocean floor consists of a slimy ooze made up chiefly of the shells of millions of creatures which for ages have lived and died in those waters. At greater depths the bottom is composed of a red clay showing the presence of meteoric iron.

Food fishes are abundant in all parts of the Atlantic, while near the surface live many varieties of sea mammals, of which the whale and the seal are conspicuous examples.

The Atlantic has currents, both warm and cold, chiefly caused by the trade winds. Along the Equator from Africa to South America the waters move westward. In the neighbourhood of Brazil they divide, one current proceeding into the Gulf of Mexico and thence northward forming the Gulf Stream, while the other turns to the south and circles back towards the African coast. The famous Gulf Stream, carrying the warm waters of the tropics, exercises a moderating influence in countries as far distant as the Scandinavian peninsula, which otherwise might be quite uninhabitable. The Labrador current is a cold stream from the Arctic regions which carries into the Atlantic the icebergs which menace ocean travel.

There are no uniformly accepted limits for the Atlantic Ocean, but if we take the Arctic and Antarctic circles as the north and south boundaries, the length is between 8,500 and 9,000 miles, and from east to west it varies between 1,600 and 4,500 miles. The total surface area is between 30 million and 34 million square miles, or more than twice the area of North and South America. It is estimated that the yearly discharge of rivers into the Atlantic is 3,400 cubic miles of water, about one half of the river discharge of the world.

A fastest crossing of the Atlantic by a liner was recorded by the Queen Mary in 1938, when she covered the 2,938 miles from Ambrose Light, off the coast of the United States, to Bishop Rock, off the Scilly Islands, in 3 days 20 hours 42 minutes. A fastest air crossing was achieved in 1945 by a R.A.F. Mosquito aeroplane piloted by Wing-Commander J. R. H. Merifield. He flew from Newquay, Cornwal, to Newfoundland in 6 hours 58 minutes (2,300 miles at 330 miles per hour), and made the return journey, with a following wind, in 5 hours 10 minutes, a speed of 445 miles per hour.

THE BATTLE OF THE ATLANTIC (1939-1945)

For sixty-eight months—until May 1945—the great fight lasted on and below and above Atlantic waters. It will always be remembered, in the words of Mr. Churchill, as 'one of the most momentous in all the annals of war.'

Barely 12 hours after the outbreak of the Second World War on September 3, 1939, an unarmed British liner, the Athenia, on its way to America, was torpedoed without warning 250 miles west of Ireland. That act by the German navy marked the beginning of the Battle of the Atlantic—which, had it gone against us, would have meant starvation and defeat for the people of Britain.

The Atlantic was, and is, the main highway along which must be carried the food we cannot produce for ourselves. Raw materials, too, essential to our successful waging of the war, and guns and tanks and aircraft had to come that way. It was Germany's aim to cut us off from all outside contacts, and in 1940 the German Admiral Doenitz boasted, " I will show that the U-boat alone can win this war . . ." On May 4, 1945, the same boasting admiral ordered his U-boats to return home, and four days later Germany surrendered.

At first, long before the shadow of defeat fell upon them, the German submarines, or U-boats, did their work singly; in the second year of the war they began hunting in groups, known as " wolfpacks," often in conjunction with aircraft. Heavily armed German liners and battleships raided far and wide. Regardless of international law the enemy laid minefields in the waters without warning. Their dive-bombers and long-range aircraft haunted our shipping lanes. In great haste we had to arm our merchant vessels to defend themselves, and put into operation a convoy system whereby many merchant ships sailed together under the command of a Naval officer, with an escort of warships and R.A.F. aircraft.

In May 1940 the British Merchant Navy was joined by the merchant navies of Norway, Denmark, the Netherlands and Belgium. But we lost the co-operation of the French navy after the surrender of France to Germany in the following month. By then, U-boats were able to operate from ports along the European coastline from North Cape in Norway to Bayonne on the Bay of Biscay. And with Italy's entry into the war on June 10, 1940, units of the Royal Navy had to be transferred from the Atlantic to the Mediterranean. The Germans then made the most of their opportunities and in the seven months from June to December 1940 they sank over 2,500,000 tons of Allied and neutral shipping.

By October 31, 1940, the German Air Force had been beaten off over Britain. But this grim struggle by sea, " a war of groping and drowning, of ambuscade and stratagem, of science and seamanship," continued unabated, and on April 27, 1941, Mr. Churchill warned us that " In order to survive we have got to win on salt water just as decisively as we had to win the Battle of Britain in the air."

In that same month, before the United States actually entered the war, ships of the U.S. Navy began to patrol the Atlantic between the North American Continent and Iceland, one of the reasons being that Germany had already committed an act of aggression against the United States in Greenland (which country the U.S. had agreed to protect) by setting up weather-broadcasting stations to assist them in timing their raids over Britain.

British aircraft by now had become increasingly active. R.A.F. long-range aircraft (American Liberators) were patrolling farther out over the Atlantic and

U-boat bases in the Bay of Biscay were mined from the air. But with the entry of the United States into the war on December 8, 1941, the Germans torpedoed many unwary targets off the east coast of North America; and early in 1942, in four weeks, 25 Allied ships were lost in the Caribbean Sea, some of them tankers with valuable cargoes of oil. To meet the danger in the Western Atlantic area the convoy system was also operated there, and the U.S. Navy and Coast Guard Service along the Atlantic seaboard was reinforced by British vessels and men.

Meanwhile, R.A.F. Coastal Command was becoming still more active in getting rid of U-boats. Though by now the Americans were escorting convoys from their side, and the R.A.F. were operating from Iceland and Northern Ireland, aircraft had not sufficiently long range to protect convoys in the mid-

Atlantic where U-boats could lie in wait for ships without fear of detection from the air. This gap, some 600 miles south-east of Greenland, was about 800 miles wide, and our shore-based aircraft were not able to cover it because they could not carry sufficient petrol.

Then, towards the end of 1942, at a time when new U-boats at the rate of 14 a month were going into service, we began sending escort aircraft carriers along with the convoys. These escort carriers were ordinary merchant vessels which had been adapted for that purpose—fitted with a flight deck clear of obstruction, and able to carry up to 30 aircraft— and by July 1943 the mid-Atlantic gap was closed.

By arrangement with the neutral Portuguese Government we were able in October 1943 to use air and naval bases in the Azores (nine scattered islands midway between Europe and North America), and Allied convoys bound for the Straits of Gibraltar sailed farther to the west than formerly, to come within protective range of our aircraft "working" from those bases. The Allied navies and air forces had now gained the upper hand. When in the summer of 1944 the German armies were swept out of France, U-boats were no longer able to use French ports, but were forced to operate from such distant bases as Bergen and Trondhjem, in Norway, whence they continued to waylay Allied convoys on their way from the United States and Britain to North Russia.

German submarines sunk by Allied forces from first to last numbered nearly 800. In British-controlled convoys 75,000 merchant ships were escorted across the Atlantic, and vessels lost in convoy amounted to 574. Altogether 2,775 British, Allied and neutral merchant ships (representing about $14\frac{1}{2}$ million tons) were sunk by U-boats during those 68 months. Our own Merchant Navy had 23,000 casualties caused by U-boats, and 4,000 men (mostly British or Commonwealth or Allied subjects) who manned the guns fitted to merchant ships were killed or wounded. Royal Navy vessels es-

British Official

ATLANTIC BASE OF GERMAN SUBMARINES
After the surrender of France to German forces in June 1940, Brest, the port on the Atlantic coast of Brittany, became a base for submarines that preyed upon Allied shipping in the Atlantic. Pens of reinforced concrete were built to protect the U-boats when in harbour, but bombs dropped by the R.A.F. tore huge holes in the shelters as shown above.

Keystone

DEPTH CHARGE DESTROYS AN ENEMY SUBMARINE

As a depth charge hurled from the stern of the British warship in the foreground explodes, a huge geyser of water is thrown up. From wreckage that came to the surface it was proved that an enemy submarine had been destroyed by the concussion. German reports disclosed that the vessel had been an Italian submarine. The Battle of the Atlantic was waged chiefly by small Allied vessels (such as destroyers and corvettes) and aeroplanes against the German U-boats.

corting convoys made over 13,000 separate voyages, and lost 172 warships to the U-boats—in the hunting of which our own submarines joined, of course.

Our aircraft flew more than 100 million miles in the course of the battle. Factories all over Germany and in countries she had overrun made U-boat parts for assembly in coastal building yards; the R.A.F. sought them out and rained down immensely heavy bombs on the enormously strong shelters in which U-boats were completing, wrecking many in their lairs.

Behind the scenes of this dread conflict the scientists were busy in many and varied ways. Our Asdic method of tracking submarines under water (the name comes from the initials of Allied Submarine Detection Investigation Committee) came into operation at the beginning of the war as a most unpleasant surprise to U-boats. By August 1940 our aircraft were equipped with a new type of radar which could detect the presence of submarines 27 miles away.

Depth charges for use by our aircraft early in 1942 replaced submarine bombs, enabling our air-craft to attack from low altitude and thus obtain greater accuracy. In June of the same year it became known that we were using the Leigh Light (a small but very powerful searchlight invented by a R.A.F. officer) along with radar, this making it possible to detect and attack a U-boat on the surface at night.

In 1943 the Germans introduced their search-receiver, which told them when their U-boats were being hunted, and they fitted their vessels with heavier anti-aircraft armament. Early the following year we were using parachute flares of 2,000,000 candle-power. When our scouting aircraft made it extremely dangerous for U-boats to come completely to the surface to recharge their batteries, German scientists devised the Schnorkel breathing tube device which enabled the U-boat to take in air for engines and men, and thus to remain in comparative safety at periscope depth, with Diesel engines running.

But there was destined to be one outcome only to it all. Our enemies were defeated in the end, and once again the Atlantic Ocean was free to our ships. Well-organized co-operation between the Royal Navy and the Royal Air Force had much to do with the victorious termination of the battle. After the German surrender in May 1945 a number of U-boats were found intact in German ports, but many more had been wrecked or scuttled.

Atlantis. An ancient tradition, recorded by (amongst others) the Greek philosopher Plato, tells of a great island west of the Pillars of Hercules (Straits of Gibraltar) adorned with every beauty. About 9000 years before his time, Plato says—that is to say, about 9400 B.C.—an attack was made upon Europe by the people of this great island of Atlantis. But these invaders were driven off by the courage of the Athenians, who expelled the invaders from the Mediterranean. Later its inhabitants became impious, and the island was in consequence swallowed up in the ocean in a day and a night.

The credulous writers of the Middle Ages, who received the tale from Arabian geographers, believed it true; they had, too, other traditions of islands in the Western Sea (as they called the Atlantic Ocean), such as the Greek Isles of the Blest, or Fortunate Isles, and the Welsh Avalon. These were sometimes marked in early maps, and more than once explorers actually set out in search of them.

The Canary Islands or the Azores, which were perhaps visited by the Phoenicians, or the thick mass of seaweed in the Sargasso Sea in the Western Atlantic, may have given rise to the legend. Atlantis, real or legendary, has given its name to the Atlantic.

When Francis Bacon described an imaginary Utopian state he gave it the name of " The New Atlantis," but he placed it somewhere in the South Seas. In that work, written on the model of Sir

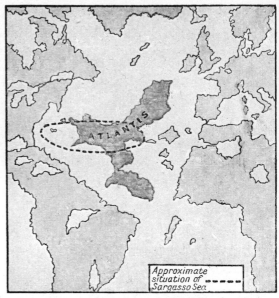

ATLANTIS, THE LOST ISLAND
Some 10,000 years ago, the Atlantic may have appeared very different from what it does today, as the map (above) shows. The position which Atlantis is supposed to have occupied largely coincides with that of the seaweed-covered Sargasso Sea.

Thomas More's Utopia, he sketches the system of government which he considers ideal, and gives a detailed picture of the application of science to the solution of the problems of human society.

SOLVING *the* MYSTERIES *of the* ATOM

It is a very ancient idea that everything in the universe is made up of tiny particles of some substance. Modern science has proved that some of the old theories contained at least a glimmering of the truth.

Atom. The ancient Greeks made some good guesses about the universe as they knew it. Democritus, a philosopher who lived in the 5th century B.C. and first suggested the idea of an " atom "— something which could not be cut up into smaller pieces—was not a scientist. He did not come to his theory by experimenting; he simply thought that if one went on cutting up some substance into yet smaller particles, there *must* come a stage when one arrived at the tiniest particle of all, which could not be further subdivided. This, said Democritus, was the atom, the unit from which all kinds of universe stuff were composed.

Of course there *were* scientists among the Greeks, and a good example was the mathematician Archimedes, who experimented and invented and has left us things like the screw for raising water. But many ancient ideas were speculations, not able to be proved.

When real chemistry began to be practised (you can read its fascinating story in our chapter on Chemistry), men like Robert Boyle and Antoine Lavoisier were able to show by experiment that many substances could be decomposed, or broken up, into simpler substances; and that some of these simpler substances were found in many different kinds of compounds. Boyle in 1661 published a book which he called The Sceptical Chymist, in

which he threw ridicule on many earlier notions which were just nonsense. He introduced the term " element " to describe a unit substance which formed part of a compound and could not itself be broken up; he pointed out what were compounds —substances formed by chemically combining different substances—as distinct from mixtures of substances in which no chemical change took place. (We can mix sulphur powder and iron filings, and afterwards draw out the iron particles by means of a magnet; but if we heat the mixture in a test tube a chemical change occurs: instead of the iron and sulphur particles we have now a different substance —iron sulphide, a chemical compound.)

John Dalton, a Manchester schoolmaster, was much interested in gases and in the composition of the atmosphere. Lavoisier and Joseph Priestley also had been experimenting on these lines, and Dalton certainly owed a great deal to them. In 1803 Dalton first put out his atomic theory : chemical elements are built of atoms, and in any particular element its atoms are all alike and weigh the same. But an atom of quite another element will have a different weight.

When different elements combine, as we saw that sulphur and iron combined, they do not do so in a haphazard way but in certain definite proportions of each. If you experimented in making compounds of these two elements you would find that you could make a number in which they combined in the following proportions :

Compound	Iron	Sulphur
No. 1	7 oz.	4 oz.
No. 2	7 oz.	8 oz.
No. 3	14 oz.	12 oz.
No. 4	21 oz.	16 oz.

Looking at these figures you would realize at once, of course, that whenever iron combines with sulphur it must act in multiples of 7, and that when sulphur combines with iron it must act in multiples of 4. You would perhaps investigate compounds of iron with some element other than sulphur — say, iron and oxygen — to see if a similar relation held good; and you would find that the proportions ran 7 to 2, 14 to 6, 21 to 8. Again the multiples of 7 for the iron, while the oxygen acts in multiples of 2. Thus you would have before you evidence in support of two great rules of chemistry— the Law of Constant Combining Weights and the Law of Multiple Proportions. Dalton saw that the refusal of one chemical element to combine with another except in units of fixed proportions must be due to the structure of the element itself. Thus iron, for example, must be made up of units that compare with similar sulphur units in the proportion of

7 to 4 by weight. You can produce compound No. 1 by combining one unit of iron with one unit of sulphur. And you could make compound No. 2 with the proportion of 7 to 8 by combining one unit of iron with two units of sulphur. But you cannot make a compound of intermediate proportions—for example, 7 to 6—because the units are not divisible. They are atoms.

Dalton developed his theory between 1803 and 1808, and before many years chemists spoke of these invisible atoms as confidently as if they had seen

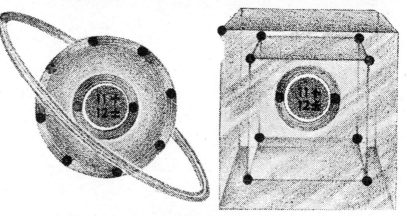

ATOMIC THEORIES OF THE SCIENTISTS: THE SODIUM ATOM
Different ideas are held by scientists concerning the construction of the atom. Niels Bohr's ' dynamic ' theory of electrons moving in orbits about the nucleus is illustrated on the left. On the right is Lewis and Langmuir's ' static ' theory of electrons at the eight corners of imaginary cubes. Numbers in circle show protons ($+$) and neutrons ($\pm$).

them. From a study of chemical compounds the relative weights of the atoms of most of the known elements were soon computed. The atom of hydrogen, lightest of the elements, was set up as the unit to which all others were compared. An atom of oxygen, for example, was found to weigh 15·88 times as much as a hydrogen atom. Later, the oxygen atom was taken as the unit, with the round number 16 for its atomic weight. On this basis the atomic weight of hydrogen is 1·008.

In general discussions, however, the hydrogen-oxygen ratio is regarded as 1 to 16. Glancing back at our previous figures, we see that the weight-proportions of the simplest compound of iron and oxygen is given as 7 to 2. This is a compound of a single atom of iron with a single atom of oxygen. Now, if the oxygen side of the proportion is raised from 2 to 16 to conform to its standard atomic weight, then the iron side of the proportion must also be raised eight times. This gives us 56 as the atomic weight of iron. Using this figure in turn for the simplest compound of iron and sulphur, we find that the atomic weight of sulphur must be 32. This illustrates how the atomic weights of all the elements are worked out.

By listing the elements in order of atomic weights and dividing the list into groups according to certain other basic chemical proportions, Dmitri Mendeléev, in 1869, constructed his famous Periodic Table (see Chemistry). In 1863–4, Newlands, an Englishman, had discovered that when he arranged the elements then known, in the order of their atomic weights, every eighth element in the list had much the same sort

ATOMS IN A CRYSTAL
This model by Sir William Bragg (1862–1942) shows us how the atoms are linked together in a molecule of a common rock salt crystal. The sodium (Na) atoms are represented by black balls, the chlorine (Cl) atoms by white ones.

of properties. The elements, in fact, seemed to fall into seven groups naturally. Mendeléev felt sure that elements to fit into gaps in the table would be discovered, and he prophesied the properties which these new-comers ought to have. In later years the gaps were filled: the list of 67 elements which Mendeléev knew now runs to a total of 94.

Although many of the elements have atomic weights which are whole numbers, some do not. You will recall that we said earlier that an atom of oxygen was found to weigh 15·88 times as much as a hydrogen atom. But if the atom itself is built up of some unit in different numbers, as the natural Laws we have mentioned must suggest, we should expect one atom of one element to weigh an amount which could be expressed as a whole number and not a fraction.

This mystery was cleared up later when chemists discovered that many elements were made up of portions having slightly different atomic weights. Ordinary chlorine, for example, consists of just over three-quarters of gas with atomic weight 35, and just under a quarter which has atomic weight 37. Together these portions give an average atomic weight of 35·46 for the mixture as found in ordinary chlorine.

The English chemist, Frederick Soddy, gave the name of isotopes to these atoms, of the same element, but having different atomic weight. The word comes from the Greek, and means " in the same place "—that is, in the table of elements. Isotopes of any particular element have the same properties, but the number of neutrons in the atom nucleus is different: for instance, chlorine-35 has 18 neutrons, while chlorine 37 has 20 neutrons. Both sorts have 17 protons in the nucleus, and it is the number of protons which affects the chemical properties of an atom.

Later researches showed that hydrogen also existed in a double-weight form, called deuterium (atomic weight 2) ; and even in a triple-weight form, called tritium (atomic weight 3). " Heavy water " and " super-heavy water" are prepared from these strange forms of hydrogen; they have come into prominence from their use in plant for splitting the atom. Again, three types of oxygen are known, with the weights 16, 17 and 18.

ATOMIC WEIGHT AND NUMBER

1. HYDROGEN

7. NITROGEN

2. HELIUM

8. OXYGEN

3. LITHIUM

9. FLUORINE

4. BERYLLIUM

10. NEON

5. BORON

11. SODIUM

6. CARBON

12. MAGNESIUM

These diagrams illustrate the theoretical arrangement of electrons (negative), and protons (positive : plus signs), and neutrons (neutral : plus-minus signs) in the atoms of the first twelve elements. Add up the protons and neutrons in the nucleus, and the result is the atomic weight of the element. Count the electrons in the outer shell and you have the atomic number. The number of electrons in the outermost shell determines the valence or combining power.

Now we must explain some of the terms we have used, and try to form a picture of the atom. In 1899 Sir J. J. Thomson gave his view that the atom of any element contained a large number of smaller bodies which for want of a better term he called corpuscles. This assemblage of corpuscles was electrically neutral—neither positive nor negative. By electrifying the atom Thomson caused it to split, so that a part of the original atom was detached and became free. Later, the name of electrons was given to the particles split off by bombarding the atom with high-voltage electricity. It is important to remember that electrons are electricity, and that—for example—the flow of 3-volt current which lights the bulb in our electric torch, or that mighty current which courses at 120,000 volts through the overhead transmission lines of the " grid " is a flow of electrons.

Thomson told us that the atom was electrically neutral, which means that any electric charge on it of one " sign "—positive or negative—must be balanced by an equal charge of opposite sign, on some other particle in the atom. It turned out that electrons were negative; the positive charges on the atom were found to be concentrated in the nucleus or " kernel," in the form of protons. The electrons were imagined as revolving in the outer region of the atom, like planets in a solar system.

Electrons and protons balanced each other by their electric charges of opposite sign—unless something happened naturally to upset the balance, or was done artificially to split off some particles and so upset the balance. Some elements, radio-active ones, break up naturally, losing particles ; when this happens the atom changes into an atom of a different element. Others can be split by high-voltage bombardment, or by exposing them to the action of radium emanations, when they too change their nature. In 1919 Lord Rutherford changed nitrogen atoms into oxygen by bombarding them with " alpha particles " (given off by radio-active substances, and consisting of nuclei of helium atoms). In 1932 Irene Curie (daughter of Marie Curie, the discoverer of radium) and her husband, Professor Frederic Joliot, found that hitherto unknown rays or particles were detached from atoms of some elements under bombardment. In the same year an English chemist, Sir James Chadwick, experimented with the new radiation, finding that the particles were not electrically charged and that they weighed about as much as protons. Since they were neutral, these particles were named neutrons. Before the year had run its course, C. D. Anderson in the U.S.A. had discovered yet another type of particle in the atom, which he called a positron. This was an electron, but with a positive electrical charge instead of a negative one.

Dr. P. M. S. Blackett

BOMBARDING THE ATOM

When an atom has been 'bombarded' by alpha rays and its nucleus shattered, free protons are driven out into space. Above, the paths of alpha rays in helium gas. The forked tracks show that an alpha particle has hit the nucleus of a helium atom.

So our present picture of the atom is something like the following: there is the nucleus with its electrons revolving around it in one or more shells. In the ordinary hydrogen atom there is one electron only; in the neon atom there are ten electrons, in two shells; in the uranium atom, heaviest of all, there are 92 electrons, revolving in seven shells. In the nucleus itself is concentrated almost all the weight of the atom, and it has a positive charge, due to its protons.

The number of protons for any given element is the same as the "atomic number" of the element in the Periodic Table (*see* under Chemistry), for in this Table the elements fall naturally into groups according to the amount of their electrical charge on the nucleus; as we have said, the charge depends on the number of protons. The atomic weight of an element depends on the number of protons, plus the number of neutrons, as we saw earlier in the case of chlorine and other elements.

This is the place to explain a fact which affects the stability of all kinds of matter, and the "holding power" of the tiny particles of which everything in the universe is made up. Albert Einstein put forth the theory of the equivalence of mass and energy. Mass means the amount of matter in any portion of substance. Energy is the capacity to do

"work"; it may be stored up in an electric accumulator. Einstein said that mass and energy in any given portion of substance were equal and convertible: by losing mass the substance could give out energy.

Here the problem of fractional atomic weights is further explained: the nucleus of the atom weighs a very tiny amount *less* than the total weight of the protons and neutrons which compose it, so that there is more energy in the added protons and neutrons than in the nucleus itself, so long as that nucleus holds together. In order to tear the nucleus apart, we must apply a comparatively immense amount of energy. In this difference of atomic weight between the nucleus and its component parts resides the binding power of the atom—and of all the substance in the universe.

At present little is known about these mighty forces which hold the atom together. When atoms break up—this means when the nuclei break up—energy is given off. It is supposed that the energy in the sun comes from the constant natural breaking up of atoms of gases and the recombining of their protons and neutrons into new elements. In the atomic bomb, about which we shall say more later, atomic nuclei of uranium are artificially split up and made to send out some of their neutrons.

The neutrons travel with enormous speed and have very great penetrative powers; they collide with the nuclei of other atoms, and break off neutrons from these. So the "chain reaction" goes on until, in a fraction of time, the whole mass of uranium is seething with heat and radio-activity—and something like an enormous explosion takes place, immensely more powerful than the explosion of the most powerful high explosive (such as T.N.T.).

So much for the atom—the smallest unit of matter in which the properties of an element can exist. As we have already seen, when elements combine to form chemical compounds they do so in definite proportions. For example, two atoms of hydrogen gas combine with one atom of oxygen gas to form ordinary water, and chemists state this reaction by the symbol for water—H_2O. Two atoms of H and one atom of O combine to form a "molecule" of water. A molecule is the smallest mass of a substance in which the properties of a compound can exist. Thus molecules are the building bricks of the universe and atoms the component units of these "bricks."

It was mainly in the study of radium and like substances that much recent knowledge was gained about the atom. First, scientists were faced with the remarkable fact that radium and other radio-active materials continually sent

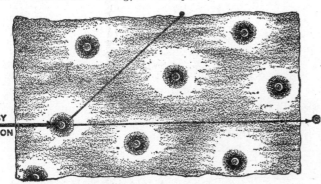

HIT BY NEUTRON

ATOMIC BOMBARDMENT : NO CHAIN REACTION

In many elements the atomic nucleus gives off an electron, a proton, or a neutron when hit by a neutron. But the nuclei of most elements do not split to release energy, and the particles they eject often fail to hit another nucleus. Hence they do not produce chain reactions.

out emanations which could be made to affect a photographic plate sealed from light, and could do other strange things such as killing disease germs. But although such emanations were sent out, the size of the portion of radium seemed not to grow less. It *did* become smaller, of course, but at such a very slow rate that in about 2000 years only half of any given piece of radium would have been dissipated in these emanations, which are in all respects identical with the nuclei of helium atoms and are named by scientists " alpha particles." Besides these, other radiations known as " beta rays " and " gamma rays " are given off by radium. All three are named from the first three letters of the Greek alphabet. Beta rays are electrons, which travel at very high speed ; gamma rays are a form of electro-magnetic radiation similar to X-rays, and the most penetrating of all three kinds.

First attempts to split the atom were made with alpha rays, and we have seen that Rutherford used this method to transmute nitrogen into oxygen as long ago as the year 1919. In 1930 two German scientists found that when they used the alpha particles given off by the element polonium in order to bombard the element beryllium, a very penetrating radiation was given off by beryllium.

At first they thought they had thus produced gamma rays, but later experiments (by Sir James Chadwick) showed that the radiation was a stream of neutrons broken off from beryllium. The neutrons, being electrically neutral, were not diverted in their passage by attraction to, or repulsion from, charged atomic particles, and proved better " bullets " for bombarding atomic nuclei. Neutrons could be slowed down by contact with substances containing hydrogen, such as ordinary water or, better, heavy water. In passing through either of these substances the neutrons lose energy and cause the emission of protons.

Many scientists of many nations helped in the subsequent discoveries up to 1939, some coming to Britain or America from Germany and Italy. Hahn and Strassmann and Frisch, with Fraulein Lise Meitner, were Germans who helped. Meitner and Frisch were refugees from Nazi Germany who worked in the laboratory of the great Danish scientist Niels Bohr, to whom many physical discoveries were due. In Paris, Irene Curie and Professor Curie-Joliot played their part. The possibilities of using atomic fission as a weapon —mainly in the construction of new bombs— were recognized by most European powers, and more or less secret experiments had been carried out on these lines, besides the researches in pure science carried out in laboratories by scientists who merely wanted to advance the world's knowledge. An Italian physicist, Enrico Fermi, worked in the U.S.A. upon the neutron experiments ; two French physicists, Kowarski and Halban, came to England in 1940 after the fall of France, and brought with them a quantity of heavy water which had been prepared in Norway by an experimental concern there. In 1943 this Norwegian installation (then under German control) was badly damaged by British parachute troops, and much of the material was thus prevented from use by Germany.

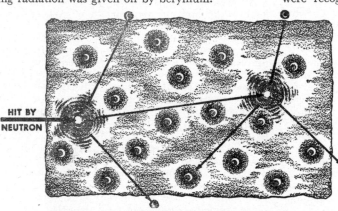

ATOMIC BOMBARDMENT : CHAIN REACTION
When an atomic nucleus of uranium-235 or plutonium splits, the shattered atom throws off several neutrons. Since each material is dense and the nuclei are large, one or more neutrons are likely to hit and split another nucleus. Hence chain reactions are possible in U-235 and plutonium.

In Britain, Canada and the United States, during the war of 1939-45, teams of scientists carried on big-scale research and experiment for the Allies. Sir G. P. Thomson (son of Sir J. J. Thomson) was appointed chairman of a band of scientists set up in 1940 to study the possibility of making atomic bombs. Sir J. D. Cockcroft, who held a high post under the Air Ministry, had invented one of the first appliances to split the atom (1932), working along with Dr. E. T. S. Watson. Later Cockcroft developed the atom-splitting machine known as the cyclo-tron, the story of which is told under its own heading. In 1942 an atomic-bomb laboratory was begun at Los Alamos, in New Mexico ; here in July 1945 the first bomb was detonated, with results which bore out to the fullest extent the scientists' theories about the enormous destruction such a weapon could wreak.

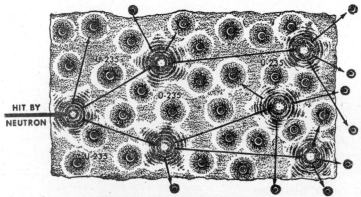

EXPLOSIVE REACTION OF U-235
If the amount of U-235 in a mass of uranium is increased by artificial means, on the average the neutrons thrown out by the splitting of one nucleus score more than one hit against other 'explosive' atoms. Then the chain reaction builds up rapidly through the mass, until it attains explosive violence.

On August 6, 1945, the first atomic bomb to be used in warfare was dropped upon the Japanese town of Hiroshima, destroying an area of about four square miles and leaving untold misery in its wake. Between 80,000 and 90,000 people were killed; a hundred thousand more were grievously wounded, while as the weeks went by other thousands showed the effects of strange diseases due to the radio-active effect of substances liberated by the bomb. On August 9, 1945, an atomic bomb was dropped upon the city of Nagasaki; here the number killed was about 40,000. Next day Japan made her offer to surrender to the Allies.

The immensity of the amount of energy liberated by an atomic bomb is difficult to realize; it is computed that a bomb in which $2\frac{1}{2}$ lb. of uranium is exploded has as much destructive power as 17,000 tons of the explosive known as T.N.T., used in ordinary aerial bombs. One of the atomic bombs dropped upon Japan contained uranium-235, an isotope of the element which is found along with uranium-238 but in smaller quantities. U-235 had to be separated from the heavier isotope in sufficient amount to make up the 8 lb. needed for the bomb. The other bomb was made from plutonium; this new element is made artificially when U-238 is bombarded by neutrons. A neutron is gained by the U-238 atom, and two electrons are lost, in two stages. U-238 thus changes into first, neptunium and secondly plutonium (Pu-239), which is more suitable for bomb making.

Along with the researches directed to making this terrible weapon there went on experiments in harnessing atomic energy to the peaceful needs of industry and manufacture. While teams of scientists were supervising the preparation of the raw materials from which atomic bombs were to be made they found difficulty in coping with the vast quantities of heat given off in the reaction. For these people were not concerned with producing power, but only with making plutonium, for use in bombs.

Central Press

AN ATOMIC BOMB HAS FALLEN

On August 9, 1945 (during the Second World War) a United States bomber dropped an atomic bomb on the city of Nagasaki, on Kyushiu Island, Japan, killing some 40,000 of the inhabitants. The smoke of the explosion did not begin to billow out until after it had passed through the clouds, when this "mushroom" formed some 20,000 feet above the ground.

Dr. H. L. Anderson, of the University of Chicago, has stated that a plant intended to produce one pound of plutonium every 24 hours would generate heat energy enough to yield 250,000 kilowatts of electricity in that period. In the smaller plants used in America for making plutonium the heat energy was removed by cooling, and was thus wasted. A quarter of a million kilowatts would provide heat and light for a whole town.

But power plants of this size are not yet within sight, and there are many difficulties in using even much smaller heat outputs. For one thing, the radio-active emanations from the materials are highly dangerous. Workers have to wear special protective clothing; the containers in which the stuff is handled (in quite small quantities at a time) are manipulated with long tongs; the appliances in which the process takes place are shielded with thick walls of concrete to screen people from the death-dealing radiations. When the metallic uranium has been prepared, it must be left for several months to lose some of its activity before the next process—purification—can be started. These dangers are nothing compared with the terrible risk that an explosion of these unstable materials may occur. But what is it that brings about an explosion? It is the starting of a chain of collisions between some kind of atomic particle and the nucleus of uranium. Alpha particles (these are helium nuclei) were used in the earliest experiments; then protons (hydrogen nuclei) and, later, neutrons. When a neutron struck an uranium nucleus it might split the nucleus into fragments which would fly apart with great speed and violence. Further, a number of additional neutrons were produced for every split or "fission." Some of the new neutrons would collide with nuclei of other uranium atoms in the mass of substance being experimented with; in a successful operation the chain of collisions would go on with ever increasing speed and violence until all the uranium was transformed. The speed of this reaction is so great that scientists use the micro-second, or one millionth of a second, to measure it.

If the piece of uranium is small, many neutrons produced in the chain reaction may escape from it without causing fresh collisions. If the piece is above what is called the critical size, the reaction will build up and cause an explosion—though this word is too feeble to describe the gigantic momentary output of energy which takes place. By providing two pieces of uranium or other fissionable material, each so small that it is safe by itself, and by bringing them together at the moment that the bomb is detonated, the reaction is made to begin.

In preparing plutonium from uranium, a plentiful supply of neutrons is produced. To make the process safe from overheating which might set up an explosion, and to prevent also a chain reaction which would have effects too terrible to contemplate, the uranium under treatment is spaced between some substance which acts as a moderator and captures harmlessly most of the neutrons. Graphite is one type of moderator. We mentioned earlier that heavy water was another slowing-down material. Certain elements such as cadmium or boron also absorb neutrons, and rods of these substances are used as controls, being thrust in farther, or pulled out more.

Attlee, CLEMENT RICHARD (b. 1883). On the corner of Barnes Street, in the heart of London's Limehouse, a group of Socialists were holding a meeting one evening in 1909. A young man mounted

the platform and began to speak, his cultured voice contrasting with the rough accents of the dockers who stood around. The speaker was Clement Attlee, who 36 years later became Prime Minister and head of the first Socialist Government in Britain with a working majority.

Educated at Haileybury and Oxford, C. R. Attlee became a barrister, but instead of practising he settled down in Limehouse and devoted himself to social work. He became a member of the Fabian Society and the Independent Labour Party. Lecturer in sociology at the London School of Economics until the outbreak of the First World War in 1914, he joined the army and served at Gallipoli, and was severely wounded at Kut-el-Amara in Mesopotamia. After further front-line service, in France, he was demobilised in 1919 as a major.

RT. HON. C. R. ATTLEE
Fox
Mr. Clement Richard Attlee became British Prime Minister in July 1945, in succession to Mr. Winston Churchill.

Mr. Attlee then returned to his work in the East End, and was for a while mayor of Stepney. In 1922 he was elected Labour Member of Parliament for Limehouse. He became Under-Secretary of State for War in the first Labour Government, under Mr. Ramsay MacDonald in 1924.

The elections of 1929 again returned a Labour Government, and in 1931 Mr. Attlee was made Postmaster-General. In the autumn of 1931 the Government was forced to resign; and Mr. Ramsay MacDonald formed a Coalition Government of Labour and Conservative members, but Mr. Attlee, with the majority of the Labour Party, joined the Opposition. As a Labour member he continued in opposition to the Conservative Governments of Mr. Baldwin (1935-37) and Mr. Chamberlain (1937-40). In May 1940 (during the Second World War) he became Lord Privy Seal and Deputy Prime Minister to Mr. Churchill in the Coalition Government, but in 1945 when the Labour Party again came into power Mr. Attlee became Prime Minister and remained in that office in 1950 when a fourth Labour Government was returned, but with a greatly reduced majority. Under his leadership independence was granted to India, Pakistan, Burma and Ceylon; coal mines, transport, gas and electricity services, and the iron and steel industry were nationalised.

Auchinleck, FIELD-MARSHAL SIR CLAUDE JOHN EYRE (b. 1884). It seemed in June 1942 (during the Second World War) that the British Empire forces in the Libyan Desert were facing defeat. The Germans and Italians, after a great victory at Tobruk, were pressing on towards Alexandria. The British commander-in-chief, General Sir Claude Auchinleck, saw one chance. Near the Egyptian village of El Alamein the enemy must pass through a gap only 40 miles wide between the sea and the impassable desert, and a concentration of our troops there might hold them. Leaving his headquarters in Cairo, "The Auk" went forward and assumed personal command of the British 8th Army. The enemy was halted, and Egypt was saved.

Field-Marshal Auchinleck was born at Aldershot, the son of a colonel in the Royal Artillery. He went to school at Wellington College, Berkshire, and after passing through Sandhurst became an officer in the 62nd Punjabis, Indian Army. In the First World War he served in Egypt and Mesopotamia, winning the D.S.O. and the French Croix de Guerre.

At the beginning of the Second World War, General Auchinleck returned to England and in 1940 was appointed G.O.C.-in-C. Southern Command. During that war it was his ill-fortune that the forces he commanded were nearly always fighting against heavy odds. In April 1940 he was in charge of the operations against the Germans at Narvik, in Norway, where a greatly outnumbered British force had to withdraw with heavy losses.

SIR CLAUDE AUCHINLECK
During the Second World War (1939–45) Field-Marshal Auchinleck was twice Commander-in-Chief in India. He was promoted Field-Marshal in May 1946.

Fox

General Auchinleck went to India as commander-in-chief in December 1940. The following July he took command in the Middle East. For a year he directed the struggle against an enemy superior in tanks and with very much shorter supply lines, but in August 1942 he was relieved by General Alexander and ordered to rest. In June 1943 he resumed his old post as commander-in-chief in India, working with Lord Wavell (then the Viceroy) for the defence of that country and the pressing home of the attacks made by British forces in Burma against the Japanese. He was promoted Field-Marshal in May 1946.

In June 1947 the Indian forces had to be divided between the two newly created dominions of India and Pakistan. Field-Marshal Auchinleck was appointed Supreme Commander and made chairman of the committee responsible for that very delicate task. In November 1947, his work accomplished, he retired.

Auckland, New Zealand. Once the capital of New Zealand, Auckland in North Island is the largest city in the Dominion and the oldest—old by New Zealand reckoning, that is, for it has grown to its proud position in a little more than 100 years.

It was founded by Governor Hobson in 1840, on the site of extinct volcanoes. Eight years later the settlement was given its present name (in honour of Lord Auckland, the British statesman who was then Governor-General of India), and became the capital and first borough of the colony. Wellington, also in North Island, took its place as the chief town in 1865, though Auckland is still the capital of the province of the same name.

The city today is famous not only for its size and history but also for its commercial importance and unique beauty of setting. Known as the " Queen City of the North," it is on the east side of a narrow isthmus, with a great natural harbour ab e to accommodate the largest ocean steamships, and wharves on the western coast only six miles away. Dotted over the surrounding hills amid the semi-tropical vegetation are the homes of those working in the city or on the huge dairy-farms to the north and south. The climate is delightful, being exceptionally even. Industries include shipbuilding, sugar-refining, and manufacture of paper, glass, bricks and rope. Butter, cheese, meat, gum, wool, coal and gold are exported. The city is the Dominion's terminal for overseas air services. Population of Auckland in 1945 was 263,500.

Audubon, JOHN JAMES (1785–1851). A great authority on American birds was John James Audubon (pron. aw'doo-bon). He was born at Les Cayes, Haiti, and taken to France as a small child after his mother died. His father, a French naval captain, wanted him to be either a soldier or an engineer; but finding that his son was not interested in either of those pursuits he sent him to America in search of a business career.

On his father's Philadelphia estate Audubon, then 18, found " a blessed spot where hunting, fishing, and drawing occupied my every moment." There too he met Lucy Blakewell, whom he married. He then sold his estate, and during the next 10 years he was clerk, merchant, miller, portrait painter, dancing master, and French teacher.

At the age of 34 Audubon decided to devote all his time to studying and sketching American birds. His wife taught in a school to support herself and their two sons. Sometimes he was penniless and hungry. Once several of his paintings were attacked and ruined by rats; undaunted, Audubon re-drew them all in three years.

Unable to find a publisher in the United States for his book Birds of America he went to England, and both there and in France people became enthusiastic over his drawings. Birds of America appeared serially, and he sold about 165 sets. The work consisted of 435 hand-coloured plates with 1,065 lifesize figures of American birds in their natural background. The descriptions of the birds appeared later in Ornithological Biography.

The first Audubon Society, organized to protect wild birds and animal life, was formed in

J. J. AUDUBON
Though of French birth Audubon won fame as one of the greatest of American naturalists. He was a pioneer in the study of bird life in America.

New York in 1886. The National Association of Audubon Societies, formed in 1905, belongs to the International Committee for Bird Preservation, which has clubs in more than 20 countries. It works also to create reservations for larger game and has charge of more than 50 sanctuaries.

Augustine,

SAINTS. (Pron. awgus'-tin). On a spring morning in the year A.D. 597, when Britain had relapsed into heathenism after its conquest by the Angles and Saxons, King Ethelbert of Kent, looking out from his city of Canterbury, saw approaching a procession of Christian monks. They bore before them a silver cross that gleamed in the sunlight. Augustine was their leader, and they had been sent

AUGUSTINE TRIES TO CONVERT THE KING
St. Augustine undertook the conversion of England to Christianity, and as a first step in his great undertaking he decided to tackle Ethelbert, king of Kent (c. 560), on the subject of the new religion. He is here seen preaching to the king and his consort Bertha, who was already a Christian, soon after his arrival in the Isle of Thanet in the spring of 597.

from Rome by Pope Gregory the Great to carry the message of Christ to the English people.

Ethelbert's wife, a Frankish princess, was already a Christian, so the king welcomed the monks. Before long he was won over to the new faith and was baptized, and his example was followed by some thousands of his subjects. Augustine was made an archbishop by the Pope, and became the first Archbishop of Canterbury. He died in 604.

Another saint of the same name was the Saint Augustine who for 35 years was bishop of Hippo, a city of Roman Africa, and upon the model of whose life with his clerics at Hippo were founded the religious orders named after him Augustinians. Of all the writers and teachers who have left their mark on Christianity none has had a greater influence than St. Augustine of Hippo. He is regarded as the greatest of the Fathers of the Church, and at the time of the Reformation his writings were referred to by Lutherans and Catholics alike.

He was born at Tagaste, near Tunis, in 354, the son of a pagan father and a Christian mother (St. Monica, to whose prayers Augustine attributed his conversion), and he died at Hippo in 430. A resolute fighter for his faith, he wrote two wonderful books which rank among the world's classics, The City of God and the Confessions. The first shows him as a formidable champion of Christianity; the Confessions tells the story of his early career.

Alinari

AUGUSTINE OF HIPPO AND HIS PUPILS
St. Augustine of Hippo was a great scholar, and here he is seen lecturing on philosophy to his pupils in the school at Rome. The illustration is from a painting by an Italian artist, Benozzo Gozzoli, who died in 1497. Italian painters of the period very often introduced a domestic animal into their paintings, and here is shown a small dog sitting among the learned students.

AUGUSTUS

Augustus, EMPEROR OF ROME (63 B.C.-A.D. 14). Julius Caesar was murdered in the year 44 Before Christ. By his will he had made Gaius Octavius, a son of his niece, his heir. At this time Octavius was a youth of 18, quietly pursuing his studies in Illyricum across the Adriatic Sea. He proceeded at once to Rome, where he assumed the name Julius Caesar Octavianus. His claim to succeed to his uncle's position was strengthened by the fact that he had been legally adopted by Caesar, and that a force of Caesar's veterans rallied to his support. With this backing Octavian was able to force Marc Antony and Lepidus, the two chief rivals for the mantle of Caesar, to come to terms with him.

The powerful trio formed a triumvirate (government of three) which overthrew the forces of Brutus at Philippi (42 B.C.), and divided the Roman world among themselves. Lepidus was soon stripped of his power, and Antony and Octavian were left to share control—Antony over the eastern provinces, Octavian over Italy and the West. But Antony neglected his provinces and spent his time in luxury and idling at the court of Cleopatra the Egyptian queen. Octavian seized this opportunity to make himself sole master. The arrogance of Cleopatra provided Octavian with an excuse to make war against her, though it was really a war against Antony. On September 2, in the year 31, Octavian's great minister, Agrippa, won a decisive victory over Antony's fleet at Actium, off the west coast of Greece, and when in the following year Octavian advanced against Egypt, Antony and Cleopatra committed suicide and left Octavian master of the Roman world.

Octavian had now reached the goal of his ambitions. He held undisputed sway over all the far-reaching domains of Rome. For the first time for 200 years Rome was at peace, and Octavian was free to devise new methods for administering her vast possessions. All hope of restoring the reality of a republic was vain. The young ruler's task was to find a workable compromise between the old republican forms and the new condition of one-man rule. Henceforward he wielded his vast powers under the titles of *Augustus* (pron. awgus'tus), the name by which he is known to the world, *princeps* (first citizen), and *pater patriae*, father of his country ; and the Senate bestowed on him the *imperium*, or supreme command of the army whence came the title Imperator or Emperor, which Augustus himself refrained from using. He was now invested by Senate and people with all the powers attaching to the old magistracies.

To Augustus the world owes the reorganization of the Roman state on a strong basis, enabling it to transmit to nations then unborn the civilization, the learning and the law of classical times. Augustus did so much to beautify Rome that it was said of him : " He found the city built of brick and left it built of marble." He established libraries and encouraged learning, especially the culture intro-

duced from Greece. Some of the greatest names in Latin literature belong to his reign—the poets Virgil and Horace, the historian Livy, and others of less renown. These writers were encouraged and helped financially by Augustus's friend and adviser, the wealthy Maecenas. So celebrated was this period that the term " Augustan Age " has come to be applied in the history of other nations to periods of great literary achievement. It was during the reign of Augustus that Jesus Christ was born in Palestine. After more than 40 years of peaceful rule (27 B.C.-A.D. 14), Augustus died, leaving his stepson Tiberius to succeed him.

Auk. (Pron. awk). At one time the great auk was found by the millions on the rocky shores and islands of northern Europe and North America. Today, there is no living specimen in existence. So far as is known the last two were shot on Fire Island, in the North Atlantic in 1844. This bird has disappeared because although so alert and swift-moving in the water, it was clumsy on land. It could neither fly

Vatican Museum; photos, Brogi, Anderson

AUGUSTUS IN YOUTH AND MANHOOD

The bust above shows Augustus in his youth, and there is every probability that it is a true portrait. Below is a magnificent statue of Augustus, showing him at the height of his power. He is wearing a cuirass ornamented with a representation of the earth rejoicing in the blessings of peace.

AUK FAMILY'S REPRESENTATIVES
The great auk (left) is now extinct, but it was once common in the Spitsbergen region. Unable to fly or run it was easily killed when it came ashore for nesting, its flesh being good for food. The crested auklet (right) lives in the Pacific, but nests in Alaska. Note the curious crest which overhangs the bill.

British Isles. Another member of the family is the little auk, which nests in the Arctic regions, but often visits our coasts in winter. The crested auklet lives in the Pacific and nests in Alaska. It has a very quaint crest which overhangs its bill. The auk family (*Alcidae*) belongs to the order *Charadriiformes*, which also includes the shore birds, gulls and terns.

Aurora. (Pron. aw-raw'-ra). This goddess of the dawn (called Eos by the Greeks), drew back every morning with rosy fingers the veil of night and heralded the coming of the sun.

One morning, according to the Greek legend, as Aurora looked down upon the world of mortals awakening to welcome the glowing dawn, she beheld the fair youth Tithonus, and his beauty won her heart. She bore him away to her bright dwelling-place at the edge of the world, and there they were wedded. Dreading the time when death must take him from her, Aurora begged the gods to allow him to live for ever. Her prayer was granted. But alas! she forgot to ask that he might stay immortally young. So, as the years passed, Tithonus grew older and older. He shrivelled and became feeble and shrill-voiced, until at last Aurora could no longer bear to look upon the husk of the man she had loved, and she changed him into a grasshopper.

Aurora Borealis. (Pron. aw-rawr'-a baw-rē-ā'-lis). In the northern hemisphere during both warm and cold weather, long waving streamers of light are often seen in the night sky. Usually they seem to radiate from an arc, and to send their rays far across the heavens. These bands of light are

nor run and was easily killed with a club. Its eggs and flesh were good for food and its feathered skin was of value to both savage and civilized man. So, when the auk came to shore for its nesting season, it was killed by the thousand; for the auk nested in colonies, the birds standing sentinel over their one egg, side by side.

The great auk (*Alca impennis*) had a thick goose-like body about two feet long, with legs set so far back that it stood quite upright, like a man, but its legs were so short that the great webbed feet seemed attached directly to the body. It had a feathered coat of black with a vest of white.

Other species of the auk family are still found in northern waters. Among these are the razorbill, the guillemot, and the puffin or sea-parrot, which nest every summer on the rocky coasts of the

AURORA HERALDS THE BREAK OF DAY
This famous painting by the Italian artist, Guido Reni (1575-1642) adorns the ceiling of the Rospigliosi Palace in Rome, and expresses the idea of daybreak as thought of in classical mythology. Before the chariot of Apollo, the sun-god, and the attendant Hours, goes Aurora, Goddess of the Dawn, scattering flowers in Apollo's path.

THE GORGEOUS CURTAIN WOVEN BY AN AURORA AS VISUALIZED BY A FAMOUS ASTRONOMER

Auroras are generally silvery white in hue, but not infrequently they display a wide range of colour. Tints of green are nearly always present, and yellow and red often appear in fiery intensity. This picture is a reproduction of a painting made by Dr. William Lockyer to convey the dramatic impression of the blazing coloured curtain sometimes drawn across the sky by this atmospheric phenomenon in high latitudes. The colours fluctuate, mix and separate, and wax and wane in brilliance before finally dissolving into luminous clouds.

To face page 304

AURORAL DISPLAYS

VERY few photographs of Auroral displays have been secured owing to technical difficulties, but the two on this page, taken by Professor Carl Stormer of Oslo, are particularly successful examples and they have the great advantage of showing the Aurora as it appears to the human eye without the intervention of an artist. That on the left, taken in Norway in 1910, shows the Aurora with ray structure, and that below is a magnificent display witnessed at Oslo in 1918.

To face page 300

hough the exact cause of the Northern Lights is still not et completely understood in all its details, the most likely heory is strikingly expressed in this picture, which shows ow discharges of electricity are supposed to stream out om the Sun and then, on reaching the upper layers of ur atmosphere, to be turned aside to the North and South magnetic poles, where, according to this theory, they produce the Northern and Southern Lights. These usually appear as long quivering streamers of white light radiating from an arc, though there are many different forms and colours. The rays often seem to move up and down so suddenly that they have been called the 'Merry Dancers.'

known as the aurora borealis or "northern lights." They are most often white, although sometimes they are red, green or yellowish. These luminous bands may be almost straight, or may wind backwards and forwards in serpentine formation. Sometimes the rays resemble a fan, or form a crown of light about a dark centre; or again long beams of light appear to fall downward somewhat like the folds of a curtain.

The aurora borealis is most frequently seen between 65 degrees and 80 degrees northern latitude. The area of visibility extends farther south in North America than in Europe. Scientists believe that auroral displays are caused by streams of electrons from the sun which excite the gases of the upper air and make them glow. These streams are deflected to the polar region by the earth's magnetic field. The aurora of the southern hemisphere is known as Aurora Australis. On the few occasions that displays are seen as far south as Southern England there have usually been signs of unusual activity in sunspots about 24 hours before.

The green and red colours are due to glowing oxygen at a height of about 100 miles. Simultaneous far-reaching disturbances in the earth's magnetic field confirm that the glow is caused by a stream of charged particles (*i.e.* by an electric current) much as in a neon sign.

Austen, JANE (1775-1817). While France was racked by the Revolution and Europe was in the throes of the Napoleonic wars, a young English girl was writing quiet stories of country life in which those world-shaking events are not

JANE AUSTEN
This charming picture shows Jane Austen as a young girl. It was painted by a German artist, Johann Zoffany (1725–1819) who came to England in 1758.

given so much as a mention. Jane Austen was the youngest of the seven children of the Rev. George Austen, rector of Steventon, Hampshire. At Steventon she passed the first 25 years of her life, and there she wrote the most famous of her novels, Pride and Prejudice and Sense and Sensibility, before she was 24, though the first to be published, Sense and Sensibility, did not appear until 1811. Besides these Jane Austen wrote only four other novels of importance— Northanger Abbey, Mansfield Park, Emma, and Persuasion. Her books depict the quiet life of middle-class country people in her own time, with no sensational incidents; but the closely observed character studies, as true to life today as when they were written, and the sense of humour displayed have won for them immortality. Until after her death at the early age of 42 Jane Austen's name never appeared on the title pages of her books. She was buried in Winchester Cathedral.

Austin, HERBERT, 1ST BARON AUSTIN OF LONGBRIDGE (1866-1941). The wonderful little Austin Seven, Britain's first " baby " car, came on the roads in 1922. Years before that, however, its creator, Herbert Austin, had been making cars.

Born at Little Missenden, Buckinghamshire, he was educated at Rotherham Grammar School, Yorkshire. After leaving school he went to Australia, where he served an apprenticeship in a foundry at Melbourne. Returning to England in 1890 with a valuable specialized knowledge of sheep-shearing machinery, he was put in charge of production at the Wolseley Sheep-Shearing Machine Co., near Coventry, when only 24 years old.

He began to experiment with motor-cars in 1895, and 10 years later founded his own car factory at Longbridge, Birmingham. Shortly before his death in 1941 that factory occupied 220 acres, employed 20,000 people and had produced nearly 750,000 motor vehicles. He was knighted in 1917 for his services in making munitions during the First World War, and from 1919 to 1924 was Member of Parliament for King's Norton, Birmingham. In 1936 he was made a baron. Lord Austin made several extensive tours of the principal motor-car works in the United States to study manufacturing processes. Many engineering societies recognized his ability and genius, conferring upon him their highest honours.

Austin Motor Co. Ltd.

SIR HERBERT AUSTIN AND HIS 'BABY SEVEN'
Designer and inventor of the Austin Seven, Sir Herbert Austin, who was created a Baron in 1936 and took the title of Lord Austin of Longbridge, was known as the 'Father of the Baby Car.' He is seen in the famous 'baby seven' which appeared in 1922 and was the first universally successful small car.

The ISLAND CONTINENT of AUSTRALIA

A great land is the Commonwealth of Australia—great in size and in natural resources, in what has been accomplished and still more in future promise. Great, too, in its fine breed of men and women.

Australia. While most of Asia and Europe were still submerged beneath the ocean, Australia was dry land. Scientists tell us that it was once connected by a land bridge with Asia, and some believe with South America also. This bridge disappeared beneath the surface of the ocean in ages inconceivably remote, before the higher forms of animal and plant life had come into existence. Isolated thus through the succeeding ages, this unique land has preserved for us, as if in a vast museum, forms of trees, flowers and animals that have vanished from other parts of the earth.

This champion ram is a splendid specimen from Australia's vast flocks of sheep.

The natives or " blackfellows " are very primitive people, still in the Stone Age of civilization, no further advanced than were the peoples of Europe more than 5,000 years ago. Yet ancient and remote as Australia is, new life has entered it and made it in some respects the most modern country of the world. It has one of the most advanced governments, and the traveller's first impression as he lands at Sydney, or one of the other fine ports, is of a busy, prosperous, and exceedingly progressive country.

This loneliest of the continents is also the most extraordinary in its physical characteristics. With all its vast area of 2,974,581 square miles, its coast is so little indented that it has only 12,000 miles of coast line, just about as long as Norway's. Along the north-east coast stretches for 1,200 miles the Great Barrier Reef, the greatest of all coral reefs, offering few safe openings for ships. There are, however, numerous spacious harbours along the south-eastern coast. The only nearby islands of importance are Tasmania, which forms one of the States of the Commonwealth, and New Guinea, the British portion of which is now a dependency of Australia.

Except for ranges of mountains in the interior and along the eastern and south-eastern coasts,

Australia is a flat lowland, with only a few isolated groups of hills to diversify it. The Eastern Mountains, or the Great Dividing Range as they are usually called, intercept nearly all the moisture of the south-easterly trade winds, so that the rainfall on the eastern coast is abundant. Here are fertile agricultural areas, where grow most of the products of the temperate zone in the centre and south, and tropical products in the north. Inland from the mountains the rainfall becomes scantier and scantier. Little but grass grows in this region, but it is here the sheep are pastured that make Australia the chief mutton and wool country. West of the grazing areas comes the huge expanse of desert that covers nearly all the rest of the continent. More than half of Australia receives less than 15 inches of rainfall a year, and more than a third receives less than 10 inches. The west coast is mostly low and sandy, but for a few patches of grazing or farm lands and forest.

The tropical northern coast is alternately drowned under summer rains so heavy that ploughing is almost impossible, and parched by winter droughts. The overheated desert draws the monsoon rains from the north during November, December and January, and tropical grasses spring up to a height of 10 feet.

Abundant moisture is brought by the " roaring forties "—the westerly winds that girdle the Southern Hemisphere between the 40th and 50th parallels of latitude—but most of Australia is too far north to benefit. The extreme south-west tip is fairly well watered, but the receding southern coastline along the Great Australian Bight receives practically no rain for half its extent, until it bends to the south and catches the moisture of the western winds. The south-eastern prolongation of the country is abundantly watered, as a rule.

Of the total land area of Australia only about one per cent is under cultivation. But irrigation has redeemed many thousands of acres in the semi-arid regions, and several great irrigating projects were completed in Victoria and South Australia during the Second World War ; the extent, however, that has thus been made available for tilling and grazing is a mere fraction of the vast tracts that must remain desert. Australia has no great system of rivers ; its streams are fewer and smaller than

Extent.—Greatest length east to west, 2,400 miles ; north to south, 2,000 miles. Area (including Tasmania), 2,974,581 square miles. Population over 8 million.

Distance from Other Points.—From New Zealand, 1,200 miles ; Japan, 3,500 miles ; India, 2,500 miles ; South America, 6,300 miles ; San Francisco, 6,750 miles ; London, 11,000 miles via Suez, 12,750 via Panama Canal.

Natural Features.—Surface, flat and largely desert except in east and south-east. Mountains: Great Dividing Range, known at various points as the Australian Alps, the Blue Mountains, the Liverpool Mountains, etc. ; highest peak, Mt. Kosciusko (7,328 feet). Rivers : Murray, Darling, Hunter, Clarence, Brisbane, Fitzroy, Burdekin, Swan, Murchison, Gascoyne, Victoria, Flinders.

Products and Industries.—Wool, frozen meats, hides and tallow ; wheat, hay, oats, barley, maize, potatoes, dairy products, sugar-cane, fruit, cotton ; gold, silver, tin, lead, coal, iron, etc. ; timber. Textiles and clothing manufactures ; smelting, metal working, flour milling, sugar refining. Motor-cars, ball bearings, optical glass, stainless steel.

States of the Commonwealth (with Capitals).—New South Wales (Sydney) ; Victoria (Melbourne) ; South Australia (Adelaide) ; Queensland (Brisbane) ; Tasmania (Hobart) ; Western Australia (Perth) ; Northern Territory (Darwin). The Federal capital is Canberra.

AUSTRALIA CLAIMED FOR BRITAIN
Though William Dampier discovered Australia in 1688 his report upon the new land was unfavourable, and it was not until Captain Cook arrived in 1770 that its possibilities were realized and it became a British colony. Captain Cook is here seen landing with the British flag in that part of Australia which he named New South Wales.

Grape-vines thrive in many parts, yielding raisins and wine, both of which are exported in large quantities. Hay, maize, oats, barley, and other products of the temperate zone are grown in sufficient quantities for home demand, and the tropical regions of the central and northern coasts yield cotton, sugar-cane, bananas and tobacco.

But far more important than the agricultural products are the sheep and cattle. Sheep raising is the main industry and wool is the great product, since sheep grazing is less dependent on rainfall than other pasturage. The flocks are kept on enormous " stations," sometimes 250,000 acres or more in extent, and, because of the mildness of the winter, wool and mutton can be produced more cheaply than in most countries. Australian wool is chiefly merino of a quality unsurpassed for length, thickness and fineness. Cattle are also raised in numbers great enough to make hides, beef and dairy products valuable exports.

The discovery of gold in 1851 marked an epoch in the history of Australia, for it brought in thousands of immigrants. There are also rich deposits of silver, copper, tin, lead and zinc. With abundant supplies of coal and iron Australian industries are being rapidly developed, and some 29,000 factories are operating. The Commonwealth produces industrial metals of many kinds, farm machinery and implements, chemicals and dyes.

During the Second World War (1939-45) Australia manufactured quantities of war material, including guns, tanks and aircraft, and was able not only to equip her own army but also to export munitions to Great Britain. New industries included the manufacture of ball bearings, extraction of nitrogen from the air, the production of magnesium, optical glass and stainless steel The first motor-car factory was opened in 1947 The pearl fisheries are among the largest known.

Australia has about 27,000 miles of government-owned railways, and 705 miles privately owned. Until recent years the railway system was complicated by the fact that the gauge, or width between the rails, was not uniform in all the States; but in 1946 an Act to adopt a uniform gauge of 4 feet 8½ inches throughout the country was passed. In 1940 a 600-mile road was built to connect the railway running south from Darwin to Birdum with the line going north from Port Augusta to Alice Springs. Numerous steamship lines link Australia with the outside world, while air mail is carried to and from England within a week.

The native plant and animal life of Australia is curious and interesting. Most of the more than 10,000 species of plants are found nowhere else in the world, and scientists have included the animals in a group of their own. In past geological ages, millions of years ago, the plant life that covered the earth was very different from that of today. In Europe and America these primitive forms are

those of any other continent, for it has no mountain snows to melt under the summer sun. Most of the Australian rivers are dry for part of the year, and few find their way to the sea. Irrigation, therefore, is obtained chiefly from artesian wells. The one great river system is that of the Murray and Darling rivers, which drain the south-eastern region.

The eastern, south-eastern and northern coasts, with a few areas in the west, are the parts of the country where the people live, and a population map shows 80 per cent of the inhabitants in a belt about 100 miles wide along the eastern, south-eastern and south-western coasts. Even in these settled portions the people are not overcrowded, for European immigration has been slow and immigration of Asiatics is prohibited in order that Australia may be " a white man's continent." Though Australia constitutes a quarter of the area of the whole British Empire, it has only about one and a half per cent of the population. Though it is larger than Europe, it has fewer inhabitants than the Netherlands.

Australia's wealth lies chiefly in its cattle and sheep and its minerals. Large wheat crops are raised in the east and south-east, and Australia is rated as one of the chief wheat-exporting countries.

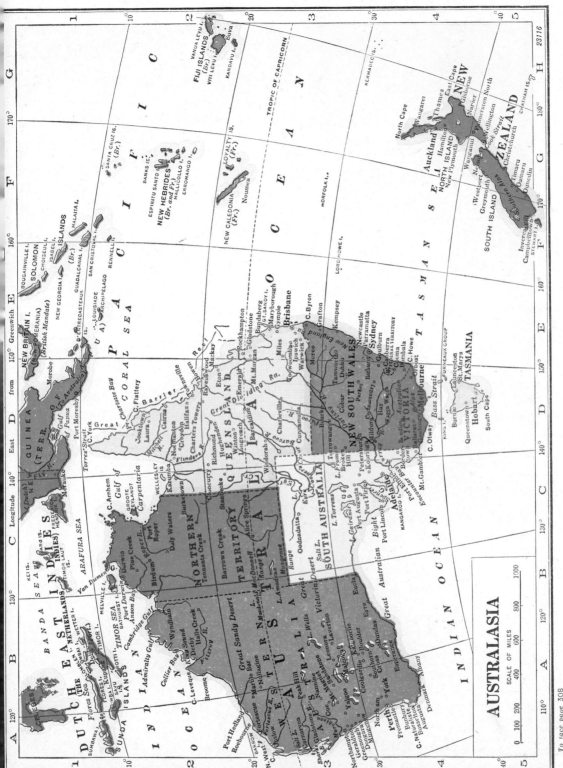

AUSTRALASIA

SCALE OF MILES

0 100 200   400   600   800   1000

23116

FACTS YOU SHOULD KNOW ABOUT THE CONTINENT OF AUSTRALIA

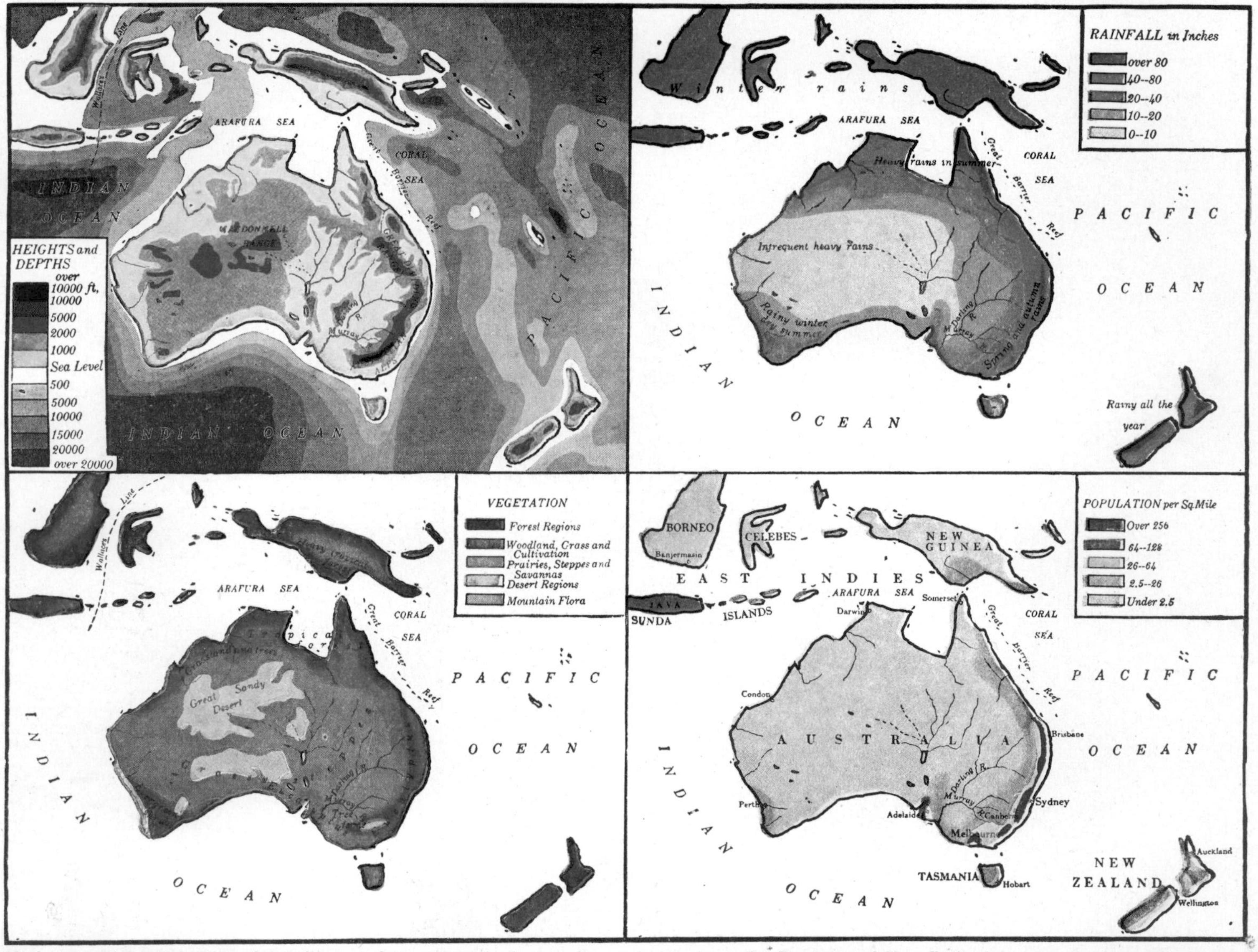
HEIGHTS and DEPTHS
over 10000 ft.
10000
5000
2000
1000
Sea Level
500
5000
10000
15000
20000
over 20000
INDIAN OCEAN
ARAFURA SEA
CORAL SEA
Great Barrier Reef
PACIFIC OCEAN
Murray
RAINFALL in Inches
over 80
40--80
20--40
10--20
0--10
Winter rains
Heavy rains in summer
Infrequent heavy rains
Rainy winter dry summer
Spring and autumn rains
Darling R.
Murray
Rainy all the year
INDIAN OCEAN
VEGETATION
Forest Regions
Woodland, Grass and Cultivation
Prairies, Steppes and Savannas
Desert Regions
Mountain Flora
Great Sandy Desert
POPULATION per Sq.Mile
Over 256
64--128
26--64
2.5--26
Under 2.5
BORNEO
Banjermasin
CELEBES
NEW GUINEA
EAST INDIES
JAVA
SUNDA ISLANDS
Darwin
Somerset
AUSTRALIA
Condon
Perth
Adelaide
Melbourne
Canberra
Sydney
Brisbane
TASMANIA
Hobart
NEW ZEALAND
Auckland
Wellington

Much interesting information about the great Commonwealth of Australia—and also about the Dominion of New Zealand—is given in these colour maps.

found only as fossils, but in Australia they are still flourishing. In the moist tropical forests are huge tree-ferns, and gigantic lilies and tulips that are not garden flowers such as we know, but large trees. In all parts of the country we see the wonderful eucalyptus tree, native to Australia, of which there are about 360 varieties—some of them measuring 400 feet in height, and including in all probability the tallest trees in the world. The wood of many varieties is remarkable for its strength and durability and is exported for building purposes. And from the eucalyptus trees come many valuable oils.

Various species of wattle, belonging to the acacia family (*q.v.*), are of commercial importance for their timber and for their bark, which is used in tanning. The blossom of the golden wattle is the national flower of Australia, and in springtime the valleys and gullies are ablaze with its radiance.

When the land bridge connecting Australia with the rest of the world was swallowed up, the continent ceased to share in the progressive development of higher forms of life, with the result that its animal life is distinctive. It has no native cats, pigs, horses, cattle, sheep, elephants, tigers, lions, camels, or other highly developed forms of animals. A few rodents and a wild dog called the dingo are almost the only kinds of the higher mammals. On the other hand it has preserved scores of primitive animals extinct in other lands for ages.

For example, there is the kangaroo, which stands on its hind legs and has a pouch in which the mother carries and nurses her babies. The wombat, the wallaby and the phalangers or opossums are the kangaroo's closer relations ; and Australia has other

creatures with the peculiar pouch which marks them as marsupials. An example is the fascinating little koala bear. Stranger still, perhaps, are the duckbilled platypus—a web-footed, beaver-tailed creature with a bird-like beak—and the spiny ant-eater (Echidna), both egg-laying mammals. They form a link between the mammals or suckling animals of today and the great family of reptiles from which the mammals and birds have both developed.

The national bird is the emu, known as the Australian ostrich, and also a very ancient creature ; related to it is the equally curious cassowary. Among others are the bower-bird, which builds a bower or playhouse, and the lyre-bird, famous for its plumage. Cockatoos and parrots enliven many a woodland scene by their chatter and their

Upper photos, Spencer & Gillen. " Across Australia " (Macmillan); lower photo, Dorien Leigh

ABORIGINES WHO STILL SURVIVE IN AUSTRALIA

It is estimated that there are about 73,000 aborigines in Australia, but, unlike the Maoris, who are the aboriginal inhabitants of New Zealand, they have not taken kindly to civilized ways and still retain their old customs and super-stitions. At top left is a magician dressed to represent a bulb in blossom, and hoping by magic power to induce the crops to bloom. The man on the right has a bone through his nose and a pattern painted on his body, both of magical and religious meaning. Lower, aborigines are performing a festive dance on Palm Island, which lies off Queensland.

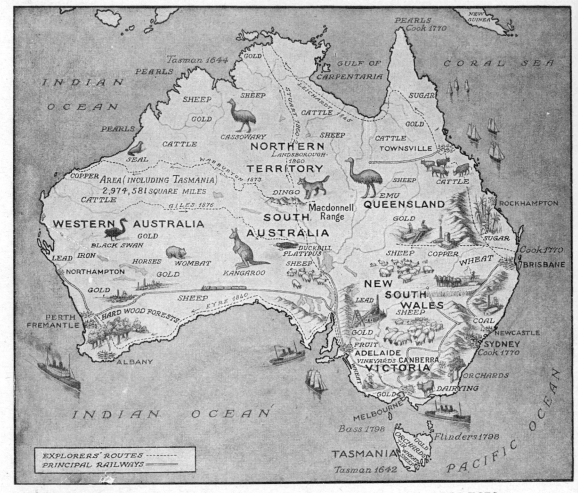

The map shows the explorers' routes and principal railways, with labels including:

PEARLS Cook 1770, NEW GUINEA, Tasman 1644, GOLD, GULF OF CARPENTARIA, CORAL SEA, PEARLS, INDIAN OCEAN, SHEEP, SHEEP, SUGAR, STUART 1860, LEICHARDT 1845, CATTLE 1845, GOLD, CASSOWARY, GOLD, NORTHERN, SUGAR, CATTLE, SEAL, LANDSBOROUGH 1860, SHEEP, CATTLE TOWNSVILLE, WARBURTON 1873, TERRITORY, COPPER, AREA (INCLUDING TASMANIA) 2,974,581 SQUARE MILES, CATTLE, GILES 1876, DINGO, EMU, SHEEP, CATTLE, WESTERN AUSTRALIA, SOUTH AUSTRALIA, Macdonnell Range, QUEENSLAND, ROCKHAMPTON, GOLD, GOLD, BLACK SWAN, DUCKBILL PLATYPUS, GOLD, SUGAR, LEAD IRON, HORSES, WOMBAT, KANGAROO, SHEEP, SHEEP COPPER, WHEAT, Cook 1770, NORTHAMPTON, GOLD, NEW, BRISBANE, GOLD, SHEEP, EYRE 1840, LEAD, SOUTH WALES, PERTH FREMANTLE, HARD WOOD FORESTS, GOLD, SHEEP, COAL, NEWCASTLE, ALBANY, FRUIT VINEYARDS, ADELAIDE, CANBERRA, SYDNEY Cook 1770, VICTORIA, ORCHARDS, WHEAT, GOLD, DAIRYING, INDIAN OCEAN, MELBOURNE, PACIFIC OCEAN, Bass 1798, Flinders 1798, TASMANIA, ORCHARDS, GOLD, Tasman 1642

EXPLORERS' ROUTES ------- PRINCIPAL RAILWAYS =======

AUSTRALIAN CONTINENT AND ITS ANIMALS AND PRODUCTS

New South Wales colony was founded in 1788, but it was not until 1896 that practically the whole of the continent had been explored. The routes of the chief expeditions are shown in this map. The largest cities are on the coast or close to good harbours, while the south-eastern states of Victoria and New South Wales contain the richest industrial areas and are the most thickly populated. The resources of the country are to be found within easy reach of the sea.

gorgeous colours. Also of interest is the famous laughing jackass, or kookaburra, a member of the kingfisher family. White ants, or termites, are a terrible plague in some districts, eating unprotected woodwork wherever they can get at it. Countless millions of rabbits, the descendants of a few introduced in the middle of the 19th century, would soon turn all the grazing lands into desert were it not for ceaseless vigilance.

The aborigines of Australia (the original dwellers in that land) resemble the Negro of Africa in colour, and, like the Negro, most of them have very broad, flat noses, but their hair is wavy rather than woolly. When first discovered they were the most primitive of savages. They wore no clothing in summer, and in winter only the skins of beasts. For shelter they had only caves or huts of the rudest sort and often were mere nomads. They ate almost any kind of plant or animal life—not only the flesh of the kangaroo and opossum, but caterpillars, moths, beetles, lizards, and snakes. They did not cultivate the soil, and could not count beyond three or four. On the other hand, thousands of years of hunting life had made them amazingly cunning in tracking an animal to its lair and killing it. Their weapons consisted of stone hatchets and spears and, most curious of all, the boomerang—a flat, curved missile of wood which they used both in hunting and in war. Only about 73,000 pureblooded and half-caste aborigines are left in the land.

Australia was the last of the continents to be discovered by Europeans. In 1606 Luis de Torres, a Spaniard, sailed along the coast and gave his name to Torres Strait. Abel Tasman, a Dutch navigator, in 1642 discovered the island now called Tasmania. William Dampier, a freebooter, in 1688 was the first Englishman to set foot in Australia. It was not till 1770 that the real nature of the land became known. Captain James Cook in that year, as head of an English scientific expedition, landed in Botany Bay, near where Sydney now stands. He explored the eastern coast northward, and planted the flag on Cape York, thus establishing the British claim to the continent.

In 1840 Edward John Eyre began a perilous journey from the Great Australian Bight, which

CHIEF SOURCES OF AUSTRALIA'S WEALTH

Australia is a great contributor to the wealth of the British Commonwealth, and is usually Britain's third best customer. Wheat, minerals and sheep are her chief sources of wealth. Wheat exports have an annual value of about £10,000,000. The principal mineral products are coal, silver, gold, copper and iron. In sheep raising, not so dependent on rainfall as is agriculture, Australia leads the world, exporting quantities of wool and mutton.

AUSTRALIA

led him through 1,200 miles of wilderness and scorching desert. More than a year later, accompanied only by a single native, he came out on King George's Sound, in Western Australia. He had traversed the whole route which is now followed by the Trans-Australian Railway.

The first settlement came soon after the loss of most of England's colonies in America, when a number of such convicts as had formerly been sent to America were landed in Australia, forming the beginning of the colony of New South Wales (1788). Other British colonies soon followed, but it was not until the end of the 19th century that practically the whole of the continent had been explored. The discovery of gold, in 1851, brought a rush of immigration, but these settlers were not of a desirable kind, and, with the convicts' descendants, caused disorder.

In 1901, after local jealousies had balked many attempts at union, the six Australian colonies became States and formed a federation under an act of the British Parliament. The name of the federal government is now the Commonwealth of Australia. All powers not delegated to the Federal Government are retained by the several State parliaments. Like Canada, Australia is self-governing and independent though the Crown is represented

by a resident governor-general. The government is conducted by a Cabinet responsible to a parliament of two houses—a House of Commons and a Senate, the members of both being elected by the people. Voting power is enjoyed equally by men and women from the age of 21. Australia was one of the first countries to enact old age and invalid pension laws. Primary education is compulsory and the State schools are free.

The temporary seat of the federal government was established at Melbourne until 1927, when a new capital at Canberra was inaugurated by the Duke of York, who became King George VI. This city is in a district set apart by the government and known as Australian Capital Territory. The Northern Territory of Australia, the most barren area of the country, is administered by the Commonwealth government at Canberra.

In the First World War (1914–1918) the Australian navy helped to clear the Pacific Ocean of German ships, and Australia sent troops to France, Gallipoli, Macedonia, Egypt, Mesopotamia and other fronts. In 1919 all Germany's Pacific possessions south of the Equator were put under the administration of Australia or New Zealand.

In the Second World War (1939–1945) Australian troops won fame in Libya, in Greece and Crete, in Malaya and the islands of south-west Pacific; over 1,000,000 men

Australian National Travel Assn.

AUSTRALIAN SHEPHERDS AND COWBOYS

There are more than 100 million sheep in Australia, and the flocks are so huge that the shepherds tend them on horseback (top). Some of the bigger sheep farms cover hundreds of square miles. Cattle number over 14 million and travel enormous distances to market, being herded across streams (lower) that may contain crocodiles.

AUSTRALIA'S UNIQUE ANIMAL LIFE

Australian National Travel Assn.

Some of the wild animals and birds of Australia are found in no other land. Here are seven of the most interesting. The kangaroo (1), is seen taking a flying leap. The koala (2) is a little native bear about two feet long, which, like the kangaroo, carries its young in a pouch. The emu (3) is the largest of all birds except the ostrich. The dingo (4) is the wild dog of Australia; it is a menace to sheep and poultry. The kookaburra or laughing jackass (5) has a cry somewhat like a human laugh. The echidna (6), an egg-laying mammal, is found also in New Guinea. Strangest of all is the duck-billed platypus (7). It is a mammal with a bill like a duck and webbed feet, and it lays eggs.

Australian National Travel Assn.

AUSTRALIAN BUSH COUNTRY OF GREAT BEAUTY

Stately giant eucalyptus or gum trees (left), of which there are about 360 species, sometimes grow to a height of 400 feet. Native to Australia, the eucalpytus sheds its bark but not its leaves. Australia's forests are light and airy and contain many varieties of wattle and tree-fern. The mountainous interior (right) of south-east Australia attracts walkers in summer ; and in winter people can enjoy winter sports on the heights of the Australian Alps.

and women enrolled for full-time service. Several Japanese bombing attacks were made on Darwin, Australia's northernmost port, the most severe being the first, on February 19, 1942. Other places raided by Japanese aircraft were Wyndham, Broome and Derby in Western Australia, Townsville in Queensland, and Katherine, south of Darwin. There was also Japanese naval activity off the East coast of Australia, though on a small scale. On June 1, 1942, a daring but not very successful attack was made on Sydney Harbour by midget submarines. Four of them were sunk, and only one Australian craft was hit. A week later the suburbs of Sydney and the town of Newcastle, 100 miles to the north, were shelled by submarines, of which at least three were sunk by Allied aircraft off the Australian coast in early June. These raids were intended as a diversion with a view to forcing the retention of Australian warships and aircraft at their home bases.

The great southern continent is famed for its artists, sportsmen and musicians, the last-mentioned

Australian National Travel Assn.

CAMEL CARAVAN IN A DESERT REGION OF AUSTRALIA

There are great stretches of desert in north-west and central Australia where agriculture is impossible. But if you went there you might see a train of camels such as this crossing the sandy waste just as they do in Arabia. The reason is that in these districts there are remote mining camps, and some fifty years ago camels were introduced into Australia to carry supplies to them. The man and woman walking at the head of the caravan are Australian aborigines.

including the composer Percy Grainger, and the great singer Madame Melba, who died in 1931. An article on Australian Literature follows. (*See also* Adelaide ; Brisbane ; Canberra ; Hobart ; Melbourne; Perth; Sydney; and the States under their own names).

Australian Literature.

Of the Australian novelists known and appreciated by English critics one of the foremost is a woman, Henrietta Richardson, who writes under the pseudonym " Henry Handel Richardson." She vividly portrayed her country of an earlier day in the trilogy The Fortunes of Richard Mahony, comprising Australia Felix, The Way Home, and Ultima Thule.

Poetry had an early flowering as inspired newcomers sang of the beauty of Australia's blue distances—frequently employing the manner of the poets they loved at home. Henry Clarence Kendall (1841–82), the first notable lyrist, celebrated his love of the bush in a style reminiscent of Wordsworth. His chief works are Leaves from an Australian Forest (1869) and Songs from the Mountains (1880). Adam Lindsay Gordon (1833–70) dealt with the adventures of squatters and horse-racers, and admirably portrayed the grim good humour and manliness of the bushman.

The Sydney Bulletin, established in 1881 by J. F. Archibald, did much to develop a literature

Australian Trade Publicity

ON AUSTRALIA'S SYDNEY BEACHES

The Sydney area is famous the world over for its glorious bathing beaches. Teams of voluntary life-savers are employed to patrol them, and above, on the right, is a youthful team at practice at North Bondi. In the lower picture is a scene on Manly Beach, at the entrance to Sydney Harbour.

Boils (1896). In the Days When the World Was Wide, a highly popular collection of his simple rhyming verse, was published the same year. A. B. Paterson, nicknamed " Banjo," wrote a similar type of vigorous racy verse, of which his Man from Snowy River (1895) is well known. Other verse writers of that period include Victor Daley, who gave to his poetry a Celtic glamour, Will Dyson, and Barcroft Boake. A later writer of power and imagination was Bernard O'Dowd, whose best work is the long poem, The Bush (1912). Later poets whose works are widely read are John Shaw Neilson, William Blocksidge and Furnley Maurice. C. J. Dennis created the typical Anzac (Australian soldier) in The Sentimental Bloke.

The first notable novel by an Australian writer, For the Term of His Natural Life (1870) by Marcus Clarke, still stands as a classic of the period of convict labour. The novels of Rolf Boldrewood (Thomas Alexander Browne) are interesting for their stories of high adventure in the newly-opened country. Henry Kingsley (1830–1876), brother of the English novelist Charles Kingsley, was the author of an outstanding novel, Geoffrey Hamlyn, the tale of an immigrant.

Louis Becke, who led a life of strange adventure, wrote sketches and stories which are regarded by

flavoured with the democratic spirit of the young colonies. It encouraged young writers and furnished the leading market for their poems and short pungent tales, discovering or bringing to the fore such writers as Henry Lawson, Rudolph Bedford, E. J. Brady and Louis Becke. Lawson has been compared to O. Henry because of the fidelity with which he pictured the types of the wild back-blocks in his book of sketches, While the Billy

many as the finest of all South Sea literature. Dr. Charles McLaurin achieved success with his Post Mortem (1922) and Mere Mortals (1925). Louis Stone's powerful stories Jonah and Betty Wayside dramatically present scenes and characters from contemporary Australian life.

Katherine S. Prichard, a notable woman novelist, achieved notice abroad chiefly through her Working Bullocks. Mrs. Aeneas Gunn wrote sympathetically of the woman of the cattle lands, and of the "blackfellows," whom she splendidly presented in

We of the Never-Never (1907). Gertrude Eldershaw, Vance Palmer, Myra Morris and Roy Bridges are among other prolific writers. Louis Esson is known for some excellent short plays, particularly Dead Timber.

Australian-born, though more English in their background, were the scholar Professor Gilbert Murray ; the poet, music-critic and writer of novels, W. J. Turner (1889-1947); and the novelist Helen Simpson (1897-1940), whose Boomerang won the James Tait Black Memorial Prize in 1932.

The REMNANT of a MIGHTY EMPIRE

Set in the centre of Europe is a little country which until the First World War (1914-18) was the heart of a great empire. Defeat in two wars and revolution and distress have worked their ruin, yet much that is charming persists.

Austria. A head without a body—this is what the Austrian republic might have been called after the treaty of St. Germain (September 10, 1919). That treaty, which ended the First World War between the Austro-Hungarian Empire and the Allied Nations, took from Vienna, the capital and manufacturing centre, the rich resources of the empire, leaving only a small Alpine country.

The country covers only about 32,000 square miles, one-eighth the area of the old empire. The population at the 1934 census was given as 6,760,233, but this figure was considerably reduced during the Second World War. Its former lands

> Area—32,369 sq. miles. Austria is divided into nine provinces, including the city of Vienna.
> **Population** (1934)—6,760,233.
> **Physical features**—The Eastern Alps, extending over nearly the whole country ; with the valley of the Danube in the north. Passes : Brenner, in Tirol, to Italy ; Semmering, between Lower Austria and Styria.
> **Products**—Wheat, potatoes, and other crops ; timber ; lignite (brown coal) and iron, copper, zinc and lead ore ; meat and dairy products ; machinery, furniture and textiles.
> **Principal cities** (populations estimated in 1945)—Vienna, 1,418,900 ; Graz (province of Styria), 152,841 ; Linz (Upper Austria) 108,970 ; Salzburg, 63,230 ; Innsbruck (Tirol), 61,000.

now under new rule surround it on three sides — Czechoslovakia on the north-east, Hungary on the east, Yugoslavia on the south-east, and the territory given to Italy on the south-west. To the north-west is Germany, related in language and blood to the Austrian people ; and to the west, Switzerland.

The eastern Alps penetrate every one of Austria's provinces. Vorarlberg, Tirol, Carinthia, and Styria are entirely mountainous. The famed Brenner Pass, lowest in the Alps, crosses Tirol, connecting Italy and Germany ; and Semmering Pass joins Lower Austria and Styria. Despite its mountain ranges, Styria has little unproductive soil. Grain grows in the northern valleys, and grapes, fruit and hops in the south, while live-stock graze on the grass-grown slopes of the higher lands.

At Salzburg, in the province of the same name, the plains meet the mountains. Upper and Lower Austria combine Alpine land with fertile farms in the basin of the Danube ; and the soil of Burgenland is almost as fertile as the basin. Industry centres in and around Vienna and in the Styrian iron belt.

Austria's weather is as varied as its scenery, for the mountains play their part in climate and

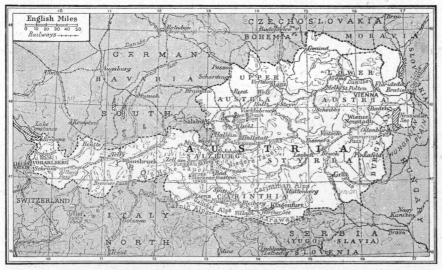

AUSTRIAN REPUBLIC IN CENTRAL EUROPE
Austria assumed its present size after the First World War (1914–18), when the old Austro-Hungarian Empire was split up under the terms of the Peace Treaty of 1919. It remained an independent republic until it was incorporated in the German Empire on March 13, 1938. After the Second World War (1939–45) it again became a republic, with the boundaries of 1937.

Austrian State Travel; Dorien Leigh; McLeish

AUSTRIAN COSTUMES SEEN IN THE COUNTRYSIDE

Even outside the Tirol, which is famed for its scenery and the picturesque dresses of its inhabitants, there is plenty of individuality and charm to be seen in the costumes of the peasants. Top left, workers on a farm in the Burgenland **province; top right, a lady from Carinthia; centre, a girl from the Salzkammergut region of Upper Austria; lower left, a costume seen in the valley of the Danube; lower right, a group of girls from Vienna in holiday attire.**

rainfall. Along the Danube and in the Alpine foothills the climate resembles that of Northern France, with an average temperature of about 47° Fahrenheit. Winters are chilly in the eastern valleys, but a warm south wind, called the foehn, tempers the northern valleys. Rainfall is greatest on the northern and southern rims of the mountains, rising to 80 inches yearly in some places. Snowfall increases with the height of the mountains, whose tops above 9,000 feet gleam white with perpetual snow, making a thousand glistening glaciers beautiful to see but dangerous to climb.

The Danube is the country's only water route to the outside world, the coast that was once Austria's, with the Adriatic ports of Trieste and Fiume, being divided between the republics of Italy and Yugoslavia. Most of the railways that traverse

the mountains—some running on suspension lines up the peaks—are state-owned. They are being electrified to utilize the country's abundant water power and save imports of coal. Omnibus lines run over the better mountain roads. Vienna in normal times was a noted hub of aviation for the Central European countries.

The Austrian people are almost entirely Germanic, related in temperament to the Bavarians of South Germany rather than to the Prussians, and, like the Bavarians, chiefly of the Roman Catholic faith. Although a third of the people are farmers they can produce less than a sixth of the country's needed food, because not quite 25 per cent of the land is fit for crop cultivation. Forests cover nearly 40 per cent of the country, and furnish timber and pulp wood for export. Austria has rich veins of

DANUBE RIVER'S WINDING COURSE
The stretch of the Danube in Austrian territory between Linz and Vienna is considered the finest in the whole length of that famous river. Below Melk the Danube winds through the long defile of the Wachau, rich in historical and legendary associations.

government put increasing pressure on the Austrians to unite with Germany, and when this proved unsuccessful their troops marched in. Austria becoming a part of Greater Germany (March 13, 1938), under the name of Die Ostmark, or Eastern Frontier District.

In the spring of 1945 during the course of the Second World War the Allies occupied Austria, the Russians taking Vienna on April 13. The country once again became an independent republic with its frontiers as in 1937, but was divided into four zones occupied by the British, Americans, French and Russians. A National Assembly was elected in November 1945, Dr. Karl Renner becoming President of the Republic.

iron ore, and mines some other minerals, but the only coal supply is a poor grade of lignite. There are extensive oilfields at Zistersdorf.

This small land, with its scanty natural gifts, must look abroad for much of its food, fuel, and raw materials for industry. In normal times the chief exports are machinery, furniture, textiles, artistic goods, and the like. Trade is chiefly with its neighbouring states, although commerce with more distant countries increased steadily after the First World War. British holiday makers made up a large share of the tourists who visited Austria in normal times for its mountain scenery and sports, its gay cities and music, its famous clinics and schools, and its magnificent art collections.

Austria adopted a new constitution in 1920, which gave more power to the people, setting up a federal government, with an assembly in each province, and a national parliament. The right of adults to vote and religious liberty were guaranteed. Economic troubles harassed the government from the start. Later the situation was complicated by the rise of a Nazi party which desired to effect a union between Austria and Nazi Germany. International rivalries added to the tension, for Mussolini in Italy did not want to see German control reach his borders. In 1932, Engelbert Dollfuss became Chancellor, with Catholic support and that of the Fascist party.

After having crushed the Socialists of Vienna in a bloody four-day fight (February 1934), Dollfuss proclaimed a new constitution, which abolished parliamentary government and made Austria a Fascist state. Dollfuss became virtual dictator. A few months later he was assassinated (July 1934) by Nazis. Dr. Kurt von Schuschnigg, who succeeded him as Chancellor, in 1936 obtained from the German government an agreement acknowledging Austria's independence. Nevertheless, the German

Austria has long been a centre of art and learning. Some famous musicians who have lived here are Beethoven, Mozart, Schubert, Johann Strauss, Haydn, Bruckner, Brahms, Mahler, Kreisler, and Hugo Wolf. Austrian opera stars who have delighted the world with their voices include

ZELL-AM-SEE IN AUSTRIA
One of the Austrian towns which in normal times is very popular with tourists is Zell-am-See. It is in the province of Salzburg, on the railway from Innsbruck to the city of Salzburg. The lake beyond the town is called the Zellersee.

Olsczewska, Jeritza, Schumann and Lehmann. Max Reinhardt and his school added much to the art of stage design. The Salzburg musical festival attracted visitors from all over the world every year.

Austria has shared with Germany in creating the literary masterpieces of the German tongue. Arthur Schnitzler and Jacob Wassermann went from Vienna to Germany. Hermann Bahr, Hugo von Hofmannsthal, Ernst Lothar, Franz Werfel and Karl Schoenherr are a few of Austria's literary notables.

Austria fosters learning in the state universities at Vienna, Graz and Innsbruck, in technical schools, and in medical schools and clinics which drew students from many lands. Medical science owes much to the work of Robert Barany, who won a Nobel Prize for his improvements in methods of diagnosis; Julius Wagner-Jauregg, another Nobel Prize-winner, who discovered the malarial treatment of paralysis; and Josef Breuer and Sigmund Freud, the founders of psycho-analysis. (*See* the following article, and also Tirol; Vienna).

Austria-Hungary.
In 1918, at the close of the First World War, the Dual Monarchy of Austria-Hungary finally broke up. Four hundred years of wars and intrigue and fortunate marriages produced the motley " crazy quilt," of a dozen or

Austrian State Travel Bureau

AUSTRIAN ALPS ABOVE FERLEITEN
In the Austrian district of Salzburg, nestling in the valley beneath the snow-clad peak of the Gross Glockner (12,470 feet), is the little village of Ferleiten. The lower slopes of the mountains in this region are covered with pine forests.

more nationalities, speaking over a dozen languages, which made up the Austro-Hungarian Empire.

This " Dual Monarchy " embraced an area of more than 260,000 square miles, with a total population in 1914, before the First World War, of some 51 millions, including such diverse peoples as the Germans, Magyars, Czechs, Poles, Ruthenians and Serbs. Its territory consisted of the empire of Austria (then including Bohemia) and the kingdom of Hungary, with its dependent province of Croatia-Slavonia. In addition, after 1908 it included the provinces of Bosnia and Herzegovina, annexed from Turkey. Four and a half years of reckless war tore the Empire to fragments and destroyed what had been one of the five Great Powers of Europe.

Do you wonder that Emperor Francis Joseph, who ruled this land from 1848 to 1916, had trouble in governing his people, when he had to publish in a number of different languages his call for a meeting of parliament? At one time Austria herself recognized this weakness and tried to make German the official language of the whole land, and, so far as possible, to Germanize the people; but the attempt was foredoomed to failure. In 1848 the Bohemians (Czechs) and the Magyars of Hungary almost won their independence, but the Magyars tried to Magyarize their Croat fellow-subjects, just as Austria had tried to Germanize them all, and as a result the South Slavs aided Austria in crushing the Magyar republic. Bohemia was compelled to submit by military force. In 1867 the Magyars were taken into partnership with the Austrians in what was called the Dual Monarchy of Austria-Hungary. This partially satisfied them, but left the Poles and the Ruthenians, Czechs and Croats, no better off.

When Austria-Hungary was defeated in the World War of 1914–18, the end came, and the old dominion of the Hapsburgs ceased to exist. Even the original nucleus, Austria, passed from the hands of this royal house, which had ruled the land since 1282, when Rudolph of Hapsburg obtained it. Hungary, deprived of Transylvania, became an independent state. Out of the remaining territory were resurrected the national states of Poland and Czechoslovakia (based on the

Dorien Leigh

STEYR IN UPPER AUSTRIA
An important centre in the province of Upper Austria, Steyr is divided into old (above) and new quarters. The principal industries, which are in the modern district, include iron and steel manufactures.

old Bohemia), while the Slav lands south of the Danube cast in their lot with Serbia to form the new state of Yugoslavia.

The real growth of the Hapsburg family began with Frederick III (1440-93), whose reign illustrates the saying that "while other states grew by wars, Austria grew by fortunate marriages." Under him Tirol was acquired, and a basis was laid for the future addition of Bohemia and Hungary. He inscribed on his buildings and possessions the five vowels " A E I O U " which were interpreted to mean *Austriae est imperare orbi universo*, that is, "The whole world is subject to Austria." Under the Emperor Charles V this boast came near to fulfilment, but his vast possessions were soon divided between a Spanish and an Austrian branch of the Hapsburgs.

When Queen Maria Theresa came to the Austrian throne in 1740, Frederick the Great of Prussia unscrupulously seized part of her territories. In the War of the Austrian Succession (1740-48) which followed, Prussia gained most of Silesia, but Austria retained the rest of her possessions. In the latter part of the same century Austria shared in the shameful partitions of Poland. In 1908 Bosnia and Herzegovina were added.

The government of Austria-Hungary from 1867 to 1918 was a Dual Monarchy consisting of the Austrian Empire and the Hungarian Kingdom. Each managed its own affairs, but they had the same ruler and ministries for common affairs.

"Autogiro." (Pron. aw'-tō-jī'-rō). Type of aircraft in which an overhead rotor takes the place of the wings. It was invented by Juan de la Cierva (1895-1936), a Spanish engineer, and shown at Farnborough, England in October 1925. The "Autogiro" has an airscrew at the nose, driven by engines in the usual manner; it has a fuselage with elevators, fin and rudder, but there the resemblance to an ordinary aircraft ends.

Standing up from the forward part of the fuselage is a mast bearing the rotor; this is really a " windmill," for although at the take-off it is turned by engine power to assist in a quick leaving of the ground, the rotor thereafter is free, and is caused to revolve only by the air stream as the "Autogiro" moves forward. The rotor acts as a sort of parachute when the aircraft is descending, slowing down the drop and enabling the machine almost to hover. When the engine is shut off in mid-air, the aircraft comes down in a steep glide, with the rotor revolving and acting somewhat as a brake.

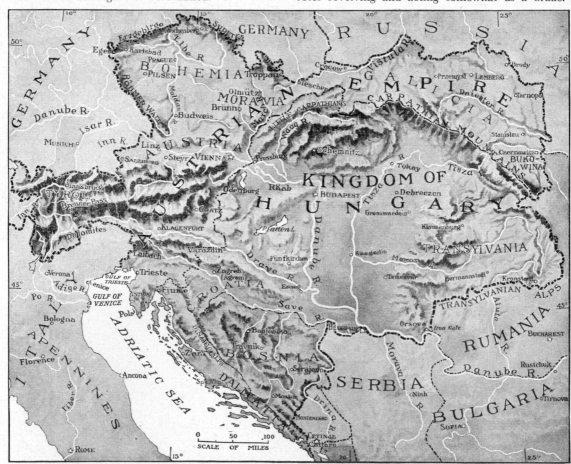

AUSTRIA-HUNGARY: THE EMPIRE THAT COLLAPSED IN 1918

If we had viewed Austria-Hungary from an aeroplane before the First World War (1914-18), we should have seen a land stretching from the lofty Alps of Switzerland on the west to the granite walls of the Carpathians on the east, and from the plains of Germany and Russia on the north to the mountainous peninsula of the Balkans on the south.

The rotor blades are hinged near the point at which they are attached to the "hub" that runs on the vertical member, or mast. As the rotor blades advance, they rise out of the horizontal, and drop back again as they pass the central fore-and-aft line of the fuselage—the action is something like a feathering one as seen in rowing. This same action gives a di-hedral effect (explained in our story of the Aeroplane), and makes for stability. Advantages of the "Autogiro" are its ability to take off almost vertically, and to land in a very small space.

Experimental work with this type of aircraft did much to enable other inventors to produce a successful helicopter—the dream of aviators for centuries. But the "Autogiro" is not a helicopter, since in the latter type of aircraft the horizontal airscrew or airscrews (there may be several) are turned by engine power, and pull the aircraft up into the air. On the other hand the "Autogiro" climbs for much the same reason that an aeroplane does, the rotors being shaped to give a similar effect to aeroplane wings. (See Aeroplane; Helicopter).

Wide World Photos

"AUTOGIRO": AN AIRCRAFT WITHOUT WINGS

In an "Autogiro" an overhead rotor takes the place of the wings used in aeroplanes. When the "Autogiro" takes off the rotor is turned by the engine, but thereafter the rotor is made to revolve by the airstream set up by the movement of the "Autogiro." The rotor acts as a sort of parachute as the aircraft descends, retarding the rate of descent.

Automatic Control. One of Man's earliest dreams, once he began to make machines, was to devise automatic controls which should make his own task easier. Thus we have the story of Humphrey Potter, who was the valve boy on the Newcomen steam engine at a colliery in Warwickshire. He had to open, one after the other, two valves which let in and let out steam. It is said that he attached cords from the valve handles to the rocking beam of the engine, above, which moved up and down like the plank of a see-saw; then the beam worked the valves.

Again, when Jacquard invented his automatic control for the loom, it did away with the task of a man or woman who had to watch the cloth pattern and to call out to another worker which threads of the warp to lift at any given time. The Jacquard mechanism selected the threads, and caused them to be lifted at the proper time.

Since those days automatic control has come to be applied for starting and stopping machines; counting the products of machines; for turning on and off shop and house lights; keeping oven temperature or room temperature at a pre-arranged level; signalling to railway or road vehicles when it is safe for them to proceed. Then we have the automatic machines for issuing tickets or selling such things as sweets or cigarettes; the machines in snack-bars and cafeterias which issue food and beverages when we insert the proper coin.

Until about 20 years ago all automatic controlling devices were *mechanical* ones, consisting of wheels

Wide World

and levers, cams, and so on. Then electricity began to be harnessed to these controlling appliances. The action of a ray of light in making some substance a conductor of electricity, or of varying the electrical resistance of the substance, has been much used. When the ray of light is interrupted by the passing of some object, the control comes into operation. It may be part of a burglar alarm; or it may be a special switch to turn on platform lights as a train comes into a "tube" station. This is an adaptation of *photo-electricity* (*q.v.*).

Some other devices depend on *piezo-electricity* (*q.v.*), which means, roughly, "pressure-electricity." When pressure on certain kinds of mineral crystal is varied, electrical variations are produced. Thus, in one type of microphone, used for broadcasting, the crystals of sodium-potassium tartrate (Rochelle salt) are utilised. If you look up the story of the Telephone, you will understand that the crystals here take the place of the carbon granules of the ordinary microphone.

The most important groups of automatic machines and control devices are described under the following titles in our volumes: Coin-Slot Machines; Electronic Devices; Photo-Electricity; Railways; Road Traffic Control; and Time Switches. Individual machines can be found by referring to the Fact-Index.

Avalanche. In mountainous regions, where great thicknesses of snow accumulate, huge masses of ice and snow sometimes slide down the mountain sides, destroying everything in their paths. These are called avalanches; smaller masses are called snowslides, and are more common.

The most frequent type of avalanche is that which occurs in spring when the snow begins to melt. Although these are dangerous, they are not so destructive to life as are the "wind" avalanches of the winter, because in the spring avalanches are expected and guarded against. In the winter, when the mountain sides are piled with loose dry snow, any slight disturbance, such as accompanies blasting, or even the wind, may start a great mass of snow towards the valley. In the summer "ice" avalanches sometimes occur. These are really parts of glaciers that have become loosened, and fall or slide down a steep slope.

Avalanches carry along trees, rocks, houses—everything that comes in their paths. Large forests planted on the mountain slopes may serve to break their force. Heavy walls are sometimes built as a protection.

AVALANCHE ON ITS WAY
No one who has not actually seen (and heard) an avalanche can imagine the destructive power of such a fall of ice or snow as is illustrated in this series of photographs taken in the Caucasus Mountains. It gives, however, a graphic enough impression of the visual effect of an avalanche rushing down from mountain top to valley bottom, where it may bury a village under thousands of tons of snow and rock.

Avebury. Everyone has heard of Stonehenge, and many have stood in awe beneath the mighty stones of England's oldest monument. Yet few in comparison go a farther 20 miles or so across Salisbury Plain, in Wiltshire, to another great relic of our ancient civilization, which, to quote John Aubrey, an antiquary who lived some 300 years ago, "doth as much surpass Stonehenge as a cathedral doth a parish church."

Aubrey wrote a description of Avebury in 1649, and it is evident that he found much that we unfortunately

W. F. Taylor

AVEBURY'S STONE CIRCLES

The picture above shows a reconstruction of the famous stone circles at Avebury, Wilts, as they probably were in prehistoric times. The photograph on the left shows two of the largest surviving stones, known as Adam and Eve, as they are today ; the cottages seen in the background enable the size of the stones to be gauged.

cannot see today. There is still a great rampart and fosse or ditch, forming a circle 1,400 feet in diameter, enclosing an area of nearly 30 acres, but dozens of the great stones which in Aubrey's day stood around the space in two circles have disappeared. It appears that a certain Farmer Green carted many away for his own use as building and road material! Even so, sufficient remain to indicate what a magnificent open-air temple Avebury must have been in its prime. Some of the stones that survive measure 20 feet above the ground and up to 12 feet in thickness. In the neighbourhood may be traced stone avenues leading to other circles on the Plain. Avebury, the biggest monument of its kind in the world, was probably erected by people of the New Stone Age nearly 4,000 years ago.

Avebury, John Lubbock, 1st Baron (1834–1912). Scientists are often regarded as men belonging to a race apart, who spend all their days in

their studies or laboratories, far removed from the hurly-burly of ordinary life. Yet it is a fact that some of the best work in science has been done by men who were not professionals but could devote only their leisure hours to their scientific pursuits. One of the most famous of these scientists was Sir John Lubbock, who in recognition of his services was raised to the peerage by Queen Victoria.

After three years at Eton, John Lubbock entered his father's bank and at 22 became a partner. He was keenly interested in business, and was also an M.P. for 30 years. During his period in the House of Commons he managed to get a bill passed providing for the setting aside of certains days as bank holidays; in England these are Easter Monday, Whit Monday, the first Monday in August and Boxing Day. He also did much to reduce the hours worked by shop assistants, and laboured long and hard to establish public libraries and protect and preserve ancient monuments. When he was made a peer he chose for his title the name of one of the grandest of these. (*See* above).

He was a keen naturalist and wrote books which may still be read with pleasure and profit, *e.g.*, British Wild Flowers (1875) and Ants, Bees and Wasps (1882). His most famous book—Prehistoric Times, published in 1865—tells of romantic discoveries of archaeology. He it was who suggested the names Palaeolithic (Old Stone) and Neolithic (New Stone), for the two great periods into which human life before written history began is divided. He loved Nature and his fellowmen, and nothing would have

Elliott & Fry

FIRST LORD AVEBURY

Lord Avebury, banker and naturalist, whose books on ant and bee life made important contributions to the study of entomology, must also be credited with the introduction of bank holidays.

AYR : THE STORIED 'AULD BRIG' OF AYR

D. McLeish

Robert Burns wrote a poem in which the 500-year-old 'Auld Brig' over the Ayr river (in the foreground above) is made to prophesy that 'I'll be a brig when ye're a shapeless cairn,' referring to its new rival, then just built. This prophecy came true, for the bridge seen behind is a modern reconstruction of the New Brig, which soon came to grief.

"Its soft tints of buff, sulphur and primrose; its dazzling shades of apricot, salmon, orange and vermilion, are always a fresh revelation of colour. They have no parallel among flowers, and exist only in opals, sunset skies, and the flush of autumn woods."

Azores. (Pron. *a*-zōrz'.) Midway between Europe and North America lie the nine islands called the Azores. Flores, the island farthest west, is some 1,300 miles from Cape Race, Newfoundland. St. Michael's Island is about 830 miles from the coast of Portugal, mother country of the Azores. The half-way station thus provided was used by the flying boat which made the first air trip across the Atlantic in May 1919 and bases are maintained by British and United States Transatlantic air services. During the Second World War Great Britain established naval and air bases there by agreement with the Portuguese.

These picturesque islands are of volcanic origin and suffer from earthquakes and eruptions. In 1522 the town of Villa Franca was buried with approximately 6,000 of its inhabitants.

Although the Azores were not located definitely by modern Europeans until the 15th century, ancient coins were found indicating visits by the Carthaginians. In the year 1431 Portuguese navigators claimed the islands for Portugal.

The Azores have a fairly heavy rainfall and, owing to this, and to the fertile soil and mild climate, vegetation is luxuriant and pasturage

pleased him more than the knowledge that the bank holidays which he did so much to secure enable people to see Nature's marvels for themselves.

Ayrshire. The Firth of Clyde washes the entire western boundary of this busy Scottish county, whose neighbours towards the east are Renfrewshire, Lanarkshire, Dumfriesshire and Kirkcudbrightshire, with Wigtownshire on the south. It is called "the Dairy of Scotland," for it affords excellent pasturage for grazing the world-famous Ayrshire dairy cattle, and its dairy products are known far and wide. There are many coal mines, and iron ore is obtained and smelted. Extensive woollen and cotton manufactures are carried on, sandstone and limestone are worked, and many thousands of earthenware articles are made.

Ayr, whose estimated population in 1940 was 41,600, situated on the river of that name, is the county town, and is loved by all literary folk as possessing the "twa brigs" (two bridges) referred to by Robert Burns, who was born at Alloway, an Ayrshire village. A portion of the old tower of St. John's church, in which Robert Bruce, King of Scotland, held his parliament in 1315, is another treasured relic of the long ago. Other important towns are Kilmarnock, Saltcoats, Ardrossan, Girvan, Irvine and Troon. Population of Ayrshire is about 299,000; area, 1,130 square miles.

Azalea. (Pron. *a*-zā'-lē-*a*). Numbered among our loveliest plants, greenhouse and garden azaleas belong to the family Ericaceae and are grouped botanically with the genus rhododendron (*q.v.*), which is widely distributed through Europe, Asia and North America, the larger number being found in the Himalayas and western China. From the rhododendron they differ in not being evergreen— they have deciduous leaves. Azaleas vary in height up to about seven feet. There are many different species and varieties, and with them plant breeders have had some wonderful results—as witness the hardy Ghent varieties. This latter class of azalea has been described in the following glowing terms:

Blanche Henrey

AZALEA IN BLOSSOM

The fragrant blossoms of this lovely shrub beautify many a British garden in the summer ; and in greenhouses the less hardy kinds of azalea flourish. There are numerous species and varieties, many from the Himalayas and China.

excellent. Large herds of cattle are kept, chiefly for dairy produce. Pineapples, oranges and other fruits, and tea, coffee and wine are produced.

The area of the nine islands is about 922 square miles and the highest point is Pico Mountain (7,612 feet) on the island of Pico. The chief towns of the Azores are Ponta Delgada, on St. Michael's Island, with a population of about 18,000, Angra do Heroismo on Terceira Island, the capital of the group (11,000), and Horta (7,000), the capital of Fayal. The total population of the islands is about 484,000.

Azov, SEA OF. Though it is commonly called a sea, the Sea of Azov is really a large gulf. Situated in southern Russia, it is an almost land-locked inlet of the Black Sea, with which it is connected by the Strait of Kerch or Yenikale. It has an area of about 14,520 square miles, a greatest length from the isthmus of Perekop to the mouth of the Don of 220 miles and an extreme width of 110 miles. Its greatest depth is 50 feet, and at some places it is only 10 feet. Small vessels use the sea, but navigation is rendered difficult by the variable currents which are set up by frequent storms. From December to March the sea is frozen.

The Don is the largest river flowing into it, and the comparatively fresh waters of the sea abound in fish, the drying of which is an important local industry. Occasional earthquakes have occurred in this area, and in 1799 an island completely

American Museum of Natural History
GORGEOUS AZTEC COSTUME
Native Aztec artists produced good representations of the life and dress of their civilization but their work is imperfectly preserved. This drawing by Keith Henderson of part of a procession, showing the rich costume of all classes of Aztecs, was based on their work and actual Aztec remains.

disappeared. There are a number of big towns on its shores, including Berdyansk, Mariupol, Rostov-on-Don, Taganrog and Yenikale.

Much heavy fighting took place between Germans and Russians on the shores of the Sea of Azov during the Second World War (1939–45). In October 1941 a German army struck east towards Rostov, while another invaded the Crimea. The Russians were compelled to retire and on November 22 the Germans announced the capture of Rostov, from which they were driven out by the Russians a week later. The city (which had to be evacuated by the Russians in July 1942) was recaptured by them in February 1943. By December 1943 the Germans had been finally swept out of the area.

The town of Azov lies on the River Don about 10 miles from its entrance into the Sea of Azov. Fishing is the chief industry, but the importance of the town has declined with the silting up of its harbour. Captured from the Turks by the Russians in 1696, it was restored to the Turks in 1711, finally becoming Russian in 1739. The population is about 17,000.

Aztecs. When bold Cortes with his band of Spaniards in 1519 reached the valley where Mexico City lies, they found in the midst of a lake an island city of high towers, temples and palaces, and across the causeways which connected it with the shore streamed busy throngs of brown-skinned people.

This was the city of Tenochtitlan (tā-noch-tēt-lahn'), where lived the great Montezuma, king of the Aztecs and emperor of the Nahua nations, whose rule extended over most of southern Mexico as far south as the isthmus of Tehuantepec. The civilization there was as far superior to that of the buffalo-hunting Indians of the North American plains and forests as was the civilization of Rome

AZTEC IDEAS OF THE BEAUTIFUL
These two illustrations show how the Aztecs adorned themselves. Top, a warrior of proven valour is having his nose ringed. Below, an Aztec man and woman; the former has his face elaborately painted, whereas the woman has refrained from such ornament.

to that of the hordes of invading barbarians from the lands of northern Europe.

Indeed, the Aztec state resembled the ancient Roman Empire in many ways. Tenochtitlan was the centre of a powerful trade system, with roads stretching to distant provinces. Commerce was protected by a large standing army commanded by the *caciques* or provincial governors, whose duty was also to collect the tribute levied on conquered tribes. The wealth which poured into the capital was used in great part to beautify the city, to spread culture and education, and to encourage poetry and painting.

Montezuma, who lived in great splendour, surrounded by his nobles and served by thousands of slaves, maintained beautiful gardens and menageries filled with rare flowers and animals.   On the lake and in the canals which cut through the city were strange "floating islands" made of earth supported on a network of branches and water grass. Here were grown herbs and spices used by the Aztec cooks and doctors. Among the Aztecs were expert stone cutters and jewellers, skilled potters, carpenters, architects and weavers. These last manufactured cotton garments, adorned with spun gold, furs and bright feathers.

A strict and wise system of laws and courts protected the citizens and even the slaves from injustice. Young men who became intoxicated or who squandered their fathers' money were put to death.

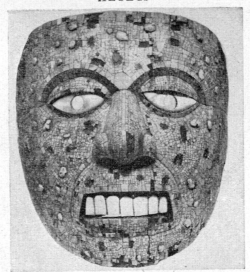

MASK OF AN AZTEC GOD
The Aztecs produced wonderful mosaics with shells, jet and ores set in resin on a wooden foundation. Above is a mask of Quetzalcoatl, the god of arts and crafts, constructed in this fashion.

AZTEC GODDESS
The Aztecs had a deity for every branch of life, each represented by an effigy. This one, now in the British Museum, London, shows Chalchihuitlicue, who was the goddess of running water.

From the very cradle children were taught courtesy and self-control. The speech used by the Aztec father when sending his son out into the world contains some admirable advice. "Revere and salute thy elders," he would say, "and never show them any sign of contempt. Console the poor and unfortunate with kind words. Do not talk too much and never interrupt others. Eat not too fast and show no dislike if a dish displeases thee. When thou walkest, look whither thou goest so thou mayst knock against no one. Live by thy work, for thou shalt be the happier thereby. Never lie. When thou tellest anyone what has been told thee, tell the simple truth and add nothing thereto. Be silent in regard to the faults thou seest in others."

Aztec women shared in most of the occupations of the men. They were taught to sing and dance, and some even learned reading and writing and the principles of astronomy and astrology. And the astronomy of the Aztecs was by no means a crude science. They recognized many of the signs of the zodiac as measures of time, and several of their calendar names bore a striking similarity to those employed by the Chinese. Their calendar system, which dated from the 7th century, seems to have been borrowed from the Toltecs (a cultured race who preceded the Aztecs), who, in turn, had borrowed it from the Mayas, who built great stone cities in northern Guatemala as early as A.D. 50.

Yet over all this learning and love of beauty and courtesy brooded the shadow of one of the most barbarous and horrible religions the world has ever known. Each year the Aztec priests sacrificed to their numerous gods many human victims. And the flesh of these victims was eaten by the nobles and the people at cannibal banquets. Thus, the principal aim of the Aztec soldier in battle was not to kill his enemy but to take him prisoner, for every prisoner was destined for the sacrifice. On the appointed day the beat of war drums sounded from the top of the tower temple. One by one the prisoners were led up the winding stairs round the outside of the temple and were put to death on the altar.

The Aztecs refused to abandon this horrible practice, which they claimed had won the favour of their gods and brought them power and greatness. Cortes overthrew their empire, and the paintings and inscriptions telling of the early history of Mexico were destroyed.

The Aztecs came originally from some country far to the north. It has been suggested that they may have been related to some of the races whose descendants now live in Arizona and New Mexico. This is partially confirmed by the fact that the Aztecs, the Piman tribes of Arizona and Sonora, and the Shoshonean family farther north in the United States are related in language. The Aztecs founded the city of Tenochtitlan about 1325, on the spot occupied earlier by the lost civilization of the Toltecs. With other Nahua tribes, which is the name given to the whole group of invaders from the north, the Aztecs formed a confederacy, but they soon subjected the other tribes to a tyrannical rule. It was with the help of rebel divisions of the Aztec empire that the Spaniards were able to overthrow the Aztec power. Indians living in Mexico City today are largely descendants of the ancient Aztecs.

WHERE AZTECS SACRIFICED TO THEIR GODS

CRUMBLE

THOUGH
wondro
mythical Asia
known for cer
to please his
Nebuchadrez
which the Ga
was enclosed
the circuit of
As picture
with earth s
flowers, and
the summit.
Yet of th
below rema
and other at

We usually associate pyramids with Egypt rather than America, yet there are many more in Central America than in Africa. The difference lies in their function—for the Egyptian pyramids were built as tombs, while the American were erected as altars. Some of the pyramids where the Aztecs worshipped are shown in this page; they are in San Juan Teotihuacan, Mexico, and were actually built by the Toltecs, a race conquered by the Aztecs, but served the same purpose under Aztec rule. On the right are the steep steps up the pyramid altar of Quetzalcoatl, the Aztec god of arts and sciences; beneath you see smaller pyramids flanking the great central Pyramid of the Sun, which appears on the left in this photo, and is seen in a closer view at the bottom of the page. This is a thousand years old, at least.

E.N.A.

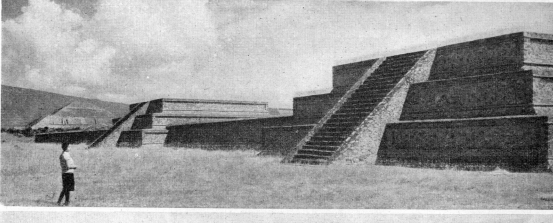

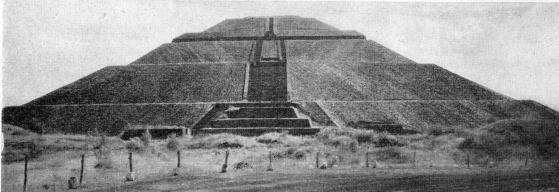

Babylon. To the a
have been very much wh
New York are to the pe
capital of the land of Baby
heart of the country we n
bank of the River Euphra
the modern town of Hilla
of modern Baghdad. T
is doubtful, but it was
of cities, for we find it
getting on for 6,000 ye
But during the first th
history it was little more
but a small part in the

Babylon began to g
some time after 3000
changed its course, des
flow past Babylon. The
point where the two
and the Tigris, were s
strip of land. From tha
creasingly great, and a
Hammurabi, it became

The next two thousa
years saw the rise and
of Babylon. Attacked a
conquered by a success
of the kings of Assyria
689 B.C. its walls, its t
ples, and its palaces
razed to the ground
Sennacherib as a pur
ment for a revolt ag:
Assyrian rule. Rebui
King Esar-haddon,
son's rule it was agair
and conquered.

King Nabopolassa
son, the famous Neb
zar, more than res
wasted glories of the
during their reigns
knew its most spler
The city revealed
cavations of modern
gists is that which
drezzar built.

At the height o
Babylon was one
magnificent cities o
It was built in the
square, enclosed
walls of great heigh
ness, defended b
towers, and surro
moat. Its palaces
gurats (temples) w
pyramid form, an
walls shone with
and tiles picturing
Babylon's history
Their sides we
either in steps o
spiral terrace win

classes in the community—a ruling class of nobles and officials, a middle class, and slaves. Much attention is given to commerce, money and banking, as well as to agriculture and the canals and ditches for irrigating the soil. Justice was insisted on for the widow, the orphan and the poor, but punishments were usually based on the principle of "an eye for an eye and a tooth for a tooth." For example, if a house fell through the crumbling of its sunbaked bricks and killed the son of the householder, the builder must also suffer the loss of *his* son. The position of women in these laws was a high one, and they frequently engaged in business.

After Hammurabi's death his kingdom went to pieces. The wild tribes again descended from the eastern mountains to the plains, this time bringing with them a strange animal which the Babylonians called "the ass of the East," but which we call the horse. The newcomers failed to benefit from the civilization of Babylonia; instead, their cruder ways became the ways of the plains. Even the old Sumerian language was forgotten and a Semitic language, related to Hebrew, took its place.

which links Mesopotamia with Egypt. Syria especially was rich in bustling cities, carrying on extensive commerce with all of the known world and spreading its system of writing far and wide. For a time these cities checked the advance of the Assyrians, and it was not until the middle of the 8th century Before Christ that Damascus, the most powerful city of Syria, fell. The conquest of the others soon followed.

Assyria not only conquered Syria and Palestine, but her rule for a time extended even into Egypt. One thing especially contributed to this military success—the organization of their whole state was based on war and conquest. One Assyrian king, Sargon II (722–705 B.C.), destroyed the northern kingdom of the Hebrews (called Israel) and took captive part of its people.

Sargon's son Sennacherib (705–681 B.C.) destroyed the ancient city of Babylon, and even turned the waters of the canal over its ruins. Sargon II had built for himself a palace far surpassing anything yet constructed. But this was not enough for Sennacherib, and he built the proud city of Nineveh, on the upper course of the Tigris.

Within the palace halls were long stretches of pictures of the emperor's conquests, cut in alabaster slabs. The men in these reliefs all looked alike, except that the king was distinguished by his curled hair and beard; and they were all devoid of expression. But the animals on slabs picturing lion hunts and the like were very natural, and on the whole the art was far in advance of the art of the Babylonians. Literature advanced with art, and there is now in the British Museum in London a great collection of clay tablets which were dis-

But in the northern part of the Tigris-Euphrates valley there had arisen a new nation, called Assyria from its chief town, Assur. At first Assur was a small city-state, usually under the control of its powerful Babylonian neighbours, from whom its people borrowed the calendar, writing, sculpture, and other improvements of civilization. By continual strife with their more advanced southern neighbours and with the wild tribes to the north, the Assyrians gained skill in warfare until they aspired to rule not only the valley of the two rivers but wider stretches to the west.

Before Assyria had reached this goal, however, there had arisen new rivals to its power. These were the little kingdoms of Palestine and Syria, situated in "the fertile crescent"

ISHTAR GATE OF BABYLON- AS IT WAS—AND IS
The ruins (top) of the Ishtar Gate of Nebuchadrezzar's fortress-palace give us very little idea of what it was really like. But by careful study of these remains archaeologists have been able to find out almost every detail of the original building, and the reconstruction (lower) shows the gateway as it was in all probability when the mighty walls of Babylon were still standing.

British Museum; Mansell

BABYLONIAN SCULPTORS' SPLENDID CARVINGS

Realism and a great sense of decorative design are combined in these bas-reliefs (i.e. carvings in which the figures stand out only very slightly above the surface of the stone ; ' bas ' is French for low) from ancient Babylon. Top left is a herd of gazelles, forming part of a hunting scene in Ashurbanipal's palace. Top right, wild asses are being captured for domestication. Lower left, a scene from camp life with the Babylonian army ; an officer has returned to his quarters, where one servant brings him water and another makes up his bed. Two camels are tethered outside. On the right, lower, are Assyrian hunting dogs—powerfully-built animals, somewhat like mastiffs.

covered in the ruins of the ancient palace of Nineveh, comprising religious, scientific and literary works.

In the gardens of the palace were all manner of strange trees, including " cotton trees that bore wool which was clipped and corded for garments." These " cotton trees " are thought to be a tall species of the cotton plant which grows today.

Interest in literature, art and industry, however, was only incidental. The Assyrian empire was still essentially military, and as conquest succeeded conquest it became more so, for a large army was needed to keep the conquered peoples in subjection. These subject peoples constantly grew more restive, for not only were they governed and taxed by the emperor at Nineveh, but they were also forced to help him fight his battles.

The end of the Assyrian Empire came in about 612 B.C. A desert tribe called Chaldeans had been creeping in from the south and had overrun

British Museum

ASSYRIAN MEDICINE BOOK

This clay tablet gives a list of plants—among them the cucumber—from which various drugs can be obtained. It is written in two languages, Sumerian and Assyrian, and was originally in the library of King Ashurbanipal.

Babylonia. Then they joined with the Medes, a tribe from the mountains to the east, and assailed Nineveh, the mighty city of Assyrian kings. The rejoicing of the world at the fall of Nineveh was expressed by the Hebrew prophet Nahum, who said: " All that hear the news of thy fate shall clap their hands over thee; for whom has not thy wickedness afflicted continually? "

The new masters of the Tigris-Euphrates valley rebuilt the old city of Babylon and made it their capital. Here for over 40 years (604–561 B.C.) ruled Nebuchadrezzar, greatest of the Chaldean emperors. He enlarged the city and built enormous walls about it to protect it from its enemies. His palace surpassed in beauty that of any former ruler, and to please his wife he constructed the wonderful Hanging Gardens of Babylon, which the Greeks counted one of the Seven Wonders of the World. This is the

ONE OF BABYLON'S GATES
These brick walls of the Ishtar Gate of Babylon, which formed part of Nebuchadrezzar's fortress-palace, were at one time enamelled, the animals in bas-relief being coloured to stand out against a blue background.

Babylon described in the Bible as the city of the Hebrew captivity, for after one of the Hebrews' many revolts Nebuchadrezzar had destroyed Jerusalem and carried away the people into captivity.

Under the Chaldean or second Babylonian Empire commerce and industry flourished and the arts were developed. Special progress was made in the science of astronomy, for the Chaldeans mapped out the sky into the 12 signs of the zodiac, and knew of the existence of the five planets we call Jupiter, Mars, Venus, Mercury and Saturn.

But the days of the Chaldean Empire were numbered, as Daniel told Belshazzar in the interpretation of his dream of the writing on the wall, and soon its lands were divided between the Medes and the Persians (538 B.C.).

This was the end of the great civilization of the Tigris-Euphrates valley, whose chequered course stretched far back down the corridors of time. It is strange to think that we are nearer today by 1,000 years to the fall of the Chaldean Empire than were the Medes and Persians of that day to the faint far-off dawn of Babylonian civilization, over 3,000 years before, on the river plain of Shinar. From 538 B.C. the country, which came to be called Mesopotamia, was subject to foreign rule—Persians, Greeks, Romans, Arabs or Turks. The Arabs took Mesopotamia from the Persians in A.D. 636 and held it for 400 years. In the 11th century the Turks overran the land, but did not settle there permanently. It suffered several invasions by Mongol armies before the Turks assumed possession in 1516. The latest chapter in its long history began when, at the end of the First World War (1914–1918), the country was made into an independent Arab kingdom under King Feisal, who had gallantly fought side by side with Lawrence of Arabia against the Turks. Now known by its Arabic name of Iraq, it is of importance for the quantities of petroleum which are obtained from its rich oilfields.

ADAM and NOAH in BABYLONIAN STORY

Just as the children of today learn about the Garden of Eden and the Flood, so long ages ago the Babylonian boys and girls listened to tales and legends that are not so very different from the Bible stories.

MORE than two thousand years before the time of Christ the ancient Babylonians had many quaint myths to explain the mysteries of life and death and Man's history on earth.

One of these Babylonian stories tells of the wonderful adventures of a shepherd named Etana who was the first of mankind to attempt to fly. It happened once that his flocks were stricken with unfruitfulness, so that no more lambs were born. But he learned of a herb in heaven which was the source of life; and to obtain this he induced a great eagle to carry him on its back to the highest heaven.

The flight began successfully, and then the eagle, bearing its shepherd passenger, mounted to yet dizzier heights. Its strength, however, now began to fail, and Etana and the eagle were hurled to earth by the jealous gods, and perished.

The mystery of death is dealt with in the story of the fisherman Adapa, who was one of the first men created. While he was busy at his trade one day, the South-wind goddess overturned his boat, and Adapa in a rage seized and broke the goddess's wing. For this he was summoned before the throne of the Sky-god. When Adapa told of the mischief the South-wind had done him, the Sky-god excused

him and even offered to him the heavenly bread and water of life. This would have made him immortal and destroyed death. But Adapa was suspicious and refused to eat or drink while in heaven, fearing that it was the bread of death and not of life. He thus lost both for himself and for mankind the precious gift of immortal life. Some scholars see in this Babylonian reference to the " bread of life " a resemblance to the Biblical " tree of life " planted in the Garden of Eden.

Several Babylonian and Assyrian records tell of a great flood which once covered all that land, and how a man named Uta-Napishtim and his family were saved by the favour of the gods.

The deluge is represented as sent upon the earth as a punishment for the sins of men. Uta-Napishtim, the Babylonian Noah, was warned in advance by the god Ea, who gave directions for the building of a great ship with strong roof or deck, in which " the beasts of the field and the birds of heaven " might be saved with the hero and his family. Then came a storm which drove the waters of the deep over the land. After seven days the floods began to subside. Uta-Napishtim sent out from his ship in succession a dove, a swallow and a raven.

When the raven came back with signs of mud on its feet, he knew that the land was beginning to appear. The ship is represented as coming to rest on the highest peak of eastern Kurdistan, instead of upon Ararat, as in the Bible account. Uta-Napishtim is then made immortal by the gods.

In its best-known form this Babylonian account is part of a long poem covering 12 tablets, found in the ruins of Ashurbanipal's palace at Nineveh. It is called the Epic of Gilgamesh. Uta-Napishtim tells the deluge story when the hero Gilgamesh visits him in a wonderful land across " the waters of death," as an explanation of his perpetual youth.

Bach, JOHANN SEBASTIAN (1685–1750). By the light of the midnight moon a little boy sat copying from a great manuscript music-book spread

BACH AT THE ORGAN
This contemporary picture shows Bach at the manuals of an organ, an instrument for which some of his finest works were composed. The great musician spent the last 27 years of his life and composed all his finest works as organist and choirmaster at the Thomasschule, Leipzig.

before him. He strained his young eyes to see the notes, and stopped at times to stretch and rub his cramped fingers; but he made no sound. The moonlight passed, and with a sigh the book was noiselessly returned to its shelf. The copy was then carefully hidden and the boy crept to bed.

This 12-year-old boy was Johann Sebastian Bach (pron. bahkh), an orphan. His brother, who was his guardian and music-master, had refused him the use of the book, telling him that its music was too difficult for one so young. But with a great music-love that would not be denied, the boy spent night after night secretly copying the coveted scores—working harm to his sight that resulted in blindness during his last years.

The life of this German musician was filled with incidents that show just such devotion to his art. When he was a choirboy he spent all his leisure hours at the organ or clavier. When he was able to fill the position of organist, he saved and skimped, and travelled many miles on foot to hear and to study with the greatest organists of the day. In later years, although his duties as choirmaster in Leipzig made demands that might have kept two musicians busy, Bach found time to compose choral, organ and piano pieces that were to become " the most universal force in the development of music." To his last days, even when, totally blind, he dictated the choral, " Herewith I Come Before Thy Throne," the passion for music governed his life. The " Well-tempered Clavier " (clavichord) was written primarily for the instruction of his sons, and some of his finest cantatas were composed for his wife and daughter to sing.

In the musical life of Germany the name of Bach is famous, for the family furnished many notable musicians. Johann Sebastian Bach was recognized both as the greatest of all this musical line and as one of the greatest organists and clavier players of the day. He had 20 children, and of these may be mentioned Karl Philipp Emanuel Bach (1714–1788), and Johann Christian Bach (1735–82), sometimes called the English Bach because he became a music master in England.

Bach perfected the tuning of the clavichord, a stringed, keyboard instrument which was the forerunner of the piano, so that its notes could be in tune to music played in any key. It was also Bach who first taught musicians to use all five fingers in playing keyed instruments. Among his greatest works are his Mass in B minor and his setting of the Passion according to St. Matthew. In Eisenach the house in which Bach was born was made into a Bach Museum.

Bacon, FRANCIS (1561–1626). One of the greatest figures in the wonderful Elizabethan Age of England was Francis Bacon, who was made a peer under the titles Baron Verulam and Viscount St. Albans. Though a great philosopher, statesman and jurist (one versed in the law), Bacon fell short of being a great man. He showed at times some of the baser characteristics of human nature, including ingratitude (so it was charged) to his patron, the Earl of Essex ; the poet Pope styled him

FRANCIS BACON
The old house at Gorhambury, Hertfordshire, once Bacon's home, is now a ruin, but in the existing house there is this beautiful bust, believed to represent Bacon at the age of eight.

" the wisest, brightest, meanest of mankind."

By birth Bacon had many advantages. His father was Lord Keeper of the Great Seal of England, and so his boyhood was spent at Elizabeth's court. At 12 he entered Trinity College, Cambridge, but he remained there only three years, because he thought " the whole plan of education was radically wrong." He was next sent to France with the English ambassador, that he might learn "the arts of state."

His father's death for a time ended all hope of advancement at Court. Cut off from the honours which he had hoped to gain, Bacon turned his attention to law. He was admitted to the bar in 1582, and his success was immediate, for he was a convincing speaker and a sound lawyer. The poet Ben Jonson declared that "the fear of every man that heard him was lest he should make an end." Through the friendship of the Earl of Essex, Bacon won advancement at the Court. In spite of writing that "there is no vice that doth so cover a man with shame as to be found false and perfidious," he later repaid the earl's kindness by helping to convict him of high treason.

Knighted by James I, Bacon rose rapidly to the positions of Attorney-General, Privy Councillor and Lord Chancellor. He was one of the profoundest statesmen of that age, but the good advice which he gave King James I was usually disregarded. In his essays Bacon gives this advice : "Seek not proud riches, but such as thou mayest get justly, use soberly, distribute cheerfully, and leave contentedly." But he himself was charged with receiving bribes in his court, was sentenced to imprisonment and to pay an enormous fine, and was prohibited from afterwards holding a public office. Bacon confessed that his punishment "was just and for reformation's sake," because the old practices which he had followed were bad.

He was soon released from prison (after about four days) and excused from paying the fine, but his exclusion from office continued in force. Cut off from his cherished career, he turned all his attention to literary and scientific pursuits. He urged that in science men should reach their conclusions only by experiment, and so is reckoned one of the founders of the modern "inductive" or scientific method of inquiry—the method which proceeds from the discovery of a number of facts to the framing of a theory to explain the facts, whereas in the *deductive* method one starts with a theory and then sees if it "holds water" by testing it against the facts.

Bacon's essays are full of shrewd, pithy, pungent observations, such as these: "He that hath wife and children hath given hostages to fortune"; and "Reading maketh a full man, conference a ready man, and writing an exact man." His life was finally sacrificed to his search for truth. On a

LORD CHANCELLOR BACON
This contemporary portrait of Francis Bacon shows him at the height of his fame, when he was Lord Chancellor (1618), a powerful statesman and a distinguished scientist.

journey by coach in winter, he stopped the driver, jumped out, and proceeded to stuff a chicken with snow, in order to test whether cold would preserve meat; in doing this he took a chill which proved fatal. "For my name and memory," Bacon said in his will, "I leave it to men's charitable speeches, and to foreign nations, and to the next ages." His trust was not misplaced, for all writers and scientists now pay tribute to his genius.

In the 19th century several writers sought to prove, on the strength of alleged "cipher" messages in Shakespeare's works, that Bacon wrote those immortal plays; but most students were not convinced. Bacon's principal writings comprise : Essays (1597); the Advancement of Learning (1605) ; Novum Organum (1620) ; New Atlantis (1626).

Bacon, Roger (1214?–1294?). A great stride forward in scientific methods was made by Roger Bacon, more than 350 years before Francis Bacon wrote his Novum Organum, in emphasizing the need of observation and experiment as the true basis of science.

After studying at the universities of Oxford and Paris, Roger Bacon became a Franciscan friar and taught at Oxford. He was able to read both Greek and Arabic books in their original tongues. He believed that knowledge could be more certainly and rapidly advanced by experimenting with real things than by poring over the books of Aristotle. He knew something of gunpowder and the magnifying glass and had an idea that by using lenses one might construct a telescope. He believed that the earth was round and that it was possible to reach Asia by sailing westward into the Atlantic.

In one of his numerous writings he suggested the possibility of some modern inventions: "Ships will go without rowers and with only a single man to guide them. Carriages without horses will travel with incredible speed. Machines for flying can be made in which a man sits and skilfully devised wings strike the air in the manner of a bird. Machines will raise infinitely great weights, and ingenious bridges will span rivers without supports."

Is it surprising that to the Middle Ages Bacon's knowledge seemed the result of magic ? Again and again he was ordered by his superiors to cease from his writing and teaching. But in Pope Clement IV he found a friend who commanded him to set forth his views. So Bacon produced in 18 months three great books (Opus Majus, Opus Minus and Opus Tertium), which he sent to the

Pope. The Opus Majus, which has been called the Encyclopaedia of the 13th century, discusses the obstacles in the way of true science and outlines the essentials of the main branches of true knowledge, referring to the chief features of the great sciences, grammar and logic, mathematics, experimental research and philosophy. The Opus Minus contains a brief review of the contents of the Opus Majus. The Opus Tertium includes detailed studies of grammar and logic, mathematics, physics, metaphysics and moral philosophy. After Clement's death in 1278 Bacon again fell into difficulties as a result of his attacks on the scholars and learning of his day, and by order of the head of the Franciscan order he was imprisoned. Bacon remained in captivity for 14 years, and during that time he wrote, among other works, a book on warding off the infirmities of old age. He sent his work to the Pope, Nicholas IV, who ordered his release. In 1292 Bacon was again working at Oxford, but he was already an old man and he died within a short time, probably in the year 1294.

Because he was so far in advance of his time, it is only in our own day that Roger Bacon's true greatness, as one of the world's most original thinkers, has been recognized.

Bacteria. These are minute organisms which play a tremendous part in the whole life of our Earth; because of their influence the science of bacteriology has important applications in the fields of medicine, veterinary medicine, agriculture and industry.

The science of bacteriology is still, relatively, in its infancy, because it is less than a century since the researches of Pasteur, Koch, Cohn, and their associates established the existence of bacteria as living things, and drew human attention to bacteria as causal agents of disease in Man, animals and plants. Bacteria were first observed by Anthony van Leeuwenhoek (1632–1723), a Dutchman of simple birth and little learning, some 250 years ago. As a hobby he kept grinding

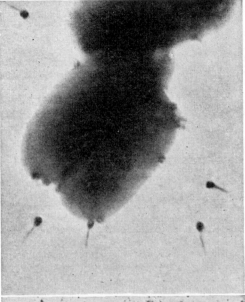

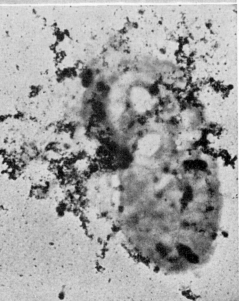

Radio Corp. of America

BACTERIA ATTACKED

In the upper picture the cloud-like mass consists of two intestinal bacteria (Bacillus coli). The objects resembling small tadpoles, which are converging on the bacteria, are particles of a virus called bacteriophage. The lower picture shows the wreck of one bacterium 30 minutes after the attack began. This 'battle' is enlarged 30,000 times by the electron microscope, the first instrument powerful enough to make these tiny virus particles visible.

lenses, mounting them as a primitive microscope, and peering at this fragment of matter and at that. One day he found a drop of rain water teeming with small organisms of different shapes and sizes, in a state of great activity. How much work has been done on these creatures since then!

The systematic study of bacteria had to wait until Robert Koch, in about the year 1878, found a way of making them easily visible by staining them with various dyes, and demonstrated that some of them could be made to grow and multiply on artificial foodstuffs in the laboratory; although, before his discoveries, the work of Pasteur, Davaine, Klebs, and others had succeeded in establishing the association of bacteria with certain diseases in Man and in animals.

We know that bacteria are abundant in all parts of our planet, except in the Polar regions and in the central areas of large desert regions. They abound in the soil, they populate water both fresh and salt, they are carried high into the atmosphere by wind and other agencies; and they are constantly present on the outside and also inside of men, animals and plants. Wherever they are found, they have these features in common: simplicity of structure, microscopic size, biological activity, and a capacity for adapting themselves to changing conditions.

To the zoologist they do not seem animal; for they have often no nucleus, no carbon element, the essential stuff of the bone and blood of organic tissue; nor do they seem vegetable to the botanist for they have none of the green colouring matter common to all plant life, nor cellulose of the very nature of plant cells; so they are given a subdivision of their own— Bacteria. It has been said that the gulf dividing bacteria from a carbon atom is greater than that dividing bacteria from Man.

A special unit of measurement, the micron—one millionth of a metre; roughly 25,000 microns go to the inch—has been invented to measure these creatures with the help of powerful microscopes. Thus

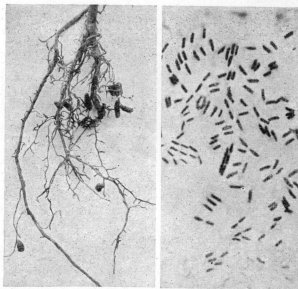

BENEFICENT BACTERIA

J. J. Ward

Not all bacteria are harmful, and some, indeed, are necessary to plant life. Above, left, are seen the roots of a laburnum bearing swollen nodules formed by bacteria that provide the plant with nitrogen out of the earth ; right, some bacteria from these nodules.

they invade the animal body, rendering it sick, but these form only a small fraction of the world of bacteria and science is learning how to control and combat their attacks.

Some great armies of bacteria on the Earth are beneficent to Man. Geologists, scientists who study the formation of the Earth's crust, teach that it was bacteria which first attacked the solid rocks of the Earth's surface, cooling as she turned through space, breaking these rocks up into soil and making them habitable by the green things of the earth—the green things which are the eventual source of all the food of the animal kingdom. Men, animals, insects, plants, all alike owe life itself to the working of bacteria.

The unending task of bacteria is to resolve all matter which they can attack into its simplest chemical structure; thus dead vegetable matter is turned again into its elements; thus, the dead body of man or animal decays by reason of their attack, and the material is used afresh by Nature for the building of new forms of life. Without them the surface of the globe would soon be hopelessly cluttered by the useless and the offensive. Many of the smells liked or disliked by us all, that of a bad egg as well as that of newly-turned earth, are due alike to gases set free by bacterial activity.

A most important part of the work of bacteria is in the field of agriculture. All plants need nitrogen to build their living cells. The greatest source of nitrogen is the air, but the nitrogen of the air is an anti-social gas unwilling to combine in a working team. Most plants are unable to grasp and use

thousands of bacteria—so incredibly small are they —could find room on a pin-point.

Bacteria are of many shapes, but they fall generally into one of three classes. A *bacillus* is rod-shaped; a *coccus* is round, a *spirillum* is curled, or spiral like a cork-screw. Some bacteria are provided with flagella, long whip-like lashes used as fins, with which the speediest ones can swim some four inches in a quarter of an hour. (This power of movement is of immense importance in the spread of such diseases as typhoid fever and cholera.) They multiply very rapidly by splitting in two. In good conditions a bacterium will reach maturity and split into two bacteria in some 20 minutes; each of these will at once proceed to repeat the performance, so that in 24 hours billions of bacteria are produced from the original parent.

Some bacteria, instead of splitting into halves, change into cells called spores. These may develop at once into full-grown bacteria, but if conditions of temperature and moisture are unfavourable they may lie in this condition for years before springing into active life. Little is known of how long they can live, but seeds of lotus found in lakes, dry for 2,000 years, have been known to sprout, as have seeds of flax found in the tombs of ancient Egypt. This explains many cases of obscure infection. Spores are capable of resisting great extremes of heat and cold ; in fact, even full-grown bacteria have been known to live comfortably in water at boiling point, while others have recovered after being frozen for days at a point below zero. Fortunately few of the disease-producing bacteria are so resistant, even when in spore form.

New varieties of bacteria are forever being discovered. The bacteriophage is a relatively new find— if one can speak of finding a thing that has never yet been seen. These "disembowel" the bacteria and devour them. Bacteria are commonly called germs when

MICRO-ORGANISMS AT WORK

Here is an odd place to find bacteria and yeasts performing a useful function ; it is a cellar where Brie cheeses are mellowing. The characteristic flavours and properties of different cheeses depend on the different bacteria and other microscopic organisms inhabiting them.

nitrogen in its ordinary state, but certain bacteria can absorb and fix it in forms on which plants can feed. Thus, nitrogen-fixing bacteria grow on the roots of plants such as peas and clover, and when these have been cut by the farmer the nitrogen still remains in the soil, to be taken up by a crop of grain if such is then next planted.

Fermentation is the special province of bacteria. Wine, cider, cheese, butter—many are the food-products directly achieved by their action. Hundreds of industries make use of bacteria.

Some bacteria can live upon inorganic chemicals, and are important in distributing the chemical elements over the Earth. Deposits of iron ore are formed by these. In the neighbourhood of volcanoes there are bacteria which can act upon raw sulphur, thus forming sulphuric acid.

Very aptly an American naturalist has written : " No picture of life today is even worth a glance that does not show the bacteria as the foundation of life itself, the broad base of the pyramid on which all the rest is erected."

Baden-Powell, ROBERT STEPHENSON SMYTH BADEN-POWELL, IST Baron (1857–1941). Only those who are old enough to remember the South African War of 1899–1902 can realize what an amazingly popular figure General Baden-Powell was at that time. While his gallant force was shut up in the village of Mafeking (October 1899– May 1900), besieged by an overwhelming force of Boers, his reports were read with breathless interest at every British breakfast-table.

Mafeking was not " B.-P's " first fight. As an officer in the Hussars he had seen active service in India, Afghanistan, Zululand, Ashanti and Matabeleland. Many were his narrow escapes, yet he never lost the boyishness and high spirits which had characterized him as a schoolboy at Charterhouse.

Scouting was one of the arts of war which specially appealed to him, and which he personally cultivated until he possessed remarkable powers of observation and deduction. Two of his earliest

Planet News
BADEN-POWELL, AS CHIEF SCOUT
Lord Baden-Powell was never happier than when he was among his Boy Scouts to whom he devoted the greater part of his life, founding the movement in 1908. He was granted a barony in 1929 in recognition of his services.

books were called Reconnaissance and Scouting (1890) and Aid to Scouting (1899).

Baden-Powell founded the Boy Scouts movement in Great Britain in 1908, but within a short space of time branches of this movement had spread to many other countries ; he became Chief Scout, and travelled widely in the interests of the movement, including a visit to India. Modern history can furnish no parallel of a Briton who has so improved the youthful imagination of the world, and rallied to his banner in a peaceful and educational movement so large an army of boys. His services were recognized by the grant of a barony in 1929 and the award of the Order of Merit in 1937. In that year he retired to Nyeri, Kenya, where he died on January 8, 1941. (*See* Boy Scouts ; Girl Guides).

Badger. In many parts of Great Britain you may see a badger "earth," or smell it—for it is often the musty odour that first betrays its existence. But unless you are lucky, you may never catch sight of the badger itself, for it is a timid animal and rarely comes out except at night. Even if you should surprise one away from its burrow, you might never notice it because of the broadness and flatness of its clumsy body. When alarmed it will often flatten against the ground, and might be mistaken for a clod of earth or a stone.

But beware of the badger when it is cornered, for it will put up a stiff fight. A badger is often a match for several dogs, and the cruel sport of badger-baiting was common in Great Britain until 1850, when it was prohibited. From this practice we get the word " badgering," meaning " persistent

A. R. Thompson
BADGER AT ITS BURROW
Badgers are rarely seen because they usually come out only at night. This full-grown specimen has been caught leaving its sett or burrow. Though normally timid, a badger will fight fiercely if molested and is a match for several dogs.

annoying." Badgers' jaws are so hinged that dislocation is practically impossible, and they can maintain their hold with great tenacity.

Badgers, which belong to the weasel family (*Mustelidae*), including skunks, otters, minks, martens and wolverines, are common in the northern parts of Europe, Asia and America. The head is pointed at the snout and the feet are armed with long claws used in digging and for defence. The thick fur is valuable, and the hairs are used in the manufacture of artists' brushes and shaving brushes.

The common badger (*Meles taxus*) is about two and a half feet long, and greyish in colour with irregular black bands on the back. The head is white with a broad black mark on each side starting from near the muzzle and passing back over the eye

court is marked out with service-lines, side-lines, etc., and divided by a net. In place of a ball, however, a shuttlecock or "bird" is used. This consists of 14 to 16 feathers fixed in a cork base. The racket, which should weigh not more than 5 oz., has a longer handle and a smaller striking area than a tennis racket. The net is much higher than that used for tennis, being five feet high at the centre. All strokes are made by volleying—that is, the shuttle is out of play if it touches the ground. Quickness of eye and agility are essential qualities. As in squash rackets, a player cannot win a point or "ace" unless he (or his partner) is serving; a game usually consists of 15 aces. A further difference from tennis is that the service must be made underhand—*i.e.* the shuttle must be struck below the level of the server's waist. The controlling body of the game is the Badminton Association of England, which holds the annual All England Championships in London; the first of these after the Second World War took place in 1947.

Bagehot, WALTER (1826–1877).

The son of a banker and shipowner, Bagehot (baj′ot) was born at Langport, Somerset, on February 3, 1826. He was called to the Bar in 1852, but in the same year entered his father's business, in which he became a partner. In 1858 he married a daughter of James Wilson, the founder of the Economist, and on the latter's death became editor of that paper, a post which he held from 1860 until his death, which occurred on March 24, 1877.

The subjects he chose to write about—political philosophy, the money market, economic questions and literary criticism—were not easy, but he illumined them all by his clear understanding and keenness of phrase. He was a master of the brief and pointed statement, and there is hardly a page of his writings which does not contain some phrase with claims to be remembered. In Physics and Politics (1872), for instance, we find the all-too-true statement that "one of the greatest pains to human nature is the pain of a new idea." His English Constitution — written in 1867, but still remarkably up to date—is filled with such apophthegms (short instructive sayings) as "a cabinet is a hyphen which joins, a buckle which fastens, the legislative part of the State to the executive part of the State"; "the women—one half the human race at least—care fifty times more for a marriage than a ministry"; and "the crown is a visible symbol of unity." In Lombard Street (1873), a study of the financial mechanism of the city of London, we come across such statements as "a panic is a species of neuralgia."

BADMINTON IN FULL SWING

Fox

In a fraction of a second the camera has taken the shuttlecock (top) just before it was struck by the racket and returned over the net. In the lower picture the layout of a Badminton court can be seen, with four women playing in a tournament at the Horticultural Hall, London.

and round the ear to the shoulder, a marking which gives the face a clown-like appearance. The throat, chest, legs, feet and belly are black. With its strong claws the badger lays open the burrows of rabbits and field-mice, feeding upon these animals and on frogs, small snakes, lizards, grasshoppers and other small creatures.

Badminton.

Evolved from the familiar nursery game of battledore and shuttlecock, badminton was introduced into England from India in 1873. The name comes from Badminton, the residence of the Duke of Beaufort in Gloucestershire, one of the first places where the game was played. Badminton is not unlike lawn-tennis in that a

Baghdad, IRAQ. On a site which has been occupied by a series of towns for 4,000 years Baghdad has stood for centuries, at the crossroads of great world highways of trade. The fertile plain of Mesopotamia, in which it lies, has been crossed from time immemorial by caravan routes connecting the Mediterranean ports with the Persian Gulf, and Turkey and south-eastern Europe with Iran (Persia) and the Far East. Where these routes met, on the banks of the river Tigris, 330 miles north of the Persian Gulf, a city grew up.

After it was made the capital of the Mahomedan caliphs, in the 8th century, it became the largest and most beautiful city in the world. The caliph Haroun-al-Raschid, poet and scholar, made it a centre of art and learning. It is known to all lovers of romance as the scene of The Arabian Nights tales.

Later, the city suffered a long decline. Civil wars and repeated sackings by Mongols, Turks and Persians humbled it; and when ocean routes around Africa were discovered, much of its trade was lost. By 1638, when it became a part of the Turkish Empire, its population had been reduced from 2,000,000 to 14,000.

As the capital of the kingdom of Iraq since 1920, Baghdad has entered on a new and more prosperous chapter in its history. Motor caravans speed over the old camel routes. In 1940 a railway linking Baghdad through Turkey with the European railway systems was completed by British military engineers, and a motor road connecting Baghdad with Haifa on the coast of Palestine was opened. Railway lines extend to the port of Basra, to Kirkuk and the Iranian border, and to the Syrian frontier.

In 1949 a railway bridge was completed over the Tigris at Baghdad to replace the railway ferry and to link the lines from Basra, Mosul and Turkey with those serving Persia and the Kirkuk oilfields. The airport, opened in 1933, is one of the principal air centres of the Orient.

Baghdad therefore is no longer the picturesque city of Haroun-al-Raschid's time. A railway station stands near the spot where that ruler built his palaces and gardens. The flat-roofed houses of sun-dried brick and the many ancient mosques still stand in a maze of narrow, winding alleyways; but in 1917 the British built a modern street straight through the city, and unromantically named it New Street. Other paved streets followed; and tramcars, taxicabs, electric lights, and a modern water system speak of Western progress. Even the covered bazaars are invaded by the wares of Europe.

The present population of Baghdad is about 270,000, one-fifth of whom are Jews, descendants of the people who were carried away into the Babylonian captivity by Nebuchadrezzar. (*See also* Iraq ; Mesopotamia).

BAGHDAD'S OLD QUARTER
All the older streets in Baghdad, the capital of the independent Arab state of Iraq, are like this—narrow, untidy, flanked by drab houses, yet somehow managing to retain an atmosphere of Oriental romance.

A PIPER OF SCOTLAND
The bagpipe is the national musical instrument of Scotland, and the pipers of the Highland regiments wear splendid uniforms. It is a very ancient instrument, and is played in several European lands.

Bagpipe. Not only in Scotland but in Ireland, in Brittany, and in various districts of Italy, the bagpipe is a popular musical instrument. Once it was common in nearly all parts of Europe. As usually made the instrument consists of a large leather bag, often covered with cloth, having a mouth-tube by which the player fills the bag with his breath. The tune is played on a pipe with finger holes (called the chanter), and two or three other pipes called "drones" each continuously sound a fixed note of the scale.

The bagpipe is spoken of in the Old Testament, and was used by Egyptians, Greeks and Romans. It is the national instrument of the Scottish Highlanders, and pipers are attached to Highland, other Scottish, and Irish regiments in the British army.

Bahamas. Columbus made this group of islands in the West Indies famous, for Watling Island, the outermost of the Bahamas (pron. ba-hah'-maz) called by him San Salvador, was

BAHAMA SPONGES BEING SORTED

At one time sponge fishing was the most important industry of the Bahama Islands, a British possession in the West Indies, but it has declined owing to disease killing numbers of the sponges. The sorting is done by Negroes at Nassau, the capital, on New Providence Island.

probably the first land sighted in the New World. They were settled by the British in 1629, but their possession was disputed by the Spanish until the final cession of the islands to Great Britain in 1783.

The Bahamas, populated chiefly by Negroes, form a line 600 miles long from a point off the east coast of Florida to the island of Haiti. Through this barrier there are but three channels for large vessels, for the islands are merely the exposed tips of a great submarine range composed of coral. In all the 20 inhabited islands there is only one running stream, which is on Andros. Fresh water is supplied by wells dug in the soft rock.

The climate is mild throughout the year, and Nassau, the capital, on New Providence Island, is a popular winter resort. Fruits and vegetables grow in profusion. The chief products are sponges, sisal hemp, timber, shells, tomatoes and pineapples. The total area is about 4,400 square miles and includes 29 islands, over 650 islets, and nearly 2,400 rocks. Population is about 69,000.

Baker, Sir Samuel White (1821–1893). Born in London, on June 8, 1821, Samuel Baker entered his father's office in Fenchurch Street, London, after leaving school, but could not content himself with city life. He hungered to see new lands. His marriage was in keeping with his romantic nature, he and his

brother, John, marrying two sisters on the same day (August 3, 1842). Soon afterwards he went out to Mauritius, where his family had sugar plantations. Two years of Mauritius were enough; he longed for other lands, and his choice fell upon Ceylon.

He returned to England after spending several years in Ceylon, where he founded an agricultural settlement. On his wife's death he resumed his travels, visiting the Crimea, Turkey and Rumania.

The most important part of his life opened when he and his second wife, after spending the greater part of the year 1861 in exploring Abyssinia, started from Khartum, at the end of the following year, to penetrate into Central Africa. Their idea was to discover the sources of the Nile. On their way the Bakers met Speke and Grant returning from their discovery of Victoria Nyanza. Speke and Grant told them they had heard from natives that there existed still another source of the Nile, in a mysterious lake called Muta Nzige. Thus encouraged, Baker pushed on, and, after months of hardship, he had the joy of being the first white man to gaze upon the waters of the great lake, which he named the Albert Nyanza. That was in 1864.

Baker was knighted in 1866, and in 1869 was commissioned by the Khedive of Egypt to suppress the slave trade and open up the districts of the Upper Nile. With the rank of pasha he organized an expedition and on the successful accomplishment of his task was made the first governor-general of the new districts, a post in which he was succeeded by General Gordon in 1874. Afterwards he travelled extensively in Cyprus, and hunted big game in Syria, Japan, India and America. He died at Sandford Orleigh, Devonshire, on December 30, 1893.

SIR SAMUEL BAKER IN ABYSSINIAN WILDS

It was in 1861 that Sir Samuel White Baker and his wife set out from Cairo to explore the sources of the Nile. Some idea of conditions experienced on their journey may be obtained from this drawing, which appeared in Baker's book, The Nile Tributaries of Abyssinia.

Baku, TRANSCAUCASIA. Prosperity came to the seaport of Baku because it is the natural outlet for one of the greatest oilfields in the world. It stands on a peninsula that juts out into the Caspian Sea, and has a fine natural harbour. A railway line connects it with Batum on the Black Sea, 560 miles away, and before the discovery of the oil it was a considerable port. As soon as oil had been found it grew very rapidly as new workers arrived.

Baku became a part of Soviet Russia on April 28, 1920, when Azerbaijan was proclaimed a Soviet Socialist Republic, of which Baku is now the capital. With a population of 809,347 it is the fifth city of the Soviet Union.

Balaclava. One of the most famous feats of arms in the history of the British Army is the charge of the Light Brigade at Balaclava, during the Crimean War, in which Britain, France and Turkey were fighting against Russia. On October 25, 1854, owing to a mistake in giving an order a brigade of light cavalry charged a mile and a half along a valley to capture some Russian guns. They were fired on by guns from all sides, and out of 673 men 110 were killed and 134 wounded. It was on this incident that Tennyson wrote his famous poem.

Balboa, VASCO NUÑEZ DE (1475–1517). When the Spanish explorer Balboa (pron. bal-bō'a) beheld on September 25,1513, from the top of a mountain in Panama, the gleaming waters of a western ocean, he was the first European to look on the Pacific Ocean, though the credit is given to Cortes in Keats's sonnet containing the oft-quoted lines:

> . . . . when with eagle eyes,
> He stared at the Pacific—and all his men
> Looked at each other with a wild surmise
> Silent, upon a peak in Darien.

Balboa was a Spanish adventurer who had been very unlucky at farming in San Domingo. When he left that settlement in 1510 to join an expedition to Darien, he had successfully arranged to have himself taken on board ship in a cask labelled " victuals for the voyage," in order to avoid his creditors. When he gained control of the colony of Darien, he started on his explorations in order to keep the favour of the Spanish king ; and for him he claimed the South Sea, as he called the Pacific, and all lands washed by it. He was too late, however, with his peace-offering, for when he returned to Darien he found that a new governor had been appointed in his place. Balboa was imprisoned on a false charge of plotting against the governor, and later beheaded.

Balder. (Pron. bawl'der). In all Norse mythology there was no god so beloved and beautiful as Balder, son of Odin, and the gods vied in showering favours upon him.

One night his sleep was haunted with dreams of dire disaster. When the gods learned of this, sorrow fell upon them. His mother, Frigga, heart-broken, roamed the earth, supplicating all things, animate and inanimate, not to harm her son, and they willingly gave their promise. The gods thereupon rejoiced, and happiness again reigned in Asgard, their habitation. Thenceforth Balder led a charmed life, and on festival days the gods hurled missiles in play at the invulnerable hero, who smiled when darts and stones fell harmless at his feet.

But among the gods was one selfish, jealous being named Loki, who wished to put an end to Balder's reign of love. Disguising himself, he sought out Frigga and obtained from her the admission that there was one little plant, the mistletoe, whose promise of protection she had neglected to get.

Loki made a spear shaft out of the toughest sprigs of mistletoe. Hoder, a blind god, loving Balder, and wishing to honour him, consented to throw the shaft. Balder fell, and his spirit journeyed to the underworld. Deeply sorrowing, the gods pleaded for the release of Balder. The ruler of the underworld consented, provided that every living thing wept for his return. The whole world wept except Loki, and that is why Balder (so it is said) still dwells in the underworld.

Baldwin, STANLEY, 1ST EARL BALDWIN OF BEWDLEY (1867–1947). Through two of the gravest crises that confronted Britain between the First and the Second World Wars—the general strike of 1926 and the abdication of King Edward VIII in 1936— the ship of state was guided by Stanley Baldwin. He was three times Prime Minister (May 1923– January 1924; November 1924–June 1929; June 1935–May 1937).

Son of Alfred Baldwin, director of the great engineering firm of Baldwins, he went to Harrow School and Trinity College, Cambridge, and joined the family business. In 1908 he was elected Conservative M.P. for the Bewdley division of Worcestershire. In 1917 he became a Junior Lord of the Treasury, and soon afterwards joint Financial Secretary to the Treasury. About that time he gave £150,000 towards the cost of the war. In 1921 he was made President of the Board of Trade, in 1922 Chancellor of the Exchequer; and in 1923 he visited the United States to arrange for the payment of Britain's war debts.

He succeeded Mr. Bonar Law as Prime Minister in 1923, but his party was defeated by the Labour Party at a general election in 1924. At the end of that year there was another general election, and for the second time he became Prime Minister ; but in 1929 the Conservatives were again defeated. In 1931, when Mr. Ramsay MacDonald, the Labour Prime Minister, formed a coalition Government (containing Ministers of more than one political party), Stanley Baldwin became Lord President of the Council. In 1935 he exchanged office with Mr. Ramsay MacDonald. On his retirement from political life in May 1937 he was made an Earl and a Knight of the Garter. He died in his sleep on the night of

EARL BALDWIN
Three times British Prime Minister, Earl Baldwin led Britain through two grave crises—a general strike in 1926, and the abdication of King Edward VIII in 1936.

December 13-14, 1947, at his home near Stourport-on-Severn. Some of Earl Baldwin's addresses have been published: On England, Our Inheritance, The Torch of Freedom, and Service of Our Lives.

Balearic Isles. (Pron. bal-ē-ar'-ik). This group of islands lies off the Mediterranean coast of Spain, to which it belongs. The five largest are Majorca (or Mallorca), Minorca, Iviza, Formentera, and Cabrera. The mild climate and beauty of the islands attract many tourists. On the terraced, irrigated slopes are olive groves and orchards of figs, lemons, oranges, and almonds. Much of their yield is shipped to Spain. Other major exports include fish, sea salt and textiles.

Palma, on Majorca, is the capital and largest city of the Balearics. On Minorca, about 25 miles east, is Mahón, one of the best harbours in Europe.

During the French occupation of Mahón (1756–63) a delicious native sauce so pleased the soldiers that they introduced it to Paris, where it was named mayonnaise—a name familiar today.

The name Balearic is due to the fact that in ancient times the people of the islands were so expert in use of the slingshot that they came to be called Baleares, from the Greek word ballein, "to throw." The islands were seized successively by the Carthaginians, Romans, Vandals, Normans and Moors. By 1235 they had been conquered by Spain. In 1276 they became an independent kingdom, but were taken back by Spain in 1349. During the 18th century they were captured by France and England, but were returned to Spain by England in 1803. The area of the islands is 1,935 square miles, and the population about 410,000.

E.N.A.

BALEARIC ISLANDS IN THE MEDITERRANEAN SEA

Situated off the east coast of Spain, to which they belong, the Balearics enjoy a mild but variable climate. Majorca is the largest island and on it is Palma (upper), the biggest town and the capital of the group. Port Mahon (lower) is on Minorca and has one of the finest harbours in Europe. The people of the islands are Spanish, with traces of Moorish blood, and in ancient times they had a reputation as slingers and fought in the armies of Rome and Carthage.

Balfour, Arthur James, 1st Earl of Balfour (1848–1930). The eldest son of a Scottish landowner, Arthur James Balfour was thought by his friends and relatives too delicate for a life of strenuous activity. Nevertheless, he lived to be over 80 and served the State in important capacities, winning towards the end of his life the reputation of being the most distinguished member of the British parliament.

Balfour entered the House of Commons in 1874, and in 1878 he went with his uncle, the Marquess of Salisbury, to the Congress of Berlin. In 1885 he joined the Unionist Government as President of the Local Government Board, and in 1887 he became Chief Secretary for Ireland, when the turbulent Irish members met their match in the "languid young aristocrat." In 1891 he became leader of the Unionist party in the House of Commons, and in 1902 he succeeded his uncle as Prime Minister, an office he held until 1905. In 1911 he resigned his leadership of the Unionist party and went into partial retirement, but when the First World War came he returned to active life and served under Asquith as First Lord of the Admiralty and later (under Lloyd George) as Foreign Secretary. He was Lord President of the Council 1919–22 and 1925–29. He was made a Knight of the Garter in March 1922, while still a commoner, and was given an earldom in the following April.

He was a distinguished philosopher, and his writings include A Defence of Philosophic Doubt, written as a young man, and The Foundations of Belief.

BALFOUR AT CAMBRIDGE
From 1919 until his death in 1930, the Earl of Balfour was Chancellor of Cambridge University. He is seen in 1921 after attending a ceremony at which degrees were conferred.

The STORM CENTRE of EUROPE

For many centuries the rugged and romantic region of the Balkan Peninsula has been one of the principal danger-zones in European politics. You will be better able to understand why after you have read what follows.

Balkan Peninsula. (Pron. bawl'-kan). The easternmost of the three southern peninsulas of Europe, its northern limit is fixed by the rivers Danube and Save and the Transylvanian Alps. On the east, at the Dardanelles and the Bosporus, it approaches so closely to Asia that it forms a bridge between the two continents. On the west it looks across the Adriatic to Italy, whose interests and ambitions sometimes have aided and often opposed those of the Balkan peoples.

For the most part the country is a wild mountainous region, with rich mineral deposits which, owing to the backwardness of the people, are still largely untouched. Running westward from the Black Sea are the lofty and rugged Balkan Mountains, from which the peninsula takes its name. These split up into other ranges, one of which—the Pindus Mountains—extends to the southernmost tip of Greece. The peaks range from 3,000 feet to 10,000 feet in height.

North of the Danube stretch the plains of Rumania, which geographically are an extension of the plains of Russia rather than part of the Balkan Peninsula. But politically Rumania is grouped with its neighbour states to the south. In these plains wheat is raised, but in the rest of the Balkans the inhabitants wrest from the soil only a precarious existence.

A part of the lack of progress of the people of the Balkans is due to the mountainous character of the country itself, but more must be charged to its history. Although the peninsula, including Rumania, has an area of only about 180,000 square miles, it contains more different peoples, with separate languages, customs, national aspirations and religions, than any other equal area.

At the opening of the First World War, in 1914, the Balkan Peninsula consisted of Serbia, Montenegro, Albania, Greece, Bulgaria, Rumania, Turkey, and the districts of Bosnia, Herzegovina and Dalmatia which had belonged to Austria for a century. At the end of the war the Balkan countries were Bulgaria, Rumania, Turkey, Greece, Albania, and the Kingdom of the Serbs, Croats, and Slovenes (renamed Yugoslavia in 1931). Montenegro, like Serbia, became a part of the kingdom, and Austria lost her Balkan possessions. If each of the many groups had been settled in one definite area, the Balkan question might have admitted of solution, but instead they are scattered over the greater part of the peninsula. Rumanians are found in Bulgaria, Greeks in Turkey, and Slavs everywhere.

During the supremacy of the Roman Empire the whole peninsula was united under Roman government. But in the 4th century successive waves of Visigoths, Ostrogoths and other people came into the country. They were pushed on farther west by the hordes of Slavs pressing upon them from the north. Then came the Turkish invasion. In

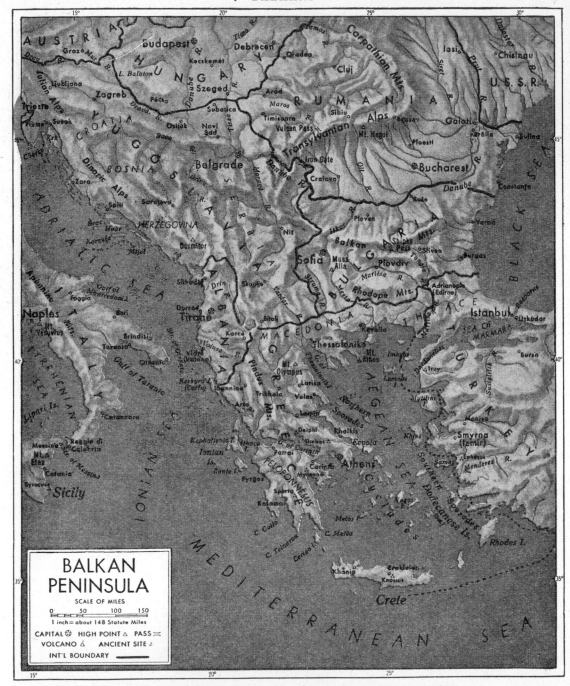

BALKAN PENINSULA

SCALE OF MILES

0   50   100   150

1 inch = about 148 Statute Miles

CAPITAL ⊛   HIGH POINT △   PASS ⤮

VOLCANO ⌂   ANCIENT SITE ⸪

INT'L BOUNDARY ▬▬▬

BALKAN PENINSULA IN SOUTH-EASTERN EUROPE

The broad plain of the Danube spreads over much of the north of the Balkan Peninsula ; mountains cover the rest of the land and divide the plain into two parts. In the east the peninsula nearly touches Asia Minor. This region has always had a troubled history and many changes took place after the end of the Second World War (1939–45).

1453 Constantinople fell, and the Turkish power was soon established up to and beyond the Danube.

A number of Balkan wars led to the break-up of the Turkish Empire. In 1828–29 Russia helped the Greeks to win their independence. Twenty-five years later the Russian demand for a protectorate over all Christians of Greek faith residing in Turkey precipitated the Crimean War (1854–56), in which Great Britain, France and Sardinia helped Turkey to defeat Russia. The troops of the Tsar intervened a third time, in 1877–78, to aid the insurgent Serbians and Bulgarians against the Turkish policy of massacre ; but the Peace of San Stefano, which Russia forced upon Turkey, was set aside by the other powers at the Congress of Berlin in place of one much less favourable to the oppressed Christians. Russia's interest in the Balkans was traceable chiefly to her desire to obtain possession of Constantinople and other parts of the inheritance to be left by the " sick man of Europe," as the Tsar once called the decaying power of Turkey. Austria began to dream of eastward expansion, and this gradually linked up with Germany's far-reaching plan for a Berlin-to-Baghdad railway and a " Middle-Europe " under her control.

In 1908 the " Young Turks " seized the government of Turkey, and sought to restore the "sick man's" waning vitality. Austria made haste to annex Bosnia and Herzegovina—two Turkish provinces which she had administered since the time of the Congress of Berlin in 1878—and Bulgaria declared her independence.

The Young Turks proved themselves, if anything, more oppressive to the Christian populations than the old government had been. After a massacre of Christians in Macedonia in 1912, Serbia, Greece, Bulgaria and Montenegro formed the Balkan League against Turkey. When that country was weakened by war with Italy over Tripoli, they declared war on it in October 1912. By striking in different places at the same time they completely overwhelmed Turkey, and the Treaty of London, signed on May 30, 1913, limited her territories in Europe to a small strip about Constantinople.

However, the peace was short-lived. Austria and Italy had insisted on the creation of Albania as a separate principality in the western part of the Balkans. This upset an agreement which had been made by Greece, Serbia, and Bulgaria for the division of the conquests from Turkey, and in June 1913 they commenced fighting among themselves. Rumania joined the other Balkan nations in opposing the claims of Bulgaria, and that country was defeated. By the Treaty of Bucharest (signed in August 1913), Serbia and Greece gained increased territory, but Adrianople (now Edirne) was handed back to Turkey.

These Balkan wars were the prelude to the First World War of 1914–18. Germany and Austria had supported Turkey against the Balkan allies in 1912, and Bulgaria against the other allies in 1913. The double defeat was a serious blow to German and Austrian prestige, so both were glad, in July 1914, to seize upon the murder of the Austrian Archduke at Sarajevo as a pretext for crushing Serbia. The First World War had, as we have seen, far-reaching effects on the peoples and states of the Balkan Peninsula.

During the 1920s exchanges of people (notably those of Greek descent in Turkey for those of Turkish descent in Greece) eased old tensions. German influence, helped by trade treaties, increased very much after Hitler's rise to power in 1933. At Easter 1939, in spite of a treaty of friendship made in 1926 and renewed in 1936, Italy occupied Albania; and in the course of the Second World War German or Italian troops occupied the whole peninsula except Bulgaria and Turkey.

Rumania joined the " Axis " in 1940, and in June 1941 sent troops to invade Russia with the Germans. Bulgaria, who joined the Axis in March 1941, hoped to remain neutral. But in December 1941, the U.K. and the U.S.A. declared war on her ally Rumania and Bulgaria then had to declare war on them. She never declared war on her old friend Russia, and eventually in 1944, after Russia had declared war on her and was on the point of invading her, she signed an armistice with the Allies, declared war on Germany, and fought against her.

After the Germans were expelled from the Balkans, Communists seized power in Albania, Rumania, Bulgaria, and Yugoslavia, the last three helping Russia to found the Cominform in 1947. Greece endured five years of civil war, the Communist rebels being aided by Albania, Yugoslavia and Bulgaria. In 1948, however, Yugoslavia was expelled from the Cominform. Thereafter she gave the Greek rebels little support, and the civil war ended in 1949.

Ballet. (Pron. bal'-ā). In 1909 artistic circles in Paris were astounded by the performances of a company of dancers (including Nijinsky and Karsavina) under the control of the Russian, Serge Diaghilev (1872–1929). In the same year audiences in London were being delighted by the dancing of another Russian, Anna Pavlova (1885–1931). These two, but especially the company of Diaghilev—the Russian Ballet, as it came to be called—were responsible for the revival of ballet which has made it enjoyed today by ever-increasing audiences.

Ballet, that is, the telling of a story by means of gestures and dancing, accompanied by music, had a long history in Europe. Beginning as a court entertainment in the 14th and 15th centuries, it developed into a theatrical spectacle, but was always associated with singing until Jean Noverre (1727–1810) conceived the idea of ballet as an art in itself. In the 18th and 19th centuries the ballet reached its height in France and Italy and spread to Russia, where the Imperial Ballet still flourished in its traditional form at the beginning of the 20th century. The ballets of Diaghilev

Dorien Leigh
BALKAN WOMAN AND GIRL
In some parts of the Balkan Peninsula the married and unmarried women are distinguished by their different headgear ; as are this girl and her grandmother, both from Dalmatia in Yugoslavia.

MAGIC OF BALLET CAUGHT BY THE PAINTER

Mansell

Above are scenes from the life of a French ballet-dancer, depicted by the greatest of all painters of the ballet, the French artist Degas (1834–1917). In the upper picture, a young member of the corps de ballet is being instructed by the maitre de ballet (ballet master), who, staff in hand, stands beside the violin-player. In the background other pupils are practising ' at the bar.' In the lower painting, a dress rehearsal of the ballet is in progress ; those who are not taking part are waiting in the wings, while on the far side of the stage is the ever-watchful maitre de ballet.

and his choreographers or ballet-designers, Fokine and Massine, were a "break-away" from this stereotyped form. Music was specially composed by Stravinsky and others, and artists and scene-designers like Léon Bakst and Pablo Picasso worked as a team with choreographers. So, when you see an original production of a great classical ballet, you are watching not merely dancing but a composite work of art, the combined efforts of perhaps four brains, interpreted by possibly as many as 40 dancers.

Other influences have affected the ballet of recent years. Diaghilev's age was influenced by Isadora Duncan (1878–1927), who revived Greek dancing, and by Dalcroze, who invented Eurhythmics (*q.v.*) and inspired the Central European ballet school, founded by Laban and interpreted by Kurt Jooss and Mary Wigman. In these ballets, called by some "expressionist," considerable symbolism is employed to aid the dramatic side of the story.

In England, a ballet school having features of its own gradually arose at Sadler's Wells Theatre, London, under the direction of Ninette de Valois.

Baron

BALLET IN GAY SPANISH COSTUMES

One of the most colourful of modern ballets is The Three-Cornered Hat (above), which is based on a Spanish story. The dances were devised by the Russian, Leonide Massine ; the music composed by a Spaniard, De Falla ; scenery and costumes were designed by the Spanish artist Picasso. First produced in 1919, the ballet was revived in 1947 by the Sadler's Wells company, at London's Royal Opera House, Covent Garden.

This school, with that of Marie Rambert, founded an almost national type of ballet, classical but with perhaps more emphasis on the literary, less on the musical side of the ballet. The idea, however, of the dance as the interpreting medium of a story, accompanied and assisted by music, remained the same as in the "Russian" ballets.

GAS-BORNE CARRIAGE *of the* AIR

Long before the dirigible airship and, of course, the aeroplane, people were experimenting with balloons and even achieving some measure of success. The modern balloon is used for scientific investigation of the air and in warfare.

Balloon. A balloon is an airtight envelope or bag made from varnished cloth, rubberised cloth, or gold-beater's skin and inflated with hot air or with a gas lighter than air. The gases most commonly used are hydrogen (*q.v.*) or ordinary household gas extracted from coal : hydrogen, lighter than coal gas, has greater lifting power, but coal-gas is cheaper.

The free passenger balloon is usually spherical or pear shaped. Over the envelope is stretched a network of thin but strong cords from which is suspended the basket or passenger car. At the top of the envelope is a wooden or aluminium valve, operated by a cord hanging down inside the balloon, and which is used to regulate the release of the gas. There is an opening at the bottom of the envelope which, by automatically releasing gas as the balloon rises, prevents gas pressure inside the envelope becoming greater than the outside atmosphere pressure.

The fabric from which the envelope is made is stitched together in long, narrow panels, extending from the top of the balloon to the bottom, and one of these panels is so arranged that, in an emergency, it can be torn open by pulling on a cord. This instantly empties the envelope of gas. The balloon also carries a guide rope, an anchor, and ballast bags filled with sand. The captive military balloon, about which more is said later, is usually cigar-shaped, and has wing-like air chambers at the rear which act as stabilisers.

Balloons are capable of controlled movement only in a vertical direction ; that is, they can go up or down, but they are without any propulsive power to drive them forward. Their forward movement depends upon the direction and speed of the wind.

Control of height is affected by two methods. Throwing ballast overboard reduces the total weight of the balloon so that it rises ; while releasing gas by means of the controlling valve increases the weight of the balloon relative to its buoyancy, causing the balloon to descend. The direction of the wind usually varies at different heights, so that a skilful balloonist can take advantage of suitable air currents to control his forward movement.

Francesco de Lana (1631–1687) had proposed building a " buoyant carriage " consisting of a canvas car supported in the air by four hollow globes of silver from which the air had been extracted. But nothing really practical was suggested until 1767, when Dr. Joseph Black (1728–1799) wrote of the possibility of inflating a bladder with the hydrogen gas (then called " inflammable air ") which had been first fully described the previous year by Henry Cavendish (1731–1810). In 1781, Tiberius Cavallo (1749–1809) filled soap bubbles with hydrogen and raised them to considerable heights.

HISTORIC BALLOON ASCENT
The first successful ascent by a free hot-air balloon carrying human beings was on Nov. 21, 1783, when Pilâtre de Rozier and the Marquis d'Arlandes floated five miles. This contemporary print shows the scene at Paris as they started.

Two Frenchmen, the brothers Joseph (1740–1810) and Etienne (1745–1799) Montgolfier, who owned a paper mill at Annonay near Lyons, sent up the first really practical balloon. They had read Joseph Priestley's (1733–1804) story of his experiments with air, and had been interested in the fact that smoke from fire always rose upwards. Eventually they began experiments with paper bags filled with smoke (mainly hot air) from a chafing dish. As these bags proved buoyant, they went on to make silken bags ; they filled a large one with 600 cubic feet of hot air, and this balloon reached a height of nearly 200 feet.

On June 5, 1783, the Montgolfiers released near Paris a linen balloon 70 feet in diameter. It rose to 6,000 feet and landed a mile and a half away. On September 19 of the same year, before the King of France at Versailles they sent up the first balloon with "passengers" ; it had suspended from it a basket containing a sheep, duck and cock.

J. F. Pilâtre de Rozier (1754–1785) was the first man to ascend in a balloon. He made his flight on October 15, 1783, in an oval captive hot-air balloon 48 feet in diameter and 74 feet high, and remained in the air for five minutes at a height of 80 feet. On November 21 of the same year de Rozier and the Marquis d'Arlandes ascended in a free hot-air balloon and made a successful flight of five and a half miles at a height of 300 feet.

In these ascents the air in the balloon was heated by means of an open brazier suspended beneath the envelope. Meanwhile, experimenters had been busy with hydrogen balloons. But the problem was how to make enough hydrogen to inflate a demonstration balloon. Money was raised by a public subscription, and the French scientist J. A. C. Charles (1746–1823) took over the task. The balloon itself was made of silk varnished with rubber, by the

brothers Robert, and was 13 feet in diameter. The gas was generated in leaden chambers by letting dilute sulphuric acid drop on to iron filings. On August 27, 1783, this balloon made an ascent and travelled 15 miles. Three months later the brothers Robert built a man-carrying balloon and on December 1, 1783, J. A. C. Charles and one of the Robert brothers ascended in it to a height of 2,000 feet and remained in the air two hours.

The first balloon ascent in Great Britain was made by James Tytler (1747–1804) at Edinburgh on August 27, 1784 ; and on September 15 following, Vincent Lunardi (1759–1806) ascended over London. The first sea crossing by balloon was on January 7, 1785, when John Jefferies (1744–1810) and Jean Blanchard (1753–1809) ascended from Dover and landed near Calais. Inflation with hydrogen was then difficult and costly, and ballooning did not attain much

Science Museum

AN EARLY ASCENT OVER ENGLAND
An Italian-born balloonist, Vincent Lunardi—he was a secretary to the Neapolitan embassy—made an ascent over London on September 15, 1784. He was accompanied by a pigeon, a dog and a cat.

popularity until 1819, when Charles Green (1785–1870) inflated a balloon with coal gas. In November 1836 Green and two companions made a journey of 500 miles by balloon in 18 hours.

Because of the difficulty of navigating a balloon on a fixed course, ballooning was never seriously considered as a means of transport by air ; but it became a popular sport for the " air-minded." There is still held an annual international balloon race for the Gordon Bennett Cup, in which the prize is given to the balloon covering the greatest distance. One of the longest voyages ever made was by E. Rumpelmayer, who took off from Paris on March 19, 1913, and landed near Kharkov, 1,492 miles away, two days later. The following year Berliner travelled 1,890 miles by balloon.

On July 11, 1897, Salomon Andrée, a Swedish scientist, took off from Spitzbergen by balloon with the object of reaching the North Pole, 600 miles away, but he and his companions were lost in the Arctic. (*See* Andrée, S. A.).

From its earliest history, the balloon was found invaluable in the scientific investigation of the upper air. In 1804, the scientist J. F. Gay-Lussac (1778–1850) ascended to a height of 13,000 feet and took notes of pressure and temperature. In 1862, an English scientist, James Glaisher (1809–1903) reached a height of over 30,000 feet.

In 1935, Professor Piccard rose to a height of over 10 miles in a balloon 96 feet in diameter which supported an aluminium, pressurised cabin weighing 2,640 lb. On November 13, 1935, two experimenters, Major W. E. Kepner and Captain A. W. Stevens of the United States Army Air Corps attained an altitude of 14 miles in a specially built balloon called Explorer II.

Unmanned balloons also are used for collecting scientific information from the upper air. These balloons carry self-recording instruments, and when the rarefied atmosphere at great heights causes the balloons to burst, the recording instruments float to the ground on parachutes. The greatest height reached by an unmanned balloon is 25 miles. Another type of unmanned, automatic-recording balloon is called the radio-sonde; as it ascends it transmits to the ground by radio the readings registered on its instruments.

Captive balloons were used for military purposes by the French Army as early as 1794. In the First World War (1914–18) " kite balloons "—oval balloons with a car slung from them and fitted with stabilising fins—were used for observation purposes. Similar balloons were used in Britain to support nets of thin steel cables as a defence against aircraft. In the Second World War (1939–45) the balloon barrage was an essential part of air defence in most countries. The British barrage balloon consists of a streamlined bag of rubber-proofed cotton fabric about 60 feet long and 30 feet high, holding about 20,000 cubic feet of hydrogen. It is flown from a flexible steel cable attached to a mobile

Science Museum

BALLOONISTS CROSS THE CHANNEL
Nearly 125 years before Blériot's aeroplane crossing, another Frenchman, J. P. Blanchard, and an American, Dr. John Jefferies, voyaged by balloon across the English Channel in two hours. The start of this historic flight, on January 7, 1785, is depicted above off Dover.

winch. When used to protect shipping the balloons are attached to winches on the ships.

Allowance is made for the expansion of gas, as the balloon rises, by fitting the envelope with a ballonet connected to the gas bag by a valve. As the balloon rises the gas expands and forces air out of the ballonet; when the balloon descends, the ballonet takes back air as the gas contracts. The balloon has three air-filled fins which keep it on an even keel with its nose into the wind.

Why Does a Balloon Float ?

If a balloon displaces more than its own weight of air it will rise until it reaches a region of the atmosphere where the air is less dense, and where the reduced weight of the air just cancels out the lifting power conferred in the first place (because the gas we then put into the balloon weighed less than the air round about at ground level). If you fill a toy balloon with *coal gas* it will rise; an *air-filled* toy balloon merely floats on air currents in the room or out of doors.

Coal gas varies in density according to the way it is made, but we can take an average figure of $\frac{40}{1000}$ lb. for the weight of 1 cubic foot. Air weighs much more than this : roughly $\frac{80}{1000}$ lb. per cubic foot. Hydrogen, much used for inflating balloons, weighs about $\frac{5.6}{1000}$ lb. per cubic foot, so that it has about seven times the lifting power of coal gas. Since hydrogen is very inflammable and many balloons have been lost by fire on this account, balloonists use helium instead whenever they can

BALLOON DEFENCE AGAINST AIR ATTACK

Keystone; Fox; Air Ministry

Balloon barrages to protect certain areas against attack by low-flying aircraft were established in Britain in 1938, a year before the outbreak of the Second World War (1939–45). Crews—at first men and later women of the Royal Air Force—were trained to handle the balloons, which were brought back to the hangars (top) at the end of the day in training establishments. After war broke out in September 1939, most balloons remained out in the open after being hauled down by the mobile winch, as seen in lower left; they were also hauled in periodically for inspection. Cylinders containing hydrogen gas under pressure (lower right) were used to inflate the balloons.

get it. Helium is plentiful in America, where it forms part of natural gas rising up in some localities; but it is scarce in other regions of the world. Its lifting power is about half that of hydrogen, but fortunately it is not inflammable.

The balloon and the ship both float for the same reason: the quantity of air which the balloon displaces (pushes aside) weighs more than the balloon ; the quantity of water which a ship displaces weighs more than the ship. If either has a reserve of lifting power or buoyancy, it can be used to enable cargo or passengers to be carried.

Ballot. The word ballot is derived from the Italian word *ballotta* meaning a " little ball," and our use of the term comes from the ancient practice of voting by means of balls. A white ball meant a favourable vote, and a black ball an adverse vote; from this comes the expression " to blackball " a person, meaning to vote against admitting him to a club or similar organization.

Some form of balloting has been in use for centuries, but the use of voting papers, or the secret ballot as we know it today, is of recent origin. Previous to 1872 the voter in Great Britain came to the polling place and announced publicly the name of the candidate for whom he voted. This method encouraged vote-buying, for the buyer or his agent could see that he received what he had paid for. But, still worse, it led to intimidation, for a voter was often influenced to vote against his better judgement because of fear of the ill-will of his landlord or employer if he dared to vote against the latter's candidate.

When a voter at a Parliamentary or municipal election asks for his paper at the polling station his number on the register of people entitled to vote is added. All that it is necessary for him to do is to put a cross against the name of the person or persons printed on it whom he wishes to vote for. Any other mark renders the document useless. Then he (or she) folds up the ballot paper and drops it into the box, so that no one sees which way the vote has been cast.

Balmoral Castle. On the banks of the Dee, in Scotland, in the loveliest of surround-

Fox

ROYAL RESIDENCE AT BALMORAL
Balmoral Castle was built for Queen Victoria in 1853, and since then the sovereign has almost invariably made a stay there in the autumn. This photograph from the air shows the castle with the stables and outbuildings beyond.

ings, stands a splendid granite castle, which has been a favourite residence of the Royal Family since the early part of the reign of Queen Victoria. The young Queen paid her first visit to Balmoral in 1848, and so pleased was she with the site that her husband, the Prince Consort, purchased the estate and planned the castle famous today as the King's holiday home in the Highlands.

Baltic Sea. The great arm of the North Sea which washes the shores of Sweden, Denmark, Germany, Finland, Poland, and the Soviet Republics of Estonia, Latvia and Lithuania, is the " Mediterranean " of northern Europe; it has for centuries been the chief highway by which the

E.N.A

BALTIC ICE-BREAKERS IN FINNISH WATERS

These Finnish ice-breakers are opening-up a passage for shipping through the ice in the Gulf of Finland, near the port of Hangö. Intense cold freezes the Baltic during three or four months of the year, partly owing to the fact that, as its waters contain only a quarter as much salt as other oceans, they freeze much more readily. The lack of salt is due to the enormous quantity of fresh water discharged into the Baltic by more than 250 rivers, many of them large.

trade of that region has been carried on. It is chiefly by way of the Baltic that Russia has its outlet to the North Sea and the Atlantic. Russia's "window to the west" was obtained by Peter the Great, who early in the 18th century built his new capital, St. Petersburg—now called Leningrad—on the Gulf of Finland.

The "window" was closed three or four months of the year by ice, due to the fact that the Baltic region has a very cold winter and that its waters contain only about a quarter as much salt as the ocean, and so freeze more readily. A fifth of the surface of Europe drains into it, through more than 250 rivers, among them the mighty Oder, Vistula, Neva and Niemen. This enormous flow of river water, and the fact that the water from the ocean has to enter the Baltic by way of the narrow passages connecting it with the North Sea, explain why the waters of the Baltic are almost fresh. The narrow straits of the Sound, Great Belt and Little Belt, and the Kattegat and Skagerrak furnished the only outlet to the Baltic until 1895,

Baltimore, U.S.A. Baltimore is the principal city in the American State of Maryland, containing half that State's population. It is the seventh city in population of the United States, and the largest city on the Atlantic seaboard south of Philadelphia. It lies on the Patapsco River, 14 miles from Chesapeake Bay and about 200 miles from the sea. The river has been widened and improved to form a land-locked harbour, over 12 miles long and three miles wide, capable of accommodating the largest steamships.

Its commanding position as a seaport is due largely to the fact that Baltimore is the nearest ocean port to the northern steel centres, to the manufacturing centres of the Great Lakes and the central western states, and to the Appalachian coal-fields. It exports large quantities of copper, coal, iron and steel, grain, flour, chemicals and cotton. Shipbuilding, and manufacture of clothing, fertilisers and aircraft are principal industries.

The greater part of the business section of Baltimore (which was founded in 1729 and named after Lord Baltimore, the founder of Maryland) was destroyed by fire in 1904. Later this fire came to be regarded as a blessing, for when the burned section was rebuilt, extensive improvements were made on the water-front; the narrow streets were widened, and a large sewer system built. The population in 1940 was 859,100.

Baluchistan. (pron. baloo'chistahn). This province of the Dominion of Pakistan covering an area of 134,000 square miles, supporting a population (1941) of 858,000, formerly consisted of British Baluchistan, tribal territory controlled by the British

BALUCHIS IN THE BAZAAR AT QUETTA
Natives of the Bolan Pass, which leads from Sibi, a town in Baluchistan about 70 miles southeast of Quetta, to Quetta itself, these Baluchis are Mahomedans and make good soldiers, but they are not so warlike as the other tribes on the North-West frontier of the Dominion of Pakistan. They have come into Quetta to buy clothes and household goods in the bazaar.

when the German government completed the Kiel Canal across the base of the Danish peninsula, between Brunsbüttel on the Elbe and Holtenau on Kiel Bay.

Even when the Baltic is open to navigation it is dangerous to seamen because of its extreme shallowness on the German coast, the ruggedness of the Swedish coast, and the frequent violent storms accompanied by sudden changes of wind. The greatest length is about 900 miles, and the width varies between 45 and 145 miles. As in other inland seas, the tides are scarcely perceptible. The broken coast line—about 5,000 miles in length—furnishes some good harbours, the most important being Riga, Copenhagen, Kiel, Danzig (now Gdansk), Gdynia and Stockholm. The north part of the Baltic is called the Gulf of Bothnia; on the east are the Gulfs of Riga and Finland.

prior to 1947, and the independent native states of Kalat, Las Bela and Kharan, all of which became part of Pakistan in 1947.

The country is largely barren desert, mountain and stony plain; its importance lies in its strategic position south and east of Afghanistan and east of Persia (Iran). The chief town is Quetta (population 900,000), a fortified town and former British garrison situated at the end of the Bolan Pass; it is also a railway junction. An earthquake devastated Quetta in 1935, 40,000 people being killed.

Balzac, HONORÉ DE (1799-1850). This great novelist was the first French writer who sought to place on his pages our entire life, to depict equally its weak, strong, happy, sad, noble and base sides. Balzac (pron. bahl'-zak) could see into the hearts of people, and show how one event dragged another with it, and how one man's life was fatally linked with another's. That is why he is said to have "a sense of the whole," and why his books are so clear, even in their wide detail. His famous series of novels called The Human Comedy was intended to be a picture of modern life.

But when we learn that he wrote 85 of these novels in 20 years, we wonder what it was that drove Balzac to such a flood of energy, when he really liked to live easily, collect old furniture, keep a good cook, and chat with a few friends.

He was born at Tours, and educated there and at Paris. Until 1829 he wrote worthless "pot-boilers" for the money they brought. Then his Chouans was published, and his real work began. In 1833 he met the lovely Countess Hanska, a Polish beauty whom he worshipped at a distance. Their great difference in social position and wealth forced him to seek fame and money. He wrote like a slave, whipped his nerves with black coffee, stayed hours at his desk, engaged in wild financial speculations to grow rich and marry his countess. He was always fighting against debt. In 1850, when his fame was so brilliant that he was the social equal of the countess, and when his finances permitted, he attained his dream of marriage with her—only to die in the same year, wrecked by overwork.

Balzac's chief works are Les Chouans (1829); La Peau de Chagrin (The Wild Ass's Skin), 1831; Le Curé de Tours (1832); Eugénie Grandet (1833); Le Père Goriot (Old Goriot), 1834; Le Lys dans la Vallée (The Lily of the Valley), 1836; César Birotteau (1837); La Maison Nucingen (1838); La Cousine Bette (1846); Le Cousin Pons (1847).

BAMBOOS' TOWERING STEMS
These giant bamboos, resembling the pillars of some great cathedral, are growing in the Peradeniya Gardens at Kandy, Ceylon. We see only quite small bamboos in Europe, but some of the Ceylon bamboos grow to a height of 120 feet.

Bamboo. The colossal tree-like grass called bamboo has been well styled "one of the most wonderful and most beautiful products of the tropics, and one of Nature's most valuable gifts to Man." It is a gift, too, with which Nature has been most generous, for nearly 500 species of it are found in Asia, Africa and America. A single root may grow as many as 100 polished, jointed stems rising 30, 50, or even 120 feet in the air. There are no limbs except at the very top. Some species are three feet round. The rate of growth is often very rapid, in some cases as much as 18 inches in a single day.

The uses of the bamboo are innumerable. Everything from a house to a pen-nib is made of it. The young tender shoots are cooked and eaten like asparagus, and they form part of the popular Chinese dish called "chop suey." The seed of those species whose fruit is a grain like barley and rye is also eaten. Some species have a fruit not unlike an apple.

But it is the hollow tube-like stem of the plant which is most useful. It is used for the posts of houses. Split into strips, it forms the planks for floors, roofs and sides. Besides the familiar fishing-rod, it is also used for water-pipes, bridges and cables, and the joints of the large stems are even used for pails and for cooking utensils Strips are woven into cages, mats, chairs, beds, cradles, and other articles of furniture. From the interior portions, beaten into a pulp, is made a fine variety of paper. The outer skin of some species is so hard that knives and swords have been made of it.

E N.A.

BALZAC, FRENCH NOVELIST
The great French novelist did not like the camera, perhaps because in his day—he died in 1850—photography was in its infancy. This daguerrotype—which is what the earliest photographs were called—was taken in 1841, and is the only photograph ever made of Balzac.

Banana. Until the end of the 19th century this fruit was a little-known luxury in temperate regions. The tall, broad-leaved plant was cultivated by white settlers and natives in tropical lands only for their own use. Then a clever business man realized the value of the fruit as food, and set to work to bring the banana within the reach of consumers in lands far removed from the home of the plant.

But the obstacles with which he contended were as discouraging and varied as the tangled forests and swamps of the tropics could make them. Transportation was only a small part of the problem, for banana plantations themselves had first to be started.

Forests had to be cleared and swamps drained ; railways had to be built, bridges thrown across mighty streams, safe harbours made, and a fleet of ships provided so that the fruit could be speedily transported. Today bananas are raised in enormous quantities on the islands of the West Indies and along the Gulf of Mexico and Caribbean coasts from Vera Cruz in Mexico to the mouth of the Amazon. Central America is the greatest banana-producing area in the world. Cities with good schools and hospitals have been built where only a few years ago were disease-breeding jungles. The banana is also an important crop in the Canary Islands, throughout the Pacific islands, parts of Africa, Malaya and the islands of the East Indian archipelago.

HOW BANANAS DEVELOP

The top picture shows blossoms turning into bananas. These blossoms grow between the overlapping scales or bracts of the big cone-shaped flower bud at the tip of the stem. From inside this bud, layer after layer of the finger-like blossoms continues to spread out. The bracts soon fall off and the tiny bananas turn upward. The next picture shows three layers or 'hands' of bananas formed in this manner. In the bottom picture, all the blossoms have emerged from the flower bud and matured into full-grown bananas, tightly clustered around the stem.

Bananas are seldom allowed to ripen on the tree. The fruit matures so quickly that the skin breaks, and ants, bees, and other insects feed upon the pulp, spoiling it. So the bananas we buy in the shop taste about the same as they do in the tropics, because they are cut green in either case. There are, however, many varieties that cannot be exported because of their tender skin, such as the little "lady's finger" banana of the Canary Islands.

Some of the numerous species known as plantains (*Musa paradisiaca*), are "cooking bananas." The fruit of one kind of plantain grows to an enormous size, sometimes two feet in length and as thick as a man's arm. Plantains constitute one of the chief foods of the natives in the tropics, taking the place of our bread and potatoes, but they are seldom exported as they are not in demand where potatoes are ordinarily available.

Banana "figs" are sold in large quantities in tropical countries as sweetmeats. They are ripe bananas which have been preserved by sprinkling with sugar and drying in the sun. Banana flour, prepared by drying unripe bananas and grinding them, is largely used in the tropics. The flower clusters of some species are considered a delicacy in India. Banana leaves are often torn into strips and woven into mats and coarse cloth, and the fibre is used for cordage and to some extent for paper.

A banana plantation is a magnificent sight, often extending over thousands of acres. The tree-like plants grow to a height of 12 feet or more, and the great leaves, 10 feet long and one to two feet wide, meet in arches that shut out the light of the sun. They are planted in rows, set about 10 feet apart.

Soon a long "bud" appears, made up of tightly overlapping purple scales, each of which protects a cluster of flowers. The lower clusters of flowers wither and only the upper ones are fertilized and produce fruit. The bananas grow round the stem in ridges called "hands," the standard-sized bunch being nine hands to a stem and 10 to 15 "fingers" to a hand. The banana plant grows and produces fruit in about nine months, each stem bearing about 12 bunches.

Bananas are 75 per cent water, but are excellent food because the starch which they contain when green changes to sugar when they ripen, and there is more of it than in most fruits, so that they are good heat producers. In addition, bananas have vitamins and alkaline salts, and so are a "protective" food. The green bunches, usually packed with banana leaves in rough crates, are taken quickly to a seaport and loaded into ships, where they are kept cold by fans and refrigerating apparatus. On

arrival in port bananas are artificially ripened by heating with gas jets for five or six days.

The bananas sold in Great Britain usually belong to the species known as "Gros Michel" (*Musa sapientum*); it is the large smooth yellow product of Jamaica and Central America. The Canary Island Banana (*Musa cavendishii*), also known as the dwarf Chinese banana, is extensively grown also in some sections of Central and South America. The red Jamaica banana is grown in various parts of the world, but it is difficult to ship because the individual bananas do not cling closely to the stem.

Import of bananas into Great Britain ceased, temporarily, early in the Second World War. On

December 31, 1945, the first resumed shipments arrived, but for some time supplies were limited to children.

Banffshire. This maritime county of Scotland has a coastline of 30 miles along the Moray Firth, and a greatest length N.E. to S.W. of nearly 60 miles, the total area being 630 square miles. The south of Banffshire is a mountainous region, with various summits of the Cairngorms culminating in Ben Macdhui (4,296 feet), on the Aberdeenshire border, and Cairngorm itself, partly in Inverness-shire. Fishing, quarrying and general agriculture are carried on. Banff is the county town and the largest place, with a population of 3,500. The estimated total population of the county is 51,900.

Bangkok. The flourishing capital and chief seaport of Siam (*q.v.*) or Thailand, Bangkok until the beginning of the 20th century was a primitive city. Its

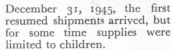

BANGKOK, CAPITAL OF SIAM
The people of Siam (or Thailand) are Buddhists, and the Wat Phra Keo temple (top) is one of their places of worship in Bangkok. Many inhabitants live in houseboats on the canals and the Menam river. One of the narrow waterways, crowded with small craft, is seen in the lower photograph.

commerce was carried by water, and a large proportion of its people lived in house-boats on the river Menam, but now wide thoroughfares, carried across the canals by bridges and traversed by electric trams, are lined with brick buildings and lighted by electric lamps. The new city, surrounded by high walls, has been laid out round the royal palace and its parks, which form the centre of local interest.

Lying only 20 miles from the mouth of the Menam, Bangkok is the centre of the foreign trade of Siam and also is the terminus of a railway from Penang, Malaya. The chief exports are rice and teak, and imports are cotton and silk goods, foodstuffs, machinery and oil. Most of its trade is in the hands of Chinese and European merchants. Population is 1,117,000, of which a large number are Chinese. During the Second World War Siam sided with the Japanese, declaring war on Great Britain in January 1942. Bangkok became an important Japanese base during the Burma campaign and was attacked by Allied bombers.

Banjo. The Negroes of the southern United States gave the world the banjo and showed that this most commonplace of musical instruments could crash out the liveliest of tunes or render soulful melodies. The banjo has a round tambourine-like body formed of parchment stretched over a frame, and a long neck. The steel wire strings, usually five in number, are plucked or struck with the fingers of the right hand, while the fingers of the left hand lengthen or shorten them by pressure against the neck. Negroes are believed to have brought this instrument with them, in a simpler form, from Africa.

Bank of England. Officially in Threadneedle Street, the Bank of England actually occupies a huge block facing four busy thoroughfares in the heart of the City of London, and it has half-a-dozen branches in the provinces.

Founded by William Paterson in 1694, it acts as banker to the Government and to all other banks, which keep large balances with the Bank for purposes of the Clearing House (*see* Banks and Banking). It has two main sections, the banking and the issue departments. The first of these manages the National Debt, in addition to carrying on most of the normal activities of a joint-stock bank, while the issue department is concerned with the maintenance of the gold reserve and is the only noteissuing bank in England. Through the Royal Mint it stamps and issues the coins forming the metallic currency. In 1937 a new nickel-brass threepenny-piece was struck. No more silver coins were struck after October 1946. In 1947 the issue began of new " cupro-nickel " coins to replace them.

In 1928 the Bank of England was rebuilt ; its imposing façade is a worthy addition to the designs of the famous architect Sir John Soane (1753-1837). An interesting sidelight on the Bank of England is the nightly picket provided by the Foot Guards. This protection was asked for after the Gordon Riots in 1780 and has been maintained ever since, despite protests in the early days from the City Fathers. That this guard is not altogether uncalled for will be realized when we remember the vast wealth contained in the Bank's vaults.

In 1946 the Bank of England came under national control. Its governor, deputy governor and directors are appointed by the Government and are collectively called the Court of Directors. The Court meets weekly, to issue a statement of both Departments (banking, and issue) and to fix the Bank Rate. By means of the latter, and by the issue of Treasury Bills and Treasury Deposit Receipts taken up by the big banks, control of the whole money market of Britain is assured.

Bankruptcy. In medieval times, when the Italian cities were the money markets of the world, it was the custom to break the bench of any money-lender or banker whose debts became greater than the amount of his property. As his bench was his place of business, the breaking of it forced him to discontinue his former pursuit, and also implied disgrace. From the Italian words describing this custom (*banca* meaning " bench," and *rotta* meaning " broken ") has come our modern word " bankrupt "; and from the custom itself comes the practice of all modern nations of forcing a man who cannot pay his debts—that is, who is a bankrupt—to discontinue his business, but this is done by means of bankruptcy laws. Those of England date from the reign of King Henry VIII, and proceedings are now taken under the Bankruptcy Act of 1914; they are heard in London in the High Court of Justice and elsewhere in the County Courts, administration in all cases being under control of the Board of Trade.

The petition may be presented by the debtor himself, or by his creditor or creditors, provided the total of the debt is not less than £50. A general meeting of creditors is first called, after which the debtor's statement of affairs is examined by the Court. If the Court makes a Receiving Order, notice of which must be advertised in the London Gazette and one local newspaper, the Official Receiver (an official of the Board of Trade who is in charge of bankruptcy proceedings) takes charge of the estate of the debtor. The debtor may make a proposal to pay so much in the pound, or agree to some other scheme, subject to the approval of the creditors and of the Court. If no such proposal is made, or if made is not accepted, the debtor will be adjudged bankrupt, and his estate vested in a Trustee and distributed among the creditors in proportion to the sum owing to each of them.

A bankrupt may start in business again, provided he does not obtain credit for £20 or more without disclosing that he is a bankrupt. He may at any time apply for his discharge from bankruptcy.

The early law of Rome gave a man's creditors, if he could not or would not pay his debts, the savage remedy of dividing his body among them, or selling him and his family into slavery.

Banks AND BANKING. In all towns and most villages in the United Kingdom there is at least one building with the word " Bank " prominently displayed above its door. Years ago each of these banks would have been as likely as not independent but now many of them are branches of one or other of the " Big Five," as they are sometimes called—Barclays, Lloyds, Midland, National Provincial, and Westminster—a series of amalgamations taking place soon after the First World War.

Banks are the places to which money goes and from which it comes. Once money has been paid in by a customer to a bank, the latter becomes the customer's agent. A cheque is simply an order to a bank from one of its customers to pay a certain sum of money to a certain person, known as the payee. Most payments nowadays are made by cheques; coins and notes play but a small part in comparison.

Let us see how the system works. Mr. Smith has some loose money—coins or notes—which he does not want to carry about in his pocket. In the old days, before banks existed, he would have placed it in a strong box buried under his floor, or hidden it in a hole in the wall, or in a secret drawer in his bureau. Today, provided he can produce at least one good reference, he takes it to a bank.

The bank opens an account for him in its books, agreeing to let him have his money whenever he wants it, either the whole or in part, and supplies him with a book of cheques. This account is known as a current account; a deposit account is one which can be drawn on only if some agreed notice is given first, and usually the banker pays interest on the amount deposited.

Now, supposing Mr. Smith wants to pay a bill, perhaps that of Mr. Snuff, the grocer. He can if he likes go to the bank and draw out some of his current account in cash and take the cash to Snuff. But he can avoid all this trouble by simply sitting down at home and writing a cheque in favour of Mr. Snuff for the exact amount he wishes to pay him. He sends the cheque to Snuff and expects to receive a receipt in due course.

G.P.A.

BANK OF ENGLAND FRONTAGE

Close to the Royal Exchange, the Mansion House (where the Lord Mayor of London lives), and Lombard Street, the bankers' street, the Bank of England stands in the heart of commercial London. Above is the front built in 1928, with, between the wreaths on the pediment, the statue of Britannia holding a model of the Bank, popularly referred to as the Old Lady of Threadneedle Street.

Mr. Snuff receives the cheque, endorses it by writing his name on the back, and takes or sends it to *his* bank, and the amount of the cheque is added to his account in the bank's books. Business transactions in Britain today are done in this way.

At the end of each day the cheques collected by the branch banks are forwarded to the head offices in London, where the amounts they represent are collected through the Bankers' Clearing House. This is an institution to which all the big banks belong. Each sends a clerk twice daily to the Clearing House with the cheques it has received drawn on other " clearing banks," and these are sorted and handed over to the representatives of the respective banks. Then a balance is struck between each pair of banks, and the bank which has received more than it has paid transfers the difference to the other bank's account with the Bank of England— the bankers' bank.

Each week the Bank of England fixes the minimum rate at which it is willing to discount bills of exchange (that is, to buy now, for cash, bills maturing at some future date). Bills of exchange are documents from one man or firm to another undertaking to pay a certain sum of money on a fixed date. This rate, known as the Bank Rate, governs the interest charged by other banks on loans and overdrafts; their rate is naturally determined to some extent by the amount of security tendered, and is approximately two per cent above Bank Rate. The Bank Rate generally rises in times of crisis, and it reached 10 per cent at the outbreak of the First World War in 1914; after 1932 it remained at two per cent except for a short period at the beginning of the Second World War.

A simple savings account may be opened either at an ordinary joint-stock bank (a branch of one of the " Big Five "), or at a special bank dealing only with accounts of this kind—such as the Post Office Savings Bank. Interest is paid on such deposits.

In addition to these normal functions the banks perform other services for their customers. They

The Midland Bank Ltd.

BANK STRONG-ROOM'S CIRCULAR STEEL DOOR

To protect the sums of money and valuable documents which they are obliged to keep on their premises in the ordinary course of business, banks place them in strong-rooms. In a big branch or head office this part of the building is practi- cally a fortress. The door (above) of the strong-room of the Midland Bank office in Poultry, London, is made of steel and weighs 35 tons. With its clock-operated combination locks, it would defy the efforts of the expert safe-breaker.

act as custodians of their valuables, and as agents for the purchase and sale of Stock Exchange securities. They make periodical payments of club and other subscriptions, insurance premiums, building society interest, and so on. They act as trustees and executors under wills. They maintain income tax departments to deal with customers' tax difficulties. They act as agents to the Government—by the mainten- ance of clothing coupon accounts for traders, by the issue of National Savings Certificates and other Government securities, by the ap- proval and issue of foreign travel documents and by their appoint- ment as "authorised depositaries" under the Exchange Control Act.

Through their Foreign Branches at home, and their Subsidiary Banks and Correspondents abroad, they can assist exporters. The strength of British banks is re- cognized abroad, and in normal times their travel documents and acceptances are current everywhere.

The history of banking goes back to the money- changers of the medieval Italian cities who con- ducted their transactions from a bench on the street ; and from the Italian word *banca*, referring to this bench, comes our modern term "bank." From these money-changers in Italy developed the first commercial bank, the Banco di Rialto of

Burroughs Adding Machine Ltd.

BANKING ACCOUNTS KEPT BY MACHINES

In the Ledger Department of big banks much of the work formerly done by many clerks is carried out by a small number of girls operating accounting machines, as above. Clients' accounts are kept on cards, instead of in bound ledgers, and the operators can tell in a moment either how much money a customer has in the bank or the sum he owes to it.

Venice, established in 1587. It was the Lombards (people of Northern Italy) who introduced banking into England. Their work is commemorated today in the name of Lombard Street, one of the principal streets in the City of London, now established as one of the centres of the world's financial system. John Stow refers to the Lombard money-changers in his famous Survey of London (1598).

Banks, Sir Joseph (1743-1820). Among the greatest benefactors of that wonderful national treasure-house, the British Museum, London, was the naturalist Sir Joseph

BANYAN, WITH BRANCHES THAT GROW PROPS
The gigantic and fantastic banyan tree must be one of the strangest things in the vegetable world, for it is not one tree but many, and its branches are supported by natural props. How it sends down shoots which root in the ground to form fresh trunks is clearly shown in this photograph of a fine specimen in the botanical gardens at Cairo in Egypt.

Banks. He devoted both wealth and time to the pursuits of science. He was an ardent botanist, and in searching for the objects that he included in his immense and carefully classified collections he made voyages to Newfoundland, and round the world with Captain Cook. On his return he visited Iceland and the Hebrides. With his friend Dr. Solander, a Swede, who had been a pupil of the great botanist Linnaeus, and was assistant librarian to the British Museum, he discovered the column-like rocks on Staffa, an island of the Inner Hebrides.

Born in London on February 13, 1743, this great naturalist became President of the Royal Society in 1778. Created a baronet in 1781 for his contributions to scientific knowledge, he continued to act as President of the Royal Society until his death. All his library and botanical collections he left to the British Museum.

Bannockburn. In the days when England and Scotland were separate kingdoms and often at war, a big battle took place between the armies of the two countries on the field of Bannockburn, two miles south of Stirling. King Robert Bruce of Scotland, with some 40,000 Scots, had barred the way to Stirling Castle against King Edward II of England. On June 24, 1314, King Edward brought against him an army which outnumbered the Scots and which included the flower of English chivalry.

The English army advanced in the belief that the Scots would be overwhelmed by weight of numbers. The Scots, however, withstood the onslaught. As the English army was brought to a standstill, it meant that those in the forefront had to bear all the fighting. Following up his advantage, the Scottish king forced home a counter-attack on the English vanguard with such fury that they began to be driven back on the masses of troops behind. Confusion led to wavering, and soon the battle became a rout. Only with difficulty did the

English King escape. Today the battlefield of Bannockburn is farming land, and the road from Carlisle to Stirling passes not far away.

Banyan. (Pron. ban'yan). One of the strangest of all trees is the banyan, which grows in India and other tropical countries. It sends down from its branches great numbers of shoots which take root and become new trunks, so that a single tree may spread over a large area. A specimen in the Calcutta botanical garden, about 100 years old, has a main trunk 13 feet in diameter, 230 trunks as large as oak trees, and over 3,000 smaller ones. It is said that once upon a time 7,000 people stood beneath it. The banyan often grows to a height of over 70 feet, and lives a very long time, though its original trunk may decay, leaving the younger ones to support the tree. It has large heart-shaped leaves and inconspicuous blossoms followed by cherry-like scarlet fruit, which furnishes food for birds and monkeys.

Among the Hindus the banyan is held sacred, and its bark is considered a powerful tonic. The wood is light, porous, and of no value. Botanically, the banyan is a species of fig, *Ficus benghalensis*; it belongs to the mulberry family, *Moraceae*.

Baptism. The name of this rite of initiation into the Christian Church is derived from the Greek word *baptizein*, meaning to dip in water. The custom of bathing the body in water, as a mark of moral and spiritual cleansing, or of initiation into a community, was a widespread one. The Christian Church took it over from the Jews, and John the Baptist made baptism a feature of his revival movement.

In the Christian Church the practice was carried on and developed. The rite expressed two main religious beliefs, the pardon of sins and the gift of eternal life, the latter being commonly described as a new birth or regeneration, or entrance into the divine family. As the Church developed, infants were baptized. The Baptist Church still adheres to the primitive view which confined baptism to adults who could make a conscious profession of faith. The practice of immersion (that is, plunging the whole body in water) has been modified in the direction of what is called " affusion " (pouring of water on the body) or of sprinkling, by many Churches, for climatic reasons. But water has always been held essential, together with a simple formula pronounced by the person performing the rite, who is in most cases the priest.

Baptism, which is regarded as a sacrament in the Anglican, Roman Catholic and Eastern Churches, implies the action of God through the Church, imparting life; the rite of baptism denotes the regenerating power of Christ. At a christening an infant is given its Christian name or names, although the giving of a name is not an essential part of baptism. In cases of urgent necessity baptism may be administered elsewhere than in a church and, in some Churches, even by a person not in holy orders. The word " baptism " is used figuratively in such phrases as " baptism of fire," meaning a soldier's first battle or any severe ordeal, and " baptism of blood," signifying martyrdom.

Barbados. (Pron. bar-bā′dōz).
One of the most densely populated regions is the self-governing British island colony of Barbados, the easternmost of the West Indies; only 166 square miles in area, it has a population of over 203,000. Its palm-shaded roads are lined with pink-tinted cottages or huts with roofs of ragged thatch. Many of the Negro men emigrate because of the pressure of population, and so three-fifths of the inhabitants are females. Negroes have equal rights in the schools, in the churches, and in politics. The natives outnumber the whites by about 13 to one.

English settlers occupied the island in about 1625 and, unlike most of the West Indies, it has never changed hands. The colony is administered by a Governor, an Executive Council and a Legislative Council, all appointed by the British Government, and a House of Assembly elected by the people. The capital is Bridgetown, with a population of about 13,000.

Coral reefs fringe the coasts of Barbados. The surface, broken by a few forests and streams, is elevated in the interior, where Mt. Hillaby rises to 1,104 feet. Over three-fifths of the island are under cultivation, chiefly for sugar-cane, but a small amount of cotton is also grown. There is a healthful climate. Barbados (Spanish for " bearded ") may get its name from the bearded fig-tree which grows here. The island has hurricanes and earthquakes.

E.N.A

BARCELONA'S WORLD-FAMED ' RAMBLA '

Through the heart of the great Spanish city of Barcelona in Catalonia runs the Rambla—a promenade, shopping street, and traffic artery all in one. Here we are looking west from the Plaza de Cataluña (Catalonia) along the magnificent extension which is called the Rambla de Cataluña.

Barcelona. Spain.
The principal seaport, chief manufacturing centre and second largest city in the country, Barcelona is one of the finest towns in Spain. Remains of its ancient splendour are to be seen in the " old town " with its narrow streets and flat-roofed brick dwellings; but for the most part Barcelona is very different from the old cities characteristic of Spain.

Built on the sloping edge of a small plain, between the rivers Besos on the north and Llobrégat on the south, Barcelona lies along the Mediterranean in the shape of a half-moon. The " new town " to the north, built on a regular plan, has wide streets, handsome modern houses of stone, and gardens of almost tropical luxuriance. The main thoroughfare of the " old town " is the Rambla, which has a fine promenade, with plane-trees planted down the centre, and on either side the principal hotels and theatres of the city. On an oval hill at the highest point of the Rambla stands a 13th-century Gothic cathedral.

Since early in the Christian era Barcelona has been one of the most important Mediterranean ports. Chief of its extensive industries are the spinning and weaving of cotton, silk and woollen goods. The First World War (1914-18) gave great impetus to the city's manufactures, for many articles which had been imported began to be manufactured here. Many textile companies and tanneries sprang up, but the greatest growth was in the output of chemical products—dyes, soaps, fertilizers, drugs—formerly imported from Germany. The chief imports of the city are raw cotton, hemp, coal, grain and foodstuffs. Fruits, wines, olive oil, textiles, leather goods, machinery and furniture are among its exports.

The city is said to have been founded by the Carthaginian, Hamilcar Barca, in the 3rd century B.C.; it thus acquired its ancient name *Barcino*. It became a colony under the Romans, and in the 2nd century A.D. was the leading trading centre in the western Mediterranean, rivalling Marseilles. It retained its importance under the Goths and the Moors, and in 801 came, with the rest of Catalonia, under Frankish rule. From the 9th to the 12th century its counts ruled as independent sovereigns. It reached the zenith of its fame in the 12th century, when its merchant ships vied with those of Genoa and Venice, trading as far north as the North Sea and the Baltic, and as far east as Alexandria. But in the early 16th century much of its importance was lost to ports of western Spain, because of the trade with America. In the 17th, 18th and 19th centuries it came several times under French rule.

Barcelona is the capital of the province of Catalonia, which in 1931-32, after Spain had become a republic, was given a large measure of self-government. During the Spanish Civil War that began in 1936 the port was an important base of the Republican Government forces, and the city was bombed by Nationalist aircraft. With the collapse of Republican resistance in Catalonia the city was occupied by Nationalist forces on January 26, 1939. Population is about 1,225,300.

Barley.

According to the Roman historian Pliny the most ancient food of mankind was barley. Barley has been found in the excavated lake-dwellings of Switzerland belonging to the Stone Age. Chinese sacred books claim that it was known in China 20 centuries before the birth of Christ, and the ancient Hebrews used the grain in Egypt, for it is referred to in Exodus.

In appearance barley is not unlike wheat, but it will grow in climates too cold for the latter grain. It is cultivated from the Arctic region of Alaska to tropical India, and it grows wild in western Asia. Barley needs a light well-drained soil, and as the roots are short the ground does not require deep ploughing. As it takes a shorter time for barley to ripen than for wheat, it is usually sown in the spring after the wheat is ripe, and is harvested before the wheat is ripe. Sometimes it is sown in autumn, this "winter barley" being the four-rowed variety.

BARLEY OF THREE KINDS

A and B are six-rowed varieties of barley, B being the true six-rowed barley. Two-rowed varieties are shown in C and D; C has had the awns or beard removed.

There are three well-known kinds of barley: the two-rowed, the four-rowed, and the six-rowed. The difference is in the number of rows of grain in the head and in the long beards or spikelets on each head. In the two-rowed variety only two rows of the spikes produce grains. In the four-rowed variety four rows of the spikes are fertile; and in the six-rowed each spikelet produces a grain of barley. The two-rowed type is most common in Europe, while in North America the six-rowed kind predominates. As the four-rowed species is of poorer quality, it is raised only in the northern latitudes, as it is extremely hardy.

Barley is not used so much as other grains for human food, for it has little gluten in it, though thousands of peasants in Europe eat the black barley bread. The round grains, called pearl barley, and the milled barley flour, are used for thickening soups, for making gruel, and for modifying cow's milk for babies. The chief human use of barley is in the preparation of malt for alcoholic drinks and malted foods. As a feeding stuff for farm animals, particularly pigs, barley, in the form of barley meal, is particularly valuable for fattening purposes.

Barnacle.

Shipbuilders and sailors must wage constant warfare against barnacles, for though, individually, these are helpless little animals, collectively they can materially lessen the speed of an ocean liner.

The common ship's barnacle, *Lepas anatifera*, starts out in life independent, active and able to swim about alone. But soon it fastens upon any support it can find—a rock, a floating log, or a wooden pile under a pier. There it develops a lime-like shell with a movable lid. Barnacles gather beneath the water-line of vessels in such immense numbers that they produce a tremendous "drag," which slows down the craft. Ships have to be placed in dry dock from time to time to have their bottoms scraped free of these salt-water pests.

Another kind of barnacle prefers to live on rocks. These may be found in large numbers at low tide, withdrawn into their small houses, waiting for the return of the water which brings them their food. The shell of this type is conical, and from the shape it is called the acorn barnacle (*Balanus tintinnabulum*).

It was believed at one time that barnacles were molluscs, like oysters, but they are crustaceans—degenerate relatives of the lobster and the crab. Born free, they attach themselves to some object and develop a hard shell and lose their power of motion, except in the six pairs of feathery feet which project from the shell and wave food into their mouths. At the base of the shell is a cement gland which provides the powerful "sticking" qualities. In natural history books one may see a picture

BARNACLES FROM THE DEEP

A barnacle spends most of its life attached either to a ship's bottom (like the stalked barnacles above) or to a rock. A scientist described the barnacle as a ' crustacean fixed by its head and kicking the food into its mouth with its legs.'

of a bird called the barnacle goose. A curious old superstition says that this goose was the product of a tree which bore barnacles as fruit ; these, on falling into the sea, turned into birds.

Barnardo, THOMAS JOHN (1845–1905). About 70 years ago, on a cold winter night, a number of ragged urchins were sitting in an old stable in the East End of London. At one end of the whitewashed room a little fire burned, and the boys sat round it, warm for the first time that day. They were members of what was called in those days a Ragged School, and their teacher was a student at the London Hospital. On this night he was tired, for he had had a stiff day at the hospital. As the school was coming to an end the door opened and a boy came in without shoes or shirt, shivering in a ragged coat. The newcomer did not want to learn anything ; he just wanted to be warm, and when the rest went away he stayed behind.

Someone had told him that perhaps they might let him sleep there by the fire ; but this the young teacher could not allow. He told the boy to go home. The boy said he had no father, no mother, and nowhere to live. All he had was his name, Jim Jarvis. The young man from the London Hospital knew next to nothing of life in slums. He questioned the boy and asked him to show him where boys who had no home spent the night.

Jim led him into a network of blind alleys and passages to a wall which supported sheds by the side of an old wharf. The young man climbed the wall after him, and saw from the top a group of lads asleep in the gutters with not a shred of covering. Horrified by what he had seen, the young man took Jim back to the stable and left him to sleep there in the warmth. He himself went to his lodgings, sick at heart.

The name of the young medical student was Thomas John Barnardo, and he was studying medicine with a view to becoming a missionary in China. What he had seen on that night, however, and on the nights that followed, convinced him that his real work lay near at hand. He gave up his intention

of going to China, and in 1866 founded the East End Juvenile Mission for the care of friendless and destitute children. Shortly afterwards, under the patronage of Lord Shaftesbury, he opened a Boys' Home at number 18 Stepney Causeway, London— the institution which developed into what are known throughout the world as Dr. Barnardo's Homes.

On one occasion Barnardo had to tell a boy that there was no room in the Home for a few days, and a night or two afterwards the youngster was found dead in an alley. After that Barnardo made the famous declaration; " No destitute child ever refused admission," which is still the proud boast of the great organization he founded.

In the course of his life he rescued 60,000 children from the most abominable conditions of poverty and sickness, and helped 250,000 more. Many of these he sent to Canada for training and settlement on the farms. Supported by men and women in all classes of society, the homes he founded continue their good work. Dr. Barnardo died at Surbiton, Surrey, on September 19, 1905.

Barometer. (Pron. ba-rom' et-er). If you have read our account of the atmosphere, in the story of Air, you will know that air has weight, and that the atmosphere reaches up into the sky above us for many miles. Everything which has weight must exercise pressure, and the atmosphere presses down upon our bodies—and of course upon everything else on our earth — with a pressure of roughly 14.7 lb. per square inch of surface.

If we climb a mountain or a high tower, or mount in the skies in a balloon or an aeroplane, the pressure of the atmosphere becomes less as we go up ; if we descend into a deep valley below sea level, the pressure becomes greater than at sea level, which is the accepted zero for measuring air pressure. In the story of Air you will have learnt

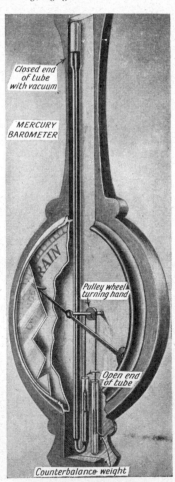

Closed end of tube with vacuum

MERCURY BAROMETER

Pulley wheel turning hand

Open end of tube

Counterbalance weight

MERCURY BAROMETER

In this type of barometer the air presses on the mercury in the open end of the glass tube and supports a column of metal about 29 or 30 inches high, according to the pressure of the atmosphere.

also that air pressure alters according to the warmth or coolness of the atmosphere at a given time and place. So if we wish to compare two or more readings of air pressure we must also state the temperature by a thermometer; moreover, we must allow for any difference in height as compared with sea level.

The principal use of the barometer is in weather observation and forecasting, and this is described in our story of Weather. But we can also use a barometer to measure heights; for this purpose the surveyor employs the type known as an aneroid barometer, made without the use of a liquid and cased up in a handy box for carrying. In aerial travel the pioneers used a barometer as a height finder and recorder; but other instruments, known as altimeters, have since been invented which are more convenient.

The ancients found that however carefully they constructed a pump, it would not suck water from a well to a height of more than 32 feet from the surface of the well water. The Italian scientist Galileo worked at this problem, but it was his pupil Torricelli (1608–1647) who solved it; he reasoned that it was the weight of the atmosphere which pressed upon the surface of the water in the well, and—when air had been sucked from the tube and the pump barrel—forced up the water to the pump spout.

Torricelli made the first mercury barometer, by sealing a glass tube at one end, emptying it of air, and plunging the other end into a bowl of mercury open to the air. He found that mercury rose in the tube to between 29 and 30 inches above the level of the mercury in the bowl. Since mercury is about 13 times heavier than water, the pressure of the atmosphere forces up the mercury in the tube to roughly one-thirteenth the height that a water column would be pushed up if we were to make a barometer of water.

Indeed, Otto von Guericke (1602–1686) made such a water barometer. Von Guericke was mayor of Magdeburg, and fond of trying scientific experiments. He astonished the town by erecting on the wall of his house a strange-looking tube more than 34 feet high, and made for most of its length of brass; at the top there was a transparent portion formed of glass. The lower end of the tube rested in a vessel of water open to the air, and the water rose in the tube to a height of about 30 feet above. On top of the water Guericke floated a little wooden manikin; in fine weather it rose with the water-level and popped up its head above the roof top (for the tube was carried out through the tiles); in bad weather the manikin dropped down the tube, out of sight.

Old-fashioned barometers of the mercury type

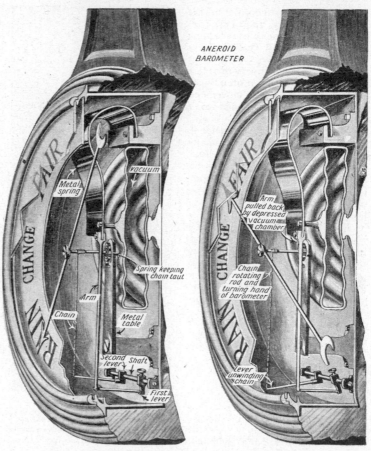

ANEROID BAROMETER AND ITS WORKING

This barometer contains no mercury, but has a metal box from which all air has been drawn. As the air pressure on the box varies, the surface of the box moves in and out, operating the indicator as shown in the diagrams. On the left pressure is low; on the right pressure is higher. For clearness the words "Rain, Change, Fair" have been brought round to the visible part of the dial.

have a little float resting on the mercury in the open end, and are of the U-tube pattern; the float has attached a fine cord which passes over a pulley connected to the indicator on the dial, the latter being graduated from usually 28 to 31 inches. At the opposite end of the cord a tiny weight keeps the tension, or there may be a fine spiral spring to do this. When the atmospheric pressure increases, the mercury rises in the tube (long arm) and falls in the short arm, letting the float drop; the cord moves the indicator around the dial. When pressure falls, the reverse motion occurs, and the indicator goes the opposite way. In another type of barometer, with a straight tube of which the lower end rests in a vessel of mercury, the reading is taken off by a graduated scale alongside the upper end of the tube.

In the aneroid barometer there is no liquid; instead there is a thin-walled metal capsule, something like the flat box used for ointments. This capsule is exhausted of air and sealed. Connected to it is a system of tiny levers which converts any rise and fall of the top of the capsule into movements of an indicator around a dial. A strong spring causes the capsule to expand again when atmospheric pressure decreases—and so the indicator follows the movement of the capsule in the reverse direction to the first movement. In automatic recording barometers, usually called barographs because they " write " the record with an inked pen, there are about half-a-dozen capsules linked together to increase the movement, which is further multiplied by a system of levers.

A word about the barometer as a weather glass. The barometer tells us if pressure is rising or falling, but we have to draw our own conclusions about what this means in terms of future weather, and we must not take too literally the legend " Fine," " Stormy," and so on inscribed round the dial. We need to know much more about prevailing conditions, such as wind strength and direction, temperature, etc., before we can begin to forecast to-morrow's weather.

We have mentioned corrections for temperature, and for height in relation to sea level. The latitude of the place also has to be taken into account, since owing to the curvature of the earth the force of gravity varies in different p l a c e s. So scientists make corrections which will compare the reading with one taken in the " standard latitude," 45 deg. North or South. Barometers may be graduated in inches or in centimetres. But there is a special unit for this measurement, known as a bar, and its sub-division of 1 millibar, or one-thousandth of a bar, is the one in which barometer readings are quoted for scientific records. A reading of 1 inch on the mercury barometer or the aneroid instrument is equal to 25·4 millimetres.

Barrie, Sir James Matthew. (1860–1937). A small man with a great heart, one of the shyest and most retiring persons, though his writings brought the world to his feet, a man of insight and wisdom who kept the freshness and gaiety of childhood, a man of tenderness, kindly humour, wit and whimsical fancy—this was J. M. Barrie.

His birthplace was the little village of Kirriemuir, Angus, described in his writings under the name of " Thrums," and there, too, he was buried. In the

SIR JAMES BARRIE
This photograph shows the great playwright and friend of children as he might have been seen any day walking in Kensington Gardens.

garret of his simple home he began to write stories of adventure before he was 12. One of his chief tasks as a small lad—and for long afterward—was to cheer his mother when she was ill. In trying to make her laugh he developed that gift of humour, touched always with pathos, which is his greatest charm. From his mother, so he tells us in his beautiful story of her life, Margaret Ogilvy, he learned all that he put into his books, and under many names and with many changes of feature she appears as the heroine in almost every one of Barrie's writings. From this Scotswoman Barrie inherited his whimsically sunny view of life.

After being educated at Dumfries Academy and Edinburgh University, Barrie b e c a m e a journalist, contributing to various English papers. He first won recognition by his stories of his native village, Auld Licht Idylls and A Window in Thrums. Later he produced a number of charming dramas, including Quality Street, The Admirable Crichton, Dear Brutus and Mary Rose. The beautiful fairy play Peter Pan won for Barrie the title of " the Hans Andersen of the stage."

" Courage is the thing," Barrie told the students of St. Andrews University. " All goes if courage goes ! The greatness of a people is founded on their moral principles; but what says one Johnson of courage: ' Unless a man has that virtue he has no security for preserving any other.' Be not merely courageous, but lighthearted, also gay." Barrie received a baronetcy in 1913 and the Order of Merit in 1922. He died on June 19, 1937.

Barrie's chief works are Auld Licht Idylls (1888); A Window in Thrums (1889); The Little Minister (1891); Sentimental Tommy, Margaret Ogilvy (1896); Little White Bird (1902); Quality Street, The Admirable Crichton (1903); Peter Pan (1904); What Every Woman Knows (1908); Peter and Wendy (1911); A Kiss for Cinderella (1916); Dear Brutus (1917); Mary Rose (1920); Shall We Join the Ladies (1922); The Boy David (1936).

The STORY of PETER PAN

ONCE upon a time there lived three children named Wendy Moira Angela, John Napoleon, and Michael. Their parents were Mr. and Mrs. Darling; their nurse—strange as it may seem —was a big Newfoundland dog, named Nana.

Mrs. Darling was glad to have this dog to watch over the children, for one night something happened which made her feel very uneasy. She woke up suddenly and saw a strange figure, no bigger than a little boy, standing just inside the nursery

window. Nana growled and sprang at the boy, who leaped lightly through the open window. But he lost his shadow, for the dog shut the window down so quickly that the shadow was snapped off. Mrs. Darling took the shadow, rolled it up carefully, and put it in a drawer. Nana was a great treasure, she thought. But one night when Mr. Darling was rather out of sorts, he said that it was ridiculous to keep a dog as nurse, and he dragged poor Nana off to her kennel in the yard.

That night, after Mr. and Mrs. Darling had gone out, Peter Pan—for he was the mysterious little boy—came back to look for his shadow. A bright spot of light darted before him, flitting about to every corner of the room, and making a tinkle as of bells. When it was still for a moment one could see that the light was really a fairy girl. The tinkling sound was her way of speaking, and she was called Tinker Bell. She stopped at the chest of drawers and told Peter that his shadow was there. The boy ran to it and snatched out the shadow. But to his dismay, when he tried to put it on it wouldn't stick to him. At last, giving up in despair, he burst into tears.

His sobs woke Wendy. She sat up in bed and asked him his name and why he was crying. She knew at once what to do: she got a needle and thread and sewed on his shadow. Peter Pan strutted up and down and danced about in glee, watching his shadow follow him as he moved.

"How old are you, Peter?" queried Wendy.

"I don't know," he replied, "but I am quite young. I ran away the day I was born, because I heard my father and mother talking about what I was to be when I became a man. I don't want ever to be a man. I want always to be a boy and have fun. So I ran away to live among the fairies."

The Daniel Mayer Co. Ltd.

WENDY SEWS ON PETER'S SHADOW

Peter Pan's shadow was found in the Darlings' nursery by Tinker Bell, but Peter could not get it to stick to him. He began to cry, his sobs waking up Wendy. When she heard what was wrong she sewed on his shadow.

"Peter, do you really know fairies?" asked Wendy, wonderingly.

"Yes, but they're nearly all dead now. You see, when the first baby laughed its laughter broke into a thousand pieces and each piece went skipping about, and that was the beginning of fairies. And now, whenever a baby is born its first laugh becomes a fairy. But whenever a child says it does not believe in fairies, then one of the fairies dies."

Then Peter told Wendy that he lived in a place called Neverland, with lost boys who had fallen out of their prams when their nurses were looking the other way. He was their captain and they had great fun. There was one thing they lacked—a mother to tuck them in at night and tell them stories. There were no girls in Neverland, for girls were too sensible to fall out of prams!

"Oh, Wendy," begged Peter, "won't you come and live with us and be our mother?"

Wendy hesitated when she thought of her own mother, but Peter won her by telling her of the wonders of Neverland, and by promising that he would teach her and John and Michael to fly, And so the two boys were awakened, and after Peter had sprinkled them with fairy dust they were able to fly far away through the depths of the starry night to the Neverland.

The lost boys, who had been anxiously awaiting Peter's return, were surprised to see what appeared to be a lovely white bird flying towards them. While they were gazing at it the fairy Tinker Bell approached, tinkling very loudly. She was telling them that Peter wanted them to shoot the bird at once. One of the boys fired at it and it fell to the ground, and then they saw it was not a bird but a girl. It was Wendy, who had come to be their mother. Tinker Bell-had told them to do this dreadful thing because she loved Peter and was jealous of Wendy.

But Wendy was not dead; she had only fainted. She soon revived, but still lay on the ground very

The Daniel Mayer Co. Ltd.

PETER PAN PIPING

Peter Pan played his pipes outside the house the lost boys built for Wendy in Neverland. The lost boys were children who had fallen out of their perambulators when their nurses were not looking.

weak and tired. The boys built around her a tiny house—

> The littlest ever seen
> With funny little red walls
> And roof of mossy green.

They stuck on John's tall hat for a chimney, and soon the smoke was rising cosily.

Peter and Wendy and their little family were very happy together. Every night Wendy went to the underground home, down among the roots of the trees, where the boys lived. She told them stories and tucked them into their beds before she went to her own little house. They had thrilling adventures, for there were wolves and pirates and Red Indians, as well as fairies in Neverland.

The Pirate and the Crocodile

Captain Hook was the wickedest and fiercest of pirates. On one arm, instead of a hand, he had an iron-pronged hook, and that is how he got his name. Some time before, in an encounter between the pirates and the lost boys, Peter had cut off the captain's arm and flung it to a passing crocodile. The crocodile had liked the taste of it so much that ever since he had wandered from land to land and from sea to sea licking his jaws for the rest of the captain. Fortunately for Hook, however, the crocodile had also swallowed an alarm clock. This clock ticked so loudly that it could be heard through the crocodile's skin, and so the pirate captain could always hear it coming. But Hook lived in terror lest the clock should run down and the crocodile come up and swallow him before he heard a sound.

No wonder Captain Hook hated Peter Pan, who was the cause of all his troubles. But so far Peter Pan and the boys, aided by the Indians who were their friends, had escaped the pirates.

One evening while the faithful Indians were keeping guard outside, Wendy, as usual, was telling the boys a story before tucking them into bed. This time the story was about her own father and mother and the children who had flown away. She told them how lonely and sad Mr. and Mrs. Darling must be, and how they would always keep the nursery window open in case the children should come flying home.

Peter Tells His Story

When she had finished, Peter gave a groan. He felt that he must tell the truth. "Long ago," he said, "I thought, like you, that my mother would always keep the window open for me, so I stayed away for moons and moons and moons and then flew back; but the window was barred, for mother had forgotten all about me, and there was another little boy sleeping in my bed."

Perhaps it was not true, but Peter thought it was, and it scared the children.

"John! Michael!" cried Wendy. "We must go back at once."

The lost boys begged her not to leave them. Peter wanted her most of all, but he refused to show his feelings.

Then Wendy suggested that the boys all come too. She felt sure that her mother and father would be glad to adopt them. The boys were delighted with the idea of having a real father and mother—all except Peter Pan. Though his heart ached at the thought of losing Wendy, he wouldn't consent to live in a real house and grow up like ordinary boys.

The last thing the little mother did before leaving was to pour out Peter's medicine and make him promise to take it. And so they said good-bye to Peter Pan.

Now a terrible thing happened. The pirates had driven away the Indians and were lying in wait for the children. They pounced upon them as soon as they came out, and carried them as prisoners to the pirate ship. Hook, annoyed at not finding Peter among them, went to the cave in search of him. Poor Peter, after a forlorn attempt to prove to himself that he was not lonely, had at last fallen asleep. Thus Hook found his young enemy defenceless. He poured into the medicine a few drops of poison and stole away.

Peter awoke and was just about to take his medicine, when he heard a voice, "Don't drink! Don't drink!" It was Tinker Bell speaking. "Don't be silly," said Peter, and he raised the glass to his lips. Just as he was about to drain it, he saw a shining light in the glass. Then he knew that Tinker Bell had drunk the poison to save him. She was dying. There was one way to save her.

"Do you believe in fairies?" he cried to all the children in the world. "If you believe, clap your hands and save Tinker Bell!"

There was a clapping of many hands, and Tinker Bell revived. She told Peter about Wendy and the boys, and immediately Peter set off to rescue them, exclaiming: "Hook or me this time!"

On the pirate ship Captain Hook had just dragged up his prisoners from the hold, and was going to make them walk the plank. Suddenly the pirate heard something that changed his look of glee to one of terror. "Tick! Tick! Tick!"

"The crocodile!" he cried. "Hide me!" The terrified crew gathered around their captain. The boys looked toward the ship's side, expecting to see the crocodile climbing over it. But instead of a crocodile they saw—Peter, coming to their aid. He had imitated the crocodile's clock!

There was a fierce fight between the pirates and Peter's band. Some of the pirates, panic-stricken, jumped overboard. The rest of the crew were cut down and Captain Hook found himself at the mercy of Peter Pan. Step by step Peter forced the pirate chief to the side of the ship, till Hook in desperation thought some fiend was fighting him.

"Pan, who are you?" he cried huskily.

"I'm youth—eternal youth!" cried Peter exultantly. "I'm the sun rising—I'm poets singing—I'm the new world—I'm a little bird that has broken out of his egg—I'm joy, joy, joy!" With that he wrenched the sword out of Hook's hand and pushed him overboard, right into the open jaws of the waiting crocodile.

Peter was now in command of the ship, and the children sailed homeward. Their home had been a very sad place while they were away. Mr. Darling, to punish himself for taking away the children's nurse, had insisted upon sleeping in Nana's kennel. Mrs. Darling had thought of them day and night, and always left the window open.

Now at last the children were enfolded in their mother's arms. Peter watched them wistfully from outside the window. He had **many joys** unknown to ordinary children, but this happiness was not for him. Mrs. Darling wanted to adopt him along with the other boys. But no. Peter wanted very much to have a mother, and he loved Wendy, but he couldn't bear the thought of growing up. Wendy's mother was so moved at the thought of Peter living all alone that she offered to let Wendy go every year to do his spring cleaning.

As the years passed the children grew up and became men and women. But not Peter. High in the tree-tops in Neverland the fairies placed the little house that had been built for Wendy, and there Peter Pan lives on and on with Tinker Bell.

(Adapted from the story of Peter Pan by Sir James Barrie, by permission of and special arrangement with Messrs. Hodder & Stoughton, holders of the British copyright.)

Barrow-in-Furness.
The fact that the engineers and craftsmen of this Lancashire town built, in 1903, the first rigid airship for the British Government would in itself give Barrow a sufficient claim to fame, but the engineering triumphs of Barrow-in-Furness have been innumerable. And only about 100 years ago Barrow-in-Furness was a small fishing village, with a score of humble cottages, and without even a railway. Within comparatively few years its manufactures became known throughout the world.

Foundations of the prosperity of this thriving and busy centre lay in the immense deposits of iron ore in the neighbourhood, which were discovered about the middle of the 19th century. The manufactures of Barrow include steamships, floating docks, armour plate and naval guns, marine oil-engines, hydro-electric power installations, rifles, sewing machines and other engineering products. The population is about 66,000.

Baseball.
It would be quite appropriate if British people played baseball, for the ancestor of the game was the old rounders which, to the early American settlers, was known as town ball; but the game has never become popular in Britain.

It is the national game of America. The first book of rules was published in New York in 1845.

The baseball field is laid out in the form of a diamond 90 feet on each side, with bases at each of the three corners and the pitcher's box 60 feet 6 inches from the home plate (or fourth base), on

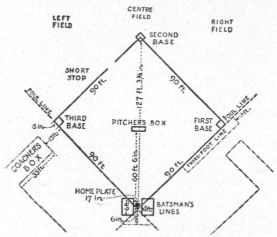

BASEBALL FIELD OR DIAMOND
You are standing behind the home plate and looking towards the centre field. The field's dimensions are 90 feet between bases, 127 feet 3⅜ inches from home plate to second base, and 60 feet 6 inches from home plate to pitcher's box.

a line between home plate and second base. At the start of the game the nine players who compose one of the teams take up their positions on the field, while the other team, in fixed succession, comes to bat. The bat is round, not more than 2¾ inches in diameter at the thickest part, and not more than 42 inches long. The official ball weighs five oz. and is nine inches in circumference. The pitcher (corresponding to the bowler in cricket) may deliver almost any sort of ball provided he remains in position and does not feint. If the batter swings at the ball and fails to hit it, or fouls it, a strike is counted, but a third foul is not a strike unless held by the catcher (corresponding to the wicket-keeper in cricket) except on an attempted bunt (this is explained in p. 368). Three strikes put him out and he retires while another player of his team takes his place. When the pitcher throws the ball across the home plate not lower than the batter's knee or higher than his shoulder and the batter makes no attempt to hit it, the umpire, who stands behind the pitcher or the catcher, calls a strike. If the pitcher misses the plate, or throws above the batter's shoulder or below his knee, the umpire calls a ball. Four balls give the batter a pass to first base. The batter's object usually is to make a fair

BASEBALL PLAYER SLIDING HOME
If the batsman can reach a base before the ball is returned to and held by the baseman, he can remain at that base. The batsman above is safe, because the baseman has not fielded the ball. The umpire watches both players intently.

hit—a ball batted within the lines that run from home to first base and home to third and beyond. A bunt is a short hit into the infield (that part of the field of play lying within the bases) without swinging at the ball; a sacrifice hit is a hit which puts the batsman out but advances a runner on bases. All other hits are fouls; they count as strikes except on the third strike, in which case they are not counted. If the fielders fail to catch a fair ball before it touches the ground, or fail to throw it to the first baseman before the batter reaches first base, he is safe. He may continue on to second, third, and home so long as he is not touched while between bases by the ball in the hand of one of the fielders, or hit by a batted ball, or forced out at one of the bases.

If the fielders succeed in catching a fair or a foul hit before it touches the ground, the batter is out. He is also out if they succeed in fielding a fair hit to the first baseman before the batter reaches first base. If a player crosses the home plate without being put out, he scores a run; if he makes the complete circuit of the bases on a single hit it is a home run.

The batting team continues to play until three of its men have been put out. It then exchanges places with the team in the field. An innings ends when a side has three batsmen out. Nine innings by each side constitute a game, except in the case of a tie score, when the game continues until one side or the other at the close of an innings retains a lead.

Perhaps the most important man on the fielding side is the pitcher, who delivers the ball full-pitch to the batsman or striker. Upon his skill depend the efforts of his team-mates to keep down the score against them. A good pitcher switches from slow to fast and from straight to curving deliveries.

The catcher, who stands behind the home plate wearing a mask, chest protector, shin guards and a large heavily-padded glove, also occupies a key position. A good catcher can detect an opposing batsman's weaknesses and signal to the pitcher what kind of ball to deliver. The basemen and shortstop prevent hits from going far out and so allowing the batter to run to first base or further. The basemen also are responsible for running out batters at their respective bases.

Basket. Birds, whose instinct taught them to weave into nests the materials which Nature gave them, were probably the first basket-makers; and men have learned from them, or may have been led by the same instinct, to intertwine branches and twigs, stems and rushes, the flexible inner bark of trees, and tough grasses. At any rate, they first used basketry, like the birds, to build their homes, for rough huts fashioned in this way were among the earliest forms of shelter.

Later, but still so long ago that we have no idea how far back in the dim and distant past it was, they learned to weave these materials into useful and beautiful vessels for storing and carrying food, and for many other purposes.

Baskets made about 6,000 years ago have been dug up from the dry sands of Egypt. When the Romans visited Britain in the first century Before Christ they found the natives already very proficient in the making of baskets of willows, or osiers. Indeed, it may be from these early Celtic inhabitants of Britain that we get our word "basket."

As the earliest form of weaving basket-making may be regarded as the parent of cloth-making and all the other textile industries. It is related to pottery,

BASEBALL IN THE UNITED STATES
Baseball is as popular in the United States as football is in Britain. The pitcher (upper right) has just delivered the ball to the batter, and the left-handed batter (lower) has hit the ball towards first base. Behind the batter crouch the catcher and umpire, both wearing masks over their faces.

Topical

BASKET-MAKING AT A WORKS IN CHESHIRE

The actual making of baskets has altered very little from the earliest times, many still being made by hand with the simplest tools. The principal material used is the willow or osier, with cane (split or whole) for extra strength. Before use, the osiers are soaked to make them pliable, the larger ones being left in a tank of water from two to seven days.

also, for the first clay vessels are believed to have been made by smearing clay on baskets and baking in the fire. Among the American Indians, especially the western tribes, basket-weaving reached its highest development and was of the greatest importance. The new-born babe was placed in a basket-work cradle, and baskets were used in the burial of the dead. Almost every domestic necessity was supplied by baskets. They were even used to carry water. "How can water be carried in a basket?" you will ask. Well, some of the water-baskets were coated with gum to make them watertight, but others were so tightly woven that even without this coating they would hold water. With or without a lining of clay, baskets were used in cooking; of course they could not be placed over the fire, but hot stones were dropped into them to bring the water in them to the boil. Fish and game traps, winnowing trays and granaries, were also made of basketry.

Basketry was also used in making various articles of clothing. Sandals made of it were worn by members of some tribes instead of moccasins of hide. Head baskets, serving for protection from the sun and rain as well as for adornment, were the predecessors of straw hats. Captain John Smith (1579-1631), the famous English explorer and adventurer, spoke of shields and armour used by the Indians in warfare which were woven so firmly that no arrow could pierce them. Basket boats were used by the Indians, as they were by the early Britons, and as they are today on the Tigris and the Euphrates.

It was the woman of the household who made the baskets. She was the burden-bearer, and she early learned to weave vessels that were light

yet strong and durable for carrying clay from the quarry, water from the spring, stones for grinding meal, firewood, fruits, seeds, roots, fish, flesh and fowl to supply the household needs. Savage and uncultured as she was, the Indian squaw had a sense of beauty, and this she expressed in her baskets. She learned to extract dyes from roots and berries to colour them. She made ornaments of shells and stones to decorate them. She used the feathers of brightly coloured birds to make more gorgeous the precious gift-baskets known as "jewels." Thongs of leather or plaited hair were frequently added for carrying.

Most beautiful of all were the designs wrought into the baskets. Many of them represent objects in Nature—the rainbow, the flowing water, the zigzag lightning, mountains, trees, flowers, birds and beasts. Others showed strange symbols, which, if you could read them, would tell of witchcraft and magic, legends of gods and heavenly beings. Into her basket-making the weaver put her feelings, her dreams, and her prayers, as well as the traditions and ideals of her race.

Basket-ball. Basket-ball originated in America in 1891, in response to a demand for a game that could be played indoors in winter instead of baseball or football, and it became increasingly popular in Britain. The game may be played either indoors or out of doors on a court ranging in size from 94 by 50 feet down to 60 by 40 feet. At each end of the court there is a goal or basket, 10 feet above the ground, in the form of a metal ring 18 inches in diameter, with a net suspended. A round, inflated leather ball is used.

There are five players in a team—a centre, two forwards, and two guards. At the start of the game the referee tosses up the ball between the opposing centres. Each team then tries to throw up the ball into their opponents' basket. It is permissible to bat or " dribble " the ball with the hands, and to throw it, but it must not be carried, kicked or punched. When a player breaks one of these rules or fouls an opponent, the opposing side gets a free throw. A goal scored from the field counts two points; from a free throw one point. (*See also* the heading Netball).

Basle, (Pron. bahl), SWITZERLAND. Besides being the second largest city in the Swiss Republic, Basle (known to the French as Bâle and to the Germans as Basel) is often the first city reached by the tourist entering the country by rail, road, air or water, for it is situated at the spot where Switzerland, France and Germany all join. It makes a very fine panorama, lying on either side of the Rhine and at the gateway to the Alps. Basle has large electrical and chemical works, and is a centre of many other industrial undertakings. The seat of the Bank for International Settlements is there. The city joined the Swiss Confederation in 1501. Basle is also the name of a canton of Switzerland; it is sub-divided into Basle-country (capital Liestal) and Basle-town, of which the city of Basle is the capital (population 162,100).

Bass. Various perch-like species of freshwater and salt-water fishes, differing in size, shape and colour, are called bass. On the angler's hook all are vigorous fighters. The common bass, or sea perch (*Morone labrax*), is a marine fish and is found in the Mediterranean as well as round the coasts of Britain. The family is *Centrarchidae*.

Bat. The bat is certainly not handsome, nor does he look very intelligent as he hangs upside-down from a rafter, blinking his beady little eyes in the daylight. But those strange wings of thin dark skin which the bat wraps round him like a cloak are perhaps the most delicate sense organs in the world. Take the bat in your hand. He is gentle enough, and you will feel him trembling

BASKET-BALL ATTACK
Basket-ball, which originated in the United States in 1891, is a strenuous game and extremely popular in America; it is also played to some extent in Britain.

all over. That is because, to those sensitive wings, the touch of your palm is like a rasping file.

The swift manner in which bats avoid flying into objects in the dark seems to us miraculous. They are enabled to do this by means of a device that is very similar to radio location, but making use of sound waves instead of wireless waves. The bats send out little squeaks, which are so high-pitched as to be inaudible to the human ear, and listen for the echo. The sound waves radiate from the flying bat and when they strike an object rebound from it. The echo is picked up by the bat's extremely sensitive ears, and in a moment the creature has changed direction. The maximum range of this warning device is about 12 feet.

Bats usually spend the day in caves, hollow trees, thick bushes, church towers, or deserted buildings. They do not alight on

Neville Kingston

BASS OF THE SALT WATER
A member of the same family as the perch, the bass or sea perch is a handsome fish in shape and colour, and is a favourite of seaside fishermen both for the sport it provides and for its tasty flesh. Bass must be handled carefully, because the spines in the first dorsal (back) fin can inflict very painful wounds.

BATS OF GREAT BRITAIN'S EVENING SKIES

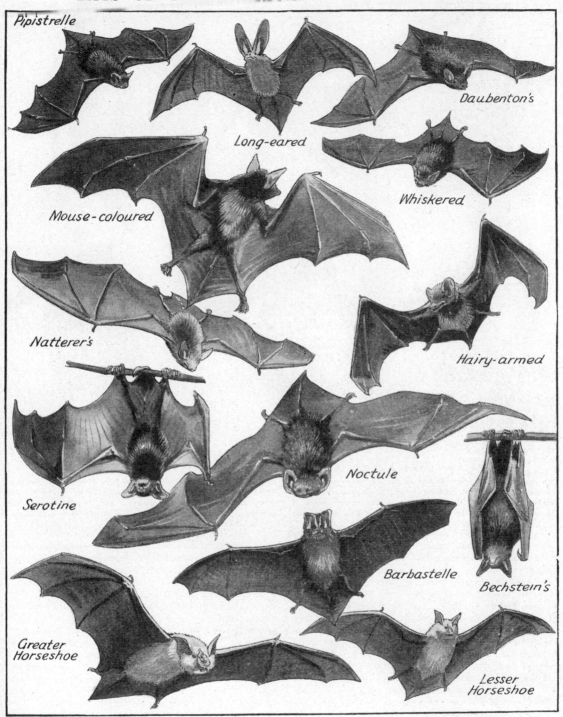

Pipistrelle

Long-eared

Daubenton's

Mouse-coloured

Whiskered

Natterer's

Hairy-armed

Serotine

Noctule

Barbastelle

Bechstein's

Greater Horseshoe

Lesser Horseshoe

Most people who have seen bats flying about as evening falls are unaware that there are thirteen species of bats found in Great Britain. They all feed on insects. The noctule is sometimes called the Great Bat and has a most unpleasant smell. The pipistrelle is the commonest of all our bats, and as it rarely hibernates for more than three months it is seen when others are in hiding. The long-eared bat is also very common. The largest British bat is the mouse-coloured. The barbastelle is rare; and the horse-shoe bats are found only in the south. Bats are mammals and are the only ones which have the power of flight like the birds. The anatomy of the bat is of great interest because its characteristics as a mammal have had to be altered to suit its existence as a flying creature. The bones have changed, and the pectoral or breast muscles have been greatly enlarged in order to operate the wings; owing to this increase in size, breast bone and ribs have had to join together to give the muscles adequate support.

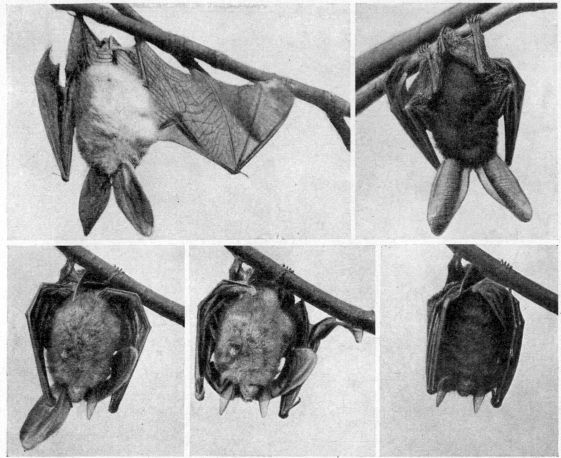

W. S. Berridge; J. J. Ward

LONG-EARED BAT TUCKING AWAY ITS EARS

This species of bat goes to bed in the daytime, and it has to find some way of tucking away its disproportionately large ears. It does this as shown in the above series of photographs. The top pictures are two views of the bat hanging upside-down by its toes on a branch; bottom (left) it tucks one ear beneath its folded wing; (centre) the other ear is also tucked away; and, finally (right) the process is complete, and the bat is ready to sleep until night.

the ground if they can avoid it, for they crawl with great difficulty, and they cannot spring into the air off a flat surface but must climb up a little distance to launch themselves on their flight.

There are many kinds of bats, distributed all over the world, except in the very coldest regions. As a rule they are small, but the flying-foxes of the Malay region have a spread of wings sometimes measuring five feet. These and other large bats found in the tropics are fruit-eaters, and do much damage to crops; but the northern bats feed on insects, and so are valuable to Man. Indeed, the bat may be looked upon as the night-watchman of our crops and gardens, for it devours enormous quantities of moths and beetles. In parts of America and also in Austria bat roosts or shelters are constructed and maintained at public expense, and the bats repay this service by keeping down the numbers of mosquitoes; where this has been done mosquitoes are rapidly destroyed.

Bats have always had an undeservedly bad reputation, and many silly tales have been told about them, such as the superstition that they take delight in entangling themselves in women's hair. There are, however, certain tropical vam-

pire bats which settle on the backs of horses and cows and even on sleeping human beings, and suck their blood, sometimes so weakening their victims that they die. These are found in parts of Central and South America.

In the north of the United States the little brown bat is the most common. These, like other insect-eating bats, do most of their hunting in the air, although they sometimes alight on the ground in search of beetles, grasshoppers and other insects.

During the cold months of the year, when insects are not available for food, bats hibernate. Before the coming of winter they have saved up a supply of fats on their bodies, which helps to carry them through the period when they do not feed. The extent of their sleep at this time seems to depend on the surrounding temperature. The colder it is, the deeper they sleep; indeed, naturalists have observed that when a number of bats are clustered together and the warmth of their bodies seems to raise the temperature slightly, they do not sleep very soundly.

The young of all bat species are born blind, and are not covered with fur until they are about a week old. The young ones grow very fast and even before they are a fortnight old are able to leave

BRITAIN'S BIGGEST BAT
W. S. Berridge
The noctule, or great bat, is the largest of the order Chiroptera (hand-winged animals) found in Britain, but its extended wing spread is only 13 or 14 inches, and its length five inches.

Bata, THOMAS (1876-1932). At the age of 18 this son of a Prague shoemaker, who worked as a child in his father's shop, started a business of his own at Zlin in Moravia, which was then a small town of 4,000 inhabitants. At Bata's death, 38 years later, Zlin had a population of 36,000 and a boot-manufacturing business employing over 13,000 people, entirely controlled by him. This feat was largely achieved by the personal supervision which he exercised and by his establishment, through profit-sharing and the creation of self-contained departments, of a community of interests among his employees.

In 1922, when the Czechoslovak currency was revalued, Bata reduced by 50 per cent not only his selling prices but also the prices he charged his workpeople for necessaries in the factory store, and at the same time cut their wages by 40 per cent. This experiment led to an immense further expansion. When he died, on July 13, 1932, he had factories in Germany, Poland, and Yugoslavia, and shops all over the world; and the site had been purchased for the British Bata shoe factory at Tilbury, Essex.

their mothers for short periods, but they are incapable of feeding themselves completely until they are about two months old. Nothing certain is known about how long bats live, but some scientists believe they occasionally attain an age of 40.

The name of the order of bats is *Chiroptera,* from Greek words meaning "hand-winged." If you look closely at a bat's wing you will see that the bones correspond roughly to the fingers of your hand, the hook at the top representing the thumb. There are 13 species of bat in Britain. Those most frequently seen are the pipistrelle (*Pipistrellus pygmaeus*), which is only about three inches in length; the long-eared bat (*Plecotus auritus*); the whiskered bat (*Myotis mystacinus*); and the large noctule bat (*Nyctalus noctula*). All of these are shown in the illustration on page 371

Bath. Readers of the Pickwick Papers, by Charles Dickens, will remember that Mr. Pickwick visited Bath in order to regain his health and spirits after the anxieties of his famous trial for

HORSESHOE BAT
The wings (above) of the bat are, as can be seen in this picture of the lesser horseshoe bat, composed of a membrane stretched over the bones of the arms and fingers. The name of horseshoe is attributable to the strange shape and marking of its face (lower).

breach of promise. The health-giving qualities of this beautiful city in Somersetshire, and the curative virtues of its waters, however, were famous long before the days of Mr. Pickwick. The Romans regarded its hot springs with superstitious veneration, and built around them a city (*Aquae Sulis*), where they went for health and pleasure during the four centuries they held sway in Britain (A.D. 44-410). Their baths, still in a perfect state of preservation, adjoin the famous Pump Room. In the 18th century Bath became again a fashionable resort, owing to the enterprise of one of its citizens, Ralph Allen, and the two architects, Wood senior and junior, who rebuilt the city in its natural amphitheatre, and made it, as it is still is today, one of the most desirable places of residence in England. "Beau" Nash, the English dandy, however, was the man really responsible for Bath's new-found importance; from 1705 until his death in 1762 he organized amusements and ruled the city and its people with autocratic rigour.

Departments of the Admiralty were evacuated from London to Bath during the Second World War. In three air-raids on the city at the end of April 1942 over 1,000 buildings were destroyed. The population is 71,000.

The greatest wonder of Bath is its hot springs, which derive their heat from some volcanic source. Bath stone, so called because it is quarried in the neighbourhood, is the material of which much of the city is built. The Bath chair originated there, having been first used to take invalids to the baths. The name of Bath is also associated with three articles of food : Bath buns, fruit buns with a knobbly sugar surface ; Bath Olivers, dry biscuits ; and Bath chaps, the cheeks of pigs cured by a special process.

Bathing.

All through the summer months the shores of Britain are thronged with bathers. Yet up to about 200 years ago hardly anyone bathed in the sea, not even those who lived a stone's throw from a splendid beach. King George III helped to popularize the fashion of sea-bathing, at Weymouth, in about 1789 ; the band used to play " God Save

the King " as His Majesty entered the water. About the same time Brighton—then known as Brighthelmstone—began to be something more than a fishing village. Margate was already a seaside resort, and it was a Margate man—Benjamin Beale, a Quaker—who about 1750 invented the bathing machine. Benjamin's machines were advertised as ensuring " strictest delicacy," and a visitor to Margate in 1754 describes them as " covered carriages, at the end of which there is a covering that lets down with hoops, so that people can go down a ladder into the water and are not seen, and those who please may jump in and swim."

A few years later Ralph Allen of Bath—said to have been the original of Squire Allworthy in Fielding's novel Tom Jones—had a bathing machine built for him at Weymouth, and we are told that his action was regarded as " so extreme and so strange that it savoured of madness." Nevertheless, the idea soon began to be widely accepted.

In course of time were invented queer little boxes on wheels which were dragged into the sea by horses;

and there are many today who remember the rumbling journey down the beach, and the door opening on to a terrible-looking sea. Then from the waves a fearsome creature— the bathing woman, as she was called—reached out her brawny arms, seized the protesting youngster and dipped him (or her) three times beneath the waves.

Among the ancients baths were very popular, but these were enclosed pools, often heated and containing medicinal salts ; in those days the baths were a kind of club where men—and sometimes women—used to meet to discuss the gossip and questions of the day. In the Middle Ages bathing went out of fashion, and there were holy men who prided themselves on never washing. It is an unpleasant

BATHING AS IT WAS AND IS TODAY
Forty years ago people bathed from machines (lower photograph) with wings on either side so that the bather could not be seen until he or she was in the water ; the men's and women's bathing stations were far apart. This photograph was taken at Dover. Top, girls with inflated cushions as bathing rafts

reflection that our ancestors' love of perfumes had its origin in their dislike of washing themselves.

There are many different sorts of bath in use in Western countries, *e.g.*, medical baths (salts, foam, mud, etc.), and Turkish baths, in which one is bathed in hot air, sweated, rubbed down and massaged.

Batten, JEAN (born 1909). Three times did Jean Batten try to fly from England to Australia—and the third time (in May 1934) fortune smiled on her pluck and ability, and she achieved her ambition of beating Amy Johnson's record by flying alone to Australia in 5 days 21 hours. Miss Batten's imagination had been fired, when quite young, by the exploits of the great Australian airman Kingsford-Smith. In November 1935, after returning to England by air, she crossed the South Atlantic in record time. The following year she was made C.B.E. (Commander of the Order of the British Empire), and won further laurels by a remarkable flight from England to Australia in 5 days 18 hours 15 minutes, and on to her native New Zealand. All these flights were accomplished alone, in a small aeroplane.

Battery. This name is used for a set of things. The electric battery is an assembly of electric cells, connected together to give a current with more pressure or more volume than would be given out by a single cell. Primary batteries or cells are those in which, as a result of chemical action, electricity is " generated " from such substances as acids or alkalis and carbon or some metals. Secondary batteries or cells (often today called " accumulators ") store up electricity in the form of chemical energy, and turn it back into electrical energy when the cell is connected into a receiving circuit and harnessed to do some work.

Let us look at a primary cell first—one of the tiny and efficient cells which light up our flash-lamp when we press or turn a switch. And for clearness of explanation we will illustrate also a wet battery of the same type, called the Leclanché after its inventor. In the wet cell there is an outer

JEAN BATTEN IN THE COCKPIT
Not many women have made great reputations as air pilots, but those who have done so have performed no less wonderful feats than those of the great men flyers. An example is Miss Jean Batten, here seen in one of the little aeroplanes with which she set up records for flights across the South Atlantic and from England to Australia and New Zealand.

glass jar, into which is put a solution of sal-ammoniac (ammonium chloride) in water. This solution is known as the electrolyte. Inside the jar stands a pot made of porous, unglazed earthenware, in which is fixed a plate of carbon bearing at its top a brass terminal screw. Around the plate in the porous pot is filled granulated carbon, mixed with manganese dioxide—the latter to act as a depolariser, whose action is later explained. The liquid electrolyte can seep through the porous pot and reach the carbon plate, the granules, and the depolariser. Also standing in the glass jar, but kept well away from the porous pot, is a rod of zinc, with a connecting wire attached to the top end.

Now look at the dry cell shown in p. 376: here the place of the zinc rod is taken by the zinc box into which all the other parts of the cell are packed, and which is insulated and protected by a cardboard or thick paper wrapping. You can see the carbon rod at the centre; it is surrounded by a package containing carbon granules and the manganese dioxide (depolariser). Sometimes, as in the cell illustrated, the electrolyte is contained in the paper or pulp layer which comes between the zinc wall of the cell and the central mass; a hygroscopic (water-retaining) liquid is added to enable it to keep moist longer. In other types of dry cell the electrolyte is in the form of a paste of sal-ammoniac filled in between the cell wall and the central package, again

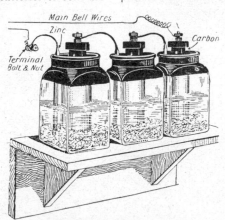

BATTERY OF THREE CELLS
Three Leclanché (the name of the inventor) cells are shown connected together to form a battery for an electric bell circuit. Compare these cells with the dry cell shown in page 376.

with something added to keep the paste moist.

The top of the cell is covered with pitch, through which is led the terminal from the carbon rod. Sometimes the other terminal wire or screw is fixed to the cell wall, or it may be that the bottom of the cell is left bare so that it may make electrical contact with the metal case of the flash-lamp. The pitch seals the cell, and insulates the terminals from one another. A certain amount of gas is generated, and a tube is often sealed in to allow it to escape. The only difference between the dry cell and the wet one, as far as electrical matters go, is that the dry cell uses a paste electrolyte and is thus more convenient and portable. But once the chemicals or the zinc are used up, the cell ceases to yield current. Often the cell fails because chemical and electrical action have caused part of the zinc wall to become eaten away. The dry cell cannot be recharged. The wet cell, however, has a continuous life; it can be kept in use if we renew the sal-ammoniac solution, and put in a new zinc rod when the old one is much eaten away.

LEAD-ACID ACCUMULATOR
Also known as secondary batteries, accumulators are really cells in which electricity is stored as chemical energy.

A wet cell or a dry one, of this type, gives out electric current because the electrolyte and the zinc begin to change chemically directly we connect the two terminals together —either through an outside circuit like that of a flash-lamp or an electric bell, or directly without any outside circuit in which work has to be done. In the latter case the cell quickly runs down, and may spoil through overheating; this kind of connexion is called a short circuit, and the cell is said to be " shorted."

By making larger cells we can get *more* current, but *not* stronger current, for the most voltage or pressure that this kind of cell will supply is $1\frac{1}{2}$ volts. By coupling two or more cells " in series "—that is, the carbon of one to the zinc of another, and so on— we can add to the total voltage. This is why flash-lamp batteries are composed of two cells (nominally 3 volts) or three cells (nominally $4\frac{1}{2}$ volts). The voltage drops off gradually as the cell is used up, and the lamps employed are a little less in voltage—$2\frac{1}{2}$ and $3\frac{1}{2}$ volts respectively —for this reason. Never leave an old spent battery in your flash-lamp, for it will become wet and corrode the case.

But we are sure you will be wondering how chemical action in the cell can cause electrical energy to be given out at the terminals. The " voltaic " cell, as it is named after Alessandro Volta, an Italian professor (1745-1827), takes different forms, with sometimes copper and zinc rods or plates, and sometimes with an acid forming the electrolyte. But the Leclanché type is the most used today. When the terminals are connected

through a circuit, the electrolyte eats away some of the zinc, and hydrogen bubbles form on and rise from the carbon, which is called the *positive* electrode.

In the older theory of electricity the current is supposed to flow from the positive electrode to the negative ; for convenience, that convention is still kept, although we know that the current—really a stream of electrons—flows from the zinc, or *negative* electrode towards the carbon one. The bubbles of hydrogen indicate that what the chemist calls hydrogen-ions are passing from the negative to the positive electrode through the electrolyte. These ions are positive, and lose their electric charge to the carbon plate. But as there must always be a state of electrical balance, the carbon electrode gives up negative charges of the same quantity, in the form of an electron stream or current which flows through the wire connecting the carbon plate to the zinc rod *outside* the cell. This stream is the energy-yielding current which works our electric bell or lights the bulb of the flash-lamp. The ions are atoms or radicals of the electrolyte which carry an electric charge, negative or positive as the case may be. So *within* the cell the current travels by the movement of these tiny charged particles.

The electrons which charge the ions are taken from atoms of zinc in the rod. The hydrogen bubbles are caused by the hydrogen-ions arriving at the carbon plate, and appear after these ions have given up their electric charge to the plate. The reason for putting manganese dioxide with the carbon granules in the cell is that without them there would soon form a coating of hydrogen bubbles on the carbon plate, and this would quickly reduce the flow of current (an effect known as polarisation). The manganese dioxide, very rich in oxygen, counteracts polarisation, but if the cell is used

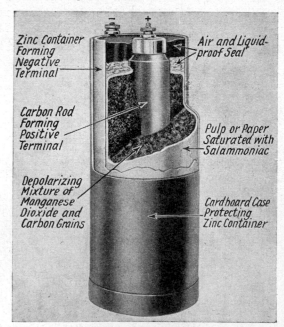

Zinc Container Forming Negative Terminal

Air and Liquid-proof Seal

Carbon Rod Forming Positive Terminal

Pulp or Paper Saturated with Sal-ammoniac

Depolarizing Mixture of Manganese Dioxide and Carbon Grains

Cardboard Case Protecting Zinc Container

DRY CELL, LECLANCHÉ TYPE
The Leclanché cell produces electricity, when the terminals are connected, by chemical action between the zinc container, carbon rod, and sal-ammoniac. Hydrogen formation is prevented by the depolarising mixture shown.

continuously, hydrogen forms quicker than it can be dispersed, and we have to give the cell a rest. It will then recover to a certain extent, though dry cells are continually weakening from the moment they begin to be used.

So remember that the proper way to use your flash-lamp or electric torch is to " flash " it on when you need it, and to switch it off directly you have finished. Of course, if it is a cycle lamp, you *must* keep it " on " when riding ; but even so, economy in use will result in a brighter light for a longer overall period.

Secondary batteries, or accumulators, are used for radio receivers, for motor-car lighting sets and, in very much larger batteries, for telephone exchanges, self-contained house-lighting plants and even for some electric locomotives. They are really storage cells. Inside the lead-acid accumulator—the most common type—there are grids made of lead and filled with a paste of either red lead (for the positive plate), or litharge (negative plate).

BAVARIAN BRIDES AND BRIDEGROOMS
These young couples of Effeltrich, Bavaria, are arrayed in their marriage finery, for there has just been a double wedding. The brides' gowns are elaborately embroidered in gold. The head-dress, which from olden times has been the chief glory of Bavarian brides, is covered with beads and trinkets.

The electrolyte is sulphuric acid diluted with water. Assuming we have a cell in proper condition, with paste in the grids and electrolyte in the container, we will in imagination connect it to a suitable source of electricity (*see* the illustration in page 376).

The cell contains two or more plates ; if there are two only, one is connected to the negative terminal (usually enamelled black), and the other to the positive (red terminal). When there are more than two plates they are connected up in two groups, one group going to the negative terminal and the other to the positive. Plates of opposite sign are insulated from one another. While being charged, the positive plate where the current goes into the cell turns brown, because the red lead in the grid mesh changes into another form of lead, the peroxide. The opposite plate, or group of plates, turns grey, because the litharge there loses oxygen and turns into metallic lead.

After charging, which takes many hours, since the current must enter slowly and in a weak form, we can begin to use the battery by taking current from it. As we do this, the previous chemical changes are reversed on the plates. The plate at which the current went in during charging becomes the positive one during discharge of current. From a lead-acid storage battery we can get current of 2-volts pressure. But there comes a time when the energy becomes used up ; before this, the voltage begins to fall. At this stage the cell must be charged again. In other types of secondary cell, different electrolytes and metals are used ; the nickel-iron cell has nickel oxide and iron oxide as the active materials.

Bavaria. GERMANY. The people of the fertile plateau and green-clad mountains of Bavaria, the most southern of the German states, are largely dark-haired, with easy-going, tolerant temper very different from the light-haired Prussians of the sandy plains of the north. They are instinctive lovers of music and colour, and their country is the true home of German art.

The Bavarian countryside has kept something of the picturesqueness of the Middle Ages. The peasants in the more remote valleys still wear quaint costumes, rich with embroidery and silver buttons. The herd-girls, in their dark full skirts and scarlet bodices with white sleeves, may still be seen guarding their flocks on the distant hills as their forebears did four and five centuries ago. Even in the towns descendants of the famous guild craftsmen of former days still labour in their little shops, turning out the skilled handiwork in wood and metals for which medieval Germany was celebrated the world over.

Cut off by wooded mountains to the north-east and north-west, and by the towering snow peaks of the Alps to the south, Bavaria had, until the past century, run a separate course in spirit and politics from the rest of Germany. When their northern neighbours followed Luther in the Protestant Reformation, the Bavarians remained Roman Catholic. When Napoleon overran Europe, Bavaria sided with the French. When Prussia and Austria fought in 1866, she helped Austria. Even after the formation of the German Empire in 1871 Bavaria kept her own army and postal system, laws and customs, and her own royal family, which continued to rule until the revolution of 1918, at the end of the First World War.

From the days of the Roman Empire, whose boundaries followed the rivers Danube and Main through the middle of Bavaria, the Bavarians have been intimately associated with Italian civilization. A rich commerce flowed northward over the Alpine passes to the ancient cities of Augsburg, Regensburg (Ratisbon) and Nuremberg. Bavaria thus early became a centre of wealth and learning. The pack-

E.N.A.

BAVARIAN MOUNTAIN TOWN OF GARMISCH

This little town in Bavaria, Germany, is about 50 miles south-west of Munich and was the scene of the Winter Olympic Games in 1936. In the mountain villages the wooden cottages very closely resemble those of Switzerland, with the roofs overhanging the balconies. The full name of the town is Garmisch-Partenkirchen. In normal times it was one of the many mountain resorts in Bavaria that attracted visitors from all parts of Germany and abroad.

mules, laden with silks, tapestries and spices of the East, which wound their way through the passes of the Alps, are today replaced by iron rails and loco-motives. Old Nuremberg remained a commercial and industrial centre of south Germany until the Second World War (1939–45), when it was exten-sively damaged by Allied air-raids. Munich, the capital of the state and birthplace of the Nazi movement, as well as the literary and art centre of Bavaria, presents a thoroughly modern appearance with its broad streets and beautiful buildings, though it also was bombed by the Allied Air Forces in the Second World War.

Northern Bavaria is noted for grapes and tobacco ; most of the crops, especially grain, hops and potatoes, are grown on the Danube's fertile plain that crosses central Bavaria from west to east. The Alpine foothills of the south specialize in cattle-raising and timber-growing. Porcelain clay, gran-ite, marble, salt, iron ore and other minerals are widely distributed. Famous for its toys and porcelain, Bavaria also manufactures chemicals, textiles, and iron and steel products.

In the mountains, wooden cottages of an Alpine type prevail; which in the more agricultural lands towards the Danube give place to tiled farmhouses. Amid the mountains of the south lies the village of Oberammergau, where every 10 years the villagers produce the Passion Play of Christ's sufferings. The villagers play all the parts and the drama takes all day, with a noon intermission, and is performed to audiences that come from all over the world. Other towns of exceptional interest are Bayreuth, where the annual Wagner Festival is held, and Rothenburg and Dinkelsbühl, both containing gems of medieval architecture.

Bavaria was organized as a duchy before the days of Charlemagne, while Prussia was still inhabited by barbarian Slavs. Napoleon in reward for its aid conferred the title of king (in 1805) on the ruling house of Wittelsbach, which continued to govern until deposed at the end of the First World War (1914–18). Bavaria then became one of the republics of the German Reich, and in 1920 the little state of Coburg was added to it. In 1935 the state was placed under the rule of a gauleiter (leader of a province) appointed by the German Fuehrer, Hitler. At the end of the Second World War Bavaria was part of the American-occupied zone; and it was the first German state to which the Allies restored the right to its own government, with its own Prime Minister and Cabinet.

Bayeux. (Pron. bah-yê′). In the museum of the little French town of Bayeux in Normandy is ex-hibited a long, faded strip of embroidery, obviously ancient but most beautifully preserved. It was called by an 18th-century antiquary "the noblest monu-ment in the world relating to our old English history."

Known as the Bayeux Tapestry (although it is not woven on a loom. but is worsted needlework), this historic relic brings to life most realistically the story of William's conquest of England in A.D. 1066. On its length of 231 feet are depicted, in eight colours, and accompanied by Latin inscriptions, no fewer than 72 scenes of life and events in that year, including the Battle of Hastings.

At one time it was believed that William's wife, Matilda, commissioned the "tapestry," but it is now generally assumed that it was made to the order of the Duke's half-brother, Odo, Bishop of Bayeux. There is a complete copy of this fascinating work in the Victoria and Albert Museum, Kensington, London.

Topical

BAYEUX'S VAST BRITISH WAR CEMETERY

A British military cemetery for those killed fighting in Normandy against the Germans in 1944 during the Second World War (1939–45) was laid out on the outskirts of Bayeux in 1946. White carnations and pinks were planted by French gardeners who tend the graves. In the distance is Bayeux cathedral, which was undamaged in the fighting.

Bayeux (population 7,200) was the first town in Western Europe to be liberated from German occupation when the Allies landed in Normandy in the Second World War. British troops captured it on June 7, 1944.

Beam. To most people this word means merely a long and stout piece of timber; but architects and engineers understand it to mean something more precise. In our story of Architecture we tell how ancient builders made doorway openings by erecting two posts, and placing on top of them a horizontal timber called a lintol. This lintol was a beam in the technical sense.

Beams are used to span openings when there is something to be supported above—for example, a wall over a door or window opening, or the roadway over a stream. But the beam may be made of various other

BAYEUX 'TAPESTRY' DEPICTING SCENES IN HISTORY

In this famous relic preserved at Bayeux in Normandy, France, history is depicted in needlework. It tells the story of English history from King Harold's departure from England for France to his death at the Battle of Hastings in 1066. Two scenes from it are reproduced here. At the top, Harold goes hunting with hawks and hounds. Lower, the keys of Dinan being surrendered to the Norman besiegers under Duke William, whom Harold accompanied.

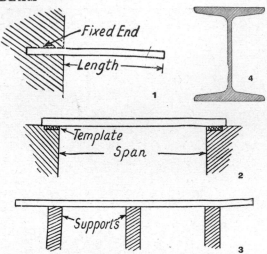

DIFFERENT KINDS OF BEAM

A cantilever (1) is fixed at one end. A simple beam (2) rests on two supports only, whereas a continuous beam has intermediate supports as well. The rolled steel joist (4) is largely used for beams.

"box girder" may be built up by riveting two separate webs to two plates, leaving a space between the webs. Another of our diagrams shows a girder built up from two flange plates, a web plate and four angles. (All these depict the joist or girder endwise, as if cut through.)

When a beam is "loaded"—that is, when a weight is placed on top of it—it tends to change its shape, or deflect; when the load is removed, the beam tends to go back to its original shape. The upper part (or the top flange) is *compressed* under the load, while the lower part of the beam (or bottom flange) is *stretched*. As we go down through the beam we come to a point where compression ceases and tension begins; this point is called the neutral axis, and in the case of rectangular-section beams and symmetrical shapes the axis is in the centre of the section. At this neutral axis there is neither compression nor tension.

It is in the top and bottom layers of a solid rectangular-section beam that the most strength is needed. If we had a solid steel bar of the same outside dimensions as the I-section joist shown in our diagram, we could cut away and thin down the top and bottom parts and the central web without losing necessary strength. Instead, the bar is

materials than timber, and today is usually of reinforced concrete or takes the form of an I-section rolled steel member. Sometimes steel beams are built up of members bolted or riveted together, and are then usually called girders.

The engineering definition of a beam is "a structural member resting on two or more supports subject to transverse stress." A "simply supported beam" is one resting on two supports—one at each end, as if you placed a balk of timber across a narrow stream to make a makeshift bridge; if this were encased in brickwork or concrete at the ends, it would be a "built-in beam."

If you fixed such a beam at one end only, and let the free end project unsupported over the stream, it would be a "cantilever beam," a form much used today in steel or concrete bridge building. If the stream were so wide that you had to drive in one or more posts to support the beam, as well as letting it rest on the banks of the stream at the two ends, it would be called a "continuous beam."

There is another form of beam which has a very old name—"bressummer," formerly breast-summer. This is a beam used over a broad opening to support some structure; today it may be a steel or concrete beam used to hold up the foundations of a house, or it may carry the load of a bay window above. Formerly the bressummer was of wood, which was the only material available to our forefathers. In fact, for many centuries there was nothing but timber for making these supporting members. In the days before machine-sawing they were often rough hewn, with axe and adze, to the shape required.

One of our diagrams shows a rolled steel joist, made from the ingot while still hot by passing it through a rolling mill. Steel plates may be riveted to such a joist to make a simple girder. Or a

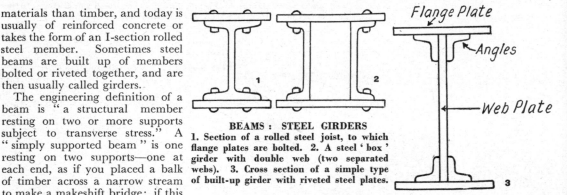

BEAMS : STEEL GIRDERS

1. Section of a rolled steel joist, to which flange plates are bolted. 2. A steel 'box' girder with double web (two separated webs). 3. Cross section of a simple type of built-up girder with riveted steel plates.

rolled to the I-section at the mill, saving metal and very greatly reducing the weight. Now you can see the advantage of the steel beam over the solid rectangular wooden one; the material is concentrated just where it is required, and the flanges and web are made just strong enough for their purpose. (*See* Bridge ; Building).

Bean. More nutriment at a lower cost is obtained from beans than from any other of our staple foods, even wheat. They were introduced from tropical countries, and many varieties are now grown throughout the world. Their clusters of flowers are followed by pods containing the seed, which are the beans. The roots are valuable soil renovators, because of the way in which they extract nitrogen from the air. The broad bean (*Vicia faba*), which was probably a native of Egypt, has been used as food for both man and beast from the remotest times. Other common beans are the runner (*Phaseolus multiflorus*), and the French or kidney bean ("French" because it was first popularised in France, and "kidney" alluding to the shape of the seed). The haricot bean is a dried kidney bean. These plants belong to the family *Leguminosae*. (*See also* Soya Bean).

YOU CAN WATCH THE BEAN PLANT GROW!

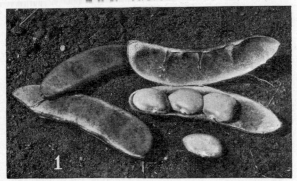

The pictures on this page were made by photographing the bean plant from time to time as the seed, or bean, began to grow. They show the plant pushing its way through the soil to the surface and extending its roots deeper into the earth. Watching a bean plant grow from the time the seed is planted is an interesting experiment as well as a very simple one to carry on at home.

Remove one side of a small wooden box and substitute a glass pane in its place. Fill the box with earth and plant a bean against the glass about an inch below the surface. Keep the glass covered with a piece of cardboard or paper to shield the seed from light except when you are observing the plant. The box may be kept in a dark place until the plant reaches the surface of the soil, but after that it should have some sunlight.

Picture 1 shows beans in a pod ready to be eaten or planted. The bean which has dropped from the pod was planted according to the directions given at the right. It was then photographed through the glass, to make this series of pictures.

The radicle starts growing first and presently breaks through the *hilum*, or scar of attachment on the seed coat.

In the soil the bean found everything it needed for rapid growth—moisture, air, and warm temperature. Now watch it grow! The skin or *testa* absorbs water quickly and is wrinkling (Picture 2). Did you ever see the inside of a bean? One has been opened in Picture 3. The two fleshy disks are the seed leaves, or *cotyledons*. Fastened to the top is the embryo plant, shown more clearly in the circle at the right. The fat, sausage-like part is the embryo root, or *radicle*. The plumule sits atop the radicle, and is made up of a stem, or *hypocotyl*, and a pair of leaves.

The radicle now lengthens out to form the primary root, which soon branches to form many secondary roots. Meanwhile the embryo stem, or hypocotyl, begins to grow rapidly and **arches its back above the soil** (Pictures 6 and 7). This **arch**, anchored by the numerous roots, **forms a power**ful lever which pulls the pair of yellow-green leaves from the earth in response to sunlight. The seed leaves have furnished all the food for the plant thus far. Now they wither and fall off, leaving the production of food to the new foliage leaves, which manufacture it with the aid of sunlight.

BEARS *of* MANY KINDS *and* MANY LANDS

Largest of the flesh-eating animals—bigger than the lion and the tiger — is the Alaskan brown bear. But bears do not feed on flesh entirely. Their diet includes such trifles as ants and grass and wild honey.

Bear. In common with many flesh-eaters, the bear has suffered in reputation from stories which greatly exaggerate his ferocity and ascribe to him many evil qualities he does not possess. The bear is naturally timid, good-natured, and in-offensive. Instead of seeking Man in order to de-vour him, the bear makes every effort to avoid Man. But he is not a coward. He knows his strength, and when occasion arises he never fails to defend himself. He fights, if need be, savagely.

In appearance the bear is a clumsy creature. The middle of his back is the highest point of his body. He has a short neck, round head, pointed muzzle, and small eyes. His legs are stout, and he walks " plantigrade," or flat-footed. The soles of his feet are bare—except in the case of the Polar bear, which has fur on its paws to prevent slipping on the ice. Each foot has five toes, armed with long stout claws which are not retractile—that is, they cannot be drawn back into a sheath like those of a cat. His hair is long and shaggy, and is shed annually. The tail is very short. The teeth clearly indicate that the bear is omnivorous—that is, he eats almost anything. The canine or " dog " teeth are long and sharp for tearing flesh; the molars are well adapted for grinding roots and vegetable foods.

The bear walks with a shambling gait, lifting both feet on one side of his body at the same time. His clumsy movements when at ease are very de-ceptive, for he can turn with surprising swiftness and deal terrific blows with his forepaws. In running he goes at a sort of gallop, and his speed is such that he can overtake the swiftest human runner or even a horse in a few minutes. In attacking, the bear frequently, though not always, stands erect and uses his forepaws as well as his teeth. Bears are good swimmers, and most kinds climb trees while young.

In the wild state most bears hibernate for a period of from two to six months, even in warm climates where food is plentiful all the year round; but in captivity they rarely do this, even in a cold climate. When the cold weather approaches the bear seeks a quiet spot and a suitable den for its winter quar-ters. Sometimes the base of a hollow tree is chosen, or a cavity under the roots of a fallen tree; or the bear may scoop out a den for himself. He covers himself with leaves, grass or dirt, leaving only an air-hole for his breathing. The bear is not always sleeping during its resting period of hibernation or seclusion, but it then takes no food or drink.

Young bears, called cubs, are born in January or February, while the mother is in hiding. Two cubs at a birth seems to be the rule, but there are exceptions. Bears are nearly hairless as babies, and ridiculously small considering the size of the parents. They are helpless for many months, and of necessity remain with their mother the first year and go into the den with her to spend the second winter.

H. J. Shepstone

BEARS OF NORTH AMERICA AT CLOSE QUARTERS

The black bear of North America is often regarded as a smaller variety of the brown bear. It is a timid and in-offensive beast, and has gradually been reduced in numbers owing to hunters coveting its valuable fur. The United States and Canadian Governments prohibit the killing of animals in their parks and reservations, and the photographer is nowadays the only person allowed to ' shoot ' the bears seen above in the Jasper National Park, Alberta, Canada.

Contrary to popular supposition, the great Polar bear really seems to enjoy the heat and to dislike cold weather, despite its warm coat and its birthplace in the Arctic regions. Unlike some animals, too, the Polar bear thrives in captivity, and often lives for 15 or even 20 years in surroundings and on food to which it has not been accustomed in its native haunts. So these two plump 'bathers' on the Mappin Terraces at the London Zoo are probably quite content with their lot. The Polar bear is to be found only in the Arctic regions, and the female alone hibernates, the male continuing to hunt fish, seals and walruses during the dark winter months. The long neck and the comparatively small head distinguish the Polar bear from all other members of the bear tribe.

Fox; G.P.A.

BEARS THAT DELIGHT THE CROWD AT LONDON'S ZOO

The London Zoological Gardens, in Regent's Park, always have a number of bears on show, both on the Mappin Terraces and in the Bears' Den, for these animals are among the most popular of those kept in captivity. Top left, a real live 'teddy bear'—actually a young Syrian bear; top right, a brown bear begging for food; and below, a trio of newly-arrived baby black bears. Like most bears they are extremely fond of milk and honey.

Though classed as carnivores or flesh-eaters, most bears subsist largely on a vegetable diet. They eat grass, grain, roots, nuts, berries, fruit, grubs, insects, frogs, snakes, mice, snails, crabs, eggs, fish, birds and any other kind of game they can capture or find in good condition. They do not eat carrion. Most bears are fond of a meal of ants, and to obtain them will tear apart decayed stumps and logs and dig up ant-hills. They are also passionately fond of honey.

Different kinds of bears are widely distributed throughout Europe, Asia, North America, and some parts of northern Africa. Only one species is found in South America. The bears of North America constitute four distinct groups. Their common and scientific names are : black bear (*Ursus americanus*);

grizzly bear (*Ursus horribilis*); Alaskan brown bear (*Ursus gigas*); Polar bear (*Thalassarctus maritimus*).

The black bear was originally found in all parts of the North American continent, except in the extreme north, and it still exists wherever there is extensive forest land sufficient to shelter it. In the autumn, when the coat of the bear is at its best, the fur is entirely black except for a brown patch on the muzzle and an occasional white spot on the breast. Its hearing and sense of smell are very keen and enable it to avoid its enemies. The least suspicious sound or odour is sufficient to start it from its lair, and it requires a skilful hunter to track it down or approach within rifle range. A black bear may weigh 500 pounds or more but normal weight is much less.

The grizzly bear formerly inhabited the western part of North America from the Arctic Ocean to southern Mexico, and from the Rocky Mountains to the Pacific, but is now chiefly found in the Rocky Mountains and Sierra Nevada. There are several varieties. In size some equal the black bear, but the largest attain a length of 10 feet and a weight of almost 1,500 pounds, and are capable of carrying off small horses and cattle. They vary in colour from yellow to almost black. The tips of the hairs are lighter, giving them a grizzled appearance, whence comes the names grizzly or " silver-tip."

The grizzly is the fiercest and most dangerous American mammal. The Indians feared it, and the warrior who overcame a large one was regarded as a great brave. The grizzly possesses greater intelligence than the black bear, and when wounded or brought to bay is a dangerous antagonist. The coming of the white man with firearms marked the beginning of the end, and the grizzly bear would be in danger of being exterminated were it not for the protection now given it in national parks.

The Alaskan brown bears are found only in Alaska. They attain the enormous weight of 1,500 pounds, and are not only the largest living bears but the largest living carnivores found on land. Yet their existence was unknown before 1898. They are afraid of Man and flee from him, but when wounded or surprised at close quarters they will fight furiously. They spend much of their time hunting for mice and other small creatures, which they dig out of their burrows. When the salmon come up the rivers, these bears gorge themselves on the fish. During the months of midsummer and autumn they present the curious spectacle of grazing like cattle.

The Polar bear is dressed in white to harmonize with its surroundings. It is completely covered, even to the soles of its feet, with long thick fur. It is a powerful swimmer, and even in midwinter is perfectly at home in the water. Only the female Polar bear hibernates. Her winter den is a cavity under the ice and snow, and there she brings forth her young. Until they are quite large the cubs remain with their mother. A well-known naturalist once said: " When a mother Polar bear scents danger she jumps into the water and her cub holds fast to her tail while she tows it to safety. But when no danger seems to threaten she wants it to ' paddle its own canoe,' and boxes its ears or ducks its head under water if it insists on being too lazy to swim for itself." The male Polar bear prowls about during the long winter nights, subsisting on fish, seals, walruses and any other food he can find. When in dire need he does not hesitate to attack Man, and many an Eskimo has fallen to his onsets. In summer, when food is plentiful, he attacks Man only in self-defence.

The brown bear of Europe (*Ursus arctus*) resembles the grizzly more than any other bear. It is larger than the black bear and more dangerous to Man, but it attacks him only when provoked or when suffering from extreme hunger. The strength of the brown bear is almost unbelievable. It has been known to kill a cow and carry it across a small stream in its forepaws, walking upright on its hind legs. Another authentic account tells how one dragged a deer weighing 600 pounds from a pit and through the woods three-quarters of a mile. The range of the European brown bear is from the Pyrenees, across Europe and Siberia to Kamchatka.

The Himalayan bear (*Ursus torquatus*) is found in Asia from Iran (Persia) to Japan. It resembles the black bear in size, colour and habits. The Malayan or honey bear (*Ursus malayanus*) is smaller. It inhabits the Malayan peninsula and the larger East Indian islands, and is called the honey bear because honey is its favourite food. It has a very long and flexible tongue with which it scoops the honeycomb out of hollow trees.

Bearings. In machinery, when a shaft has to turn in some plate or support, it may have a plain bearing, which is merely a hole made in the support, just loose enough to let the shaft turn freely. In bearings which have to stand a lot of wear the hole for the shaft may be lined with brass or some other fairly soft metal; usually the brass lining is made in two halves, the upper and lower halves being separated at the joints by two or three slips of very thin metal. When the brass lining wears and becomes too loose, one or more of the thin slips (which are called shims) can be taken out to bring the brass closer down to the shaft.

In large plain bearings the brasses are often lined with a thin coating of a soft bearing metal such as Babbitt metal, which has a low melting point;

G.P.A.

HIMALAYAN BEAR UP A TREE

This is the Himalayan bear, which is very similar in colouring and habits to the American black bear. In Whipsnade Zoo, in Bedfordshire, the authorities have provided a tree-top perch where this bear can make believe that it is back home among the mountains of Central Asia.

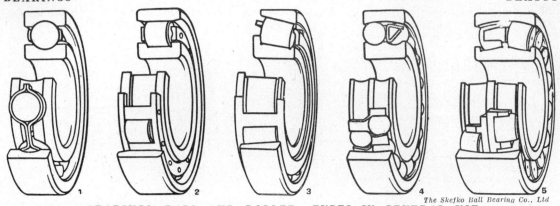

The Skefko Ball Bearing Co., Ltd

BEARINGS, BALL AND ROLLER: TYPES IN GENERAL USE
Shown here and described below are (1) a single-row radial ball bearing ; (2) a cylindrical roller bearing ; (3) a taper
roller bearing ; (4) a double-row self-alining ball bearing ; and (5) a double-row self-alining roller-bearing.

this softer lining allows a closer fit to the shaft and,
if it should become overheated, it will "run."
Lubrication with oil is intended to prevent bearings
becoming overheated by friction: the shaft actually
rotates on a very thin film of oil which coats the
surface of shaft and lining. Adjustment of the plain
type of bearing we have described is done by
screwing down the cap of the bearing to tighten it,
or by unscrewing to loosen it.

Today much machinery is provided with ball
bearings or roller bearings instead of with plain
ones. The wheel hubs, crank bracket and pedal
spindles of your bicycle have got ball bearings,
probably. There is a grooved ring known as the
ball race, in which are a number of hard steel balls,
free to roll and turn, and they are in contact with
the shaft or axle, which actually runs on them.

In the cycle wheel hub there is an enlarged
conical part which you can screw in or out to
adjust the wheel, and it is upon these cones that the
balls run; the ball race or "cup" is pressed into
the shell of the hub. This kind of bearing (usually
called a cup-and-cone bearing) deals with load
mainly exerted in a radial direction, from the circumference to the centre of the bearing. In the
steering head of your bicycle, where the handle
bars enter the head, there is a bearing of another
type, called a thrust bearing. This is to take up
endwise pressure.

Apart from these cycle bearings, the main types
of ball and roller bearings in general use are shown
in the "cut-away" diagrams Nos. 1 to 5. The
rolling elements are kept correctly spaced by means
of a "cage." First we have (1) a single-row radial
ball bearing; then (2) a cylindrical roller bearing
for heavier loads; (3) shows a taper roller bearing.
The next one (4) is a double-row self-alining
ball bearing in which the construction allows for the
inner ring cage and balls all running slightly out of
line if the shaft should be bent or deflected under
load. No. 5 is similar in principle, being a double-
row self-alining roller bearing, designed to carry
the heaviest radial loads combined with some
amount of end thrust.

Needle roller bearings are similar to the type
shown in (2) above, but have longer rollers of very
much smaller diameter in proportion to their length.
Ball and roller bearings are used instead of plain

(sliding) bearings for the following reasons: the loss
of power by friction is smaller, especially at the
start of rotation; there is almost no danger of the
bearing becoming overheated; the scraping and
fitting needed with the brass linings of plain
bearings is avoided.

Beatty, DAVID, 1ST EARL BEATTY (1871–
1936). The British Grand Fleet was commanded
during the last two years of the First World War
(1914–18) by Sir David Beatty, who was largely

BEATTY'S GREAT MOMENT
On November 21, 1918, Admiral Beatty witnessed the surrender of the German High Seas Fleet in compliance with the
conditions of the Armistice. He is here seen at this supreme
moment on the bridge of his flagship, H.M.S. Queen
Elizabeth, with Flag Captain Chatfield behind him.

WHAT A BEAVER LODGE LOOKS LIKE FROM INSIDE

The artist here shows us a beaver lodge with one side cut away so that we can see how cleverly it is built both above and below the water line. Notice that the bedroom, for more warmth, is higher than the dining room. The hall leads down under water to the front door, which is designed to be below the thickest ice that may cover the pond in winter. The beavers drag down and anchor near this entrance a supply of green branches and bark for winter feed. Observe that the main dam is protected by two others which relieve the pressure of water on the first one.

responsible for defeating the German submarine campaign. Born at Howbeck, Cheshire, of Irish stock, he entered the navy in 1884, becoming a Commander in 1898 and Admiral of the Fleet in 1919.

At the battle of the Dogger Bank on January 24, 1915, the forces under his command sank the German battle-cruiser Blücher, but unfortunately the Lion, his flagship, was obliged to leave the line with an ugly rent caused by a shell that stopped the working of one of the engines. Signalling a destroyer alongside, Beatty transferred his flag to her and tried to rejoin the squadron. His last signal was, "Engage the enemy more closely." He met his ships at noon retiring, the explanation being that the engagement was broken off when the squadron had " reached an area where dangers from German submarines and mines prevented further pursuit."

In the battle of Jutland on May 31, 1916, Beatty commanded the battle-cruiser squadron, and engaged the enemy in spite of heavy losses until the arrival of the battleships of the Grand Fleet. Soon after this, in November 1916, Beatty succeeded Sir John Jellicoe as Commander of the Grand Fleet, and in that capacity he received the surrender of the German fleet off Rosyth, on the Firth of Forth, east coast of Scotland, in 1918. He was made an Earl (Earl Beatty of the North Sea and of Brooksby) after the Armistice and given the sum of £100,000, and from 1919 to 1927 was First Sea Lord. He died on March 11, 1936.

Beaver. Where we say " as busy as a bee," a Canadian might say " as busy as a beaver." These are among the most intelligent and industrious of

animals, and the dams and houses which they construct display amazing skill. The scientific name of the North American beaver is *Castor canadensis*. The European beaver, *Castor fiber*, was common in England and all over Europe, but is now practically unknown except in some parts of Scandinavia, Germany, Poland and France, and also in northern Asia. The beaver belongs to the group of " gnawers," or rodents, and is the largest and heaviest of that family. A large beaver measures about two feet from the tip of his nose to the root of his tail, which adds about a foot more. The weight of such a specimen is about 35 pounds, but old animals may weigh as much as 75 pounds.

The tail is broad and flat with a horny covering resembling scales ; it serves as a rudder when swimming. The fore feet are small and hand-like. The hind feet are large and webbed for swimming. The front teeth are very large, and like those of squirrels and rabbits are hard in front and soft behind, so that they become worn to the shape of a chisel edge.

Beavers are social animals. A family of several members usually lives in one house, and sometimes a large number of families collects together in a community. They usually work at night and build their houses or " lodges " well concealed in small lakes made by damming a forest brook.

Their lodges are nearly dome-shaped and built of sticks, grass and moss, woven together and plastered with mud. The room inside may measure eight feet in diameter and two or three feet in height, and the floor is carpeted with bark, grass and wood chips. There are two entrances, both under water. One

BEAVERS AT WORK
The beaver is often described as the greatest natural engineer in the world. It is certainly astonishing how these animals fell the trees they need for building or food by gnawing at the trunks, as seen above.

entrance is often winding in its course, as a protection against enemies. The other is straight, and is used both for taking in the wood for winter food and as a means of escape in case of invasion by a mink or other water enemy. Both entrances open into a moat too deep to freeze solidly, so that the beavers are not likely to be shut in.

In order that they may easily pass to and fro under the winter's ice, and that they may have room to store food, the beavers build dams to deepen the water about the lodges. These dams are often of great size. The first step in dam-building is the selection of a suitable site, a narrow place in shallow water with firm bottom. Then the work of felling trees is begun. Standing on their hind legs, the beavers gnaw round and round the trunk with their chisel-like teeth until the tree is ready to fall. Sometimes trees 18 inches in diameter are thus cut through by these sagacious animals.

Some say that they arrange for the tree to fall towards the water; others declare that they work

haphazard. After the tree is down the beavers set to work lopping off branches and cutting the trunk into lengths which they can drag into the water. The short logs, dragged or floated to the desired spot, are sunk parallel with the current, and if the water is deep they are kept down by means of stones, grass and mud loaded on by the beavers. Mud and stones and heavier timbers are carried in their forepaws, and smaller timber between their teeth. There is no superintendence in their work, but each beaver does what seems to him best. The result is that the dam is usually a tangled heap, but it serves its purpose.

The beaver feeds mainly on the bark of trees (willow, poplar, birch, etc.), and on roots, buds, berries and leaves. A store of green logs is always sunk in the water at the doors of their houses for winter feeding. When the trees near the water are used up and the land is too uneven for rolling, log-slides and canals are cut in the banks and bottom to carry down the timbers. These channels may be hundreds of feet long and about a yard in width and depth. One of the chief uses of the beavers' dam is to ensure sufficient water to float these logs.

The soft, thick, grey under-fur of the beaver has long been highly valued by Man, and during the 17th and 18th centuries beaver skins held first place in the world's fur trade. At that time, before the invention of the silk hat, men's tall hats were made from beaver skins; hence the word " beaver " often meant " hat." So great was the demand for beaver fur that in the western part of Canada and the United States beaver skins at times were used as money. Formerly hunted practically out of existence, the beaver is now rigidly protected in eastern Canada and most American states.

The beaver has been blamed for the damage it sometimes causes by flooding tracts of valuable timber land. Its good deeds, however, outweigh the bad. By building a series of dams in mountainous districts, the beavers form ponds which hold the waters of the melting snows and give them out gradually during the summer, thus helping to irrigate the land.

Beaverbrook, WILLIAM MAXWELL AITKEN, 1ST BARON. This British newspaper proprietor and politician was born in New Brunswick, Canada, on May 25, 1879, made a considerable fortune, and then transferred his activities to England. From 1910 to 1916 he was Unionist member for Ashton-under-Lyne.

Max Aitken, who had been knighted in 1911 and created a baronet in 1916, was made a peer in the next year and in 1918 became head of the Ministry of Information, entering the Cabinet as Chancellor of the Duchy of Lancaster. He resigned after the Armistice in November 1918 and then took complete control of the Daily Express, which he raised to the position of a journal of great circulation and popular appeal. In 1921 he founded the

Criterion Press
LORD BEAVERBROOK
Canadian-born, Lord Beaverbrook, created a baron in 1917, was the first British Minister of Aircraft Production during the Second World War (1939–45).

Sunday Express and later secured a controlling interest in the London Evening Standard.

In 1929 he led a movement for free trade within the British Empire. During the Second World War he was successively Minister of Aircraft Production, 1940–41 ; Minister of State, 1941; Minister of Supply, 1941–42 ; and Lord Privy Seal, 1943–45. In 1947 he passed over control of the Express group of newspapers to his son, the Hon. Max Aitken. Among his writings are Success (1921), Politicians and the Press (1925), Politicians and the War (2 vols., 1928 and 1932) and The Resources of the British Empire (1934).

Becket, THOMAS, ARCHBISHOP OF CANTERBURY (1118–1170). The shrine of the murdered Archbishop Thomas Becket, which once stood in Canterbury Cathedral, was destroyed by Thomas Cromwell in 1538, but the steps which led up to it still stand, worn into hollows by the knees of countless pilgrims. For three centuries this was one of the most sacred spots in Christendom, and streams of religious pilgrims constantly thronged the road from London to Canterbury. It was to this shrine that the pilgrims of Chaucer's Canterbury Tales were journeying from Southwark.

The saint at whose shrine they came to worship was a London merchant's son, who had risen to be chancellor, chief minister and bosom friend of King Henry II. Thomas was about 15 years older than his royal master, but had endeared himself by his love of fun and sport no less than by his sagacity in matters of state.

BECKET'S VESTMENTS
Becket was canonized in 1173, three years after his murder, and every relic of him was regarded as sacred. What are said to be his vestments are preserved at Sens, in France.

But this friendship was soon to turn to bitterest enmity. Wishing to bring the Church under the power of the State, Henry appointed his boon companion to the highest Church office in England, that of Archbishop of Canterbury. Thomas protested, for he had been the pupil of the former Archbishop, and in that office he would be forced to resist the King's attempts to weaken the Church's power.

But Henry blindly persisted, and Thomas straightway became a devout and jealous defender of the privileges of the Church. The clash was not long in coming. The burning question of the time was whether churchmen should be subject to the King and his courts or only to the Pope and the ecclesiastical courts. Unfortunately this " benefit of clergy," as it was called, extended not only to priests but to everyone who had ever been a monk; it thus permitted many persons who were practically laymen to escape due punishment for their misdeeds, for the Church law forbade the death penalty.

Becket boldly stood out against Henry when he tried to lessen the independence of the clergy, and a furious quarrel began. One night Becket fled in disguise to appeal to the Pope. Henry seized Becket's revenues and exiled his relatives; but after several years a peace was patched up and Becket was allowed to return to England. His first act was to cut off from the church membership those who had illegally, as he believed, executed the King's commands in his absence. This act of defiance stung the quick-tempered monarch to fury.

" My subjects are sluggards, men of no spirit !" he cried. " They keep no faith with their lord; they allow me to be made the laughing-stock of a lowborn clerk !"

Four of the King's knights, hearing these words, took passage hastily across the Channel—for the King was in Normandy—proceeded to Canterbury, and slew the Archbishop with their swords on the altar steps of his cathedral on December 29, 1170. This savage deed shocked the Christian world. Henry was forced by Pope Alexander III to do penance. The Pope declared Becket a saint, and

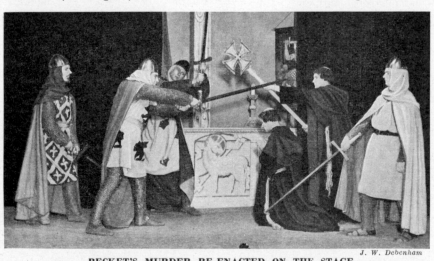

J. W. Debenham

BECKET'S MURDER RE-ENACTED ON THE STAGE
A play, Murder in the Cathedral, by the poet T. S. Eliot and first produced in 1935, has for its theme the tragic end of the great Archbishop. Here we see the final scene, as it was staged in Canterbury Cathedral and in London. The actual spot on which Becket was struck down may be seen in the cathedral, and along the Pilgrim's Way from Winchester to Canterbury we may tread the path worn by the feet of countless thousands of pilgrims to his shrine.

BEDFORDSHIRE DOWNS AS A GLIDING GROUND

Many gliding clubs meet at Dunstable Downs, in south Bedfordshire, where the highest point is about 800 feet above sea-level. The glider above has left the ground but is still being towed. The rate of towing is about 30 m.p.h., and the gliders leave the earth almost at once.

Graphic Photo Union

Midlands, the county town Bedford (population about 56,000) being only 50 miles from London. It is mostly flat country throughout its 473 square miles, but in the south are Dunstable Downs (the chief centre of British gliding), and in the N.W. a ridge of low chalk hills. Wheat, barley and market-garden produce are grown, and sheep rearing, straw-plaiting for hats, lace-making and quarrying are other local industries. The Great Ouse river passes through the town of Bedford, the county gaol of which is famed as John Bunyan's place of imprisonment (1660 to 1672). Bedford School is only one of several important places of education. Other towns are Luton and Dunstable, centres of the hat trade. Population of the county is 275,000.

his shrine remained the most hallowed spot in England until the Reformation, when it was destroyed by Henry VIII's orders.

Bedfordshire. This is one of the most fertile of the English counties. It is in the south

BUSY BEES *in their* WONDER WORKSHOP

Some bees live in vast and well-ordered communities, some by themselves. Some help our fruit crops to be abundant by assisting the fertilization of the flowers. There are nectar-gatherers (who make us our honey), and others.

Bee. The structure of a honeycomb nears perfection in the way of strength and space for holding fluid contents, for the bee—especially the honey-bee—has a skill in architecture unsurpassed in the animal kingdom. Maurice Maeterlinck, the renowned Belgian poet, in his The Life of the Bee, describes the inside as it would look to us if we could see it through the eyes of the bee:

"From the height of a dome more colossal than that of St. Peter's at Rome, waxen walls descend to the ground gigantic and manifold vertical and parallel geometric constructions, to

This humble-bee is enjoying one of its favourite foods— the nectar of the clover.

which, for relative precision, audacity and vastness, no human structure is comparable. Each of these walls contains thousands of cells that are stored with pro visions to feed the whole people for several weeks. In the centre there stands the royal domain of the brood cells, set apart for the queen and her atten dants—about 10,000 cells wherein the eggs repose, 15,000 or 16,000 chambers tenanted by larvae,

40,000 dwellings inhabited by white nymphs to whom thousands of nurses minister, and, finally, in the holy of holies of these parts, are the three, four, six or twelve sealed palaces, vast in size compared with the others, where the adolescent princesses lie, wrapped in a kind of shroud, all of them motionless and pale, and fed in the darkness."

Wonderful structures like this can, of course, be made only by highly developed communities, such as are formed by the honey-bees. Honey-bees and humble-bees are called the social bees, because they live all their lives in great colonies containing sometimes in the case of honey-bees as many as 50,000 individuals. All the other families of bees, which nest by themselves, are called solitary bees. Each mother of these species provides a nest for her young. which no longer live together when grown up.

The honey-bees which we see flitting from flower to flower in the garden and meadow have the most complicated social organization of all the animals with the possible exception of the ants. They live in a republic where the citizens do all the governing without voting, where the many kings are powerless, and the one much cherished queen works as hard as any of her subjects, and longer. Honey-bees are perfect socialists; they labour without competition or personal reward, and they have everything in common. They are divided into castes as workers, queens and drones; but these castes exist for the benefit of all, and not for their own private advantage. The worker honey-bee is an undeveloped female specially changed physically in order to carry on the labours of the colony. Her brain is much larger than that of the queen or the drone. She has combs on her hind legs to collect pollen from the flowers, and baskets to store it in. She has a system of chemical laboratories within herself, in one of which she changes the nectar of the flowers to honey. In another she produces food for queens, and in another she changes honey into wax. Her duties are many.

E. Fiedelholz

BEES OF THREE DEGREES

In the kingdom of the honey-bees there are three well-differentiated castes—those illustrated here. On the left is the queen, large of body but lacking in strength. In the middle is the worker, an infertile female, small-bodied but long-winged. On the right is the drone, the fertile male bee.

When she first matures she has to feed the little bee grubs, or larvae, and keep the hive clean and ventilate it by fanning with her wings. Later she learns how to take wax and build it into a honeycomb, or to hang up claw in claw with her sisters and gorge herself with honey in order to give forth little scales of wax from the glands on the lower side of her abdomen. She gathers nectar from the flowers, changes it into honey, and then stores it in the honeycomb.

She gathers pollen in her leg-baskets and then scrapes it off into a cell, where she flattens it down with her head to make it into solid " bee-bread " to be fed to young larvae. If the colony is attacked she must join in the battle to defend it. She may help in exiling her drone brothers when the time comes to get rid of them ; or she may be waiting-

maid to the queen, feeding and caring for her tenderly and producing from her own glands the rich food necessary to the royal mother. She may also have to gather bee-glue from leaf-buds to caulk the crevices of the hive.

Whatever her duties, she works with all her might and without any consideration for herself. She will starve herself to feed the queen; she will fight any enemy with recklessness; she will work at bringing in food until her frayed wings can no longer carry her. And at the end of her short and laborious life she falls by the wayside to die, neither expecting nor obtaining any help from her sisters. There is no gratitude or pensioning in the bee colony; death and oblivion is the fate of the most ardent workers when they fail. The individual is of no account; the community is everything.

The life story of the bee begins with the tiny white egg that the queen lays in a cell of the honeycomb. The egg stands up straight and is glued at one end to the bottom of the cell. After three days a little white grub or larva hatches from it, and is continuously fed by the nurse bees. It grows until it fills almost the entire cell. The bees then cap the cell with a mixture of wax and pollen which is porous enough to allow the air to circulate. Meanwhile, the larva lines the cell walls with a fine silken

Rev. C. Metcalfe, Neville Kingston, Clarence Ponting

CHAPTERS IN THE LIFE-STORY OF THE HONEY-BEE

The bee is the only insect which Man has to some extent domesticated. Left to themselves honey-bees would make their nest in the hollow of a tree or even in the open, hanging their combs from the first spot where the queen alighted after her flight from the hive, as in the photograph on the left. Centre, is a swarm of bees, a mass of workers crowded round the queen, and this swarm may be captured and placed in a hive. But a queen may settle in a hive, and then other bees, as on the right, will follow her, ready to start a new colony now that she has chosen her home.

cocoon, within which it changes to a pupa. After gnawing through cocoon and cell-cap, the full-grown bee emerges.

During the first three days the little larva is fed in abundance. It actually swims in the rich creamy food which is prepared by the nurse bees. For the next day or two the diet changes in quantity and quality. Only honey and pollen serve as food, and these are fed to the larva in measured quantities. Six days of larval life are followed by 12 days in the pupal stage, so the development from egg to fully-formed worker bee lasts about 21 days.

The queen takes only 16 days to develop. She comes from the same kind of egg as the worker, but is reared in a different cell, the so-called queen cell. A queen cell, which is much larger than a worker cell, is attached vertically to the comb. The queen larva, during the six days of larval development, is fed with a rich substance called " royal jelly," which is deposited at the base of the queen cell in such abundance that after the larva ceases to feed a great quantity of royal jelly still remains in the cell. Seven days after the cell is sealed a young queen emerges.

After a short time, on some sunny day, the queen will fly from the hive seeking her mate. After mating she returns alone to the hive, capable of laying fertilized or unfertilized eggs at will. The fertilized eggs develop into workers and queens, the unfertilized into drones. She soon begins laying, thrusting her abdomen into cell after cell and leaving an egg glued at the bottom of each. When the honey season is at its height, she sometimes lays as many as 3,000 in a day. When the honey harvest runs low she lays fewer eggs. The queen may live for several seasons, while the worker may wear herself out in six weeks.

Bee colonies spread by swarming—to remedy an overcrowded condition of the hive. Young queens are reared early in the season, but before they are allowed to emerge from pupal life, swarming has taken place. The old queen, followed by a large

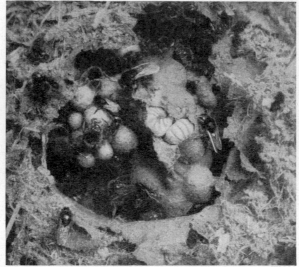

J. J. Ward

HUMBLE-BEES IN THEIR NEST

Here is the inside of a humble-bee's nest, with several bees still at work. From two of the cells the tops have been removed to show the grubs inside. The outside of the nest consists of moss, grass and straw, while the papery lining is of the bees' own manufacture.

that one drone may fulfil his destiny of mating with the queen, many are born only to be slain when the food supply runs low. The drone is a clumsy, broad, blunt-ended bee. He has no pollen baskets on his legs, no wax glands or honey stomach in his body ; he has no sting to protect himself, and his tongue is not long enough to reach nectar in the flowers. But his wings are large and strong and carry him miles in search of a queen, and his equipment for finding her is most complete; he has very large eyes—with 8,000 to 10,000 facets—and his antennae are fitted with smelling glands so that he has more than 2,600 tiny organs wherewith it is said he detects the fragrance of his consort's person.

The drone is hatched from an unfertilized egg laid in a cell larger than that of the worker. He is at first fed on rich food of pollen and honey. Twenty-four days from the laying of the egg he cuts a circular lid in the cap which the workers have made over his cell and crawls out, to move about on the comb and eat his fill of honey. After about two weeks he begins making flights, hunting for a queen; but when he finds her his happiness is brief, for he dies immediately after mating. If he finds no queen consort, his lot must puzzle him ; for his sister workers, so kind before, on a day when the food supply is low, hunt and

number of workers, departs for another home, which, unless controlled by Man, will be probably a hole in a roof, in masonry or in an old tree. The reason for her departure before the emergence of the young queens is that she would at once kill them if they put in an appearance, and their cells are therefore actually guarded by workers who prevent them emerging until the coast is clear. Even then, of course, they will fight amongst themselves, for the first thing a fertilized queen does on her return to the hive is to slay all possible rivals.

The drone or male bee has the least fortunate lot of all the bee citizens. In order

LANGUAGE OF THE BEE'S FLIGHT

Here we see (A) the circuitous course of a bee approaching a blossom, but when it has taken on its load it will go home in a ' bee-line.' Back in the hive, it may perform the honey dance (B), which means ' I have found nectar ' or the pollen dance (C), which means ' I have found pollen.'

ALL IN T

1

Gathers nectar
and turns it into
honey

3 Stores the hon

5 Manufactu

6 F
aff

Cells
to devel

The picture
facturing a
of wax, ar
picture-bi
begins as
parts of t
these mar
most care
shows th
amazing

From a painting by Bruno Ertz

Forcing its way into the 'mouth' of the snapdragon flower to get at the nectar, the humble-bee becomes dusted with pollen—which it transfers to the next snapdragon it visits and thus ensures cross-pollination.

Five times actual size

To face page 392

harry him, driving him outside the hive to perish.

The products of the honey-bee are honey and beeswax, the honey being marketed either in the comb or extracted and bottled. The beeswax remains when the honey is extracted from the comb. Honey is the most healthful of sweets, and before the 17th century was the only generally used substance for sweetening food.

Many cultivators of orchards realize the value of bees in carrying the pollen of fruit blossoms and find it profitable to keep bees for that purpose. In favourable seasons bees seldom find it necessary to go more than two miles from the hive for nectar.

The bumble- or humble-bees are also social, but have not reached the efficiency of the honey-bee. However, they are very important as pollen carriers for thousands of plants, because they have long tongues and are, so able to take nectar from deep flowers which the honey-bee cannot reach. This fact has proved very important to growers of red clover, for only the humble-bee can reach the nectar and thus carry the pollen.

In early spring we may often see a great humble-bee queen or mother flying low over the meadows, hunting for the deserted nest of a field-mouse or some other suitable cavity for a home. Finding a cosy place, she toils early and late gathering pollen and nectar from all flowers in bloom. This she mixes into an irregular mass of solid bee-bread, upon which she lays a few eggs, about 12 at a time, roofing each batch of eggs with wax and gradually adding to the pollen mass until the first brood is hatched.

The bee grub as soon as it is hatched burrows into the bee-bread, making a cave for itself as it eats. After it is fully grown it spins a silken cocoon about itself, and later comes out as a worker humble-bee. She and her sisters then relieve the queen-mother from the work of providing food, so that the queen can give all her energies to the duty of laying eggs. These daughters tend the growing family, and later strengthen the silken cocoon cradles with wax, making them into cells in which they store honey. Late in the season a few queens are developed from the eggs laid by the queen, and a few drones to be mates for the queens. The queens are the only members of the whole colony of hundreds of workers and drones that are strong enough to endure the cold of winter. Thus each humble-bee colony lasts only one season, in contrast to the honey-bees, which pass the winter in a semi-dormant state.

The hairy body of the humble-bee is particularly useful in brushing and holding the pollen when she is working on flowers. After she is well powdered she

alights on some leaf, and with the most strenuous efforts combs the pollen out of her fur with special combs on her legs, and packs it in her pollen baskets on her hind legs.

Among the most common of the solitary bees are the carpenters, the leaf-cutters and the miners. The mother carpenter-bee bores a tunnel in soft dead wood by cutting out the chips with her jaws. The tunnel leads straight in for a short distance and then downward, and it is just large enough for her to move in comfortably. After the tunnel is completed she gathers pollen and nectar from flowers and mixes them into a ball. Then she lays an egg upon this pollen mass. Next she gathers some of the chips cut out in making the tunnel and glues them together with saliva, making a little partition above the pollen mass. This acts as a floor for the next cell, in which she places another pollen ball and another egg. She thus makes several cells, in each of which a young bee hatches from the egg and develops to maturity upon the bee-bread she has provided. When they are fully grown each young bee tears down the partition above him, and they all come out into the world in single file. Not all carpenter-bees bore into solid wood, for many species bore out the pith in the dead twigs of bramble, elder, raspberry, and other bushes.

The leaf-cutter bees line their nests with pieces cut out of leaves, especially rose leaves, separating the cells with circular pieces cut from leaves. Some leaf-cutter bees save themselves the trouble of boring out a nest by using crevices between boards. Others line their nests with pieces cut from the petals of pansies and other flowers. These carpenter and leaf-cutter bees vary in size from that of a small humble-bee to a tiny creature which is little more than a quarter of an inch in length.

The miners bore tunnels into the ground instead of into wood, and make tiny cells branching off the main tunnel to receive the eggs. The walls of the cells are glazed, so that they look like the inside of an earthen jug. In each cell is stored pollen and nectar paste; then an egg is laid and the cell closed until the pupa is grown up and pushes out. While each mother miner digs her own nest, many of them may live as neighbours in "villages." Some of the miners are as large as honey-bees, but one species is less than a quarter of an inch in length—the smallest of all the bees.

Lord Avebury (q.v.) once made an interesting experiment to try to ascertain whether the colour of flowers attracted bees. Placing honey on slips of paper of different shades, he found that the insects which visited them seemed to have a marked preference for blue

CARPENTER-BEE

The carpenter-bee lays one egg in each cell. When the young bees emerge from the pupal stage they tear down the partitions and file out.

H. Bastin

BEECH TREE IN ALL ITS SUMMER BEAUTY

The smooth grey bark and glossy leaves of the beech are sufficient to distinguish this noble tree of our woods and forests. It is also cultivated in our gardens and parks. Its habit of retaining its dead leaves all winter—until they are pushed off by the new foliage—makes it specially useful as a windbreak and for hedges. The leaves are seen, close up, at the top left. At lower left are the flower clusters, resembling little tassels, which are followed by the beech nuts.

after which came white, yellow, red, green and orange. This test was repeated frequently.

Bees constitute the section called *Apoidea* of the order *Hymenoptera*, which includes the ants, wasps and saw-flies. The hive-bees constitute the genus *Apis;* the scientific name of the common honey-bee is *Apis mellifica.* Humble-bees belong to the family *Bombidae.* The bee has two pairs of wings, the hind pair being the smaller; its mouth parts are fitted for biting and sucking, and the basal segment of the foot is broadened and fitted for carrying pollen.

Beech. Not until it is fairly old does the beech tree produce its nuts, but it makes a beautiful shade tree much earlier. Its leaves are so arranged on the twigs that very little sunlight can pass between them, and that is one of the reasons why there is little or no undergrowth in a beech wood; often even the nuts of the beech are unable to germinate beneath their parent trees. The life of the tree is about 250 years. The common beech (*Fagus sylvatica*) often grows 100 feet high or more, and has dark grey bark and shining leaves, which in autumn change to beautiful shades of yellow and brown. During the winter the beech may easily be recognized by its buds, which are long and narrow and are covered with a number of brown scales.

The beeches of England have long been famous, as are the beech forests of Denmark and Germany. One of the most handsome varieties is the copper beech, distinguished by its coppery-purple leaves.

Beechnut oil is sometimes used on the continent of Europe in cooking, salad dressing, and for lighting purposes. The wood is almost impervious to water, and is used in France and elsewhere for making wooden shoes. It is also used for flooring and as building timber, and for charcoal, and is distilled to make creosote for medicinal purposes.

Beecham, SIR THOMAS (b. 1879). To this great musician, in his capacity of opera impresario and conductor, England owes a debt of gratitude, for it was he who introduced many operatic works as well as Russian ballet to this country before the First World War (1914-18).

His perfect control of the orchestra, his expressive gestures and commanding personality have made him one of the most famous men in the musical world of his time. Many years ago he established a rule that late-comers at his concerts or operas must wait for admittance until the interval.

The son of Sir Joseph Beecham, a wealthy business man, he was born on April 29, 1879, and educated at Rossall School and Wadham College, Oxford. In 1910 he gave a series of opera performances at Covent Garden, London, at which the finest singers of the day appeared. Under his direction the famous Russian baritone Chaliapin appeared in Boris Godunov at London's Drury Lane Theatre in 1913, and in the same year Der Rosenkavalier by Richard Strauss was first produced at Covent Garden.

Then came the First World War, and Beecham maintained a regular series of operatic performances in English. In 1922 he was associated with the founding of the British National Opera Company,

SIR THOMAS BEECHAM AT REHEARSAL
Topical
This famous British conductor founded the London Philharmonic Orchestra in 1932 and did more than anyone to revive opera in Britain. He succeeded his father, the 1st baronet, in 1916.

introducing such works as Holst's Perfect Fool, and Vaughan Williams's Hugh the Drover to the stage. This movement for the permanent subsidising of opera in England proved financially unsuccessful, but Beecham was not a man to be easily defeated by the indifference of the public. In 1932 he became musical director of the National Opera Council, a body which provided for co-operation between the Covent Garden Opera Syndicate, the Imperial League of Opera, the Vic-Wells Theatre, and the B.B.C., a position he held until 1938. It will thus be seen that opera in England was moving in the direction of being sponsored by the State—as in most European countries.

Apart from his immense contribution to ballet and opera, Beecham was responsible for a higher standard of orchestral playing. He conducted the Royal Philharmonic Society's concerts, and in 1932 founded the London Philharmonic Orchestra. He was responsible also for introducing the work of Delius to the concert-hall during the years 1907-09, at a series of concerts at the Queen's Hall, London, and in 1929 he conducted the festival of that composer. His fame as conductor was established in the U.S.A. during the 1920s, and during the Second World War he was director of the Seattle Symphony Orchestra, 1941-42, and later conducted the New York Metropolitan Opera.

He received a knighthood in January, 1916 and succeeded to the baronetcy on the death of his father in the same year. His autobiography, A Mingled Chime, published in 1944, gives a vivid and fascinating picture of his activities.

Beefeater. The quaint name given to the old soldiers who act as a bodyguard to the Sovereign on state occasions means what it seems to mean—an eater of beef. The name was suggested by a grand duke of Tuscany, Count Cosimo, who was visiting England in the year 1669. Commenting on the magnificent physique of the corps, he wrote : " They are great eaters of beef, of which a very large ration is given them daily at court, and they might be called Beefeaters." And the name stuck. It used to be thought that " beefeater " was derived from the French *beaufetier*, meaning one who attends at a sideboard, but there is no evidence for this.

The corps, whose official title is the King's Body Guard of the Yeomen of the Guard, was constituted in 1485 by Henry VII. They wear a scarlet uniform of the Tudor period, and carry a partisan, which is a long-handled axe. Yeomen of the Guard still attend Court ceremonies. The Yeomen Warders of the Tower, though their uniform is in almost every detail the same as that of the Yeomen of the Guard, are now a separate body and their duties are performed wholly within the ancient precincts of the Tower of London.

CHIEF WARDER OF THE TOWER
Fox
The King's Bodyguard of the Yeomen of the Guard and the Yeomen Warders of the Tower are popularly called Beefeaters ; but the Warders do not wear the crossbelt of the Bodyguard and they perform their duties wholly within the Tower of London. The chief warder wears four gold stripes on his right arm.

Beet. Napoleon's two contributions to the greatness of France have been said to be the set of laws called the Code Napoleon and the sugar-beet. It is true that the great emperor did much to encourage beet-growing in France, because of England's practical monopoly of the colonies which produced sugar-cane ; but we are chiefly indebted to the scientists of the 19th century, who developed the beet from a root producing only seven per cent sugar to one which is 16 per cent sugar, and who are still working to improve the sugar content by seed selection. This remarkable advance in the last few years is proof of what can be done by scientific methods. Many thousands of acres are devoted to the cultivation of sugar-beet in England, particularly in East Anglia Sugar-beet residues are used in the feeding of pigs and cattle, particularly dairy cattle.

The beet (*Beta vulgaris*) belongs to the family *Chenopodiaceae*. It is found growing wild in sandy

'BEEFEATERS' IN THE DRESS OF TUDOR DAYS

The King's Body-Guard of the Yeomen of the Guard is the proper title
of these picturesquely-clad veterans, though they are popularly known
as Beefeaters. The Yeomen of the Guard number one hundred, and
are recruited from military pensioners with a record of distinguished
service in the field.

'BEEFEATERS' BRING THE MAUNDY MONEY

AMONG the duties still remaining to the King's Body-Guard of the Yeomen of the Guard are attending the Sovereign on certain ceremonial occasions and—a quaint survival, this—searching the cellars of the Houses of Parliament on the first day of every fresh Session lest a modern imitator of Guy Fawkes be concealed there with intent to blow up our legislators.

The Beefeaters have also an ornamental part to play in the distribution of Maundy Money, on Maundy Thursday—the day before Good Friday. This takes place at Westminster Abbey, where the specially-struck coins are distributed by the Lord High Almoner, deputizing for the Sovereign. A detachment of the Yeomen of the Guard is seen in this picture arriving in the Abbot's Courtyard at Westminster, having escorted the Maundy Money from St. James's Palace. One of them carries the money on a flat dish on his head, where it is contained in purses of which the strings hang down all round the edges of the dish.

Tattersall; The Times

SUGAR-BEET INDUSTRY IN EAST ANGLIA

Cultivation of the sugar-beet in Great Britain is carried on chiefly in East Anglia. The plants require a good deal of attention ; and at the left men are hoeing, while girls are hand-weeding around the plants. After the roots have been taken out of the ground they are delivered to factories, where they are sliced and steeped in water to extract the sugary juice. The factory on the right, at Peterborough, Northamptonshire, deals with 3,000 tons of sugar-beet daily.

soil in the neighbourhood of the Mediterranean, and has been cultivated for about 2,000 years. Besides the sugar-beet, which is usually whitish or yellowish, several other species are cultivated. Of these the garden beet—" beetroot "—is the best-known. Mangels, or mangel-wurzels, are very large varieties of beet for cattle feeding. Foliage beets, which have beautifully coloured leaves, are often grown for decorative purposes in gardens.

Beethoven, LUDWIG VAN (1770–1827). Tragedy and triumph played equal parts in the life of the great musician Beethoven (pron. bā′-tō-ven). At the age of four, weary, hungry and cold, he was compelled by his father to spend hours at the violin and clavier (a forerunner of the piano).

His life's climax came at the memorable concert at which, after the performance of his Choral Symphony, the great master, totally deaf, had to be turned to the audience to *see* the frantic applause. His story closes with a great funeral pageant, in sad contrast to the death-bed scene in which the lonely artist passed away, his longing for intimate companionship unsatisfied.

Beethoven, while credited to the German nation, came of Flemish stock, his grandfather having removed from Antwerp to Bonn. His father, a singer, was both poor and intemperate, and the household was always in need. The father planned to make of his son a child musician whose concert perform-

ances would fill the family purse, and gave him the best available instruction. At nine Ludwig was the pupil of the court organist at Bonn ; at 11 he made his first concert tour, and at 12 became assistant court organist.

When Beethoven was only 15 his mother's ill-health and his father's incompetence forced him to take entire charge of the large family. Nevertheless he made such progress in music that his friends, impressed by his genius, enabled him to settle in Vienna, then the world's musical centre. There he studied under Haydn and Salieri. His brilliant piano-playing at once established him in musical circles, and publishers eagerly sought his compositions. Soon he was the foremost musician of the day.

These should have been bright years for Beethoven, but over his success hung the shadow of a great grief. He was growing increasingly deaf. With this affliction came periods of intense suffering caused by a digestive ailment and aggravated by his highly emotional temperament. He became nervous and irritable, and at last withdrew entirely from society. His brothers, attempting to manage his business affairs, entangled him in lawsuits and estranged him from his best friends. A nephew on whom Beethoven lavished his affection proved a burden of sorrow and bitterness.

He worked in the greatest disorder, quite unmindful of

LUDWIG VAN BEETHOVEN

This master of music was not only one of the greatest musicians who ever lived but also a great man. His strong personality is vividly portrayed in this painting.

the passage of time. He quarrelled frequently with his housekeepers and landlords, and never knew the comfort of a real home. Loving the country, he spent much time in the fields, wandering about, singing and muttering to himself. Though he was below medium height, his friends said that in moments of inspiration his diminutive figure seemed to tower to the gigantic proportion of his mind. In the letter known as his will he tells his brothers of the physical conditions under which he struggled, and begs them to forgive his seeming harshness, which he declared was partly caused by his hopeless longing for human intercourse and sympathy.

Pitiful as Beethoven's isolation was, it seemed a source of inspiration. Composition after composition flowed from his pen. All forms of vocal and instrumental music, from dainty " bagatelle " to grand symphony, from simple songs to opera and mass, are included in the list of his 138 works. In all these varied forms Beethoven showed his skill. His 32 piano sonatas alone would entitle him to a foremost rank among musicians, for he gave to this musical form a freedom unimagined by his predecessors. It is his nine symphonies, however, that make him incontestably pre-eminent. Richard Wagner wrote of them, " He developed the symphony to such a fascinating fullness of form, and filled this form with such an unheard-of wealth of enchanting melody, that we stand today before the Beethoven symphonies as before the boundary-line of an entirely new epoch in the history of art; for with them a phenomenon has appeared in the world, with which the art of no time and no nation has had anything to compare."

Statues have been erected to the memory of the great Beethoven both in his birth-place, Bonn, and in Vienna, and the house in which he was born is preserved as a museum.

ARMOUR-BEARERS of the INSECT WORLD

Beautiful or forbidding in appearance, peaceful or warlike by nature, the beetles are all provided with a tough covering that safeguards them from most mishaps. In size they range from a mere pin-head to giants of the insect world.

Beetle. If a contest of strength were held among insects, the beetles would undoubtedly carry off the prize. Nearly all of them are covered from head to foot with strong, tough " armour-plate," which is their skeleton worn on the outside. In addition to this great advantage they have drawn on nearly all the rest of Nature's bag of tricks for their protection and support. They are powerful flyers, some are strong jumpers, fine climbers, swift runners. Some excel in digging and boring, swimming and diving; and as weight-lifters they number in their ranks unquestioned champions. Some of them, like the fire-flies, have the power of giving off glowing light in the dark.

The stag beetle, with its mandibles, is one of the most striking British insects.

It is the armour of the beetles that chiefly makes them different. As you know, it is a distinguishing trait of most of the insects to have four wings, like butterflies, moths, bees and wasps. In the case of the housefly and other true flies, the hind pair has been lost. In the beetles, something has happened to the front pair; they have turned hard and thick, folding down over the back. These front wings, or " wing-covers," are not used for flying, but are raised on high to permit the filmy, delicate hind wings to spread out when the beetle wants to take a trip in the air. Then, when it alights again, the hind wings fold up, the armoured wing-covers fall into place over them, and you would never know that the beetle was ever meant for anything except running, climbing, digging or swimming.

It is from this peculiarity that the beetles get their scientific name *Coleoptera*, which means " sheath-winged." Another of their qualities is suggested by their English name, which comes from the Anglo-Saxon word *bitel*, meaning " the biting one." Most beetles are indeed great biters, having strong jaws, which some use for killing living prey, some for devouring plants, others for gnawing timber, leather, fur, cloth, books, etc., and others for tearing apart the dead things they eat.

In battle, beetles use no stings or poison fangs, but grapple with jaws and claws. So, despite the fact that many beetles look fierce and dangerous, you may pick them up without fear, provided you dodge their " pincers " and don't mind the unpleasant smell many of them can create when frightened or angered. Because beetles have so admirably adjusted themselves to nearly all conditions of life in almost all quarters of the world the number of their species is believed to be greater than that of any other insect group, with the possible exception of the flies. Scientists have classified more than 200,000 different kinds.

The life cycle of all beetles has a complete metamorphosis, that is, the beetle egg turns first into a grub or larva, then into a pupa, then into a full-grown insect. Beetle larvae, which are usually soft-bodied and often worm-like, with hard heads and strong jaws, are generally very active.

The smallest beetles are the feather-wings, no larger than the head of a pin; the largest are the African goliaths and the elephant beetles of the West Indies, which reach six or seven inches in length and are the giants of the insect world. Between these two extremes are found beetles of all shapes and sizes, long and slim, short and fat, and with all the colours of the rainbow. It will be possible to mention only a few of those remarkable for some trick or habit or curious formation.

Perhaps the most handsome are the tiger beetles (family *Cicindelidae*), wonderfully graceful and active

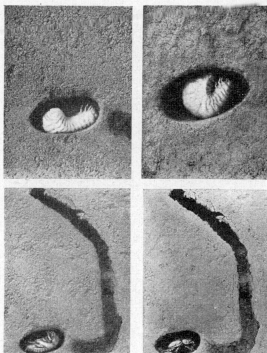

Hugh Main

FROM GRUB TO BEETLE
From each egg hatches a grub, or larva; and the two upper photographs show (left) a female lunar dung beetle at this stage, and (right) a male. Lower (left) the larva has changed into a pupa, and (right) it has become a beetle.

insects with long slender legs for swift running, and coloured with brilliant metallic greens and blues, sometimes marked with stripes or spots. They are fierce creatures, an inch or more in length, always ready to pounce on some fellow-insect and devour it. The tiger-beetle grubs have a strange way of trapping prey. They lie in holes in the ground, with their large ugly heads blocking the entrance. When an unwary insect steps upon its head the grub drops suddenly to the bottom of the hole, and the victim tumbles after, to its fate.

There is a much smaller beetle, called the bombardier, one of the ground beetle family (*Carabidae*), which has a way of making the hungry tiger beetle look foolish. Just as the tiger beetle's jaws are about to close upon it, the bombardier fires a little cloud of acrid, irritating vapour from the rear of its abdomen. If one dose is not enough to discourage the pursuer the discharge may be repeated several times, each accompanied by a faint pop.

In contrast to the savage tiger beetles are those peaceful, lumbering members of the scarab family (*Scarabaeidae*), perhaps the most famous of all the beetles, because their ancestors were held sacred by the ancient Egyptians, who buried them with their mummies and carved gems in their likeness.

One of the scarab beetles carves out a mass of manure bigger than itself and rolls it into a ball, then stands on its head with its hind legs upon the ball and pushes it along backwards. Up hill and down it goes, stumbling and kicking, crawling round and under its treasure, lifting it over stones, pulling it out of pits, until it finds a spot to suit it. There a

hole is dug and into it the beetle goes with its ball, remaining until the latter is entirely eaten. The eggs of this beetle are laid in similar balls buried in the ground. The scarab, like many other beetles, has a very hard time getting up if it falls on its back on a smooth, flat surface.

There is a group of beetles, however, which has solved this difficulty admirably. They are the click beetles (family *Elateridae*), so named because, if they are upset, they double up and then suddenly straighten out with a click, which tosses them high into the air. Like cats, they usually land on their feet and scurry away. These acrobats are also called skipjacks. Their larvae are the wireworms so destructive to farm and garden crops.

On the whole, the order of beetles is harmful, for although the tiger beetles, the ground beetles, the lady-birds (family *Coccinellidae*), and many other varieties destroy enormous numbers of plant-eating insects, and the scavenger and carrion beetles (family *Silphidae*) dispose of a great quantity of decaying matter, there are far more beetles which feed upon trees, plants, fruits, grain and other valuable foodstuffs. Among the worst offenders are the rose-chafers, the leaf-chafers—both of them closely related to the scarabs—nearly all of the long-horned beetles, the dreaded Colorado beetle—which attacks potato crops—the tortoise beetles, raspberry beetles, asparagus beetles, and, most destructive of all, the countless hordes of weevils (family *Curculionidae*).

It has been said that there is no animal or vegetable substance that is not preyed upon by some member of the beetle family. As an example of varied diet consider the menu of the tiny " drug-store beetle," an American species, which not only eats any form of dry groceries, but delights in such things as red pepper and in at least 45 different drugs, including aconite, belladonna and ergot—

Ray Palmer

TIGER BEETLE SEEKING PREY
The wood tiger beetle is, as its name implies, a fierce little creature. This specimen, magnified 2½ times, is on the alert for any morsel to satisfy its flesh-eating appetite.

all three poisonous to Man. Printed books are not too dry for it, nor paraffin too oily. A near relative, the spider beetle, one of the varieties often called bookworms, has a record of having " penetrated directly through 27 large volumes in so straight a line that a string could be passed through the opening and the whole series of volumes suspended." It is to this group of small beetles that the famous death-watch belongs. Spending its life in tunnels bored in timber, this creature calls to its mate by tapping its head against the sides of its corridors. This faint knocking sound was formerly believed to be a warning of the impending death of a member of the household. Other obnoxious pests are the *Dermestidae*, or " skin-devouring " beetles, including the larder beetle, which feeds on smoked meats, hides, feathers, hair and horn; and the leather beetle, with similar tastes. One of the strangest of beetles is the blister beetle, sometimes called the Spanish fly; besides the fact that its body contains cantharidin, a substance which is used medicinally for raising blisters on the human skin, it has a most unusual life history. After the larva hatches from the egg it does not go directly into the pupa form but passes through no fewer than five intermediate larval stages. The oil beetles have a similar experience, which is called by scientists hypermetamorphosis.

Among the most interesting English beetles are the large carnivorous water beetles, family *Dytiscus* (from the Greek word *dytes*, meaning diver). Shaped like big water-melon seeds, their smooth boat-shaped lines and paddle-shaped hind legs make them excellent swimmers, enabling them to capture and devour almost all of the smaller inhabitants of ponds, including young fish. When at rest they float head down with the tips of their bodies sticking out of the water. In this way their spiracles, or breathing tubes, situated at the rear of the abdomen, have access to the air. When they dive they carry down a supply of air beneath their water-tight wing-covers. Their larvae, sometimes called " water-tigers," are even fiercer creatures than the adults.

The most amusing of the water beetles are the whirligigs (*Gyrinus*), which may be seen on still waters dancing in rapid circles over the surface, as though gone mad. If disturbed they make a queer squeak by rubbing the tip of their abdomen against their wing-covers. These whirligigs have " split " eyes, the upper half for seeing above the surface, the lower for looking through water.

The burying beetles (family *Silphidae*) lay their eggs in the bodies of dead animals. They are undertakers for mice, frogs, rats, birds and moles, and they usually carry out their labours at night. A male and female of this family have been known

'POCKET HERCULES' OF BEETLEDOM
This unpleasant-looking insect, the male of the lunar dung beetle, is not so fearsome as it looks ; it is shown here enlarged to 3 times life size. The dung beetles are related to the scarab, the famous sacred beetle of the ancient Egyptians and often found buried with their mummies.

J. J. Ward

to work for many hours digging such a grave with their heads, and afterwards covering the body.

A strange family of creatures called stylops is sometimes included in the beetle order. Only the male has wings; the female spends her life in the body of some other insect, the tip of her body projecting through the segments of her host's abdomen.

The stag beetle, *Lucanus cervus*, with its great hooked mandibles half as long as the rest of the insect, is perhaps the most startling of northern species; the tropics have even more remarkable species, such as the centaur beetle, with huge cow-like horns; the five-horned rhinoceros beetle ; and the hercules beetle, with dangerous-looking projections from its head. Curiously enough, these are nearly all harmless.

Some beetles recognize their own species by sound ; others emit a bright light for the same purpose. The luminous beetles belong to the families *Cantharidae* and *Elateridae*, a familiar member of the *Cantharidae* being the common European glow-worm, *Lampyris noctiluca*. The wingless female emits a bright light near the hind end of the body, the winged male showing a much feebler light. The luminous *Elateridae* include the fire-flies of the tropics, both sexes of which display brilliant lights.

There are several theories as to the cause of the light, one being that it is produced by luminous bacteria in much the same way as is the phosphorescence seen on dead fishes. The purpose of the glow-worm's light is almost certainly to show the male where the female is; because the insect comes out only at night, and since the female cannot fly she is obliged to depend on the male finding her. The male glow-worm is about half an inch in length and greyish brown in colour. The female is slightly browner than the male.

SEXTON BEETLES AT WORK
The bright colouring of these burying or sexton beetles is somewhat inappropriate to their grim task of burying a dead bird. The reward of their industry is to lay their eggs on the carcass under the soil.

H. Bastin

In this picture the artist has included quite a number of the beetle family—not drawn to scale. Two wasps are flying above a pair of scarabs, who are engaged in moving a ball of dung far larger than themselves. The beetle coming down the tree is a wasp's nest beetle, which lays its eggs near wasp holes and whose young devour the wasp grubs. Walking up the tree are a timberman and a long-horned musk beetle. At the foot of the tree a hercules beetle is watching a group of golden ground beetles attacking an earthworm. Behind the hercules beetle is an oil-beetle. Arriving on the wing at the extreme left is a blister beetle, and below it appears a member of the scarab family. Beneath the scarab is the curious caliper beetle, just thrusting its head into the picture. The spotted one in the left centre is a tiger beetle in search of prey. The big black three-horned beetle is next, and below are the rhinoceros beetle and the elephant beetle. In the pond are two water-beetles; a third is flying over the water. Scientists have classified over 200,000 different kinds of beetles.

Carters Tested Seeds

BEGONIA PLANTS SPANGLED WITH BLOOM

Magnificent displays of begonias planted in summer flower-beds in our parks and gardens are perhaps more familar than begonias flowering in pots. The free-blossoming habit of these plants makes them of great value for greenhouse and conservatory decoration. There are many varieties and an extensive range of colours.

Begonia. This beautiful plant has several forms, some of them with fibrous roots and some with tubers. The flowers of some varieties are very large and showy, reaching from four to six inches in diameter, and vary in colour from pink to scarlet and from white to yellow. The fleshy leaves of some begonias, large and variegated, are curiously unequal-sided. A winged capsule containing the numerous minute seeds constitutes the fruit.

The begonia is native to the tropics of both hemispheres, excepting Australia. The plant was named in honour of Michel Begon (1638-1710), a French administrator and patron of botany, and the family name is *Begoniaceae*.

Belfast. This great city, which is in County Antrim, is the capital and seat of government of Northern Ireland. Many of the inhabitants are Scots-Irish and Protestant — descendants of Scottish and English colonists of the 17th century—and they have built up a city which, in population, manufacture and trade, ranks first among the cities of Ireland. Situated where the River Lagan enters Belfast Lough or Bay, the city has large shipyards; during the Second World War (1939-45) their output exceeded a million tons. A big aircraft factory produces flying-boats and bombers. Belfast is famous for its linen, has an important tobacco industry, and its rope-works are the largest in the world.

In the 16th century there was only a little fishing village where Belfast now stands, and not until the introduction of machine spinning and weaving, in the latter part of the 18th

century, did it begin to thrive. It is now a city of fine churches and of imposing public buildings; it is also the seat of Queen's University, and has a number of church schools. Among the most prominent of its buildings, in addition to the university, which was erected in 1849, are the Parliament buildings at Stormont, just outside the city; the fine City Hall, St. Anne's Protestant Cathedral, opened in 1904; and the law courts given by Great Britain in 1922. Severe damage was done to all quarters of the city in five German air-raids in the spring of 1941. Population of Belfast is about 438,000.

On the outbreak of the Second World War (1939-45) Belfast, with large graving and floating docks, became a naval base and later an Admiralty dockyard. During the Battle of the Atlantic many of the operations directed against German submarines were controlled from the port. It was also the chief connecting link between Great Britain and the United States, huge quantities of foodstuffs and munitions of all kinds being landed there. At the approaches to the port enormous convoys assembled for the Atlantic crossing and for operations in the Mediterranean and North-West Europe. The port was so extensively used by the Admiralty that sometimes as many as 82 vessels were in harbour at the same time ; in 1944 the tonnage of the vessels which used the port amounted to nearly five million.

Belfast Telegraph

BELFAST'S IMPOSING CITY HALL

The home of Belfast's municipality stands at the top of Donegall Place, the great business thoroughfare of the city. The building was completed in 1906, and is encircled by gardens. It is one of the finest city halls in the United Kingdom. In front of it stands a statue of Queen Victoria. The city is the capital of Northern Ireland ; but the Parliament buildings are just outside, at Stormont.

The WAR-WORN LAND of a BRAVE PEOPLE

Romans, Spaniards, Austrians, French, British and Germans at some time have fought over the low-lying fields of Belgium. By the efforts of her peoples she has been restored to a position among the leading industrial nations.

Belgium. The shape of Belgium may be roughly compared to a triangle with the long side lying along the French border; the base resting against Luxembourg, Germany and Dutch Limburg; and the third side bordering on the shallow North Sea and the kingdom of the Netherlands (Holland). Such is the little kingdom of Belgium, a land which has probably played as important a part in the world's affairs, in proportion to its size, as any other country since the far-off days of ancient Greece and Rome.

Menin Gate, Ypres, memorial to 58,600 British soldiers of the First World War (1914–18).

During every one of the centuries which intervene since the Roman conquest, Belgium has been one of the battle-grounds of Europe. The struggle has been not only with hostile Man but with unfriendly Nature as well. Like the fields of Holland, many of those of Belgium are, in part, the product of careful cultivation of barren sand-dunes; and dikes and windmills are still necessary to prevent constant encroachment by the sea.

In this struggle with Nature the Belgians have succeeded wonderfully well. Today we find, fringing the sea, only a narrow belt of dunes. Behind this bleak region lies verdant country in which are red-roofed cottages of the peasants. The green fields, watered by running streams and sluggish canals, are rich with harvests of wheat and rye. In some of the fields men in smocks, with loose baggy trousers tied below the knee with a cord, are digging. In others, men and women kneel and weed the flax ; while in the streams they beat the ripened stalks of the harvested flax to separate the fibres so that they can be spun into linen thread.

The ground is made to produce the utmost possible, and grain and sugar-beet are largely cultivated. Even so, Belgium is not able to supply food enough for all her people, for it is the second most densely populated land in Europe. There are a score of thriving cities, and a hundred little villages dot the fields ; on every side rise the towers and spires of churches. Belgium is richer in these monuments of medieval architecture than any other country except northern France.

In the 14th and 15th centuries Flanders—as Western Belgium was then called—was the richest part of Europe. The rivers Scheldt, Meuse, Yser and the Lys, were busy with vessels from all parts of the known world. The wharves of Ghent were piled with bales of wool from England and with casks of wine from southern France. The vast Cloth Hall of Ypres was crowded with merchants eager for the products of the Flemish looms and the handiwork of the lace-makers. It is said that merchants from 17 kingdoms had settled homes and businesses in Bruges, the great northern market of Europe. Much of the money gained from this commerce was used in building churches, but more was used in the construction of the town halls and belfries. The people were jealous of the glories of their towns. No one spoke of being a citizen of Flanders but of being a man of Bruges, of Ghent or of Ypres.

The gateway to Flanders is now Antwerp, which in the 15th century wrested from Bruges its commercial supremacy. It lies on the winding course of the River Scheldt, 55 miles from the sea, and the inhabitants of the city say that " the whole world is a ring, in which Antwerp is the diamond." To the south of Antwerp lies Brussels, the modern capital of the kingdom. Down its streets clatter

BRUGES'S OPEN-AIR MARKET
Every Belgian city and town has its market, where produce from intensively-cultivated smallholdings is sold. Here, in the picturesque city of Bruges, the market-women have displayed their wares and wait for the housewife to purchase her supplies for the day.

the Flemish milkmaids in their wooden shoes and their big white caps. Occasionally you may see dogs drawing little carts filled with milk-cans. From the houses comes the hum of looms, for although Belgium has many large textile factories much of the work is still done in the homes of the people.

In Brussels hundreds of women sit all day long patiently weaving in and out the threads of fine Brussels point-lace. For more than 400 years the country has been famous for its lace manufacture, not only of Brussels lace but also of the airy Mechlin lace and the fine Valenciennes. The well-known Brussels carpets are made not in Brussels but at Tournai, on the Scheldt, 50 miles to the south-west.

Ostend is the great seaside resort, and one of the playgrounds of all Europe. Indeed, the whole Belgian coast is one long series of seaside towns and villages which in normal times are visited every year by thousands of British holiday-makers. But Ostend has its industrial side, for it is the second port in the kingdom, connected by canal with the quaint old cities of Bruges and Ghent, and it is the centre of the Belgian fishing and oyster industry.

To the south-east of Brussels the skies at night are aflame with the glare of iron furnaces and glass and other factories at Liége. This is one of the busiest parts of the great workshop of Europe, because of the gifts which Nature has lavished upon this section. It is Belgium's rich mines of coal and iron—supplemented by the near-by iron ores of Luxembourg and northern France—which make her an industrial country. Even the sand of her dunes is made use of in the manufacture of glass.

But this region is poor in beauty. The earth is scarred by refuse from the mines. The villages, stretching over a grey country, are hidden behind mountains of coal ash, or they crouch beside the towering chimneys of factories. Even the people are different from those in the northern half of Belgium, and they speak a different language. They are known as Walloons, and their speech is a dialect of the French; while about Antwerp and Brussels and throughout the north the people are Flemish, and speak a tongue closely akin to Dutch. These differences in race and language and culture cause some political friction.

To the south of the factories and the mines of the "Black Country" lie the woodlands and the swiftly-

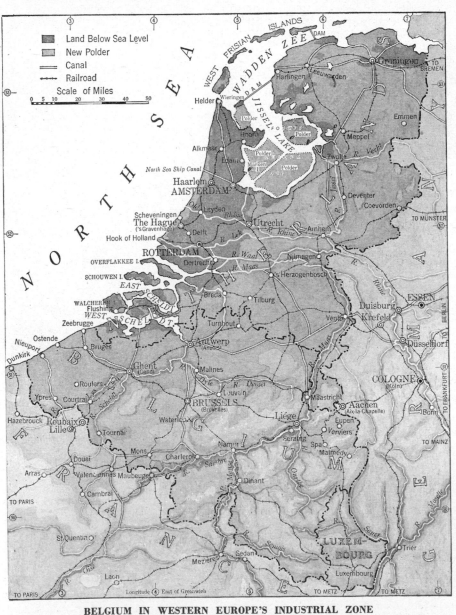

BELGIUM IN WESTERN EUROPE'S INDUSTRIAL ZONE

Belgium's own industries make it the most densely populated country in Europe, and the industrial portions of France and Germany border it on each side, while the fertile fields of the Netherlands lie to the North. In the Ardennes to the south-east the land rises to two thousand feet above the sea, but the northern region is mostly flat and low-lying.

BELGIAN SCENES FROM NORTH SEA TO MEUSE

Belgian Railways and Marine; Dorien Leigh

Dinant (1) stands in a beautiful situation on the banks of the Meuse ; it was practically destroyed during the First World War (1914–18), but was rebuilt. Mons (2) has the beautiful Gothic Cathedral of St. Waudru, begun in the 15th century. On a hillock on the field of Waterloo—about ten miles south of Brussels—stands the Belgian lion (3) commemorating Napoleon's final defeat. One of the beauties of Namur (4) is the old bridge over the Meuse, with the town and remains of the citadel rising above it. A typical Belgian seaside resort is Le Zoute (5) with its splendid expanse of sands. Ostend harbour (6) was very badly damaged during the Second World War (1939 -45).

This fine old city, one of the greatest seaports in the world, has a history reaching back at least to the 6th century A.D. In the centre of the oldest part of Antwerp stands the cathedral of Notre Dame (above), which was begun in 1352 but not completed until 1518. In the foreground is a statue of the Lion of Belgium. Many of the buildings in this quarter are ancient guild houses, dating from the 16th century when Antwerp became the most important commercial city in Europe. After a decline to insignificance in the 17th and 18th centuries, it recovered its importance in modern times, as the Continental Atlantic seaport nearest to the heart of Europe.

in September 1944, the Belgians once more set about the task of reconstruction.

In a little over a century Belgium had only four kings, Leopold I, Leopold II, Albert I, and Leopold III, who succeeded him in 1934. During the Second World War King Leopold remained in Belgium, a semi-prisoner of the Germans, until taken to Germany in 1944. Many Belgians felt he had betrayed his country, and after the war he lived in exile, his brother Charles acting as regent. In 1950 Leopold returned to Belgium, but was persuaded to relinquish his royal power to his elder son Baudouin, called the Prince Royal, until he should have reached his majority and become king.

flowing rivers of the Ardennes, where the land in places is some 2,000 feet high.

During the Middle Ages the towns of Flanders had built up an industry and commerce which rivalled that of the early 20th century. But in the time that followed, when the land was handed about from one country to another—when the Duke of Burgundy sought to repress the free spirit of the towns; when Philip II of Spain, through his general Alva, drenched the land with blood; and when Austria, after obtaining these provinces by the treaty of Utrecht (1713) tried to crush the liberties of the people —the industries suffered severely. Belgium was annexed to France at the time of the French Revolution, but handed over to Holland as part of the kingdom of the Netherlands in 1815.

Not until 1830 did the kingdom of Belgium, as we know it, come into existence. Then, with its neutrality guaranteed by that treaty which Germany tore up as a "scrap of paper" in 1914 (the beginning of the First World War), the land entered upon a period of peace and prosperity. This lasted until 1914, when the Germans entered and overran the country, of which, except a very small portion, they retained possession until the end of the war in 1918. It is remarkable how rapidly and courageously Belgium tackled and overcame the problems which beset it when the time came to put its house in order after four years of destruction and oppression. Belgian neutrality was again violated by the Germans in May 1940, and on May 28 of that year the Belgian army was compelled to surrender. Liberated by the Allies

Imperial War Museum; Central Press

YPRES RISEN FROM THE RUINS OF WAR

No place in Belgium suffered more severely from continuous shelling by the Germans during the First World War (1914–18) than Ypres, and when the Armistice came in November 1918 all that was left of the famous Cloth Hall was a few ruins (top). In 1934 King Leopold III inaugurated the new belfry (lower) close to the cathedral, on the right. Ypres escaped serious damage during the Second World War (1939–45).

Belgium is a constitutional monarchy and its legislature consists of two houses, a Senate and a Chamber of Representatives. Since 1893 all males have been allowed to vote, and in 1919 certain women were given the same right. A general election is held every four years for the Chamber of Representatives and the Senate.

The Belgian constitution was framed in a spirit of true liberty and has been termed one of the best of modern times. All religions are equal, there being no State religion, but as the overwhelming majority of the people are Roman Catholics, the sovereign must be a member of that

LACE-MAKERS IN BELGIAN FLANDERS
In the old quarter of Bruges you may still see (as above) women sitting outside their cottage doors making their fine pillow lace. The people in this part of Belgium speak Flemish, which is similar to Dutch. In the south of the country are the Walloons, who speak French.

church. This law, however, was not enforced in the case of Leopold I, who ascended the throne in 1831 and was a Protestant, but his children were brought up as Roman Catholics.

Belgium's only colonial possession is the Belgian Congo, which, until 1908, was the property of the King and was called the Congo Free State.

The area of Belgium (including Eupen and Malmédy, annexed from Germany in 1918), is 11,775 square miles; population is about 8,300,000.

Belgrade, (Pron. bel-grād'), YUGOSLAVIA. The capital of the Balkan republic of Yugoslavia has a dominating situation on a ridge at the junction of the Danube and the Save. On a chalk cliff at the apex, overlooking the broad blue lake formed by the meeting of the rivers, stood the once white walls and towers of the ancient citadel. It is from this citadel that Belgrade got its name, which means in Serbo-Croat, "White City."

Though the people of Belgrade have adopted the sober dress of Paris and London, the streets of the city are gay with picturesque and brilliant peasant costumes, for Belgrade is the trading centre as well as the capital of Yugoslavia.

Most of the buildings in Belgrade are new, but above the city stands the old citadel, now used as barracks, and in the Turkish quarter are some old houses. Newer build-

ings, erected before the Second World War (1939–45), included the opera house, the cathedral, the university, two palaces and those for government purposes. Belgrade has a considerable trade both along the river and by rail. It is a junction on the lines from Paris, Berlin and Vienna to the East and is served by international air lines. During the Second World War, although declared an open city, it was heavily bombed by German aircraft in April 1941. The Germans occupied it until October 1944, when it was taken by Russian troops and Yugoslav Partisans. Its population is about 267,000.

Bell, ALEXANDER GRAHAM (1847–1922). This famous scientist rendered many public services and gave us many inventions, and he was honoured by universities and learned societies throughout the world. His fame, however, will always rest on the invention of an apparatus which eventually developed into the telephone of today.

Alexander Graham Bell was born in Edinburgh and educated at the Universities of Edinburgh and London. In 1870 he removed to Canada with his father and the rest of the family. His father and his grandfather before him had devoted their lives to the study of human speech and teaching the deaf and dumb to speak, and this became his profession, too.

During 1874–75 he worked at the problem of the telephone. It was on March 11, 1876, that the first spoken message successfully transmitted by wire was sent by him to his assistant in a Boston hotel. He filed his application for a patent for his invention on March 14 of that year, just two hours before Elisha Gray filed a notice in the Patent Office covering some of the

Black Star

BELGRADE, CAPITAL OF YUGOSLAVIA
Situated on the south bank of the Danube at its junction with the Save, Belgrade has lost much of its former Oriental appearance, having many modern buildings. It experiences very cold winters, and peasants drive into the city in sleighs, like the one seen here, to sell firewood, many of the houses having wood-burning stoves.

BELL AT THE TELEPHONE HE INVENTED
Alexander Graham Bell was the inventor of the first practical telephone, in 1876, and here we see him opening the line between Chicago and New York with a later though still antiquated-looking apparatus.

same principles. In 1876 he erected the first real telephone line, at Brantford, Canada, where his father resided. (*See* Telephone).

Belloc, HILAIRE (born 1870). Usually one can say of a writer that he is a novelist or a poet, an historian or an essayist. Belloc is all these and more; he has written a history of England, several biographies and The Bad Child's Book of Beasts (1896) and More Beasts for Worse Children (1897), and many witty novels.

Perhaps his French birth and English education have much to do with this extraordinary ability to write—and write well—on almost every subject. He is seldom dull and often challenging; he thinks that most of the people who have written English history before him have made colossal mistakes in their interpretation of the facts, particularly of the Reformation period and the years of the Whig supremacy in the 17th and 18th centuries.

Many a youth has been inspired to tramp by Belloc's book Path to Rome (1902) in which he tells of his experiences on a walking-tour. And such books as Danton (1899) and The Girondin (1911) have awakened in many the realization that history can be as fascinating as a novel.

Belloc was a great friend of G. K. Chesterton who illustrated some of his books. The latter may be counted by the score; perhaps the most important, in addition to those mentioned above, are The Servile State (1912), a criticism of the British political system, inspired by his own experiences as an M.P. from 1906 to 1910; History of England, the first volume of which appeared in 1925; Wolsey (1930); and Cromwell (1934).

Bells AND BELL-RINGING. From the early centuries of the Christian era the ringing of big bells has been used to mark the divisions of the day, to summon the faithful to prayer, and to announce tidings of joy or sorrow. They have sounded the alarm of fire and the tocsin of war, and have given the signal for many a deed of terror and blood. At Eastertide in 1282 the vesper bells of Palermo, in Sicily, marked the beginning of one of the most atrocious massacres in history, which has ever since been known as the "Sicilian Vespers." On that occasion 8,000 Frenchmen were killed by Sicilians. On St. Bartholomew's Day in 1572 church bells gave the signal for the massacre of thousands of Huguenots in France.

In the days of ancient Greece and Rome bells of this sort were unknown. The only bells the ancients had were small handbells, often shaped like the square-mouthed bells sometimes used to tie to the necks of sheep and cattle, or they were closed bells like those fixed on harness. Such small bells were hung about the necks of dogs and cattle, and small tinkling bells of gold were attached to the dresses of Jewish high-priests.

By the 5th or 6th centuries of our era, when Christianity had firmly established itself in the Roman Empire, bells were in use in Christian churches. At first they were of small size, but gradually they became larger and were placed in high towers so that they could be heard throughout the city. Sometimes these towers were built as a part of the church; but often they were quite separate structures, especially in Italy, where the bell tower or *campanile* (pron. cam-pa-nē´-le), from Latin *campana*, meaning "bell", developed into a building of extraordinary beauty. Among the most famous and beautiful of existing bell-towers are the campanile of Saint Mark's at Venice, which collapsed in 1902 after standing a thousand

The Lion

The Lion, the Lion, he dwells in the waste,

He has a big head and a very small waist;

But his shoulders are stark, and his jaws they are grim,

And a good little child will not play with him.

Courtesy, Gerald Duckworth & Co

ONE OF BELLOC'S 'BEASTS'
One of the lighter products of Hilaire Belloc's versatile genius is The Bad Child's Book of Beasts, which he not only wrote but illustrated himself. This page from the book is typical of Belloc's delightful humour.

It has long been customary to hang several bells of different pitch together, which are made to sound one after the other and thus play simple tunes; these are called a " peal " of bells, or " chimes." Each bell is rung by pulling on a separate rope. As the number of bells increased from three to eight, or even 12, an elaborate art of bell-ringing was developed. With three bells, only six " changes," or sequences, are possible, while eight bells give the enormous number of 40,320 changes. With 12 bells the number is so great that it has been calculated that to ring the changes at the rate of two strokes to the second would require approximately 91 years.

Bell-ringing became a popular amusement in England in the 17th century. Societies which were formed all over the kingdom performed wonderful feats of accuracy and endurance in competition. The patterns or tunes were worked out by experts and received many queer names, such as " Kent treble bob major," " Grandsire Triples," " Treble bob royal." The art is still much practised.

In " ringing," properly so called, the bells are swung through a complete revolution, resting bottom-upward at the end of each swing. " Chiming " is the technical term for swinging the bells in their normal position just far enough to be struck by the clapper, or for producing tones by striking the stationary bells with small hammers. The latter method is used in all mechanically operated chimes or *carillons*. Sometimes as many as 60 or 70 bells are thus struck by means of a keyboard or levers, so that any tune may be played with its accompanying harmonies. Carillon-playing has been practised for centuries on the Continent.

The curfew (from the French *couvre feu*, " cover fire ") has rung in some parts of England every night since the time of William the Conqueror. At Oxford 101 strokes are rung on " Great Tom " over the gateway in Christ Church every evening to warn undergraduates to return to their colleges.

HOW CHURCH BELLS ARE HUNG

Here is a view inside the bell tower of a church Eight of the bells are attached to the wheels in the top room, where is also the rope of the ninth, or Sanctus, bell, which is lodged in the steeple and is rung from the bell chamber.

years but was rebuilt in 1912; the leaning tower of Pisa; and Giotto's campanile at Florence.

The earliest bells preserved in the British Isles, like the famous Saint Patrick's bell at Belfast, which is supposed to date from the 6th century, were of the ancient rectangular shape and were made of thin plates of metal riveted together. Gradually men learned the art of casting bells in one piece, and of the familiar curving bell-shape.

The process of casting bells is much the same now as it was many centuries ago. A core of bricks is built up and covered with soft clay, moulded to the outline of the *inside* of the bell. Then an outer mould or " cope " of clay is made, shaped to the outline of the *outer surface* of the bell, but kept at the proper distance away from the core to allow for the thickness of the bell. Into this space between the two moulds the molten metal is poured and left to harden. When the moulds are removed the bell may be tuned to the desired tone by taking off thin shavings from the inside. From the earliest times the metal most used was an alloy of copper and tin in various proportions.

'YOUTHS' IN THE BELFRY

The curiously-named Ancient Society of College Youths, which was founded in 1637 and first practised in a church in College Hill, London, is the senior body of bell-ringers in England. Above are two members at work with the ropes in the belfry of St. Paul's Cathedral, London.

Perhaps the largest bell ever made is the "Tsar Kolokol" (Emperor Bell) at Moscow, which weighed nearly 200 tons when it was cast in 1733 or thereabouts. It has never been rung, however, as soon after it was cast a fragment was broken out of it. This great bell is more than 22 feet in diameter and stands 19 feet 3 inches high; it now rests on a raised platform. Another Moscow bell weighs 128 tons. There is a great bell of about 87 tons in a pagoda at Mingoon in Upper Burma, and one of 53 tons at Peking. Beside these monarchs the other famous bells of the world are dwarfs. "Great Paul" in St. Paul's Cathedral, London, weighs 17 tons; "Big Ben" in the Westminster clock-tower of the Houses of Parliament, 13½ tons; "Great Peter," at York, 12½ tons; and "Great Tom," at Oxford, 7½ tons. The largest bell in America is in Riverside church, New York, and was cast at Croydon in Surrey; it weighs 18 tons.

Benares, INDIA. (Pron. ben-ah'rez.) The city of Benares is the holy city of all Hindus. Its very air is held to be holy, its soil so sanctified that to carry away its dust on your feet is a sin. Pilgrims in countless numbers visit it to wash their sins away in the sacred Ganges, and many of the wealthy spend their declining days there, for it is said that he who dies at Benares is sure of immediate admission into heaven.

From the river you see Benares as a richly coloured jumble of temples, mosques, palaces, domes and minarets flung haphazard along the steep bank. Many of the houses are painted with pictures of gods and goddesses, flowers and symbols of Hindu mythology. At the water's edge run the famous *ghats* (pron. gahts, and meaning steps), a four-mile curving row of stone terraces. You cannot see the city from a carriage; its

E.N.A.

GIANT BELL THAT NEVER TOLLED
This is one of the largest bells ever cast—the 'Tsar Kolokol' in the Kremlin at Moscow. Its weight was nearly 200 tons. Before it had been hung, it was cracked and rendered useless and was exhibited as a gigantic curiosity.

You arrive at the Golden Temple, its floor paved with silver rupees, and go into a crowded sanctuary, where burning camphor-laden leaves are dropped by worshippers, crowding round the mouth of a pit, to illumine far below a flower-enshrined image of the god Siva. You stop to watch one who has stepped aside a moment from the surging throng to worship before a shrine at which he leaves two *pice* (copper coins).

Go to the ghats—what a sight greets the sun each morning as it rises out of the richest plain in India! Grey granite and red temple walls, the golden shafts of slender spires, the stately minarets of a hidden mosque, a *mullah* (Mahomedan priest) counting his beads while he drones a passage from the Koran, monkeys gambolling over temple walls, *fakirs* (holy men) clothed in ashes, fat Brahmin priests thumbing sacred texts beneath flame-coloured umbrellas. The sweeper's wife (a sweeper is a low caste servant), knee-deep in "Mother Gunga," as the Ganges is piously called, dabbles at a copper pot, her prayers finished; three feet away a high-caste banker, filling his cupped hands with Ganges water, sends his praises to the sun.

Naked children dart in and out of the water near a great pyre or funeral fire, where wreaths of smoke rise about a smouldering corpse. Women, their ablutions over, patter off up the steps, straight of limb, like slim goddesses. The tinkle of their

A BELL IN THE MAKING
The process of casting bells is much the same as it was centuries ago. Here is the scene as molten bell-metal is poured from a huge cauldron into a mould of the required shape. The bell can be tuned to the desired tone by shaving strips of metal from the inside. The metal most used is an alloy of copper and tin.

canyon-like streets, rising in narrowing flights of steps, are barely wide enough for a single horseman. You must go on foot through the slippery passage ways, threading your course amid pilgrims making the rounds of the sacred road and thus being cleansed from all sin. Now and then you will have to give way to a sacred bull, which wanders nibbling from one grain-seller's stall to another.

BENARES ON THE HOLY RIVER GANGES

Benares, which lies in the United Provinces of the Republic of India, is very ancient and the holiest city of the Hindus. On the banks of the Ganges, which is a sacred river, are lines of temples and burning ghats (steps) where Hindus come to wash away their sins by bathing in the waters, and where they cremate the bodies of their dead on huge funeral pyres. Devout worshippers believe that he who dies at Benares is sure of immediate admission into heaven.

silver anklets mingles with the chatter of monkeys, the muffled murmur of worshippers, and the deep booming of the holy temple drums.

The chief manufactures of Benares are silk brocade and metal goods. The Benares brass for which the city was once famous has greatly degenerated and much of it sold there is manufactured elsewhere. Benares was a centre of importance when Buddha came there, six centuries Before Christ, but its buildings are all comparatively modern. The Hindu University was founded in 1916. The houses are generally shops on the ground floor; their upper storeys, often as many as five or six, have projecting balconies and verandas, and their walls are garish with bright colours. The population of Benares is about 263,000.

Benedict, SAINT. The founder of the order of Benedictine monks was born of a wealthy Italian family at Nursia, near Spoleto, about the year 480. He was sent to study in the schools of Rome, but was repelled by the wickedness of the city and dissatisfied with the teaching. As his biographer, Gregory the Great, writes : " He despised the literary studies (of Rome) and departed knowingly ignorant and wisely unlearned." It is strange that one who was so little of a scholar himself should have been the founder of the Benedictines, the most learned of the monastic orders.

The earnest-minded boy was appalled by the sinfulness of the times; he felt that he must find a cure for all the wickedness he saw about him. He fled to the mountains, and at last came to Subiaco, where he found a cave in which he took up his abode. There he remained for three years—during which his mind was being made up and his character was forming—living an austere life of prayer. The monks of a neighbouring monastery chose him for their abbot; but he soon left them, with the parting words : " Choose ye some other abbot suitable to your own conditions," for their lives were far from holy. He went back to his cave,

but disciples flocked to him, and before very long he had established 12 monasteries. His success gave rise to jealousy and persecution from the laxer clergy, so, leaving his monasteries in safe hands, he travelled southwards and finally arrived at Cassino, midway between Rome and Naples. There, on the mountain overlooking the town, he founded his monastery of Monte Cassino, which was the mother house of the Benedictines and became, in a sense, the monastic capital of the West. The Monte Cassino monastery was destroyed in 1944, during the Second World War. Benedict died about 544.

Benedictines. The order of monks known as Benedictines was established by St. Benedict (q.v.) in Italy about A.D. 530. Because of the colour of their robes they are sometimes called " Black monks." There is also an order of nuns of the same name. The principal monastery during the lifetime of St. Benedict was that of Monte Cassino, between Rome and Naples.

Benes, DR. EDUARD (1884–1948). Until the end of the First World War (1914–18), Czechoslovakia was not a separate nation but formed part of the kingdom of Austria-Hungary. The leader of those who worked for independence was a Dr. Thomas Masaryk (q.v.), and among his chief supporters was Dr. Benes (pron. ben-esh).

Eduard Benes was born on May 28, 1884, in the Bohemian village of Kozlany. Although his father was only a poor farmer he was sent to the university at Prague, and afterwards studied in Paris and London before becoming a doctor of law at the university of Dijon, in France, in 1908. He returned to Prague as a teacher in the university, and entered eagerly into the struggle for Czechoslovakian freedom. In 1915, with Austria engaged against the Allies in the First World War, he saw his chance; escaping into Switzerland, he joined Dr. Masaryk in Paris and helped him to form a Czechoslovak National Council.

In 1918 Austria was defeated, and among the terms of the peace treaty was the granting of independence to the Czechs. The new republic's first government was formed by Dr. Masaryk, and Dr. Benes was Foreign Secretary. He held that post continually until 1935 ; in 1921–22 he was Prime Minister as well. He brought about an alliance between his country and Yugoslavia and Rumania, and took a leading part in the activities of the League of Nations.

In 1935 President Masaryk resigned,and Dr. Benes succeeded him. In 1938 began the shattering of that peace for which he had laboured so hard. The German dictator, Hitler, demanded that the district of Sudetenland, which lay in the north of Czechoslovakia and whose inhabitants numbered many Germans, should become a part of Germany. Poland and Hungary joined in threatening the little republic, and on the advice of British and French representatives Dr. Benes yielded. Resigning the presidency, he went to America. The following March, Germany invaded Czechoslovakia and proclaimed it a part of the German Empire.

Dr. Benes did not give up. Soon after the Second World War broke out (September 1939) he formed in London a government of Czech statesmen who had escaped from their enslaved country; and with the otherthrow of Germany in 1945 he returned to Prague. The people received him joyfully, and in November 1945 he was once more elected President of the Czechoslovak republic. In February 1948 the Czechoslovak Communist Party seized power from the Coalition Government; and Dr. Benes, ill and dispirited, resigned the presidency on June 7. In September of the same year this great patriot died, broken-hearted at the shattering of his life's work. (*See* Czechoslovakia).

Bengal. A district to the north-east of the Indian sub-continent, now divided into the state of West Bengal, republic of India, and the province of East Bengal, Pakistan, with a total area of 77,442 square miles, Bengal was one of the earliest British settlements in India, the first factories being established there in 1633. In 1699 it became a separate Presidency. The " partition of Bengal " in 1905 was revoked in 1912 when a new Presidency was established reuniting all the Bengali-speaking districts. With the division of Bengal between India and Pakistan in 1947, West Bengal became a part of India and East Bengal with the Sylhet region of Assam joined Pakistan. The two principal cities, Calcutta and Howrah are both in West Bengal, while the third city, Dacca, is in Pakistan.

Bengal as a whole stretches from the Himalayas to the Bay of Bengal and consists mainly of an alluvial plain, watered by the delta of the Ganges and Brahmaputra. It is densely populated, over 90 per cent of the inhabitants belonging to the Bengali races and speaking the Bengali languages.

The staple crop is rice; about four-fifths of the cultivated area is devoted to this crop, and a large surplus is normally available for export.

Some 80 per cent of the people are engaged in agriculture, and in particular Bengal produces an immense crop of jute and supplies the fibre from which most of the world's sacks are made. Cotton is also grown. There are many jute and cotton and flour mills operating, most of them being clustered on the banks of the River Hooghly. Bengal also produces coal and iron ore.

The only hilly district in Bengal is in the extreme north. There, in the neighbourhood of Darjeeling, in Western Bengal, are many tea plantations producing very large crops. Darjeeling (population about 23,000), set amidst magnificent mountain

Paul Popper; Associated Press

PRESIDENT BENES OF CZECHOSLOVAKIA
In the grounds of his palace on Hradcany Hill in Prague, Czechoslovakia, President Benes and his wife (top) take a rest with their dog. During the Second World War (1939–45) the President on many occasions addressed Czech soldiers (lower) training in Britain to help in the liberation of their country.

BEN NEVIS IN INVERNESS-SHIRE
R. M. Adam
Nearly 20 miles away to the west, at Glenfinnan, looking across the mountain slopes of Inverness-shire and Argyllshire, the view afforded of snow-capped Ben Nevis is exceptionally fine. This granite mountain is the highest in the British Isles, rising over glens and lochs to a height of 4,406 feet.

scenery, is the summer resort of the Europeans in Bengal. Of the railways the most important is the East Indian, serving the densely-peopled districts in the Ganges valley. The Bengali are intelligent and politically active. Total population of E. and W. Bengal is about 64 millions.

Bennett, ENOCH ARNOLD (1867–1931). It would be difficult to find a less inspiring piece of England than the Five Towns, the Potteries of Staffordshire, a district given over to the china and earthenware industry. But it was against this smoke-grimed background that Arnold Bennett wrote some of his best novels.

These studies of life in the Potteries began in 1902, with Anna of the Five Towns. The Old Wives' Tale appeared in 1908, but it was not until 1923 that the author again touched the same high level in Riceyman Steps, of which the setting is London.

Arnold Bennett was born on May 27, 1867, near Hanley, in the Potteries. He worked at law for some time, but later turned to journalism and then to fiction. With two plays he had great success: Milestones, which he wrote with Edward Knoblock, and The Great Adventure, which was based on his novel Buried Alive.

University College Committee
BENTHAM'S SKELETON
The clothed skeleton of Jeremy Bentham, celebrated philosopher, is kept at University College, London. Between his feet, under a glass bell, is his mummified head.

Ben Nevis. The highest mountain in the British Isles, Ben Nevis is situated in Inverness-shire, Scotland, between Loch Leven and Loch Eil. The summit is 4,406 feet above sea-level, and the circumference of the mountain exceeds 25 miles at the base. The nearest town is Fort William, which is 4½ miles away. The top of the mountain is a plateau of some 100 acres in extent, with a slope towards the south, but on the north-east side there is a sheer drop of 1,500 feet.

Snow is to be found in the deep gullies all the year round although as much as 43 inches of rain has been registered at the summit. Ben Nevis is bounded on the north by Glen Spean, on the east by Glen Treig, and on the west and south by Glen Nevis.

The lower half of the mountain is composed of granite and gneiss, whilst the upper half consists of porphyritic greenstone. A great number of minerals are scattered over the whole. In 1883 a meteorological observatory was built by public subscription. For a time it was maintained by the Scottish Meteorological Society; but, funds sufficient for its upkeep not being forthcoming, it was closed down in 1904.

The ascent may be made from Achintee, in Glen Nevis, by means of a bridle-path, the gradient of which is never greater than one in five.

Bentham, JEREMY (1748–1832). " The greatest happiness of the greatest number "—this is the phrase we generally associate with Bentham's name, and this was the keynote of his life work. Many of the reforms urged by Bentham—for instance, universal suffrage, voting by ballot, and paid Members of Parliament—have since been achieved.

Born in London; educated at Westminster School and later at Oxford, Bentham was called to the bar in 1772, but never practised. Instead, he became one of the most vigorous and constructive critics of legislation ever known. In his later works he showed a fondness for coining words; some of them, for instance " international," " codify," and " minimize," have become part of the English language. For years his greatest concern was his inspection house, or Panopticon (" see all ") as he called it. This was a penetentiary building for the reformation of criminals, so arranged that the governor could see all the occupants. In the end the scheme was abandoned, but Bentham was paid £23,000 by the Government for all his trouble and expense.

In his London house, in Queen's Square Place, there was a piano in every room. As a young man he had fallen in love with Caroline Fox, Lord Holland's sister, and when he was not far short of 60 had proposed to her and been refused. At the age of 80 he showed his friend Samuel Rogers the withered remains of a flower which Miss Fox had given him when she rejected his proposal of marriage. In accordance with his directions his body was dissected in the interests of science, and his skeleton, in the form of an effigy, is to be seen at University College, London.

Bentham's writings include A Fragment on Government (1776), an attack on Blackstone's praises of the English Constitution ; Principles of Morals and Legislation (1789) ; Discourses on Civil and Penal Legislation (1802); and Rationale of Punishments and Rewards (1825).

Beowulf. (Pron. bā′o-woolf). The early English, like all primitive peoples, delighted in the songs of their minstrels or poets. From Denmark and Germany they brought the songs of the hero Beowulf, and these were later woven together into the great Anglo-Saxon epic or heroic poem which bears his name. The poem tells how the " battle-brave " Beowulf came over the sea from Geatland (possibly the Sweden of today) to the land of the Danes and freed that country from the ogre Grendel ; how he was forced to battle with Grendel's mother, who came to avenge her son's death; and how, long afterwards, when Beowulf had been king of the Geatas for half a century, he came to his death in killing a fire-breathing dragon.

Beowulf is the earliest English epic poem, and the language has undergone such changes since the time when it was written that only those who have studied the old Anglo-Saxon language can read the story in the original. It has been translated into modern English, however, and in this form may be read by anyone who likes a story of heroism and adventure. Scholars do not agree as to how old the epic is or when it was first put into writing, but the oldest form in which it has come down to us is in a manuscript written in the 10th century, and now preserved in the British Museum as the only known copy of the first English epic.

New York Times Photos

BERING SEA MEMORIAL TO MISSIONARIES
This bronze statue of Christ was erected in 1937 on King Island, about 85 miles west of Nome, Alaska, to commemorate the heroism of Roman Catholic missionaries who worked amongst the Eskimos of this and other lonely islands of the Bering Sea.

A small parchment book of 140 pages, old and worn and discoloured, it has suffered from fire, there are holes in several leaves, and some of the pages have crumbled away. It is written in the clear, beautiful hand which the Irish monks introduced into England during the 7th century. There is no attempt at illumination or ornament, except that the capital letters beginning a fresh division of the poem are larger and blacker than the others.

Bering Sea. The sea and strait of this name were first discovered by a Russian Cosssack, Deshnev, in 1648; but they were named in honour of Vitus Bering (or Behring), a Danish navigator, in the employ of the Russian Tsar, Peter the Great, who made the first systematic explorations (1725 to 1741). Bering died in 1741 on an island near Kamchatka which also bears his name. This island, which belongs to Siberia, is also called Avatcha.

Bering Sea is part of the North Pacific Ocean, and is bordered by Alaska, the Aleutian Islands, Kamchatka, and Siberia. It extends about 1,250 miles from east to west and about 950 miles from north to south; on the north it leads to the Arctic Ocean through Bering Strait. It is a sea of almost perpetual fogs, and for a large part of the year it is obstructed with ice in packs and floes. Navigation, however, is usually possible from June to November. Bering Sea receives several large rivers, including the Yukon from Alaska and the Anadir from Siberia. The average depth is 4,700 feet. Bering Strait, lying between the projecting peninsulas of Siberia and Alaska, is 45–55 miles wide and has an average depth of 160 feet. A dispute between the United States and Great Britain over the fishing rights in the Bering Sea, known as the Bering Sea Question, was settled by arbitration in Paris in 1893.

Berkshire. This county has few historical associations to distinguish it, except those connected with Windsor, but it is a stretch of typical English agricultural country. It is separated from Oxford-

There was little in modern Berlin, the capital of the Prussian republic and of the German Empire, to remind one that its history dated from the 13th century. Until 1920 Berlin consisted of a number of independent boroughs, having certain public services in common; in that year they were united into a sprawling city covering 340 square miles, bigger in area than any other city in the world.

The streets were broad and straight, the buildings up to date and imposing, if not especially elegant.

shire and Buckinghamshire by the Thames, and adjoins Surrey, Hampshire, Wiltshire and Gloucestershire. About one half of the area of the county (725 square miles) is devoted to pasture and grain crops, while there are great areas of forest, heaths, commons and waste land in general.

. In the west of the county are high chalk hills, known as the Berkshire Downs, but geologically forming a continuation of the Chilterns. The Vale of the White Horse has, carved on the face of a hill, the finest of all the "white horses," the origin of which is lost in the mists of antiquity. This part of the county is mentioned in Thomas Hughes' book, Tom Brown's Schooldays.

Keystone

BERLIN'S FAMOUS BRANDENBURG GATE

Five years of Allied air-raids during the Second World War (1939–45) and intense bombardment preceding the final Russian assault in May 1945 left most of Berlin in ruins. From the Brandenburg Gate (pre-war, at top) the Sieges Allee, or Victory Avenue, ran through the Tiergarten, a large park in the centre of the city formerly containing a Zoo.

The principal towns include the county town of Reading (population about 117,800)—famous for biscuits, seeds and aeroplanes—Maidenhead, Newbury, Windsor (with its castle, from which our Royal House takes its name), Wokingham, Wallingford and Wantage. Population of the county is 361,000.

Berlin, GERMANY. Never in history has a great city been so utterly laid waste as Germany's capital. Five years of Allied air-raids during the Second World War (1939–45), culminating in the siege and final assault by the Russian armies in May 1945, reduced the third city of the world to a vast expanse of ruins. Of a pre-war population of more than 4,332,000 scarcely more than half remained. The buildings were shattered, the underground railway, the buses and trams destroyed, the drainage, water, gas, and electricity systems put out of action.

The main thoroughfare, called Unter den Linden, stretched westwards from what was once the Imperial Palace to the Brandenburg Gate, hard by the Reichstag or parliament building. Crossing this street at right angles were the two-mile-long Friedrichstrasse and the Wilhelmstrasse, Berlin's Whitehall, with the enormous Chancellery built by the dictator Adolf Hitler in 1939 and destroyed by the Allies in 1945. In this quarter were the main buildings of the capital—the university, the cathedral, the opera, the museums, the picture gallery.

Beyond the Brandenburg Gate the Sieges Allee (Victory Avenue) ran through the Tiergarten, a 630-acre park in the heart of the city, site of many statues mostly of little artistic worth. In 1945 and onwards the trees were cut down for fuel.

Berlin dates its foundation from 1230. During the 15th century the Elector of Brandenburg built a

BERLIN'S LARGEST STORES

In Neukölln, a district on the east side of Berlin, was built in 1929 this gigantic structure to house one of the world's biggest department stores—the Karstadthaus. The large 'U,' in the middle distance on the right, denotes one of the entrances to the Untergrund-Bahn or underground railway.

and Elbe rivers, and the development of the city's industry by Frederick the Great, led to further expansion, and by the end of the 18th century Berlin had some 150,000 inhabitants.

When the German Empire was created in 1871 Berlin, numbering then over 800,000 citizens, became its capital. From then on the city and its loose confederation of suburbs grew swiftly, and by the end of the 19th century Berlin was second only to the Ruhr as a centre of German industry. Engineering, electrical, chemical, optical, and clothing works were among its activities. By 1914, when the First World War broke out, the population had reached 4,000,000.

The National-Socialists, or Nazis, who seized power in 1933, built on an ambitious scale. Besides the Chancellery, the Avus motor-racing track, the great broadcasting station, the vast Air Ministry, and the immense stadium built for the 1936 Olympic Games—all more or less damaged in the Second World War—are memorials of the regime which brought destruction on the city it sought to glorify.

Berlin has several airports, of which the largest, the Tempelhof, is near the heart of the city; it was much used for Nazi parades. In the western suburbs are the lakes of the meandering Spree, notably the Wannsee, where the Berliners bathe and go boating.

Berlin held out stubbornly against Allied air and land attacks in the Second World War, but at last, on May 2, 1945, it fell to the Russian forces under Marshals Zhukov and Koniev. The battered city was divided into four zones for the British, American, French, and Russian allies. The British were allotted the western suburbs of Spandau, Charlottenburg, and Wilmersdorf; the Americans the south-western districts of Tempelhof, Steglitz, and Neukölln; the Russians

castle there; and later, Frederick William, the Great Elector, paved and lit the streets of the city and encouraged immigration. The building of canals from Berlin's river Spree to the busy Oder

Black Star

BERLIN'S FAMOUS UNTER DEN LINDEN

The Unter den Linden, which may be regarded as the centre of Berlin, formerly contained many fine buildings. Most of them were ruins (above) at the end of the Second World War (1939–45). The thoroughfare took its name from the lime (linden in German) trees planted along it. Nearly all the city's principal streets resemble the Unter den Linden, being wide and straight. After the Ruhr, the Berlin district was Germany's chief industrial centre.

BERMUDAS' GREEN ISLETS IN THE ATLANTIC

The Bermudas, a group of small islands in the Atlantic, about 580 miles from the nearest point on the North American continent, form a British colony of some importance, being valuable as a naval base half-way between Canada and the West Indies. There are about 360 islands, but all except 20 are merely small coral reefs like some of those in the photograph. The islands, with their pleasant climate, are a popular holiday resort with Americans.

the eastern half of the city ; the French zone was subsequently created from parts of the British and American zones. In Berlin the Allied Control Council was set up ; but unified control failed. In 1948 the Russians stopped surface traffic between the western zones of Germany and Berlin, and as Western Berliners were thus faced with starvation the British and U.S. authorities began, in June 1948, to fly in necessities, this " air lift " continuing until the blockade was raised in September 1949.

The West German Federal Republic was formally proclaimed on May 23, 1949, with Bonn (*q.v.*) as provisional capital; and on October 7 was announced the decision to form an East German Democratic Republic (Soviet-dominated), its seat of government to be in the Russian zone of Berlin. (*See* Germany).

Bermudas. In this delightful group of coral islands forming a British colony midway between the West Indies and Nova Scotia, frosts are unknown, the winter temperature ranging between 50 and 70 degrees.

Only 20 of the islands are inhabited, though there are about 360 islands, islets and reefs in all, with an area of about 19 square miles. Bermuda, or Main, Island, which occupies three-fourths of the total area of the group, is connected by causeways and bridges with some of the smaller islands. Regular air services are maintained with Europe and the United States. There is a railway between St. George's Island and Ireland Island; the line is about 22 miles long, and numerous bridges and causeways span the channels separating the intervening islets. The chief town, and seaport of Bermuda, Hamilton (population 3,000), is the seat of the government, which is in the hands of a Governor, who is assisted by two councils, an executive and a legislative. There is also an elected assembly.

The islands get their name from the Spaniard, Juan Bermudez, who discovered them in 1515. They are sometimes called the Somers Islands, from Sir George Somers, who first settled them early in the 17th century. Population is about 34,000, of whom over one-third are whites.

Berne, SWITZERLAND. This capital city of the Swiss Confederation lies in western Switzerland, on a plateau round whose base flows the River Aar, one of the upper tributaries of the Rhine. The city's name comes from the German word *Baern*, meaning " bears," and was adopted, according to legend, because of the great number of bears that were killed there the day the city was founded. The bear is the heraldic emblem of Berne, and bears in wood and stone are used as decorations for the buildings. A curious old town clock heralds the striking of the hours by the crowing of a cock and a procession of tiny bears. The city maintains a den on the right bank of the Aar in which there are always a number of fat, sleek bears.

The Aar flows completely round the old town, except for a narrow neck to the west. Among the public buildings is a great cathedral, begun in 1420. Its tower was restored in 1894. The council building (*Rathaus*) is another structure dating from the Middle Ages. The Parliament House, in which are held the sessions of the Congress of the Confederation, commands a splendid view of the Alps.

BERNE'S CLOCK TOWER
The charm of the city of Berne, Switzerland's capital, is shown in this photograph of the Marktgasse or Market Street. The clock tower was formerly the western gate of the city. In the foreground is the Schützen-Brunner, or Archer fountain, surmounted by the figure of an archer carrying the banner of his guild.

The city is an industrial centre, noted for its manufacture of scientific instruments and chocolate. It is the headquarters of the Universal Postal Union and of associations dealing with world problems of telegraph services, transport and copyrights.

Berne was founded in 1191, and entered the Swiss Confederacy in 1353, becoming the capital in 1848. Population, mainly German-speaking, is 130,000.

Bernhardt, SARAH (1845–1923). "Temperament and quick intelligence, passion, nervous mobility, grace, smile, voice, charm, poetry—Mademoiselle Sarah Bernhardt has them all." That is what a critic said of Sarah Bernhardt, the greatest French actress of her time. Though unable to sing in tune, she had a glorious speaking voice, a "voice of gold." Her hands were almost as expressive as her features. But she never lost her own personality in any part she played. She won applause for the brilliance of her acting rather than for making her audience forget they were watching a play. She achieved distinction also as a sculptor and painter, wrote plays, a novel and memoirs.

Sarah Bernhardt, whose real name was Rosine Bernard, was born in Paris on October 22, 1845, of French and Dutch parentage and Jewish descent, and was brought up in a convent at Versailles. At the age of 13 she became a pupil at the Paris Conservatoire. Her first successes were as Zanetto in Coppée's Le Passant in 1869, as Cordelia in a French version of King Lear, and as the Queen in Victor Hugo's Ruy Blas in 1872.

As Phèdre in Racine's play of that name she scored a triumph. This was her greatest part, and one in which she required so much concentrated passion that she would never play it twice running. In 1877 as Doña Sol in Victor Hugo's Hernani she was acclaimed as a genius. After a season in London in 1879 she toured Denmark, America and Russia. In 1899 she opened her own theatre in Paris, producing Hamlet in French and, in 1900, Rostand's L'Aiglon. At the age of 55 "the divine Sarah," as she had come to be called, was impersonating young men with astounding success.

Even in her crippled old age she could still hold her audiences spellbound. In 1915, during the First World War (1914–18), one of her legs had been amputated, but she gave performances to the troops at the front, made a further tour of America and, in 1922, of Italy. She was engaged in a film production when she was taken ill on March 21, 1923. Three days later she died.

Berwick-on-Tweed. Many think that when they cross the high bridge over the Tweed and come abreast of the red-tiled roofs of Berwick-on-Tweed they are in Scotland. They are wrong. Berwick-on-Tweed is not in the Scottish county of Berwickshire, but in England, and "a county of itself" attached to

SARAH BERNHARDT
One of the most famous parts played by this great French actress was that of Phèdre (lower) in Racine's play of that name. Upper, a painting of her by the French artist, Bastien-Lepage (1848–84). As famous in Britain as she was in France, Sarah Bernhardt was also an accomplished sculptor and painter, and wrote several plays.

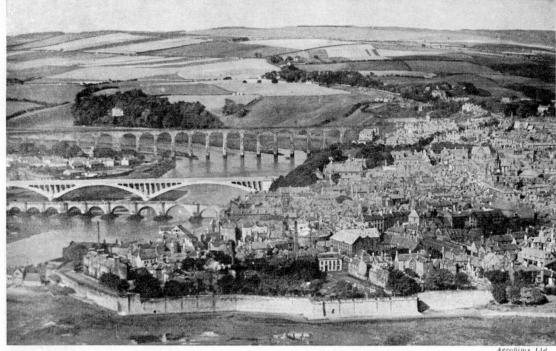

Aerofilms Ltd

BERWICK-ON-TWEED, TOWN AND COUNTY

Though Berwick stands on the north bank of the Tweed, it is not in Scotland but forms a " county of itself," and used to be mentioned separately in Acts of Parliament. From this arises the fact that, technically, Berwick was, up to 1914, at war with Russia ! For when the Crimean War began (1854–56) she was mentioned, along with Great Britain and Ireland, in the declaration of war against Russia, but through an oversight was not included in the peace treaty.

Northumberland. Its ancient status as a free borough is still recalled in certain proclamations, in which the town's name is inserted after Wales.

Owing to the importance of its situation over-looking the border between England and Scotland, Berwick was in olden days strongly fortified. Its castle at one time was regarded as one of the strongest fortresses on the border, but its site is now largely taken up by the railway station. A complete line of ramparts still stands, however, and there are the slight remains of the castle.

There is a very old and narrow bridge of 15 arches carrying a roadway across the Tweed. This bridge was built in the reign of James I, and it is peculiar in having its largest arch near the northern shore. The railway bridge which crosses the Tweed was constructed by Robert Stephenson, and was considered such a triumph of engineering at the date of its completion—in 1850—that Queen Victoria was invited to open it. A ferro-concrete road bridge was brought into use in 1928. The population of Berwick is about 12,000.

Berwickshire. As explained in the Berwick-on-Tweed article, Berwickshire is a Scottish county, although Berwick-on-Tweed is in England. The Tweed forms part of the border between Berwickshire and Northumberland, and is the only river of any size in the county. Berwickshire is rich in historical associations and can tell many tales of border warfare, but is now above all a pastoral county. Sir Walter Scott lies buried in Dryburgh Abbey, and many of his works, notably The Bride of Lammermuir, are derived from Berwickshire

history. Duns (population 1,780) is the county town; other towns are Eyemouth, Coldstream—from which the Coldstream Guards received their name—and Lauder. Estimated population of Berwickshire is 26,100.

Beryllium. This is a metallic element (symbol Be). Its atomic number is 4; atomic weight, 9·02; melting point, 1280° C. It is very light (density only 1·8, as compared with 2·7 for aluminium), but unlike some other light metals its melting point, it will be noticed, is high. When a small percentage is alloyed with copper it forms the beryllium bronzes, which are very strong—six times as strong as copper alone, and twice as strong as mild steel.

When, in the 1930's, scientists began experimenting to split the atom, it was discovered that by bombarding beryllium with alpha particles a stream of " neutrons " was liberated by the beryllium. (See Atom).

Bessemer, SIR HENRY (1813–1898). Inventor of a process of making steel, he was born at Charlton, in Bedfordshire, the son of Anthony Bessemer, an engineer, and very largely educated himself while pottering around his father's metal works. Before he introduced his process, in 1856, cast iron and wrought iron were the only materials fit for structural use, or in the construction of ships, locomotives, and so on. Cast iron is brittle and could not be shaped after casting.

Wrought iron could be welded and shaped by the smith, but needed a long and costly process to produce it, and was used mainly for sheets and plates, and the large forgings needed as engine or boiler parts. Steel was used mainly for tools, and was made in small pots or crucibles by heating bars of wrought iron along with a mass of charcoal.

Bessemer showed the world how to make steel from molten pig iron (this is the product of smelting iron ore in a blast furnace) *without fuel*, in lots of ten tons at a time—the whole process for a batch taking about half an hour! No wonder the steel makers of his day were sceptical. Bessemer's invention ushered in the Age of Steel, for he was able to reduce the cost from £80 per ton to a tenth or less of that figure. Henceforth steel was cheap and plentiful, for sheets and plates, bars, railway and tram rails, locomotives, ships, columns and stancheons and girders. Thousands of things, from fine steel wire to big guns, were now made of steel.

The difference between various forms of iron, and between iron and steel, is mainly in the percentage of carbon contained in the metal. Pig iron contains $3-4\frac{1}{2}$ per cent but structural steel had to have only about half to three-quarters of 1 per cent of carbon; furthermore, various impurities in the pig iron had to be got rid of. Bessemer did these things in a very simple fashion in his "converter." This was an egg-shaped vessel of steel plates lined with heat-resisting bricks made of silica or a similar material. The vessel was pivoted on trunnions so that it could be swung down from the upright position to a horizontal one which would bring the open mouth ready for the charge to be poured in from a ladle. Near the base there were holes to which were led pipes through which a blast of hot air could be forced in.

A charge of molten pig iron was put in the converter, the latter was tilted towards the vertical, when the liquid metal covered the air-blast holes in the base, and the blast was turned on. The air entering stirred up the contents; the oxygen in the air reacted with the metallic impurities and with the carbon of the pig iron, turning the former into oxides and the carbon into monoxide. This chemical reaction actually made the molten iron hotter, so that, as Bessemer said, the conversion was done without fuel. In less than half an hour all the carbon was expelled; most of the metallic impurities floated on the top of the metal as a slag, but some were blown out from the top as fumes. The steel actually seemed to boil towards the last stage, and this was accompanied with a vivid and intense white flame which spurted up 20–30 feet high; the dying down of the flame showed that the process had been completed, leaving only pure iron.

Bessemer's early attempts failed because the iron had not enough carbon, was porous, and was brittle; some iron oxide remaining dissolved in the molten metal had to be removed, and the other defects made good. Robert Mushet, another

BESSEMER CONVERTER DURING A 'BLOW'
A revolution in metallurgy was brought about by Sir Henry Bessemer's invention of the steel-converter seen here. The converter is here seen in the upright position with the fiery blast that purifies the molten pig-iron emerging like the beam of a searchlight at the top.

experimenter with steel, suggested that Bessemer should add to the mixture a quantity of an iron containing manganese and carbon and known as "spiegeleisen" (German, mirror-iron). This did what was necessary, and Bessemer steel began to play its important part in industry. Today a carefully measured amount of pig-iron is added to the molten iron after the converter has done its work; this puts back enough carbon.

Bessemer's process had defects, and later inventors improved upon it and also introduced other ways of making steel cheaply. But the world's debt to Henry Bessemer is an immense one. His first converter was set up at the Dowlais ironworks in South Wales. In 1879 he was knighted by Queen Victoria. (*See* Iron).

Betatron. This is a machine for producing and speeding up electrons so that they can be used in research into nuclear physics. The machine was invented by an American, D. W. Kerst, about 1941, and used in atom-splitting experiments. In 1945 a much larger and more powerful betatron was built in the U.S.A. for research work; this is able to produce electrons having an energy of 100 Mev (a Mev equals 1,000,000 electron-volts). Other similar machines are described under the heading Cyclotron.

The betatron acts like an electrical transformer or an induction coil (*q.v.*), but instead of the primary and secondary coils of these apparatus it has a primary only; the secondary is replaced by a ring-shaped tube of glass or a similar substance, in which the circulating electrons are urged round by electro-magnetic action time after time, the stream increasing in speed at each circuit until the enormous energy of up to 100 Mev is attained.

Bethlehem. The little town of Bethlehem in Palestine shares with its neighbour Jerusalem the distinction of being the most sacred spot in Christendom. At the end of its long straggling street, lined with low, flat-roofed houses, is the shrine to which millions of pilgrims have turned their steps—the Church of the Nativity, erected in about A.D. 327 over the grotto where Christ is believed to have been born. The nave of this church is said to be the oldest monument of Christian architecture in the world. In the grotto below, a marble trough marks the traditional spot where the manger-cradle stood. A famous altar, the Altar of the Innocents, marks the reputed burial place of the 2,000 children who, according to the New Testament account, were slain by Herod.

But even before the birth of Christ Bethlehem was a place of great fame, for it was the scene of the romance of Ruth, whose story is given in the

Old Testament, in the Book of Ruth; and of the death of Rachel, who is mentioned in the Book of Genesis and First Book of Samuel in the Old Testament. It was also the birthplace of David, the second king of Israel (*c.* 1030–990 B.C.). Population is about 9,000.

Bevin, ERNEST (b. 1881). An unschooled farm-boy who took his place in the highest councils of the world; a labourer who rose to be one of his country's most eminent statesmen; such was Ernest Bevin, Great Britain's Foreign Secretary in the critical years after the Second World War.

The son of an agricultural labourer, he was born at Winsford, Somerset, and went to work on a farm at the age of 10. Later he moved to Bristol, where he obtained employment successively as errand-boy, page-boy, and tram-driver. He joined the Dockers' Union and was soon an active member, later becoming assistant general secretary. He worked tirelessly for better conditions of employment for dock labourers, and at a court of inquiry held after a dock strike in 1920 he won for himself the name of "the dockers' K.C." (K.C. stands for King's Counsel).

He took a big part in reforming the Trades Union Congress in 1919, and when the Transport and General Workers' Union (one of the biggest trade unions in the world) was instituted in 1922, Mr. Bevin became its general secretary. He was among the organizers of a general strike in support of the coal-miners' demands in 1926, and in the same year was a member of the Government's Industrial Committee to inquire into disputes between workers and employers. In 1937 the general council of the Trades Union Congress elected him chairman.

Topical

RT. HON. ERNEST BEVIN
Great Britain's Foreign Secretary in the difficult years of peace after the Second World War (1939–45), the Right Honourable Ernest Bevin had started out in life as a farm-boy in Somerset.

Mr. Winston Churchill, who became Prime Minister in May 1940, recognizing that Mr. Bevin enjoyed the confidence of the mass of trade union members, appointed him Minister of Labour and National Service. Mr. Bevin speeded up production, and kept labour disputes to a minimum. At the time of his appointment he was not an M.P., but soon at a by-election he was elected Labour member for Central Wandsworth. In October 1940 he joined the War Cabinet and was sworn a Privy Councillor.

When a Labour Government was formed in 1945 the Prime Minister, Mr. Attlee, made Mr. Bevin his Foreign Secretary, and he retained this post when, at the General Election in 1950, the Labour Party remained in office. Prominent in the councils of Europe, he quickly established himself as a stalwart representative of the British viewpoint in international conferences during the disturbed years of the post-war era.

The GREATEST BOOK in the WORLD

How the sacred Jewish and Christian Scriptures have come down to us over more than two thousand years and, though written in ancient tongues and in lands far distant, still speak to all in the language of the soul.

Bible. Some 1,200 years ago in a narrow cell in an English monastery the Venerable Bede, the most famous scholar of his day in Western Europe, lay dying. Feebly he dictated his translation of St. John's Gospel, for although desperately ill, he would not rest.

"Go on quickly," he commanded the scribe. "I know not how long I shall hold out or how soon my Master will call me hence." All day long they worked, and when the rays of the setting sun glided into the quiet room the task was almost done.

"There remains but one chapter, master," said the scribe. "Will you not rest now?"

Oliver Cromwell's Bible, which measures 4½in. by 2½in.

"Nay, we must go on," Bede replied. "Take up thy pen again and I will translate."

His eyes blinded with tears, the young scribe wrote on. "And now, father," said he, as he set down the last sentence from the quivering lips, "it is finished."

"Ay, it is finished," echoed the dying Bede. And, turning his face to the window, he died.

This saintly scholar is only one of the many great men who have spent their lives in making available to all the Bible, the sacred book of Christianity. Translated into Latin, its lessons were the basis of all the church services of the Middle Ages. That its message might be carried to the heathen Teutons and Slavs, Ulfilas devised the Gothic alphabet and Cyril the Slavonic. An English translation of the Bible was the chief treasure of that little band of Puritans who set sail for America to find "freedom to worship God" in their own way. Explorers have carried it into the frozen North and into the heart of the tropical jungles for consolation on their hard journeys; and missionaries, many times at the cost of their lives, have brought its message to heathen lands.

But the Bible is more than our great sacred book; it is also our greatest literary heritage. There is no other book worded with more beauty than our English Bible. Merely as literature it has made a deeper impression upon the human mind than has any other book, and the extent to which it has helped to shape the world's ideas cannot be estimated. However much you know of poetry and prose, you cannot consider yourself well read unless you have an intimate acquaintance with the Bible.

It is a library rather than a book, for it is a collection of 66 books, each distinct in itself, abounding in literature of the highest type. Almost every phase of life and thought is dealt with, and every form of literature is included in its pages—stories, biographies, letters, orations, prayers, hymns of praise, and much else.

The Bible has two great divisions, the Old and the New Testaments. Testament means "covenant" or mutual understanding—a covenant between God and His people.

The Old Testament is the record of the history and religious literature of a little band of people, the Jews, who believed in one God who was loving and just. All about the little country of Palestine were great and powerful nations, who worshipped many gods, but Israel managed to retain its belief in only one God. In the New Testament is the story of the life of Jesus and His teachings, and the acts and epistles (letters) of the Apostles. All through the Old Testament are promises that God

BEDE DICTATING HIS VERSION OF ST. JOHN
The touching scene when the Venerable Bede lay dying, described in this page, is here portrayed in a painting by J. D. Penrose. Bede passed his life—from the age of seven until his death—in the Benedictine monasteries at Wearmouth and Jarrow in Co. Durham, and he died in Jarrow monastery in 735, at the age of 62.

would give His people a deliverer ; and these promises, which Christianity teaches were fulfilled in the life and death of Jesus, give the thread of unity binding the Old Testament to the New.

The Old Testament as we know it is by no means the whole of the sacred writings of the Jewish people. It was not until 200 years after Christianity had been founded that the rabbis and

THE CODEX SINAITICUS
In 1933 the British Museum bought the Bible manuscript known as the Codex Sinaiticus for £100,000. Above is Sir George Hill, then the Director of the Museum, receiving the MS. from Mr. Maggs, the intermediary in the purchase from the Soviet Government. The Codex, found in a monastery on Mt. Sinai, dates from the 4th century after Christ, and is written in Greek, as is seen from the extract reproduced.

PSALM ON PAPYRUS
One of the earliest existing manuscripts of any part of the Bible is a papyrus in the British Museum, a portion of which is shown above. It contains a translation of the Twelfth Psalm from Hebrew into Greek. Much of it has perished, but even such a fragment as this is prized by scholars.

teachers of the Jews finally decided which of their books should be regarded as " canonical " in the Jewish Church. " Canon " means literally a rule or measure, and, applied to the Bible, it means a list of books which were accepted as inspired. These " canonical scriptures " of the Jews became the Old Testament of the Christians. But the early Christian Church put 14 of the rejected books in a separate group at the end of the Old Testament. These we call the Apocrypha—which is the Greek word for " hidden " or the " hidden books."

The Roman Catholic Church still uses these Apocryphal books. They include the books of Tobit, Judith, the remainder of Esther, the remainder of Daniel, the Wisdom of Solomon, Ecclesiasticus (called " The Wisdom of Jesus, the son of Sirach "), Baruch, Maccabees 1 and 2. All the leading English translations down to the King James Version included these books, and the scholars who gave us the Revised Version revised these books with the rest, although they were published in a separate volume. Some of the passages are equal in nobility of thought and language to portions of the Old Testament books included as inspired.

Similarly, there was for a long time a difference of opinion as to which books should be included in the New Testament. There are no fewer than 109 of the New Testament Apocryphal books, whose very names are unfamiliar to most Christians today; examples are the Epistle of Barnabas, the Teaching of the Twelve Apostles, and the Shepherd of Hermas. The canon of the New Testament was not decided until A.D. 382 at a council held at Rome.

The oldest manuscripts of the collected books of the Bible go back only to about A.D. 350. There are only a few of these. The one known as the Codex Vaticanus is kept in the Vatican Library at Rome; it contains almost the whole of the New Testament. The oldest manuscript of the entire New Testament is the Codex Sinaiticus. Discovered in St. Catherine's monastery at the foot of Mt. Sinai in 1844, it was purchased from Russia by Britain in 1933 and placed in the British Museum, London. The Alexandrine manuscript, written after A.D. 400, was presented to King Charles I of England and is also in the British Museum ; it contains the greater part of both the Old and New Testaments. Some of these old manuscripts are called " palimpsests " (from Greek terms meaning to rub away again), the original writing on the parchment sheets being erased to make room for later writing. By using chemicals and photography, however, scholars have been able to restore the old letters so that they show up faintly.

The New Testament was written in Greek. There are nearly 2,000 ancient manuscripts of the whole or different parts of the New Testament written in this language, but none is older than the manuscripts described above. In the past 30 years, however, in excavations made in Egypt, there have been found several pages containing " sayings of Jesus," which are probably a full century or more older than the oldest New Testament manuscripts we have.

The work of comparing such early manuscripts and correcting the text and revising the translation has gone on from early days. When the Temple at Jerusalem was burned in A.D. 70 much of the sacred literature of the Jews was lost; but a school of rabbis was formed at Tiberias to restore it. Alexandria in Egypt early became a centre for the study of the Christian writings. All through the Middle Ages patient monks busied themselves with the labour of copying and so preserving the sacred texts. With the publication of the printed Greek text of the New Testament by Erasmus in 1516 the modern study of the Bible began.

The Old Testament was written in Hebrew (except for a few passages in the Aramaic dialect), and was translated into Greek about 270 B.C. by a committee of 70. Their version is known as the Septuagint, from the Latin word meaning " 70." In every country where Christianity spread, the Bible was translated into the language of that country—first into various eastern dialects, then into Latin, the language of the Romans, and then into the languages of Western Europe. No other book has been translated into so many languages.

The greatest of the early translations was that into Latin made by St. Jerome, who lived about 400 years after Christ. This translation, known as the Vulgate (from a Latin word meaning to make public) is today the official Bible of the Roman Catholic Church throughout the world. It was also the basis of the earlier translations into English and other European tongues and of the Douai English translation which is used by English-

THE BIBLE IS BROUGHT TO THE PEOPLE

For centuries the common people were deliberately kept in ignorance of the book on which their religion rested, and it was not until the first great English reformer, John Wycliffe, translated the Latin version into English in 1382 that they were allowed to realize all that it meant to them. In this painting, by W. F. Yeames, R.A., Wycliffe is sending out his wandering disciples, each with a hand-written copy of the Bible.

speaking Catholics. When printing was invented in the 15th century, the Latin Bible was the first complete book printed.

Parts of the Bible were early rendered into English. The first writer to do this was Caedmon, though it is true he did not translate the Bible at all in the usual sense, but sang its divine stories so that the ignorant people of his time could understand them. Other translators, including Bede, gave the people of England fragments of the scriptures in their own tongue, but not until about 1382 was the whole Bible translated into English.

This first English Bible, translated from the Latin Vulgate and copied out by hand, is considered by many to be the work of the group of early reformers headed by John Wycliffe, and bears his name. Great opposition arose to it because its authors translated many passages in a sense not approved by the Church. Nevertheless, it was so

READING THE BIBLE IN OLD ST. PAUL'S

When the majority of people in England were illiterate, and, moreover, the cost of the book was very high, many could get to know the Bible only by listening to a scholar reading to them in church. Here a nineteenth-century artist, Sir George Harvey, has painted such a scene in Old St. Paul's Cathedral in London. You will notice that the precious Book is chained to the pillar.

result of their labours was the King James Version, published in 1611, which has been for over 300 years the "Authorized Version" of the Protestant English-speaking people. It is the greatest book in the English language. "Its simple, majestic, Anglo-Saxon tongue," says one writer, "its clear, sparkling style, its directness and force of utterance, have made it the model in language, style and dignity of some of the choicest writers of the last two centuries, and its reverential and spiritual tone have endeared it to the hearts of millions."

Its language is not that of the early 17th century but of the Tudor Age, for the translators depended very largely on the Bishops' Bible, which in turn was based on Tyndale's.

widely circulated that, in spite of the fact that its reading was prohibited by law, there are more than 100 manuscript copies of it preserved today. William Tyndale, who was born 108 years after Wycliffe's death, went back to the original Hebrew and Greek versions, and his translation of many passages is so good that much of it is preserved in the English Bible of the present time. But Tyndale, too, was a "heretic," and when his books first reached England from the Continent they were burned as "pernicious merchandise." The new art of printing, however, spread his Bible far and wide. In the end Tyndale was condemned as a heretic on the Continent, and was strangled and burned at the stake in Belgium in 1536.

Miles Coverdale's Bible (authorized in 1535) was founded in part on Tyndale's translation; while the "Great Bible," ordered by Henry VIII in 1539 to be placed in all the churches, was partly based on Coverdale and partly on the work of John Rogers, later a martyr. A revision of the Great Bible was issued in 1568, and known as the Bishops' Bible.

When James I came to the throne, the Reformation had been accomplished in Great Britain and the church services were all in English. He desired an English Bible more perfect than any then existing, so he instructed 47 Biblical scholars to prepare a new translation. They were divided into small companies, each company translating a book or several books of the Bible. They kept the earlier versions, especially that of Tyndale, before them, so that there are whole sentences in their version which are the same as in earlier translations. The

For English-speaking Catholics, a similar place is held by the Douai Version. This was first produced at the University of Douai, in France, by Catholic refugees from England in Elizabeth's day.

TYNDALE : TRANSLATOR AND MARTYR

So strong was the objection of Church and State to people learning the true foundations of the Bible by reading its words in their own tongue that Tyndale, its second great English translator, was strangled and burned as a heretic. In this well-known painting by A. Johnstone, William Tyndale (the seated figure) is shown working at his task.

Dr. Gregory Martin, formerly of Oxford, played the chief part in the translation, which was revised by William Allen and others. The New Testament was published in 1582, and the whole Bible in two volumes in 1609 and 1610.

The Revised Version, made desirable by the discovery of new manuscripts, was produced by a committee of English scholars co-operating with a similar committee appointed in the United States. Its translations are more accurate, but it lacks the beauty of language of the King James (or Authorized) Version. The New Testament was published in 1881, the Old Testament in 1884.

A number of further revisions have been made to obtain a more accurate translation and to express the Bible in more modern speech. Thus we have Weymouth's New Testament in Modern Speech; the Twentieth Century New Testament; the translation by Dr. James Moffat; R. A. Knox's translation of the Latin Vulgate; and the Basic English New Testament. In 1949 work began on a new translation from original texts under the direction of a joint committee of churches in Great Britain.

There have been many editions of the Bible possessing some particular interest. The Mazarin Bible was the first complete book printed from movable types (1452–56); the first copy discovered was found among the books of Cardinal Mazarin. The Complutensian Polyglot, published by Cardinal Ximenes in 1522, prints the Greek of the New Testament in one column and the Latin of the

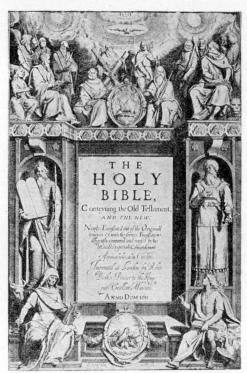

' KING JAMES BIBLE '

It was King James I who ordered the preparation of our great ' Authorized Version ' of the Bible, which has been and still remains the finest literary treasure of our language. Here is the title page of the first edition of the book, completed, by nearly half a hundred scholars, in 1611.

Vulgate in the other. For the Old Testament it gives the Hebrew on one side and the old Greek translation (called the Septuagint) on the other, and the Latin Vulgate between—"like Christ crucified between the two thieves," so the preface says.

The Bug Bible (1551) was so called because of the translation of Psalm xci, 5, which read, "afraid of bugges by night," instead of the present " terror by night." The Breeches Bible is an English version published at Geneva in 1560, and is named from its translation of Gen. iii, 7, which reads, " making themselves *breeches* out of fig leaves." The Wicked Bible, printed in England in 1631, left out the word " not " in the Seventh Commandment. The Thumb Bible, published in 1670 at Aberdeen, was one inch square and one-half inch thick. The Vinegar Bible (1717) has as the heading of the 20th chapter of Luke " The Parable of the Vinegar," instead of " vineyard."

The Devil's Bible is the name give to a manuscript of the Bible taken to Stockholm after the Thirty Years' War (1618–48). It is beautifully written on 300 asses' skins, and legend says it is the work of a monk condemned to death, who by selling himself to Satan was enabled to save his life by meeting the condition that he should copy the whole Bible on asses' skins in one night.

One of the smallest Bibles in the world was printed in Glasgow in 1901. Without the cover it is 1¼ by 1¾ inches, and seven-sixteenths of an inch thick, containing 876 pages and several illustrations. It is provided with a small magnifying glass which slips into a pocket in the cover.

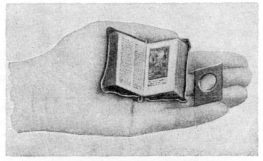

ONE OF THE SMALLEST BIBLES

This is the little Bible referred to in this page. Made in Glasgow in 1901, it is so small that it may be slipped into a waistcoat pocket. It is provided with a magnifying glass, which slips into a pocket in the cover.

Bibliography. (Pron. bib-li-og'-rafi). There are said to exist in printed form about eight and a half million separate writings, each long enough to be called a book. No one can, of course, read more than a few thousand of them in the course of his lifetime. It is, therefore, important that one should select for one's reading the books which will best serve one's particular needs. Bibliography is the science which has been designed to assist in making such a selection.

The word comes from two Greek words meaning " book " and " to write." Thus, in the broadest sense, any literary composition about books might be called a bibliography. In ordinary use the word is applied only to instructive lists of books, concerned with special subjects or branches of subjects.

Necessarily, there are all sorts of bibliographies to meet all sorts of different needs. There are author bibliographies, as, for example, a list of all the writings of Charles Dickens; subject bibliographies, such as lists of useful books about chemistry; bibliographies of literary form, like lists of one-act plays; local bibliographies, such as a list of the works dealing with Kent or Wessex; period bibliographies, like lists of the literary productions of the Age of Elizabeth; language bibliographies, as a list of books written in Spanish. There are even bibliographies of bibliographies. The British National Bibliography founded in January 1950, and compiled at the British Museum, provides for librarians throughout the world an up-to-date guide to British books.

For the convenience of the reader, a good bibliography distributes its subjects under logical subdivisions. A bibliography should divide and subdivide its subjects until only a few books are included under each topic, and arrange these topics so logically that a reader can turn quickly to the particular section he wants.

What a Title Page Tells the Reader

The bibliographer must also be accurate. When he mentions a book he must do so in such a way that his reader can be certain of just what book he means. To achieve this he will do well to use the conventional system which has proved well suited for the purpose. This system records certain facts about each book which may be regarded as the indispensable elements of detailed bibliographical description. In their simplest form these are: author, title, place of publication, date of publication, and size of the book. All except the last two of these appear on the title page of every ordinary book.

In the record of size conventional usage varies. Usually approximate indications are sufficient. It makes little difference to the ordinary reader whether a book contains 272 or 288 pages, but it makes a great difference whether it is a slender pamphlet or an extensive treatise in many volumes. Similarly, most readers will want to know whether a book is a portable volume or is of the size of an encyclopedia.

Every librarian, by the very nature of his profession, must be something of a bibliographer, and through the science of bibliography he is able to make out lists of books dealing with many subjects without being an expert on the subjects in question.

Bihar. A province of former British India, west of West Bengal and bordered on the north by Nepal, Bihar was joined administratively to Orissa until 1937. In 1947, when the two Dominions of India and Pakistan were created, it became a state of India. With an area of 69,745 square miles, it has a population numbering over 36 millions, chiefly engaged in agriculture. Owing to the density of the population Bihar formerly suffered severely from famine, but an increase of railway and canal transport has averted such disasters.

In the district of Chota Nagpur there are large deposits of coal yielding 15 million tons annually out of India's total output of 28 million tons. At Jamshedpur in the south of Bihar (population 83,000) are the famous Tata Iron and Steel

Works. Mica is also produced, and about 154,000 persons are employed in the coal, iron ore and mica mines. Nine million acres are devoted to the cultivation of rice, while maize, oilseeds, wheat and barley are also grown. The capital, Patna, on the Ganges, has a population of 175,000, and other important towns are Gaya (105,000) and Bhagalpur (69,000). Near Gaya is Buddh Gaya, where Buddha sat beneath the sacred bo, or fig, tree, and became " enlightened." The Government is moved to Ranchi, in the hills, during the hot weather. Communications in general are good; several railways now traverse the province.

Bilberry. There are three names for this plant (*Vaccinium myrtillus*). In some parts of the country it is called the blaeberry and in others the whortleberry. It is a low shrub about the same height as heather, to which it is related, and grows in similar places, that is, on heaths and hills. It is usually found in great quantities, hiding the ground with a dense covering of small oval, tough, leathery leaves; in some localities it makes such a carpet under oak trees or other woodland.

In spring it has a beautiful little flower, which looks like a tiny pink inverted globe tinged with green. But the plant is seldom noticed except in autumn, and then its attraction is its delicious round berry, which is covered with a blue " bloom " like that of the sloe. It makes a delicious jam.

Billiards. This game has been played in many different ways at various times, and even today there is a marked difference between the English, French and American styles. In whatever style it is played it requires a steadiness of touch and accuracy of eye needed by no other game.

The full-sized table is 12 feet long and 6 feet 1½ inches wide, and has a perfectly level green baize surface surrounded by rubber cushions. Pockets are placed at the four corners, and one in the centre of each side.

The game is played by two players, each of whom has a cue, which is a wooden rod generally about five feet long and varying in diameter from half an inch or less at the point to an inch and a half at the butt. Upon the point is fixed a leather tip. Three balls are used, two being white and one red, one of the white balls having a black spot. Hence one player is " spot " and the other " plain."

Scores are made by cannons, winning hazards and losing hazards. A cannon is scored when the striker's ball hits the other two, a losing hazard when it enters a pocket after hitting either. A winning hazard is scored when either the red or white ball is " potted " or sent into a pocket by the striker's ball. A cannon counts two; a winning or losing hazard off white ball two, and off red three. Having scored with his first shot, a player continues his " break " until he fails to score.

Labels on illustration: Red spot, Pyramid spot, 12¾", 12', Middle spot, Balk line, 6', The "D", 2'5"

The markings used in the games of billiards, pyramids and snooker.

Also played on a billiards table is the game known as snooker pool. It is played with 22 balls, 15 of which are red, and the others of various

BILLIARDS PLAYED BY MASTERS OF THE GAME
Above are two modern players of billiards making cannon shots, which will score two points each. Both keep their heads as low as possible, so that their eyes look straight along the cue to the ball, thereby assuring an accurate stroke.

Biochemistry.

The chemistry of life and living matter, of bodily processes and functions, is known as biochemistry. It is a very wide branch of chemistry, and all we can do here is to give one or two examples. Many small organisms such as bacteria and moulds manufacture chemical substances which they give out to the substance on and in which these organisms live. Certain of these chemicals will kill, or at least hinder the growth of, other tiny organisms—for instance, those which cause disease.

When Sir Ambrose Fleming was making experiments with a certain bacterium which causes boils on human beings, he accidentally stumbled on the discovery of penicillin (*q.v.*). It chanced that when Fleming took off the lid from a glass dish in which he was growing the bacterium, a stray spore of some mould (this is a form of fungus) must have fallen into the culture dish and begun to grow. As the colony of mould organisms grew stronger it destroyed the bacteria round about. The next step was to cultivate colonies of the new germ-killer; after a very great deal more of experiment, penicillin—for that was the name coined for the substance made by the mould, *Penicillium notatum*—was able to be manufactured in large quantities and used in combating disease all over the world.

Another instance of the imitation of living chemistry is in the artificial production of antibodies. These are substances manufactured naturally in the living body when a disease germ or a strange ("foreign") protein gets into the blood. Thus some persons cannot eat duck eggs without ill effects, because the protein sets up a disturbing reaction. The body then manufactures an antibody which acts as an antidote to the "poison." Today biochemists are experimenting in their laboratories with artificially made antibodies for many of these peculiar reactions. Synthetic penicillin, too, has been made in the laboratory.

So you see how immensely important is biochemistry. There is hardly a field of human endeavour in which it does not promise us benefits—from agriculture, where soil chemistry is enabling farmers to grow bigger and better crops, to the prevention and destruction of locust plagues, the improvement of health and the conquest of disease.

colours and values. Winning hazards are the only means of scoring in snooker, cannons being ignored and losing hazards penalized.

Bill of Rights.

After Magna Carta the great bulwark of English liberty is the Bill of Rights passed by the English Parliament in 1689, after William and Mary had been brought to the throne by the revolution of 1688. The Bill contained a number of clauses to protect the freedom of the people. It guaranteed a fair trial in the courts, frequent meetings of Parliament and freedom of debate therein, freedom from taxation except by Parliament, the right of petition, etc. Several of the first 10 amendments to the constitution of the United States, including the one forbidding "cruel and unusual punishments," are taken from the Bill.

The most important statement of rights which the State may not take from the individual is the Declaration of the Rights of Man issued by the French Assembly at the time of the French Revolution in 1789. It laid down the principles of the freedom and equality under the law of all citizens and the sovereignty of the people, as well as the rights of the individual to freedom of speech, of religion, and of the press. This declaration passed beyond the frontiers of France and became an important factor in the growth of democracy in the 19th century. The new French Constitution of 1946 reaffirmed its policy, and introduced new principles, including the equal rights of women with men in all spheres.

Biography AND AUTOBIOGRAPHY. A book that relates a man's or a woman's life-story is called a biography, and when a person tries to set forth his own life in a book it is known as an autobiography. There are innumerable examples of both classes.

Biography is a useful handmaid to history, and there is no better way really to understand any period than to study the lives of people who lived during that period. There could, for example, be no pleasanter approach to an understanding of the men and movements that led to Italian unity than through Trevelyan's three great works on Garibaldi.

One of the earliest biographies is that in which the Latin writer, Tacitus, describes the life of his father-in-law, Agricola, a famous soldier who fought and conquered in Britain. The Greek writer, Plutarch, also left a collection of biographies, numbering nearly 50; and from these, in an English translation, Shakespeare drew many of the incidents and characters in his great tragedies.

Biography has flourished in more recent times, and in our own language. Boswell's Life of Johnson is one of the greatest books in English, and is by some regarded as the greatest biography ever written. Dr. Johnson himself wrote several biographies, which were published as Lives of the Poets. The famous writer, Thomas Carlyle, devoted many laborious years to writing the lives of Oliver Cromwell and Frederick the Great. The life of Thomas Carlyle has in turn been described by a dozen writers since his death—notably by James Anthony Froude, a friend of Carlyle, whose biography of him aroused a storm of controversy, and David Alec Wilson, who for 40 years collected material of all kinds about Carlyle.

The 20th century brought a fashion for biographies, many of them written in a critical and cynical spirit, sometimes disparaging instead of praising the people with whom they deal. This new method of biography is generally regarded as originating with Lytton Strachey, who employed it effectively in his Eminent Victorians (1918). Lytton Strachey's books were always the product of wide reading and research, so that, while his interpretations are often original, they are founded upon a deep knowledge of facts. Those who have tried to copy his style have not always imitated his industry and accuracy.

Autobiography was not practised as a form of literature by the writers of ancient Greece and Rome. But the spread of the Christian religion, which encouraged people to consider more carefully their own thoughts and actions, gave a stimulus to the writing of autobiographies. Thus in the 4th century St. Augustine wrote his Confessions, telling of his life, his inward struggles, and his final conversion to Christianity. This book was very popular throughout the Middle Ages, and inspired a great many people to write their lives as Augustine had done. In the 18th century the Frenchman, Jean-Jacques Rousseau, wrote his Confessions, which, when they were published after his death, created a great and lasting impression.

Book That Sowed the Seeds of War

Today it is almost taken for granted that anyone who has reached eminence will write his autobiography. The first volume of the novelist Beverley Nichols's life-story appeared (1926) when he was only 21. Among outstanding autobiographies published since the First World War are those of the statesmen Lloyd George and Winston Churchill, of the authors H. G. Wells and Laurence Housman, of the sculptor Eric Gill, the composer Dame Ethel Smyth, and the Swedish doctor and philanthropist Axel Munthe. There is one book of this kind which has had an influence for evil beyond measure— Mein Kampf (My Struggle), by the German dictator Adolf Hitler, who in this account of his life's work and aims sowed the seeds of the Second World War (1939–45).

WONDROUS SCIENCE of LIVING THINGS

Here are summarised the chief facts of Biology, the science which teaches the essential " oneness " of Life throughout its more than two million forms— ranging from microscopic bacteria up to Man himself.

Biology. This, in brief, is the "science of Life." But this study is so vast that it is broken up into departments of which the primary ones are botany, the science of plant life; and zoology, the science of animal life. Each natural scientist usually specialises further in some less wide field of study, such as anatomy, physiology, embryology, genetics. However, biology, as such, takes account of living things especially in their larger aspects, and seeks to harmonise and correlate all the divisions of this wide subject.

The old-time " natural history " was mainly a great accumulation of somewhat disconnected facts about plants and animals. Modern biology, on the other hand, takes account of the detailed facts mainly as they illustrate the principles and laws that govern life. We still use the term natural history, but keep it for the out-of-doors study of the habits, modes of life and activities of plants and animals as opposed to laboratory research.

At the bottom of the scale of life we cannot make a clear distinction between plant forms and animal forms, since these two kingdoms converge. Some simple organisms, which need a microscope to see them, possess some characteristics of both.

Most plants contain the green colouring matter known as chlorophyll; but some do not, because they do not manufacture their foodstuff (sugar), but get it ready made from other plants or from decaying matter. Chlorophyll is a catalyst (q.v.), a kind of substance which brings about chemical changes without itself altering, as far as we can see. When sunlight or some substitute falls upon the leaves of a green plant, carbon dioxide and water in the cells are changed into sugar, and this the plant turns into starch and other substances which it needs for its life and growth. This process is called photosynthesis (q.v.).

Among plants without chlorophyll are the parasites such as dodder, which live on other plants;

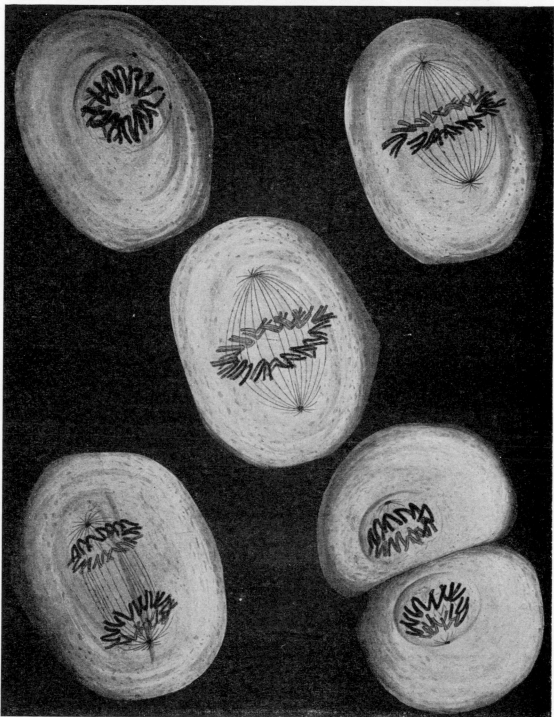

Here you see a new life developing from a fertilized cell. In the upper left-hand corner is a cell, enormously magnified; the sphere in the centre is the 'nucleus.' The black rods shaped like bent pins inside the nucleus are 'chromosomes,' made up of the substance 'chromatin,' half of which comes from the mother and half from the father. On the edge of the nucleus are two black specks, 'centrosomes.' In the upper right-hand corner the centrosomes have separated and an arrangement of fibres has been formed to which the chromosomes have attached themselves. The cell in the centre shows a further stage; each of the chromosome rods has split length-wise into equal halves! In the next cell at the left, half of each rod has been pulled away from the other half by those centrosome fibres, forming now two separate groups, each made up of mother and father elements. In the last picture the cell walls have split, forming two new cells. These will in turn split into two, and so again and again, and the new life will grow to become a plant, fish, bird, elephant, or a man, depending upon the nature of the parent chromatin.

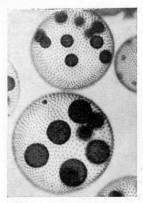

Specimens of volvox globator, representing a stage in life higher than a one-celled animal like the amoeba. The spheres are colonies of plants.

and the fungi, which get their nourishment from decaying matter. This is an aspect of biochemistry (q.v.), but as yet no chemist has been able to repeat the wonderful process artificially. Then—another difference—plants have the cell walls made of the woody substance cellulose, but animal cells are made of quite another material.

But despite their many differences, plants and animals are alike in some fundamental things. The living substance in both is protoplasm, and though it may differ in animals and plants, or even in different parts of the same organism, it contains always the same twelve chemical elements: carbon, oxygen, nitrogen, hydrogen, sulphur, calcium, magnesium, sodium, potassium, phosphorus, chlorine and iron. It may contain others, including copper. All forms of protoplasm are sensitive to certain outside influences, such as touch, or temperature changes.

All living organisms, whether plant or animal, feed and grow. They all " breathe," in the sense that they take in oxygen and give off carbon dioxide. They are all made up of cells—some have only a single cell— and reproduce themselves by one cell dividing to form two cells, and so on.

We have seen that sunlight and water were necessary to enable plants to manufacture sugar. They are necessary for animal life, also, since protoplasm is largely made up of water; and sunlight is the only source of energy for plant growth, on which animals depend directly or indirectly for food. The general essentials for life are light and warmth, an atmosphere, and water or moisture. But even here we have to allow for exceptions, for some lowly forms of life can exist without oxygen obtained from the air; some can bear being frozen, and others are none the worse for being dried and shrivelled up.

In fact, the biologist has found out that life is so stubborn that it can exist in conditions where one would think it quite impossible. In Arctic regions, where the ground in winter is frozen many feet deep, the coming of the brief summer will bring a myriad insects and plants to life. Russian scientists who camped on an ice floe at the North Pole discovered that the icy sea was plentifully supplied with plankton, the tiny forms of animal life on which fishes feed. The plankton, in turn, fed on tiny plants, certain forms of algae.

In general the greatest variety and wealth of plant life is on land; but the sea holds the greatest abundance and multiplicity of animal life. The liberal vegetation in the fields and woods provides the basic food supply for animal life—in our own country, for insects, birds mice and other small mammals, rabbits, and squirrels. Indirectly, plant life furnishes food for the predaceous animals which live on their smaller or less fierce brethren. These inter-relations of life are more complicated in tropical regions, where vegetation is more luxuriant and dense, and where the warmth and moisture combine to further the growth of insects, birds and animals in a bewildering variety. Here the web of life is so intricate as to baffle imagination.

In the sea all is different. While there is often much plant life in the form of seaweeds (flowerless plants), especially along rocky shores, the wealth of plant life of the open sea consists of tiny forms only to be seen with the microscope, especially the diatoms whose flinty skeletons, though so small, form deep and vast beds of ooze upon the ocean floor.

THE STORY OF THE TRANSMISSION OF LIFE

IN thinking of living things it is most important to realize that they are all made up of tiny units of protoplasm which we call ' cells.' These cells are of many kinds, each with a special task to perform. There are blood cells to carry oxygen from the lungs to all parts of the body, muscle cells for movement, gland cells to produce digestive juices, nerve cells to convey messages to and fro. But all of the cells that form a plant or an animal have come from a single cell at the beginning of its life. By a beautiful and mysterious process this single cell divides into two, and each of these into two—always two—and so on, until there have been formed the millions and millions of cells that make up its body.

Within the walls of each cell is a nucleus containing tiny threads of a substance called ' chromatin.' This chromatin is the most wonderful of all living matter, for it controls all life. The picture in the preceding page shows how the chromatin threads form tiny rods, which split in halves. It shows how these halves divide into two equal groups, and how each of these groups becomes the centre of a new cell. The cells of an acorn multiply into a giant oak in just this way, and when you use up muscle cells in work or in play, new cells to take their place are produced in the same manner.

But more wonderful still is the process at the beginning of a new life which keeps the vital flame burning. Consider a flowering plant, for instance. Down in the flowers, sheltered from harm, are many tiny delicate egg cells—the mother cells. A gust of wind or an insect roving in search of nectar, brings to one of these a pollen grain from another flower. This pollen grain is the father cell. Left alone by themselves the mother cell and the father cell would die. But now the chromatin in the tiny father cell, following a mysterious ' instinct ' which lies at the very heart of life's secret, grows down into the flower and unites with the chromatin of the mother egg cell, and fertilizes it. At that moment the new life of the plant begins. The fertilized cell divides again and again, as described above, until it forms the tiny embryo plant, which lies folded up within the seed and is ready to unfold and grow when the seed germinates.

The process is similar among animals—a single tiny male cell penetrates and fertilizes an egg cell, and causes it to develop into a new animal. Half of the chromatin in that first fertilized cell is given by the mother and half by the father. That is why the new life resembles both parents. As the cells go on dividing, each of them has material from both of the parents.

Can you think of anything more wonderful than this strange power, locked up in a cell so small that the eye cannot see it—the power to multiply and create bone and muscle, nerves and brain, the power to create new life, and to carry out to that new life those complex details of face, features, complexion, and even of mind and character which the parents possessed ?

Through geological changes in the earth's configuration, such beds of diatomaceous material are now found inland. One in Germany, 150 feet thick, provides the material known as kieselguhr (pron. kē'zl-goor), used as a polishing powder, and as the absorbent material in making dynamite.

There are animals everywhere in the sea. Even the colder seas are populated by immense numbers in great variety. Along the rocky shore, or by

LUMINOUS FISH OF THE DEPTHS
In the dark ocean depths live luminous fish, one class of which, Photo-blephron (above), is found off Banda Island in the Netherlands East Indies. To obscure its light when necessary it is provided with a curtain of pigment to draw over it. There are luminous sharks, too, at depths of 500 to 1,500 fathoms (3,000 to 9,000 feet).

big fish are marine ones, a few (such as the sturgeon) are found in our bigger rivers. Biology shows us many contrasts such as these. Most of the life of the sea is fed ultimately by the tiny plant forms that grow and live near the surface. Small sea creatures feed upon these, and bigger fish eat the smaller ones.

So it goes, through the scale of marine life. But here again we have contrasts, for some of the whales (these, like the dolphins, are mammals and not fishes) feed upon tiny creatures, which they sift out from sea water through their whale-bone strainers. Other kinds of whale eat cuttlefish; and others still attack fellow members of their own order, the Cetaceans, as well as seals.

Biology, as we have said, has a number of important branches. A few words upon the chief divisions will be helpful. *Embryology* is the study of the reproduction and development of animals and plants—from the spore or seed or egg or embryo to the adult creature. Though all forms originate from a single cell, the manner of their coming into being, and their later development, presents amazing differences.

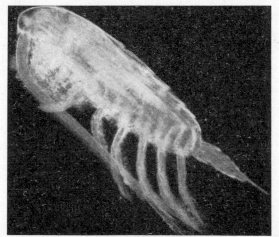

muddy or sandy beaches, there are those which live near tide level—crabs and the small crustaceans we see scurrying about as the water comes up. The open sea has many peculiar forms near the surface; there are still stranger forms near the bottom, even as deep down as five miles. In the icy cold and utter darkness of these great ocean depths, under the tremendous pressure of 5 tons on every square inch of surface, there live weird creatures unlike anything we can conceive, when thinking of ordinary fishes. Some of them have a mechanism for producing phosphorescent light.

Genetics is the branch dealing with the laws of inheritance. Gregor Mendel (*q.v.*) discovered some of these laws, but it was not till nearly half a century later, in 1900, that scientists realized the importance of Mendel's experiments. Since then men like Luther Burbank have applied these dis-

All the food and energy for this wonderful population at the sea bottom comes from or near the surface. We have already mentioned the tiny animals called plankton; there are tiny plant forms also, whose remains as they die (and the remains of fish which have fed upon other of these minute creatures). all fall to the bottom to make up the deep ooze we have mentioned. The chalk cliffs and downs of our own islands are built up of the shells and other remains of sea creatures which lived in long-past ages.

In the oceans there are living forms which have never made their way into our fresh water lakes and streams. Such are the starfishes, the jelly-fish family, most of the sharks, and a number of others. On the other hand we have some, such as the crayfish, which have near relatives in our rivers. Though most of the really

F. M Duncan: E A Botting

MARINE ANIMALS TOO SMALL TO SEE
Here are two classes of microscopic sea animals, whose functions vary widely. The upper one is Calanus finmarchieus, the shrimp-like creature that forms the chief food of whales. The lower photo shows Radiolarians, whose shells help to form the rocks of the sea. Both animals are here highly magnified, being invisible to the naked eye.

Geological Museum

ANCIENT FERN LIKE TODAY'S

This prehistoric fern, found in a coal seam in Somersetshire, tells us something of the vegetation that covered England long before the great Ice Age. The study of fossils (palaeontology) is a most fascinating pursuit, for it enables us to see how living forms of millions of years ago are linked to those which flourish at the present time.

regions where no daylight ever penetrates, things are altogether otherwise: the plants are those such as fungi, which have no leaf organs containing chlorophyll, since they do not make their own food by photosynthesis, but live on decaying matter. The animals include queer creatures, almost colourless and generally blind—worms, crustaceans and fishes, and the strange amphibious newt known as the proteus. Ecology is especially valuable to agriculture, since it teaches us how to preserve the balance of natural life in a region. By unwisely killing off certain insects or animals we may inadvertently destroy this balance and bring about a worse state of affairs !

Palaeontology is the branch of biology dealing with ancient life forms as shown by fossil remains. It is more often associated with geology, or the study of rocks, but very much has been learnt about the history of life in the world by examining the fossil remains which have come to light. We have mentioned the tiny sea forms found in chalk; on the other hand, palaeontology has revealed much about the gigantic land animals of long ago, such as lizards fifty feet long, enormous elephants preserved by the ice in Siberia, and giant mosses as big as present-day trees.

Physiology is the study of the properties, activities and functions of living things. At one time this study was devoted almost entirely to Man, and was mainly a part of medical study. With the general widening of biology, physiology was extended to the study of all living things. A fuller knowledge of plant physiology in recent years has brought enormous benefit to agricultural science.

Taxonomy (from Greek words meaning " arrangement " and " law ") is the name given to the branch of science devoted to the classification and orderly arrangement of living things in natural groups, showing the relationships which exist between them. It is probably more familiar to the reader in plant names than in those of animals. Thus the Lesser Celandine, one of the first of our

coveries to improving our domesticated animals and plants, to the great benefit of the world. In Russia agricultural scientists have begun to grow cotton plants which produce red or yellow and other coloured fibres instead of the familiar white cotton of America.

Ecology is the study of the relations of living organisms to their surroundings. We all know that certain types of plant or animal are found in some localities, where there are conditions not present in other places. Thus whole groups of plants, or " plant societies," inhabit marshy places; the birds and insects of the same region are specially adapted for life in such a region. Ecology also studies the manner in which organisms have adapted themselves to life in certain circumstances: an example is the study of the plant and animal life of caves and subterranean streams.

Near the mouth of caves the animals or plants may not differ very greatly from those found outside, but when we explore further, into the

S. V. Waters

DESTRUCTIVE FUNGUS OF THE WOODS

Quaintly shaped but harmless looking, these honey coloured fungi are flourishing on the stump of a tree which they have helped to kill. They are members of the parasitic group of fungi, getting their food from living matter—in this instance a tree. Their presence resulted in its gradual weakening and ultimate death.

spring flowers, has the name *Ficaria verna* : *Ficaria* is the generic name, or name of the genus ; *verna* is the specific name, or name of the species. There may be many genera (plural form of genus) in one family, and many species in one genus, each species being given a different specific name to distinguish it from others of the same genus. The family in this case is Ranunculaceae, which includes also the buttercup and the spearwort.

There is also the Greater Celandine, with the scientific name of *Chelidonium majus*; but this celandine belongs to the poppy family (Papaveraceae). Popular names are given generally because of some outside

Thos. Fall

DOGS, BUT HOW DIFFERENT !
The streamlined racing greyhound of England is seen top right, while lower is the aristocratic Pekingese. Despite the great and obvious difference between these animals, they are only breeding variations of the same genus, Canis.

Sub-order Phaneroglossa (having a tongue); in the Order Anura, of tail-less amphibians; in the Class Amphibia, including frogs, toads and salamanders; in the Sub-phylum Vertebrata (backboned animals); in the Phylum Chordata (backboned animals and their kin); and, finally, in the Kingdom Animalia (all animals).

Remember that these are not mere names: at every step they tell us of the relationship of the frog—to other amphibians, especially those having no tails; and to other backboned animals; and they point to the frog's place in the wider scheme of the animal kingdom. The genus-and-species naming of particular kinds of animal and plant is called the binomial or " two-name " classification. Until Carl von Linné, the eminent Swedish naturalist, introduced this way of naming plants and animals, there was no precise method of identifying them. Naturalists in different places might be using quite different names for the same individual, which was very confusing when they tried to share their knowledge. Linné, whose name is often given in its Latinised form of Linnaeus, was a great explorer, visiting America, Asia and Africa. His system is the basis of present-day classification.

resemblance or character of the flower; but scientific names show the *real* relationship of the plant, to others of the same family, when the more important characters are considered. Just two examples from the animal kingdom will help us: the common British frog is *Rana temporaria*; its relative which is bred in France for food is *Rana esculenta*. You will have noticed that it is usual to write the name of the genus with a capital letter, but not so in the case of the species.

If we go higher in the frog's relationship we find that it is classed in the Family Ranidae (true frogs); in the

FROM JUNGLE FOWL TO DOMESTIC BREEDS
Every one of the numerous breeds of domestic fowl, widely different in appearance as some of them are, is derived from the Indian jungle fowl (left). In the centre is a gamecock, which in some countries is still bred for fighting and closely resembles the jungle fowl in a number of details. Vastly different is the Buff Orpington (right).

Birch. With its grey bark, slender spreading branches and delicate foliage, this tree, widely distributed through Europe, North America, and Asia, is both beautiful and graceful. There are several species of birch, most of them hardy and rapid of growth. The wood is close-grained, often with a beautiful " figure," and is used for making furniture and for ornamental and other purposes; it also makes excellent fuel.

The bark is much more durable than the wood because it is proof against water, and long after the fallen trunks have rotted away the encircling bark remains sound. Baskets, boxes, and many other articles are made from the bark, including the birch canoes of the North American Indians. Large sheets of birch bark are used for roofing purposes in Scandinavia.

The silver birch is well named, for if you were to go into the woods to search for it you would know it at sight by its silvery bark, marked with dark horizontal lines. It is always thin, for as the tree grows the older bark peels off in long papery strips, leaving exposed the fresh young bark that meanwhile has formed underneath it.

Two kinds of birch are found in England, the species *Betula alba* being divided into the common birch, *B. pubescens*, and the true silver birch, *B. pendula*. The bark of the latter usually becomes dark and rugged for three or four feet from the ground. In the common birch the bark is smooth and reddish at the base. In the silver birch the ends of the branches tend to hang down, so that it has a very beautiful drooping appearance. When these branches are very long and feathery the tree is known as the weeping birch.

The leaves are small, and roughly triangular in shape, with uneven saw-like edges and a sharp point. In autumn they become golden yellow. The buds of the male catkins may be seen in winter like twin fingers at the tips of the twigs. In spring these develop into long tails. About the same time the leaves begin to appear, and among them the female catkins. The latter are much smaller than the males, and at first stand upright, but later they thicken and hang down; and in autumn they remain after the leaves have fallen. As these female catkins are shaken by the winter winds they gradually shed their tiny winged seeds.

H. Bastin

SILVER BIRCH : BEAUTY OF THE WOODLANDS

Though small in girth, the white or silver birch (Betula pendula) grows to a height of fifty feet ; its drooping masses of foliage, which never entirely hides the branches, make a lovely cloak for its slender form. On the left above, the sharply-toothed, wedge-shaped leaves are seen ; they are arranged spirally on the stem. Beneath are the birch's male catkins, which are in pairs and hang downwards : the female catkins at first stand upright, but droop later.

CONTRASTS *in the* FEATHERED WORLD

Perky sparrow and trilling skylark, brilliant humming bird and gaunt vulture :
the birds each have their own kind of life to lead, their own homes to make,
their own food to find.   Here is the story of the feathered kingdom.

Birds. All creatures which bear feathers are birds. Feathers are out-growths from the skin, like the scales of reptiles or the hairs of mammals, but they are much more beautiful adaptations to the life which birds lead. Birds, with the fishes, reptiles, amphibians, and mammals, make up the division of the animal kingdom known as Vertebrates or back-boned animals.

On this perky house-sparrow the black of the chin and head contrasts strongly with the white of the cheeks.

Because of the modifications necessary for flight, however, the backbone of a bird, like the rest of its skeleton, seems very different from those of the other vertebrates. If you examine the skeleton of a bird and compare it with that of a reptile or a mammal, you are impressed by the way Nature adjusts structures to suit different needs. Birds are believed to have evolved from a reptile-like ancestor; and the differences in their structure which seem so great today have been brought about by the birds learning to fly. Birds now do not have teeth, but many fossil birds had teeth.

A bird is a flying machine, and its skeleton is its framework ; and Nature has transformed each part to adapt it to the bird's needs. The backbone, for example, has been shortened, and the separate vertebrae of the trunk have been fused with one another and with the pelvis to give it greater strength. The ribs are firmly attached to the backbone and also to the breastbone, and they have overlapping appendages to give the trunk great solidity. All the bones are hollow, to make them light but strong.

In an aeroplane the engines and the passengers and all the heavy parts are placed as near the centre of gravity as possible, and with a bird it is the same. The outlying parts, such as the head and tail, wings and legs, are extremely light, and the heavy muscles that work them are attached to the trunk,

only the tendons extending to the outermost parts. When one examines the skull one is immediately impressed with the thinness of the bones. There are no teeth, and the jaws, therefore, need not be heavy; for the work of chewing, which would require muscles and weighty bones, is performed by the gizzard, a modified portion of the stomach.

When we examine a bird's tail, we see that the numerous vertebrae which in a reptile make up the tail are here shortened and fused into one little bone called the *pygostyle*. It is noticeable that the largest muscles of the legs are located about the thigh bones, which are held close against the trunk and thus near the centre of gravity. As if to make up for the shortening of the leg which this position causes, the ankle and foot bones are fused and drawn out into a long slender bone called the *tarsus*, which is the only part of the leg that is usually not covered with feathers, and to which the toes are attached.

A bird's wing is the arm or front leg modified for the purpose of flight; few heavy muscles are borne upon it. The strong muscles that manipulate the wings are attached to the keel of the breastbone, and are thus brought close to the centre of gravity. The unnecessary bones of the wrist and hand are fused, only one finger remaining well developed. Thus the portions which were originally reptilian have been so transformed as to make the bird a perfect flying machine.

Another great difference between birds and reptiles is that birds, in common with mammals, are warm-blooded animals. The warm-blooded animals have a constant temperature, while the temperature of the cold-blooded animals varies with that of their environment. It is for this reason that reptiles become very sluggish in cold weather, a characteristic that would not fit in well with the needs of a flying bird.

We may assume, therefore, that one of the most important changes that took place in the development from the reptile was the change from a cold-blooded to a warm-blooded condition. This change brought with it many accompanying changes in the life of the bird, for it ordained that the bird's eggs, also, should be maintained at a constant temperature, and that the temperature of the young should not fall below normal. This resulted in the need for " incubation " of eggs, the building of

British Museum

A BIRD WITH TEETH

These fossil remains of an archaeopteryx (Greek word meaning ancient wing) show that it had teeth as well as a beak, and fingers and feathers on its wings. It was a link between modern birds and those ancient reptiles we know only as fossils, being half a lizard.

Birds' eyes are equipped with a third eyelid, so that they can see without being dazzled. This can be observed in the Harpy Eagle, above.

hibernate during cold weather. It is also the reason for their enormous appetites. It is because Nature developed in them a bodily temperature much higher than that of Man that their life processes go on at a much more rapid rate, causing their ceaseless search for food.

The eyes of birds are very highly developed, so that they can see great distances and follow rapidly moving objects. Thus a swallow swooping through the air is able to keep its eyes on a tiny insect which is also moving rapidly. The bird, like many mammals, has a third eyelid which is blinked rapidly to clean the surface of the eye. The eagle or vulture, soaring almost out of sight in the air, can shade its eye when flying into the strong sun, and yet still see. And these and other birds of prey will dart with the speed of a bullet to a tiny object a human eye would hardly notice at a distance of 100 ft. Birds can adjust their eyes for different distances quicker than can other animals, and in general their powers of vision are far greater than ours.

Their never-ending search for food gives some birds great economic value, in keeping down hoards of insects. "Without birds, not only would successful agriculture be impossible, but the destruction of the greater part of the vegetation would follow." We can appreciate the meaning of this statement by a famous naturalist if we stop to consider the great reproductive capacity of most insects, particularly those that feed upon vegetation and are therefore dangerous to crops.

nests, and the care of the young— duties which occupy so much of the bird's life.

This is likewise one of the reasons for the comings and goings, or the "migration," of birds, which makes their study so fascinating; for if they were still cold-blooded animals they would undoubtedly

The Colorado beetle which is so destructive to potato plants, if left undisturbed, is capable of producing 60 million offspring in a single season— not, of course, all its direct children, but some of them its grand-, even great-grand-children, since there are several generations a year under favourable conditions. A common plant aphis, which brings forth living young, has such a short life cycle that there may be 13 generations in a single season; and inasmuch as each female brings forth at least 50 young, the number in the 13th generation alone would be a million multiplied by a million six times and then by 10. If left undisturbed and given plenty of food, it would take any insect only a few years completely to cover the earth with its offspring. The need of birds and of many other enemies of insects is, therefore, very apparent.

The astonishing number of insects consumed by birds has been revealed by scientists in several ways, including examination of the contents of crops and stomachs of birds that have been shot while feeding; and by watching birds at their nests and observing the food brought to the young. An American bird called the scarlet tanager was watched feeding in a tree infested with gipsy moths, and in 18 minutes was seen to consume 630 caterpillars.

A pair of great tits was once watched while they were feeding their family on the caterpillars of the winter moth, which do an immense amount of damage to apple trees. In one hour the pair visited the apple trees 47 times and each time they carried back to their nest two or three caterpillars. A wren was seen to feed her young 38 times in an hour, and the food she brought them consisted of aphids, which suck the juice of plants ; caterpillars, which eat the leaves; and daddy-long-legs, the grubs of which destroy corn and grass by devouring the roots. Starlings, which feed largely on leather jackets (grubs of daddy-long-legs) and on wireworms (grubs of click beetles) which also do immense damage to crops, bring food to their young about 30 times in every hour, both parents cooperating.

The common sparrow, which is detested by farmers because it devours their grain, is a real benefactor at nesting time. Seeds are not a suitable food for its young, so it brings them caterpillars instead, and in this way destroys hundreds of these pests in a day. But probably the most remarkable case of

STRUCTURE OF BIRDS
The upper drawing shows the anatomy of the wing : a, humerus ; b, radius ; c, ulna ; d, hand ; e, bastard wing ; f, primary quills ; g, secondary quills. Below is the skeleton of a fowl showing the principal bones and joints. The figures indicate the toes.

feeding on record is that of a wren, which fed its young 1,217 times in 15 hours and 45 minutes.

It is not only by the destruction of insects that birds play an important part in the economy of Man. Many of them derive a large part of their food from the seeds of weeds, and so help in keeping down these also. Here again the amount which they consume is remarkable. From the crops of two seed-eating birds were taken 1,700 and 5,000 weed seeds respectively.

Another way in which birds help Man in his pursuit of agriculture is by eating the small rodents which are very destructive to grain and forage

E. Hosking
ROBIN REDBREAST AND WREN
Robins are amongst the most useful of our birds for they eat noxious insects ; the one above has a caterpillar in his beak. At the top right, a wren, one of the smallest of our birds, climbs back into her neatly-fashioned nest with a daddy-long-legs for her evening meal.

few that usually prove troublesome at certain seasons of the year. Most birds, for example, are fond of small fruits, so that strawberries, raspberries and cherries often suffer from their plundering. Where there is a plentiful supply of wild fruits, however, the cultivated fruits are sometimes left alone. Other birds, that customarily feed upon weed seed, often prove destructive in grain fields, so that it is necessary to frighten them away. Crows, and some hawks, are enemies of the poulterer and the game breeder, but they serve an important function as destroyers of vermin which would otherwise kill far more poultry than the birds themselves ever do.

As soon as one begins to observe birds one discovers that the different kinds are mostly found in different surroundings. Some, like the robin and thrush, are widely distributed in woodlands, orchards, and gardens throughout the country, while others are restricted to certain localities or to particular environments. Thus the nightingale nests only in the southern half of England, and the grouse is to be found only on the heather-clad moors. If we wish to see moorhens and coots we go

crops, and which frequently do much general damage in farm and garden. The common field mouse is so prolific that in five years, if all the offspring of a single pair lived, they would number several millions. A check upon their numbers is provided by the hawks and owls.

Each hawk or owl requires the equivalent of a good many mice a day in order to live, or several thousands a year. These birds, therefore, have a considerable money value to the farmer upon whose land they take up residence. It is a noteworthy fact that following so-called plagues of mice, when these pests overrun districts by the thousands, there is always a flight of owls, usually of the short-eared species. Nature thus regains her balance.

Certain birds, such as grouse, snipe, pheasants, woodcock, ducks and geese seem to serve Man best by providing him with food. None of them is particularly important as a destroyer of insects, and many of them become harmful to agriculture if they occur in large numbers.

Although practically all birds are valuable to Man in some one of the ways mentioned, there are a

W. A. Ramsay
SCREECH-OWL AND HIS DINNER
It is generally thought that all owls hoot, but the word hardly describes the cry of the barn-owl or screech-owl. The screech-owl seen here carries his dinner—a vole—in his beak. The bird is the best known of all our owls.

SWALLOWS READY TO MIGRATE

Such a scene as this may be seen in the south of England in late autumn. The swallows are preparing for their winter migration to a more temperate clime, probably North Africa. They have lined up on telegraph wires and soon they will be off, not to return until spring comes to Britain again.

of North and South America or between those of Europe and Africa than between those of Europe and North America.

When we study the birds of the East Indian Islands we discover some of the strangest facts of distribution, for some of the islands lie in the Australian region and some in the Indian, and the line between the two is very sharp. Thus the islands of Bali and Lombok (in the Malay Archipelago just east of Java), though but 20 miles apart differ as greatly in their animal life as do Africa and South America, suggesting that the two islands had never been united and that the deep strait separating them marked the dividing line between the Australian continent and that of Asia—Bali belonging to Asia and Lombok to Australia.

In consideration of the geographical distribution of birds, the home of each species is considered to be that place where it builds its nest and raises its young, but many species migrate with the change of seasons from one region to another. Many of our nesting birds spend the winter in Africa.

The swallow that visits Britain in summer travels 5,000 miles over land and sea to his winter home in South Africa. The golden plover wings a 2,000-mile flight over the Atlantic from Labrador and Nova Scotia to South America without a stop; while his relatives on the Pacific coast each year travel the 2,000 miles from Alaska to the Hawaiian Islands, and back again. Not all birds migrate beyond our shores, for our woodpeckers, nut-hatches, tits, grouse, and others are permanent residents. But swallows, swifts, ducks, warblers, fly-catchers, thrushes, and many other species join the yearly migration.

During the winter the birds travel about in scattered groups searching for food, the sexes sometimes in different flocks, as often in the case of the chaffinch. With the approach of spring the birds begin to feel the urge to move northward. Southern birds, of course, as for instance those migrating from southern to northern Australia in autumn, move southwards. The males are usually the first to start north, and arrive on the nesting grounds from a few days to a few weeks before the females. Once arrived, the males usually select the general locations where they wish to nest, and drive all rival males from these areas; at the same time they try to entice the females to remain and to mate with them. As a rule, birds nest at the northernmost point of their migrations.

Even birds which do not migrate, and are therefore called residents, often move from one part of a country to another. Thus the curlew, which mates and spends the summer on the upland moors, commonly comes down to the shore to live in

to the ponds; and if we wish to see skylarks, meadow pipits, and lapwings we go to the upland fields. The study of local distribution offers many interesting problems to the amateur as well as to the scientific naturalist.

The study of the distribution of birds over the surface of the earth, or their geographical distribution, offers many other fascinating problems. If the world could be charted according to its families of birds rather than according to its races of people or its governments, it would make a strange map, because all the birds of the Northern Hemisphere are more closely interrelated than are the birds of adjacent islands of the East Indies.

Six main divisions or geographical regions have been recognized by naturalists when dealing with birds: New Zealand, Australian, Neo-tropical (South America), Indian, African, and Palaearctic (North America, Europe and Northern Asia). While a few birds are found all over the world, and others in two or more of these regions, the vast majority of species and many whole families are restricted to some one of these geographical regions. In travelling round the world, therefore, one would expect to find greater difference between the birds

winter. Often a male returns to the same spot year after year, and frequently his former mate returns also and they remate for another year. This may occur until the death of one bird, when the surviving member ordinarily finds a new mate and often returns to the same nesting site.

Although monogamy, or a single mating for the year, is the rule, a few birds, akin to our common poultry, such as the turkey, the grouse, the pheasant, and others, are regularly polygamous—that is, each male is mated to several females. Polygamy occasionally occurs among other birds, especially the wrens and blackbirds. Cuckoos do not have permanent mates, even for a single season, as they do not take care of their own young but lay their eggs in other birds' nests. A bird of tropical America, called the Anis, is regularly communistic—that is, the members of this species build a common nest in which several females lay their eggs, and all care for the young.

Mating is never accomplished without a more or less elaborate courtship. It is during this period that the birds are seen and heard to the best advantage, for the males try to make themselves as conspicuous as possible, both by their songs and by the display of their plumage. Of course, all birds do not sing, and a few—such as the storks, the pelicans, and the frigate birds—seem to be voiceless in adult life. True song is confined to the higher families of birds and reaches its best development among the thrushes.

The vocal organs of a bird are somewhat different from those of a man, for instead of having vocal cords located in the larynx at the upper end of the trachea or windpipe, they have simple membranes which vibrate, located at the lower end of the trachea in a structure called the syrinx. The shape of this structure and the number of muscles which control the tension of the membranes vary with the different families and produce the different songs.

Apart from songs we have other sounds. The woodpeckers produce a loud vibrating sound by

The males of t... turkey (lower)... their intended... beautif...

SOME FINE SPECIMENS OF BRITISH BIRDS' EGGS

Painted specially for this work by Percy J. Billinghurst

The normal position of eggs in a nest is with their small ends pointing inwards; thus they occupy the minimum space, making it easy for the sitting bird to cover them. The space occupied would be much greater if the small ends pointed outwards. When there is no nest and the egg is laid on a bare ledge of rock from which the wind might roll it, as in the case of the common guillemot, the egg is very much elongated so that instead of being rolled away when disturbed it merely spins round. When eggs are laid on pebbles, or sand, as in the case of the ringed plover, their colouring and marking make them practically indistinguishable.
A key to this plate appears overlea...

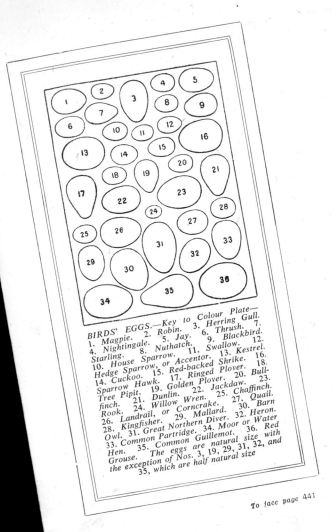

To face page 441

E. J. Hosking

SPARROW'S ROUGH NEST

Sparrows build their nests wherever there is a solid foundation, as in this nesting-box, where the material consists chiefly of feathers. In building, birds do not always use those materials which are nearest at hand but may go quite a distance to get those they fancy.

already selected the nesting area, the female usually selects the exact nesting site, and builds the nest, the male standing guard near by or accompanying her in her search for nesting material, and permitting no other male bird to approach within his territory. The character of the nest depends upon the species of bird and its zoological family.

When birds evolved from their reptilian ancestors they at first laid their eggs as do the turtles and lizards today, burying them in the sand or hiding them in holes in trees. But as they became warm-blooded creatures and the need for incubation arose to keep the eggs at a constant temperature, it was necessary to lay the eggs above ground so that they could be brought into contact with the bird's body. At first the birds probably did not even scratch depressions to keep the eggs from rolling about, but laid them on the flat ground. The next stage was doubtless the scratching of depressions to keep the eggs from rolling, and we find this stage represented today by the nests of some of the plovers.

An advance from this stage was the addition of a lining to the depression, such as in the nests of the lapwing. Such nests, however, give little protection against long spells of wet weather, or against enemies. It is easy to imagine that the birds which learned to raise their nests above the ground, first on heaps of vegetation and then in bushes and trees, were more successful in raising their young.

It is not difficult to select from the nests built by birds today a series which shows the probable

evolution of nest architecture, from the crudest to the most elaborate. Thus, the simplest platforms of sticks are built in trees by some pigeons and the herons, while the crows and hawks build more substantial structures of sticks with deeper hollows to hold the eggs and usually with linings of softer materials. Continuing up the scale we find twigs discarded for finer and softer materials, until we come to nests which are made almost entirely of woolly substances.

The highest type of nest is that of the weaver bird, with its long overhanging tube entrance; but those of our longtailed tit, golden-crested wren, and reed warbler are very wonderful structures. Many of the simpler nests, too, show specializations. The nest of the humming-bird and that of the chaffinch, for example, are covered on the outside with lichens and bits of bark, so that they resemble the surface of the tree in whose branches they are built.

In selecting their nesting material birds ordinarily take that which is nearest at hand, so long as it conforms to the type of the nest which that species builds. Field birds ordinarily use grasses and hair, woodland birds use leaves and rootlets, and marsh birds use sedges and reeds, while birds nesting in ready-made holes often use no lining.

The time taken to build a nest depends upon how much time the bird has before its first egg is ready to be laid. With ordinary birds the time required is about a week; but there have been instances—as when the first nest has been destroyed and the eggs are ready to be laid—of birds building their entire nests in a day. Occasionally birds that are permanent residents, or that arrive early in the spring, begin their nests long before eggs are due to be laid; they may spend several weeks in building a structure that could be completed in a few days if necessary. At times certain birds simply mend old nests left over from the year before.

The eggs of birds are among the most beautiful creations of all Nature. They vary in colour from those that are as white as snow to those that are almost black; but the majority have a delicate ground colour and are spotted or streaked with darker colours.

Many theories have been advanced to account for the coloration of eggs. It is almost certain that the colour, as originally developed, was of some value to the eggs, probably in rendering them less conspicuous; for eggs like those of the woodpeckers and kingfishers, that are laid in dark holes where the colour would not be seen, are pure white. Eggs such as those of the plovers and terns, on the other hand, that are laid in exposed places with no protecting nest, are coloured like the soil or gravel and are very difficult to find. The majority of eggs, however, that are laid in nests, seem to be conspicuously marked rather than otherwise, for they are white or some light tint in ground colour. In such nests there is no need for protectively coloured eggs, because the bird ordinarily selects a site where the nest will not be readily seen. So it has come about that, with the evolution of nests, the need for

ARCHITECTURE IN THE FEATHERED WORLD

A. R. Thompson; F. Jefferson; S. Crook; I. M. Thomson

Birds have widely-differing ideas as to what makes a comfortable home, as may be seen from the selection of nests illustrated in this page. The nightjar (1) builds no nest and lays her eggs on the open ground. The ringed plover (2) has primitive notions of architecture, and only scrapes a hole in sand or shingle. The linnet (3) makes an ordinary nest of twigs and grass lined with wool. The reed-warbler (4) fashions what seems to us a rather unsafe home, for it is built around swaying reeds well above the ground. The golden-crested wren (5) slings its nest from a branch. The long-tailed tit (6) builds a domed nest of moss, covered with lichen and lined with feathers.

protectively coloured eggs has disappeared, and the pigment has lost some of its quality, causing the many variegated but conspicuous eggs found today.

Ordinarily, one egg is laid each day, until the normal number for the species is complete; and this number varies according to the dangers to which the eggs and young are exposed. Many sea birds that nest on very high cliffs lay but a single egg, while the majority of game birds and water fowl, that have numerous enemies, lay from 10 to 20. The usual number for most birds is from three to five in each brood.

The size of eggs is fixed for each species. It varies from that of the humming-bird, little bigger than a pea, to that of the ostrich, which is between five and six inches in diameter. Occasionally, with very old domestic fowls or at the close of the egg-laying period, very small eggs are laid. Occasionally also two or even three eggs become enclosed in a single shell, forming the so-called " double-yolked eggs." In general the size of the eggs varies with the size of the bird, but birds whose young are hatched blind and helpless lay much smaller eggs than those whose young are able to run about when hatched.

With the laying of the last egg most birds begin to incubate, but a few, like the owls, begin to in-cubate with the laying of the first egg, causing the young to hatch on different days. The time required for eggs varies with the size of the egg, though for some reason a few small eggs require a longer time than some of the larger ones. While the eggs of the white-throat require but 12 days, and the eggs of the robin but 14, the eggs of the humming-bird require 15 days to hatch. Hens' eggs require 21 days, ducks' 27, and geese's 35. In addition to being maintained at a constant temperature by the heat of the bird's body, the eggs are regularly turned by the old bird, and occasionally moistened to keep the pores in the shell open and the membranes which line the shell moist so that the embryo can breathe.

With most birds the work of incubation is performed entirely by the female, the male either feeding her on the nest or standing guard by the nest while she flies off to feed. With some species, usually those in which the males are as dully coloured as the females, the males share the duties of incubation; the cock birds of some species actually sit most of the time, whilst the hen does the foraging.

There are two types of young birds—those that remain helpless in the nest for some time, and those that can run about as soon as hatched. The first type are hatched blind and helpless, with only a scant covering of down. Their parents build well-formed nests in which they remain for varying lengths of time—from a week in such ground nesting species as the skylark, to a year in such birds of flight as the condor and the wandering albatross. The young of the second type, like those of the domestic fowl, are fully covered with down when hatched, have their eyes open almost immediately, and are able to follow their parents about in their search for food. The parents must, of course, be birds that live on the ground or in the water.

Most young birds are fed at first on partially digested food brought up from the crop of the parent bird. Doves, petrels, albatrosses, and a few other birds continue this method of feeding as long as the young require care; but the majority of birds soon begin to bring fresh food to the young. This is usually carried in the bills or in the talons of the old birds; but to this, as to all rules, there are again exceptions.

Most parent birds put the food into the open mouths of their young, and are careful to pop it well into the throat so that it cannot fail to go down. The young pigeon, however, thrusts its head into the open mouth of its parent and sucks a milky fluid secreted in the crop of the old bird. The young cormorant acts similarly, but

E. J. Hosking

ENJOYING A READY-MADE HOME

Most nest-building birds show considerable ingenuity in avoiding conspicuous sites for their homes, preferring these to be as little in evidence as possible. Others, less scared of human beings and possible enemies in general, will eagerly occupy a nest-box such as this, and within its snug confines will rear a family. Its exposed position counts less than its ready-made usefulness. Sparrows are in occupation here.

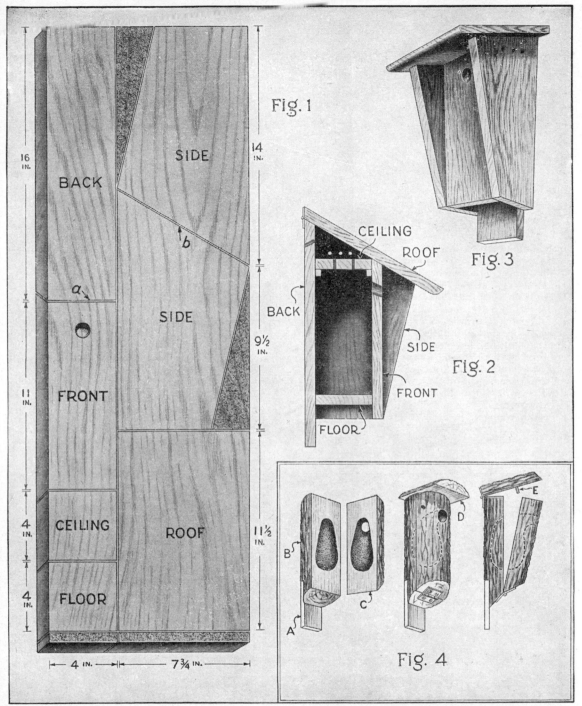

Fig. 1

SIDE

BACK

14 IN.

16 IN.

SIDE

b

a

FRONT

9½ IN.

11 IN.

CEILING

ROOF

11½ IN.

FLOOR

4 IN.

4 IN.

4 IN.

7¾ IN.

CEILING

ROOF

BACK

SIDE

FRONT

FLOOR

Fig. 2

Fig. 3

A   B   C   D   E

Fig. 4

The first of these is designed for wrens. Notice in Fig. 1 that all the parts of this house could be cut out of a single 3-foot board. It might be easier to procure *two* boards, one 8 in. wide, one 4½ in. wide, and plane them to the proper width. The drawings make the design clear. The saw-cut marked *a* in Fig. 1 must be made at an angle of about 60 degrees. The two sides are identical and the difference between the long edge (14 in.) and the short edge (9½ in.) will make the angle of the saw-cut marked *b* almost exactly 60 degrees. Figs. 2 and 3 show how the parts are assembled. Distance between ceiling and floor should be about 8½ in. The ceiling should rest on cleats so that, when the hinged roof is raised, the ceiling can be removed when necessary. The entrance hole for the wrens must not be more than 1¼ in. in diameter, to prevent larger birds from trespassing, and it should slope upward so that rain will not run in. Ventilating holes around the top and through the ceiling will help to keep the house cool in hot weather. Fig. 4 shows another type, made by splitting and hollowing out a small log. The board A is used to fasten the house to a post. B and C are hinged at the bottom; the roof D holds the two together at the top by means of the short pin E.

After feeding, the parent bird inspects the mouths of the young, which usually remain wide open, and if any food remains unswallowed she removes it and gives it to one of the other young. As stated earlier, the amount of food taken by young birds is surprising, for they require from one-half of their own weight to their full weight in food each day in order to grow. To keep up the supply both parents work from early morning until nearly dark. In a few instances, like that of the humming-bird, the male bird never assists in the care of the young;

instead of milky fluid it takes tit-bits of half-digested fish from its mother's crop.

The food of most young birds consists of insects at first, this being varied later by fruits or seeds. The insects are placed far down into the throats of the young birds, which normally stretch up their necks and open their mouths widely at the approach of their parents. Swallowing is entirely automatic, and unless food is placed beyond the base of the tongue, the muscles do not act and the food remains in the open mouth unswallowed. There is likewise a nervous adjustment to prevent the young from being overfed, for after each has received sufficient food, the throat muscles refuse to work and any further food remains unswallowed.

H. Mortimer Batten; W. F. Cassie

TABLE MANNERS DIFFER

As there are many different bird-foods, so there are ways of feeding. The young starling above, with wide-open beak, is just waiting for its parent to push food into its mouth. The young of some birds help themselves from the parent's gullet ; a shag is seen (top left) feeding in this fashion, which the young cormorant also adopts.

but in most cases the male is even more industrious than the female. After each feeding the nest is scrupulously cleaned, except with flesh-eating and fish-eating birds.

A few young birds of the helpless type, such as kingfishers and swifts, are absolutely naked when hatched, but the majority have a scant covering of down on the back and on the top of the head. Feather growth starts immediately, and within a week or 10 days the majority of small birds are fully covered with feathers, and within 10 days or two weeks are able to fly. The largest birds of flight, however—the condor and the albatross—do not learn to fly for nearly a year.

The first covering of all young birds is called the nestling plumage. The covering of the fledgling is called the juvenile plumage, and it is worn only a short time after leaving the nest. It is then replaced by the first winter plumage. These feathers are worn throughout the winter ; but, in the case of most birds, towards spring they are replaced by the first breeding or nuptial plumage. This is replaced in the autumn by the winter plumage.

The gradual change from one plumage to another is called a moult. When a bird is in good health only a few of its feathers are shed at a time, and these are replaced before

E. J. Bedford

THE OWL PUFFED-UP

Some birds have a strange habit of ruffling-up their feathers when angry or alarmed, as this young long-eared owl. The whitish, downy breast-feathers are evidence of its youth. As is customary with most birds, it will change its plumage gradually by moulting.

others are shed, the whole process requiring from one to two months. The moult begins at a definite place on the bird's body, and the feathers are lost in a regular order.

Thus, in the wing, the first feather to be lost is always the innermost primary feather, and when the new feather replacing it is about half-grown, the next one is shed; and so on, so that the bird is never deprived of the power of flight. But in a few swimming and diving birds such as the mallard or wild duck, that are not entirely dependent upon their wings for escape, all of the flight quills are shed at one time, and for a period the birds are unable to fly. This

J. T. Newman; A. H. Willford

READY FOR THE FIRST VENTURE
Here we see a group of young blackbirds, on the great day when they must try their wings for the first time, poised on the edge of their nest. On the left, a newly-hatched sandpiper leaves its nest.

is, however, a quite exceptional form of moulting. The summer moulting season as a rule begins in August and continues through a part of September. This is the most difficult season of the year to study birds, because during the moult they stop singing and seek seclusion, many species seeming to disappear altogether. During this moult every bird changes every feather on its body, and most birds that have been brightly coloured during the breeding season now assume sober colours, usually like those of the female. For example, the male linnet, which during the summer has a red breast, appears with a buff breast like the female. During the spring moult, only such feathers are replaced by birds as are necessary to bring them into breeding colours ; the black-headed gull, which has a white head in winter, sheds only the feathers of its head.

Some birds appear to change their colours without moulting by a process called feather wear. This occurs only with such birds as have their new feathers edged with brown or grey; for these edges, by their overlapping, conceal the underlying main colour of the feather. The blackbird appears largely rusty brown in its winter plumage; but as spring approaches and the brown edges wear off it gradually becomes blacker and blacker until, by the time the breeding season has arrived, its feathers are shiny black. Often some prominent mark is concealed in this way during the winter, as for example the black throat-patch of the male house-sparrow.

It is impossible to imagine a colour that could not be matched by the plumage of some bird, but in spite of this fact there are only four pigments of colour substances found in the feathers of most birds—black, brown, red and yellow. In a small group of African birds called touracos, a green pigment also is present; but all other greens, and all blues and metallic colours, are due to the structure of the feathers rather than to pigments. It is usually the superficial layers of cells that are prismatic in shape and cause the refraction that gives the colour to the feather. To see the colour at its best, therefore, the observer has to be in good light with the sun at his back. It is for this reason that it is often difficult to identify the birds one sees under unfavourable light conditions.

Occasionally birds are seen whose feathers are deficient in pigment. There may be only a few white feathers in the plumage, or the entire bird may be spotted, or it may be entirely white. In the latter case it is said to be a pure albino. Such birds must not be confused with those in which the feathers are normally white, such as the gulls and certain northern birds in their winter plumage. A true albino has no colour and can be distinguished by the pink eyes and pale beak and legs. Albinism may occur in any species.

In a few species the red pigment occasionally becomes over-developed and the birds appear much redder than the normal coloration, irrespective of age or sex. This is well shown in the red and grey phases of the American screech owl and in certain other dull-coloured species, but it is a phenomenon of a different type from albinism.

When there is a difference in the coloration of the male and the female bird, it is usually the male that is brighter. Among British birds, the phalaropes (a group similar to the sandpipers) are exceptions to this rule, the females being brighter than the males. It is interesting to note in this case that the males incubate the eggs and care for the young.

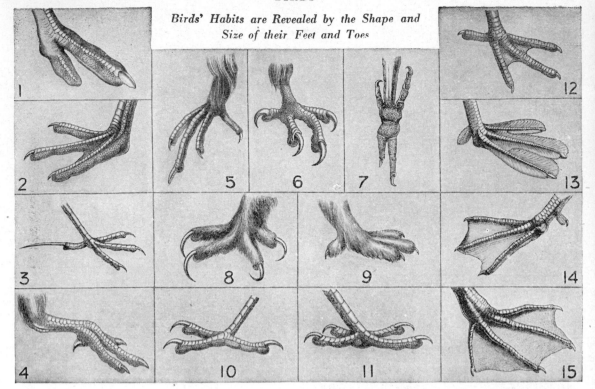

Birds' Habits are Revealed by the Shape and Size of their Feet and Toes

WHY BIRDS' FEET DIFFER SO WIDELY

Here is what a bird ' palmist ' might say to an Ostrich on looking at its foot (1) : ' Your ancestors of millions of years ago had five toes. The other three have disappeared because your family have put in so much time running. The third toe has grown very big, while the fourth toe, the only other one you have left, is dwindling. In the case of your descendants it will probably disappear altogether.' Another thing the ' palmist ' would say to all these birds whose feet we see before us is : ' Your early ancestors were reptiles.' He knows it by those scales, except in the case of the Tawny Owl (8) and the Ptarmigan (9), whose legs and toes are covered with feathers. All the other feet are scaled : Plover (2), Skylark (3), Apteryx (4),

Night-jar (5), Sea Eagle (6), Toucan (7), Three-toed Woodpecker (10), Green Woodpecker (11), Stork (12), Grebe (13), Merganser (14), Pelican (15). Feet 12 to 15 are clearly those of birds that frequent the water. In the Stork (12) the web reaches only to the first joint. In the Grebe (13) the web is attached to each toe, but these toe webs do not join ; this makes it convenient for walking as well as swimming. Plovers (2) have long toes to distribute their weight as they walk over sand and mud. A Woodpecker's feet (10 and 11) are arranged to give them a grip on tree trunks. Toucans (7), like the Green Woodpecker. have two toes projecting forward and two backward. The Owl (8) is able to turn his third toe either backward or forward.

while the females go off by themselves; for it is believed that the dull colour of most females is due to the need for being inconspicuous on the nest.

When the males and females are coloured differently in the breeding season, the male in its winter plumage usually takes on a coat very similar to the female. It is for this reason that so few brilliantly coloured birds are seen during the autumn migration and during the winters spent in the south.

When the male and female differ in colour, the young birds in juvenile plumage usually resemble the female. If both sexes are alike, the young are similar, unless the adults differ in coloration materially from the other members of the family. In such cases the young often show the characteristics of the family.

When one begins the study of birds one very soon realizes that some birds are much more easily seen than others; for certain birds, such as the tits and finches, are quite conspicuously marked, while others, for example the sparrows and shore-birds, are protectively coloured. The conspicuously marked birds are ordinarily shy birds and do not

permit of very close approach, while those that are protectively coloured are quite the reverse. Moreover, plumage that seems conspicuous when we see the bird close up, or in unfamiliar surroundings, may be really protective in its favourite haunts. This form of " camouflage " among birds is an interesting example of the manner in which Nature safeguards animals from their foes.

There are today between 13,000 and 14,000 species of birds in the world. Before anyone can handle conveniently any such large group of objects or facts it is necessary that they be systematically arranged, and this arrangement is called classification. In the classification of birds similar animals are put together in groups and similar groups together in larger groups, etc., their classification being based upon their structure rather than upon external similarity. Thus, all birds comprise the Class *Aves* of the Phylum *Vertebrata*. Below this they are grouped into Orders, with the termination -*formes*, as for instance *strigiformes*, the owl-like birds (*strix* is the Latin for an owl) ; and, finally, they are grouped into Families, with the termination *idae*.

BEAUTY IN THE WORLD OF WINGS

No wonder these two swans look proud, with their family of ten cygnets swimming along so charmingly behind them. Although they are so very small, the little ones are quite capable of looking after themselves in the water, as is indeed the case with most true water-birds that build close to their natural home. They are still wearing the first fluffy down which covered them when they hatched only a day or two ago from the big nest of reeds and rushes—probably on the bank, or perhaps on an island in mid-water—and will not acquire the adult plumage for a year or more.

SUPPER TIME IN THE NIGHTINGALE'S NEST

Here is a mother nightingale at her nest, wondering what to do for those wide-open little beaks that are gaping up at her. She appears not to have any food for the youngsters, and perhaps that is why they are making such a fuss. There is something very reminiscent of the robin in the pose of the nightingale and the way in which its tail is held stiffly up, while the head is a bit on one side with a bright eye looking perkily at you; and, as a matter of fact, the nightingale is a brown cousin of the robin with a wonderful voice, which is heard by night as well as by day.

ROOKERY IN THE SWAYING BEECH TREE TOPS

We all know the rook, with its loud and cheerful "caw" and its broad blue-black wings, and here we see one of these birds at home, in the act of feeding its hungry family. You can tell it's a rook, by the way, and not a carrion crow, because the base of its beak is covered with pale, bare skin; if it was a crow, this part would be as black as the rest of the bird. The rookery here is in the tops of beech trees, safe from most climbers and strongly made to withstand the swaying there must be when the wind rises. Sociable birds, rooks nest in colonies.

SPARROW-HAWKS AT HOME IN A TALL PINE

The business of feeding the young takes up all the time and energy of most birds, and this cock sparrow-hawk must have a very hard time with such hungry youngsters to provide for. You can see the remains of a bird on the edge of the nest, and one of the fledgelings is still picking at a last morsel. The sparrow-hawk, unlike the kestrel seen opposite, builds a large nest of its own—usually, as here, towards the top of a tall pine or other tree, where foliage provides shelter and hides the nest from above and below. Speedy on the wing, this hawk flies rather low.

Three young kestrels, almost ready to fly, are having what looks like their breakfast, for the clear light and the angle of the shadows show that it is an early-morning photograph. While one is receiving portions of a small bird from the parent, another is sitting looking out from the decayed tree-trunk, within which you can just see the third young hawk bending over some food. Down in the hollow, hidden from view, is the nest, probably the former home of some other bird, for the kestrel seldom makes a home of its own. Another name for the kestrel is windhover.

FOR THIS THE HEDGEROW SONG IS STILLED

Two of our commonest birds, the hedge sparrow (top) and the chaffinch (lower) do their share to swell the chorus of song in spring and summer. But silence falls when the nestlings gape. The hedge sparrow (which is not a true sparrow and should be called the accentor) normally has a quiet little warble in keeping with the subdued greys and browns of its plumage. The chaffinch, one of the smartest and gayest of our birds, makes a loud, insistent, cheerful whistling and clatter which one cannot fail to hear—until such time as it becomes busy rearing a family. Both are seen at their neatly constructed and cleverly concealed nests, silently engrossed with the cares of parenthood. The materials of their nests are mostly moss, wool and hair with an outer layer of lichens in the case of the chaffinch.

HANDSOME RAIDERS OF OTHER BIRDS' NESTS

Coloured black with green and blue gloss, and white, with a long tail, the magpie builds a domed nest with the entrance at one side. It feeds on all manner of vegetable and animal oddments—including other birds' eggs and nestlings. The fledgeling magpies in the top photograph are almost ready to begin foraging for themselves. The baby jays in the lower photograph are being reared on the same kind of food as magpies enjoy. The nest is a flat structure of sticks, grass and fragments of root, and two broods are reared in a year. The jay's harsh scream of alarm when disturbed is more often heard than the bird itself is seen. Its colour is reddish brown in general, with blue on the wings, and a whitish-grey head-crest spotted with black. Like magpies, jays are inveterate egg-thieves.

In livery of black and white and chestnut, with scarlet beak and pink legs, the sheldrake or sheld-duck (top), feeds on mussels and similar fare. It nests usually in colonies, in old rabbit burrows, sometimes in rock-crevices or dense undergrowth, and its large cream-coloured eggs number eight or ten. The young birds walk and swim as soon as hatched. The oyster-catcher (lower) is also black and white, with a long, stout orange coloured bill and pinkish legs. Its natural food is not oysters (as the name would suggest), but mussels, limpets, winkles and small crabs. Its nest is a mere depression among pebbles and shells of the seashore or the shingle of a riverside, and it lays three yellowish eggs. The young are able to fend for themselves in about three weeks.

Birkbeck, George (1776-1841).

One of the colleges that make up the great University of London is the Birkbeck College. George Birkbeck, after whom it is called, was the son of a banker, of Settle, Yorkshire. He was educated at Edinburgh, studying medicine, and for a few years he was a professor at Glasgow. In that city he started the Glasgow Mechanics' Institution, the first of its kind in the country.

Later, he began to practise medicine in London, and while there had a good deal to do with the foundation of the London Mechanics' Institution, which was opened in 1824. Of this institution he was the first president, and to it he lent £3,700 in order to build a lecture room. After a time the name was changed to Birkbeck Institution or College, and a home was found for it in Breams Buildings, Chancery Lane, London, E.C. Birkbeck was also one of the small group who founded University College, London. He died on December 1, 1841.

Birkenhead.

One of the most important seaports in the north of England is Birkenhead. It stands on the Cheshire or southern side of the estuary of the Mersey, opposite Liverpool, the two places being connected by the magnificent road tunnel opened by King George V in 1934, as well as by a railway tunnel. The town is quite modern and it was only in 1847 that the first dock was constructed, but after that its population grew rapidly and there are now 171 acres of docks with 12 miles of quays. Many persons who work in Liverpool make their homes in the surrounding districts, crossing twice a day either by the tunnels or on the ferry boats. There is an observatory on Bidston Hill near the town. The population is about 116,000.

Birkenhead, British Troopship.

The story of the Birkenhead affords one of the most wonderful examples of discipline and bravery in the face of death that has ever been told. During the Kaffir War in South Africa, this paddle steamer was dispatched with nearly 700 troops on board as reinforcements to the British regiments on active service in Cape Colony. After a voyage of 48 days from Cork, the Birkenhead arrived at Simon's Bay on February 24, 1852. There it discharged a few troops, and the following night again put to sea in order to proceed to Algoa Bay.

Perhaps because the captain wished to make a quick passage the vessel was kept too close to the shore, and within only seven hours from the time she left the harbour the Birkenhead struck a rock, at two o'clock in the morning. Immediately a great hole was torn in the bottom of the ship. The bugles sounded, and while the sailors were ordered to the pumps or their stations all the soldiers were mustered on deck. Everyone stood steadily in rank.

Seven women and 13 children were placed in a small boat, which was safely launched within 12

BIRKENHEAD END OF MERSEY TUNNEL

In the centre of this aerial view of Birkenhead is the entrance to the road tunnel under the Mersey, connecting the town with Liverpool on the opposite bank. The tunnel is nearly three miles long and was opened in 1934. Birkenhead's first dock was built in 1847.

minutes from the time the vessel struck. What a heart-rending ordeal it must have been for these to pass silently into the boat, leaving husbands and fathers standing there so silently that even a word of farewell might not be said ! No sooner had this boat been got away when the ship broke in two, and the stern half sank.

Still the men stood in rank awaiting the end, and the two senior officers who commanded them told them not to jump overboard, as any attempt to get into the boat containing the women and children would certainly swamp it. Soon after this the deck sank beneath the British soldiers and within 20 minutes of striking the rock the Birkenhead had foundered None of the women's and children's lives was lost, and altogether 192 persons were saved ; but 454 officers and men were drowned.

Birmingham.

The great manufacturing centre of Birmingham, 111 miles north-west of London, is the second city of England. It was in existence before the Norman Conquest, and its manufactures date at least from the early 16th century, as evidenced by Leland's Itinerary (1538), in which he writes of Birmingham : " There be many smithes in the towne that use to make knives and all manner of cutlery tooles, and many loriners that make bittes (for horses), and a great many naylors (nail makers) so that a great part of the

Centre was completed early in the Second World War (1939–45), during which the city suffered severe damage from bombing. The municipal airport was opened in 1939.

In 1904 Birmingham became the seat of a bishopric with St. Philip's Church as the cathedral. St. Martin's Church, in the Bull Ring, another fine building, is the parish church. There is a Roman Catholic Archbishop of Birmingham, whose cathedral is in Bath Street. All three of these churches were damaged by German bombs in 1940–1. Birmingham's water supply is drawn from a great reservoir at Rhayader in Wales, about 80 miles away. It was completed in 1905.

The city extends over 79 square miles and includes Aston Manor, once a separate borough, and other outlying districts. It possesses many parks and open spaces, one being Aston Park, and land on the Lickey Hills in Worcestershire. It is governed by a lord mayor and a council and sends 13 members to Parliament. The population was 1,020,500 in 1945.

Until 1769 Birmingham was ruled chiefly by the lord of the manor through his two manorial courts. In the court baron by-laws for local government were made; in the court leet cases were tried, bailiffs to superintend the markets were

towne is maintained by smithes, who have their iron and sea-cole (ordinary coal) out of Staffordshire."

The leading industry today of the district of which Birmingham is the centre is metal-working of all sorts—founding, rolling, stamping, plating, drawing, etc. ; and the products include machinery, engines, iron roofs, girders, and all kinds of industrial wares. The manufacture of railway carriages, and of motor-cars, tyres, and other accessories is extensively carried on.

Small arms, watches and clocks, electrical apparatus, brass work of all sorts, gold and silver articles and jewelry, screws and nails, and steel pen-nibs are manufactured in huge quantities. and buttons, hooks and eyes, pins, etc., are also produced. It is said that over 1,500 trades are carried on in the city. Near Birmingham the steam engine was perfected by James Watt and Matthew Boulton, and their famous Soho works are one of the most precious heritages of the city. Four miles away is Bournville, with its famous cocoa and chocolate works, and scene of a pioneer town-planning enterprise.

Birmingham claims to be one of the best-governed cities in the world, a reputation it began to win when Joseph Chamberlain was mayor (1873–74), and to the same man it owes its university. This was founded in 1900, and has a fine range of buildings at Edgbaston, where all the requirements of a modern seat of learning are found. King Edward's grammar school, an old foundation, was moved to a site away from the centre of the city. There are several technical schools, including one at Aston and another at Handsworth. The first section of a new Civic

Dixon-Scott

BIRMINGHAM : CAPITAL OF THE MIDLANDS
The great industrial city of Birmingham is reputed to be one of the best governed in the British Isles, and it is justly proud of its fine buildings and spacious streets. The City Museum and Art Gallery (top), opened in 1885, is housed in a wing of the Council House. Below is Corporation Street, one of Birmingham's chief business thoroughfares.

elected, and constables appointed. The affairs of the parish were looked after by the church-wardens and overseers, and the surveyors of highways were chosen at parish meetings. There were two bailiffs. The high bailiff saw that order was kept and that no " unlawful games to the injury of ignorant persons and thoughtless youths " were played. The low bailiff summoned the juries.

Bismuth. This is a metallic element (symbol Bi) with a pink or reddish lustre. It has a low melting point, 518° F., and is therefore used to make alloys which melt easily. One of them, Wood's metal, was much used in the early days of radio reception to cement the crystal into its cup. Since

Wood's metal melts at about 158° F., or two-thirds the temperature at which water will boil, it could be fused by a moderate heat which would not damage the crystal.

A famous practical joke was to cast a teaspoon in Wood's metal and put it among the tea things for the table. When someone tried to stir their tea, the spoon quickly melted! This strange alloy is made up of 4 parts bismuth, 2 parts of lead, and 1 part each of tin and cadmium. More practical uses of such alloys are for the plugs in automatic water sprinkler nozzles: when fire breaks out in a warehouse, the heat melts the plugs, and water spurts out just where it is wanted.

Compounds of bismuth are used in medicine for stomach ailments. Some bismuth salts are opaque to the X-rays, so when a patient in hospital is to have his food canals examined, he is first given a meal containing the bismuth salt. Then the passage of food through the stomach and intestines can be watched on a fluorescent screen by the doctors. Other bismuth salts are given as germ-killers.

The atomic number of Bismuth is 83; its atomic weight, 209; and its density, 9·8.

Bison. Commonly called "buffalo" in the country of its origin, the American bison (*Bison americanus*) is the largest and most celebrated of all American hoofed animals. Originally it was found on two-thirds of the continent of North America. Its range extended from Mexico to the region of the Great Slave Lake in Canada, and from Pennsylvania and the Carolinas to the Rocky Mountains. Its food was the herbage of the plain.

The number of bison at the time America was discovered has been estimated at from 30 million to 60 million. In 1870 the number of survivors was estimated at 5,500,000. The vast herds sometimes derailed trains in the west and stopped boats on the

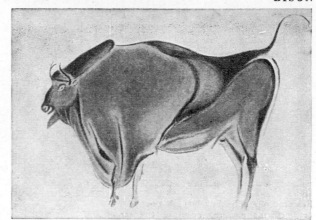

BISON OF 20,000 YEARS AGO
In prehistoric times bisons wandered all over Europe, and fossil remains of them have been found in the Thames valley. This drawing shows how a bison appeared to prehistoric Man, for it is one of the marvellous wall paintings in the Altamira cave at Santander, in Spain, which were made in the Old Stone Age.

Yellowstone and Missouri rivers. The completion of the transcontinental railways and the introduction of the repeating rifle about this period soon almost completed their destruction.

To the Indians of the great plains the bison was the most important game animal. The hides furnished him with the material for tepees, or tents, and robes. He lived a good part of the time on the fresh meat, which is almost as good as beef; and for winter the northern tribes made a preparation of the dried meat with berries and fats, called "pemmican." This furnished a nutritious and well-balanced ration in small space.

In 1883 the famous Sioux chief, Sitting Bull, and his band of warriors are said to have slaughtered the last 1,000 head in south-western Dakota, leaving less than 1,000 head then alive on the American continent, two-thirds of those being in Canada.

The bison's massive head is his most characteristic feature. His bow-shaped back, different from that of the ox, and the unusually long vertebral spines increase the size of the shoulders. The convex shape of the frontal bone makes the forehead bulge. Over all the bulk of bone and powerful muscles of the neck and shoulders is the great shaggy coat of curly brown fur. The hair on the head falls over the eyes in a thick mane. The forequarters are heavier and higher than the haunches.

The adult male stands 5½ feet high at the shoulders, is 9 to 10 feet long, and weighs from 1,600 to 2,000 pounds. The female does not exceed 1,200 pounds. The horns are short and black, and in the males are thick at the base, tapering abruptly to a sharp point as they curve outward and upward. The hoofs are short, broad and black. The general colour is pale brown, darker on the head and shoulders and underneath. The hair on the forepart of the body is 10 to 15

AMERICAN BISON OF TODAY
In America bisons were once so numerous that a single herd was estimated to consist of 4,000,000 animals, and to cover an area 50 miles by 25 miles. Now the few that remain are carefully guarded. This one was photographed in the Buffalo National Park, Alberta, Canada.

VANQUISHED MONARCHS OF THE PLAINS

This herd of stampeding bison is re-enacting for a cinema camera scenes of the early pioneer days when great hordes of these beasts roamed the prairies of North America

The Aurochs or European bison was common in Europe some two or three thousand years ago, but now there are few survivors, several herds having been destroyed during the two World Wars. The animals in the small herd below are not pure-blooded stock.

The Royal Bison (above) roamed the earth during the Stone Age. We know of him from pictures drawn by cavemen artists who hunted this beast thousands of years ago, and from his fossil remains. The illustration is from a painting by Charles Knight in the American Museum of Natural History, New York.

The train hold-up shown in the old engraving on the right took place in the United States in 1869, at a time when bison frequently blocked the lines for hours. At first the engine drivers used to try going through the herds, but the weight of the beasts often derailed the engine.

inches long on the head, 6 to 8 inches long on the neck, shoulders and forelegs, and 10 to 12 inches under the chin, where it resembles a beard and is so called. The hinder and lower portions of the body are covered with short, soft, woolly hair. The tail ends in a tuft of coarse hair 12 to 18 inches long.

The long hair on the forepart of the body is permanent, but that on the hinder portions is shed annually, beginning in March. By early summer this part of the body is bare in patches and very sensitive. In order to escape the attacks of flies and other insects, the bison seeks out muddy sloughs and shallow ponds, where it wallows until its body is covered with mud, which bakes in the sun and forms a protective armour, lasting for days.

The new coat is fine by October, and at its best in November and December. The hide is then valuable as fur. A half-century ago " buffalo coats " —overcoats made of the fur of young bison—were in common use and remarkably cheap. A prime " buffalo robe " could be obtained from the Red Indians in exchange for a pound of tobacco.

Under primitive conditions bison herds moved from one feeding ground to another, going northward in the spring and southward in the autumn. The migrations occurred in herds numbering millions of animals. They travelled hundreds of miles, swimming mighty rivers and climbing or descending steep banks, cliffs and precipices. They followed the same routes year after year, making paths that became lasting trails two or three feet deep. The northward movement began in the spring after the calves were strong enough to travel. In this movement they separated into smaller herds, the bulls occupying the outer circle and the cows and calves the inner. When danger threatened the herd closed in, the bulls facing outward, ready to protect the weaker members.

The principal enemy of the bison, apart from the Indians, was the grey or buffalo wolf which roved in packs about the outer edge of the herds, and often succeeded in isolating and capturing a calf in spite of all vigilance. The grizzly bear was the only animal that could ever vanquish a buffalo bull in single fight. It required heroic efforts to save the bison from complete extinction. It was not until 1902 that the U.S.A. Congress took the first steps towards preservation when it voted a sum of money for the purpose of assembling survivors in the Yellowstone National Park. As the bison breeds readily in captivity its numbers have steadily increased. The Canadian herds now contain over 13,000 head, chiefly in a vast park in Alberta; and there are, besides, many thousands of bison in the United States, the largest single herd being in the reservation on the Yellowstone. The " cattalo," part buffalo and part common cattle, has been bred for experimental purposes in Canada.

The European bison was common in Europe two or three thousand years ago, and later in the Harz Mountains, but is now reduced to a few herds in the Zelentschek district of the Caucasus Mountains and in a few private preserves. The herds in Poland suffered at the hands of the German invaders during the two World Wars of 1914-18 and 1939-45. Thus the herd at Bialowieza, which numbered 700 in 1914, was reduced to 200 by the end of the First World War; and it suffered again in the Second World War, only 23 remaining in 1945. Of another herd, in the Pszczyna area, only 19 were alive after the Germans had been driven out of Poland in 1945. Happily, the Polish government has again taken over the protection and breeding of these rare animals.

The European bison is somewhat smaller than the American, and since it lived in forest country it ranged in smaller herds: it is sometimes called the *aurochs*, but this name is more properly reserved for the long extinct wild cattle of Northern Europe. It is stated on good authority that male bison outlive the females by about 10 years. If this is true of the American species, it explains why in every herd the bulls always outnumber the cows. No effort has been made to tame the bison.

By an unusual mischance the first skeleton of an American bison, exhibited in Paris in 1819, contained 15 pairs of ribs. As a result of this freak, which probably occurs only once in many thousands of specimens, the report became current that the American bison has 15 pairs of ribs, while his European cousin is blessed with only 14 pairs. The true buffalo (*q.v.*) belongs to India and Africa, and differs from the bison in the absence of the hump on the shoulders and the long hair on the forepart of the body.

Bittern. The bittern was once a common bird in the eastern counties of England, but the draining of the fen country deprived him of most of his nesting haunts and so drove him to seek a home elsewhere. A few pairs remained for a number of years, but these were gradually reduced by hunters and egg collectors, despite the efforts of bird-lovers, till about the middle

E. J Hosking

BITTERN ACTS AS UMBRELLA
The bittern makes its nest among the reeds, and here one has been photographed as she stands over her nest to protect the young bird which has just hatched and the remaining eggs from a drenching shower of rain.

of last century the bittern could no longer be counted as a breeding species in Britain.

For about 50 years he was known only as a casual visitor to this country, but he has been encouraged to nest again by certain landowners who have strictly preserved the reed beds on their property and so have provided him for a number of

Bastin; Dennis

BITTERSWEET

This plant, also called woody nightshade, is often confused with deadly nightshade and, like deadly nightshade, is poisonous. The berries (right) turn from green to red or orange.

seasons with a sanctuary in which he could live and breed in peace.

The bittern, *Botaurus stellaris*, belongs to the same tribe as the heron, *Ardeiformes*, but he has a much shorter neck and is more stoutly built than that bird. He spends his days among the reeds, and his plumage, which is buff marked with brown and black, is so well suited to his surroundings that, though he is a large bird, over two feet in length and about three feet high, he is difficult to see. His protection is made all the more complete by his strange habit of standing, when he is alarmed, with his long bill pointing straight up in the air.

Like the heron he feeds on fish, frogs, water insects, etc. The nest is placed on the ground among the reeds, and, of course, is made of reeds. The eggs are laid in April or May, and so soon as one is laid the hen bird starts sitting, so that the young in the nest are of varying ages. Unlike the heron, the bittern is a migratory bird. The American bittern, *B. lentiginosus*, sometimes visits this country, and so also does another species called the little bittern, *Ardella munila*. The bittern's spring call is a very distinctive loud booming note. He also has another call which is a kind of double croak.

Bittersweet. This common plant of hedgerows and waste places throughout Europe, North Africa and Asia may be recognized at once by its purple and yellow flowers, and also by the peculiarly shaped leaves. These have a large lobe like the blade of a spear, and two smaller ones more or less at right angles to it.

The bittersweet (*Solanum dulcamara*) is a member of the nightshade family (*Solanaceae*). It is also known as woody nightshade. The blossoms give place to tempting-looking but poisonous egg-shaped berries about half an inch long, which turn from green to red or orange.

Björnson, BJÖRNSTJERNE (1832–1910). The famous critic Georg Brandes once said of Björnson (pron. byêrn'-son) that "when his name is mentioned it is like hoisting the flag of Norway," for he was the most loved and the most representative of Norwegian writers. The author of Norway's national hymn, her greatest novelist, and, next to Ibsen, the greatest dramatist of his country, Björnson embodies the finest qualities of the Norwegian people. He was born in Kvikne, a little village in central Norway, where his father was a Lutheran pastor. He was educated at the University of Christiania (Oslo), but left without taking his degree in order to devote himself to journalism.

His first novel, Synnöve Solbakken, published in 1857, made a deep and lasting impression. It was the first of a series of tales of Norwegian peasant life, written in the simple and charming style of the old sagas, or traditional stories. Arne, published in 1858, is perhaps the best of all these stories; it contains the beautiful song Over the Lofty Mountains, which first showed Björnson's ability as a poet.

Björnson was also deeply interested in the drama. Two years after writing his first play he was made director of the theatre at Bergen, later becoming director of the National Theatre at Christiania (Oslo). In 1863 he was granted a government salary to enable him to travel in Italy, France and Germany. He wrote a number of dramas based on the history of Norway, and then he turned, like Ibsen, to the social problems of the day. He took a more hopeful view of these problems, however, than did Ibsen. As someone has said, while Ibsen expressed the doubt, Björnson expressed the faith of his people. He was less stern and cold, more gentle and sympathetic, than Ibsen.

As a newspaper writer and editor, and as a political orator, Björnson kept in close touch with the life about him. A strong Nationalist, he helped to bring about the separation of Norway from Sweden, which took place in 1905. In 1903 he was awarded the Nobel prize for the most important literary work of that year. Long before his death his books had been translated into English and into many of the continental languages. Among Björnson's best stories and novels are: Synnöve Solbakken (1857); Arne (1858); The Heritage of the Kurts (1884). His dramas include Between the Battles (1855); Sigurd Slembe (1862); Sigurd Jorsalfar (1872); The Gauntlet (1883); Beyond Our Powers (Part I, 1883; Part II, 1895).

Blackberry. It may surprise some people to learn that the blackberry plant or bramble is a cousin of the rose. Compare its flower with that of the common wild rose and you will see how alike they are, apart, of course, from size. You will also see a strong likeness between its leaves with their three or five large-toothed leaflets, and those of the rose with five or seven similar but smaller ones.

A still closer relative of the blackberry, *Rubus fruticosus*, is the raspberry, *Rubus idaeus*, which also grows wild in England. More than 25 varieties of blackberry have been developed for garden and commercial purposes, one thornless with white berries.

Blackbird. The sweet songed blackbird, whose scientific name is *Turdus merula*, belongs to the thrush family — *Turdidae*, of the order *Passeriformes*—though in colour it differs so much from the common thrush. The two birds are somewhat similar in size and form, and also in habits. Even in the plumage we can still find traces of their descent from the same forefathers. The adult cock blackbird has a beautiful black plumage and a bright orange bill; the adult female is not black but brown, and her breast is lighter brown with dark markings. The young birds also are brown above, but this is profusely marked with buff spots, and their breasts are light brown with a dark tip to each feather. This spotted breast and the lighter markings on the upper parts, which are also possessed by the young thrush, may lead you to confuse the two species in the immature state.

The blackbird is one of our commonest birds, and for this we may well be grateful, for his song is the most beautiful of all our bird notes. He begins to sing at the end of February, and very soon afterwards is mated and making preparations for nesting. The nest is built of grass and mud, and lined with finer grass, and is usually placed in a hedge or low bush. The eggs are bluish-green, speckled with brown. There are usually four or five in a full clutch. As a rule a pair of blackbirds will raise two broods in the course of a season; in mild springs they may have three and sometimes even four families.

Blackburn. An important part in the cotton trade has been played by this Lancashire town. It was one of the earliest towns in England where the factory system grew up, and it has always been in the front rank as regards improvements in manufacture. James Hargreaves (*q.v.*), inventor of the spinning-jenny, was a Blackburn man, and although his invention at first aroused much opposition, it was afterwards acknowledged to mark a wonderful advance in the process of manufacture. The city has also important engineering works.

C. W. Teager

BLACKBIRD SONGSTER

There is no more welcome visitor to our gardens than the blackbird, because his song is one of the most musical of those we hear from British birds. The cock (above) is all black save for his yellow bill. The hen is dark brown.

Unlike many modern factory towns, Blackburn was an important place long before it became one of the chief centres of the cotton trade. It is mentioned in Domesday Book, and it is believed that there was a Roman station, or camp, in the locality. Blackburn possesses a grammar school dating back to 1567, and boasting Queen Elizabeth as its foundress. The Gothic church of St. Mary, completed in 1826, is now the cathedral of the Bishop of Blackburn. The public buildings (which include a fine town hall) and public services are of the most modern kind. Population is 105,700.

Black Death. "I leave parchment for continuing the work if haply any man survive and if any of the race of Adam escape this pestilence." So wrote a despondent English monk in his chronicle while the terrible plague called the Black Death raged in England in 1349. And well might he despair, for this epidemic swept off at least one-quarter of the whole population of Europe.

The plague raged from 1348 to 1357. In France the ravages were as great as in England. "It is impossible to believe the number who have died throughout the whole country," wrote a French monk. "Travellers, merchants, pilgrims, declare that they have found cattle wandering without herdsmen in fields, towns and waste lands. They have seen barns and wine-cellars standing wide open, houses empty, and few people to be found anywhere. In many towns where, before, there were 20,000 people, scarcely 2,000 are left."

A person began to shiver, his temperature rose, swellings appeared in neck, armpits or groin, and frequently death resulted in 12 hours. In many ways the Black Death helped to bring the Middle Ages to a close. In England before the plague there were about four or five million inhabitants; when the pestilence had passed away there were only about half that number. Field labourers had become scarce, and those who were left demanded greatly increased wages. Many peasants left the estates of their masters and fled to the towns. Parliament passed laws to keep wages and prices at their former levels, but these could not be enforced. The old manorial system of labour and agriculture broke down to some extent in England; in the new system the land was either rented to tenant farmers, or else it was retained by the lord and put into pasture for sheep and cattle.

The Black Death was only one of the many visitations of that disease which today we call the "bubonic plague." During the Peloponnesian War it broke out in the city of Athens (430 B.C.). In the reign of the Roman Emperor Justinian grain-ships from Egypt brought it to Constantinople. Boccaccio, the Italian writer, places the scene of his book, the Decameron, on the hills about Florence, Italy, during the epidemic of 1348. Defoe describes the outbreak of 1665 in London in his Journal of the Plague Year, published in 1772.

The home of bubonic plague is in Asia, and we now know that it is carried by a certain kind of flea which lives on rats. With the advance of medical science and sanitation its ravages have been checked in the western world, but constant vigilance is required on the part of health officers at sea ports to prevent its revival.

Black Forest, GERMANY. Scores of German nursery tales tell of the dwarfs and elves and fairies that were supposed to haunt every valley and wooded height in the famous Black Forest of Germany. The Black Forest lies in the elbow formed by the River Rhine as it flows westward from Lake Constance and turns sharply to the north. Stretching away to the north—mile after mile— are the rounded mountains, crowned with stately

pines and firs. The trees support a dome of dark-green foliage, giving in the half-light an appearance not unlike the interior of a great cathedral, although no human craftsman ever fashioned so magnificent a temple. Two lakes, both ancient volcanic craters, give a perfect reflection of the trees around.

In the narrow valleys lie hamlets scattered along the streams, while here and there are isolated dwellings, partly hidden by fruit trees, looking down from sunny slopes or projecting their quaint gables from a forest background. The length of the forest is about 100 miles and its average width is 24 miles. The loftiest elevation is the round-topped Feldberg, 4,898 feet high. To one coming from the towering snow-capped peaks of the Alps, the Black Forest seems but a mass of gentle wooded hills.

Here and there are nurseries in which each spring are planted the seeds of a future forest. The pine

and fir predominate, but in order to provide for every locality other varieties are sown, such as maple, ash, birch, walnut, and even fruit trees. The groves planted by one generation are cared for by the next, and are cut down and sawed into lumber by the third.

The Danube and Neckar rivers rise in the Black Forest mountains. Along these and other streams are manufacturing towns where wooden articles, cuckoo-clocks, musical-boxes, and toys are made. Cattle graze on the grassy slopes, and the beauty of the region made the Black Forest a favourite summer tourist resort. The greater part of the Black Forest is included in the state of Baden.

Black Sea. This great sea, one-sixth as large as the Mediterranean—with which it is connected by way of the Bosporus, the Sea of Marmara (Marmora) and the Dardanelles—lies between Asia Minor on the south and Russia on the north, and between Bulgaria and Rumania on the west and the region of the Caucasus Mountains on the east, and so plays its part in separating—and in uniting—Europe and Asia.

For over 2,000 years its waters have been traversed—by ships of early traders, pirates and settlers, and by vessels of modern commerce and war. For Russia the navigation of this sea, with its Mediterranean outlets, is a vital necessity, and it has figured since the 18th century in that country's history. The fact that the Turks were able to block the entrance at the Dardanelles in the First World War (1914-18) tended to prolong that contest and contributed to the discomfort of Russia, because the Allied nations could not send supplies by this route.

BLACK FOREST COSTUMES

In the valleys between the forested slopes of that part of southern Germany called the Schwarzwald (Black Forest) are many little villages and towns that seem to have changed little in life, or architecture, or dress, for hundreds of years. In such villages live these girls, wearing the old traditional costumes.

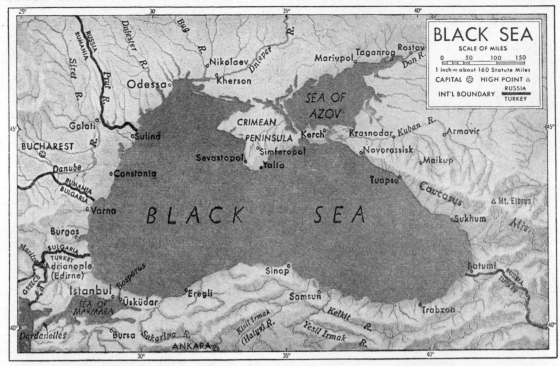

BLACK SEA BETWEEN EUROPE AND ASIA MINOR

Draining nearly a quarter of Europe, the Black Sea receives such a large inflow of fresh water that it is much less salt than the Mediterranean, with which it is connected by the Bosporus, the Sea of Marmara and the Dardanelles. It has an area of about 150,000 square miles, no islands of importance and no tides. It is usually free from ice during the winter.

Including the Sea of Azov, which is really a gulf of the Black Sea, almost enclosed by the Crimea and entered through the Strait of Kerch or Yenikale, the surface area is about 150,000 square miles, that of the Sea of Azov being 14,500 square miles. Its greatest length is 720 miles, its greatest width is 350 miles, and its greatest depth 7,360 feet.

The Black Sea drains nearly one-quarter of the surface of Europe. This large inflow of fresh water makes it much less salt than the ocean or even the Mediterranean, and sets up a peculiar current. In the upper level of the Black Sea the fresh water flows outward towards the Bosporus, while in the lower levels the current from the Aegean Sea flows in the opposite direction. Some of the great rivers which find their outlet in the Black Sea are the Danube, the Dniester, the Bug, the Dnieper, the Don (through the Sea of Azov), and the Kuban. The larger ports include Odessa, Kherson, Sevastopol, Constanta, Trebizond (Trabzon) and Sinop.

The Black Sea has the reputation of being dangerous to navigation, especially during the season of winter storms. But it is now believed that the Black Sea is no worse in this respect than other inland seas. It is usually free of ice, even in the coldest weather. It has been navigated from very early periods. The Greeks colonized its shores as early as the 7th century B.C. After the Turks captured Constantinople in 1453, they closed the sea to all but their own ships, though later Russia obtained certain rights. By a convention signed in 1936, merchant vessels even of non-Black Sea Powers may pass through the refortified Dardanelles into the sea at all times.

Blake, ROBERT (1599-1657). The memory of the great Admiral Blake is dear to the British people, not only for his naval glory and success but even more for the tradition of his chivalrous character and his unselfish patriotism.

Like Sir Francis Drake, Blake grew up in the West Country—at Bridgwater, in Somerset—but spent some years studying at Oxford University. He left Oxford in 1625, and little is known of him for the next 15 years; probably he was trading at sea. In 1640 he was chosen by his fellow-townsmen as their representative in the Short Parliament.

Blake's great qualities of leadership first shone with brilliance when the Civil War broke out in 1642. He at once joined the Parliamentary forces and drew favourable attention to himself, chiefly through the seizure and year-long defence of Taunton, which enabled the Parliamentary party to maintain itself in the west of England for a considerable time. Blake was now asked to assume a high command in the Navy and pursue the royalists who had taken to the sea. He built up a fleet and proceeded to hunt the royalists from the high seas. At Cartagena, Spain, he caught and destroyed the greater portion of their vessels and succeeded in capturing their last stronghold, the Scilly Islands.

Blake was then called upon to lead the English fleets in their mighty struggle for the mastery of the seas against the Dutch under De Ruyter—and Van Tromp, who was cruising, according to the story, with a broom at his masthead to indicate that he had swept the seas clear of Englishmen.

In battle Blake showed the same daring and heroic endurance that had already marked him

Permission of City of Plymouth Museum and Art Gallery

ADMIRAL BLAKE PROTECTS A SEAMAN

" I would have you and all the world know that none but an Englishman shall chastise an Englishman ! " These are the words that Blake is addressing to the Spaniard who has demanded the right to punish a British seaman guilty of ungentlemanly conduct on shore. The incident occurred during Blake's operations against Moorish pirates in the Mediterranean Sea in 1655. The original painting is by the Irish artist A. D. McCormick, R.I. (1860–1944).

out. He was repeatedly in the most extreme danger, was once severely wounded, and much o the time he suffered from disease. In spite of all, however, Blake and the other English leaders triumphed, and Van Tromp was defeated. The English, for the time being, had established their naval supremacy. The last exploit of the great admiral was his greatest and most daring—the crushing defeat in 1657 of a Spanish fleet off the Canary Islands under the guns of a castle and six or seven forts. This exploit excited great enthusiasm in England and admiration throughout Europe. But the admiral was a sick man, and after this his health failed rapidly, so that he died on his way home as he was sailing into the harbour of Plymouth. Blake received a magnificent public funeral and was buried in Westminster Abbey, but in 1660 his body was exhumed and re-interred in the churchyard of St. Margaret's, Westminster.

T. Phillips

WILLIAM BLAKE
The creator of etchings of great beauty, William Blake printed a unique series of books written, illustrated and decorated by himself.

Blake, WILLIAM (1757–1827). In a single room in a humble part of London, William Blake, by a process of his own, etched words on copper, decorated the plates with designs of singular beauty, and added an occasional full-page picture. The book was Songs of Innocence, a collection of poems written by Blake himself. The illustrations were from his paintings. He blended the ink, ground the colours, and mixed his own paint. Catherine, his wife, made impressions, tinted the prints, and bound them neatly in boards. They must have laughed together when the first volume was finished, for they had made everything but the paper ! In 1789 the book sold for a few shillings. Today a copy is worth hundreds of pounds.

William Blake, poet, artist, designer and mystic, was born in London on November 28, 1757, the son of a hosier. He developed his talent for sketching at a drawing school and by collecting prints of old masters. At 14 he was apprenticed to an engraver; at 24 he had married and opened a print-seller's shop. In the poetry and painting of his leisure hours he developed a mysticism whose beauty was not appreciated until long after he was dead. All his life he had visions. When he was four years old he remarked that he " saw God put His forehead to the window," and three years later he barely escaped a flogging from his father for saying that he had seen a tree full of angels.

When he grew older these visions gave to his painting extraordinary power, for he saw everything before he put his designs on paper. Publishers took advantage of him; rival artists stole his ideas and reaped rich profits while Blake himself fared poorly. He died on August 12, 1827, and was buried in an unmarked grave. Not until 100 years later, in 1927, was a tablet erected over his supposed resting place.

Songs of Innocence and its later companion volume, Songs of Experience, are his best-known works. The second includes his famous Tiger, Tiger! Burning Bright. In 1804 Blake published Jerusalem, later set to music as a hymn by Parry.

Blake's fame as an artist and master of design rests largely on a set of copperplate etchings, his dramatic interpretation of the Book of Job. He illustrated Richard Gough's massive work, Sepulchral Monuments of Great Britain, produced between 1786 and 1796. For his models he spent hours in the dim vaulted aisles of Westminster Abbey, copying the figures.

Blast Furnace.

This is a tower-shaped furnace in which iron ore is smelted to produce pig iron. About 100 feet high and nearly 30 feet in diameter, the furnace is built of steel plates and has a lining of fire-brick. In old-fashioned furnaces the gases produced used to be allowed to burn off at the open top ; but today the furnace mouth is sealed with a double bell which allows the charge of alternate layers of iron ore, limestone and coke to be fed in without the escape of the hot gases.

A ring-shaped bustle pipe encircling the furnace base carries the blast of hot, dry air to a number of openings called tuyères. From near the mouth of the furnace the hot gases are led off to pass first through huge cylindrical towers in which the dust is trapped ; thence the gases go to one of several hot-blast " stoves." These, again, are tall towers, divided up into many compartments by fire-brick which absorbs the heat as the products of the gases rise up from the base of the stove, where there is a combustion chamber in which the gases are burnt.

The fire-bricks are thus made red-hot. Two or three stoves are worked together : after one has been heated in the way described, the gas inlet is shut off and a hot-air outlet some way up the stove is opened. At the same time a cold-air inlet near the bottom is opened, and the air supply for the furnace is forced in. The air takes up heat from the hot bricks and passes on to enter the furnace under pressure through the ring-shaped bustle pipe and the tuyères. While this is happening the hot gases from the top of the furnace are passing now to another stove, to heat it in turn. In former days a cold blast of air was used, and it took eight tons of fuel to smelt enough ore to yield one ton of pig iron. The hot-blast method cut down the fuel con-

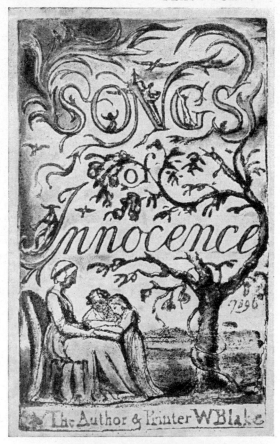

EXAMPLE OF BLAKE'S WORK
Here is the title page, drawn by William Blake, from Songs of Innocence, one of his two famous books, the other being Songs of Experience. First editions of these works are very valuable ; though they are little larger than a pocket-book the two volumes have been sold for £1,700.

sumption to half this figure, and today it takes roughly a ton of coke to make a ton of iron.

In the U.S.A. interesting experiments have been made to cut down the coke consumption yet more, by feeding the air at greater pressure while checking the drop in pressure in the furnace. By this means the output of pig iron has been made larger and the consumption of coke has been reduced by 10 per cent. A big blast furnace will consume as much as 1,000 tons of coke per day, so that a saving of 10 per cent means a great deal.

The air fed to the furnace enables the coke to burn and melt the iron ore; the limestone acts as a flux, and is broken up by the heat into calcium oxide and carbon dioxide. The weight of air consumed is greater than the total weight of the ore, coke and limestone. The oxygen of the air " reduces " (as the chemist puts it) the iron oxide in the ore. The iron melts, and a coating of slag floats on top of it. When sufficient molten iron has accumulated in the base of the furnace, one or more of the tapping holes are opened, and out gushes a fiery stream which is led into moulds. In the older method the moulds were arranged in rows, and from a fancied resemblance of these to a litter of little pigs suckling a sow, the name pig iron was given to the cast ingots of metal. Today the moulds travel past in two rows on a conveyor, while the molten iron pours into one after another. Pig-iron is re-melted for casting into machinery parts as cast iron. Henry Bessemer (q.v.) invented a process of making pig-iron directly into steel, in his converter. Pig-iron contains about 3–4½ per cent of carbon, whereas steels contain much less : from a quarter of 1 per cent (mild steel) up to 1½ per cent (high-carbon steel). Besides heating the blast stoves, the gases from the furnace mouth drive gas engines for working the air compressors and other machines.

The coke used as fuel in blast furnaces and in other smelting processes is somewhat different from ordinary coke which we obtain as a by-product of gas making, where coal is distilled in retorts to drive off the gas. "Metallurgical" coke is made in coke-ovens by heating coal to 1,300° C. with a controlled entry of air. The older method was to distil the coal in a beehive-shaped brick oven; only part of the fuel actually burned, with a limited supply of air, and the heat penetrated to the rest and turned

it into coke. But this method was disadvantageous in that it wasted the by-products, such as gas, tar and ammonia; they were burnt uselessly at an opening at the top of the oven.

Today most coke for smelting is made in brick ovens built side by side and with steel doors at back and front, the coal being heated indirectly by gas burnt in flues underneath and at the sides of the

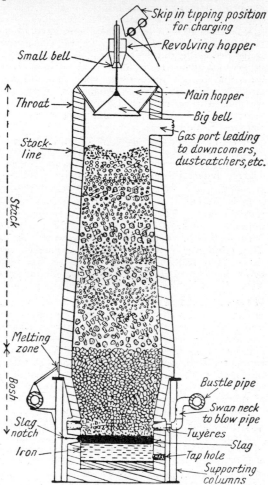

BLAST FURNACE EXTERIOR

This illustration in conjunction with the diagram alongside explains what goes on in a blast furnace. The ring-shaped bustle pipe conveying the hot blast is seen near the base ; hot gases from the furnace mouth are taken away to the stove by the slanting downcomers. The conveyor (left) takes up ore, limestone and fuel.

BLAST FURNACE INTERIOR

A blast furnace is in effect a vertical cylinder, varying from 80 to 100 feet in height, lined with fire-brick. The lowest part is called the hearth, and this is where the molten iron collects, sinking downwards through the coke.

oven. The air needed is also warmed before it enters the ovens. The coal is fed in at the top, and after about 15 hours' heating has become red-hot coke; the end doors are then opened, and the mass of coke is pushed out mechanically and conveyed by a car to be quenched with water.

Coke-oven gas is sold to gas companies for distribution through their mains ; or is used in steel works for heating furnaces. Some of the gas is utilised to heat the coke-ovens themselves. The reason why coke is used for smelting is that it gives a higher temperature than coal ; the moisture and volatile products have been driven off beforehand, and none of the heat is taken away in vaporising these substances. Metallurgical

Stewart and Lloyds, Ltd.; British Iron and Steel Federation

BLAST FURNACES PRODUCING BRITAIN'S PIG-IRON

From the blast furnaces (top left) gases are led to the washing towers (in foreground), where they are cleaned before being used. Huge mounds of iron ore (top right) rise up in front of the furnaces and stoves. To draw off the molten metal the tapping hole at the base of the furnace is opened (lower left), the metal flowing into pig moulds (lower right).

coke is columnar in structure, of a silvery grey colour, and gives out a metallic ring when struck; the coke which is familiar to the domestic consumer is usually black and dull, and less dense.

Bleaching. The old-fashioned way to whiten cotton or linen is to lay it out in the sunshine. Sunlight and air oxidise the natural colouring matter and turn it into a colourless compound of oxygen. This is an example of photochemistry (*q.v.*) or the chemical action of light.

Straw hats are sometimes whitened in this manner, though the process is too slow, and sunlight too uncertain, for general use. Formerly cotton and linen were bleached by repeated boilings in caustics and lyes and, after this, by exposure to sun.

After the discovery, about 1790, that chlorine gas and its compounds were good bleaching agents, chloride of lime came into use and shortened the process from months to days. The chloride is generally known as bleaching powder; it is made by the action of chlorine on quicklime. Chlorine or its compound act in this way only in the presence of moisture, and the gas will not bleach a dry rag.

When bleaching powder is dissolved in water it releases oxygen freely, and the oxygen combines with the natural colouring matter (or the dye in dyed fabrics), producing a colourless compound and so taking out the colour. Repeated treatment may be necessary, and all the chlorine or bleaching powder has then to be removed by washing or by immersing in chemical solutions which neutralise the bleaching agent. Instead of bleaching powder, laundries often use sodium hypochlorite. Since chlorine would damage or destroy such substances as wool or straw, the bleachers use hydrogen peroxide, sulphur dioxide, and other agents with similar properties.

The same property of releasing oxygen makes bleaching powder and chlorine valuable as disinfectants, germ-killers or water purifiers.

Blenheim, BATTLE OF. Blenheim village, in Bavaria, on the Danube, is not so well known, perhaps, as the mansion of Blenheim, and its princely estate, the home of the Duke of Marlborough, in Oxfordshire. The estate, together with £500,000, was granted by England to the first Duke of Marlborough for his services in defeating the French and the Bavarians at the Battle of Blenheim on August 13, 1704. Robert Southey wrote a poem on the battle, and he very truthfully and wittily hits off its importance in the last verse:

" And everybody praised the Duke
　　Who this great fight did win."
" But what good came of it at last ? "
　　Quoth little Peterkin.
" Why, that I cannot tell," said he,
　　" But 'twas a famous victory ! "

Marlborough began the battle by ordering his infantry to attack the French, who had taken up their position behind a strong defence of palisades. The British suffered severe losses in the earlier encounters, and it seemed as if the French would be the victors. Marlborough, however, asked the Austrian leader, Prince Eugene, to send assistance. The united forces checked the French and made it possible for the cavalry to advance, and the French army was driven from the battlefield.

Blériot, LOUIS (1872–1936). On July 25, 1909, Britain lost much of the security from attack that it had previously enjoyed as an island, for on that day Blériot (pron. blār´-iō) crossed the English Channel in his aeroplane.

At dawn Blériot was ready on the beach at Baraques, near Calais, beside his frail monoplane, the product of 10 years' experiments. " Dîtes-moi, où est Douvres ? " (" Tell me, where is Dover ? ") he asked, and on being shown its rough direction he took off and headed out to sea with nothing to guide him but an escorting destroyer.

Soon, however, Blériot left even the destroyer behind and his safety now depended on his aeroplane and its 25 h.p. engine. He remembered the almost tragic result of Latham's attempt six days before—engine-failure and a descent into the Channel. But all went well with Blériot, and 40 minutes after the start he landed on the cliffs near Dover at a place now marked by a stone tablet.

In after years Blériot became famous as an aircraft constructor, and many of his machines were used by the French in the First World War (1914–18). He died on August 1, 1936.

Blind, EDUCATION OF THE. No more pitiful plight for a two-year-old child can be imagined than to be blind, deaf and dumb. This was the situation of a little American girl, Laura Bridgman (born in 1829), after an attack of scarlet fever; but, nevertheless, she became a cheerful, happy citizen and did a great deal for the happiness of others.

Daily Mirror

BLÉRIOT: FIRST MAN TO FLY THE CHANNEL

A Frenchman, Louis Blériot, made the first aeroplane flight over the English Channel, on July 25, 1909, landing on the cliffs near Dover, where a memorial tablet marks the spot. Here is the airman (in flying suit) standing beside his monoplane. The machine was fitted with a 25 h.p. engine and the flight of some 20 miles took 40 minutes. The sea had ceased to be Britain's sure defence against attack which henceforward could come by air.

When she was eight years old Dr. Samuel G. Howe, superintendent of the Perkins Institute for the Blind in Boston, U.S.A., undertook successfully the untried task of developing a mind thus trebly barred. First, the child was given a spoon and a fork on which were labels with the raised letters F-O-R-K and S-P-O-O-N. Gradually the connexion dawned upon her, and when the labels were removed she could replace them on the proper articles. Then the letters were separated, and patiently she was taught to assemble them so that they would spell the words. This process was repeated with other articles, until finally she was familiar with the whole alphabet.

Now she was ready to learn finger-spelling. A raised letter would be given to her, and, with Laura's delicate fingers " watching " closely, the deaf-and-dumb sign of that letter would be formed by the teacher. Soon she was " writing her thoughts on the air " with astonishing rapidity, and by feeling with her hands the signs made by the person conversing with her, she was soon " talking " with them. This education continued until she was 20 years old, and she developed into a skilful teacher of blind children and was happily employed earning her own living until her death in 1889.

Laura Bridgman did not have the brilliant mind of another famous blind deaf-mute, Helen Keller, who was also trained by Dr. Howe, and did not achieve such spectacular results. But her education was the greatest accomplishment of the comparatively new art of teaching those similarly afflicted. Up to the beginning of the 19th century scarcely any attempt had been made to ease the lot of the blind and to teach them to support themselves. Today, by far the greater number of blind persons in progressive countries are educated, independent, self-supporting citizens. For this change much of the credit is due to the blind themselves—to their eagerness to learn and their untiring devotion to their appointed tasks.

Books for the blind are now for the most part not printed in raised letters, but in an alphabet of raised " points." This method was invented in

BLIND MAN READING BRAILLE
Sightless people may read with their fingers by means of the Braille system, which consists of raised dots representing the alphabet, numerals, punctuation marks and various contractions. A varying arrangement of six dots is used.

1829 by Louis Braille, who became one of the best organists in Paris, and a noted educator of the blind. As a child he delighted to play in his father's saddlery shop, punching holes in the scraps of leather with an awl. One day, when he was three years of age, the sharp tool slipped, injuring his eyes so severely that he became totally blind.

Becoming first a pupil and then a teacher at a Paris school for the blind, he thought a great deal about the little marks the awl left in the leather, and the idea came to him that if the awl were punched only half-way through, a dot would be raised on the other side. With this as a basis Braille worked out a system whereby different variations of groups of little, raised dots represented letters of the alphabet, special word and syllable signs, and punctuation marks. Educators seized upon this system, and with modifications it is taught in every country where there are schools for the blind.

To persons whose fingers are not sensitive, it seems as it did to the newly-blinded soldier, who, running his fingers over the page, exclaimed disgustedly, " It feels just like a sheet of sand-paper." But to thousands who have mastered its characters it has opened a new world of happiness. Books printed in Braille, besides being much bulkier than ordinary books, are much more expensive, so that the vast majority of the blind depend for their literature on libraries.

Typewriters have been invented for writing Braille, and machines for embossing the characters on zinc plates, so that any number of impressions may be printed. For writing Braille by

MAP FOR SIGHTLESS EYES
Physical geography can be taught to the blind with the aid of maps on which mountains, coastlines and frontiers are indicated by raised outlines. Sensitive fingers of the blind soon become highly skilled at ' reading ' such a map.

VARIED CAREERS OPEN TO THE SIGHTLESS

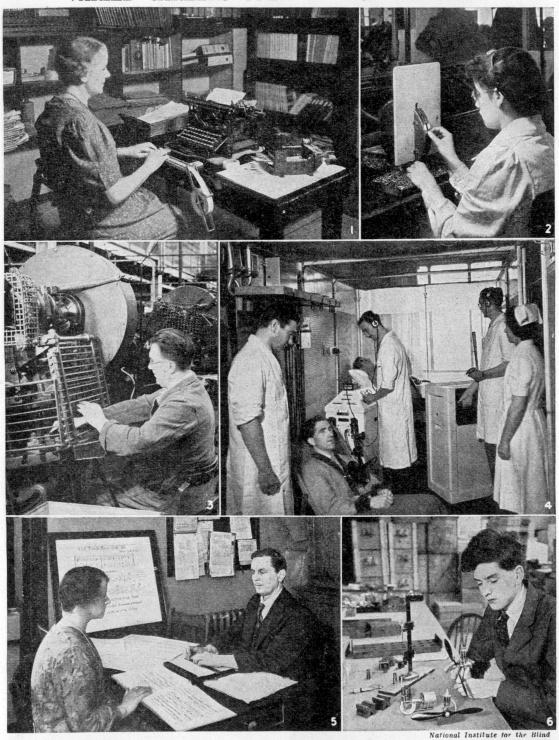

A blind shorthand typist takes down dictation in contracted Braille on a special machine which embosses the notes on a paper ribbon. and then when she 'reads' the ribbon (1) she types the notes on an ordinary typewriter. In (2) the worker is operating a machine that renders metal components less brittle by first heating and then cooling them slowly; the parts are placed in holes on the edge of a revolving wheel. The power-press (3) cannot be operated until the gate on which the man's left hand is resting is shut. Blind students (4) give electrical treatment under the eyes of a Sister. To prepare Braille music the woman reader dictates the notes to the blind transcriber (5) who transliterates the music into the symbols of the Braille musical notation. The young inspector (6) of a small petrol engine makes use of a Braille micrometer for checking his measurements.

hand, a grooved board is used with a perforated metal rule to serve as a guide, and the points are impressed on manila paper with a metal pencil. This is read on the reverse side. Writing Braille is a tedious process, so in most institutions for the blind the use of the Braille typewriter is taught as well. Some pupils are also taught to use an ordinary typewriter. The " touch " system. now universally used by typists, was originally devised for the blind. Special touch devices are employed to teach geography, arithmetic and natural history to the blind. Trained guide dogs have proved invaluable to a number of blind persons.

Not a few blind persons are engaged in farming. Many of them excel as musicians, and a considerable proportion become piano-tuners. Basketry and broom-making are other occupations especially suited to the blind, while many blind persons take to healing their fellow men and women by becoming masseurs. In Great Britain the four principal institutions wh ch look after the welfare of the blind are the National Institute for the Blind, which co-ordinates all the efforts to assist those without sight; the Royal Normal College, which gives a good general and technical education to blind pupils of both sexes; the National Library for the Blind, which makes and circulates Braille books ; and St. Dunstan's, which was founded in 1915 by Sir C. Arthur Pearson to look after the welfare of soldiers blinded in the First World War (1914-18). The first chairman of St. Dunstan's, Sir Ian Fraser, who was himself blinded in the First World War, was subsequently called to the Bar, and became a Member of Parliament and a Governor of the British Broadcasting Corporation.

Blockade.

When the coast of a country at war is patrolled by enemy ships to break its sea communications it is said to be blockaded. During the Civil War in America (1861-65), the most daring sea captains of the Confederacy (the Southern States) were employed in trying to break through the lines of northern warships which blockaded the southern seaports. At night their low black-painted ships, usually loaded with cotton for the British market, would steal out of the harbours and dash for the open sea. The war measure which closed the southern ports and ultimately starved out the Confederacy is an historic example of the naval operation known as blockade. It extended even to neutral ships, which were liable to seizure if they tried to break into one of the blockaded ports.

In the Declaration of Paris, agreed to by the Great Powers in 1856, the principle was laid down that fighting nations could not declare an enemy port blockaded unless they actually carried out the blockade with warships patrolling the approaches to the harbour. " A blockade, in order to be binding, must be effective, that is to say, maintained by a force sufficient really to prevent access to the coast of an enemy," was the way that particular agreement read.

During the First World War (1914-18) sea-mines, submarines, and the development of long-range guns for coast defence made it impossible for the Allies to carry out an actual blockade of the ports of the Central Powers. So the principle of 1856 was modified, and an " embargo " or " long-range blockade " of the enemy countries was declared. In February 1915 the Germans declared a submarine blockade of the British Isles. This meant that their submarines would sink without warning all ships entering the North Sea and other surrounding seas. Great losses were caused to British and neutral shipping, for submarines unlike surface ships, cannot take seamen prisoner and put them in safety ; but after a tremendous effort the danger was largely overcome. This ruthless action on the part of Germany did a great deal towards inducing the United States to join the Allies. In the Second World War (1939-45) the German occupation of all the Western European states from Norway to France gave the Allies a very long stretch of coastline to blockade. The Allies granted permits, known as navicerts, to neutrals trading with Europe when the cargo could be shown to have a genuine neutral destination. The laying of mines and the use of aircraft to co-operate with submarines added to the effectiveness of the blockades of both sides.

BLONDIN ABOVE NIAGARA
Blondin's most famous feat was to walk on a tightrope over Niagara Falls carrying a man on his back. It required perhaps greater courage on the part of the passenger than on that of the rope walker !

Blondin,

CHARLES (1824-97). The name of Charles Blondin—his real name was Jean François Gravelet—will go down in history owing to the marvellous feat which he successfully accomplished in 1859, when he walked on a tightrope across the falls of Niagara. Blondin was a Frenchman, a born showman, and such was the world-wide fame which he gained that he repeated the feat a good many times, with variations—blindfold, pushing a wheel-barrow, carrying a man on his back, and so forth.

Blondin made a great deal of money by this and similar acrobatic performances, and afterwards spent most of his life in England. He gave many performances at the old Crystal Palace at Sydenham, Surrey, and elsewhere. Notwithstanding the dangerous nature of his work, Blondin was 73 years of age when he died at Ealing, Middlesex.

The BLOOD STREAM in our BODIES

The drop of blood that appears when you prick your finger marks a leak in the circulatory system of your body. Here we are told of the wonders of blood of what it is made and the work it has to do.

Blood. "The Blood is the Life" in the Biblical phrase, and in the most exact sense blood is the life stream. It carries food and energy to all parts of the body; it scavenges the waste material of living which would otherwise poison us; it helps to keep our temperature within the narrow limits in which our cells can stay alive; it fights off the unceasing attacks of the bacteria of disease and of decay. When the blood ceases to flow, life ends. Let the supply of blood to the brain stop for only a second and consciousness stops. The airman levelling-out after a power-dive suffers a "black-out" because the violent change of direction momentarily drains blood from his head.

Blood normally accounts for about 1-13th of our total weight. A man weighing 155 pounds thus has about 12 pounds of blood, making about 5½ quarts. How it is pumped by the heart into the arteries which branch and become smaller like the branches and twigs of a tree, which twigs are the capillaries (Latin, *capillus*, a hair, because they are so very fine in bore), and how the blood leaves the capillaries for minute veins which become bigger veins returning the blood to the heart and lungs—all this is told in our articles on Heart, Lungs, and Respiration. Here we shall see of what the blood is made and examine some of its tasks.

The blood is a mixture of liquid and solid particles. Most numerous of the particles are the red corpuscles, which give the blood its colour. There are about 300 million of them in a drop. Thinly scattered among them are the larger white corpuscles, about one to every 700 of the red, and the tinier platelets, about one to every 20 red corpuscles. The liquid in which these particles are suspended is called the plasma. Each part of the blood is adapted to the special work it has to do. The red corpuscles (called erythrocytes, "red cells"), are button-shaped, slightly concave on each side. They are so small in diameter that 3,200 of them, placed edge to edge, would measure hardly an inch. They are so thin that it would take more than 11,500 of them to make a stack an inch tall. Each red corpuscle is a sac, enclosing a material called haemoglobin. This consists of haematin, a substance containing iron, and globin, a protein. Because there is iron in the haematin, the haemoglobin unites readily with oxygen.

The work of the red corpuscles is to carry oxygen from the lungs to the tissues and cells throughout the body. In the lungs, the haemoglobin picks up the oxygen to form oxyhaemoglobin. This is what makes the blood in the arteries (arterial blood) bright red. As the red blood moves on from the arteries into the capillaries, the corpuscles give up their oxygen, which diffuses out through the capillary walls and is used in the activities of the cells. In exchange, the cells give up carbon dioxide, a waste product, and the red corpuscles carry it back to the lungs. When the oxygen leaves them the red corpuscles turn purple, and this is the colour of the blood in the veins.

It is amazing to reflect that the red corpuscles are formed in the red marrow, deep in the bones. At first, each has a nucleus but it loses this on entering the blood stream. There the cells last from 10 to 30 days. When worn out by knocking against their fellows and the vessel walls the cells break up, passing through the spleen, and their iron content is carried to the liver. Here the iron is stored until the bone marrow needs it for making new red corpuscles.

There are two chief kinds of white corpuscles. About 74 per cent are the kind called leucocytes, and 22 per cent are the kind called lymphocytes. A leucocyte is a round semi-transparent cell, consisting of a many-lobed nucleus surrounded by protoplasm (*see* Cell). It is about one-fourth larger than a red corpuscle. Unlike a red corpuscle, which is circulated only by the blood stream, the leucocyte can move independently. It moves like an amoeba by changing its shape. It can even work its way through the walls of the capillaries.

The work of the leucocytes is to police the blood. They engulf and devour and carry away harmful bacteria and other foreign substances. Because eating is their main task they are called phagocytes

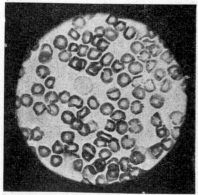
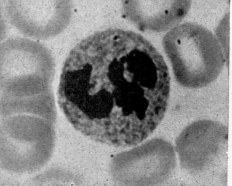

Right photo. courtesy F. Davidson & Co.

RED AND WHITE CORPUSCLES OF THE BLOOD

On the left are seen red corpuscles (erythrocytes) and on the right a white corpuscle (leucocyte) in the centre, surrounded by reds. Note that the white corpuscle has a nucleus, while the non-nuclear reds are concave on both sides. These photographs are highly magnified, that on the right being 5,000 times actual size. Some 10 million red cells are formed every second.

(from the Greek *phago*, " I eat "). When bacteria enter the tissues the leucocytes come out by the thousands from the near-by capillaries and attack them. Many leucocytes die in the battle, but reinforcements move in constantly. The resulting accumulation of dead bacteria, leucocytes, blood, dead tissue cells, and cell fragments is called " pus." The leucocytes, like the red corpuscles, are formed in the red marrow of the bones. They spend their lives in the blood stream and in the lymph, the fluid which surrounds the cells. A lymphocyte is a smaller white cell and helps to repair damaged tissue. The tiniest particles in the blood are the

body. All vaccines, antitoxins and the blood antiseptics of the " sulpha " group do their work as they are borne by the plasma stream.

The plasma carries all these things along with the corpuscles and platelets. It is like the water of a great river, and the body's cells, tissues, and organs are like ports where the stream picks up some cargoes and discharges others. It transports wastes, and delivers excess foods into the liver and other storage regions of the body.

Throughout all these transactions, the chemical composition of the plasma remains almost constant. This is necessary to maintain life. Should the blood

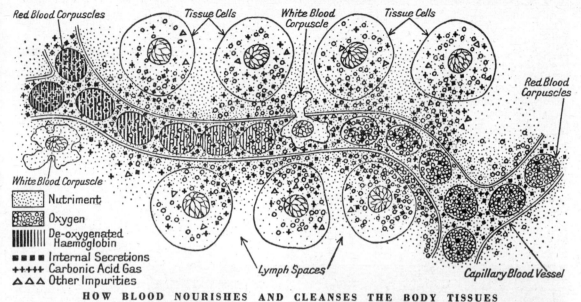

Red Blood Corpuscles   Tissue Cells   White Blood Corpuscle   Tissue Cells

Red Blood Corpuscles

White Blood Corpuscle

▦ Nutriment
▩ Oxygen
▥ De-oxygenated Haemoglobin
■■■ Internal Secretions
++++ Carbonic Acid Gas
△△△ Other Impurities

Lymph Spaces

Capillary Blood Vessel

HOW BLOOD NOURISHES AND CLEANSES THE BODY TISSUES

This diagram explains the important roles played by the circulation in the microscopic blood vessels known as capillaries. On the right are red corpuscles full of oxygen, nutriment and internal secretions which they give out to the tissue cells lying outside the capillary. In return they receive carbon dioxide (carbonic acid gas), de-oxygenated haemoglobin (colouring of red corpuscles) and other impurities which they carry to the veins on the left. Note the white blood corpuscle on the left which has passed through the capillary wall, and another, in centre, passing through.

platelets. They are only from one-fifth to one-tenth the diameter of the red corpuscles and have scalloped edges. When platelets come into contact with air or with any other foreign substance they disintegrate, liberating an enzyme (thrombokinase), which causes the blood to clot (*see* Enzyme). The origin of the platelets is unknown. They may be fragments of red corpuscles or they may be made independently in the red bone marrow.

The red and white corpuscles and the platelets make up together somewhat less than one-half the volume of the blood. The rest of the blood is plasma. About 90 per cent of this plasma is water, in which are dissolved at one time or another virtually all the tissue-building materials, the life-controlling chemicals, and the wastes of the body.

The complete story of the plasma is the story of respiration, because it transports both oxygen and carbon dioxide (*see* Respiration). It is the story of digestion and body chemistry (metabolism), since the stream carries food and wastage alike; it is the story of the glands and of the hormones, because it is through the plasma that all these substances travel to the cells, tissues, and organs, to regulate and co-ordinate the activities of the

become more dilute, the red corpuscles would swell and burst. Should it become more concentrated, the red corpuscles would shrivel. Thus the water taken by the plasma from the intestines is balanced by the amount it gives off through the kidneys. Most of its exchanges are made through the walls of the capillaries.

When normal blood is exposed to air, as by a cut, it clots and forms a scab. The reason for its clotting are two substances—prothrombin and fibrinogen. Prothrombin reacts with an enzyme supplied by the blood platelets in such a way as to form thrombin. This goes on to react with the fibrinogen to form a thread-like substance called fibrin, which traps the red corpuscles, as in a net, preventing further out-flow of blood from the cut. Serum is simply plasma from which fibrin has been removed.

Closely allied to blood is lymph, a clear, yellowish liquid which surrounds all the body cells. It is through the lymph that the cells receive oxygen and food from the blood and send waste products back to the blood. Lymph is made up of those parts of the blood which seep through the walls of the capillaries into the surrounding tissues. It has no red corpuscles and contains much less protein than blood plasma. The lymph circulates constantly.

After reaching the cells, it returns to the blood stream by two routes. It may simply pass back through the walls of the capillaries or it may return through the lymphatic system. This consists of a network of vessels draining all parts of the body and converging finally in a large duct (the thoracic duct), which discharges into a vein in the upper part of the chest. Pressure on the walls of the lymph vessels, caused by breathing and other bodily activities keeps the lymph in motion. But it can flow only in one direction, since these vessels are equipped with one-way valves.

Along the lymph vessels lie the lymph glands, specially abundant in the neck and under the arms. They are a friendly mechanism which filters out bacteria and poisonous material, preventing them from gaining a footing in the body. When we get a sore throat and the glands of the neck swell, it is because lymphocytes in these glands are repelling the invaders; similarly if we get a septic arm and the glands under the arm-pit swell, it is because battle is being done against an enemy.

The body is continually transforming energy into heat, which is carried off by the air coming out of the lungs and by radiation from the skin. To maintain the normal temperature of 98·6 degrees Fahrenheit the main mechanism is the surface capillary system, shrinking in the cold and dilating in the heat, working in combination with the sweat glands of the skin.

Much can be learnt by the physician by examination of the blood. About five million red cells per cubic millimetre is normal. A "differential count" shows the proportion of the different types of corpuscles, the specimen being treated with dye to make the white corpuscles visible. Anaemia is the general name for deficiencies in the number of red corpuscles or in the amount of haemoglobin they carry. Some anaemias are characteristic of serious disease of the blood, such as pernicious anaemia, which was invariably fatal until the liver extract treatment was discovered in 1925.

An increase in the number of white corpuscles is called leucocytosis. It is a normal response to invasion by bacteria and is a protective mechanism. White corpuscles also multiply enormously in a dangerous disorder of the bone-marrow and lymph glands called leucaemia.

Haemophilia is a condition in which the blood does not clot sufficiently to stop bleeding, so that minor wounds may prove fatal. It appears only in men, but is transmitted only by women. Thus the sons of a haemophilic father will be normal; but the daughters, while apparently normal, will hand on the disease to their sons.

Early experiments in replacing blood lost by one person with the blood of another sometimes succeeded and at other times proved fatal. Long investigation revealed that there are sharply different types or groups of blood. One classification recognizes four types, called for convenience, A, B, AB, and O. Between persons of the same blood type, blood can be exchanged safely. But where blood types differ, the following rules apply: Persons of Types A or B can receive blood from those of Type O and can give blood to those of Type AB; but persons of these first two types cannot exchange blood. Type AB can receive from persons of all other types (universal receivers), but can give to none outside their own group. Those of Type O can receive from no other groups, but can give to all others (universal donors).

The wrong type of blood introduced into a patient causes his red cells to clump and clot together, blocking the capillaries and killing him. The fluid meant to help him starts off the disaster, and the reaction of the victim towards incoming help encompasses his death.

In giving transfusions, hospitals prefer to use blood of the same type as the patient's, but in emergencies will use blood suitable according to the foregoing rules. Blood plasma, from which all

HARVEY DEMONSTRATES THE CIRCULATION OF THE BLOOD
William Harvey, an English physician, discovered the circulation of the blood in 1616. Here he is seen explaining his discovery to King Charles I. Previously it was thought that blood moved irregularly throughout the body, but Harvey showed that the heart is a pump systematically and regularly circulating the blood through the arteries. Harvey, like many pioneers in science, received much criticism and contradiction before his theory was accepted.

the red corpuscles have been removed, is often adequate for transfusions and does away with the problem of matching blood types. Whole blood for transfusion may be kept in refrigerated " blood banks " from two to three weeks; liquid plasma can be kept for several years. Dried plasma may be kept indefinitely without refrigeration and requires only the addition of sterile water.

Knowledge of pressure of blood in the arteries is very helpful to the physician in diagnosis and in treatment. An instrument invented by German scientists is in common use. Pressure measured when the heart is contracting is called the systolic pressure; that recorded when the heart is relaxing is known as the diastolic pressure. The diastolic pressure is very important because it is the measure of the only rest which the heart can ever obtain. High blood pressure is of great interest in modern life. Its cause is unknown.

But some substance elaborated by the kidneys outweighs a substance elaborated by the liver, and up goes the blood-pressure. The bore of the arteries is narrowed, the heart enlarges because it has to work harder against the increased pressure, and the patient tends to suffer from fatigue, sleeplessness and irritability. The essential treatment is rest. Low blood-pressure is an inherited condition often aggravated by sepsis, such as bad teeth or septic tonsils.

The ancients believed that the arteries contained air, and only the veins blood. The Greek physician Galen, in the 2nd century A.D., demonstrated that both arteries and veins contain blood. A direct connexion between the arteries and veins was not thought of. The year 1628 was an epoch-making date, for then William Harvey, of London, published a book in which he proved that the quantity of blood leaving the heart and the rate at which it leaves made a return to the heart necessary. He did not, however, actually see the capillaries which connect the small arteries and veins. (Harvey had made his discovery in 1616, and had begun to teach his theory before the publication of his book.)

It remained for the Italian Malpighi, in 1661, and the Hollander Leeuwenhoek, in 1669, to demonstrate, with the microscope, the existence of these minute tubes connecting arteries and veins. If the foot of a live frog is placed under a microscope, the blood may actually be seen flowing through the capillaries which lie in the webbing between the toes. The walls of these capillaries are immeasurably delicate and thin. Compared with them a sheet of tissue paper would be as the hide of an elephant.

Blood, THOMAS (died 1680). Having been deprived of his estates at the Restoration in 1663, this Irish soldier of fortune, who was known as " Colonel " Blood, tried to seize Dublin Castle and to carry off Ormonde, the Lord-Lieutenant. The plot failed and some of his associates were executed, but Blood himself managed to escape. He made another attempt on Ormonde's life, but this also was unsuccessful. His next and most famous exploit was stealing the crown jewels from the Tower of London. Disguised as a clergyman, he entered the Tower and carried off the crown under his cloak, while two of his associates made off with the orb and the sceptre. Meanwhile, the keeper of the jewels, who had been maltreated by the ruffians, recovered sufficiently to give the alarm, and the gang were captured with the jewels in their possession. One would have thought that Blood would be executed for this dastardly attempt, but instead of paying with his life he was rewarded. He insisted on seeing the king, and so contrived that Charles pardoned him and restored his estates.

Blowlamp. You may have seen a painter using a roaring, hissing type of lamp to soften the old paint on a door, after which he scrapes off the layer of paint with a broad scraper. Or you may have seen a plumber making a new soldered joint to a lead pipe and using the same sort of lamp to melt and soften the solder, while he moulds the new metal neatly around the joint with a wiper made of moleskin cloth.

The blowlamp gives a hot flame because it uses extra air really extra *oxygen* from the atmosphere, and this extra oxygen is mixed with the fuel vapour *before* burning. The principle is the same as that of the Bunsen Burner (*q.v*). The blowlamp is portable and handy; it can be used out of doors since its flame, once started, keeps alight even in a wind. It burns paraffin, alcohol, or petrol or benzine, though the lamps using the more volatile fuels are differently constructed from the paraffin lamps. Blowlamps burn vaporised fuel: the paraffin, etc., is turned into a gaseous form by heat and pressure; the fuel issues from a very tiny hole in the burner; air, on the contrary, can get in through several large holes in the outer tube of the burner. The jet of vaporised fuel, coming through the tiny hole issues with great velocity, and this produces a state of lowered pressure in the burner tube. Air rushes in to balance the pressure.

BLOWLAMP AT WORK
In the diagram, A is the fuel container; B the burner; C the air-pump; D the filler; E the air-release valve; F the handle; G the priming recess.

This, of course, is what takes place inside the Bunsen Burner, where a stream of coal-gas is burned with extra air. In the blowlamp, when properly working, the flame does not start from the fuel-jet, but from a point farther forward, where the tube contains a mixture of vaporised fuel and air. But if the pressure inside the lamp reservoir should fall too low, then the flame may ignite at the tiny jet, and liquid paraffin will then probably gush out in a luminous, smoky flame. The proper flame of the blowlamp, like that of the Bunsen Burner is a non-luminous one which we call atmospheric, because it burns air mixed with fuel.

Paraffin blowlamps are provided with an air-pump to generate the inside pressure needed to start them; lamps burning methylated spirit or

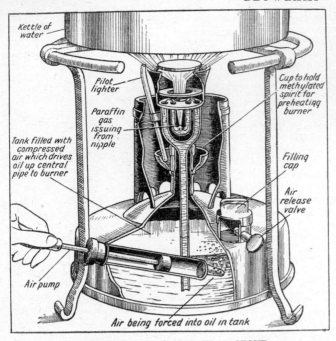

Kettle of water

Pilot lighter

Paraffin gas issuing from nipple

Tank filled with compressed air which drives oil up central pipe to burner

Air pump

Cup to hold methylated spirit for preheating burner

Filling cap

Air release valve

Air being forced into oil in tank

BLOWLAMP PRINCIPLE IN A STOVE
A pressure oil stove works on the same principle as a blowlamp ; the diagram explains how it functions. The stove is wickless and burns paraffin, and providing the burners are kept clean there is no more trouble with this type of stove than with any other.

benzine or petrol are " self-blowing." This means that, once the lamp has been warmed up sufficiently, the heat from the flame maintains the pressure needed to gasefy the fuel and force it to the jet, where it burns.

Our illustrations (p. 477) show a lamp being used to strip paint from a door ; also a diagrammatic drawing of a blowlamp as if cut through vertically. In the diagram, A is the steel or brass reservoir to contain the paraffin; a tube leads up from it to the burner B, inside which is the fuel-jet. C is the air-pump, underneath which you can see the air-release valve E. This valve is closed when the lamp is working; to extinguish the flame, the valve E is opened to release the pressure inside the reservoir, and the flame then dies down. D is the filler opening, with its screw cap. Around the base of the vertical tube leading to the burner is a shallow recess G to hold methylated spirit for " priming " the lamp. F is the handle.

In use, the paraffin lamp is three parts filled with fuel, and the air-release valve is shut; a little methylated spirit is poured into the recess G, and lit with a match. The flame from the spirit gradually warms the burner and also the body of the lamp; enough pressure is thus generated to force out vaporised paraffin at the jet. The size of the recess G is calculated to be such that, before the spirit burns out, the paraffin will have begun to gasefy, and the mixture of fuel and air will catch light and begin to hiss in the familiar manner. Now one or two strokes with the pump are given, to force in air and increase the pressure inside the reservoir. At this the flame begins to sputter and to roar—finally, in nine cases out of ten, settling down into a steady note, the flame meanwhile getting hotter and bigger.

If pumping is begun too soon—before sufficient heat has been generated to warm and vaporise the paraffin—a fiery fountain of liquid oil may spout from the burner ; in this case the pressure must at once be released, and we have to start all over again ! In lamps burning spirit there is no need for an air-pump; the heat from the priming flame starts them; and, since these more volatile fuels are turned into the gaseous form more readily, they continue to burn and make enough pressure.

Instead of an air-release valve there is a fuel-valve which shuts off the supply of spirit. Usually this valve is of the " needle " type in which a fine rod with a conical, pointed end, is screwed farther into a conical hole in the valve socket to shut off the supply, or is drawn back to allow spirit vapour to pass through. Spirit-burning blowlamps are less easy to manage than paraffin lamps, though they start up more quickly. In the paraffin blowlamp the flame can be immediately extinguished by opening the air release, so that no explosive mixture exists. In petrol or benzine lamps, on the contrary, the vapour is explosive, as well as the fuel itself.

The same principle is used in oil stoves for boiling water. We all know the handy pressure-stove which is so useful at picnics. It has a shallow, flat brass reservoir for the paraffin, and this supports three or four steel uprights which carry the plate or ring on which we stand our kettle or saucepan. Standing up vertically from the centre of the reservoir is the burner. Usually this is somewhat more complicated than the burner of the small blowlamp, since the actual jet is a nipple screwed into a coiled copper tube, the rear end of this tube being fixed into the top of the upright burner tube (*see* diagram).

As a result, the flame plays upon the copper coils and keeps them hot enough to vaporise the fuel—

The Tilley Lamp Co. Ltd.

PRESSURE LAMP AND HEATER
The pressure table lamp (left), burning paraffin, gives an excellent light and can be used in the open air. The heater (right) has a polished copper reflector which throws forward heat from an asbestos mantle.

which is pre-heated in passing around the coils before it goes to the burner nipple. The pressure-stove is tended in the same way as the blowlamp, and needs occasional pump-strokes while burning. An important point with all these appliances is to make sure that the tiny hole in the jet is clear; special prickers are supplied for this purpose, and wise people clear the jet each time before using.

Pressure-lamps, on much the same principle, are very handy. The hot flame plays upon a mantle and makes it white hot. Heaters, in which the mantle is made of woven asbestos, are also used.

Bluebell AND HAREBELL. The " bluebells of Scotland," about which the song was written, are the common harebell. In England the flower that is known as the blue-bell is the common wild hyacinth. In the harebell the petals are all united so as to form a complete bell-shaped corolla, whereas those of the hyacinth are separate or only joined at the base, and the flower itself is more tubular ; the advantage of these bell-shaped blossoms to the plants is that by drooping they protect the pollen from the rain.

Harebells grow wild on pasture-land and heaths, and the slender stems bear two or three dainty, drooping bell-shaped blossoms. The harebell belongs to the genus *Campanula* which includes about 300

H. Bastin

BLUEBELLS AND DAINTY HAREBELLS
In England the flower known as the bluebell is the common wild hyacinth (left). The bluebells of Scotland are harebells (right). The bluebell grows in woods, and each stalk has up to 12 flowers. Harebells are to be found in pasture-land and on heaths, and the slender swaying stems bear two or three dainty, drooping, pale blue blooms.

species, among them the familiar Canterbury bells, all of them popular on account of their bell-shaped, blue, violet, or white flowers and the ease with which they are grown. Its scientific name is *Campanula rotundifolio.*

The true English bluebell, *Scilla nutans*, grows in profusion in woodland glades, over most parts of the country; the flowers are usually a lovely misty blue colour with a tinge of purple ; occasionally they are a creamy white, but even then there is a faint suggestion of purplish-pink. The blue-bell, together with the primrose and, to a lesser extent, the wood violet, is a member of a group of flowers that are especially to be found in the oak woods of southern England.

Boadicea (died A.D. 61). Beneath the shadow of the Houses of Parliament, at the western end of Westminster Bridge, there stands a majestic bronze statue group. It depicts the figure of a woman erect and fearless, standing in a war-chariot drawn by two horses, with a spear in her hand, and crouching at her feet two girls, her daughters. The inscription on the pedestal reads : "Boadicea, Queen

of the Iceni, who died A.D. 61, after leading her people against the Roman invaders."

Tens of thousands of people daily pass this work of art, and although Londoners are proverbially indifferent to statues, this one is so striking and so spirited that many must admire it. Probably, however, the names of Boadicea (pron. bō-*a*-dis-ē'-*a*) and Iceni have such a foreign look that many who read them never dream that the statue commemorates a heroic queen who fought and died for Britain.

When the Romans invaded Britain in A.D. 43 they quickly reduced the more southerly portion to the outward form of a Roman province. But the shoulders of Britons were never fashioned to wear a foreign yoke, and beneath the surface of the national life there smouldered the fires of rebellion that only awaited a favourable opportunity to burst forth.

The Iceni, a warlike tribe which inhabited that portion of England which is now Norfolk, were far from subdued. While Suetonius Paulinus was Governor of Britain, and had gone north to make fresh conquests, the Iceni rose, under their queen, Boadicea, and but for the speedy return of the Roman legions the invaders would have lost Britain at the hands of a woman.

When the Romans took possession of Britain, the practice here, as elsewhere, was for Roman veterans, on being released from active service, to settle down in the conquered lands as country gentlemen of their day. These men were a law unto themselves, not being under military discipline like the soldiers, and when they coveted a farm they had few scruples about turning out the rightful owners. In the country of the Iceni, although the people there were nominally under Roman protection and regarded as allies, the violence of these foreign immigrants, and even that of their slaves, surpassed anything ever previously known in Britain. During the absence in the north of the governor and the army, these settlers drove the Iceni from their homes, stole their lands, made slaves of those they could capture, and committed fiendish atrocities. Even the royal house of the Iceni was invaded and despoiled by the ruffians. Queen Boadicea herself was scourged.

These insults roused the Iceni to fury, and under the command of Boadicea, her back still " bleeding from the Roman rods," as Tennyson puts it in his poem, an immense host of Britons for a time swept all before them, and put every Roman they came across to the sword.

Several Roman garrisons were wiped out, and the victors swept down on London – then little more than a trading village – and burnt it to the ground. When a sewer was made in Lombard Street a little more than a century ago, the trench cut through the ancient Roman tessellated pavement, above which lay the charred ashes and debris of this, the first fire of London.

Verulamium (St. Albans) was the largest Roman city in Britain at that time, and it was now attacked by Boadicea and utterly destroyed. In all, so it is said, about 70,000 of the Romans and their allies were killed in the battle.

It has to be remembered that these victories were gained while the main body of the Roman legions was engaged elsewhere. That army had still to be met. Suetonius came south as quickly as he could, and with some 10,000 armed men awaited the onslaught of the Britons. It is not certain where this battle took place—it may have been fought on Watling Street, between London and Chester, or at Battle Bridge (now King's Cross), in some fields to the north of London, or at Chester.

Before the battle Queen Boadicea, with her daughters beside her in a chariot, rallied her warriors, who included many women, urging them to strike a blow for freedom. " If you weigh well the strength of the armies, and the cause of the war," she cried, " you will see that in this battle you must conquer or die. This is a woman's resolve ; as for men, they may live and be slaves."

Alas ! for Britain's freedom ; the trained legions of Rome, with their better weapons, proved too strong. The battle was long and fierce, but the Romans had the advantage from the first, and many thousands of Britons were slain. When all was lost Boadicea put an end to her life by poison rather than fall into the hands of the Romans. Our information about the queen is obtained from the Roman historian, Tacitus. The name is more correctly spelt Boudicca, and is supposed to be connected with the Welsh buddugol or victorious, so that as a proper name Boudicca may be considered practically equivalent to Victoria.

Boar. Hunting wild swine was once one of the favourite sports of kings and nobles, and a special breed of dogs (boar-hounds) was developed for it. The wild boar is larger than most breeds of the domestic pig, and its formidable tusks and savage spirit make it a dangerous foe when brought to bay. It is still preserved for hunting on some great estates in Europe. " Pig-sticking," as it is called in India, is one of the most popular sports in the sub-continent.

This powerful beast is about four feet long and covered with bristles and greyish-black hair. The great tusks of the lower jaw in the adult curve so far over the snout as to become useless, and their place as weapons is taken by the protruding teeth of the upper jaw. The boar lives in the forest and comes forth at night to feed on roots, herbs, grains, and small animals.

The wild boar (*Sus scrofa*) is found in Europe, Northern Africa, and Central and Northern Asia ; it is fairly plentiful in Spain, Russia, and Germany, but is extinct in England. The Indian wild boar, *Sus cristatus*, is slightly taller than the European.

BOADICEA RIDES BESIDE THE THAMES
One of the finest of London's statues is that by Thomas Thornycroft (1815-85) near Westminster Bridge representing Boadicea, the queen who led the Iceni tribe of eastern Britain in a vain attack on the Roman invaders. Though her end was tragic, her name lives in our nation's story. This photograph was taken from the top of a flight of steps leading down to the riverside

From LOG RAFT to RACING YACHT

Thousands of years have passed since Man launched the first boat. But still today as we pull on oar, glide beneath a billowing sail or dash along in a motor-boat, we recapture some of the thrill of that first brave venture.

Boats AND YACHTS. Each age has contributed something to the development of boating, so that now there are all manner of craft that plough through the water or glide over the surface. But the pleasure of boating has not greatly changed—it is essentially the same now that it was thousands of years ago, when Man first discovered that he could contrive a craft that would support him upon the water.

From the raft to the dug-out canoe, made from the hollowed-out trunk of a tree, was a big step, from the dug-out to the skin- or bark-covered craft a smaller one, and no one knows when or how these steps were first taken. The earliest white man who set foot on the shores of America found the Indians paddling their birch-bark canoes up and down the streams and even venturing out upon the ocean. A great deal of the exploring which was done by the pioneers was accomplished by the aid of such canoes.

Racing dinghies, each with a crew of one man only, carry a big spread of canvas, calling for really expert handling.

They were so light in weight that the travellers could carry them long distances over rough trails in the wilderness, and at the same time could transport in them considerable loads of equipment.

The Canadian canoes which we use for pleasure today are modelled upon the type that the Red Indian devised when he fashioned his craft of birch and cedar and filled its seams with the pitch of the spruce. The light construction of the ordinary canoe makes it extremely sensitive to movement on the part of the paddler. For that reason every canoeist should be a good swimmer, though it is true that a capable paddler is not likely to capsize, for he has learned to adjust his body to the craft.

Boats differ from canoes chiefly in being propelled by sculls or oars instead of by paddles. Greater force, of course, can be exerted with oars than with a paddle, but the rower is at the disadvantage of having to face backward instead of forward. The types of boats for pleasure and use range from narrow racing skiffs to lifeboats and the heavy "dories" of the Newfoundland fishermen. Lighter boats used on inland waters are generally called skiffs, and

the heavier ones used on the sea, rowing-boats. A dinghy is shorter and of much broader beam than a rowing-boat and generally has but one pair of rowlocks. Dinghies are carried by small yachts as tenders and are used as pleasure boats on inland waters. Boats are either carvel- or clinker-built, a carvel-built boat having the edges of the planks laid flush, while in a clinker-built boat they overlap.

One-man skiffs are extremely light boats of a long, narrow build, with sliding seats and outrigger rowlocks. Sliding seats are set on rollers and move forward as the oarsman pulls at his oar, thus giving him a longer stroke. In the eight-oared shells, such as are used in the Oxford and Cambridge Boat Race, each man pulls a single oar. Much time is spent in training for such races, for there is probably no sport in which technique and physical

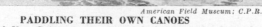

American Field Museum; C.P.R.

PADDLING THEIR OWN CANOES

This canoe of New Guinea is so uncertainly balanced that it needs a roughly constructed outrigger to keep it from capsizing. Natives do not hesitate to venture far out to sea in such craft. In the upper right photograph a fishing party is setting out on the St. Maurice river in Canada in a Canadian canoe, the design and structure of which were learned from the Red Indians.

QUAINT PRIMITIVE TYPES OF NATIVE CRAFT

One of the most extraordinary-looking craft ever built is the canoe (4) used in the Santa Cruz Islands, a group near the Solomon Islands in the South Pacific. It has a long platform erected at right angles to the dugout, with a little house at the end supported by the outrigger. The strangely shaped sail is peculiar to the Santa Cruz Islands. Others shown are an Eskimo kayak (1), which, except for the paddler's compartment, is completely decked over; a goofah (2), a circular boat of water-proofed hides, used on the Tigris in Iraq; a coracle (3) such as the early Britons made; a dugout canoe with an outrigger (5); an inflated hide (6) on which natives in parts of the sub-continent of India cross rivers; a balsa, or large raft (7), used by some natives of South America.

Topical

OXFORD AND CAMBRIDGE ROWING NECK-AND-NECK

The eight-oared boats used in the University annual boat race, and in all other eight-oared events, are frail craft, the woodwork being so thin that if you stepped in the wrong place you might put your foot through it. These boats are also known as racing shells and cost well over £200 to build. This photograph shows the Oxford and Cambridge crews at Hammersmith. The race is rowed annually from Putney to Mortlake, Surrey, the distance being a little over four miles, and an oarsman must be superbly fit to take part in such a gruelling contest.

condition are of greater account than in rowing. The person who combines strength with such a mastery of the stroke that he gets the full power of his body into each sweep of the oar is the one who " makes the crew." Weight is an advantage, of course, but sometimes candidates who are light win races from rivals of much greater weight but less skill.

In the ordinary rowing-boat the rower uses two oars or sculls, the difference between oars and sculls being that sculls are shorter, lighter and have a more concave blade. Sculls are always used in pairs.

Sailing does not offer, perhaps, so much opportunity for exercise and physical development as rowing, but there is no question about the fascination of the sport. Between the sailing-boat 12 to 15 feet long and the great Bermudian-rigged racing yachts are many gradations in size, speed and amount of sail carried. The smaller boats usually depend upon a " centre-board "—a kind of additional keel that can be lowered at will—to enable them to sail " in the wind," which the larger ones do not need, because they are already well provided with the necessary weight of lead in their deep " fin " keels.

The great event of the English yachting season is Cowes Week, held in August, when the pick of the racing yachts may be seen competing for the King's Cup and other coveted trophies. The premier British club is the Royal Yacht Squadron, with headquarters at Cowes. Crews trained in all the

knacks of sail handling, helmsmen who know how to steer their boats with extraordinary skill, and skippers who have an uncanny way of finding wind streaks and of manoeuvring their boats into favourable positions, handle the competing yachts.

The most technical problem in sailing is handling the sails to take advantage of the wind. The simplest sail action occurs when a sail is spread so that the boat is driven square before the wind. But suppose a wind from the north is blowing upon a boat headed west. If the boat's sail were in line with the hull, so that everything was " broadside on " to the wind, the wind would press the boat and sail sidewise to the southward. To sail westward, the sail must be set to extend approximately south-eastward from the mast. The wind now will exert a glancing pressure upon the sail, tending to force it south-westward. This south-westward pressure can be considered as operating in two directions—southward with the wind, and westward, the direction in which the boat is headed.

Water resistance against the side of the hull keeps the boat from going more than a little to the southward (the amount it does go is called " leeway "); but the water offers little resistance to westward movement. The exact set of sail and rudder needed varies with the design of the vessel and other factors.

The handling of sails may be understood from considering the Bermudian or triangular sail used on many sloops. The vertical forward edge of the sail is fastened to wooden rings, which slide up the mast as the tip is drawn upward by a halyard. The bottom edge is fastened to a boom, or horizontal spar, so attached at its forward end that it can swing from side to side about the mast, moving the sail with it, much as a door turns on its hinges. The other end is fastened by block and tackle to a convenient mounting on the deck, so it can be let out (" paid out ") to either side, or hauled close in to the centre line. A jib (the triangular sail before the mast) is handled similarly, save that it has no boom, and the hoops on which it runs are mounted on the forestay, a rope from the tip of the mast to the bow.

Every large sail bears on each side one or more horizontal rows of short lengths of cord, called " reef points." If, owing to high wind, the yachtsman does not want to hoist his entire sail, he hoists as much as desired, then by tying reef points from each side firmly under the boom, he lashes down the unexposed portion of the sail. Because the sails of " square-rigged " ships were attached to spars high above deck, the crew had to go aloft to reef sail—instead of being able to do so from the deck, as they can on craft with " fore-and-aft " rig.

Motor-boats have won great favour. While they do not offer the challenge to skill presented by a sailing-vessel, they are less dependent upon weather, and easier to handle in narrow waters, such as rivers. They range in size from launches no larger than a rowing-boat to ocean-going cruisers usually driven by Diesel engines.

Such boats are classified broadly according to the type of hull and position of the engine. The traditional hull is the " displacement " type, which has a prow that cuts through the water, and always sits low enough to displace its own weight. For achieving high speed on relatively calm water, the " hydroplane " hull is widely used. The hull is flat-bottomed, with or without " steps." At high speed the forward portion rises clear of the water, and the craft skims over the surface, rising on the " heel "

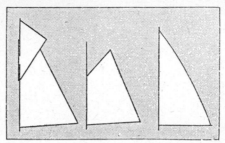

RIGS OF SMALL CRAFT
Each of these rigs has the same area of sail. The gaff and topsail rig, left, is the steadiest ; the single gaff mainsail, centre, is used in small boats, while the Bermudian rig, right, is used on racing craft of all types.

of the hull. As it capsizes easily, only skilled helmsmen can handle this type of vessel at high speeds.

Motor-boats are further classified as those which have the engine inside the hull, connected by a shaft to the propeller, and those which have the engine and propeller in one unit, hung overside from the stern. The latter engine is known as an " outboard." Rowing-boats can be made into motor-boats by attaching an outboard motor, and can be used in extremely shallow water, since the engine is pivoted on its mounting and can be swung up to clear obstructions. Outboard motors are suited only to smaller craft. Larger ones must have their motors mounted farther forward, not only because of the greater weight but also because the powerful action of the propeller has a tendency to force the stern of the boat down into the water.

One of the most curious of primitive boats was the round coracle which Caesar found in use when the Romans invaded Britain, and which, very nearly 2,000 years later, is still used on certain lakes of Ireland and by some Welsh fishermen. It is an open saucer-shaped vessel, usually large enough for one man only. A skin or other waterproof covering is stretched and fastened over a frame made of thin strips of wood laid across one another, tied together, and bent upward.

A boat similar to the coracle is the goofah, a queer circular basket-like craft of the East, still in use in the region of Baghdad on the Tigris and Euphrates rivers. It is about six feet in diameter, woven from willow twigs, and made watertight with bitumen.

Boats of a very different type are made by Eskimos. Those used by a single man for sealing or fishing, called kayaks, are made by covering a strong but light framework of bone or wood with skins. The boat is decked over except at the centre, where a hole is left for the occupant, who, when seated, laces himself in tightly with a skin apron, to prevent the water from entering. Though frail, these boats are very buoyant, and a skilful boatman can capsize his kayak with a twist of the paddle and

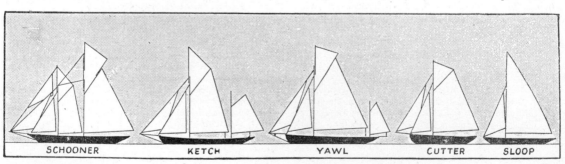

SCHOONER KETCH YAWL CUTTER SLOOP

FIVE CHIEF TYPES OF SAILING YACHTS
The schooner was once a popular rig for yachts but is not very often seen nowadays. This rig has two masts with fore-and-aft sails, the main mast being higher than the foremast. The ketch and the yawl reverse this order, and the ketch carries its smaller mast (mizzen) before the wheel or tiller and the yawl aft of it. The cutter carries a mainsail, topsail, jib and foresail. The sloop has only a foresail and mainsail. The sloop here is Bermudian rigged.

JET-ENGINED SPEED-BOAT AND RACING YACHTS

The jet engines which had proved so successful in military aircraft during the Second World War (1939-45) were later tried out in boats. Sir Malcolm Campbell, who set up a world's water-speed record of 141·7 m.p.h. on Lake Coniston, Lancashire, in 1939, fitted a Goblin jet engine to the hull of the motor-boat which he had then used. The Blue Bird II, as it is called, is just over 27 feet in length, nearly 11 feet in beam and is largely built of timber. During trial runs (top) at Poole Harbour, Dorset, in 1947, the boat was estimated to have reached a speed of 150 m.p.h. The headquarters of British yachting are at Cowes, Isle of Wight, and annual regattas (lower) are held there in August. The three yachts in the foreground are Bermudian rigged, with mainsail and spritsail.

TO see how a yacht is manoeuvred, let us follow this cutter as she leaves port (at the top of the picture), sails around the island (in the centre of the picture) and comes home again. The positions of sails and rudder illustrate the theoretical mechanics of sailing ; they will not necessarily correspond exactly to those required for sailing any particular boat, for each boat has its peculiarities, requiring individual allowances in steering and setting of sails. At first the vessel 'quarters' with her mainsail, jib and rudder all set to starboard (right). The wind presses on the sail and jib, and tends to turn the yacht counter-clockwise—that is, to turn its nose to the left. To counteract this, the rudder is set to turn the bow to the right, with the result that the boat sails as shown. When it becomes time to head south, the yachtsman, knowing that later he must turn west, probably will choose to 'jibe' into his southerly course, by hauling his mainsail and jib from right to left, and then sail before the wind as shown, with the wind pressing his sails forward. When it is time to sail west, he hauls in on his mainsail a little, throws over his jib to the port (left) side, and sets his rudder to port. Now he is 'reaching,' or sailing across the wind. The wind presses slantwise on the sails, wedging them forward, and the rudder is set as shown to counteract the tendency of the bow to turn northward. In this case, he is sailing on a 'starboard reach.' so called because the wind is on his right, or starboard, side. When it is time to turn north, the yachtsman faces his most difficult problem. Since he cannot sail directly north, he must 'tack'—that is, pursue a zigzag course, keeping as near north on each tack as his boat will sail. Here the shape of the open water makes it advisable to start north on the starboard tack, so he 'goes about,' by setting the rudder and sails to the starboard. Now the wind presses on the sails, trying to turn them so they will lie north and south. The rudder prevents this, and the boat, held between these opposing controls, slips slowly forward as shown. After sailing this tack as long as desirable, the yachtsman changes to the port tack, and continues alternating tacks—that is, 'beats to windward'—until he 'goes about' to reach his anchorage.

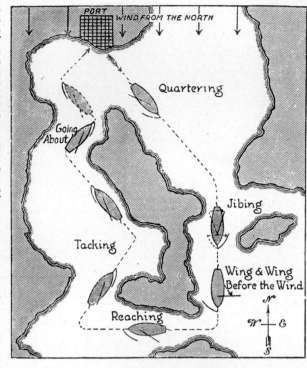

HOW TO SAIL A YACHT

turn completely over under water. A large undecked boat constructed of skins, called the oomiak or woman's boat, is also made. While clumsier, it has the advantage of carrying a larger number of persons and considerable loads.

In the Pacific Islands and elsewhere a sort of raft called the catamaran is much used; it is made by lashing together three or more logs. Though crude, it is able to travel through rough seas where modern craft would be unsafe. The name catamaran is also applied to boats with outriggers of varying forms, which serve to stabilize them. It is practically impossible to capsize such craft, and long sea voyages have been made in them.

In 1865 John MacGregor, a Scotsman, invented a wooden canoe known as the Rob Roy, built somewhat like the Eskimo kayak, being entirely decked over with the exception of a cockpit in which the paddler sat. Strong and light enough to be carried over land, it was propelled by a paddle grasped in the middle and with a blade at either end. Canoes on these lines are still built, and sometimes the wooden frame is covered only with canvas. Collapsible canoes, which can be taken to pieces and so carried about, are also made.

The making of a dug-out canoe by savages without adequate tools required much skill. Usually a suitable log was shaped roughly on the outside with axes, and the interior was then burned out. A week or more was required for this operation, as the coals had frequently to be renewed or shifted from place to place, while the wood was dampened here and there to guide the course of the fire. The final shaping was then completed with the aid of various crude tools.

Boer War. On October 11, 1899, war broke out in South Africa between the independent Boer republics of the Transvaal and the Orange Free State on the one side, and Great Britain on the other. Only after three years of the hardest fighting were the British able to conquer their sturdy opponents. The Boers were descendants of Dutch colonists in Cape Colony who had trekked northward in 1836 and afterwards, following the passing of Cape Colony into British hands.

A conflict with the Transvaal Boers had occurred in 1881, in which the British suffered a defeat at Majuba Hill ; this was followed by treaties (1881 and 1884) in which it was agreed that the Transvaal should have complete self-government in internal affairs, though in external affairs it should be under the guardianship of Great Britain.

Meanwhile came the discovery of rich gold mines in the Transvaal, and a flood of adventurers poured in. The Boers remained chiefly farmers and stock-raisers, and friction with the "uitlanders" (foreigners) followed. A futile raid by Dr. Leander Jameson (in December 1895) to aid the uitlanders against the oppressive measures of President Paul Kruger, only made matters worse. A cablegram sent by the German Emperor to President Kruger on the day after Dr. Jameson's surrender led the Boers to believe that they might count on German assistance, and in 1899 war ended the long-drawn-out negotiations. The Orange Free State joined the Transvaal in arms.

The vigour of the Boers and the distance of the conflict from Europe taxed the resources of Great Britain as they had never been taxed since the days of Napoleon. Her foes had been trained to the use of weapons since boyhood, and fought in a country where they knew every pass and kopje (hill). There were no great battles, and the war was mainly a series of ambuscades and sieges—of Ladysmith, Mafeking and Kimberley especially. For the British, Lord Roberts, with Lord Kitchener as chief of staff, was eventually put in supreme command, while the Boers fought under Cronje, Christian de Wet, Louis Botha, Joubert, Smuts and Delarey.

Excellent marksmen and horsemen though they were, the Boers were unable to resist forces that Great Britain poured into the war. On February 27, 1900, Cronje surrendered with 4,000 men. On March 13, Lord Roberts entered Bloemfontein. On May 1, the advance began on Pretoria, the Boer capital. At Spitzkop, on September 8, General Botha fought the last set battle of the war. Towards the end of the year Lord Roberts returned to England, and the command of the British army was taken over by Lord Kitchener. From that time until the war's actual end, the Boers, led by De Wet, Smuts and others, harassed the British with guerrilla tactics. Because of the obstacles placed in the British path by the non-combatant population, concentration camps were established for them.

By the treaty of Vereeniging (May 31, 1902), the Transvaal and Orange Free State became British colonies. But self-government was soon restored, and in 1910 these former enemy countries became equal members with Cape Colony and Natal in the Union of South Africa, and General Louis Botha became the first Prime Minister. The British had employed 250,000 men in the war, losing 5,774 killed, 22,829 wounded, and 43,616 sent home as invalids. The total Boer force was about 95,000.

Bohemia. This chief part of the Czechoslovak republic lies very nearly at the centre of the European continent, and is roughly rectangular in shape. At the time of its incorporation into Czechoslovakia, in 1918, it had an area of 20,060 square miles and a population of just over 7,000,000. It is bounded on three sides by mountain chains (the Bohemian Forest, Ore Mountains and Sudetic range), and on the fourth side by the Moravian hills. Since early in the Middle Ages it has been inhabited mainly by a Slavic race called Czechs, but there was a numerous German minority in the north (Sudetenland).

The king of Bohemia early became one of the seven electors of the Holy Roman Empire. In the 14th century Bohemian kings of the Luxembourg line were also emperors, and Bohemia was one of the most flourishing countries of Europe. The University of Prague or Praha (the capital), dating from this period (1348), is one of the oldest in Europe. The Hussite wars of the 15th century, which grew out of the religious teachings of John Huss, left the power of the kingdom greatly impaired. After 1526 Bohemia was a possession of Austria. The Thirty Years' War, which started in 1618 with a Protestant revolt in Prague, left the land wasted and Protestantism crushed.

In the 19th century there was an unsuccessful revolt against Austrian rule—in 1848; and in 1918, after the First World War, Bohemia became part of the new state of Czechoslovakia.

In 1938 the Germans incorporated the Sudetenland region into the German Empire; and the following year the rest of Bohemia, with Moravia, was forced to become a German protectorate. With the victory of the Allies in 1945, which terminated the Second World War, Czechoslovakia regained its independence and the lost territory.

The principal products of Bohemia are glass, gloves and textiles. (*See* Czechoslovakia).

Bohr, NIELS (born 1885). This Danish scientist was born at Copenhagen, and was destined to win a world-wide reputation by his theories of

BOHEMIAN PEASANT GIRLS IN GALA DRESS
These girls are wearing the traditional Bohemian costume which is seen on Sundays and holidays in the villages. Bohemia became a part of the republic of Czechoslovakia in 1918, at the end of the First World War (1914–1918), when Austria-Hungary was broken up.

SIMPLE BOILER FOR HIGH PRESSURE ENGINES
In this water-tube boiler the water in the large drum at the top circulates through the tubes ; the hot gases pass around the tubes and heat the water, the steam accumulating in the drum.

the construction of the atom. He studied in England, and while working at Manchester under Lord Rutherford, who was professor of physics at the university, he proposed his theory that the atom consisted of a central nucleus with rings of electrons revolving about it. Rutherford, who had already begun his own experiments on bombarding atoms with alpha particles, had done a good deal to clear the way for a theory of the kind which Bohr worked out for the atomic structure.

With Bohr he now suggested that the atom of hydrogen consisted of one particle of the kind which we now call the proton, and of one negative electron revolving around the central core or nucleus. This theory was soon accepted by physicists. Bohr went on to make more discoveries and to evolve theories which did an enormous amount to help us to understand radiation and the atom. In 1939 he spent some months in the U.S.A., where he conferred with Albert Einstein on atomic energy projects.

At this time Bohr was giving his time to the possibility of splitting the uranium atom and so releasing the vast amounts of energy stored up in uranium. In 1943 he escaped from German-occupied Denmark in a small boat, and put his immense knowledge and experience at the disposal of Britain and America. Bohr played a very important part after this in solving some problems of the atomic bomb. In 1922 he had been given the Nobel prize in Physics; many other honours came to him, including election to the Royal Society in 1926. (*See* Atom).

Boiler. We boil foods in order to soften the tissues and make them tender and appetising, and to render them digestible. In an " open " vessel—one which is allowed to take the same pressure as the atmosphere outside, water boils at 212° Fahrenheit. We cannot

make the water any hotter, since any added heat merely makes more steam come off. But this temperature of boiling water is a good one for preparing foods. and it is only when we especially want to get a higher one that we need close in the top of the saucepan or boiler, and seal it against loss of steam.

There is a kind of boiler called an autoclave (when it is used for scientific work or for industrial processes), or a pressure cooker. This was invented by a Frenchman, Denis Papin (1647–1710), and consists of a very strong vessel with a steam-tight lid which can be fixed on by clamps or screws. It has a safety valve which can be set to blow off at a desired safe pressure. Papin called it a " digester," and big ones are used for softening or cooking things in factories and canneries.

Smaller pressure cookers are used in domestic cookery—for example to make a " boiling-" fowl tender; the cooker also saves time in preparing food, and by using a small pressure above that of the atmosphere we can reduce the cooking time by half. Papin had no idea of using his boiler for raising steam to drive an engine, which is one of the most important ways in which we use the same principle today, in high pressure engines.

Early steam engines had simple " tank " boilers and took off the steam at very low pressure—2 4 lb. per square inch—and such engines as Newcomen's really used the pressure of the atmosphere to drive the piston in the cylinder. James Watt (1736–1819) used what was then called a " wagon " boiler, and indeed it was something like a covered wagon in shape, and was heated by a fire *outside* it underneath. The pressure was only five pounds per square

YARROW BOILER AS USED ON SHIPS
In this Yarrow boiler, used for some marine engines, there are three drums with many water tubes connecting them. Some boilers have four or five drums and work at pressures of 1,500 lb. per sq. inch.

inch above atmospheric pressure. When Richard Trevithick (1771–1833) invented his high-pressure steam engine and steam carriage he needed a boiler to withstand at least ten times the pressure used by Watt. So he built a cylindrical boiler, horizontal, with the furnace *inside* it and running through to a smoke stack at one end.

The great aim henceforth was to get a bigger surface at which the water was exposed to the heat of the fire, and of the hot gases as they made their way to the chimney. George Stephenson (1781–1848) used a fire-tube boiler, in which the hot gases passed from the firebox at the back to the smokebox at the front through a number of tubes. The fire-tube boiler came into general use for steam locomotives; but for stationary engines a boiler on the lines of Trevithick's, with a furnace tube inside it, was usual for many years. This was called the " Cornish " boiler; by making it longer, more heating surface was provided. A similar cylindrical boiler but with two furnace tubes became known as the " Lancashire "; many are in use today for small installations.

Meanwhile inventors had been busy making boilers in which the water flowed in many tubes and the hot gases from the burning fuel circulated around these water-tubes. During the few years when steam road carriages had their hey-day, before restrictions drove them out of business, other types of boiler were attempted. Sir Goldsworthy Gurney designed one in 1826 which had many U-shaped water-tubes, and the lower limbs of the U-tubes formed the actual fire-bars. Walter Hancock, who also put steam coaches on the roads of England, used a boiler made something like the modern hot-water radiators commonly used for warming rooms.

On the ocean the steam boilers went through much the same development, except that, at first, they missed the fire-tube stage and used large flat-sided flues as high as a man and about 18 inches wide. Rectangular " box " boilers did for low pressures, but when higher pressure engines came in, the boiler had to be made cylindrical, since this shape is much stronger against internal pressure. But both on land and on sea the tank type of boiler gave way to others of very different construction. A Babcock & Wilcox water-tube boiler as used on land is shown in page 488. You will notice that the water in the large drum above circulates *through* the tubes; the hot gases pass *around* the tubes and give up much of their heat before going to the chimney shaft. Inside the drum, steam accumulates and builds up the pressure needed.

Another picture in page 488 shows a Yarrow boiler for ships. Here there are three drums arranged in a triangle, with many tubes connecting them. The Babcock & Wilcox boiler in different forms is used both on land and at sea. The diagram reproduced above, of a fairly big installation, on land, shows many interesting things about boilers generally. Thus at the bottom there is the travelling grate which takes the coal gradually through the furnace and then discharges the ashes into a pit

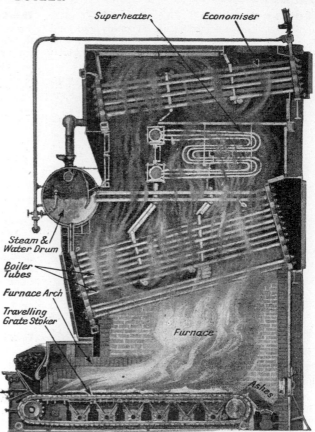

Babcock & Wilcox, Ltd.

BOILER WITH A MECHANICAL STOKER

Here is shown the mechanical stoker which takes the coal gradually through the furnace and then discharges the ashes into a pit. In the superheater the steam is made so hot that it becomes dry.

at the end. Above the boiler tubes is the superheater, a nest of tubes in which steam from the drum is made so hot that it becomes dry and loses its water vapour. In the top part of the casing are the long tubes of the economiser (really fuel economiser, or feed-water heater). In these tubes the cold feed water is heated before entering the boiler. Note that both superheater and economiser are in the path of the furnace gases, from which they extract all possible heat before these gases pass on to the chimney stack.

And now we will say something about a really big boiler, which generates a million pounds of steam every hour. It was built for a generating station of the Edison Company of New York, and consumes 40 tons of powdered coal per hour. Such a boiler is as high as a ten-storey house, and as wide as two main roads. When this one was completed, and before it was put into use, a luncheon was given in the main chamber, walled in by the water tubes, and 60 persons sat down to table!

A few words about the hot-water boiler many of us have in our houses is necessary. It is not really a " boiler," for the water does not—or should not —boil. Unlike a steam boiler the water fills it, and there is no steam space. It is intended to make cold water hot, so that we can use it for baths, etc. (*See* Steam ; Steam Engine ; Water).

Boleyn, ANNE (1507-36). The grim Tower of London has witnessed many sad and moving scenes—not least the imprisonment, trial and execution of Anne Boleyn, Queen of England and mother of Queen Elizabeth.

ANNE BOLEYN AS QUEEN
When Anne Boleyn was Queen of England (Henry VIII married her in November 1532 or January 1533) her portrait was painted by the German artist Hans Holbein (c. 1497-1543). A contemporary writer described her as being of ' swarthy complexion, long neck and wide mouth.'

The second queen of Henry VIII, she was the daughter of a noble of Henry's court, spent some three years at the French court, and soon after her return from France, about 1522, was so unfortunate as to attract King Henry by her gaiety and charm. Having divorced Catherine of Aragon, Henry married Anne. But she failed to give him a son, and he was ready to believe scandalous tales which were whispered of his young wife. Condemned on the charge of unfaithfulness to her royal husband, Anne protested her innocence to the last. The Lord Mayor of London—worthy representative of a noble line of Lord Mayors, who for centuries were among the few public men in England who had the courage to defy unjust kings—said that he could not observe anything in the proceedings at her trial " but that they were resolved to make an occasion to get rid of her."

She went to her death with pathetic courage. " My neck is small enough," said she, spanning it with her fingers, when assured that the headsman would do his work skilfully. On the day following the execution, Henry was betrothed to Jane Seymour.

Bolingbroke, HENRY ST. JOHN, 1ST VISCOUNT (1678-1751). Statesman and writer, Bolingbroke was also, to all intents and purposes, a traitor. He was born at Battersea, Surrey, on October 10, 1678, the only son of Sir Henry St. John, and was educated at Eton. In 1710 he was appointed Secretary of State for Foreign Affairs; was created Viscount Bolingbroke in 1712; and in the following year he concluded the Treaty of Utrecht between England and France and Spain.

Peace being restored, the succession to the British throne became a question of the first importance, Queen Anne having no surviving children. Bolingbroke got into communication with James, the Stuart Pretender to the British throne, and it is believed Bolingbroke was prepared, in so far as it lay within his power to do so, to offer the crown to James on Anne's death.

Anne's sudden death in 1714 and the promptitude with which George I was proclaimed king shattered Bolingbroke's plans. He was dismissed from office and fled to France, where he became Secretary of State to James the Pretender. Bolingbroke was pardoned in 1723 and returned to England, where he wrote essays upon history in the form of letters to his friends. He died on December 12, 1751.

Bolivar, SIMON (1783-1830). The great South American statesman and general, who organized and led the revolutions which, after centuries of misrule, freed Venezuela, Colombia, Peru and Bolivia from the power of Spain, was Simon Bolivar (pron. bol-ē'-var), known as the " Liberator." Born in Caracas (now the capital of Venezuela) of a wealthy Spanish colonial family, he was studying law in Madrid when Napoleon overran Spain and temporarily broke her power. All the Spanish American colonies realized the opportunity and struck for their freedom.

Hastening home, Bolivar put himself at the head of the patriots of Venezuela. The successful insurrection in Caracas, in April 1810, was followed within a month by rebellion in Argentina and Chile. Soon the continent boiled into revolution. For the next 20 years Bolivar was alternately a conquering hero

SIMON BOLIVAR
Liberator of several of the South American states from the Spanish yoke, Simon Bolivar (1783-1830) is held in high honour in the Latin republics. Here is his portrait on a Venezuelan stamp, value one bolivar (coin).

with an army and autocratic power, and a fugitive pursued to the West Indies by hired assassins. He reached the pinnacle of his glory in 1828, when he was president of three countries which he had liberated: the republics of Colombia (then comprising Venezuela, Colombia, Panama and Ecuador), of Peru, and of Bolivia—the last formed in 1825 from South-Eastern Peru and named in Bolivar's honour.

Obliged for a time to assume dictatorial powers, Bolivar was a sincere patriot, devoted to the cause of liberty and equality. His private fortune and the large sums voted to him were spent on military supplies and in liberating slaves. Bolivar died in Colombia, but in 1842 his remains were taken to Caracas, where a statue of him occupies the centre of the gardens of the Plaza de Bolivar.

ANDEAN LAND *of* SNOW *and* SUNSHINE

Largely because it has no seaboard, Bolivia is one of the less-known of the republics of South America. When we come to study it, we find that it is a land of the most interesting contrasts.

Bolivia. The history of this South American republic has been a stormy one. Under the Spanish rule it formed part of Peru. After about 15 years of insurrection the Bolivians gained their freedom in 1825, and took their name in honour of Simon Bolivar, who drafted their new constitution. Disputes and civil wars were many during the 19th century ; a disastrous war with Chile, which ended in 1883, stripped Bolivia of its rich nitrate-bearing province on the Pacific seaboard, together with the port of Antofagasta, and since then the country has had no coastline.

In 1932 fighting broke out between Bolivia and Paraguay as a result of a long-standing dispute over the Gran Chaco, a stretch of territory between the Pilcomayo and Paraguay rivers, to which both countries laid claim. It continued with increasing intensity until May 1933, when Paraguay formally declared war on Bolivia. The troops engaged endured terrible sufferings, for most of the fighting took place in swamps and dense forests. Several attempts at mediation were made without avail, and the war went on until June 1935, when an armistice was signed. A treaty of peace was concluded in July 1938.

Although Bolivia is the fourth political division of South America in size, its population is reckoned

to be just over 3,500,000. Boundary disputes with its neighbour Paraguay make its area uncertain; official estimates vary from 506,000 to 562,000 square miles. The population is about six to the square mile, and is distributed principally through the lofty plateaux of the Andes Mountains, which here reach their greatest width and tower to enormous heights. Although Bolivia lies in the torrid zone, these high table-lands, most of them more than 12,000 feet above sea-level, have a climate almost arctic in its severity.

Potosi, where Bolivia's greatest silver and tin mines are situated, is one of the highest towns in the world (13,600 feet above sea-level), and frosts occur there every night. Sucre is the nominal capital, but La Paz is the actual seat of the government. It is the loftiest of the world's capitals, its elevation of over 12,000 feet giving it an annual average temperature of 50 degrees. There is no coal or timber at these heights, and fires are rarely used, except for cooking. The only fuel is a large woody-rooted plant called yareta. The great central table-land is extremely arid.

Lake Titicaca, a great inland sea of about 5,817 square miles, lies partly within Peru and partly within Bolivia. It is the largest lake of South America, and one of the loftiest in the world, having

BOLIVIA'S CAPITAL, LA PAZ, AMONG THE MOUNTAINS

La Paz, capital of Bolivia, lies in a valley between mountains rising to 15,000 feet and dominated by the snow-capped peak of Illimani, seen in the centre of this picture at the top. The city itself stands 12,120 feet above sea-level ; it is a curious mixture of ancient and modern, for it has cobbled streets and some adobe (sun-dried brick) houses, yet is reached from Buenos Aires by a railway journey taking only about three days. Another odd thing about La Paz, is its cathedral, which, though it was begun in the 17th century, was not completed and dedicated until 1933.

BOLIVIA

swamps, vast grassy pasture-lands, and dense, impenetrable virgin forests.

In the valleys, known as yungas, and in the lowlands the climate is sub-tropical and tropical. The soil is amazingly fertile, and with the development of transportation and increase in population these regions, which comprise about three-fifths of the country, can be made one of the garden spots of the world. Here are grown Bolivia's principal crops — sugar-cane, coffee, cocoa-bean, maize, wheat, beans, rice and fruits. Rubber forests and timber abound.

Of the Bolivian animals the most interesting are the guanaco, the llama, the alpaca and the vicuña —all of the camel family, but smaller than their relatives of Africa and Asia. The llama (q.v.) and the alpaca (q.v.) have been domesticated, the llama as a beast of burden, the alpaca for its fine wool, which is a staple export. All the characteristic animals of the Amazon tropics occur in the localities of the river basins.

Mineral wealth of incalculable extent lies buried in the Bolivian Andes. Much of the gold and silver of the ancient empire of the Incas came from the Bolivian mines, and the yield since the days of the Spanish conquerors exceeds in value a thousand million pounds, it is said. Bolivia ranks third among the tin-producing countries of the world, and has also valuable deposits of copper, wolfram (tungsten), lead, antimony, bismuth, and other metals, besides precious stones. Indications of very rich oil deposits have been found in many places.

To serve her vast area Bolivia has less than 2,000 miles of railway. Construction is exceedingly costly, because of the difficulties of the Andean routes. Most of the recently-constructed lines connect the uplands with the eastern lowlands, so that crops raised in the fertile valleys and plains adjoining Brazil and Argentina may be more

REED BOAT OF BOLIVIA
This is what the Bolivians call a balsa, which is a Spanish word meaning raft but is applied in this South American State to craft of all shapes and sizes. Above, we see one made of tree trunks bound with straw and reeds, and having a matting sail of loosely woven reeds.

an elevation of 12,900 feet. Its intensely cold waters are frequently swept by furious gales. Regular steamer services are maintained on the lake. Not far from the Bolivian end lie the vast ruins of Tiahuanaco, one of the most remarkable megalithic sites in the world, the work of a mysterious Indian race of unknown antiquity, antedating by centuries the Inca semi-civilization. (See Incas).

On the eastern slope of the Andes the river valleys fall away in fertile slopes. Between 9,000 and 5,500 feet the temperature is mild and the vegetation is varied and abundant. Below 5,500 feet great undulating plains or pampas stretch away east and north-east to the borders of Brazil, and southeast to Argentina and Paraguay. Here lie trackless

ON THE SHORES OF LAKE TITICACA
Copacabana, the city shown above, is on a peninsula that runs out into Lake Titicaca at its south-eastern end, and is only just inside the boundaries of Bolivia, for that country's frontier with Peru runs down the length of the lake. Copacabana's famous cathedral can be seen in the centre foreground of this photograph.

BOLIVIAN DANCES IN HONOUR OF PAGAN GODS

Though the Indians of Bolivia are nominally Christians, they still celebrate many of the old pagan festivals. In the top photograph a number of men are engaged in a dance on one of the feast days. They wear stiff breastplates made of the skins of animals, and their strange, looped hats would be uncomfortable on a windy day. In the lower photo another ceremonial dance is taking place, and the headgear worn is even more weird, being made of ostrich and macaw feathers dyed yellow, red, and blue, and fastened to long canes radiating from a peaked cap. More than half the population are Indians, chiefly Aymaras, Quichuas or Guaranis, who speak only their own languages.

BOLIVIAN INDIANS OF THE QUICHUA TRIBE
In ancient days when the Incas ruled Bolivia and Peru, a man's clothes were supplied to him by the State, and a marked uniformity of dress resulted. Something of this clings to the Quichuas seen above, whose striped cloak-like ponchos are almost a uniform. They live in a hamlet near Lake Poopo in the department of Oruro.

many of which date back to the 11th and 12th centuries, thriving factories turn out silk and linen, glass, leather and machinery. The well-known Bologna sausages are sold in the markets where the Guelphs and Ghibellines (two political factions) long fought for supremacy in the 13th century.

One of the most noted churches in the city is that of San Domenico, where lies the body of the founder of the Dominican order of friars. The art collection includes Raphael's painting of St. Cecilia.

The University of Bologna was founded in 1088, and its fame drew students from all parts of Europe. It began as a law school, but soon expanded to include faculties of arts and sciences, and in 1262 is said to have had 10,000 pupils on its rolls. It was here that Luigi Galvani discovered galvanic electricity in 1789.

speedily transported to the bleak barren mountains to support a larger mining population. Seven thousand miles of navigable rivers provide the chief transport in the eastern regions. Air transport is widely used, and the Bolivian air line was nationalized in 1941.

Of the population of Bolivia 50 per cent is of pure Indian blood, about 12 per cent is white, and the remainder are *cholos*, a term which is used in Bolivia to designate those of mixed white and Indian blood. Eighty-five per cent of the population is distributed over the great central plateau, where the enormous distances prevent the development of a unified national spirit. Probably fewer than 40 per cent of the people can read and write, but in recent years a determined effort has been made to improve this state of affairs. All illiterates under 21 must attend school.

The government of Bolivia is a highly-centralized republic. The electorate is small because it is restricted to those who can read and write, and own land, or have a fixed income. Married men may vote at 18 and unmarried men at 21. There is a Congress with two Houses, but the chief power is the President, who appoints the ministers and prefects (governors) of the nine departments.

Bologna, (Pron. bol-ō'-ny*a*), ITALY. Presenting a vivid contrast between picturesque medieval days and the busy commercial life of modern times, the city of Bologna lies in a fertile plain at the base of the Apennines. It is the centre of a network of railway lines which follow roughly the course of the ancient roads from Florence, Milan, Genoa and Venice.

Along the arcaded streets, laid out by the Romans in the 2nd century B.C., busy shopkeepers ply their prosperous trade. Motor-cars move rapidly up and down before the doors of the oldest university in Europe, where the great Italian poets Dante, Petrarch and Tasso studied. In the shadow of the 130 churches,

McLeish

BOLOGNA'S LEANING TOWERS
Though they are less well-known than the leaning tower of Pisa, Bologna's two leaning towers are of great interest. The unfinished Torre (tower) Garisenda is 160 feet high and nine feet out of the perpendicular, while the Torre Asinelli (right) is 320 feet high and four feet out of the perpendicular. They date from 1110.

Bologna was incorporated in the Papal States in 1506 by Pope Julius II. By a popular vote in 1860 it became part of the kingdom of Italy. Population about 330,000.

Bolshevism. The words Bolshevism and Bolsheviks were first used in 1903, when the radical wing of the Russian Social Democratic party, led by Lenin, gained a majority (Russian, *Bolshinstvo*) in a meeting to shape the policies of that organization. Thereafter Lenin's group was called the Bolsheviki or Bolsheviks (" majority men "), and their policy Bolshevism, their opponents being known as the Mensheviki (from *Menshinstvo*, minority).

Both these groups were followers of the theories put forth by Karl Marx (*q.v.*), commonly known as Communism. But they differed in their idea of how these theories were to be made to work. The Mensheviks thought that the overthrow of Russian tsardom and the building up of a Socialist state should be a smooth and gradual evolution, and that the existing liberal democratic movements in Russia should be used in beginning this work. The Bolsheviks, on the other hand, wanted a violent and immediate overthrow of the Russian system of rule ; they regarded the moderates as enemies to be ruthlessly destroyed along with the Tsarists.

When the workers of Petrograd (later named Leningrad) rose in revolt, in March 1917, and a provisional government was formed under Prince Lvov and Alexander Kerensky (March 16), the Mensheviks gave their support. But in September of that year they were ousted from the soviets (councils) by the Bolsheviks who, in November, brought about the second revolution of that year and seized power, driving out Kerensky's government. The Mensheviks continued to oppose the bigger party but steadily lost influence.

The Bolsheviks, led by Lenin, believed in the seizure of power by a small group of trained professional revolutionaries, using armed insurrection as the weapon against all opponents. In what they themselves call the "October Revolution "—because Russia at that time still used the out-dated Julian Calendar, in which our date November 7 was reckoned as October 25—the Bolsheviks founded the modern Soviet Russian State. A Congress of Soviets met on November 7, 1917, and issued proclamations and decrees; it created the Council of People's Commissaries as the Provisional Workers' and Peasants' Government. (*See* Russia).

Bolton. This Lancashire town (population, 153,000) has been connected with the manufacture of cotton since the middle of the 17th century, and before that was an important centre of woollen manufactures. It is the centre of the cotton-spinning trade, particularly as regards fine yarns made of Egyptian cotton. The introduction of the spinning frame and mule, the respective inventions of Sir Richard Arkwright, a resident, and Samuel Crompton, a native, led to the building of many factories in the town. There are also large dye works, bleaching works, paper mills, foundries, and chemical, steel and iron works. Many fine buildings include the parish church and the town hall. A very early recorded fact in the history of Bolton was the granting of the manor of that name to Roger de Poitou by his cousin, William the Conqueror.

Bombay, (Pron. bom-ba'), REPUBLIC OF INDIA. The city of Bombay, on the western coast of the vast sub-continent, has been called " the gateway to India," for here most of the Europeans bound for India have entered the country. On the Apollo Bunder, where kings, princes and viceroys have landed, stands a handsome arch built in commemoration of the visit of King George V and Queen Mary in 1911. The harbour is one of the finest natural shelters in the world, and is only rivalled in beauty by the harbours of Naples, Rio de Janeiro, Sydney and San Francisco. The city is on an island 11 miles long and three miles broad, but causeways and breakwaters connect it with the mainland so that it is practically a peninsula. Along the coast-line to the southward a range of mountains, the Western Ghats (" stepping stones "), looks down on the city.

The Portuguese in 1534 formed the first settlement, but it passed to the English in 1661 as part

BOMBAY'S GATEWAY TO INDIA
On the Apollo Bunder in Bombay stands this archway, known as the Gate of India. It was built at the wish of King George V to commemorate his visit to India in 1911, though it was not opened until 1924. This picture shows the ceremony on the occasion of the arrival on a state visit of the King of Afghanistan.

BOMBAY: CENTRE OF INDIA'S COTTON INDUSTRY

Bombay has been called the Manchester of India because it is there that the cotton industry is concentrated; the first Bombay mill was erected in 1857. The city's tram service daily transports thousands of mill-workers to and from their homes, many of the people living in one or two rooms in houses such as those seen here with washing drying on the balconies.

persecution. Though they number fewer than 90,000, they are the richest and most influential group in the large native community. Population of the city is about 1,500,000.

Bombay City is the capital of the province of Bombay, which has an area of 76,443 square miles and a population of 20,850,000, mainly Hindus. Over 60 per cent of the population are engaged in agriculture, the textile industries being centred on Bombay Island, on which the city stands. Bombay province stretches along the west coast of India from Gujarat in the north to Kanara in the south. Bombay, previously a presidency, became an autonomous province in 1937, Sind having been detached in 1936. When India became a republic in 1950, Bombay, like other former provinces, became a state. Geographically it includes a number of former native states. Among these was Baroda (8,000 square miles), whose Maharaja (the Gaekwar) played a leading part in Indian politics. The chief cities besides Bombay are Ahmedabad (population, 591,267), Poona, which was the hot-weather residence of the Governor

of the dowry of the Portuguese wife of Charles II. It is the capital of the state of Bombay, one of the largest administrative divisions of India. The name Bombay has been said to be derived from Mumbai (also known as Parvati), a Hindu goddess and the wife of the god Siva.

The city is the second largest in all India. It is the terminus of important railways, and its cotton mills, dyeing, tanning and metal works make it a great manufacturing centre. Bombay boasts many of the finest buildings in the republic, both public and private, the chief of them being Elphinstone College, the Government Secretariat, the Museum, the Courts of Justice, and the Public Works Office. The university is one of the oldest in India or Pakistan, and the city is a great educational centre. To the docks come vessels from all parts of the world. In the bazaars are folk of many races, both Asiatic and European. Over 60 languages and dialects are spoken.

The main European quarter was the old district, which grew up around the Fort, though there are many pleasant hilly districts overlooking the sea that are full of handsome modern villas. On Malabar Hill are the old Towers of Silence, where the Parsees deposit their dead to be devoured by vultures. The Parsees are descendants of a body of followers of the ancient Zoroastrian religion who fled from Persia to India about the 8th century because of Mahomedan

STATE ELEPHANTS IN A BOMBAY PROCESSION

Within the state of Bombay is the former state of Baroda, 8,127 square miles in area, forming part of the Republic of India. Its Maharaja, or Gaekwar, maintained the pomp customary with Indian princes. Here are his elephants on a state occasion, their heads painted in vivid colours and wearing elaborate trappings. Leading the procession is the Gaekwar's own elephant, carrying a golden howdah.

of Bombay (population, 258,197) and Sholapur (213,000).

In the south of Bombay state is Portuguese India, which consists of Goa, with the islands of Angediva, São Jorge and Morcegos on the Malabar coast. The total area of the colony is 1,537 square miles, with a population of 624,000. Goa has belonged to Portugal since 1510. (*See* India).

Bonaparte.
The characteristics which made members of this Corsican family rulers of a great part of Europe were probably inherited in the main from their strong-willed mother. Her husband, Carlo Buonaparte (it was the Emperor Napoleon who changed the spelling of the name from the Italian style to the French), was a lazy, pleasure-loving, unpractical man, who afforded her little aid in the rearing of their eight children; he died in 1785. But she, according to her famous son, Napoleon I, had " a man's head on a woman's body." She was endowed with good health, ceaseless energy and a resolute will.

Letizia Bonaparte (1750–1836) lived to witness his glory and his fall, and even survived him by 15 years. But she never fitted into the altered family fortunes. Though given immense wealth and the title Madame Mère (Mother), she lived in such retirement and strict economy as to make her unpopular in France. Her last days were spent in Rome, whence she wrote a pathetic letter to the powers assembled at Aix, begging for her son Napoleon's release from captivity.

The eldest of her family, Joseph (1768–1844), was a man of culture and talent. When he was made King of Naples by his brother, Napoleon, Joseph introduced many much-needed reforms into that land. His troubles began when his imperious brother took the throne of Naples from him and gave him that of Spain. Joseph was unable to suppress the rebels of that kingdom, and was driven from his throne in 1813. After the Battle of Waterloo, with the crash of the family fortunes, he found a place of refuge in America for some time. He died in Florence. Next in the family came Napoleon, whose career is described under Napoleon I.

Bowes Museum

NAPOLEON'S MOTHER

Letizia Bonaparte was a woman of great character. Her husband died in 1785 when Napoleon was but a youth, so that in his most impressionable years it was she who guided his life. She survived her famous son by fifteen years.

Engraving after Mme. Kinson, British Museum

JOSEPH BONAPARTE

As virtual ruler of the greater part of Europe, Napoleon made his eldest brother Joseph (1768–1844) King of Naples in 1806, and in 1808 King of Spain, where Joseph reigned until the Duke of Wellington's victory at Vittoria in 1813.

Napoleon's next younger brother, Lucien (1775–1840), was an ardent republican; he took little interest in his imperial brother's conquests, and often quarrelled with him. He never ruled a kingdom, although he held the papal title of Prince of Canino. He died in Rome.

Next to Napoleon I, the fourth son Louis Bonaparte (1778–1846) ranks in interest. He was King of Holland by gift of his great brother, and was father of Napoleon III (*q.v.*), second emperor of the French. When King Louis could no longer rule his country in the interests of its people he resigned his throne and retired to Italy in 1810. A sentimental interest also attaches to Louis as the husband of Hortense, daughter of the Empress Josephine, Napoleon's consort. A man of kindly and sensitive nature, he was noted for his philanthropy.

The youngest son of this illustrious family was Jerome (1784–1860), at one time King of Westphalia, a kingdom created by Napoleon in Western Germany. Before attaining this royal dignity Jerome had been in the French navy, and on one expedition had taken refuge from his English pursuers in the United States. While in that country he married Elizabeth Patterson of Baltimore. The marriage was soon annulled by order of his imperial brother, and Jerome married a German princess. From the first alliance sprang the Bonapartes of Baltimore, whose best-known member, Charles Joseph Bonaparte, became attorney-general of the U.S.A. in 1906.

There were, besides the five boys, three girls in the family—Elise, Marie Pauline and Caroline—all of whom shared in their brother's glory. Caroline (1782–1839) married Napoleon's general, Murat, and attained to the dignity of Queen of Naples, for Murat was given that throne by Napoleon when Joseph Bonaparte was transferred to Spain. Elise (1777–1820) married a Corsican who was made Grand Duke of Tuscany. Pauline (1780–1825) was married to Prince Borghese in Italy, but with her mother joined Napoleon at Elba, in 1814, and is said to have expressed a desire to share his exile in St. Helena.

Bond. When a corporation or a government borrows money, it often issues written or printed promises under seal to repay it at the end of a stated period, and to pay in the meantime a specified rate of interest per year. Such an evidence of debt is called a bond. The word comes from the verb " to bind," and is used in other senses also —*e.g.*, fidelity bonds given by officials who handle money, as a guarantee of their honesty; bonded warehouses where imported alcoholic liquors, tobacco, silks, and other articles are placed pending payment of revenue taxes.

In building, bond is a system of ties of galvanised or other rust-proof metal by which bricks are held together ; also the system by which the bricks themselves are overlapped so that no continuous weak vertical joints occur.

Bone. This is the very dense and durable substance which forms the skeleton of Man and of animals. The skeleton is a permanent framework; its flat and very hard bones protect that structure of paramount importance, the brain; the backbone or spine shepherds downwards the important nerves which run off at intervals to supply structures at the various levels.

The schoolboy's description of the spine is not a bad one. " His head sits on one end of it, and he on the other." From the spine spring the ribs, six a side, making a safe bony cage for the lungs and heart. The attachment of muscles to the long bones of the leg makes movement and locomotion possible, while to the long bones of the arm we owe all our skill in handicraft and trade.

When Man first got on his hind legs, in ages infinitely remote, the whole picture of his development began to take on new values. Now he could walk on his two hind limbs; with his two front limbs thus set free, and with the fingers increasing in sensitivity and skill, he could develop and achieve along lines hitherto impossible for him. This upright position also gave new significance and importance to the human face. While Man was on all fours it was the top of his head which met the impact and gaze of the world. (*See* Brain).

Calcium and phosphorus are of essential importance in forming the hardness and unyieldingness of bone, while soft substances which infiltrate the material of bone lend toughness to the skeleton. In a child there is much of this soft substance, and so the bone is elastic and not easily broken; in the older person the soft material has been absorbed, and so the bone is brittle. One tends to think of bone as " dead," but on the contrary it is very much alive. It is traversed and pierced by a net-

work of very fine vessels carrying lymph, by nerves, and by very fine blood-vessels which branch and ramify through all its structure. Bone marrow is formed and is found in the hollows contained in the long bones (as of the arms and the legs), and in the flat bones such as the breast-bone. Here, strange as it may seem, are the blood-factories of the red cells and of some of the white blood cells (*see* Blood). When mature, these cells drift themselves into the minute blood-vessels and thence into the general blood stream. Marrow is a valuable food, rich as it is in blood-forming elements.

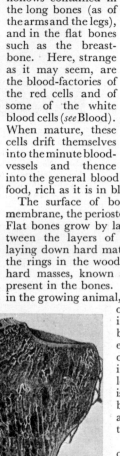

BONE MEMBRANE
This membrane, richly supplied with blood vessels, is shown covering the femur or thigh bone. A flap of membrane has been turned back, exposing the bone.

The surface of bone is coated with a fibrous membrane, the periosteum (*peri*, around; *os*, a bone). Flat bones grow by laying down hard material between the layers of periosteum; long bones by laying down hard material in cartilage—rather like the rings in the wood of trees. Before birth, little hard masses, known as centres of ossification, are present in the bones. Before birth, after birth, and in the growing animal, the ossification centres stretch out bony tentacles till, by their infiltration, the whole bone becomes hard and dense. The ends of the long bones have only a lacy network of bone inside them. But this does not lessen their strength, and one is reminded of an arch which, by some strange law of stress and strain, is even stronger than the adjacent solid wall.

Increase in height is possible only while the growth of the long bones is not yet complete, a completeness which occurs at varying ages. A long thigh bone is of great advantage to the appearance of men and women, lending them swing and grace in movement and enabling them to wear clothes to advantage. At puberty— the stage of growth at which a boy or girl leaves childhood— the growth of the thigh bone ceases; and if the thigh bone is short, the owner is destined to " waddle," ducklike. But extracts of certain suitable endocrine glands are now given at once by the doctor in such cases if the growth factor in bones is judged to be lacking. (*See* Gland).

BONE'S BLOOD SUPPLY
Blood is supplied to the interior of bones partly by a main artery and partly by a membrane known as the periosteum. The blood vessels lie in minute channels which traverse the bone in all directions.

Because of war, and as a result of the increasing hazards of modern life, fractures of bones are common and make a fascinating chapter in surgery. When the ends of a broken bone are held together in proper position the living bone cells join the ends together, and the bone may become as adequate as before. But a splint is not the only means of holding the ends together. A metal plate may be applied to the bone itself; or a pin of metal or of bone may be introduced. Moreover, a graft of living bone and periosteum may be inset, either from the patient himself or from the body of another, and these alien bone cells will multiply and repair the damage. The X-ray has been of untold value in assessing any injury to bone.

Rickets is a disease of bone which in the past has caused much deformity and distress. It is due to a defect in the chemistry of calcium and phosphorus on which the hardness of bone depends, a defect depending on a shortage of vitamin D. Vitamin D is found most richly in the unpleasant tasting cod-liver-oil and in halibut oil. Contrary to popular belief, the best dose of cod-liver-oil is a half tea-spoonful to one teaspoonful three times daily after meals. Larger doses stop the flow of the gastric juices. Such small doses can well be taken in tasteless capsules. It took scientists many years to find out the real cause of rickets. Sunshine has the power to make vitamin D out of fat when it plays on the body, and this confused their researches.

Bones can be attacked by the tubercle germ, but the condition answers well to rest and treatment. A form of cancer called sarcoma also attacks bone.

Bone has many industrial uses, such as making buttons and so on. But the synthetic chemist, working in his laboratory, has devised other hard and durable materials which are far more suitable. In another respect, however, bone keeps its age-old supremacy: this is as a fertiliser of the soil, in the form of bone-meal. Animal charcoal, or bone-black, is made by distilling bones in iron retorts.

Bonheur, MARIE ROSALIE (1822–1899). Many know the animal pictures of the French-woman, Rosa Bonheur (pron. bon-êr′), though all may not know that young lions followed her about like dogs and pined during her absence, or that wild chamois, goats, deer, gazelles, monkeys, and other animals had their quarters in her country home at By, in the forest of Fontainebleau near Paris.

This painter studied her animals at first hand. Her father, a struggling artist of Paris and her only teacher, was so interested in the art of his children that he always provided some pet for Rosa and her sister and two brothers to sketch. They spent hours in art galleries copying pictures of the great artists, but Rosa liked best to catch the quick movements and changing expressions of living creatures. So, dressed in her brother's clothes, she went often to the stock-yards of Paris ; there with her short hair and strong features she easily passed as a boy and was freely admitted even to the slaughtering pens, where she studied the anatomy of the animals until she knew their bodily structure perfectly.

When she was only 18 years old her picture of two rabbits was accepted for the Salon, the annual exhibition of works by French artists, in Paris. Eight years later she received a gold medal from the same institution. When it was presented to her in the name of King Louis Philippe, the girl replied, " Thank the king for me and tell him I expect to do better." Four years later she ranked as the leading animal painter of the day.

By the time she was 34, the income from her pictures enabled Mademoiselle Bonheur to establish a beautiful country home at By, where, except for occasional sketching trips, she spent the remainder of her life. Many medals and honours were bestowed upon her, and she was the first woman to be made an officer of the Legion of Honour.

Among the paintings that have brought fame to Rosa Bonheur are Deer in the Forest, Weaning the Calves, and the well-known Horse Fair. The

ROSA BONHEUR'S FAMOUS PAINTING OF A HORSE FAIR

Most famous of Rosa Bonheur's pictures is the Horse Fair, painted when she was only 31. The original now hangs in the National Gallery (Tate Gallery) at Millbank, London, but engravings of this spirited picture are to be found in many homes. From time immemorial horse fairs have been held all over Europe, but the great French painter and lover of animals has somewhat idealized the scene, for sorry nags as well as the fine beasts depicted above are bought and sold. Rosa Bonheur was the first woman to be created an officer of the Legion of Honour, in 1894.

British Museum

POPE BONIFACE AMONG HIS CARDINALS

Of the nine Popes Boniface, the one who is given most space in the history books is Boniface VIII (c. 1230-1303), seen in this picture presiding over a meeting of his cardinals. He was a very determined character and was so prone to simony, i.e., selling Church appointments, that the great Italian poet Dante gives him a place in his Inferno.

breeze stirred, and suddenly the wide branching top was broken off and the oak crashed to the ground in four pieces, while Boniface stood unharmed. The awed multitude accepted this as proof of the superiority of the Christian God, and agreed to forsake their heathen deities and to become true Christians. Out of the wood of the fallen oak Boniface built a Christian chapel.

Boniface, POPES. Nine different Popes have borne the name of Boniface, beginning with BONIFACE I (418-422). BONIFACE VIII (1294-1303) was the most important of their number. In his pontificate occurred a bitter conflict with King Philip IV of France, in the course of which brutal agents of the king seized the aged Pope at his summer home at Anagni, and treated him with such indignity that he died about a month after his release. Shortly afterwards Avignon, on the River Rhône, became, and for about 70 years remained, the seat of the Popes. BONIFACE IX (1389-1404) was one of the Popes in the period of the "Great Schism," the division in the Roman Church which followed the return of the Papacy to Rome, while anti-Popes still reigned at Avignon.

Horses Threshing Corn, showing 10 life-size horses, was at the time of its execution the largest animal picture ever known to have been painted.

Boniface, SAINT (680-755). In 716 the German worshippers of Woden and Thor were being won to Christianity through the labours of a Devonshire man, whose real name was Winfrid or Winfrith, but whom we know more familiarly as Saint Boniface (pron. bon'-i-fās).

For nearly 40 years he worked in Southern Germany — preaching, baptizing, consecrating churches, founding monasteries, and everywhere imposing better order on the clergy and establishing the authority of the Pope. He and his companion monks bore hardship without number, from fire and flood and famine in a savage land; and at last he crowned his life of heroic labour and sacrifice by suffering martyrdom at the hands of the heathen in what is now The Netherlands.

Here is one interesting scene out of many in the life of this great missionary. The place is a gloomy forest at Geismar, in the heart of Germany, in which stood a sacred oak whose massive trunk and branches made it an object of wonder to every beholder. Under it priests, supposedly Christian, still performed rites of heathen worship.

"Down with that tree," cried Boniface, "for it is an altar to false gods!"

But the Hessians called down the curses of their pagan deities upon anyone who should touch the tree, and no one dared to lift the axe against it.

Then said Boniface: "Behold, I will chop it down myself," and fearlessly he applied the axe. When he had cut into the trunk only a little way, a

Bonn, W. GERMANY. The provisional capital of the West German Federal Republic (formally proclaimed on May 23, 1949), Bonn was once famous for its university and the charm of its old buildings. It is situated on the left bank of the Rhine, about 15 miles to the south of Cologne.

The finest of its buildings was the former palace of the Electors of Cologne, which was occupied by the university, founded by King Frederick William III in 1818. Prince Albert, the consort of Queen Victoria, studied at Bonn. Prior to the Second World War (1939-45) during which it was destroyed by bombing, the university was well equipped for the teaching of science, medicine, theology and agriculture, and had a splendid observatory. The city is also the birthplace of the composer Beethoven whose house (slightly damaged during the war) is preserved as a museum. The minster, which suffered comparatively little, is famed for its great central tower. Much of the town was destroyed by Allied air raids in 1944.

Bonn had manufactures—chiefly of porcelain and stoneware—and up to 1939 carried on an active trade. The population was about 100,000.